INTERNATIONAL CONFERENCE ON HUMOUR & LAUGHTER

HELD IN CARDIFF, 13-17TH JULY, 1976

IT'S A FUNNY THING, HUMOUR

Edited by
ANTONY J. CHAPMAN

and

HUGH C. FOOT
Welsh Branch, British Psychological Society

Illustrated by
Roy R. Behrens

PERGAMON PRESS
OXFORD · NEW YORK · TORONTO · SYDNEY · PARIS · FRANKFURT

U.K.	Pergamon Press Ltd., Headington Hill Hall, Oxford OX3 0BW, England
U.S.A.	Pergamon Press Inc., Maxwell House, Fairview Park, Elmsford, New York 10523, U.S.A.
CANADA	Pergamon of Canada Ltd., 75 The East Mall, Toronto, Ontario, Canada
AUSTRALIA	Pergamon Press (Aust.) Pty. Ltd., 19a Boundary Street, Rushcutters Bay, N.S.W. 2011, Australia
FRANCE	Pergamon Press SARL, 24 rue des Ecoles, 75240 Paris, Cedex 05, France
WEST GERMANY	Pergamon Press GmbH, 6242 Kronberg-Taunus, Pferdstrasse 1, Frankfurt-am-Main, West Germany

First edition 1977

Library of Congress Cataloging in Publication Data

International Conference on Humour and Laughter, Cardiff, Wales, 1976.
It's a funny thing, humour, the International Conference on Humour and Laughter, held in Cardiff, July 13th-17th 1976, under the auspices of the Welsh Branch of the British Psychological Society.

Bibliography: p.
1. Wit and humor--Psychology--Congresses. I. Chapman, Antony J. II. Foot, Hugh C. III. British Psychological Society. Welsh Branch. IV. Title: It's a funny thing, humour ...
PN6149.P515 1976 152.4 76-53731
ISBN 0-08-021376-6 (Hardcover)
ISBN 0-08-021377 (Flexicover)

In order to make this volume available as economically and rapidly as possible the authors' typescripts have been reproduced in their original form. This method unfortunately has its typographical limitations but it is hoped that they in no way distract the reader.

Printed in Great Britain by A. Wheaton & Co., Exeter

Contents

Contents

Preface

It is always difficult to trace the origins of an idea, and the idea for the International Conference on Humour and Laughter is no exception. Suffice it to say that we became aware of the rapidly increasing academic interest in humour and laughter, and that it was the Welsh Branch of the British Psychological Society which provided the opportunity to organize an international gathering. Delegates from sixteen nations were in Cardiff between July 13th and July 17th 1976, and this book contains reports of the papers that were presented.

Guest comedian, Ken Dodd, endeared himself to other delegates with an address that was scholarly and informative. It was also very funny. He argued that no-one can 'make' anyone else laugh — laughter, he said, is a gift. He concluded his address with a plea that nobody should ever discover or disclose 'the key' to humour. He can rest assured that no sane person could currently be harbouring any such irreverent ambition.

To date, analysts have barely begun to scratch the surface, revealing the vast complexities in humour and in responsiveness to humour. We are still at the stage where close examination seems only to enhance the elusiveness of humour, and that is especially the case when closer scrutiny involves mingling with researchers having other orientations and interests. If we are to make worthwhile statements about humour, then there is no doubt that much more than at present, we need to exchange ideas and communicate knowledge across disciplines. Moreover, within the discipline of we Editors — Psychology — we need to be extremely catholic in the types of methodologies employed.

The majority of delegates at this Conference were academics and most were psychologists, but other academic disciplines were represented too: for example, Anthropology, Communication, Education, English, French, Mathematics, Philosophy, Politics, Psychiatry, Social Work, and Sociology. Then there were school teachers and there were others from outside the world of teaching and research. Hopefully, the balance across disciplines will be spread more evenly at any future international humour conference.

In general terms, the structure of the book reflects the structure of the Conference Programme, with contributions falling into ten main sections. Eight of these sections correspond to the eight symposia presented during the Conference; they are sandwiched between two sections arising from the various sessions of 'individual' papers. The papers comprising the opening section are somewhat more theoretical in focus than those in the closing section, although to some extent the division is arbitrary. Certainly many of the 'individual' papers were suitable for symposia and we were often spoilt for choice when designing the Programme.

Each of the 'symposia sections' has an introductory chapter, a short series of papers, and some brief evaluative comments. Opening chapters are based upon the Symposia Chairpersons' introductory talks, and they constitute overviews of the areas under discussion. Symposia Discussants have supplied the concluding comments, and some of them allude directly to points made from the floor during open discussion. Only a handful of all the contributions here appear in the form read at the Conference; most have been modified.

The bibliography is extensive and has been drawn up over a number of years. It is intended to contain all analyses of humour, laughter and comedy published in English. We should be grateful to be told of any errors and omissions, and also to be kept informed of new work.

The Conference was the first of its kind and it provided rich material for the press and broadcasting media. In 1977, the BBC is to present a television programme on the Conference, produced by Derek Trimby. The press comments have been reproduced and are available from Pergamon in 'scrapbook' form.

On the whole, press coverage was fair and unprejudiced but some was flagrantly dishonest. For example, 'Time' was one magazine which reported a paper that was not in fact presented. The Speaker was in hospital and consequently his paper featured in the Programme only! Then again, a writer in 'Punch' was guilty of the same howler and was also inaccurate on a number of 'details'. His analysis was couched in a curious mixture of past and present tense — that article appeared on the bookstalls immediately before the Conference was underway!

Most journalists did attend those papers about which they chose to write. However, it is evident from some reports that they did not always follow what was said, but we must hasten to admit that, on some occasions, this does not reflect any inadequacies on their part! Some of the jargon issued from the platform was unfortunate and served to inhibit communication. We regret that a degree of this creeps over to the book. Some of the extensive publicity received before the outset of the Conference and during it, brought home the fact that 'humour' and 'laughter' are not yet recognized by many as legitimate topics for serious study, and the unnecessary jargon may sometimes have slipped in as a form of defence against anticipated criticism. Of course, the jargon itself then became the subject for fun. You have only to thumb through the Pergamon 'scrapbook' to see this.

The smooth, day-to-day running of conference events resulted in no small part from the resourceful and assiduous assistance given by our students, graduates and friends. Jean Smith, Mary Jones and Liz Pritchard worked cheerfully through endless hours during July and, at the Conference, were joined by Pauline Corbett, Ann Davies, Isabelle Davies, Nick Gadfield, John Haigh, Brenda Klug, Rob Mason, Kathie Osborne, Alison Turnbull, and Paul Twynham. For more than a year we had the solid backing of the clerical and technical staff in UWIST's Applied Psychology Department. It was a pleasure working with all these people and with those from Traherne Hall of Residence. We can imagine no finer group of fellow-workers and friends.

In the production of the book, Liz Clarke was magnificent. All of it was typed in camera-ready-copy during her 'spare-time' over a period of two months, and readers can see for themselves the superb quality of her work. Pam Morris, again in 'spare-time', provided some support towards the end when alterations were necessary and the deadline had been brought forward by several weeks. Jean Smith and Liz Pritchard proof-read the typed plates with us, and they were of enormous help in this respect.

We are grateful to the BPS Welsh Branch and, particularly to our friend and colleague Tony Gale who formally proposed that the Conference be convened. We are also grateful to the Social Science Research Council for allowing us to grant nominal travel awards to newly established research workers in attendance. Otherwise, the Conference financed itself.

The book should provide interesting reading to people from all backgrounds. Within humour and laughter, it covers a very wide range of issues, and it contains many insights and much fresh information. But there is certainly no single 'key' to be found in these pages, and we do not believe that such a key exists. For those who have not begun to study humour in a systematic or serious fashion, the book will illustrate if not confirm, Ken Dodd's words: 'It's a funny thing, humour.'

Welsh Regional Office
British Psychological Society   Tony Chapman
c/o Department of Applied Psychology   Hugh Foot
UWIST Cardiff

September 1976

Foreword

In this book are assembled the papers, or abstracts of papers, delivered at the Conference on Humour and Laughter held in July, 1976. During the last session of that Conference, the audience was asked if the Conference might end up by trying to produce a definition of humour. The response was overwhelmingly negative; nor was any attempt made to work out a taxonomy of laughter, though of course individual authors did talk about their own definitions and taxonomies. So, as far as this book is concerned, humour and laughter must be defined in terms of what the authors have chosen to talk about. There does seem to be some measure of agreement, perhaps because the large majority of contributors have English as their first language. Also the contents of this book may be taken to represent a fairly good sample of the work English-speaking psychologists (mainly) are doing, since the conveners of the Conference, Dr. Chapman and Dr. Foot, were very successful in their preliminary publicity. Anyone interested was almost certain to hear about it beforehand, and as Editors they have tried to give all-comers a platform, whatever the focus of the work or the idiosyncracies of the authors.

It should be said that there may have been another unifying factor. Chapman and Foot's excellent survey "Humour and Laughter: Theory, Research and Applications" was published earlier in 1976. Many contributors to this present book were familiar with it and had been brought up to date with current work, and, of course, with the viewpoints of the Editors. In their Introduction to that book, the Editors make it clear that there are many kinds of humour and laughter, and that there are no simple one-to-one connexions between them. It is still worth referring back to Flugel's classic 1954 survey for a scholarly discussion of definitions and taxonomies. Comparing his study with the contents of these proceedings it is instructive to find how little change there has been in the concerns of those trying to analyze humour. There are more experiments being done and some of the jargon is different, but many of the hypotheses are similar, though Flugel's own background thinking was more influenced by psychoanalysis than is the case for most of the present contributors. Also, he was concerned with laughter as much as with humour, whereas here there are five times as many contributions on humour.

Why study humour? As Chapman and Foot have pointed out, the lack of psychological and related research on humour is noteworthy, especially since so much everyday behaviour and conversation involves humour and laughter. That fact alone should be enough to start anyone with an inquiring mind. If psychologists are to do the job properly, then it seems to me that they should attempt to find answers to the following, with respect to both humour and laughter: the probability of their occurrence under various conditions; their ontogeny and, according to some contributors, phylogeny; individual differences in reactions, and differences between cultures and sub-cultures, and changes over time; neurophysiological correlates; the effects of humour and laughter on other people; their relation to social structure and group dynamics. On the applied side, as this book shows, there is growing interest in the use of humour and laughter in therapy and in persuasion. If the work is to be done rigorously, it needs careful categorising of the various kinds of humour and laughter, sophisticated experimental and observational techniques and new methods of measurement are still needed; and one of the main problems in this kind of research, as contributors have shown themselves to be well aware, lies in translating results from controlled experimental settings to what might be expected in day-to-day behaviour.

Since probably before Plato there have been theories about humour and laughter. At present the theories seem to be particularly related to developmental stages, to understanding the functions of humour and laughter, and to explaining what is psychologically different about a humorous situation. The theories have three main orientations – cognitive, social and deriving from psychoanalysis – and of course one needs all three if all aspects are to be covered. Functional explanations attract a great deal of attention and disagreement, not surprisingly since they are intended to answer the most interesting questions and yet are in practice untestable.

The writer has to admit that his main interest lies in trying to understand the functions of humour and laughter, with related interests in developmental changes and changes with fashion. Laughter is easier to deal with than humour, possibly because there are not so many definitional problems. It is obvious that there are many different kinds of occasion when laughter may occur. In his early (1942) study of laughter in young children, Valentine listed fifteen categories. They are worth recording, to show the need for a taxonomy, and because they are suggestive of explanations of adult laughter, and humour. They are: (1) expression of delight, (2) response to laughter or smile of another, (3) sight of a bright or pleasing object, (4) tickling or jogging, (5) mild shock or surprise, (6) repetition, as in the peep-bo game, (7) the incongruous, as of the child's own name or the sight of his face in a mirror, (9) accomplishment of some new form of activity, (10) teasing, (11) mild discomfiture of another, (12) laughter in the course of social play, (13) laughter to make another laugh, especially after doing something naughty, (14) incongruity in words or ideas, as in puns, (15) laughter at mere coincidences. The list is rather comprehensive but there have been longer ones. Another important category might be (16) laughter as a more socially desirable response to be substituted for crying, as for instance when the child has fallen down. Presumably this last is an example of what Ludovici (1932) called 'the expression of superior adaptation', one of the 'superiority theories' which are said to derive from Hobbes (1651). How many functions of laughter are there? Are they as numerous as are the occasions for laughter, or can they be reduced to one, for example, superiority? As in most cases where there is this kind of apparent polarization between multiplicity and unity (for example, how many drives are there?), it may help to think in terms of a hierarchy. The level chosen will depend on what the taxonomy is to be used for, but the various levels must be compatible with each other. In the writer's view, the most general remark to be made about adult laughter is that its functions are social, the evidence being that people do not laugh when they are on their own. The exceptions prove the rule in that they occur when one has forgotten that one is alone. At another level of analysis I have speculated that laughter has a most important function in determining and maintaining group cohesion and in distinguishing between the mores of one's own group and that of the outgroup - laughing with and laughing at. It can be argued that these functions have played an important part in cultural evolution.

The links with humour are not obvious. While attending this Conference I came to the conclusion that laughter has a lot to do with social development whereas many kinds of humour have more to do with cognitive development. This latter point has been made by many theorists and experimenters, and seems particularly applicable to those kinds of humour which involve 'playing with cognitive categories', the kind of thing epitomised in the pun. It would be expected that this kind of humour cannot be appreciated until a child can see that a thing or word or occurrence can be categorised in more ways than one simultaneously, and the experiments which are based on Piagetian theorizing do seem to support this. (Is it too much to expect that 'condensation' in dream work does not occur until then?). Similar unconventional uses of categories are found in some forms of thought disorder, as for instance 'overinclusion', and many kinds of humour are thought of as being nearly psychotic. In fact, if one did not know that the setting (for example, of a cartoon or the comic performance) was a humorous one, then one would be faced with the 'Buffery problem', funny peculiar or funny ha-ha! (see Buffery, this volume). The response of laughter then means 'I know you don't really mix up categories in this way'.

The Conference reported here received a good deal of attention from the British press and broadcasting. The usual reaction was of amazement and amused disbelief that scientists would be coming from all over the world to Cardiff to have a Conference on Humour and Laughter, and that was also the reaction, though perhaps a bit mollified, of many psychologists. But is it not generally the case that all psychologists have some niche of behaviour or experience which they are unwilling to analyze? The musician does not really want to know why he likes music or the religious person why he is religious. Or the humorous person why he is humorous. Oh dear!

The difficulties involved in analyzing humour and laughter introspectively suggest that there is something early and basic about them, like trying through introspection to work out how language is acquired. It looks as though both humour and laughter are concerned with boundary phenomena, with making discriminations between what is done and what is not done, between them and us, between sanity and insanity. To be aphoristic about it, and like most aphorisms this one is ninety per cent untrue: laughter is a defence against neurosis, humour is a defence against psychosis.

The Conference ranged the whole gamut from devout seriousness to obscene hilarity. It was most enjoyable, and participants would want me to express our thanks to the University of Wales Institute of Science and Technology for its hospitality, and to the Welsh Branch of the British Psychological Society and especially Tony Chapman and Hugh Foot for having the idea and organising it.

B.M. Foss
Professor of Psychology
Bedford College
University of London

REFERENCES

Chapman, A.J. & Foot, H.C. (Eds.), Humour and Laughter: Theory, Research and Applications.
    Wiley, London (1976).

Flugel, J.C., Humor and laughter. In: G. Lindzey (Ed.), Handbook of Social Psychology.
    Volume II. Addison—Wesley, Cambridge,Massachusetts (1954).

Hobbes, T., Humane Nature. Anchor, London (1651).

Hobbes, T., Leviathan. Penguin, Harmondsworth (1968). (Originally published 1651)

Ludovici, A.M., The Secret of Laughter. Gordon Press, London (1932).

Valentine, C.W., The Psychology of Early Childhood. Methuen, London (1942).

INDIVIDUAL PAPERS

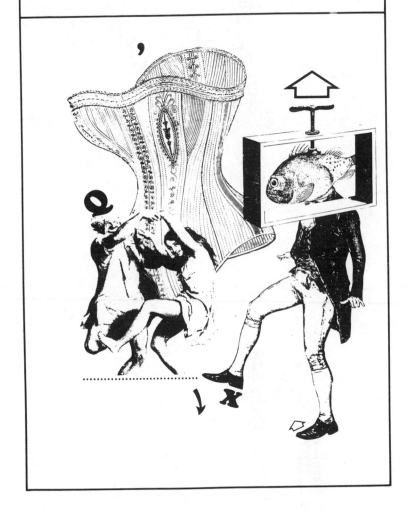

ESSAYS ON THE NATURE OF HUMOUR, LAUGHTER AND COMEDY

If Hamlet Had Had A Sense of Humour

Harvey Mindess

Antioch College/West

Ladies and gentlemen of the jury:

The case I intend to argue in this courtroom is simplicity itself. If there are any wits amongst you, they may conclude, when I have done, that that is because it is over-simplified, inspired by simple-mindedness, and conceived by a simpleton. Before the rest of you pronounce your verdict, however, I ask you to simply listen to the very simple points it undertakes to make.

Our lives, I propose, extend between the poles of tragedy and comedy, but we possess more freedom than we realize to experience our circumstances and ourselves in tragic or comic guise.

Some events, it is true, are so unrelievedly dreadful that one would have to be out of one's mind to find them amusing. Other events, it is equally true, are so undeniably funny that one would have to be pathological to find them grim. Most of the happenings in which we engage, however, reside at neither pole. Our family ties, our friendships and loves, our marriage arrangements and occupational activities, our personal strivings no less than the public events of the countries to which we belong, are riddled through and through with both tragic and comic elements. Our experience of them, therefore, depends at least in part on how we choose to perceive them.

I use the word 'choose', I confess, with malice aforethought, for I wish to contend that we have it within our power to focus on one or the other aspect of our lives and thereby to turn them in one or the other direction. Just as we are capable of replacing, or at least augmenting, despair with resolve, fear with anger, impulsiveness with thoughtfulness, we are capable of adding humour to our repertoire of self-perceptions – indeed, of giving it a central place in our conceptions of ourselves – and in this act, I say, we may exert a greater effect on the course and outcome of our struggles than anyone has yet envisualized.

Not only may a humorous view of ourselves help lighten a mood of gloom; not only may it promote an appreciation of the tininess of our individual complaints within the broader scheme of things; it may, I suggest, transform the very texture of our lives, rescuing them both from horror and banality by its refusal to buy into either a tragic or a flatly objective outlook.

Members of the jury, if you judge this a debatable notion, let me hasten to agree with you. Although I intend to develop it, I am not at all certain that I can muster enough evidence to convince you of its validity. I would readily admit, in fact, that everything I have to say may be irrelevant and immaterial. And yet I feel compelled to pursue it. Why? I will tell you. It is because I sense – dumbly, dimly – that the thesis that self-directed humour can radically alter our lives may be true, and it is because I believe that the promulgation of this thesis could be so significant that even the weakest effort expended on articulating it would have been well worthwhile.

I do not intend, however, to argue the case on theoretical grounds. Nor do I have any research data to present to you. There are some anecdotal reports I could mention, but rather than do that today I thought I would simply illustrate the notion in a somewhat fanciful fashion. Since it is nothing more at this stage of its development than an intuitive fancy itself, I hope you will not find it insulting to the stature of this gathering if I invite you to join me on an imaginary journey into the world of drama and literature. If you come along, I will try to show how the spirit of humour can penetrate the edifice of tragedy and reduce it to something less substantial than it at first appeared.

As we all know, many great plays and novels have been created in which the leading characters endure tragic fates. Dostoevsky's Raskolnikov, Shakespeare's Othello, Bronte's Heathcliff and Catherine Earnshaw, Medea, Prometheus, and others in Greek mythology are only the first that come to mind. Not only are their destinies heartbreaking, however; their authors also convince us that their tragedies are inevitable. Having read their stories or seen them performed, we are left with the ominous feeling that certain individuals, often admirable and enviable in other respects, are doomed to live out a destructive sequence of events culminating in a dreadful or horrifying death.

Perhaps the most eloquent of all these tragic heroines and heroes is Shakespeare's 'Hamlet'. He is certainly amongst the most well-known and the most universally acclaimed in the persuasiveness of his plight. Almost everyone, I think it fair to say, is convinced that Hamlet cannot be other than he is and that the havoc he wreaks on himself and those about him is therefore unavoidable.

As a student of humour, I doubt it. Despite his trenchant wit, what Hamlet lacks is a grasp of himself as a mortal fool. In this lack, he is kin to the vast majority of tragic characters in literature and life. Taking themselves and their plights with utmost seriousness, they invest in their own destruction and compound it with added interest. In order to explore the possibilities the Prince of Denmark would have had if he had perceived himself and his circumstances with humour, let us take a moment to review the play from that unusual perspective.

Imagine, if you will, that you are young Prince Hamlet. (Well, not so young; you are thirty years of age and still unmarried, so already you should be ashamed of yourself). Nevertheless, your father, a noble king, has expired under suspicious circumstances. (But perhaps we should not say expired; it makes him sound like a library card. No, let's face it: he has kicked the bucket, passed away, gone to meet his Maker, breathed his last, and also died). Barely two months have passed since the sad event and already your mother has cast off her mourning gown, and probably her nightgown as well, and hopped into bed with your uncle Claudius. They have also been legally married, so the swine has taken possession not only of your father's wife but of his realm as well.

You are, to put it mildly, perturbed. In more contemporary terms, you feel bummed out, ripped off, dumped on, fucked over, and generally unappreciated. In fact, you have a strong urge to shout, 'Something is rotten in the state of Denmark!' But you don't. You don't say it because you are moody, disconsolate, and lost in thought – and besides, it's not your line. Your line is, 'The time is out of joint. O cursed spite, that ever I was born to set it right'. But you don't say that either. Not yet at least. You may be disconsolate, but you are not dumb enough to throw away good material before you have made your entrance.

So you go to meet a strange apparition that claims it's your father's ghost. And what does it do? It tells you he was murdered by his brother Claudius, who performed the foul deed by pouring poison in his ears, and directs you to seek revenge.

Well, here I would say is your first opportunity to exercise your sense of humour. True, the murder of one's father is hardly a laughing matter, but the manner of this crime is hardly the stuff of tragedy. Poison in the ears, indeed! The villain must have gotten his degree in otolaryngology. But never mind. Let us say that this chink in the armour of destiny, this unbuttoned fly on the trousers of tragedy, escapes your attention. What then?

You return to the royal palace, where you find your mother concerned about your sulking (as well she should be), your uncle solicitous of your welfare (or so he shrewdly claims), and other friends and acquaintances, not excluding your sweetheart Ophelia, anxious to rouse you out of your grief.

Do you allow them to do so? Not on your life. Having discoursed with a ghost, you are now consumed with suspicions about your uncle's treachery, your mother's lust, and your friends' friendliness, so you deliver a few verbal sallies to show them all what you're made of. 'Frailty, thy name is woman!' Get thee to a nunnery!' 'O what a piece of work is man!' And at one particularly desperate moment, wishing that you could at least have had a barmitsvah, you mourn, 'Oh, that this too too solid flesh would melt, thaw, and resolve itself into a Jew'.

But nothing helps. You are pinioned on the cross of hesitation, goaded to avenge your father's death and yet restrained by some mysterious mixture of doubt and despair, uncertainty and ennui.

Now once again, I suggest, your sense of humour could come to your aid. It could show you that not only mother and uncle but also you are a little offbase (that's American for, 'off your wicket'). I mean, what's with this walking around acting crazy, poking your sword into other people's arrasses, and muttering, 'The play's the thing?' The time may be out of joint, old pal, but what makes you think that you're in any shape to set it right? If you'll forgive my saying so, you would be well advised to call in Columbo, let Ophelia relieve your misery, learn to bake Danish pastry, or at least consult a shrink.

Alright, I know what you're going to say. What kind of a shrink? A Freudian, a Jungian, a behaviour modifier, or an existential humanist? They're all terrific, goodness knows, but which is the best for your case? Well, I can tell you this. A Freudian would help, because you can bet your mother's couch that he would tell you you have a terrible Oedipus complex. Like all normal boys, you wished that you yourself could poison daddy's ears and climb into bed with mom, so you're only mad at your uncle because he got there first. I don't say that would cure you, but think what it would do for your sense of humour. Just compare that foxy Ophelia with your old saggy mom and tell me, wouldn't you crack a smile?

Or how about taking a different tack? Instead of telling the shrink what's really bugging you, you could start with a cover story to test him out. You could say, 'I have this strange compulsion to go BEEP BEEP all the time. So wherever I am, whatever I'm doing, I'm obsessed with the question, TO BEEP OR NOT TO BEEP.'

In other words, Prince Hamlet, instead of taking yourself and your plight so seriously – though I admit that it is in many respects a terribly serious matter - you could try to see the ludicrousness that is, or could be, a part of it. Although, or because, the attempt would lead you to step off your moral podium and mingle in the playground of common silliness, I believe it would help you immeasurably. You would, it is true, lose some of your gloomy grandeur, but consider how many people you wouldn't have to kill. Yes, your father is dead, perhaps murdered, and your mother is behaving badly, but as my grandmother would have said, you still have your health and a lovely girlfriend, so why not try to enjoy?

Ladies and gentlemen of the jury, I suggest that we are all Hamlets to the extent that we are undone by the injustices in our lives and the lives of those about us. And it is surely part of our nobility, as it is Hamlet's, to attempt to right the scales. But it is short-sighted to believe that we can accomplish this goal in any enduring sense, for the time is always out of joint. Treachery and greed, stupidity and lust are always on the loose, and every avenging angel partakes of those qualities too. Hamlet's predicament is real, but he compounds it by his inability to perceive it in broad enough perspective. While as seekers of justice we may applaud him, as psychologists of humour we must admonish him. You take yourself too seriously, young Prince. Like most of us most of the time; you fail to register and cultivate the humorous dimension of your plight. As you told Rosencrantz and Guildenstern before you got all befuddled, 'There is nothing either good or bad but thinking makes it so'. Would that we all, in our own times of trial, could remember those words.

Ladies and gentlemen (place briefcase on lectern), in the immortal words of that great Shakespearian scholar, Groucho Marx, 'I rest my case'.

The Psychoanalytic Theory of Humour and Laughter

Paul Kline

University of Exeter

In this paper I make no apology for examining in some detail the Freudian theory of wit, humour and the comic. This is because, as can be seen even in as thorough a survey of the field as that of Goldstein and McGhee (1972a), the psychoanalytic theory of humour is generally cursorily described, missing out some of the most significant aspects.

Fortunately from our point of view, there are effectively only two sources for Freud's work on humour (a generic term which we shall use, except where obvious, to include humour, laughter, wit and the comic): the 1905 work 'Jokes and their Relation to the Unconscious', which is a lengthy volume and the brief 1928 paper entitled 'Humour'.

Before we begin any analyses of the contents of these papers, their historical context in terms of the development of psychoanalytic theory has to be appreciated. In the same year as the first work on humour there appeared the celebrated and theoretically important work 'Three Essays on Sexuality' in which the notions of pregenital sexuality and psychosexuality were first clarified. Three years before this had been written 'The Psychopathology of Everyday Life' preceded (by a year) by 'The Interpretation of Dreams'. Thus it is no idle speculation to argue what is in fact clear from the text, that at the time of writing 'Jokes and their Relation to the Unconscious' uppermost in Freud's mind was the psychical significance of every piece of behaviour no matter how trivial; and the equal importance of pregenital sexuality and its repression on personality development was already current in his mind. Notice, however, at this stage, Freud's supreme discovery, (described by Sears, 1943, as a grotesquerie), the Oedipus Complex, had not yet been made as had not the topological division of the mind, like Gaul, into three parts. By 1928 this was no longer the case and the paper on 'Humour' may be interpreted accordingly.

One further point needs to be made. For some reason Freud regarded his work on humour as something of a byway on psychoanalysis, one that had led him from its main track. Certainly this aspect of Freudian theory, although integrated with the whole which as we shall see is what makes it attractive, could be proved wrong without thereby destroying the rest of the theoretical structure.

Although perhaps contrary to psychoanalytic theory and refuting it, Freud tries to account for interest in jokes, to explain his motivation for studying them: there were two influences at work, first that of the philosopher, Lipps, who was interested both in jokes and the unconscious, and secondly, as Fleiss had pointed out, the interpretation of dreams had involved a large number of jokes. Furthermore it may be hazarded that talking about jokes appealed to the somewhat cumbrous style of twentieth century Germany academe, with no racial overtones intended.

The first part of the 1905 work is taken up with a study of the technique of jokes. A number of techniques, with examples, is enumerated. By 'techniques' Freud simply refers to the mechanics of the joke, the way the joke is constructed. They refer to the psychical phenomena of making jokes — joke-work. The main techniques are:

1(a) Condensation — Examples quoted by Freud are: from De Quincy, 'old people fall into their anecdotage'. Of an ex-farmer, 'Return to your place before the plough', that is, be an ox.

(b) Dividing up Words — 'Have you anything to do with masturbation?' 'On na nie'. With this technique the smaller the change, the more effective is the double use or double meaning. This is effectively the technique used by the script-writers, Muir and Norden.

(c) Multiple Use — Battle scared and bottle scarred warrior is an obvious illustration.

(d) Double Meaning — Here puns are a sub-species of this technique. The double meaning is
     probably the easiest form of joke to make. On the radio again, to mention 'have it' or
     'want it' seems guaranteed to produce laughter.

All these last three techniques are special types of condensation and Freud regards them as
examples of economy. However, not all economies of expression are jokes, although it has
been remarked elsewhere that brevity is the soul (not the whole) of wit. A laconic
expression is not a joke.

2.   Displacement — This is the next joke technique discussed by Freud. Displacement, as
     the name suggests describes that event where the emphasis changes to a different meaning
     of the word. Freud's example is clear: 'Have you taken a bath? ..... Is there one
     missing?' One Galatian Jew (reputedly a filthy group) to another. Here we must note
     that two techniques are used. Displacement where the emphasis is shifted from both to
     take, and of course double-meaning of the word take.

3.   Absurdity — The absurd punchline points up some previous absurdity. One of Aristophanes'
     dead characters in Hell: 'Strike me alive ...'

4.   Sophistical Reasoning — A man accused of stealing a kettle: 'I didn't borrow it: it
     had a hole in it: I returned it undamaged'. This is a clear example.

5.   Unification (similar to condensation) — Unexpected unities are pointed out. On an ode
     to posterity 'This ode will never reach its destination'. Definition of a tromba
     marina as a 'Trumpet in C'. Unification according to Freud is the basis of repartee.

6.   Representation by the Opposite — Freud's examples are: 'You can conjure up spirits?'
     'Yes, but they don't come'. 'I have a bath once a year whether I need one or not'.
     However, not all representations by the opposite are jokes. Some are irony.

7.   Reference to the Similar — Two Jews (again) outside the bath-house: 'Another year gone
     by already'. Not all allusions, however, are jokes.

These two last could be described as indirect representation.

Finally, there is a sub-species of these techniques — representation of something small — a
technique to be found in certain cartoons. Freud did not claim that this list of techniques
was complete. Nevertheless, it represents a wide variety of mechanisms found in jokes.

I have enumerated these mechanisms of joke-work, for a reason which I hope has gradually been
dawning upon you. All the mechanisms appear in dream-work, the process by which the latent
content of a dream (the wish fulfilment) becomes transmuted into the manifest content of our
dreams, to avoid the censoring superego. Indeed, Condensation, Displacement, Representation
by the opposite (like reaction-formation a red rag to the Maudsley Bulls) and representation
by something small are all highly important mechanisms of dream-work.

Now there are several points in this comparison of jokes and dreams that need immediate
elucidation. First, if joke-work is unconscious, how can we make jokes deliberately — as
comics can? Freud agrees that in jokes a pre-conscious thought is given over for a moment to
unconscious revision (by the techniques of jokes) and the outcome of this is at once grasped
by conscious perception. It is noteworthy that jokes normally appear involuntarily, they
'occur' to one as one speaks. If I decide at any particular moment to make a joke
deliberately, I am unlikely to be able to do it, although as I continue some may come into
my mind, probably, ideas, to be consciously censored before my audience as too banal or
obscene. All this, the involuntary genesis of jokes, supports their unconscious provenance.
Script-writers work long hours for relatively few jokes: they, like the proverbial
Englishman, need time. Thus, then, the actual techniques of jokes, even if we can consciously
imitate them are basically unconscious.

Note also that the conscious imitations of joke-work of script-writers such as Norden and
Muir who do it rapidly in panel games on the radio utilising condensation and double-meaning
are funny in a different way from natural jokes: one admires the verbal ingenuity and skill
but that is usually all. The purpose of the jokes which we shall examine in a moment is
usually missing. They are all technique.

Joke-work differs from dream-work in another important respect. The dream-work was designed
to hide the meaning of the dream. The joke-work must allow the joke to be intelligible, or it
is no joke at all. There is a further interesting point that has not been seriously studied
as yet. Fairbairn (1938) claimed that a further equivalent to dream-work, but in the realm
of art — art-work — was fundamental to the visual arts. The greatness, the universal appeal
of art lay in the disguised portrayal of the oedipal wish. The more complex the art-work,

Fairbairn argued, the greater the work of art. Although this does not always seem to be the case, as Pickford (1969) has shown, it still might be true of the joke-work. Is the quality of a joke related to the richness of its joke-work? This question remains to be answered. Or is it, perhaps more likely, related not to the technique but to the content and purpose of the joke? What is the purpose of jokes? Let us now examine the psychoanalytic view of the purpose of jokes. With respect to purpose, Freud divides jokes into two classes: innocent or trivial and what are called for lack of a better English word 'tendentious' jokes. In the innocent joke it is the technique that makes us laugh, as we have discussed before with reference to deliberate joke-making. In the tendentious joke on the other hand there are two major purposes: (1) a hostile purpose (aggression, satire or defence) and (2) an obscene purpose (exposure). The joke, like the dream, makes possible the satisfaction of an instinct, sex or aggression, that would otherwise be banned. The barrier is repression. Then Freud delightfully illustrates, mature and free from hypocrisy as he thought himself to be, that he too was a prisoner of his time. The barrier is a woman's incapacity to tolerate undisguised sexuality - the refined laugh at sexual jokes: the peasant at obscene smut. Thus the tendentious joke has two bases of humour: purpose and technique. Freud distinguishes sub-classes of tendentious jokes: cynical jokes v. institutions - the mother-in-law used to be popular, and sceptical jokes v. the certainty of knowledge itself.

With this teleological formulation the joke then becomes an important defence mechanism in one's personal adjustment. To prevent joking, as dreaming, should have dire psychological consequences. It should lead to psychopathic outbursts of rage and sexual activity, or on a less spectacular level to increased dreaming. As far as I know, there are no experiments putting this Freudian hypothesis to the test.

In tendentious jokes, the purpose is the expression of sexual or aggressive feelings which would otherwise be barred. This gives us a clue to what, in Freudian theory, is the source of pleasure in the joke. So far we have examined the technique and the purpose of the joke but have not explained the laughter. Why do we laugh? Our yield of pleasure (hence laughter) at a joke corresponds to the psychical expenditure saved by not having to repress. This saving of energy is transferred into laughter in tendentious jokes. Notice too how this accounts for individual differences in response to jokes, perhaps most often obvious in sexual jokes. What convulses one listener, in this theory, is what fits his own conflicts. 'In joco veritas'. For another the technique alone may be amusing. This, of course, sufficiently accounts in our culture for the emphasis on sexual and anal jokes and for the fact that such jokes are crude; that is, lack technique. Because of their content they need but little technique.

This, of course, applies only to tendentious jokes. With innocent jokes the saving of psychical expenditure lies in the acoustics rather than the semantics: the acoustics short-circuiting, as it were, the link between two normally distant ideas. Other sources of pleasure in jokes are mentioned by Freud who seems to regard them as almost basic instincts: rediscovering a relationship, joy of recognition, rediscovery of the familiar (the basis of topicality in jokes); the love of nonsense - a childish pleasure - when we were free of the criticisms of logic and reason. All these gain their power as sources of pleasure from the fact that we economize on psychical expenditure.

One other important aspect of pleasure in tendentious jokes needs to be mentioned. In the sexual joke, for example, the pleasure in the technique allows the joke which therefore allows us the sexual pleasure. This pleasure in technique Freud regards as forepleasure and he posited an analogous process in aesthetics where pleasure in the technique allows us to look at the picture, and thus increasingly experience the oedipal conflict.

Thus, just as the mechanism by which jokes are formed was analogous to that whence dreams originate, so the pleasure to be obtained from jokes resembles that to be found in the arts. Both express what is normally forbidden as again do dreams, although the specifically humorous pleasure has in the economy of psychical expenditure. In this way Freud has neatly encompassed the nature of humour within his more general theory. This relationship between humour, art and aesthetics implied in the Freudian theory of humour has been extensively developed by Grotjahn (1957) in 'Beyond Laughter'. Here it is pointed out that just as Freud postulated that the essence of great tragedy lay in the portrayal of the tragedy of the oedipal conflict, as in Hamlet or Oedipus Rex, so too is the case with comedy. However, in comedy the tragic guilt of the son is displaced onto the father. As once the son tried to interfere with the lovemaking of the father, so now the father attempts to interfere with the son.

The clown too is a similar depreciated important father figure, bedecked in the symbols of impotence: the huge tie, the enormous baggy trousers, the phallic nose. Only when the clowning is skilful (clown-work analogous to joke-work) and the disguise is good can we laugh. Notice how many comics have canes. Fields had a flexible billiard cue. Groucho Marx leers, cigar in mouth. This leering is the symbol of the primal scene.

Mention of the primal scene leads us on to the phenomenon of Kilroy. This according to Grotjahn is yet another oedipal disguise. Kilroy, called by some Chad, that enigmatic figure with phallic nose inviting castration, with staring eyes (drawn as + or - in some depictions) is the impudent son, the peeping Tom, who appears where he should not. The phallus erect is in his upraised thumb, the hope of the subservient soldier. Even his name (Kill roi) is oedipal.

There is a further aspect of jokes which in Freud's view differentiates them psychologically from dreams and perhaps from art. Jokes are necessarily social. One should not, indeed cannot, laugh at one's own jokes. Jokes are for other people. The third person laughs because he gets free the effect of the joke-work and thus gains the maximum economy of expenditure. However, this economy will only be effected if his inhibitions are those of the joker (as already discussed). In addition there must be the distraction of the joke-work from the real meaning of the joke or he cannot laugh. For all these reasons, Freud argues, the best jokes are short and easy to understand. For intellectual consideration kills a joke. Reading Aristophanes is not funny when every reference has to be explained. Such scrutiny leads to the meaning of the joke and it is thus rejected. Something in the technique of the joke must divert our attention from the meaning, as we argued above. This accounts for the fact that (a) only new jokes are funny, and (b) we often cannot say why a joke amuses. As in art 'I know what I like' is true of jokes although its obverse is false, that I like what I know.

The final part of this early work on humour is of less interest today being an attempt to distinguish between jokes, the comic, humour and wit. Certainly no usefully clear distinctions can be made in that Freud has difficulty in clarifying some of the examples which were previously treated as jokes. It will be sufficient to summarize the distinctions that were finally concluded.

Pleasure in jokes lies in the economy of expenditure on inhibition, as we have seen. Energy freed from repression is expended in laughter.

Pleasure in the comic lies in economy of expenditure on ideation.

Pleasure in humour lies in the economy of expenditure on feeling. This last definition of humour is of some importance because in Freudian theory humour is considered to be one of the highest defences. That is why in more than one place Freud has commended the man who can produce Gallows humour (a saving on pity). Such a man, Freud argued, is truly mature; the balance of id, ego and superego, is complete. Freud, indeed, had a taste for this himself as evidenced by his forced description of the Nazis when he finally left Vienna. 'I can thoroughly recommend them'.

All three varieties of humour, then, it may be concluded, in Freudian theory attempt to recapture that first, fine, careless rapture of childhood when our psychical energy expenditure was small when we were incapable of humour or wit and had no need of it to make us happy. Through humour our repressions may be lifted and the mechanisms by which this is brought about are analogous to those of dreaming.

At the beginning of this paper I pointed out that this first formulation on humour appeared before some of the fundamental postulates of psychoanalytic theory, notably the topological concept of mind. In his later discussion of Gallows humour Freud (1928) argued that the superego was projected onto the ego. This enables the ego to look at itself (as the superego) like a little child and thus resist the grimness of reality. This, then, is a further mechanism to facilitate the joke-work.

Such, then, is the Freudian theory of humour. As I have shown it is truly integrated into psychoanalytic theory in general. So, we may well ask, what follows? What implications does it have for the study of humour? One important feature of a theory is held to be by many philosophers of science (e.g., Popper, 1959) its capacity to generate experimentally verifiable hypotheses (perhaps the sole defence now left, incidentally of Hull). On this criterion psychoanalytic theories of humour are powerful. For example, as I have discussed elsewhere (Kline, 1972), the following hypotheses are easily derived:

(1) Individuals finding aggressive jokes funniest will be those in whom aggression is normally repressed.

(2) Individuals finding sexual jokes funniest will be those whose sexuality is normally repressed. In this instance we can be more specific:

    (a) Anal jokes will appeal most to those fixated at the anal level (this is partly supported, in any case, by the commonplace observation of primary school humour).

(b) Oral jokes will appeal most to those fixated at the oral level. (To
    quote Brigid Brophy: in air-cunnilingus you meet a better class of
    fellatio).

(c) Homosexual and transvestite jokes will appeal to those with the
    relevant repressed tastes.

(3) Those whose main defence mechanism is repression and who have a strong superego will
     be humourless (they will not laugh at jokes).

(4) Psychopaths should not find jokes amusing for they have no need to lift their
     repression in this way.

(5) Since most wit is hostile, wits will tend to have powerful unconscious aggression.

(6) Wits will be more neurotic than the normal population.

All these hypotheses, it will be noticed, refer to the best-known aspect of psychoanalytic
theories of humour, namely, the purpose of jokes. However, hypotheses can be derived from
the theories of joke-work. Thus:

(7) Highly repressed individuals should prefer jokes with complex joke-work to 'simple'
     jokes; and

(8) Joke deprivation should produce increased dreaming and/or direct expression of impulses,
     a hypothesis derived from both aspects of psychoanalytic theory.

For the most part, alas, these hypotheses have not really been put to the adequate scientific
test. In my 1972 study of the objective evidence relevant to psychoanalytic theory, 'Fact
and Fantasy in Freudian Theory', I surveyed much of the work that had been done. In a paper
of this sort it would be inappropriate to describe the experiments in detail. Generally,
however, there has been moderate support for a number of hypotheses but nobody could argue
that any of them was in any sense proven. The Cattell Humour Test of Personality (Cattell &
Luborsky, 1947) is relevant to psychoanalytic theories only in the most tangential way:
that humour does reflect differences in personality. O'Connell in a number of investigations
(e.g., O'Connell, 1964a) has put certain psychoanalytic hypotheses to the test using the 'Wit
and Humour Appreciation Test'. This consists of ten examples of hostile wit, ten of nonsense
wit and ten of humour. Adjusted subjects (as distinct from maladjusted) did prefer humour,
in accord with theory, but the question remains, of course, whether such large categories could
be sampled by ten items. A factor analytic investigation also showed that there was a factor
of gallow-humour jokes, as discussed by Freud. But this does not demand a psychoanalytic
theory to explain it. Gollob and Levine (1967) found that intellectual analysis decreased
the enjoyment of aggressive jokes, a psychoanalytic hypothesis, as we saw: the superego
theory seeing through the bribe of the joke-work. Finally Lamb (1968) was able to relate
sex guilt to the enjoyment of sexual jokes. Generally, it must be admitted that this is but
meagre support for Freudian theories of humour. It is not that they have been rejected,
rather that the experiments do not exist. This, however, is attributable in part to a severe
problem in the testing of the hypotheses.

Custom stales humour so that in any test consisting of jokes the subject may find unfunny
the very jokes that he himself knows best because he is familiar with them through use!
This would not matter in factor-analytic studies since it would mean that loadings would
emerge negative rather than positive were it not for the fact that such unfunny jokes would
be confounded with those that made no appeal because they touched no relevant repressions in
the unconscious (to assume the theory to be correct).

Some readers may feel that the title of this paper ('The Psychoanalytic Theory of Humour')
is misleading in that I concentrate solely upon classical psychoanalysis. However, there
are two reasons for this. In the first place the Freudian view of humour and wit constitutes
a number of separate hypotheses, which only careful examination can disentangle. As we have
seen there are basically three theories: (1) that jokes are formed through the mechanism
of joke-work; (2) that the laughter reflects an economy of psychical expenditure; and
(3) that the purpose of the joke is the expression of repressed wishes. Now the statement
of these three distinct theoretical claims has enabled us to clarify the Freudian view of
humour in as much as it is now evident that most of the empirically tenable hypotheses
derived from it relate to the third of these theories, while the remainder relate to the
first. The second theory seems hard, indeed, to verify and will remain so until some way is
found of quantifying psychical energy (an event unlikely in the near future). Thus I would
argue, as does Farrel (1951) in relation to Freudian theory as a whole, that in reality the
Freudian theory of humour is best considered not as a unified theory but as a collection of
hypotheses.

A second and more cogent reason is that, unlike Freud, many of the other analysts had little to say on humour, especially the major figures. Minor analysts, of course, had more to say but without objective scientific evidence there is little reason to discuss what are essentially but speculations.

In conclusion then it seems to me that Freud's theories of humour and laughter still constitute a notable attempt to integrate specific theories of how jokes are constructed, what purposes they serve, and why they make us laugh, into a general personality theory with almost no new concepts. This is what is meant by describing psychoanalytic theory as essentially parsimonious. Careful examination of these theories indicates that most workers in the field if they have been interested at all in the psychoanalytic view have concentrated their efforts on only one of the three basic theories accounting for humour. The more general and interesting proposition that links humour with aesthetics and the arts and with the origin of dreams has hardly been investigated. It is my hope that should there be another conference in a year or two, this situation will have changed.

REFERENCES

Ses Bibliography for publications on humour, laughter and comedy

Fairbairn, W.R.D., Prolegomena to a psychology of art. British Journal of Psychology, 28, 298-303 (1938).

Farrell, B.A., The scientific testing of psychoanalytic findings and theory III. British Journal of Medical Psychology, 24, 35-51 (1951).

Freud, S., The Interpretation of Dreams. Standard Edition, Volumes 4-5, (1900).

Freud, S., The Psychopathology of Everyday Life. Standard Edition, Volume 6 (1901).

Freud, S., Three Essays on the Theory of Sexuality. Standard Edition, Volume 7 (1905).

Kline, P., Fact and Fantasy in Freudian Theory. Methuen, London (1972).

Pickford, R.W., Dream-work, art-work and sublimation in relation to art therapy. Paper presented to the Annual Conference of the British Psychological Society, Edinburgh (1969).

Popper, K., The Logic of Scientific Discovery. Basic Books, New York (1959).

Sears, R.R., Survey of Objective Studies of Psychoanalytic Concepts. Bulletin 51, Social Science Research Council, New York (1943).

Humour as a Tool of Social Interaction

Thomas R. Kane, Jerry Suls, and James T. Tedeschi

State University of New York at Albany

Much of the available research and theory on the topic of humour focuses on identifying and examining factors that cause target persons to judge humorous stimuli as funny or amusing. In general this emphasis has illuminated us with regard to the intrapsychic functions of humour. There has, however, been a general neglect of the social functions that humour serves. Although the present paper cannot exhaustively cover the social aspects of humour, it is the precursor of a more comprehensive treatise examining the social functions of humour for both the source and target. The present prospectus is designed to jog readers' consideration of humour as an instrument of social influence. Thus, we briefly consider the generally unattended question of why humour is initiated. At least a partial answer focuses on the social influence functions that humour serves.

Psychologists have long assumed that persons do not initiate actions unless there is apt to be something gained from it - either the pull of an incentive or the push of punishment. Consistent with this assumption is the assertion that a source does not emit humorous statements unless he expects to achieve some interpersonal purpose by so doing. Humour is unique to humans. It is essentially a social psychological phenomenon and not merely a biological release or a cognitive process. Once the question is asked regarding why a source of communication directs a humorous statement at a particular target, intuition can be put to work to develop some hypotheses that might be worthy of investigation. In any case, a shift of emphasis would encourage more research concerning the source of humour and his purpose in using it.

It might be worthwhile, before we discuss the social influence functions of humour to mention how the present analysis differs from Martineau's model, as the latter is prototypical of other social analyses of humour. Martineau's analysis focuses on how humour is used to initiate and facilitate communication and how it fosters the development of social relationships, for example by esteeming one's ingroup and disparaging the outgroup. We have no disagreement with this model; however, it fails to take into account or explain why humour should be used where praise or criticism would seemingly serve just as well. In addition, Martineau's theory, because of its sociological cast, focuses on the importance of humour for group behaviour. The present analysis is equally applicable to the relationship between the individual and his group and with other single individuals.

SOCIAL INFLUENCE FUNCTIONS OF HUMOUR

What interpersonal goals can humour help the source to achieve? Answers to this question will illustrate our contention that humour serves as an instrument of social influence. Its use can help the source to claim or disclaim responsibility for his actions, can reveal courage or relieve embarrassment, may invoke normative commitments or release the individual from commitments. Humour can serve such purposes because it generally can be interpreted in several different ways at the same time. The reason for this is that humour carries with it a cue that it is non-serious, that it is play. This means that the source can communicate a message and then take it back if need be by simply saying 'it was only a joke'. In fact, since everyone is aware of the ambiguous nature of humour the disclaimer may not even be necessary. At any rate the source can to some extent decide how he wishes his statement or action to be interpreted if he couches it in humorous terms.

The notion that because humour can be interpreted in several different ways it allows the source, target or audience substantial flexibility of behaviour is suggested by the results of several studies. For example, in an investigation by Suls and Miller (1976) subjects read a description of a group discussion in which a man told an anti-women's liberation joke

to either a group of conservative women or to a group of liberated women. The group of
women either laughed or glared at the joke source. Subjects were then asked to estimate the
man's actual opinion of women's liberation. The results were somewhat surprising; when the
man told the joke to the liberated audience and they laughed, he was seen as liberated but
when the same audience glared he was seen as most chauvinistic. Less extreme attributions
were made when the man addressed the conservative audience. The authors suggest that the
man was seen as most liberated when the liberated audience laughed because the subjects
assumed that the group knew he was teasing and that he did not really agree with the content
of his joke (otherwise why would they laugh?). When the liberated women reacted negatively,
the subjects used this as an indication that he was in dead earnest and was critical of
women's liberation. It would appear that the ambiguity that surrounds humour allows for the
rather substantial shift in its perceived meaning depending on situational factors. Below
we consider some of the social functions that can be achieved by humour precisely because of
its ambiguous nature.

Self-disclosure and Social Probing

Persons continually explore their social environments in order to ascertain what values or
incentives exist for them and what other persons are significant, powerful or expert in terms
of mediating rewards or information. Persons are also naturally interested in fathoming
what intentions, motives, and values these relevant others possess. Standards of propriety
may prohibit a person from directly asking others about these matters. A less direct approach
would be to make a humorous remark that communicates the source's interest: presumably, if
the target laughs and later reciprocates with a similar form of humour, the social
relationship has moved toward more intimacy without committing either party in such a way
that he or she could be called to account for their actions.

Davis and Farina (1970) reported an experiment which demonstrated subjects' use of humour as
a self-disclosure tactic, and as a probe to elicit reciprocation from the target. Male
subjects were exposed to either a rather plain female experimenter or the same person made
up to be sexually attractive and provocative. The subjects were presented with aggressive
and sexual jokes and asked to rate how funny they were. Half of the subjects performed the
ratings on pencil and paper scales and the other half provided their ratings orally to the
experimenter. An interaction was obtained showing that the male subjects rated the sex-
related materials as most funny when their ratings were made orally to a sexually provocative
female. The authors suggested that these males wanted the attractive experimenter to know
that they were sexually interested in her and when they were given a socially sanctioned
opportunity to indicate that they enjoyed sex, they did so.

Of course, sex is not the only taboo subject that may be most delicately approached through
indirect and noncommital means. During time of danger, such as occurs in warfare and
concentration camps, the individual might want social comparison information about the
extent of danger, the imminence of death, and the degree of fear experienced by others.
Standards of bravery and manliness prevent many men from asking direct questions about fear.
Gal'ows humour may serve to manage the impression of courage in the presence of others and
to elicit information regarding the situation and the feelings of others. In these
circumstances failure by the target to laugh may serve to indicate that he or she is deeply
afraid and may create more concern in the source. On the other hand, hearty laughter by
others may serve to indicate less danger and fear, thereby increasing the resolve or morale
of the relevant parties to the interaction.

While lack of space prevents consideration of all circumstances in which humour might be
used as a self-disclosure and probing tool, clearly the common feature of such occasions is
that the source wishes to communicate a value, intention or motive to another in such a way as
to allow a disclaimer that the communication had any serious purpose.

Emerson (1969) has similarly proposed that jokes contain implicit messages about serious
topics and that underlying the exchange of humour is a negotiation regarding whether to
transpose the repartee into a more serious discussion. A question remains concerning which
party should accept responsibility for giving interaction a serious purpose. Thus, the
ambiguity associated with the 'real' meaning assigned to humorous statements by the source
allows him or her to take interpersonal initiatives that otherwise would be too risky.

Decommitment

When a person faces failure, a false identity is about to be unmasked, an inappropriate
behaviour is discovered or a lie uncovered, he may attempt to save the situation by
indicating that the proposed or past action was not serious, but was instead meant as a
joke. Children are unskilled at turning a social disaster into a joke and hence allow too

long a time interval to transpire between the action in question and the revelation of its
nonserious purpose. Hence, timing seems to be important to the success of this tactical use
of humour.

The use of humour as a decommitment tactic is essentially one of denying any harmful
intention for an action. For example, if a source threatens a target and provokes a counter-
threat, he may smile and indicate that he had been kidding all along. This tactic might
also take the source off the hook when a target fails to comply and it comes time to back up
the threat (put up or shut up). If the source does not want to incur the costs that are
associated with harming others, he might lose his reputation for credibility; however,
converting the situation into one of playful banter both saves the relationship from
deteriorating into one of conflict between the parties and removes the source from a critical
test of his credibility. Laughter by the target indicates a tacit agreement by him or her
to treat the source's prior behaviour as nonserious. Of course the target might take the
initiative in a threat-laden situation by refusing to treat the source's threat as a serious
influence attempt. This tactic might cause the source to reconsider his initiative, and if
he then laughs, both parties can then act as if no threat had been issued.

The use of humour as a decommitment tactic amounts to a declaration by the source that he
did not have any intention of maintaining or carrying out or treating seriously an action
that had been initially started. In a complementary way, laughter by the target person or
other observers indicates that they did not, or would not make, or would reverse an attribution
of serious intention to the source. However, the longer the delay between initial action
and later humorous attempts to decommit the source, the greater the suspicion that the action
did have a serious intention behind it.

A sense of relief often accompanies a decommitment from a potentially disastrous social
interaction. This relation of tensions has often been noted by theorists and interpreted as
catharsis.

Face-saving

Tolstoy tells of a particularly resentful cossack who encountered a commissar in what could
have been a serious altercation; however, a rather well-respected cossack made a joke in
the middle of the hostile exchange between the two. This had the effect of making those
around him laugh and it served to defuse the situation so that no face was lost by either of
the contending parties backing off from the confrontation.

People are embarrassed when an identity they are fostering in front of others is seriously
undermined by events. A dignified and stately senior ambassador may be embarrassed if he
spills food on his clothing during a formal dinner engagement because such a faux pas
indicates lack of social grace. One way to save the situation is to joke about it. That
is, the persons present (either the ambassador or anyone else) can treat the event as a
trivial one, merely an accident that could happen to anyone - and hence allow the ambassador
to maintain his identity as dignified and stately. Of course the ambassador would owe a
social debt to anyone who helped him preserve his image, and the hope of gaining the
ambassador's special favour would serve as a motivation to help him. It could be expected,
therefore, that the more powerful, prestigeful, or attractive the person whose identity is
endangered by an embarrassing event, the more likely it would be that a bystander would use
humour as a device to help restore his identity. Failure by others to laugh may suggest
that their image of the embarrassed person has been changed by the incident.

Humour as an Unmasking Tactic

Ridicule, sarcasm, caricature, cartoons, and satire are used to reject an identity preferred
by particular persons, groups, institutions, or nations. Often, as in Aesop's Fables, these
uses of humour are disguised in symbolic form so that no one can clearly hold the source
accountable for embarrassing them. The political cartoon may isolate a statement or impute
an intention to an important authority to highlight what the author believes to be the
essential motivation for his or her behaviour. A satire may have the purpose of showing the
absurdity of certain mannerisms, class privilege, professional pretensions, institutional
rules, etcetera. Laughter by an audience indicates acceptance and agreement with the
source's interpretations.

In face-to-face interactions poking fun at or ridiculing or putting down another person
amounts to a refusal to accept the identity projected by the target and the meaning of the
social situation that the identity implies. While persons normally act in such a way as to
negotiate and agree on each other's identity and the definition of the social situation,
the source may believe the target's identity (if accepted at face value) would give the
latter such an advantage in the interaction that it becomes unacceptable. If the situation

is a competitive one, and each person is seeking to form coalitions with others, it may be important to puncture a particularly positive identity projected by competitors.

Humour as an Antecedent of Interpersonal Attraction

Given the advantages of being liked (cf. Tedeschi, 1974) it is understandable why persons engage in considerable effort to get others to like them. With regard to humour, a cheerful demeanour is an invitation to interaction. Ready humour indicates a spontaneity and joy in relating to others, indicates a willingness to explore alternatives with others prior to making serious overtures, reveals an ability to see through pretensions and the deceptions of others, and conveys the goodwill and benevolence of the source. A jovial person is often perceived as a socially sensitive person, who is personable and fun to be with. In a very real way humour breaks down affectations and conveys a basic honesty in a relationship. Thus, much fun can be generated in an interaction where the parties want each to like the other(s).

There is empirical evidence suggesting that individuals who use humour are seen as likeable. Mettee, Hrelec, and Wilkens (1971) had undergraduate subjects rate a job candidate who gave a short lecture. Half of the subjects were told the candidate was reputed to be aloof and detached, the other half were told he was reputed to be clownish. At the end of his lecture the candidate told a joke. The results indicated that liking for both communicators tended to increase with increases in humour.

There is also evidence that when people are feeling good (i.e., experience a positive arousal state), they judge others as more attractive and are more likely to engage in prosocial behaviour. Humour also serves to attract and hold the attention of others. The combination of these effects encourages orators to begin their speeches with a humorous story and to sprinkle witticisms throughout.

Humour as Ingratiation Tactic

Serious attempts at ingratiation, including self-enhancement, other-enhancement, opinion conformity, self-deprecation, and feigned interpersonal similarity are intended to garner special favours from a powerful other person. The risk of ingratiation, however, is that one's insincerity will be unmasked, and this risk increases with the mount of advantage that can be gained and the degree of power held by the target. If ingratiation tactics are carried out in a humorous fashion, such as in a self-enhancing story, it makes no sense for the audience to seriously question the identity presented in the story and yet the positive image does get conveyed.

Since laughter is often a sign that the audience has accepted the source's humour for its intended purposes (whatever they are), laughter can be used as a form of ingratiation (a form of opinion conformity). Observation suggests that the higher the status of a dignitary, the more likely the same joke, story, or pun is to evoke laughter from the audience.

CONCLUSION

In summary, we have proposed that the source's use of humour serves as a rather safe way of self-disclosing taboo interests or values and to probe the values, intentions, and/or motives of others, is a decommitment tactic allowing the source to dissociate himself from responsibility for performing a prior action, is a face-saving device that helps preserve a person's identity after an embarrassing incident, is an unmasking tactic that reveals the hypocrisy and pretensions of persons, groups, institutions, and nations, provides a basis for forming positive and long-standing relationships with others, and allows for safe practice of ingratiation of powerful others. In each instance, laughter can be used to initiate a cognitive transformation of a situation into a non-serious one or it may indicate acceptance of the meanings conveyed by a source of humour. Finally, obtaining scientific knowledge about the source of humour may have a revolutionary impact on current views about the target since the latter's responses may in fact be related to the source's purposes and thus not be the product solely of intrapsychic processes.

REFERENCES

See Bibliography for publications on humour, laughter and comedy

Tedeschi, J.T., Attributions, liking and power. In: T. Huston (Ed.), Foundations of Interpersonal Attraction. Academic Press, New York (1974).

American Humour and the Spirit of the Times

Lawrence E. Mintz

American Studies Program, University of Maryland

However deep-seated and universal the psychology of humour may be, clearly most of its manifestations are culture-bound — connected to realities of time and place. Humour as a cultural and historical phenomenon is not merely a matter of content; such elements as form, style, structure, and convention reveal values, beliefs, and concerns.

For this reason, just as the psychologist, anthropologist, and sociologist find humour useful to the study of thought and behaviour, the historian is tempted to use it as a source of insight into the past, or as an index to the development of a national character, a public opinion, a 'Zeitgeist'. Knowing that the comprehension and appreciation of humour is often particular to a nation, region, or social group, and that yesterday's hilarity is often merely bewildering today (while conversely, interestingly, the tragedy and melodrama of the past frequently seems funny in the present), he assumes that humour is a potentially useful tool.

But how is this tool to be used? The problems of material and method are enormous, perhaps even overwhelming. To be sure, scholars such as Constance Rourke (1953), Walter Blair (1960), Norris Yates (1964), and Jesse Bier (1968), among the many others working with American humour, have been undeterred, drawing broad conclusions and generalizations from often rather arbitrarily chosen sources, and assuming without much, if any, methodological questioning that the literary humourist is a valid spokesman for his audience, which is in turn representative of the population of the time.

Recent examinations of the methods of intellectual history and the so-called 'American Studies Approach' challenge effectively such carefree relationships with documentary sources. What do we know about the significance of the joke anthology, novel, newspaper column, platform lecture, play, poem, short story, film, television programme, comic strip, cartoon, nightclub performance, record or other such source of humour upon which our cultural analyses rest? How was the material received, by whom, why? Who laughed at what, with what degree of intensity? Was laughter generated by a recognition of the foolishness of the world perceived as realistically portrayed, or by a sense of fantasy which was comic because of its incongruity with the world as the audience knew it? Who knows? How will we ever know? In short, the student of the history of humour is troubled, or at least he should be troubled, by the theoretical problems of both humour studies and historiography.

So far, at least, the theoreticians in both fields have come up with little to resolve these problems, but their negative critique is not without value. If nothing else, it encourages caution and humility. The researcher must beware of generalizations based upon single or too few sources, of sources chosen for aesthetic or personal reasons rather than for the likelihood that they are representative, and he must be careful not to phrase his speculations, hypotheses, and generalizations as though they were empirical results or logical proofs. And then, having exercised such caution and humility, he can say the hell with it, plunge right in, and have fun. Since we are not scientists, we can define truth as that which is acceptable to the 'intelligent community' (which is unofficially defined as those who agree with me), and try to make as much sense as we can. Provocative arguments are certainly as interesting, and probably as useful as more limited, tightly-controlled scientific forays into the world of humour.

An examination of American humour over the years prompts many generalizations including the search for basic fundamental, identifying characteristics, and the exploration of the differences in the humour of various periods. It is apparent that while some aspects of American humour remain constant, or at least reappear regularly and frequently, some significant changes can be noted. It is with one of these changes, the reversal of the positive attitude toward the democratic hero, that this paper will deal as an example of the kind of historical and cultural insight the study of humour might suggest.

The thesis presented here is that American humour reveals an ambivalent attitude toward democracy, and toward the faith in the common man, and the idea of progress which has been so closely connected with the democratic system, and that this ambivalence has leaned increasingly toward cynicism and disbelief. This paper does not try to account for the change in attitude, not does it argue that the reflection of a theme in humour is self-sufficiently a proof of a national character or attitude, but what it does imply is that, because humour is a significant expression of belief, disposition, and concern, the increasingly negative portrayal of the common-man is an important and interesting phenomenon. It should be pointed out that the thesis is neither entirely original nor particularly surprising to students of American humour. Many historical overviews - particularly those of Bier and Yates - suggest, if they do not state, the position offered here. But the connection between trends in humour and the social situations with which they deal is too often treated as tangential, peripheral rather than as central, and the emphasis is most frequently an aesthetic rather than a cultural appraisal.

Another qualification is necessary. While this paper maintains that the negative attitude toward democracy and the cynical stance toward the efficacy of our system grows steadily over the history of our humour, it is recognized that the basic ambivalence was there in the beginning - that is, that anti-democratic humour exists in the earliest humour - and that it remains in the present; that is, that positive, pro-democratic humour can be found today. However the continual counterbalance does no more than particular exceptions to repudiate the recognition of the trend. It should also be pointed out that since this is an exploration of one particular premise rather than itself a survey of the history of American humour, the examples which are referred to are intended to illustrate rather than to substantiate the contentions. The legitimacy of the thesis cannot possibly be upheld in so brief an exercise whose purpose must be to suggest and to describe that which can only be confirmed by a thorough, inclusive study.

Despite the existence of some early, imitative Tory satire, and some anti-bumpkin humour in Colonial and early national journals and plays, the thrust of pre-twentieth century American humour is clearly democratic (cf. Blair, 1960; Rourke, 1931). The central figure of much of the material is the wise fool, and while this character is hardly original, having his origins in Old Testament, mediaeval, Shakespearean, and even primitive, tribal traditions, the use to which he is put in nineteenth century American humour is revealing (cf. Mintz, 1969). In his first, most simple phase, the wise fool is essentially a negative figure, exposing folly through his reflection of it in his thoughts and action. The use of this first-stage wise fool is not unknown in American humour (e.g., Seba Smith's Jack Downing), but for the most part the figure evolves toward a second stage in which the naif, the innocent, exposes folly by his simple, honest, matter-of-fact purity and good nature (e.g., Brother Jonathan in Tyler's 'The Contrast'), and a third stage in which he becomes the positive model - the commonsense philosopher. Understandably the third stage wise fool figure is most important to nineteenth century American humour. He is the vehicle by which the norms, values, opinions and attitudes toward democracy, progress, and social goals can be expressed; an archetypal hero articulating the core of America's self-definition.

As my own above-cited work on the wise fool figure demonstrates, Brother Jonathan and his cousins do not disappear in the twentieth century, but they are steadily replaced in prominence and significance by two new central figures, who are, to use Yates' terms, the 'solid citizen' and the 'white collar neurotic' or 'moral bumbler'. Yates considers these characters to be developments of the wise fool. But if the solid citizen resembles the commonsense philosopher, the latter's honest observations begin to sound pompous, cliched, and unrealistic, and if the antihero, loser figure has much in common with the negative fool, the naif, and even the trickster, at times, it is quite clear that the archetypal 'middle-American' has become the butt rather than the vehicle of the humour.

Needless to say the change does not take place overnight, nor does it conveniently fit into neat periods by starting exactly in 1900 and lasting exactly twenty years, but it is possible to view the years from the late 1890's to the mid-1920's as a distinct phase in the development of American humour. One can give countless examples from literature, journalism, comic strips, and the silent film of the point that democratic man is no longer viewed as the confident, controlling, debunking, exposing figure but is now, rather, seen as the victim, the weakling, the confused, and the oppressed. To be sure, the portrait is not yet entirely negative; Chaplin's tramp does survive, retain his dignity and jauntiness, occasionally even prevail, and our sympathies are clearly with Jiggs despite his helplessness in the face of his wife and mother-in-law. But authority figures - universally the butt of humour, now include the typical American father, and the hero begins to get lost amidst the victims. The silent films and the comic strips are transitional elements in this process. The Katzenjammer kids do triumph over the bully (the father), and the mother is quite the commonsense philosopher, Keaton and Langdon as well as Chaplin redeem their weak heroes, but we are heading toward Dagwood Bumstead, a victim without redeeming features in a world without any admirable figures, toward the mood of Chaplin's 'Modern Times' and the cartoons of Rube Goldberg, where the machine is master and man exists to make a fool of himself while trying to cope. The popular humour magazines, 'Life', 'Puck', 'Judge', 'Vanity Fair', begin to provide a social satire that will contribute considerably to the next phase of the evolution of twentieth century American humour, the so-called 'golden age' of the nineteen-twenties and thirties.

The two terms that typify the humour of the 'golden age' are aggression and insanity. It is interesting that two decades so different in economic and political climate produce a humour which, while displaying some definite differences (e.g., Mencken's fall from grace in the thirties), provides a distinct period of similar trends. Again the same themes, moods, and tones emerge from many different media sources. In literature the work of the Algonquin/ 'New Yorker' school, in films the Marx Brothers and W.C. Fields, in the comics, Herriman's 'Krazy Kat', in the social-satire cartoons in the magazines, and in radio humour, one finds an aggressive, cynical, combative, iconoclastic spirit merging with nonsense, chaos, 'anarchy', and destructiveness. Thurber, Parker, Benchley, White, and Marquis grow progressively more bitter, more negative, and more unredemptive as the thirties era develops, but the seeds of all of their work have been clearly sown in the twenties. The aggressive wit of Mencken, Groucho, Fred Allen, Herriman, and numerous other humourists is not a reaction to the depression years, but to a new, and pervasive anti-social mood. It is true that the romantic, 'screwball' comedies of Lubitsch, and the social comedies of Sturges and Capra are, to some extent, an exception to the trend, but as several film critics have noted, the redemptive, positive, 'happy ending' aspect of the comedy films of the period is an artificial element grafted on to an essentially negative social satire (the reasons for this phenomenon are variously explained, but even if we were to accept the idea that a totally different comic principle is at work in those films, the exception would disturb, not damage the thesis (cf. Durgnat, 1970; Hansen, 1974, this volume; Nast, 1973). It is interesting to note that the lampooning of the democratic hero is by no means entirely an elitist, or 'tory' phenomenon. While one might want to categorize the New Yorker school, Mencken, and some of the others as essentially Rightist, the Marx Brothers, Will Rogers, Sinclair Lewis (in Babbitt, particularly) and others come to a similar conclusion from an opposite point of departure.

During the 'golden age' American humour becomes increasingly self-deprecating. It is true that Mencken, Parker, Will Rogers and other wits still take out after the fools, prudes, hypocrites, and other villains, but in the words of Walt Kelly's Pogo (used in this context before his birth, of course) 'we have met the enemy and he is us'. Chaplin recognizes the difference when he laments:

> Modern humor frightens me a little. The Marx Brothers are frightening. Thurber, Stewart, Joe Cook, Benchley - yes, all of them. They say, 'all right, this is how we live and we'll live that way'. They go in for being crazy. It's a soul- destroying thing. They say, 'all right, you're insane, we'll appeal to your insanity'. They make insanity the convention. They make humor a premise. Acquiescense in everything disintegrating. Knocking everything down. There's no conduct in their humour. They haven't any attitude. It's up to date, of course - a part of the chaos. I think it's transitional. (cf. Eastman, 1936).

Again we must be reminded that negativism, chaos, nihilism, and hostile, aggressive wit were not entirely new elements in American humour; they are readily found in folk and literary humour a century before the golden age - but Chaplin is right in his last few sentences - there is an absence of 'conduct' and 'attitude' in the newer humour, that is, an absence of a moral norm, or specific satiric focus. And he is right that it is transitional, at least in the sense that it stands mid-way between a budding social criticism and a basically defeatist world view.

Interestingly Chaplin's criticism of the humour of the thirties sounds exactly like Jesse Bier's criticism of more modern humour, offered in defence of the thesis that the twenties and thirties were golden years followed by a 'decline' and 'fall'. Bier (1968), along with many other critics of American humour, argues that the humour of the forties and fifties represents a distinct low point in the history of humour in America and from an aesthetic point of view, at least, it is not easy to assail that position. The humour of the forties, fifties, and early sixties is alternatingly silly (banal, escapist - the romantic film comedies carried to the worst possible conclusion) and sick (the rage of 'sick jokes' the most obvious example).

Without even entering into the decline/fall debate, it is important to recognize that a social view of the humour of this period is consistent with the evolutionary trend of twentieth century American humour. Some of the decline/fall critics argue that it was impossible to laugh after World War Two, the Cold War and 'the bomb', but this position ignores the humour of the period, and the fact that laughter is evident in equally threatening and perilous

times (e.g., the Depression, and perhaps our own era). What one does find in this period is
a continuation of many of the same trends of the previous one, with perhaps less imagination
and enthusiasm, and the continuation of the drift toward an even more thorough negativism.
The radio, film, and literary humourists walk the same ground, a bit more wearily; there are
a few bright lights in the comic strip and cartoon (Kelly, Mauldin, Herblock), and there is
the birth of television comedy.

Among the more interesting developments of this period in American humour are the films of
Jerry Lewis and the birth of 'Mad' magazine. American critics find both of these subjects
more suitable for adolescents, but one should not ignore their significance. The clown-zany-
child-grotesque created by Lewis, more appreciated in France than in the States (perhaps
because he's less painful at a distance, but with French critics, the real reason is anyone's
guess) is in the tradition of the European jester, but he looks exactly like a normal, healthy,
all-American teenager — until he moves or opens his mouth. It is my opinion that the French
could appreciate his clowning because they view him as an exception, a grotesque in the
literal, traditional sense, but Americans — expecially intellectual, adult, 'responsible'
Americans — are scared by him because he is too real, believable, and in an exaggerated way,
of course, too typical.

'Mad' magazine's motto, 'What, me worry?', is also a threat to an optimistic, positive outlook.
Melvin is very much a Jerry Lewis type, and what is worse, he mocks the verities which earlier
kiddie-literature worked so hard to inculcate. Perhaps Theodore Roszak overstates the case
when he credits 'Mad' with a great role in creating the iconoclastic, cynical, sceptical mood
in the counter culture of the late-sixties, but 'Mad' did reveal a popular social satire whose
target is often the mainstream of American life and belief.

The variety comedians — Berle, Caesar, Skelton, Buttons et al — offer little that is new,
borrowing from radio, vaudeville and film for almost all of their output, but the much-
maligned situation comedy (also a borrowed format — from radio), illustrates that the decline
is not so much one of the humour as it is the continuing fate of modern man. Critic John
Leonard describes, in an amusing, if over-simplified way, the history of this genre:

> In the fifties, that flabby decade, the sitcom proposed as a paradigm the
> incompetent father, the dizzy mother, the innocent child. In the sixties, it
> proposed the incompetent father, the dizzy mother, the innocent child, war as
> a fun thing, and young women with supernatural powers (witch, genie, magical
> nanny, flying nun) who could take care of their men and their children, look cute
> and never leave the house. In the seventies it proposes the incompetent father,
> the dizzy mother, the innocent child — all sitting around discussing abortion,
> infidelity, impotence, homosexuality, drug addiction and death — and the career
> girl (have talent, need sex). The inability of the American father to lace up
> the shoes of his own mind without falling off his rocker has been constant,
> perfectly reflecting and perpetuating our cultural expectations. (Leonard, 1976).

In this sitcom we have the ultimate in self-deprecating humour. The brilliant Lucy struggles
valiantly for success, stardom, excitement — and gets chaos and confusion. The helpless,
hapless fathers are no longer shocking in their ineffectuality — as Leonard suggests, we
have come to expect their failures. If, as in the film comedies, there is a redemption
brought about by the 'happy end' and the fact that they are loved despite their worthlessness,
it is a cosmetic and a palliative, not an alternate view.

Contemporary American humour perhaps reveals the completed process. Since the mid-1960's there
has been something of a renaissance (in terms of both quantity and quality) of American humour,
and the trend toward a social satire ridiculing the norm rather than the aberration has
continued. Again almost every comic genre presents a similar picture, from the stand-up
comedians who are either self-deprecating or unrelentingly hostile (Alan King, Bill Cosby,
Godfrey Cambridge, Woody Allen, Don Rickels and a host of others) to the 'National Lampoon',
'Doonesbury', films such as 'Dr. Strangelove', 'M.A.S.H.', and 'Nashville', to the devastating
political humour, 'legitimate' and 'underground', prompted by the war in Vietnam and
Watergate. In literature the prevalence of absurdist or 'black humour', to-be-sure a
phenomenon neither American nor contemporary in origin, attests to the final stage of an
anti-democratic, anti-optimistic, anti-progressive humour. Samuel Beckett describes this
mood:

> The bitter laugh laughs at that which is not good, it is the ethical laugh.
> The hollow laugh laughs at that which is not true, it is the intellectual
> laugh.... But the mirthless laugh is the dianoetic laugh, down the snout —
> Haw! — so. It is the laugh of laughs, the _risus purus_, the laugh laughing at
> the laugh, the beholding, saluting of the highest joke, in a word the laugh
> that laughs — silence please, at that which is unhappy. (From Watt, quoted by
> Rudy Cohn, In: Corrigan, 1965).

One has little difficulty applying Beckett's description to the writings of Bartholeme, Pynchon, Donleavy, Friedman, and a number of other modern American writers.

Popular humour, however, is not so obviously nihilistic. 'Black humour' does influence the more popular forms (a Carole Burnett television hour of a few seasons ago offered the spectacle of two husbands murdered in two separate sketches – hardly rose-coloured humour), but the more typical negation is that of the modern situation comedy – that, for example – of the 'House of Lear' ('All in the Family', 'Maude', 'The Jeffersons', 'Sanford and Son' and so on). What we have here is neither a new form (it is basically identical to the old sitcom), nor an original concept (two of the programmes are English in origin), nor significantly new themes (the 'issues' are treated superficially and are mere excuses for the characters to behave in their expected manner). The maturation of the sitcom is due to the recognizable, believable characters. In the fifties and early sixties the ideal, mythic American family was exposed, in the contemporary social satire (in the other genres as well as in the sitcom) as another step in a process of self-examination that began around the turn of the century.

We are left, of course, with the problem of accounting for, and assessing the significance of these changes in American humour. Do they indicate that Americans have lost faith in the democratic ideals, or do they reflect an audience secure enough, confident enough to laugh at a situation to which they consider themselves to be distant, superior? Is the humour a critical appraisal of the contemporary reality, a ritualized escape from it, or a means of de-fusing it with laughter?

Humour is so complex a phenomenon that perhaps it is all of the above. An historical appraisal suggests that American humour has provided both an opportunity to express ideals and beliefs, and an opportunity to examine, critique, and question whether these ideals and beliefs are valid and whether they have been achieved in reality.

REFERENCES

See Bibliography for publications on humour, laughter and comedy

Leonard, J., And a picture tube shall lead them. Playboy, June (1976).

Mintz, L.E., Brother Jonathan's city cousin: the urban wise fool in twentieth century American social and political satire. Unpublished doctoral dissertation, Michigan State University (1969).

The Appeasement Function of Mirthful Laughter

William F. Fry, Jr.

Stanford University, California

One of the secondary findings of my research on the respiratory components of mirthful laughter posed an apparent paradox. This paradox was precipitated by the finding that mirthful laughter causes a consistent and complete disruption of the usual physiological respiratory cycle.

Mirthful laughter, like cyclic physiological breathing, consists of varying combinations of expiration, inspiration, and interval pause. These basic elements are affected in their occurrence in each individual laugh by the influence of seven parameters. These parameters are: duration (both of total laugh and of each component element), magnitude (of component expiration and inspiration), predominance of component elements, element frequency, element sequence, element rhythmicity, expiration/inspiration respiratory excursion level. Each laugh can be systematically described by analysis of its basic elements, according to the influence of these parameters.

When mirthful laughter intervenes, its respiratory pattern completely replaces that of the usual regular, rhythmic respiration. With its complexity and multiformity, laughter appears to precipitate utter respiratory chaos. This disruptive effect presents a paradox. Laughter, a frequent and ubiquitous human phenomenon, disturbs one of life's most basic survival activities - physiological respiration cycling. Obviously, the degree of disturbance is not crucial, or there would be no laughing or no life. But, laughter thus seems to come into conflict with the evolutionary tendency. How has laughter escaped the pruning axe of unrelenting evolution?

Other respiratory behaviour may affect physiological cycling, to varying degrees. Most professional speakers and vocalists learn breath control measures to minimize the impact on respiration of the extreme forms of articulation which are their stock-in-trade. But the usual effects of speech and singing are relatively small. Their articulation rides on the expiratory side of the breathing cycle and little modifies inspiration - so that modification of expiration takes place but the underlying expiration/inspiration alternation experiences modest variation. Sobbing approaches laughter in its disruptive impact. On the other hand, sobbing occurs less frequently during ordinary life than does laughter.

Man's direct ancestry has now been shown by the Leakeys in Africa to extend back at least three-and-a-half million years. First hints of hominid anatomical features exist in fossils twelve to fourteen million years old. This extended lineage proves the contemporary human race is no recent upstart mutant, and has been exposed to the same evolutionary pressures as other organisms. The slow, unrelenting selection process pertains for human development.

Fossils of several human-like species demonstrate the process in actual operation. These species were contemporaries, at various times in prehistory, of Man's direct ancestors, but were different in some crucial way and did not survive evolutionary culling. Richard Leakey stated: '(these fossils destroy) the notion that all early fossils can be arranged in an orderly sequence of evolutionary change.' A relatively recent example of this elimination process is the gradual disappearance of the Neanderthal during the period 50,000 to 20,000 B.C.

Laughter also, like Mankind, is certainly no newcomer to the evolutionary arena. This likelihood is substantially indicated by several factors. One derives from the increasing scientific belief that human cognitive abilities began their emergence prior to the evolutionary separation into distinct species of man and the higher apes - at least chimpanzee and gorilla. This belief is based in part on the now well-established knowledge that both chimpanzees and gorillas are capable of symbolic communication and manipulation of abstract concepts. An ever-increasing band of apes carries on ever-increasing volumes of communication with humans, with proficiency and even with what might pass for humour in some unsophisticated circles.

Another indication of this long history of laughter in the human behavioural repertoire is found in information about the beginnings of human language, which no doubt postdated the beginnings of human laughter. Data from several sources suggest that language was gradually established during a prolonged epoch one to two million years ago. Stone tools dated to that period manifest a level of technological development considered by anthropologists to be impossible without language. Anatomical features of the interior walls of fossil hominid skulls are compatible with brain features related to speech production. Handedness — a pre-requisite for language skill — is indicated by ancient artifacts. And the 'common ancestor' dating factor is again brought into play by a recent study reported by Yeni-Komshian and Benson. This study revealed that the brain left-right Sylvian fissure asymmetry — indicative of language function — approaches similarity for man and chimpanzee, whereas rhesus monkey brains show no difference of significance between left and right fissure lengths.

Also significant is the affirmation by several contemporary scientists — Jane Goodall, Arthur Riopelle, R.J. Andrew, Dian Fossey, Francine Patterson, and Lawrence Pinneo and myself — that man shares laughter with gorillas, chimpanzees and orangutans. This information is no surprise to anyone who has carefully studied Darwin's 'Expression of the Emotions.' In that volume he wrote, 'If a young chimpanzee be tickled ...... a more decided chuckling or laughing sound is uttered....' 'Young orangs, when tickled, likewise grin and make a chuckling sound...' I, myself, have heard this 'chuckling or laughing sound' produced by all these three primate species mentioned and can state that the behaviour is similar in all three, and its basic characteristics are similar to those of a common form of human laughter.

Combining the conclusions from these three areas of study — cognitive skill, language acquisition, and laughter behaviour — results in an integrated argument for the early appearance of laughter in the behaviour of the evolving human species. And that early appearance of laughter indicates its unquestionable exposure to the irresistible pressures of natural selection. This long-term exposure underlines the paradox inherent in laughter's persistence and expansion in human affairs, despite its disruptive effect on the life-sustaining normal respiratory cycling.

But we know that there are really no paradoxes in Nature, only insofar as humans conceive them. Paradox marks the frontier boundary of human intelligence. What is paradoxical is only what humans do not as yet understand. Some paradoxes are presently unassailable, requiring some evolutionary advance before they can be resolved. Others are subject to resolution with ingenuity, or new information, or both.

I was tantalized and stimulated by the challenge of this paradox presented by laughter's effect on respiration. I believed that any factor resolving the paradox would have to be of powerful influence in human life, would probably provide significant information about humour, and must address the survival issue. The matter could be compared with that of eating. The immediate digestive response to ingestion of food creates a temporary disadvantage for other body systems — such as the muscular system, through competition for primacy of blood circulation. But the survival benefit of food intake is so obviously powerful, no question can exist as to its evolutionary status. The factor resolving laughter's paradox would be of a comparable importance to, at least, human existence, but would not be of such basic importance as nutrition since laughter presents itself in much more narrow scope than does nutrition. Also, considering laughter's relatively primitive origins, it must be assumed that the function of the resolving factor is primitive, existing as an active force today beneath our complex and sophisticated contemporary behaviour.

During my investigation of this paradox, I discussed its nature with linguist Thomas A. Sebeok. He contributed the observation, in response to my presentation, that the phenomenon conformed to some characteristics of 'appeasement behaviour.' I have given his observation careful attention and concluded that his intuition points in the correct direction. As already stated, laughter's disruptive effect on respiration is not, in itself, a vital matter. Laughter does not cause people to die from suffocation. Laughter does not cause tissue death, resulting from oxygen deficiency. In another research project, I have demonstrated that even prolonged laughter does not cause significant oxygen decrease in peripheral circulating blood. On the other hand, laughter does create a disadvantage to human functioning. There are many things we can not do, or can not do so readily, when we are laughing, which present less difficulty when we are not laughing. And this effect is correlative: the harder and longer we laugh, the greater is the disadvantage. Experimental data consistent with this common observation was provided in Paskind's finding that skeletal muscle tone diminishes as a result of laughter. The folk expression of this experience is, 'I'm weak with laughter.'

These two qualities — non-lethal, but creating a functional disadvantage — are hallmarks of appeasement behaviour. Although there is controversy about one specific act or another serving an appeasement function, extensive information has provided a well-established, detailed description of the appeasement display/sparing response behaviour throughout a wide range of living creatures. The general principle involved in all forms of appeasement is that the subordinating creature is placed in a position of even greater jeopardy vis-à-vis the dominant, than already existed.

At this juncture, there are two matters I wish to emphasize. The first is the widely accepted biological principle that almost all human behaviour serves not a single function alone, but rather a multiplicity, and usually at the same time. What I mean to emphasize here is that I am not suggesting that laughter is solely an appeasement display — and nothing else. It appears that it is appeasement display, but many other functions are involved as well. As with most other behaviour, laughter should be regarded as a node in a complex nexus of impulse and motivation.

Second, I wish to emphasize that I do not propose that laughter originally developed in the human repertoire in its appeasement role. Because of the very primitive nature of that role, it might be tempting to conclude that it was that primitive role which ushered laughter into human behaviour. The Darwinian position is different, and it is the one I prefer. Darwin's presentation on the development of displays is that a behaviour bit pre-exists its signalling function, and is either functionally inconsequential or has some other adaptive value. The signalling function is subsequently picked up through generations by virtue of its producing some survival value, usually within a social context. I see no reason to characterize laughter differently.

Using as a foundation the concept of laughter as appeasement behaviour, several general considerations become appropriate. One deals with the flawed interpretation of Darwinian evolution as emphasizing a picture of almost-continuous combat and violent competition for basic biological necessities, including mates, nutrition and territory. This view is flawed in its essence. Little actual combat takes place, as life is generally lived by all creatures; little violence is committed. This is true even of that most contentious - the human - species, where notable exceptions to non-violence can easily be brought to mind. Survival and selection are not, by and large, mediated by combat and violent extermination of adversaries. Survival and selection are primarily mediated by stereotyped displays - threat, challenge, appeasement, avoidance.

Laughter's function as appeasement display evokes the concept of its survival value. And in this fashion, its evolutionary rationale can be identified. Thus, laughter functions as a valuable contributor to the economy of natural selection. Specifically, laughter's appeasement display obviates violent competition sparing individuals. And it also enhances opportunity for the cooperative, gregarious behaviour which is responsible for so much human productivity and which is one of man's greatest biological assets.

Hierarchy plays a significant part here. In my book 'Sweet Madness,' I have discussed at length the multiform role of humour behaviour (laughter included) in hierarchy transactions. Generally, hierarchy ranking is communicated by species-specific signals. In those animal species where hierarchy is rigid, these signals are primarily involved in the maintenance of rank structure, which is originally established by social inheritance or aggression. Human hierarchy is mostly fluid, and dynamic, with the result that display-signalling both maintains and establishes.

In the hierarchy arena, humour and its associated phenomena have many functions. Easily recognized are its roles in hierarchy threat and attack - establishing and maintaining the hierarchy structure, in submission, in defence, in acclaim of victory, and in acceptance of defeat. A jest may serve as a challenge in hierarchy conflict. A laugh may be a signal of accession - 'a laugh of triumph' - or of appeasement, as with mirthful laughter. A smile may express establishment of one's dominance. Numerous anthropological and sociological studies detail the actual realization of these roles in many different settings, both private and public.

Certain aspects of the relationship between laughter and smiling are brought into focus by this consideration of mirthful laughter as appeasement display. Tradition and extensive observation by many scientists indicate a close relationship between human smiling and laughter.

Several developmental scientists - notably Wolff, Freedman, Ambrose, Andrews, and Spitz - have delineated a complex, but integrated, picture of the ontogeny of smiling and laughter. A brief, simplified summary of that delineation describes two basic smile entities - the earliest smile being that facial behaviour which occurs in the neonate during irregular sleep or drowsiness. This behaviour is characterized as a spontaneous reflex, stimulated when the infant is exposed to 'mild surprise' or 'an ambivalent situation'. Wolff stated, 'The most general necessary and sufficient condition in the neonate seems to be a mild level of tension which is neither so intense as to produce a state of waking arousal, nor so minimal as to be compatible with regular sleep.'

This congenital reflex smile is presented as precursor of the later-appearing 'social' smile; and both smiles, as precursors of laughter. Spitz commented, '.... what was previously a (meaningless) motor pattern..... is integrated on a higher level into a pattern syndrome embracing the motor pattern on one hand and a psychic pattern on the other.' '..... the motor anlage is integrated into the nascent pattern of the child's emotional relations with its human partners.'

Pinneo and I have devoted some study to that social display of primates which is labelled 'social grimace' by primatologists. It is a common phenomenon among communal primates, and occurs in those situations which can be characterized as 'ambivalent' for the signalling individual. The social grimace has several anatomical and structural similarities to infantile 'reflex' smiles.

A prominent function of the social grimace is appeasement. The display is presented at times of moderate threat, and results usually in modification of the threat elements in the social situation - decreased speed of approach of threatening individual, increased interpersonal distance, decreased intensity of threat behaviour, etcetera. Speculation suggests that the reflex smile and the social grimace may represent a set of homologues, genetically determined, susceptible to use as appeasement display in broadly-defined ambivalent social situations. A 'common path of development,' rather than a 'common ancestry,' is the mechanism we prefer to invoke as explanation for the similarity.

Ekman and Friesen have examined smiling behaviour in their study of facial behaviour. Their observations made it possible to present several conclusions. One was: 'Our theory holds that all human beings share the same neural programming, which links facial muscles with particular emotions. The specific events which activate an emotion and the rules for managing the display of the emotions are learned and culturally variable.'

In its appeasement role, laughter presents a somewhat different picture. Here, rather than a variation of its character indicating a specific social context for a laugh, the social context is related to an effect caused by the general act of laughing, upon another physiological activity. This difference could be interpreted as being associated with the very fundamental part appeasement plays in our social interactions.

Certainly a complex relationship exists between smiling and laughter and the many functions to which they are applied in human life. It is awe-inspiring to contemplate the multitude of roles and functions performed by humour and its attendant phenomena. Laughter's potential for appeasement is but one of many ways our daily experiences are affected by this mirthful magic. There can be little question that humour and its associates constitute one of the few, basic sectors of human existence.

A Model of the Origins and Early Development of Incongruity-Based Humour[1]

Paul E. McGhee

Fels Research Institute, Ohio

The present developmental model is designed to apply to occasions for humour based on incongruous relationships between stimulus events (sometimes described as violation of expectancy, stimulus discrepancy, etcetera). This restricted model stems from my belief that our limited understanding of humour might be best overcome by initially developing theoretical models designed to provide very molecular levels of explanation of humour phenomena. Only after numerous such models have been advanced will it be possible to achieve the integrated level of explanation required for more global models. It is not being suggested here that all cases of humour may be reduced to cases of incongruity. Rather, incongruities are considered to provide both the earliest and simplest forms of humour experienced by children. It would seem fruitful, then, to initiate one's study of humour development by examining these simple forms of humour, uncluttered by the addition of such tendentious (Freud, 1960) qualities as sex and aggression. Once a satisfactory understanding of the development of pure incongruity as a basis for humour has been achieved, the combined contributions of incongruity and tendentious elements can be studied more effectively.

EARLIER VIEWS

Theoretical models concerned with the origins and early development of humour have been rare. A considerable amount of theoretical and empirical attention has been given to the smiling response, but the relationship of these efforts to the development of humour has been neglected. This trend has only recently begun to be reversed. McGhee (1971a), for example, distinguished between smiling, laughing, and humour, proposing that incongruities do not become associated with humour until the acquisition of class concepts at three or four years of age. McGhee drew attention to the general importance of cognitive mastery, arguing that children do not possess a sufficient level of certainty about expected relationships between events to perceive distortions of the 'normal' relationships as humorous until words begin to be used as class concepts. He further suggested that a 'reality-fantasy' dimension is important in this respect, in that children perceive expectancy violations as being funny only when they have acquired a stable enough conceptual grasp of the 'real world' that they can construe the violation as being only a play on reality; only at that point could they recognize it as being 'pretend' or 'make-believe'. Psychoanalytically-oriented theorists have also emphasized that mastery over a given idea or physical movement is necessary before a discrepant depiction of it becomes a possible basis for humour (e.g., Grotjahn, 1957; Kris, 1938; Wolfenstein, 1953, 1954). (See McGhee, 1974a, for a general discussion of the role of cognitive mastery in children's humour).

Two additional attempts have been made recently to explain laughter in infants and young children, although neither of these efforts are extended specifically to humour. Rothbart (1973) proposed that:

> Laughter occurs when a person has experienced heightened arousal but at the same time (or soon after arousal) evaluates the stimulus as safe or inconsequential. Emotional responses other than laughter to arousing stimuli are likely to occur if arousal increases to a very high level or if the stimulus is identified by the person as dangerous.

This model clearly specifies that laughter results from the tension release which follows heightened arousal. Given a nonthreatening context or a judgment of safety, the level of evoked arousal determines whether laughter or smiling is likely to occur. When arousal is too high, however, laughter is likely to be replaced by some defensive reaction, such as fear. Sroufe and Wunsch (1972) advanced a similar model, which was revised and extended by Sroufe and Waters (1976). Adopting Berlyne's (1960, 1972) notion of an 'arousal jag,' Sroufe and Waters proposed that a tension increase followed by a decrease is required in order for smiling or laughter to occur. 'In comparison with smiling, laughter ... requires a greater and typically more rapid build up of tension.' They further emphasize the importance of contextual factors in determining whether underlying arousal fluctuations are associated with positive or negative forms of affect.

Shultz (1976) recently proposed that the onset of 'pure incongruity' humour occurs at about eighteen months, the age at which the infant first demonstrates a capacity for symbolic play. This position is similar to the view outlined in the present chapter. However, Shultz also suggested that several more primitive forms of humour antedate such incongruity humour. One such form of humour is 'characterized principally in terms of pleasure in cognitive mastery'. This position is derived from Piaget's (1952, 1962) view that infants derive pleasure from the successful assimilation of discrepant events (i.e., where some accommodation is required). Other forms of humour in the first year are found in connection with certain games, such as peek-a-boo, the tickling game, and chasing games. The laughter and smiling which accompany these activities are considered by Shultz to constitute early forms of humour because they share the biphasic sequence of arousal increase followed by a decrease which is assumed to characterize the identification and resolution of incongruities among older children and adults.

The Meaning of Infant Smiling and Laughter

The major problem confronting any attempt to specify the developmental origins of humour concerns the meaning which must be attributed to early cases of smiling and laughter. There appears to be general agreement that not all smiling and laughter in the first year is suggestive of humour. The question is whether a case can be made that any instance of smiling or laughter in the first year reflects the cognitive experience of humour. In my view, the arousal-plus-context explanation offered by Rothbart (1973), Sroufe and Wunsch (1972) and Sroufe and Waters (1976) is capable of accounting for most instances of infant smiling and laughter to strange or discrepant events without invoking the concept of humour. While humorous events may share the types of arousal fluctuation and contextual influences described within this position (see Berlyne, 1960, 1972), the concept of humour is not necessary to explain such laughter-arousal relationships.

At another level of analysis, McCall and McGhee (in press) reviewed the research literature dealing with determinants of attention and affect in infancy and concluded that both attention and positive (not negative) affect occur as an inverted-U function of the degree of physical or conceptual dissimilarity (discrepancy) from a well-familiarized standard stimulus. Presumably, as a given stimulus is repeatedly encountered a schema or memory engram is developed. Any new stimulus is related to the infant's growing store of schemas. The bulk of research evidence suggests that if a 'match' between the incoming stimulus and some already developed schema is either very easily made (due to only slight discrepancy) or extremely difficult to make (due to high discrepancy, without being totally novel), both attention and smiling are likely to be minimal. Attention and smiling are maximal when some optimal moderate level of discrepancy occurs between the stimulus event and previously established schemas.

Piaget (1962) noted that smiling in such circumstances appears to reflect the achievement of some new cognitive mastery over the environment. Kagan (1967, 1971) extended Piaget's view, proposing that smiling occurs when the infant successfully matches a new stimulus to the memory of a familiar standard, but only if that match is accomplished via some optimal moderate amount of cognitive effort.

> When the child encounters an event that is not immediately assimilable, a special state of tension is generated by the psychological uncertainty. If the child can relate the event to available cognitive structures, the uncertainty and tension are relieved and the smile is an epiphenomenon of that process. (Kagan, 1971).

The data on smiling in response to graded levels of discrepancy are in accord with this view. Thus, it appears that effortful processing of new information may be intrinsically pleasurable, and that this pleasure is reflected in the infant's smile. Studies of problem solving in young children (e.g., Harter, 1974; Kagan, 1971) support this view, demonstrating that smiling tends to occur following problem solution, and is more likely to occur following solution of more challenging problems. Sroufe and Wunsch (1972) interpreted some of their findings for infant laughter along similar lines.

If the effortful processing (when successful) of new information is experienced as pleasurable, this explanation is sufficient to account for any occurrence of smiling or laughter in response to discrepant events. As noted by Rothbart (1973), Sroufe and Wunsch (1972) and Sroufe and Waters (1976), contextual factors may play key roles in determining the direction of the affective response; but, it is not necessary to postulate a humour experience in order to account for the data obtained. This should not be taken to mean, however, that similar processes are not operating in genuine humour experience. Studies using older children (e.g., McGhee, 1976a) have demonstrated that moderate levels of cognitive challenge are also associated with maximal appreciation of the humour in jokes.

It is clear, then, that overt responses such as smiling and laughter cannot be used as a basis for postulating the age of onset of the perception of humour in incongruous events. Similarly, humour cannot be anchored in the stimulus event itself, since the same discrepant event has been found to be associated with both laughter and crying, depending on contextual factors (for example, mother putting on a mask either while the infant is watching or is not watching; see Sroufe and Wunsch, 1972). If the essential properties of humour cannot be found in either the stimulus event or the reaction to that event, it follows that humour must be defined in terms of some organismic variable. That is, humour, like beauty, must be found in the cognitions of the perceiver-thinker.

THE MODEL

The views advanced below are intended to apply only to cases of humour based on incongruity or stimulus discrepancy. No implications are drawn regarding the origins and development of tendentious bases for humour.

Definition of Incongruity Humour

Humour is considered here to be most essentially a type of cognition; it does not exist in objects or events, or in any form of relationship between them. Of course, certain stimulus properties, such as incongruity, are more likely to lead to such cognitions than others (see Berlyne, 1960, 1972). This undoubtedly accounts for the frequent attempts in the past (see Keith-Spiegel, 1972) to equate humour with these properties. But, the fact that incongruity, surprise, novelty, etcetera often lead to confusion, fear, or interest or curiosity is sufficient to defuse any attempts to define humour in terms of such properties.

One might choose to operationally define humour in terms of measurable responses, such as laughter, which are known to be evoked in the presence of stimulus events commonly agreed upon as sources of humour (for example, jokes or cartoons), but the circular nature of this approach is immediately apparent. We must then define the peculiar properties of jokes and cartoons which lead to the common agreement that they are humorous.

Humour is often conceptualized as a form of emotion. As in the case of associated stimulus properties, this may have resulted from the fact that characteristic arousal fluctuations do appear to accompany the perception of humour. However, comparable processes may be demonstrated to accompany nonhumorous events, so the properties which serve to distinguish humour from other experiences or events must be sought elsewhere. Others might be tempted to define humour as an emotion because of its relationship to specific emotional states. Individuals are more likely to appreciate humour, for example, when sexually or aggressively aroused than when not so aroused. While moderate states of anxiety may enhance one's appreciation of humour, high levels of anxiety are likely to interfere.

Humour might best be defined as a cognitive-affective experience, in that it consists of a characteristic set of cognitions, and is accompanied by characteristic forms of arousal fluctuation. Two properties are proposed here as essential in the definition of incongruity-based humour; these properties serve to distinguish humour from other cognitive-affective experiences. First, humour involves a characteristic manner of processing discrepant information; this might be referred to as a 'make-believe,' 'as if,' or 'fantasy' interpretation of the discrepant event. That is, while perceiving any incongruous event as humorous, the child is for the moment pretending that certain of its elements have relationships or characteristics which they do not, in fact, possess. This fantasy element is essential to the humour experience of young children, and to much of the incongruity humour of adults. The specific manner in which this fantasy element is manifest varies as the child's cognitive capacities increase during development.

Given this type of fantasy activity, a second characteristic is essential to perceiving incongruities as humorous; a playful set or 'frame of mind'. This emphasis on play, of course, is not new; many writers have pointed out that a playful mood is somehow important in humour (e.g., Berlyne, 1972; Flugel, 1954; Fry, 1963; McGhee, 1972b; Piddington, 1933). Without this playful set, the same incongruous event may be generated (or encountered), but will be accompanied by some reaction incompatible with humour, such as curiosity, puzzlement, or fear. Some sort of play signal is required to initiate the set of information processing events leading to the perception of humour. In some cases these signals are provided externally (for example, by another person, seeing the incongruity in the form of a cartoon drawing etcetera), but they may also be provided by the child him/herself.

A prerequisite for all forms of incongruity-based humour is a high level of mastery over the stimulus elements which compose the incongruity. That is, the child must have a high level of certainty that the incongruous event could not (or at least does not) occur as constructed or encountered. The event is funny only if the child can feel confident that it is in some way 'wrong' or impossible. As will be noted, it is much easier to have this confidence when the incongruity is constructed by oneself than when it is encountered in the external environment. This accounts for the fact that the earliest forms of incongruity humour are self-generated.

Impact of Acquisition of Symbolic Capacities

McGhee (1971a, 1972b), drawing from Piaget's (1950) equilibration model of development, distinguished between two different modes of cognitively processing events which are discrepant with the child's prior experience; reality assimilation and fantasy assimilation. Reality assimilation refers to the standard adaptation process, described by Piaget, which occurs when a child encounters an event containing some novel characteristics which are not immediately assimilable into the child's existing cognitive structures. The child accommodates those structures or concepts judged relevant to the new event in order to incorporate the discrepant information. If the discrepancy from previous knowledge is only very slight, little accommodation is required for successful assimilation. It has already been noted that such minor discrepancies generate minimal attention in the infant and are not likely to produce expressions of positive affect. In the case of larger discrepancies, the child struggles to fit the new information into appropriate schemas, but may or may not be successful in this effort. If the infant is eventually successful in assimilating (i.e., understanding) such a highly discrepant event, however, smiling or laughter may be expected to occur as a reflection of the pleasure derived from finally gaining some meaning from the discrepant event.

In make-believe or fantasy activities, this chain of events does not occur in reaction to perceived incongruities. Rather, as noted by McGhee (1972b), a new set of 'rules' seems available to the child, such that discrepant ideas or events may be assimilated into a given concept of schema without attempting to accommodate the schema to fit the peculiar properties of the new event. In other words, the assimilation-accommodation process of adaptation is not initiated. McGhee referred to this process as 'fantasy assimilation' in order to reflect the fact that the discrepant event is momentarily assimilated into some schema as if it provided a perfect match. Piaget (1962) referred to these make-believe assimilations as 'symbolic play,' emphasizing the relative predominance of assimilation over accommodation in such instances. The child is aware that the discrepant event is not compatible with the schema he has brought to bear on it, but chooses to link them together anyway. For the moment, the child sees object and schema in his/her imagination as being quite compatible, and does not even consider accommodatory attempts. It is this capacity for pretending that an object or event has certain characteristics, with full awareness that it does not, which enables the child to perceive certain such juxtapositions as being humorous.

Infants first begin to reality-assimilate events during the first month. That is, by the end of the first month they are beginning to adapt their reflexive sensori-motor structures to fit newly encountered objects (Piaget, 1952). This reality-based equilibration process continues throughout the first year, taking on different forms as development proceeds. Only with the initial development of the capacity to represent sensori-motor schemas symbolically (usually early in the second year) does the child begin to show evidence of a capacity for fantasy assimilation. Prior to this point, the infant automatically attempted to accommodate existing structures to fit discrepant encounters with familiar objects. Early in the second year, however, the infant begins to assimilate apparently 'inappropriate' objects into well-established sensori-motor schemas without initiating accommodatory efforts (Piaget, 1962). The child is aware that such objects do not satisfy the set of criteria normally used to determine the appropriateness or relevance of objects to a given schema, so that no permanent accommodation of that schema is made when the inappropriate object is assimilated into it. Rather, the infant appears to temporarily dismiss the normal rules for inclusion of objects into the schema by 'pretending' that the discrepant object is, in fact, an example of an object appropriate to that schema. Consider the following example:

'At 1:3(12) Jacqueline ... saw a piece of cloth whose fringed edges vaguely recalled those of her pillow; she seized it, held a fold of it in her right hand, sucked the thumb of the same hand and lay down on her side, laughing hard. She kept her eyes open, but blinked from time to time as if she were alluding to closed eyes.' (Piaget, 1962).

According to Piaget, this early symbolic play represents the first attempt by the child to assimilate objects into existing schemas in the absence of the object. These pretend assimilations occur at a representational level, presumably based on images.

Piaget (1962) gives an additional example of a child in the second year holding a leaf (as well as other objects) up to her ear and talking into it as if it were a telephone. Again, the child is fully aware that the leaf does not meet the normal requirements for assimilation into a 'telephone-speaking' schema. This initial capacity for fantasy-assimilation of inappropriate objects into existing schemas provides the child with the cognitive prerequisites for the most primitive form of incongruity humour. It is important to note at the outset, however, that this fantasy-assimilation mechanism serves several functions in both younger and older children. It may be initiated as a means of exploring the range of applicability of schemas, out of a sense of curiosity, as a means of relieving boredom, etcetera (see Singer, 1973).

Stages in the Development of Incongruity Humour

Four distinct childhood stages in the development of incongruity humour are distinguished below. Each stage corresponds to a specific cognitive acquisition originally described by Piaget (1950, 1952, 1962). These stages reflect the assumption that as new cognitive capacities are acquired, they immediately begin to contribute to the child's humour perceptions. The model proposed here is not intended to apply beyond the middle childhood years.

Stage 1:   Humour in Action-Based Discrepancy During Object-Image Matching. The first two stages of incongruity humour correspond to the two initial stages of symbolic play described by Piaget (1962). The earliest perceptions of humour occur early in the second year and derive from the execution of actions previously established during the sensori-motor period (Piaget, 1952). During this first stage, the actual behaviour exhibited by the child does not differ from that demonstrated prior to the acquisition of symbolic capacities. What does differ is the object toward which the action is (at times) directed. Before the child acquired the ability to use images to represent objects symbolically, similarity of the perceptual properties of the present object to those of objects previously assimilated determined which schema(s) might be brought to bear on the object. With the onset of representational capacities, however, objects bearing no similarity at all to those previously assimilated into a schema may, nonetheless, be assimilated into that schema. Thus, a leaf has none of the outstanding perceptual properties of a telephone, but by keeping an image of a telephone in mind while activating the actions appropriate to the telephone-speaking schema, the child is able to maintain a clear and meaningful link between schema, object, and action. Piaget referred to this early form of symbolic play as 'projection of symbolic schemas on to new objects'.

The key factors which lead the child to perceive this incongruous juxtaposition of action, object, and image as humorous are a set to engage in playful forms of activity and the knowledge that the present object does not match the properties which serve to define the action schema into which it is assimilated. It is important to note here that not all such fantasy constructions of incongruous events are perceived by the child as being humorous. While assimilation may predominate over accommodation (hence qualifying as play within Piaget's system) in most fantasy operations, curiosity and exploration are sometimes the prime focus of the child's fantasy activities. (See Singer, 1973, for a review of forms of fantasy behaviour shown by children). Without actually accommodating schemas to fit the new events assimilated into them, the child may, nonetheless, display differential inclinations toward information processing and affective display at different times of engagement in fantasy activities.

During the early preschool years, children frequently engage in activity at the fantasy level comparable to that demonstrated at the earlier sensori-motor period of 'tertiary circular reactions' (Piaget, 1952). This constitutes the last true stage of sensori-motor functioning, and usually occurs during the early months of the second year. According to Piaget, this marks the first point at which the infant actively searches for novelty 'for its own sake'. Infants are especially curious about objects at this age and often engage in repetitious activities in which the action directed toward the object is repeatedly altered to see what new effect on the object can be produced. In a similar fashion, children in the last half of the second year, and in the third year, sometimes repeatedly change the schemas (now available as memory images) brought to bear on familiar objects. Many different objects may be fantasy-assimilated into particular schemas simply in order to 'see what happens' when they are brought together. As in the tertiary circular reactions stage, children during this period are very curious about the range of fantasy application of their schemas, and may generate endless sequences of incongruous action-object-image juxtapositions. Within this relatively more serious cognitive set, then, the child derives pleasure from the mere activity of processing challenging forms of new information. While smiling or (less frequently) laughter may be expected to accompany such fantasy activities, the intensity of any affective responses will be relatively more restricted as long as the child remains in an information-processing or novelty-seeking frame of mind. Within this frame of mind, curiosity and learning are the child's primary focus.

Children spend a great deal of time engaged in the activities described above, but a significant amount of time during the second year is also spent in a more playful frame of mind, in which curiosity about the effect of extending familiar schemas to varying new objects is markedly less pronounced. During these more playful times, the child may engage in activities very similar to those characteristic of more serious fantasy activities. That is, the same type of discrepant action-object-image juxtapositions may occur. In this case, however, the child's attention is primarily directed toward confirming the fact that the object does not match the schema. Acknowledgement of this discrepancy, given the playful set the child brings to the fantasy activity, characteristically produces more intense and extended forms of laughter and constitutes the most primitive form of incongruity humour. This humour is reflected in the frequent observation of laughter by Piaget (1962) during the one- to two-year-old's symbolic play using objects. This laughter reflects the fact that the child derives pleasure from constructing in his own fantasy a set of conditions known to be at odds with reality. It is precisely this knowledge which makes the idea of the discrepant event funny.

Verbal descriptions may or may not accompany the action-object-image discrepancies providing the basis for humour in Stage 1. In Stage 1, verbal accompaniments simply describe the ongoing action-image sequences, whereas in Stage 2 the verbal statement takes the place of action. For example, Piaget (1962) noted that at about twenty-two months of age, Jacqueline 'put a shell on the table and said "sitting", then she put it on top of another, adding delightedly: "Sitting on pot."' If this was perceived by Jacqueline as funny, the important role of object manipulation indicates that it should be categorized as Stage 1 rather than Stage 2 humour.

The humour of Stage 1 is more likely than that of subsequent stages to be a solitary experience. Since private images form the underlying basis for humour at this stage, the experience is simply not available socially. When verbal descriptions do accompany the action, observers will usually be provided with sufficient information to identify the image being brought to bear on the action. As the child becomes increasingly skilled at transmitting fantasy constructions verbally, (s)he tends to become increasingly interested in sharing the humour thus brought about.

Stage 2: Humour in Discrepant Identification of Objects. As the child becomes increasingly competent in the use of language during the second year, verbal schemas become more involved in make-believe activities. The second stage of incongruity humour is marked by a reliance on statements about an object in the absence of any action directed toward the object. That is, in addition to engaging in an incongruous act toward an object, the child can now also say something incongruous about the same object. Piaget (1962) proposed a second category of play along these lines, arguing that the child might either identify one object as another, or identify his/her own body as another person or thing. For example, Jacqueline at twenty-seven months 'pointed to a big rough pebble: "It's a dog" - "Where's its head?" - "There" (a lump in the stone). - "And its eyes?" - "They've gone."' In an example with stronger affect evident, Jacqueline at twenty-four months 'opened the window and shouted, laughing: "Hi boy!" (a boy she met on her walks and who was never in the garden). Then, still laughing, she added: "Over there!"' Similarly, eight days later 'she laughed as she pretended to make a seagull, painted on a box, fly: "Come" (opening her arms)'. In these cases, the incongruities are created at a purely verbal level, without any imitative or other action being central to the fantasy event.

These examples suggest that language may serve humour in two distinct ways during Stage 2. It may be used either to give one object a different name or to posit the existence of an object that does not exist (at least in the suggested place). Although actions are no longer (necessarily) involved in this stage, image manipulation continues to play a key role in creating the incongruity perceived by the child. In the example just mentioned, the verbal statement 'it's a dog' takes the place of an action which might relate to dogs. The incongruity is created by combining this statement with both the present object (a stone) and the image of a dog. Again, this statement is funny simply because the child knows it is at odds with reality.

By virtue of the use of a language medium, humour experiences in Stage 2 are frequently more social in nature, and may even be shared by another child. While the incongruities perceived as humorous in Stage 1 were exclusively self-initiated, the Stage 2 child shows the first signs of being able to respond with humour at incongruous relationships suggested by others. However, the child's sense of mastery over what is possible and not possible with respect to familiar objects is still very limited. In any given case of an incongruous relationship suggested by another person, then, the child cannot be certain that the suggested event really is at odds with reality. Accordingly, some form of strong play signal is required before the discrepant event can be confidently fantasy-assimilated and perceived as humorous. In most cases, smiling or laughter on the part of the child issuing the discrepancy provides this signal.

Stage 3: Humour in Violation of Language-Mediated Class Concepts. Until age three, children's incongruity humour consists of distortions of actions and verbal schemas brought to bear on objects. While these continue to provide opportunities for humour during the balance of the preschool years, a new form of discrepancy begins to lead to humour perceptions between three and four years of age. This new level of humour stems from the achievement of a more advanced level of understanding of words. During the first three years, the child operates in terms of 'preconcepts' (Piaget, 1962). During this period, (s)he doesn't realize that a given word refers to a class of objects or events sharing certain key characteristics which serve to define the class, but differing in certain other nonessential respects. Word labels tend to be used in reference to specific objects or events, without any underlying set of criteria by which examples are either included in or excluded from assimilation into a given verbal schema.

As the child begins to organize objects into true concepts between the third and fourth year, (s)he acquires a new sense of confidence regarding what is possible and what is not possible within the set of concepts already mastered. For example, a cat might be conceptualized as a small animal with fur, four legs, two ears, a tail, which 'goes meow,' etcetera. If the child encounters (at a fantasy level) a cat with two heads and no ears, and which makes a 'moo' sound, such a fantasy creation is likely to be perceived as humorous, because it violates the child's conceptual understanding of reality. This form of humour is more complex than simply saying, for example, that a cat is a cow, a stone is a dog, etcetera, in that any number of, or combinations of, characteristics serving to define the concept might enter into the humour process. A given characteristic, however, must be considered essential to defining the class before distortion of that characteristic may be expected to trigger humour perceptions. For example, a cat with red fur is not likely to be funny, while a cat with no fur or two tails will be funny.

It is assumed here that language plays a central role in all of the child's humour based on violation of class concepts. Several species of animals have demonstrated the capacity for acquiring simple concepts (form, colour, etcetera); that is, they are able to respond to a single stimulus dimension while overlooking others. The lack of a representational anchoring of these concepts, however, interferes with these animals' ability to utilize such concepts in the perception of humour.

Although language-mediated class concepts form the basis for the child's humour during this stage, it is not necessary for violations of a concept to be communicated verbally in order for humour to occur. Thus, either seeing a cat with two heads in a cartoon, having another child describe a cat with two heads, or thinking up such a cat oneself may trigger humour. The important thing is that the child knows that cats do not have two heads. Of course, as we have already noted, the circumstances under which such a discrepant event is encountered may determine whether curiosity and surprise results, or whether humour occurs. Even though the child now has a high level of confidence in his/her knowledge of what cats must be like, seeing one in real life might cause a sudden questioning of that certainty. Similarly, if a parent tells the child with a serious expression that, in fact, cats can have two or more heads, interest and puzzlement are more likely to occur than humour. In short, some sort of play signal must accompany the perception (whether visually or verbally) of the cat as having two heads. Only in the presence of such a play signal will the child automatically fantasy-assimilate the event and perceive it as being funny. Because (s)he can still be easily fooled (by convincing external cues) into thinking that a given concept violation really is possible, the child should most consistently find humour in discrepancies which (s)he creates. Only by constructing concept violations oneself can one be absolutely certain that a fantasy mode of assimilation is more appropriate than a reality mode.

Wolfenstein (1954) noted that children at this age (three-four years) begin to take great delight in suggesting changes in another child's gender. For example, one boy might laughingly call another a girl, or call him by a girl's name. The beginning of this type of humour at this age reflects that children are just mastering the concept of what it means to be a boy or girl. Wolfenstein's observation with respect to gender changes is not atypical. That is, once a child acquires a true conceptual understanding of a given object or event, (s)he tends to enjoy initiating fantasy distortions of it. Again, these distortions may or may not be expressed verbally.

Throughout Stage 3, lasting until age six or seven, the child's humour remains very perceptually oriented. Empirical support for this view has been provided by McGhee (1971b, c, 1974c), Shultz (1972, 1974) and Shultz and Horibe (1974). Although the acquisition of class

concepts does lead to some increase in abstraction in the child's thinking, it is actually
the perceptual features of objects which are used to define concepts. Thus, it is inevitably
an inconsistency with a child's understanding of the perceptual properties of objects which
forms the basis for humour in this stage. Piaget (1950), of course, initially drew attention
to the fact that children's thinking and reasoning during this period are characterized by
a strong perceptual 'centeredness'. That is, thinking and judgments are heavily influenced
by perceptually dominant features of an object or event. It is not surprising, then, that
humour during this period is based on violations of such perceptual features.

Stage 3 contains some of the features of both Stages 2 and 4. The image manipulation which
provided the basis for humour in both Stages 1 and 2 continues to be involved in Stage 3.
While part of the humour in Stage 3 derives from the conceptual awareness of discrepancy,
Piaget (1950) notes that the child continues to manipulate images in many problem situations.
It seems likely, then, that images corresponding to prominent perceptual features combine
with the child's conceptual understanding of those features to produce the humour of Stage 3.
In Stage 4, such image manipulation makes no contribution at all to the perception of humour
in double meanings.

Gesell and Ilg (1946) noted that a common form of children's humour during the preschool
years consists of repetitious rhyming of words, in which changes in pronunciation are gradually
introduced (for example, 'itsy, bitsy, witsy, mitsy,' 'happy, dappy, sappy,' etcetera). The
humour in this case derives from distorting the familiar sound of a given word, rather than
distorting some aspect of the meaning of the word. This kind of humour may appear any time
between ages two-four, and does not clearly fall into any of the Stages defined here. It may
be that while the incongruous event itself (sound distortion) does not tap the child's
conceptual understanding of the distorted word directly, it simply does not occur to the
child to play with the sounds of words until (s)he begins to understand them in a conceptual
sense.

Finally, Stage 3 marks the onset of a new form of social influence on incongruity humour.
During the later preschool years, children begin to issue incongruous statements in an attempt
to 'trick' another person into believing them. This form of humour activity does not become
a main focus, however, until the following stage when formal jokes begin to be understood.
Part of the 'fun' of verbal humour, then, derives from tricking another person into believing
a discrepant communication, and avoiding being tricked in this fashion oneself.

To this point, the focus of this model has been directed exclusively toward intrinsic bases
for experiencing pleasure in incongruities. While the central components of the humour
experience are considered here to evolve in this manner, social factors also play an important
role in the overall development of humour responsiveness. As children in the second and third
years of life proceed to engage in fantasy creations of incongruous events, a parent or an
older child may recognize the nature of the pretend behaviour and exhibit great laughter and
merriment as a result. This type of reaction along with other forms of positive reinforcement,
should serve to reinforce the child's fantasy activity and lead to a sharing of the positive
affect shown by others witnessing the event. It should also have the effect of increasing
both the frequency of occurrence of the child's creation of such discrepant fantasy events
and the amount of laughter and other forms of positive affect accompanying such creations.
Singer (1973) has also proposed that such early social reinforcement experiences play a
central role in the child's early experiences of humour. However, it must be remembered that
children might begin to repeat those fantasy behaviours which arouse adult laughter without
themselves having any genuine understanding or appreciation of the humour involved.

Stage 4: Operational Thinking and the Humour of Multiple Meanings. Several lines of research
suggest that a major transition in children's perception of humour in incongruity occurs at
about six or seven years of age. McGhee (1974b) directly examined children's ability to
understand riddles based on word play or double meanings. First graders were not able to
discriminate between a joking and a nonjoking (factual) answer to riddles, when asked to
choose the funnier of the two. The ability to make this discrimination began in grade two,
and improved progressively through grade six. Prentice and Fathman (1975) obtained similar
findings. Similarly, Shultz and Pilon (1973) found that children are not able to detect
linguistic ambiguity until after age six. Even though the younger child understands both
meanings of a word, riddles and other forms of jokes require a simultaneous acknowledgement
of the two meanings in order to appreciate the humour depicted. Consider the following joke
used by Shultz and Horibe (1974): 'Order! Order in the court!' 'Ham and cheese on rye,
your honour.' It is impossible to understand or appreciate this joke without being aware of
both meanings of the word 'order'.

According to Piaget (1950), children begin to lose their perceptual 'centeredness' at about
the age of six or seven. Instead of focusing attention on only one meaning of a word or one
prominent perceptual feature of an object, the child begins to be able to keep one meaning

or feature in mind while thinking about another. This capacity, along with the capacity for reversibility in thinking and the tendency to focus on transformations leading from one event to another rather than on the final state resulting from such transformations, accounts for the child's sudden ability to understand humour involving dual interpretations of words during the sixth or seventh year. Piaget referred to the combined changes in cognitive functioning occurring at this time as a transition into concrete operational thinking.

The acquisition of concrete operational thinking appears to have a number of additional influences on the child's comprehension and appreciation of incongruity humour. McGhee (1971b) tested children at the age of transition (age seven for the sample tested) in acquiring concrete operational thinking and found that children who were further along in developing operational capacities showed better comprehension of more abstract incongruities which did not involve perceptual discrepancies from the child's exsprience. They also gave more frequent interpretive (as opposed to descriptive) explanations of why the jokes or cartoons were funny. Degree of acquisition of operational thinking was not significantly related, however, to comprehension of simpler jokes and cartoons based on perceptual incongruities (a Stage 3 form of humour). Similar findings were reported by McGhee (1971c).

In another approach to demonstrating the role of operational thinking in children's humour, McGhee (1974c) tested children operating at two different levels of moral development (heteronomy and autonomy) described by Piaget (1932). The transition from the less to the more mature level occurs with the onset of concrete operational thinking. Humorous stories were presented in which intentionality of damage and amount of damage to objects were manipulated. Among morally heteronomous children (pre-operational) more damaging outcomes were funnier than less damaging ones, apart from whether they were intentional or accidental. Among morally autonomous (concrete operational) children, on the other hand, accidental damaging outcomes were funnier than intentional ones, apart from the amount of damage occurring. The prominent perceptual feature in these stories was the damage to the objects depicted; as this perceptual characteristic was exaggerated, humour increased accordingly in the less mature children. But with the (assumed) acquisition of operational thinking, children were able to utilize the more abstract information about intentions in forming judgments of funniness.

Shultz has completed a number of studies (Shultz, 1972, 1974, 1976; Shultz and Horibe, 1974) suggesting that children below six years of age respond to incongruity alone in their appreciation of verbal humour. That is, no difference in appreciation was noted as a function of the presence or absence of information required to resolve or understand the incongruity depicted. For instance, in the 'Order in the court' joke presented earlier, a resolution-removed (pure incongruity) version would be as follows: 'Silence! Silence in the court!!' 'Ham and cheese on rye, your honour.' While eight-year-olds rated the original joke as funnier than this version, six-year-olds gave the two versions comparable ratings. Pien and Rothbart (see this volume) have recently obtained data showing that four- to five-year-olds do appreciate the resolution information in certain types of humour stimuli, so that the role of operational thinking in this transition remains uncertain.

It can only be concluded, then, that concrete operational thinking enables the child to understand and appreciate forms of verbal humour based on ambiguity of meaning, and to generally perceive humour in more abstract forms of incongruity. As the child approaches adolescence, the perceptual features of objects and events become decreasingly important as contributors to humour. However, earlier bases for humour are not totally lost. They may contribute in a secondary fashion to the appreciation of humour in incongruities which are primarily represented at higher levels. In a cartoon, for instance, several different forms of incongruity varying in degree of abstractness may simultaneously contribute to the overall humour experience. Vivid images might, in some cases, even make a greater contribution to funniness than the identification of more subtle implied meanings. Similarly, as individuals get older, certain forms of incongruity may become especially favoured and sought out in preference to forms requiring more advanced cognitive skills.

FOOTNOTE

[1] This paper contains only a portion of the contents of an address delivered at the conference, entitled 'Phylogenetic and ontogenetic considerations for a theory of the origins of incongruity-based humour'. An abstract describing the balance of the address is presented at the end of this paper.

REFERENCES

See Bibliography for publications on humour, laughter and comedy

Gesell, A. & Ilg, F., The Child From Five To Ten. Harper and Brothers, New York (1946).

Harter, S., Pleasure derived from cognitive challenge and mastery. Child Development, 45, 661-669 (1974).

Kagan, J., On the need for relativism. American Psychologist, 22, 131-143 (1967).

Kagan, J., Change and Continuity in Infancy. Wiley, New York (1971).

McCall, R.B. & McGhee, P.E., The discrepancy hypothesis of attention and affect in infants. In: I.C. Uzgiris & F. Weizmann (Eds.), The Structuring of Experience. Plenum, New York, in press (1977).

Piaget, J., The Moral Judgment of The Child. Kegan Paul, London (1932).

Piaget, J., The Psychology of Intelligence. Harcourt, Brace, New York (1950).

Piaget, J., The Origins of Intelligence in Children. International University Press, New York (1952).

Piaget, J., Play, Dreams, and Imitation in Childhood. Norton, New York (1962).

Shultz, T.R. & Pilon, R., Development of the ability to detect linguistic ambiguity. Child Development, 44, 728-733 (1973).

Singer, J.L., The Child's World of Make-Believe: Experimental Studies of Imaginative Play. Academic Press, New York (1973).

CONFERENCE ABSTRACT

This paper will be primarily of a theoretical nature and will use available research and theory to develop a position regarding the point in both phylogenetic and ontogenetic development that it makes sense to begin talking about the capacity to experience humour. Considerable attention will be given to the meaning of smiling and laughter in animals, young infants, and older children, with a view toward examining how one decides whether laughter is indicative of humour or some other underlying process (e.g., arousal fluctuations). Previous relevant theories and conceptions along these lines will first be reviewed. I will not spend time discussing such issues as the adaptive significance of laughter, or the evolution of the laughter or humour response.

It will be proposed that in both humans and infrahumans some evidence of symbolic functioning must be present in order to experience humour. The aptness of this position with respect to both tendentious and nontendentious (i.e., stimulus discrepancy or incongruity) humour will be discussed. Relevant research on animals will be brought to bear on this issue, with special focus on recent work with Sarah, Washoe, and other chimps. Similarly, research on smiling and laughter in human infants will be discussed as a basis for distinguishing between humorous and nonhumorous laughter. It will be proposed that laughter first becomes associated with humour in infants at eighteen months of age. This corresponds to the point (with Piaget's system) at which sensori-motor schemas first become available on a symbolic basis. Various types of 'pretend' or 'fantasy' assimilations of 'inappropriate' content will be discussed as cognitive prerequisites for the capacity to experience humour. Finally, a discussion will be provided on the relative onsets of tendentious and non-tendentious humour and internally versus externally initiated humour, along with the role of context in humour. The implications of the position developed for humour research with adults, and research methodology in general will be discussed.

Elephants and Marshmallows: A Theoretical Synthesis of Incongruity-Resolution and Arousal Theories of Humour

Mary K. Rothbart and Diana Pien[1]

University of Oregon

Many current theories of humour have stressed the importance of incongruity and resolution as determinants of humour appreciation. Both arousal (Berlyne, 1969; Rothbart, 1973) and cognitive processing theories (Shultz, 1972; Suls, 1972) propose that resolution of incongruity can lead to humour; in addition, arousal theories (Berlyne, 1969; Rothbart, 1973) propose that incongruity alone can produce humour. Both kinds of theories, however, have been largely limited to predictions that each component will in fact contribute to humour, and only rarely have they dealt with more complex issues. Shultz' treatment (1972) of possible developmental changes in the contributions of incongruity and resolution to humour appreciation is an exception.

We would like to suggest that a major limitation of current theories has been an overly simplistic classification of humour elements of jokes, cartoons, and stories into just two categories, incongruity or resolution. In the present paper we will argue in favour of a more detailed classification system and propose a model of the humour process incorporating such a classification system. In addition, we will describe an example of the research predictions possible using the more refined system.

Let us now consider some currently popular definitions of incongruity and resolution. Shultz (1976) defines incongruity as 'a conflict between what is expected and what actually occurs in the joke'. Resolution is a 'second, more subtle aspect of jokes which renders incongruity meaningful or appropriate by resolving or explaining it'. Shultz then distinguishes humour from nonsense by characterizing nonsense as 'pure or unresolvable incongruity', and humour as 'resolvable or meaningful incongruity' (Shultz, 1976, pp. 12-13). At first glance, the distinction seems simple enough to apply. The following riddle, for example, would fit the criteria for humour: 'How far can a dog run into a forest?' 'Only halfway. After that he'll be running out of the forest'. The initial incongruity of the question and the punchline is made entirely meaningful by recognizing that the unexpected answer is definitionally correct. However, in many jokes, resolution of incongruity may not make the incongruity completely meaningful and may sometimes add new elements of incongruity. For example, the joke 'Why did the elephant sit on the marshmallow?' presents an incongruous situation, and the answer 'Because he didn't want to fall into the hot chocolate' provides some explanation of the incongruity, but also introduces a new element of incongruity – an elephant sitting in a cup of hot chocolate. An even more complex situation is presented in the joke 'Why did the cookie cry?' 'Because its mother had been a wafer so long'. There are two elements of incongruity, the fact that cookies don't cry and the initial incongruity or surprisingness of the answer to the riddle. The answer contains its own resolution – the phonological ambiguity of 'a wafer' (i.e., away for), but also adds the additional incongruity of a cookie having a mother.

An isolation of incongruity and resolution elements in these jokes requires at least the following two categories of incongruity and two categories of resolution:

1. Impossible Incongruity: elements that are unexpected and also impossible given one's current knowledge of the world, for example, cookies crying.

2. Possible Incongruity: elements that are unexpected or improbable but possible, for example, a dignified man slipping on a banana peel.

3. Complete Resolution: the initial incongruity follows completely from resolution information.

4. Incomplete Resolution: the initial incongruity follows from resolution information in some way, but is not made completely meaningful because the situation remains impossible.

Each of the two resolution categories can be further elaborated to include instances when a resolution adds new incongruous elements, for example, the new information that the elephant is sitting in a cup of hot chocolate, which partially explains why the elephant is sitting on a marshmallow while adding an even greater incongruity, the idea that the elephant is sitting in a cup of chocolate. These new incongruities may themselves be either completely or incompletely resolved within the joke.

The reader will note that incongruity and resolution elements in any given joke may not be completely independent. An Impossible Incongruity element cannot be completely resolved, and partial resolution is only possible if one willingly suspends disbelief and accepts the impossible incongruity for purposes of enjoying the joke (this situation may be similar to McGhee's, 1972, 'fantasy assimilation'). In contrast, a Possible Incongruity element can be either completely or partially resolved. In terms of the classification system described in Figure 1, the dog running into the forest joke would be classified as $R(I_1)$, involving complete resolution of a single incongruity. The elephant on a marshmallow joke would be classified as $R(I_1) + I_1 + I_2$ (partial resolution of one incongruity with addition of a second, unresolved incongruity). Classification of the latter two jokes as either humour or nonsense would be extremely difficult; they seem to include a mixture of both humour and nonsense. We would like to suggest that both incongruity, and incongruity with resolution elements contribute to humour appreciation, in addition to other arousal-enhancing elements such as the fearful, sexual or aggressive subject matter of jokes.

Fig. 1   Types of incongruity and resolution

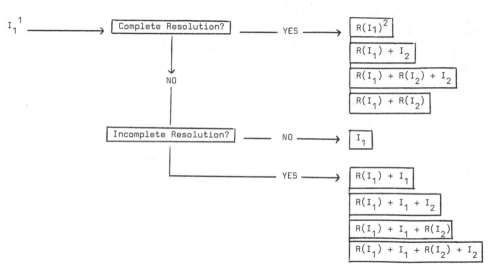

[1] Each Incongruity symbol refers to either impossible or possible incongruity, but only possible incongruity can be completely resolved. For simplicity, we are assuming only one initial incongruity element even though there may be more than one element.

[2] $R(I_1)$ means full or partial resolution of I_1 incongruity element.

This type of classification system can be combined with Rothbart's (1973) arousal-safety theory of laughter to produce a general model of humour accounting for differences in the contribution of incongruity and resolution to arousal and humour appreciation. Cognitive aspects of humour would be seen as a function of (a) the number of resolved incongruous elements, (b) the number of incongruity elements remaining unresolved, (c) the degree of incongruity of each element, (d) the difficulty of resolution, and (e) the degree of resolution. Increases in the first three factors should lead to increases in humour appreciation, while the difficulty of resolution may be curvilinearly related to humour (McGhee, 1974a). In connection with degree of resolution, theorists such as Suls (1972) and Shultz (1972) might predict that complete resolution in a joke would lead to more humour appreciation than incomplete resolution. We would suggest that remaining unresolved incongruity elements would also add to the humour response.

This classification scheme allows us to develop research designs for investigating questions rarely examined in humour research, such as repetition effects (Goldstein, 1970; Suls, 1975). For example, we propose that repetition of jokes and cartoons may differentially affect resolution and incongruity elements. If incongruity elements that have not been resolved in the joke are repeated, they are no longer unexpected or surprising to the subject in the context of the joke, but they remain incongruous with respect to events in the real world. So, for example, the image of an elephant sitting in a cup of hot chocolate remains incongruous no matter how many times we may think about it. Familiarity decreases novelty of the elements in the short-term joking context, but does not affect their long-term novelty. Whatever humour is based on long-term novelty should not decrease with repetition.

The effect of repetition of resolution elements, on the other hand, that is, the effect of cognitive processing in 'solving' the joke, should depend on the difficulty of resolving the incongruity. Repetition of jokes having difficult resolution components may produce appreciation of humour based on satisfaction or mastery in having understood the joke the first time it was heard (Suls, 1975); repetition of the joke may also require additional processing to the extent that an original complex resolution has been forgotten. In contrast, there may be little feeling of satisfaction or mastery associated with easy to understand resolution components. With repetition, easy resolution of incongruous elements becomes even easier, resulting in less humour due to the resolution component. This account of the effects of repetition predicts that humour from unresolved incongruity should decline less with repetition than humour from easily-resolved incongruity. In addition, humour based on very difficult resolution should decline less with repetition than humour from easily-resolved incongruity.

Fig. 2 Cartoon for repetition study

A. Incongruity Alone

B. Incongruity and Partial Resolution

'He won't be in today. He's in bed with a bug.'

Part of this proposal can be tested by using humour stimuli having easy, partial or complete resolution but where resolution does not introduce new incongruities. Referring to Figure 2, if the incongruity components of each stimulus (A and B) are presented separately, we can compare the effects of repetition of incongruity components alone (A) with the effects of repetition of the same incongruity components with at least partial resolution (B). We predict that ratings of stimuli with only incongruity components will decline less than ratings of stimuli with both incongruity and moderately easy resolution components.

The present model may also be useful in explaining other questions such as analyzing the differences between jokes and riddles, and testing the effect of difficulty of problem solving on humour appreciation. While changes in the model are undoubtedly necessary, we hope the model will be useful in clarifying some complex issues in humour research and providing a method for future examination of such issues.

FOOTNOTE

[1] Both authors have made an equal contribution to this paper. The authors wish to express their appreciation to Myron Rothbart for his helpful comments on earlier versions of this paper.

REFERENCES

See Bibliography for publications on humour, laughter and comedy

Cognitive and Disparagement Theories of Humour:
A Theoretical and Empirical Synthesis

Jerry Suls

State University of New York at Albany

This paper focuses on two different perspectives that have received attention from psychologists studying humour- incongruity- resolution theory and what I will call disparagement theory. It is argued here that these apparently disparate models may be usefully integrated. To accomplish this, we first review the tenets of each theory.

THE INCONGRUITY-RESOLUTION MODEL

Many simple cognitive-perceptual theories of humour have been proposed, but all apparently share one critical element, that is, the key impact of incongruity, surprise or paradox in eliciting humour responses. Other more complex cognitive-perceptual theories (Jones, 1970; Shultz, 1972; Suls, 1972) have argued that incongruity is only the first stage and that resolution of the incongruity is necessary for eliciting humour responses. In brief, the two-stage incongruity-resolution model assumes that the humour respondent typically has expectations about the verbal or pictorial material to which he is attending. The humour stimulus is deliberately constructed to play-off these expectations and thus generates incongruity. After this stage has occurred, the respondent is motivated to resolve or make sense of the incongruity. This second stage involves the retrieval of information, either from the joke or from any other source, which can effectively explain the joke punchline in the light of the material that preceded it. Finding a satisfactory resolution results in humour. Lacking a satisfactory resolution the respondent cannot 'get the joke' and does not find it funny. Another element recently appended to the model is that the respondent must have a humour set or some cue so he realizes that the stimulus is to be processed as a joke, as play or fantasy.

Despite the relative simplicity of the two-stage model, a considerable amount of research supports it. For example, Shultz (1972) reported that humour appreciation is impaired in children if they are not able both to perceive the joke incongruity as well as to find a solution or reason for the appearance of the incongruous information. Shultz (1974) in another study used a self-report technique to demonstrate that the information in verbal jokes is processed in the order specified by the two-stage model. For example, resolutions were nearly always detected after incongruities. Other research has shown that if the information or rule needed for the incongruity resolution is too challenging or complex then humour appreciation declines (McGhee, 1976a) and that when resolution is made easier by making the joke material salient, appreciation of the humour stimulus increases (Goldstein, Suls & Anthony, 1972; Suls & Shaw, 1976).

DISPARAGEMENT THEORIES

By disparagement theories we mean those theories of humour based on the observation that we laugh at other people's infirmities, particularly those of our enemies. Variously known as superiority theory, vicarious superiority theory (La Fave, 1972; La Fave, Haddad & Maesen, 1976) and dispositional theory (Zillmann & Cantor, 1976), all focus on humour communications in which one party is disparaged or aggressed against by another party. A recent statement of the theory comes from Zillmann and Cantor (1976) who posit that:

> '...humour appreciation varies inversely with the favourableness of the disposition toward the agent or entity being disparaged and varies directly with the favourableness of the disposition toward the agent or entity disparaging it. Appreciation should be maximal when our friends humiliate our enemies, and minimal when our enemies manage to get the upper hand over our friends'. (pp100-101).

Numerous studies have supported this humour model. For example, La Fave (1972) reported that pro-male males preferred pro-male-anti-female jokes over pro-female-anti-male jokes. Also pro-female females (members or sympathizers of Women's Liberation organizations) tended to find pro-female-anti-male jokes funnier than pro-male-anti-female jokes. In another study Zillmann and Cantor (1972) presented to male undergraduates and male professionals cartoons depicting exchanges between a superior and a subordinate. Their results indicated that subjects with primarily subordinate experiences exhibited greater appreciation for humorous communications that showed a subordinate temporarily dominating a superior while subjects with primarily superior experiences appreciated humour showing superiors dominating subordinates.

A SYNTHESIS OF THE TWO MODELS

At first thought the incongruity-resolution model and the disparagement model appear quite different since they focus on different variables and processes. The first theory seems linked to cognitive processes, the second to affective reactions toward social groups or individuals. It is contended, however, that a closer examination reveals some important commonalities which may lead to a possible synthesis.

Let us consider an example of disparagement humour:

    Question: If your son flunks out of school and is illiterate and anti-social, what
               can he grow up to be?

    Answer: An Italian policeman.

The disparagement model handles this quite simply. It would argue that someone who dislikes Italians would enjoy this joke since it disparages Italians and more specifically Italian policemen. However, an Italian would not find the joke funny since it disparages a group whom he presumably likes. Some important considerations are, however, not included in this disparagement analysis: it says nothing about the joke punchline as information and it does not explain why we fail to laugh at other (non-joke) occasions of disparagement. Zillmann and Cantor (1976) recently confronted this issue and suggested that without cues to establish the joke setting individuals are inhibited about expressing euphoria when others undergo misfortunes. It is unclear, however, why one should inhibit laughter when misfortune befalls an enemy.

How does the incongruity-resolution model consider this joke? In brief, the material preceding the punchline serves to set up the joke. As the respondent listens he attempts to predict the outcome. A well-constructed joke leads the respondent astray so that the punchline comes as a surprise. The answer 'an Italian policeman' should be at least somewhat surprising. The two-stage model proposes that the respondent then needs to make sense out of the punchline, to find a way to make it follow from the information preceding it. In our example, the respondent could obtain the necessary resolution if he believes that Italian police are illiterate and anti-social. The two-stage model dictates that without a satisfactory resolution (from the respondent's perspective) the humour response should not result.

It may be obvious by now how the disparagement process can be conceptualized in terms of the incongruity-resolution model. An Italian should not be able to provide the information necessary to resolve the joke. For him the information provided should not fit and not make sense of the punchline since Italian police are not illiterate or anti-social as far as he is concerned. Even if our hypothetical Italian is aware that others believe these things of Italian cops, he should not personally perceive the resolution as satisfactory. In short, from his perspective the incongruity should not follow from the joke premises. Hence the joke material would be unresolved and the process would terminate at this point.

In short, the present analysis proposes that the affect associated with joke protagonists in the joke influences the extent to which the respondent can find a satisfactory resolution for disparagement humour stimuli. However, these comments should not be construed to mean that the variables examined by disparagement theorists are trivial or irrelevant, not that the model that they propose is incorrect. Rather, it is proposed that these variables and the disparagement theory can be incorporated into the broader incongruity-resolution model which considers not only aggressive and sexual humour (which also typically employs putdowns) but nonsense humour as well.

Before proceeding, it should be noted that the present formulation would appear to have difficulty in accounting for those occasions when an individual is amused by a joke which disparages his own membership group[1]. Of course, disparagement theories have difficulty with this point also. However, the difficulty is resolved at least partially by La Fave (1972) who noted that an individual's membership group may not be his reference group. For example,

some Blacks may appreciate anti-Black jokes because they identify with Whites rather than
Blacks (Middleton, 1959)[2]. This explanation can also be incorporated into the present analysis.
Specifically, it is argued that Italians who do not identify with their membership group
should have little difficulty with the resolution structure required by the policeman joke.

Thus far only the relevance of the resolution phase to the disparagement process has been
emphasized. The incongruity phase also has importance in disparagement humour. In humour
communications involving disparagement, the joke incongruity usually takes the form of some
hostile behaviour or statement. It is conceivable that at this first stage the humour
perception process may terminate for those who sympathize with the disparaged party. The
reason is simply that the depiction of a sympathetic character being teated badly may cause
the respondent to interpret the communication as not being a joke. The outcome may instead
be seen as hostility. At this point resolution may not be perceived as necessary since the
respondent may simply 'leave the field'. McGhee (1972b) has proposed that for humour to be
appreciated the respondent must have a fantasy-assimilation set; he must see the events
depicted as occurring in play. A respondent who identifies with the disparaged party may not
process the hostile joke incongruity in a fantasy mode and therefore not find it funny.

RELEVANT EVIDENCE

At present there is no empirical evidence specifically linking the two-stage model to
disparagement theories, however, there is evidence that suggests such a link.

First, let us consider a study undertaken to test the disparagement notions. Zillmann, Bryant
and Cantor (1974) varied the brutality of assault in political cartoons and measured humour
appreciation. They also obtained an independent index of the respondent's political preference.
The results indicated that mirth was reduced when the magnitude of the mishap befalling a
resented candidate was extreme. In another study, Cantor and Zillmann (1973) also reported
that increased severity of misfortune impaired humour appreciation in jokes depicting a
resented victim. Interestingly, disparagement theory predicts that such situations would be
the funniest. These results are easily explained, however, if we assume that even a hostile
respondent might have difficulty resolving or explaining extreme brutality.

A study by Gutman and Priest (1969) also supports our suggestions. Gutman and Priest
manipulated the perceived character of a verbal aggressor and a victim who got squelched in
a punchline. Their results indicated that when the aggressor's overall behaviour was
perceived as socially acceptable, the hostile punchline was perceived as both more justifiable
and more humorous than when the aggressor's behaviour was perceived as socially unacceptable.
These results are interpretable within the disparagement framework since the humour was
greatest when the 'good guy' aggressed against the 'bad guy'. Note, however, that the authors
interpreted their results in terms of the social acceptability of the actions described in
the joke. Presumably, it is more acceptable for a 'good guy' to aggress, and therefore more
funny. The results are just as easily interpreted in terms of the incongruity-resolution
model, that is, it is reasonable to assume that when a 'good guy' squelches a 'bad guy' the
squelch appears justified, makes sense, and is acceptable, but not the converse.

The influence of acceptable behaviour on humour appreciation has received recent attention
from McGhee. McGhee (1974c) examined the relationship between moral development and
children's appreciation of humour. McGhee found that heteronomous children (those who give
less attention and weight to the intentions of a transgressor) perceive jokes more funny as
the amount of damage that occurs increases. Autonomous children (who give weight to
intentions in moral judgments), in contrast, find jokes less funny if the joke outcome is
perceived as being the result of morally unacceptable behaviour. That is, if the initiator
is perceived as intentionally destroying some property the event becomes naughty or wrong
rather than funny. The incongruity-resolution interpretation of these data would be that
older children find it difficult to resolve or justify the events described in the joke when
they are the result of bad intentions and thus they do not find the joke funny. The younger,
heteronomous children, however, are not attuned to intentions and therefore apparently do
not need to justify or resolve the action. It is interesting in this regard that Shultz and
Horibe (1974) reported that children under the age of eight or so need only to perceive joke
incongruity to find a cartoon funny, while older children need to find an explanation or
resolution for the incongruous events described. As it turns out, it is at about the age of
seven or eight when children shift from heteronomous to autonomous morality.

There is one source of data which seems at first to contradict the present analysis. In
their 1972 study Zillmann and Cantor reported that jokes that disparaged superiors were
found funnier by subjects with subordinate experiences than were jokes that disparaged
subordinates. Novelty ratings of the joke outcome were also taken and indicated that the
situation in which superiors dominated subordinates was seen as most novel. In fact Zillmann
and Cantor state because these results are inconsistent with an incongruity model they

eliminated the incongruity notion as a possible alternative account of their results. However, incongruity according to the present analysis is only a necessary not a sufficient condition for the humour response. A clear test would have subjects rate disparagement jokes for humorousness and would collect information on subjects' perception of incongruity and satisfaction with their resolutions.

The last empirical study to be discussed is the most relevant to the present analysis. In a recent paper Zillmann and Bryant (1974) directed their attention to humour communications which involve an exchange of insults between two protagonists identified only by commonly occurring names. The authors reasoned that the disparagement model should not apply here since the respondent has no appreciable degree of negative sentiment toward the victim. To explain these cases Zillmann and Bryant argued that mirth in this case depends on the perception of the behaviour enacted by the antagonistic parties. Specifically, Zillmann and Bryant proposed that mirth is maximal when the exchange of negative consequences is about equal, that is, when the victim's retaliation is of similar magnitude as the damage he suffered. In a study which manipulated the retaliatory equity of the joke events, Zillmann and Bryant found that fair retaliation provoked the greatest mirth while under- or over-retaliation impaired mirth, thus supporting their hypothesis.

In discussing their retaliatory equity notion, Zillmann and Bryant argued that their results are consistent with Piaget's notion of retributive justice. Mirth is impaired in inequitous situations because the respondent's intuitive sense of justice is disturbed.

A moment's thought suggests the congruence of this formulation with our earlier discussion. It is suggested by Zillmann and Bryant, consistent with the two-stage model, that adequate and justifiable reason must be perceived by the respondent for the actions portrayed in the joke, specifically the incongruous and hostile outcome. Either over- or under-retaliation will not allow the respondent to formulate a satisfactory or adequate resolution for the events described in the humorous communication.

SUMMARY

In this paper we have attempted to relate two supposedly different theories of humour appreciation. The two-stage model has been primarily stated in cognitive terms, while the disparagement theories are generally couched in social terms. It is our contention, however, that the incongruity-resolution model may be capable of incorporating much of what has been reported by disparagement theorists and researchers. This does not mean we are disparaging their efforts. On the contrary, work drawn from the disparagement perspective has helped all researchers to focus on crucial variables that influence humour appreciation. It may nevertheless be useful, for future theoretical and empirical development, to interpret disparagement research in terms of the two-stage incongruity-resolution model. This approach has several advantages since it suggests a more global theoretical framework which incorporates both cognitive and social dimensions involved in humour appreciation.

The present author readily concedes that this analysis is speculative and further that the terms 'incongruity' and 'resolution' may have been stretched to an extent that is undesirable. It is conceivable that disparagement and incongruity-resolution are parallel processes each having separate influences on humour appreciation. In the last analysis, only empirical research can determine whether one process subsumes the other. If this paper motivates such research, it will have achieved its purpose.

ACKNOWLEDGEMENTS

The writing of this paper was supported by a SUNY Research Grant. The author is grateful to Howard Tennen for his comments on an earlier draft.

FOOTNOTES

1. The author is indebted to Gary Alan Fine who brought this point to the author's attention.

2. Other explanations for this phenomenon have been proposed by Goldstein (1976) and by La Fave and Mannell (1976).

REFERENCES

See Bibliography for publications on humour, laughter and comedy

Jones, J.M., Cognitive factors in the appreciation of humor: A theoretical and empirical
    analysis. Unpublished doctoral dissertation, Yale University (1970).

Suls, J.M. & Shaw, E., A further examination of the salience hypothesis in humor appreciation.
    Unpublished manuscript, SUNY-Albany (1976).

Operationalization of Incongruity in Humour Research: A Critique and Suggestions

Göran Nerhardt

University of Stockholm, Sweden

This paper opens with three points that emerge from traditional views on incongruity and humour. This is followed by a brief recapitulation of a formal model proposed in Chapman and Foot (1976). In the main part of the paper some empirical investigations are criticized with respect to the operationalization of incongruity, and the model is applied to some of them.

The first point is that humour is seen as a consequence of the discrepancy between two mental representations, one of which is an expectation and the other is some other idea or a percept. This view is expressed in many formulations, usually referred to as incongruity theories of humour. Examples are the formulations by Kant, Schopenhauer and Spencer (see Piddington, 1963). It is evident that incongruity defined in this way is a highly personal variable and that we should be cautious when treating it as a more objective or interpersonal stimulus variable.

The second point is that the constituents of incongruity in humour are seen as similarity and dissimilarity. This is the case in, for instance, the formulations by Addison, Beattie and Schopenhauer (see Piddington, 1963). Similarity is not defined in these formulations, which therefore, leave room for a liberal interpretation. Similarity and dissimilarity must, of course, be seen as highly personal variables, too, although not to the same extent as incongruity (Consider, for instance, similarity in terms of common verbal labels).

The third consideration is that the incongruity considered theoretically in relation to a certain humour stimulus is the incongruity that is specific to that humour stimulus. This is implied in all well-known definitions of humour in terms of incongruity, an example being Koestler's (1964) definition. From this it will be appreciated that a humorous situation may include incongruities which are not relevant to the humour stimulus under consideration.

THE MODEL

The model has already been detailed in Chapman and Foot (1976). The essential features of it are as follows: An event is referable by an individual to several mental classes. In a situation where the event constitutes a stimulus, these classes are psychologically available to different degrees, due to recency and frequency of usage. It is considered, however, that when this availability is held constant, an event is referred to a class with a probability which is a positive function of the event's 'total similarity' (that is, similarity dependent on all 'unidimensional similarities', among other things) to typical members of the class (or to a 'class type'). This in turn rests on the assumption of a positive relationship between frequency of represented events in the class and total similarity to the class type. Within a class the distribution of the frequency of different degrees of unidimensional similarity to a typical quality is likewise a positive function. (Folding a normal distribution of qualities yields the similarity distribution exemplified in Figure 1, but there are also dichotomous and other distributions). Now, funniness of an event is seen as a function of the divergence from expectations of qualities in a dimension, and this divergence in any one dimension is a direct function of the frequency in the class of the event's similarity to a class-typical quality. Thus, referring to Figure 1, an event with the similarity B to a typical quality in its class diverges more from expectations in this dimension and is funnier than another event, with the similarity A — because the frequency in the class of similarity B is lower than that of similarity A.

When two events (or two elements of an event) are perceived or thought of together or in close succession, each will actualize respective classes in which they are fairly close to class types and class-typical qualities. If one of the events is perceived as similar to the types in the other event's classes (and as these classes are highly available), they will become reference classes for the former event. If an event in this manner becomes a member of a certain class actualized by another event and at the same time diverges enough in unidimensional similarity from a typical quality in that class, it will be found funny. If, on the other hand, the event does not have sufficient total similarity to the second event, it will not become a member of the class, there will be no expectations about it as a member of that class and there will be neither divergence from expectations nor funniness. Thus, if unidimensional similarities of an event with another event decrease, and consequently also total similarity decreases, the funniness of the event will increase at first and then decrease.

OPERATIONALIZATION OF INCONGRUITY: CRITIQUE OF EMPIRICAL INVESTIGATIONS AND ANALYSES IN TERMS OF THE MODEL

Mull (1949) analyzed the formal qualities, among other things, of passages in music that were judged to be funny. This study represents an uncomplicated approach to the problem of formal elements of humour. A more deliberate attempt to penetrate the matter was made by Kenny (1955), whose subjects were asked to tell how 'expected' different joke endings were. In Kenny's case, it must be borne in mind that a joke is typically constructed so as to contain incongruity. The punchline diverges from expectancy built up by the body of the joke, and the extent of this divergence varies the humour value among jokes. At the same time it is conceivable that a joke is very funny when, as a joke, it contains exactly the expected amount of unexpectedness. In other words, the expectancy relevant to the main funniness of the joke may differ from the expectancy concerning the joke as a member of the class of jokes. It is conceivable that the 'relevant' incongruity was not operationalized in Kenny's experiment. Similarly, the study by Pollio and Mers (1974) does not contain a test of the incongruity hypothesis. These authors defined predictability of joke endings (continuations of what was said in a jocular situation) in terms of how well the endings were actually predicted by subjects.

Shurcliff (1968), Dodd and Lewis (1969), Lewis and Goldberg (1969), Lewis and Harwitz (1969) and Nerhardt (1970) presumably manipulated relevant divergence from expectations. These experiments all belong to the category where, when applying the model, either one classification class or several classes with equal distributions as to similarity must be assumed for the event whose funniness is studied. In the experiments by Lewis and co-workers, children were presented six identical visual stimuli prior to a seventh, which was different, and smiling was observed. Values for a seventh identical stimulus were obtained by extrapolation. It is seen in these experiments that the specific (seventh) event presumably varied in similarity to a type in a constant class which existed as a consequence of the presentation of the preceding six events. The relationship in one dimension between the specific stimulus and the class is illustrated in Figure 1.

In Shurcliff's experiment, on the other hand, along similar lines of reasoning, one of three classes was made psychologically available to the subjects by means of instruction and visual arrangements, before a specific event was presented. The classes can be described intuitively as handling a docile rat in an experimental situation, taking a small amount of blood from a rat in an experimental situation, and taking a large amount of blood from an 'aggressive' rat in an experimental situation. The specific event (whose funniness was studied) was the sudden presentation of a toy rat. This specific event, it is postulated, immediately belonged to a class which had been made available in the situation, on account of its total similarity to the class type in it. The event still belonged to the class when perceived in its entirety, but at that moment it was also found to diverge in several unidimensional qualities from the typical elements in the class. If, now, it can be assumed that the three classes in the experiment were equally distributed as to total and unidimensional similarities, the divergences, which were a function of the unidimensional distributions, should increase with decreasing similarity of the class-evoking events (specified by the instructions) to the specific event. And the funniness, too, should increase, as in fact it did in Shurcliff's experiment. The case is illustrated in Figure 2. In my experiment, (Nerhardt, 1970) both ways exemplified above of getting at divergence from expectancy were practiced.

Ertel (1968; referred to by Berlyne in Goldstein & McGhee, 1972) conducted an experiment in which the results are readily explicable in terms of incongruity, when it is postulated that some of the stimuli fell within a certain class and some fell outside (fell into a broader class with less precise expectations). Texts representing different approximations to German served as stimuli and the subjects judged their funniness. It can be reasoned here that language which is little removed from normal language represents little divergence from expectation as a member of the normal language class. Language which was moderately removed

Fig. 1 Distribution in a class of the frequency of different degrees of
        unidimensional similarity to a typical quality.

        A stimulus at position B represents more divergence from expectancy
        than one at position A because there is a lower frequency of that
        degree of similarity in the class.

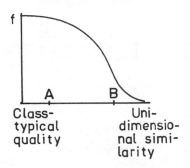

Fig. 2 The position of a stimulus with a certain degree of a quality
        (SQ) on similarity in that dimension with class-typical qualities
        in three classes.

        The curves stand for frequencies of degrees of similarities in
        the classes. It is seen that the stimulus (for example, the toy
        rat in Shurcliff's experiment) diverges greatly from expectations
        (as to difficulty, for instance) as a member of the class with
        the A distribution (the aggressive rat class), less in the class
        with the B distribution (sampling blood from a normal rat) and
        less still in the class with the C distribution (the handling-of-
        rat class).

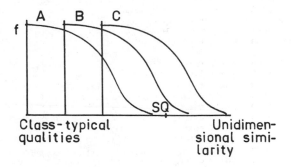

represents substantial divergence. Language, finally, which was far removed does not represent any divergence at all because it is too dissimilar to be referred to the class of meaningful language and is thus not subject to expectations as a member of that class. Ertel found that moderately distorted language was judged funnier than slightly or highly distorted language. This might therefore represent not an unverted-U-shaped relationship between incongruity and funniness but a monotonically increasing one.

Jones (1970) in an experiment on cartoons, argued that the caption of a cartoon implies a certain situation and the picture represents a different situation. Incongruity exists between the caption and the picture. It is negatively correlated, over cartoons, with similarity between the 'caption situation' and the visual situation, and so is degree of funniness. The model presented here can be readily applied to a single cartoon; both events - the situation implied by the caption and the situation in the picture - actualize classes in which the respective event is fairly close to class types and class-typical qualities. One event then becomes a member of a certain class actualized by the other event and eventually diverges in similarity in some dimensions from typical qualities in that class, and is funny. The funniness may increase when the similarities diminish but it finally decreases when these diminishing similarities make the total similarity of the event to the class type so small that the event leaves the class. The incongruity and funniness are a rising and falling function of diminishing total similarity between the events. When several different cartoons are used, however, one cannot predict the relationship between similarity and funniness or incongruity. The reason for this is that although similarity between elements may be assessed, classes actualized by, say, the captions in different cartoons cannot be assumed to have equal distributions. There was no correlation between similarity and funniness in Jones' experiments.

The concept of 'explanation of incongruity' and related concepts as used in humour research tend to be confusing. Jones (1970), using cartoons, conducted an experiment with children. One of the cartoons pictures three giraffes, two standing with heads high, the third with its head close to the ground. The caption reads: 'heights make him dizzy'. According to Jones, incongruity was present between the giraffes with their heads in the air and the one with its head low down, and the caption explained this incongruity. It is clear, however, that the incongruity relevant to the main funniness of the cartoon is not that between the giraffes but rather the divergence of the particular manifestation of dizziness from the more common forms. The caption, far from explaining the incongruity, is an integral part of it.

Shultz (1972) in two investigations on cartoons, worked with a variable which he called 'solution of the incongruity'. As an example of the material used, a cartoon is given depicting a little girl, with an empty bucket, angrily leaving a cow bearing the sign, 'out of order'. A fundamental mistake, in terms of traditional incongruity theory, is committed in the reasoning around this cartoon. The little girl in the picture is said to afford a resolution of its incongruity. The resolution implies that 'the subject discovers that the two incongruous elements (the sign and the cow) share some important characteristic (malfunction) which he had not previously noticed'. It is evident that malfunction is not a characteristic of the sign but rather of the machine implied by the sign. Also the incongruity relevant to the funniness of the cartoon does not lie in the relation between the sign and the cow but in the relation between the idea of a machine and the cow. In other words, the relevant incongruity lies in the divergence of this particular cow from typical cows on the machine dimension, typical cows being close to 0 on'machineness'. Thus, if by resolution is meant that the subject discovers this relationship, the girl in the cartoon is just an aid to that discovery or a commentary on the incongruity. The solution in this sense does not constitute a structural part of incongruity.

To test the model, a series of studies was carried out with nonrepresentational figures (Nerhardt, 1975). With reference to the results, it can be concluded that more work is needed before the model can be considered substantially supported. In any event a uniform definition of incongruity is much needed among researchers.

REFERENCES

See Bibliography for publications on humour, laughter and comedy

Dodd, C. & Lewis, M., The magnitude of the orienting response in children as a function of changes in color and contour. Journal of Experimental Child Psychology, 8, 296-305 (1969).

Jones, J.M., Cognitive factors in the appreciation of humor: A theoretical and experimental analysis. Unpublished doctoral dissertation, Yale University (1970).

Lewis, M. & Goldberg, S., The acquisition and violation of expectancy: an experimental
    paradigm. Journal of Experimental Child Psychology, 7, 70-80 (1969).

Lewis M. & Harwitz, M., The meaning of an orienting response: a study in the hierarchical
    order of attending. Educational Testing Service Research Bulletin, Princeton, New
    Jersey, April (1969).

Humour as a Form of Social Control:
A Deviance Approach

Chris Powell

University of Stirling

It is my intention in this paper to suggest that it is possible to interpret jokes and joke situations as having significance in terms of what can be claimed to pass for 'order'. I want to argue that the process of distinguishing 'deviance' from 'normality', or in some cases 'deviance' from 'the ideal' (which I maintain is the most crucial aspect of humour), operates at several different levels - of most importance those of interpersonal order, group or sub-cultural order, and finally societal order.

My fundamental argument, that humour is concerned with ideas/behaviours in some ways separate from, or deviations often in conflict with 'normal order', has been implicitly recognized by most classical theorists of humour. The joke, for Freud, fulfilled an equilibrium function for the individual monitoring system, which was given a 'temporary holiday' from its primary purpose of clarifying the serious nature of everyday life. Hobbes' 'superiority' approach, in suggesting that individuals respond with humour to attack a target whose status is thereby diminished, similarly emphasizes the 'separateness from normal order' angle, given Hobbes' somewhat naive belief that 'normality' involved being sufficiently good-mannered not to denigrate fellow human-beings. The 'incongruity' theories of writers such as Kant, taking the view that humour hinges upon perceiving 'anything out of the ordinary' when unaccompanied by a sense of danger (to which I shall return) can be seen to fit my interpretation, as does Bergson's essential distinction between spontaneous and automatic behaviour, where individual automatism is ridiculed by a generalized audience for failing to measure up to the natural spontaneous and alert dimensions of a 'normal' human.

Most of the afore-mentioned theorists gravitate towards, but fail to make explicit two interconnected ideas. (A) The interpretation of any fragment of experience as 'humorous' depends on the recognition from someone, some group or some society, that certain ideas and behaviours are in certain contexts and situations 'deviant', and (B) that such a recognition implies that the 'recogniser' holds certain ideas and behaviours to be 'normal' within such contexts: that is, representative of 'normal' order. Thus the entire 'humour experience' is in a constantly fluctuating but always present form, a commentary on order. Following on from these points, it could be further suggested that any target of humour is simultaneously a target for invalidation.

A major theoretical advantage of this kind of an approach is that it is capable of providing at least some kind of an explanation as to why some people find certain aspects of 'social-happenings' 'funny' whilst others do not, and indeed may even feel nauseated by apparently the 'same' event stimulus. Whereas Bergson and Kant, for example, were implying that certain events were almost objectively comic, and Freud seems to have found any exterior social object virtually irrelevant, this 'normality' versus 'deviance' or 'rule-breaking' approach solves the problem by recognizing that different individuals, groups and societies recognize different norms and rules and thus find a wide variety of events and ideas funny and worthy of humorous comment. Many variables are involved, in terms of 'time' for a brief example, it is commonplace to make mockery of past fashions of dress, fashions treated with great seriousness at the time. We respond with humour where our attention is drawn to 'events' in the widest sense, which from our perspective seem to break some kind of rule, be it of 'rational' opinion, taste, manners or behaviour. What it is that constitutes 'our perspective' is constantly fluctuating and is therefore probably incapable of ever being fully defined or described.

Since, according to this 'rule-breaking' framework, there is no reason why different people should not respond in widely divergent ways to what are apparently the same stimuli, neither is there any reason why different people should not respond in apparently the same way to overtly the same stimuli. I shall use a short example to make clear that it is indeed the case that even individuals or groups with widely diverse values, perspectives and identifications can laugh at stimulation derived from the same fragment of experience. Given that the interpretation of the next event is to be one of humour, information passed on by a varied series of signals, prepares or cues the audience for the 'appropriate' response. These cues may take a linguistic or para-linguistic appearance at the informal 'everyday in the office' level or 'comic' music, or an announcer describing a television or radio programme as a comedy at a more formal or 'canned' level. Provided with the predisposition for reacting with amusement, the potential for recognizing different rule-breaking as the comical one 'par excellence' exists. I'll use Chaplin's 'Modern Times' to show how this could operate given purely hypothetical ideal-types of audience, in this case from overtly diametrically opposite ends of the political spectrum — radical left and radical right.

A probable marxist interpretation of Chaplin's antics in an American factory of the 1920's is to see Chaplin acting legitimately as both film-maker and character by exposing the dehumanizing working conditions inherent under capitalism. Chaplin's Tramp responds sanely and rationally by acting against the interests of the factory as a focus for production. Chaplin, the film-maker, has pointed to the activities commonplace within the factory situation and argues that such activities deviate from his personal standards of fairness, which he is implying should be regarded as absolute standards. People laugh because they applaud the sentiments of this assessment. A right-wing interpretation might see Chaplin as film-maker portraying the factory situation as representative of a legitimate normality and Chaplin the tramp as a deviant. We laugh because the tramp fails to measure up to the required level of competence in the factory situation. The causes of laughter are quite different, but nevertheless both audiences have found something humorous; each has discovered a deviant. However, if our left- and right-wing hypothetical friends were to be provided with supplementary information, for example that Chaplin is a 'socialist', a different interpretation might have to be found, in this case from the right-wing viewer. Chaplin the 'tramp' and Chaplin the 'film-maker' now merge whilst originally they were regarded as quite separate. Chaplin, far from being humorous is now to be categorized within a serious framework and is to be considered a threat to the normal social order. This is, of course, what actually happened to Chaplin and is indeed something which comedians from Lenny Bruce to Billy Connelly are constantly threatened by, that their rule-breaking is interpreted as serious or their topics are considered too serious to joke about (placed within a joke framework). As an aside, one could have predicted that Claude Faraldo's film 'Themroc' would have been interpreted similarly to 'Modern Times'. As with Chaplin's film, there was no dialogue to provide supplementary information. I would like to emphasize that the question of misinterpretation as such does not, in my opinion, have to arise. We are not talking of absolute realities, but rather of a world of multiple realities and constructed meanings.

I believe the general 'rule-breaking' framework holds good not only for situations where we are provided with apparently direct evidence to suggest that a given experience is funny, but also where people laugh without such direct evidence, but again for widely diverse reasons. Two people may laugh at a piece of modern art, one because he believes it is making a valid point in ironically commenting upon the imperfect nature of contemporary life, the other because he believes it deviates from his standards of what it is that constitutes art. The crucial point is that people respond according to what they think is the meaning of a given event.

We have been talking so far predominantly of interpreting messages in joke form. If we adopt the model of an individual as a transmitter as well as a receiver of messages, we confront the other major dimension of humour as a topic for study. Not only do people interpret messages according to their predisposed perspectives and then process them according to their system of classification and categorization, but they also send out messages based upon their same categorization of meaning. If we argue that everyday discourse is a reflection of the individual's or group's recognition and consciousness of self or group identity, humour can be seen to be a part of that constructed self or group. Humour, with its dependence upon stereotype and exaggeration can be regarded as an indication of an overall world view. On the topic of feminism, for example, an individual or group can use the tools of humour, stereotype and exaggeration, to equate feminism with bra-burning. Thereby two things are achieved. On the one hand, reinforcement of the individual or group attitude that feminists deviate from 'normal' women; political demands are thereby reduced to an irrelevant gesture. At the same time, that idea can be communicated to any given audience. Humour is used as a tool for attempting to control our thought-processes and our environment. Professional comedians, in trying to emphasize their separateness from 'normal' people, routinely use exaggeration techniques to achieve the impression they are aiming to construct, indeed regularly go out of their way to neutralize their 'normal' physical characteristics. Harry Langdon, for instance, refused to be filmed from behind, believing that he was insufficiently 'baby-like' from that angle.

So far I have been arguing chiefly at the interpersonal level, of individuals using and interpreting humour of learning about what constitutes 'normality' and communicating those ideas whether they be of balance or deportment (slapstick) of language (puns) or other forms of social experience. In so doing, there is a danger of overemphasizing the relative and arbitrary nature of social life, at the expense of the recognition that we live within a political system, the dominant members of which, like those of any other ruling or established group, have an interest in sustaining and maintaining their ideas of what constitutes 'normal'/ 'legitimate' actions, beliefs and demands, and those which do not. Because the 'Establishment' has far wider access to the instruments of mass-communication, it is their ideas which retain dominance. I would argue that humour is quite regularly used in a generally unsystematic, almost certainly non-conspiratorial though routine manner, to reinforce the 'world-view', values and norms of the 'Establishment' and to ridicule and invalidate those who constitute a threat. There are many examples of this, ranging from media response to the early feminists, through to C.N.D., hippies, homosexuals, and Asians in luxury hotels 'at tax-payers' expense'. I would suggest that a 'humour' reaction is an initial response to a deviation not perceived or thought of as being too serious. When circumstances become defined as serious, with suffragettes making stringent attacks on property, or French student demands and arguments being given a general degree of credence and legitimacy in 1968, an altogether harsher reaction is adopted and different social labels are used. The establishment is not alone in responding initially with rather patronizing humour and later more seriously. To quote an International Socialist pamphlet on the perceived threat of the National Front, 'Ten years ago the people who founded the National Front could be considered as nutters and cranks. Not any more'. The distinguishing factor is of course that in the final analysis the dominant political groupings have the ultimate powers of invalidation, and arguably retain somewhat of a stranglehold over interpretations of joke meanings and associated implications in the wider society. Conventional humour can be regarded as fundamentally ideological in character.

To conclude, humour can be regarded as a cornerstone of everyday social order, where appropriate and non-appropriate behaviours and ideas are demarcated at a generally informal level, by routine invalidation of the 'unconventional'. When the deviation is judged to be serious, social order is reinforced at a more systematic level with more severe repression for the deviant by the official agencies of social control - the judicial system, and more controversially the medical and psychiatric professions. 'Crime', 'mental-illness', 'sickness', and 'the comic' are all social labels for various forms of perceived rule-breaking in any given social order.

Black Humour in the Modern Cartoon

Robert Barshay

Prince George's Community College, Maryland

Perhaps one common characteristic of black humour applicable to all the genres in which it is found is the transformation of the invisible to the starkly visible. By wilfully attacking the jugular vein of culture, by becoming the lightning conductors of common anxiety, and by embodying the moral outrage in reaction against an outrageous world, the radical sensibility exorcises the private fears, submerged fantasies and repressed taboos from the collective unconscious of society (cf. Goldman, 1968).

Cartoonists, like their black humour cousins in standup comedy, drama and literature, make public that which is ordinarily private through comic confrontations. What they must expose, clarify and finally exorcise are the insanities, absurdities and contradictions of contemporary post-industrial society, the very conditions which have spawned, nourished and midwifed this thriving, but most ungenteel form of comedy. Limited, however, to a few words or to none at all, the cartoonists of the modern sensibility must express visually that which has been suppressed imaginatively; they must render pictorially the dissolution of all enduring touchstones in the cosmos for, at best, the conditional and the whimsical, and for, at worst, the sinister and the hostile. In perhaps the most compressed and elliptic genre of black humour, the cartoonist must suggest in a single frame the chaos and amoral relativity of contemporary living by an image which to be successful has to be simultaneously funny.

The cartoonist, then, is a modern shaman who must perform the magic of exorcism with almost magical finesse. He reveals the precarious situation in which modern man is rooted in a rootless world, exposes the uncontrollable forces against which man is ignorantly pitted, magnifies the impotence of man's will against arbitrary change and concerted hostility, and hopes to exorcise his all too frequent shrinkage from a being with dignity to an insensible object of manipulation. And this he accomplishes with the power of an image packed with meanings and associations.

The forerunner of the fully developed black humorists of today is undoubtedly Charles Addams, whose earliest collection of cartoons was first copyrighted in 1940. The title ('Addams and Evil') is significantly revealing, for the evil suggested by these cartoons is to be seen in the everyday life of contemporary society, and is not embodied in any specific social or political institution, idea or movement. Addams' vision comprehends evil as woven inextricably into the cultural fabric of life, the same material that garbs our bodies from morning to sleep.

The fifth cartoon in this volume, for example, depicts an obviously well-to-do lady sitting in the back of a taxi, with only the back of the driver's head visible. The passenger's look of astonishment is caused by the picture of the driver's face on his licence, attached to the car visor, which is visible both to her and to the reader. It is the kind of face which combines the most conspicuous features of a sex fiend and an uncommonly sinister monster. Though the cartoon is humorous, the implication of it is decidedly grave; the normal events of the day can and often do turn out to be unexpectedly abnormal and even fraught with indefensible dangers.

That such unnatural and unanticipated occurrences can intrude in our lives may not be altogether disturbing. But that they happen during special times set aside for pleasure and relaxation is particularly disconcerting, since it is precisely at these intervals that we are caught with our guard down, in positions of extreme vulnerability. For in another cartoon of this collection, Addams depicts a typical family on the beach, the father being buried by his son, while the mother is sitting on the towel near by. Again, a look of astonishment reveals something basically wrong in this otherwise happy family setting. The mother is dismayed by what appears to be a suspension of the ordinary laws of reality when she observes her son digging a path through the middle of her buried husband, who is shown divided into two separated parts - the covered legs on one side of the active boy and the covered chest on the other. This image suggests that cosmic absurdity can arbitrarily strike innocent scenes and disorient average people to cause intolerable anguish. His technique – the superimposition of sinister impossibilities upon the laws of reasonable experience – is, as I will demonstrate, developed and refined by Howard Shoemaker, a newer artist to this medium.

Grotesqueness and absurdity, the trademarks of Gahan Wilson's cartoons, are the devices by which this brilliant artist develops his themes. For example, the diminution of the 'little man', which, according to Norris Yates (1964), is the major motif in twentieth century American humour, is a staple in the menu of Wilson's art. In this century, the little man has been dethroned from the Newtonian universe of order by the forces of Darwinian social strife and competition, Freudian irrationality, and the unpredictable and random changes of a material environment in which man is merely another particle indifferently treated. More frequently, he is being subjected to even greater anguish, and one does not have to turn to the black humour of contemporary novelists to appreciate or, perhaps, despair over, the results.

In the December 1965 issue of 'Playboy' magazine, Wilson depicts the little man – perhaps a white collar clerk, wearing a conventional overcoat and hat, glasses, and carrying a brief-case – walking into an elevator. This is a common enough scene, except for the large bestial teeth at the entrance and the ceiling of the elevator, with just a drop of saliva visible. Not only has the little man shrunk in relation to his environment, now he is threatened with destruction by a malevolent universe in which the known and familiar objects of everyday life have become unpredictable and even evil.

Leonard Feinberg, in 'Introduction to Satire' (1967), observes that, '... the basic technique of satire is distortion ... and distortion implies disorder. A popular satiric method of achieving distortion is incongruity, which also results in disorder.' Gahan Wilson uses incongruity to express the disorder implied in another variation of the little man in the modern world; the psychological insecurity resulting from identity crisis, or the swift and unexpected reversal of roles. For example, Wilson shows a touring middle-aged couple, 'straight' from Middle America – the golfing hat, bermuda shorts and glasses unmistakably reveal their status – being accosted by a native huckster pandering a shrunken head. The caption reads: 'I'm sure of it, Harry – it's that nice Mr. Bently we met on the tour'! One source of irony in this cartoon is that Mr. Bently, undoubtedly a former prototypal American middle-class tourist, has become himself a tourist souvenir, or the kind of exotic curio that American tourists prize so dearly.

On a more terrifying level, however, Harry and his wife are suddenly confronted with the precariousness of their own status in this universe; the change from the role of free and conscious agents to whom others cater, to the one of insensible objects which others manipulate for their own interests, is unexpected and swift, the transformation of which is outside the will and control of the victims. The surprise of Harry and his wife, stemming from their recognition of whom the shrunken head was, is a short step away from the fear which must consequently accompany the recognition of their own psychological insecurity in a universe which acts arbitrarily, unexpectedly, and, too often, malevolently.

In many ways, the cartoons of Howard Shoemaker are closer to black humour than those of Gahan Wilson. Whereas the inspiration of the latter derives from a world hostile and unpredictable to man, Shoemaker's art evolves from a universe in which laws governing the most common events are upset or reversed, the results of which are phenomena physically impossible. In short, rational expectations are unfulfilled, in lieu of which the impossible and the absurd become the norm.

For example, in one cartoon a businessman walks up to a sun-dial to check the accuracy of his own watch ('Playboy', February 1966). Suddenly the triangular measure on the dial turns into the protruding dorsal fin of a shark, the rest of which emerges from within the dial to attack the gentleman. As a variation on the little man motif, there is a peculiarly sinister quality about this cartoon. That the man's environment will attack him unprovoked is clear enough in Wilson's work; but that such an attack emanates from a situation defying all the laws of reasonable experience has a new implication. No one and nothing can be taken for granted. Not only is everything in the universe to be distrusted, but all reality is to be assumed illusory unless proven otherwise.

An hilarious, but gruesome, cartoon shows a dentist who, while attempting to extract a tooth from his patient's mouth, pulls out his whole skull. This morbid absurdity has just enough illusion of credibility to work – the tooth, after all, is attached to the jaw which, in turn, is part of the skull. The irrelevance of the patient's and, inferentially, everybody's experiences is the most painful aspect of this cartoon. 'If you cannot trust your dentist, who can you trust?' is a question which must grow out of this picture.

In a world of flux and uncertainty, one marked by the impermanence of things and the instability of institutions, the fragility of values and the fetish of change; life is insecure, vulnerable to the anguish of disorder and surprise, and constantly threatened by the illusion of familiarity. When what is new becomes valued as an end in itself, and the dissemination and packaging of every shade of ideas become popularly accessible through the mass media, then cartoonists like Charles Addams, Gahan Wilson and Howard Shoemaker are justified in presenting a world in which absolutes, conventions, and standards are shattered, and in which things are not what they appear to be.

The physical threat to life is partially due to modern technology: pollution of the air and water, accidents from cars and other vehicles, wholesale death from new, improved methods of war, ad infinitum. Psychological disintegration is often the modern counterpart to physical destruction. The mechanization of work often implies alienation, discontent, and a sense of meaninglessness. Routinization of life and an inability to use and enjoy leisure are frequently translated into boredom and despair.

It is precisely these aspects of the contemporary world, in addition to the impersonality and incomprehensibility of science, government, and economics and their attendant bureaucracy and corruption, which make the little man feel so little and inconsequential. For all of these reasons and more, the pessimism and gloom implied in Addams', Wilson's and Shoemaker's humorous cartoons over man's cosmic status is the logical product of an illogical world. That we still laugh at them is our brightest hope, for it suggests that we are sane enough yet to appreciate the insanity of our condition.

Perhaps we are indebted more to the talent of these philosphers of popular culture than we are to the scholarship of professional academics in understanding emotionally and concretely the painful existence of our lives. By their art they have provided us with the means with which to perceive the madness of life and the fragility of physical and psychological well-being. And perhaps it is only through this recognition of the precariousness of the human condition in modern society that man can develop a strategy of survival, the appropriate emotional equipment with which to confront his problems without fear and trembling, but rather with a smile.

REFERENCES

See Bibliography for publications on humour, laughter and comedy

Goldman, A., The Comedy of Lenny Bruce. In: E. Quinn & P.J. Dolan, The Sense of the Sixties. New York (1968).

Verbal Jokes as De-Transformed Utterances and as Speech Acts

John Bradshaw

University of Aston, Birmingham

The theory of jokes presented here originated in three insights of Freud (1960), namely:

1. Humorous pleasure arises from both cognitive appreciation of the joke structure and the fulfilment of motivated purposes; the latter being facilitated by the former (p117).

2. Jokes are social processes and their success is conditional upon the observance of social rules (p150).

3. Joker and audience are unconscious of the psychological processes entailed (p176).

Two hypotheses are offered. H_1 is informed by the first and the third of Freud's insights. It is expressed in psycholinguistic concepts derived from Chomsky (1957), Fodor and Garrett (1967), Fodor, Garrett and Bever (1968), and Miller, Galanter and Pribram (1960). H_2 is informed by the second and third of Freud's insights. It is expressed in concepts derived from Searle (1969). H_1 is as follows: From deep structures and their explicit meaning (M), the joker (A) generates the joke-utterance (JU) about the butt (C). The audience (B) de-transforms JU and so guesses the deep structures, their collative meaning and A's intention. A and B are unaware of the psycholinguistic processes and of the knowledge of linguistic rules involved. H_2 is as follows. A performs a Speech Act, the non-defective performance of which depends on A's observance of conventional constitutive rules. A and B are unaware of the constitutive rules.

The general theoretical setting of these hypotheses is that B can guess M, and A's intention reliably provided that: (1) A and B have overlapping perceptions of themselves, of each other, and of C. (2) A and B have mastery of the semantic, syntactic and phonological rules of language (L) and of the dialect and special register in which JU is transmitted. (See the present author's concept of language mastery, 1974). (3) A and B have unimpaired speech, hearing and memory systems. (4) A and B have mastery of the conventional constitutive rules for Speech Acts. (5) B has the capacity and opportunity to attend selectively to JU.

H_1 and H_2 concern complex language skills and consequently are inapplicable to cartoon jokes and to trivial puns. Their application is restricted not merely to verbal jokes but to verbal jokes that do not depend on verbally triggered mental pictures as in 'Have you tried the famous echo in the reading room of the British Museum?' Hoffnung's joke belongs to a large excluded class of jokes which depend on incongruity between JU and the pictured situation. The emphasis in H_2 on observance of conventional rules for joking also excludes unannounced minor witticisms both intended and unintended.

JOKES AS DE-TRANSFORMED UTTERANCES (H_1)

Freud discovered that if JU is subject to post-hoc analysis it expands into two or more statements which are not humorous. He concluded that condensation occurs in joking as it does also in dreaming. It is now suggested that A works from these deep-structure statements; that he conjoins them or embeds them one within another and transforms the result mainly by deletions, in this way:

(1) Unperceptive persons are termed philistines.
(2) Stupid persons are termed donkeys.
(3) Academics are unperceptive persons and stupid persons.
(4) The academics are divided into students and professors.
(5) The academics are inhabitants of Göttingen.

1-5 are the deep structure statements having a collative meaning (M). Embed 5 in 4; conjoin the result and 3, generating:

(6) The academics who are inhabitants of Göttingen are divided into students and
    professors who are unperceptive persons and stupid persons.

Embed 1 and 2 in 6 generating:

(7) The <u>academics who are</u> inhabitants of Göttingen are divided into students <u>and
    professors <u>who are unperceptive persons who are termed</u> philistines and <u>stupid
    persons who are termed</u> donkeys.

Statement 7 is the prosaic product of 1-5. If it were uttered as the surface structure, B
could not fail to guess M. However, 7 is now subjected to massive deletions of the underlined
parts, yielding the 'super-surface-structure'. This phrase is borrowed from Leonard Bernstein
(in press). The result is:

   The inhabitants of Göttingen are divided into students, professors, philistines and
   donkeys.

This is JU and is one of the jokes quoted by Freud. Since B hears JU and not statement 7, he
must perform a piece of linguistic problem-solving in order to guess 1-5 and so, M. However,
the transformational deletions helpfully place students, professors, philistines and
donkeys together. This provides B with a clue, that the deep structure contains statements,
some of which are analogies, like 1-4, from which M can be guessed. Successful problem solving
is pleasurable in itself, but laughter results from the discovery that the superficially
innocent JU was generated from a concealed deep structure having a tendentious meaning M. B
is aware that A's intention was to amuse B and to express mild aggression at the same time.

The hypothesis that some verbal jokes are de-transformed utterances applies also to jokes with
a long build-up followed by a terse JU, the punchline. For example, in a joke about a man
who plays golf with an archbishop, there is a lengthy account of the game during which the
archbishop repeatedly warns his opponent not to say 'Damn it, I missed!' when failing to sink
putts. But the blasphemy is repeated at the eighteenth hole, whereupon there is a flash of
lightning, the archbishop is left writhing on the ground while a great voice from heaven
says 'Damn it, I missed!'. During the build-up a deep structure statement meaning 'mortals
are fallible' is elaborated, but it is not until JU itself is nearly complete that a clue is
offered which permits B to guess the other, parallel, undeveloped deep-structure statement,
meaning 'God is fallible'.

Returning now to the short joke about the inhabitants of Göttingen, M has a 'denotative'
component (it clearly refers to certain people), a 'logical' component (it clearly relates
four classes) and a clear 'affective' component of aggression. By contrast, JU in itself is
vague referentially and logically; it is affectively neutral. Thus JU and M are cognitively
and affectively incongruous. If, as appears likely, many jokes base emotional incongruity on
cognitive appreciation of linguistic structure, it is unnecessary in such cases to choose
between the two types of incongruity in order to explain the humorous effect of jokes, as has
often been supposed. Obviously it is no accident that 'students','professors','philistines'
'and donkeys' occur together in the JU; so also with the inversion contained in Churchill's
remark 'The Right Honourable Member is a sheep in wolf's clothing' and the portmanteau-word
in Disraeli's quip 'When a man fell into his anecdotage it was a sign for him to retire'.
Hence, if these surface features of JU are transforms of deep-structure statements, the
generative process is heavily guided toward a crucial surface structure feature. Yet, in this
respect, jokes are not exceptional, as the following transcription of part of a student's
speech shows:

   '.... we discussed whether <u>we</u> - <u>it</u> would be better "more app" for us ...'

At the time when <u>it</u> was selected in preference to <u>we</u>, the target was better or more appropriate;
thus the execution of the speaker's plan for expressing M was guided by his choice of a
particular lexical feature in the end-product, that is, the surface structure. More generally,
particularly since Friedman (1971) discovered that, unless a computer which has been programmed
with Transformational-Generative Rules of Syntax, is heavily steered by the operator, it
produces grammatically impeccable nonsense, it has been recognised that the speaker's intention
to communicate M guides his choice of phrase-structure rules, of lexical items, of transformations and of phonological rules. However, since the particular features of the surface
structure are crucial when joking, it may be that the generative process for a good joke is
unusually slow, complex, or both. Indeed, the present author takes leave to doubt that there
are any spontaneous jokes, and would not be surprised if it were discovered that A incubates a
novel JU for longer than his average time for prosaic utterances of equal length.

JOKES AS SPEECH ACTS

   '..speaking a language is performing speech acts, acts such as making statements...
   and...these acts are in general made possible by and are performed in accordance
   with certain rules for the use of linguistic elements'. (Searle, 1969, p16).

However, Searle labels play-acting and jokes 'parasitic forms of communication' and does not
regard them as speech acts. In the case of play-acting the ground for rejection is firm, since
the constitutive rules for stating p include:

It is not obvious to both A and B that B knows p.

The act counts as an undertaking that p represents an actual state of affairs.

Now, in play-acting, the actors already know p, and p is fictitious. Hence, statements in plays are not speech acts.

In the case of jokes, however, the ground for rejection is weakened by Searle himself when he points out that it is in the deep structure and 'we can often identify those elements that correspond to the illocutionary force' of a speech act (pp. 30,31, 64). Now the JU about the inhabitants of Göttingen does not represent an actual state of affairs at its surface level. But at its level of deep structure it does represent a state of affairs that A has reason for supposing to be actual, namely that the academics are unperceptive and stupid. Moreover, even if B knew this, he did not necessarily know that A knew it, and even if B did know that A knew, B did not necessarily know that A felt strongly on the subject. Hence, whereas JU does not imply a statement so straightforward as that implied by 'it's stopped raining' it does imply a statement in a roundabout manner. Hence, A's utterance of JU to B may be regarded as a speech act. Likewise, the jokes by Churchill and Disraeli mentioned earlier may be regarded as speech acts. Indeed, since all tendentious jokes will tell some B something about A, they may be regarded as complicated speech acts. However, many nontendentious jokes do not satisfy Searle's rules and turn out to be pseudo-statements, pseudo-questions, pseudo-promises and so forth. A clear example is the pseudo-statement: 'Two caterpillars were crossing the road. A butterfly flew overhead. One caterpillar said to the other "You won't get me up in one of those!"'

Few, if any, jokes are simple speech acts; some jokes are complicated speech acts while others are pseudo speech-acts, parasitic on the corresponding true acts. Nevertheless it is helpful to adopt Searle's approach, that is, to state the rules observed by A when he engages successfully with B in the social activity of joking. The rules are suggested below, bracketed ones being optionally applicable to long jokes.

Intention: A intends to achieve X, where X = amuse B, state p about C....by means of a joke, J.

Occasion: A knows that B can hear him and is paying attention.
A has reason to believe that B is not likely to be distracted and that B is not unwilling to be amused.

Audience: A believes that B can 'take a joke' (and that B can recognise a joke-commencement cue such as 'Have you heard...?', 'Did I tell you....?', 'There's a story about...!'
(A believes that, on recognising the cue, B will remain silent and attentive until JU is uttered, and that B will suspend judgment until JU is uttered).

Joke: A believes that B has not heard J before or recently, will not find J trivial, and will prefer his telling J to his not telling J.
A believes that B has sufficient intelligence to guess M from JU, has sufficient knowledge of C and has sufficient knowledge of the idiom or figure of speech particular to J.
A believes that B will not be merely embarrassed by J.

Skill: A knows that if the foregoing rules are observed and if his beliefs are justified he has the skill to utter J in such a manner as to stimulate B's interest about C, while preventing him from guessing M until JU is complete.

Laughter: A knows that he may laugh if B laughs, provided that M is implicit and not explicit.

Fulfilment: When all the above rules are observed, where relevant, the utterance of JU is the clue to M and hence is the token of A's intention to achieve X. The intention is fulfilled if B's laughter is triggered by JU and not adventitiously.

DISCUSSION

Two hypotheses about verbal jokes have been offered within a general, five-point theory of successful verbal joking. Each hypothesis narrows the gap between joking and other forms of verbal communication. In turn, this raises the issue as to whether some of the questions that are asked about verbal communication in general can be asked about joking in particular. The first hypothesis was that verbal jokes are de-transformed utterances; it encourages the following questions:

1. What syntactic features of joke utterances serve as clues to deep structure, and hence as clues to meaning?

2. Since, in child language development, comprehension of syntactically complex utterances precedes their production, does appreciation of verbal jokes precede their production?

3. Carol Chomsky has shown that mastery of transformation rules is not complete until at least about ten years after the onset of speech. Does appreciation and production of verbal jokes develop in early teenage?

4. Since degree of lateral cerebral dominance differentially affects performance on tasks requiring visuo-spatial ability as compared with tasks requiring formal analytical ability, is this also reflected in preference for picture jokes compared with preference for verbal jokes?

The second hypothesis was that verbal jokes have varying degrees of resemblance to speech acts; it encourages the following questions:

1. The constitutive rules for stating, greeting, asking, etcetera, are culture-free and language-free, and in those senses universal. Are the rules for successful verbal joking universal? For instance, are there societies in which it is not necessary that B has not heard the joke before or recently? Are there societies in which A laughs before B, or in which the response takes the form of some activity other than laughter?

2. To know the rules for effective joking is to possess a skill. Can the skills of joking and of joke-appreciation be taught?

3. The process of transforming several statements into an utterance terminating with a JU which stimulates the audience to guess what 'lies behind it' is, in principle, of wide application. Since, moreover, successful guessing is pleasurable, A is imparting knowledge to B under reinforcing conditions of learning. Is this a possible teaching technique? Can joking and similar verbal activities increase teacher-effectiveness? For example:

Johnny, finding life a bore, drank some H_2SO_4;
Johnny's father (an M.D.) gave him $CaCO_3$;
Now he's neutralised — 'tis true,
But he's full of CO_2.

4. It is forty years since the present author heard his Chemistry teacher recite this. Yet it is more readily retrievable from permanent memory than information imparted prosaically. Why?

REFERENCES

See Bibliography for publications on humour, laughter and comedy

Bernstein, L., The Unanswered Question. Norton Lectures, Harvard, in press (1976).

Bradshaw, J., What is language mastery? Audio-Visual Language Journal, 12, 129-133 (1974).

Chomsky, N., Syntactic Structures. Mouton, The Hague (1957).

Fodor, J.A. & Garrett, M., Some syntactic determinants of sentential complexity. Perception and Psychophysics, 2, 289-296 (1967).

Fodor, J.A., Garrett, M. & Bever, T.G., Some syntactic determinants of sentential complexity, II: verb structure. Perception and Psychophysics, 3, 453-461 (1968).

Friedman, J., A Computer Model of Transformational Grammar. Elsevier, New York (1971).

Miller, G.A., Galanter, E. & Pribram, K.H., Plans and the Structure of Behaviour. Holt, New York (1960).

Searle, J.R., Speech Acts. Cambridge University Press, Cambridge (1969).

The Psycho-Logic of Political Humour

Charles E. Schutz

Albion College, Michigan

This paper explores humour as a unique kind of reasoning or argumentation – almost an illogical logic of social thought. Humour is termed a psycho-logic, because, at least in its higher reaches, it is a highly rational form of thought, building upon psychological drives and emotional needs of men in society to fulfil social purposes. The thesis is concentrated on p itical humour. Because of the peculiar nature of politics (rule, authority, competition, conventionality, etcetera), political humour attains a complexity and intensity seldom achieved elsewhere. In short, the psychological causes of humour are stimulated and their expressions are rationally refined to the greatest peak by the nature of politics. Finally, under political rule, the psychology of humour develops a social form and social functions that endow it with a high survival value for social man.

THE SOCIAL NATURE OF HUMOUR

Few studies, with the notable exception of Koestler (1964), have probed the uniquely social nature and attendant logic of humour[1]. Yet, its psychology cannot be fully comprehended unless this dimension is charted, for original motivations may be radically altered by their humorous social expression. In effect, in humour, man's psychology must co-operate with his social rationality in a distinctive partnership.

The basis of the humorous partnership is a consubjectively transmissible communication between men. However idiosyncratic are the humorist's motivations, his humour must be consubjective in that it must cause 'parallel impressions in different human beings' (cf. Brecht, 1959). Humour requires a social sharing of private experiences. The social sharing is possible because of the uniformity and continuity of the objects of humour in the experiences of most people. But humour remains dependent upon its rational transmissibility between social creatures of like dispositions.

Political humour exemplifies these objective characteristics. Humour can choose an infinity of objects for its exercise, but social authority and man's response to it afford a constancy of objects that are intrinsically related to the psychology of humour. The objects are the essentials of man's governance in society, and given social man, governance is omnipresent. Governance requires social conformity. The biological individuation of man as a learning animal results in human diversity. The conflict between social man's conformity and biological man's individuation constitutes the heart of the comic agon – a perpetual conflict between society and man who retaliates humorously (cf. Cornford, 1914[2]). The comic agon can also take a reversed form in that the humorist may become society's censor against the socially deviant. In this instance, the participants in the humour (often a caricature or verbal exaggeration of some deviant feature of its target) are more threatened or repelled by the deviation from their group behaviour or beliefs than by social conformity. But the agon remains.

Man, the social animal, is a speech animal. He builds and maintains his societies through speech. He does not think with direct perception of phenomenological reality but with conceptual perception (speech-derived) of socially defined reality. Thus, his very reason is a rationality of words. In turn, all but our most simple humour[3] is a humour of words; its transmission is dependent upon a pattern of symbolic communication. No transmission, no humour. Obvious? Yes, but it adds a complex rationality to humour. Word construction requires rules of grammar; humour flaunts them by reversing or twisting premises, by adding conclusions which are contradictory or incongruous, by ignoring contextual meanings, and so on. Here are two examples: (1) The late United States Senator Langer, ill and aged at the time of U.S. President Eisenhower's 1966 candidacy, said that he deserved the presidency over the ailing incumbent. He was older, sicker, and needed the rest more. The conventional premise of strong leadership is replaced by a shocking one of convalescence. (2) In 1972, U.S. presidential candidate, Senator George McGovern, was characterized as a humble, self-effacing egomaniac. Two adjectives build an expectation shattered by a concluding and contradictory noun.

This is also word play (cf. Farb, 1974). Its humour is such that concealed aggression or repressions can be surmounted by the enjoyment and appreciation of word usage. In the 1972 presidential campaign a bumper sticker read, 'Vote for Nixon in '72. Don't change Dicks in the middle of a screw'. Aside from taboo violation, it presents rhyme, pun, word ambiguity, and a parody on an axiom. Even a Nixon partisan can take delight in the verbal virtuosity. Psychological sources remain, but the perverse logic adds an independent factor to the pleasure – our rational faculty.

The puzzle or problem-solving character of much humour (recognition of axiom in the above) also appeals to our rational faculty. Then, our pleasure in the covert expression of the aggression in humour is preceded or supplemented by our pride of superiority in a successful exercise of our reason. In fact, the target of the humour can become secondary to the manner of its expression. One can be the target and, nevertheless, appreciate its rational expression.

Often, the humour of word play has to do with taboo words or subjects. Their use is permissible because the speech act of humour skirts the formal rules of taboo, and the wordiness of humour allows even further camouflage of the violation.

Speech taboos are conventional prohibitions imposed on us by social authority. They repress our sense of freedom and primal urges which society frowns upon. The violation of taboos in humour provides a cathartic release from 'civilization and its discontents'. Their use is spice in the meat of political humour, but also functional in the maintenance of society[4]. The humour of taboo words is a humour of logic – rational word play. The psychological connotations of the taboo words provide the thrill of pleasure, but their deliberate employment is an objective word construction requiring rationality. The stock ploy is the double entendre, ambiguity in word or expression. The humorist constantly seeks the ambiguity in order to accomplish the taboo violation in a socially acceptable manner.

Finally, the most complex rationality of the humour of man, the speech animal, is to be found in the constant disparity between man's words and the phenomena to which they refer. All words are symbols denoting other things, some reality 'out there'. Then, our social world that ordains our symbolic representations is another reality grounded in the words as basic to our existence. Thus, there is the ultimate reality of the universe, the social realities of men, and the conceptual realities of men's words whereby they express to one another their realities. To add to the confusion, the Western world poses a Platonic or Christian 'reality' of an ordered universe beyond all apparential realities.

Humour often plays with the disparities between these levels of reality (in the divine comedies of Plato, Dante, Cervantes with the deepest seriousness; see Feibleman, 1939, for divine comedy), pitting the verbal inadequacy of symbols of one reality against the comic aggressor's verbal vision of another reality. Though each is necessarily a word construction of man, their effects are 'real' enough in their feedback on man's feelings, actions, and humour.

In short, words are conventions that contain social conventions and express them in a conventional logic – ripe targets for the unconventional or anti-conventional humorist. In his 'Republic', Plato ridicules the corrupt world through his vision of the good. In like manner, Jules Feiffer, playwright-cartoonist satirist, ridicules politics with a child-like vision of nature. When he was called a writer of adult cartoons, he replied that he writes for children. He said, 'the questions I seek to raise are always questions a young, not very bright, child might ask. Questions like "what is good and what is bad?" "Is good always good?" "Is bad always bad?" A child would answer "Yes"' (Black, 1960).

The reality posed by Feiffer against social conventionality is also one of words – a rational construction and itself a social convention. But its critical standard, posing a relationship of socially unadorned man to life's necessities, leads back to a new premise opposed to socially acceptable ones from which Feiffer deduces 'absurd' reasoning on social issues, culminating in shocking conclusions. The pleasure for the audience or humour participants lies in the shared anti-social biases, successful defiance of social authority, and the harmless release of aggressive tensions. But it all takes place in a word reality requiring our social rationality[5].

The radical 'childish' perspective of Feiffer's humour is a rational manner of comic invention. Its psychological causation remains, but his humour is rational and deliberate. Sociologically, his comic perspective is that of the marginal man, one who exists within a society but is not fully a part of its culture. Generally, the marginal man possesses social attributes opposed to the dominant culture or lacks attributes vital to it. Either way, the 'reality' of society fails to fasten its logic (conventions) on him.

Most marginal man humour is attached to some sub-culture within a larger society[6]. All subcultures endow their marginal men with a comic advantage. They possess a vantage point with alternative ways of thought from which to observe critically society's conventions and ways of behaviour. In some men these observations are channelled into the humour of social satire. Most importantly, all marginal men are enabled to see social conventions as merely one reality among others.

In the end socially critical humour parallels the philosophic issue of nature versus convention or 'what is real?' The humorist as ironist takes one side, then the other, depending on what he and his audience perceive to be the antagonist of the moment. This classical agon of man-against-society is rooted in the dual nature of man - social and individual, each natural and necessary, but both a threat to each other. Humour serves as a peaceful reconciliation of opposites, making the strains of the human agon bearable.

THE POLITICAL PSYCHOLOGY OF HUMOUR

The most common types of political humour in the United States are comic invective, dirty political jokes, and comic stories. Each one, in different degrees, has the agonistic form and employs the counter logic of word play. Yet, each type exploits and retains basic drives of man. Comic invective is the most aggressive of political humour, but it may be the most typical humour of democratic politics and the least dispensable to it. Its very aggressiveness makes it so politically necessitous. Democratic politics continues men's rivalries, but it requires their peaceful expression and resolution. Words become the action of politics, and comic invective, as a humorous verbal abuse, ridiculing, or insulting of someone or thing, becomes the substitute for violence. Political man can express his rage, contempt, sense of difference without disrupting the fragile peace of political societies. The mock warfare of comic invective is a continuation of aggression by other means - the genius of humour. If comic invective cultivates language to covertly aggress through it, dirty political jokes seem to degrade language to escape social repression. Sex-related humour is the most popular, continuous, and, probably, ancient of comic forms. If politics requires a sublimation of aggression, and if our socialized sexual behaviour demands a repression of even more basic drives, then dirty political jokes, releasing the tension of both aggression and repression humorously are bound to be winners.

In fact, the popularity of obscene political humour may be grounded in a relationship between their vulgarity and the egalitarian ethos of the 'vulgus-populus'. Freud termed obscene humour an 'unmasking'. In politics that unmasking performs a levelling function for the subjects against the rulers. It is a comic calling-to-common-humanity of the high and mighty. In effect, humour which employs references to our basic biological drives and functions strips away cultural superficialities to reveal man's common and continuing animality. When it is employed against personages who have attained social eminence, obscene humour gives the pleasure of permissibly expressing the sex drive and flaunting its taboo, and politically the obscenities level the superiors to a common equality. They too are vulnerable and, thus, inferior. We are all equal!

In levelling our rulers back to a common humanity, obscene humour restores a psychological equality and facilitates democratic equality. In sum, dirty political jokes, by the very nature of their initial employment of taboos, engage in a primary form of social criticism. A dirty joke may be a mere witty crudity, but in its initial rejection of moral conformity, obscene humour challenges convention with man's primary nature. George Orwell once wrote, 'but the point is that the modern emphasis on what is called "clean fun" is really a symptom of a general unwillingness to touch upon any serious or controversial subject. Obscenity is, after all, a kind of subversiveness.' (See Orwell & Angus, 1968, Volume 3, pp286-288).

The third form of political humour is the most social in the psycho-logic of humour. In fact, when most analyses of humour find aggression and superiority to be its concealed motivations, the benevolence of the comic story should receive far greater attention. Moreover, throughout the ages, comic stories have been a means of education through entertainment. Comic stories are probably the most rationally communicable of all political humour.

In the United States comic political stories flourished on the farm and frontier (and remain popular in the South). In these areas man, lacking the graces of civilization, re-developed the ancient art of story-telling. The story falls back on a fundamental characteristic of men, their talking to each other. Its comic element entertains and heightens the interest of the audience but the story can record experiences, point up a moral, and develop thought itself. Abraham Lincoln, President and America's greatest politician-humorist, succinctly stated its qualities:

I often avoid a long and useless discussion by others, or a laborious explanation on my own part, by a short story that illustrates my point of view. So, too, the sharpness of a refusal or the edge of a rebuke may be blunted by an appropriate story so as to save wounded feelings and yet serve the purpose. No, I am not simply a story-teller, but story-telling as an emollient saves me much friction and distress. (See Gross, 1912, p210).

In addition, to the charitability and educational purposes of the comic story, Lincoln refers to its economy of effort. His friend, Ward Lamon, said that his stories were most often 'labor-saving contrivances' (Sandburg, 1936, p305). Thereby, Freud's characterization of humour as 'economy of expenditure of thought' was anticipated by years.

The logic of the comic story is also economical, being analogical and utilizing metaphors and emotions to short circuit the reasoning to the desired conclusion. The comic story begins with a present situation about which the teller wishes to make a point. The teller recounts a story about some past event or fictional experience with a crucial similarity to the target situation. The basis of the humour lies in the story, but the conclusion concerning the present must be drawn by transference by the audience. The point is made by indirection (the story) and inference (conclusion by transference). The humorist-teller has camouflaged the message and cushioned any personal rebuke by having the analogue serve as the butt of the humour and by muting the practical conclusion.

Lastly, the humour and logic of the comic story is a matter of group participation. The group contributes its emotional set, common knowledge, stereotypes and perceptions, and the 'natural' logic of analogical reasoning. The comic story can, then, transcend its origins, attaining a group consensus and goodwill. Humour can be a political response to a possibly disruptive situation.

THE SOCIAL SENSE OF HUMOUR

Humour in politics springs from the encounter of man's psyche with his sociality: the sublimation of aggression, the continuing resentment of social authority, the necessary repressions of society, the levelling impulse against social hierarchy, and, even, man's creativity against social conformity. Our voluntary subordination to social authority is always strained by the rules which mould man-the-animal into man-the-citizen. Humour, like dreaming, gives us a socially tolerable outlet for 'the discontents of civilization'. A political regime should welcome comic invective and obscene humour, however overtly anti-social. While the humour accomplishes catharsis, it persuades acceptance of necessary conformity.

To sum up: The basic structure of almost all political humour is the comic agon - a competition between two or more contestants in which one is perceived as the antagonist and the other, the ironist who retaliates humorously. The agon pervades man's existence, and, most acutely, his politics. Humour is our psychological response and rational construction to resolve the tension of the struggle peacefully. The rationality in agonistic humour is, then, dialectical - an arguing against someone or thing, an exposing of its defects, fallacies, above all, its contradictions. Humour is a negative response; it proceeds against something, but its contribution is positive. Through humour, man achieves personal and social balance and maintains a mean between his individuality and his social necessities. The reconciliation or marriage in the agon of ancient Attic comedy is for all political humour the attainment of this mean.

Within the comic agon the essential device of humour is contradiction. As logic too begins in the perception of contradiction, the rationality of political humour is solidly based. We have spoken previously of the contradictions which plague man's existence and bless his humour: words versus things, words versus themselves, nature versus convention, spirit versus nature or convention, and so on. But there is a logic to the comic sense that contradicts the seeming illogic of its contradictory approach; the logic of formal rationality is an artificial imposition on man's rational comprehension of the illogic of our chance existence. Contradiction is the consequence of the agon between chance and order in man's reason.

The logic of political humour seizes upon all forms of contradiction as the stock ingredient of humour. The pattern of the comic rationality in politics is to use contradiction to strike against excess or defect. As political humour is negative, the genuine humorist will find the claim or stance which deviates most from a basic norm the best target for comic counter-aggression. To the extent that deviation is perceived by the audience as a threat or claim of superiority, they will identify with comic retaliation. The success of the humour lies in the restoration of equilibrium. Unlike overt aggression, humour does not destroy or disrupt, its gentle retaliation is reconciliatory.

Thus, the comic claim is a compromise. To view something humorously is to lessen hostility. That at which one can laugh is no longer fully threatening. To laugh at someone and with others in political humour is a step toward community. It is enough to say that, finally, there is a social sense in man which cultivates humour for the sake of community, and that successful political humour requires knowledge and rational construction.

FOOTNOTES

1. Oddly, Freud's concept of humour as 'economy of expenditure in thought' is invaluable for a logic of humour, but he never placed it in the social context of his 'Civilization and Discontents' or of 'Totem and Taboo'.

2. I have generalized Cornford's notion of the agon into a theory of humour in my forthcoming book: 'Political Humour'.

3. Childish miming or repetition might be an exception, but there is often the suggestion of a social norm in it.

4. Peter Farb's (1974) 'Word Play' explores the conventional character of taboo words. There are no objective standards which fix them. Yet, they are the stock ingredients of obscene humour.

5. cf. Martin Gardner's brilliant discussion of logic and reality of words in his note on Humpty Dumpty's defiance of word reality in Gardner (1976) pp268-270.

6. In the United States, Jewish humour is the most pervasive of marginal humour. Jews create humour about themselves and gentiles because of the friction between their sub-culture and the dominant culture. Thereby, they sublimate potentially dangerous aggressions and assert their superiority and uniqueness boldly but harmlessly.

REFERENCES

See Bibliography for publications on humour, laughter and comedy

Black, S.M., Sokolsky, Meet Feiffer. The New Republic, 17-18, June 6th (1960).

Brecht, A., Political Theory: The Foundations of Twentieth Century Political Thought. Princeton University Press, Princeton (1959).

Farb, P., Word Play. A. Knopf, New York (1974).

Gardner, M., (Ed.), The Annotated Alice: Alice's Adventures in Wonderland and Through the Looking Glass (by Lewis Carroll). Penguin, Harmondsworth (1976).

Gross, A., Lincoln's Own Stories. Harper Brothers, New York and London (1912).

Orwell, G., Funny, but not vulgar. In: S. Orwell & I. Angus (Eds.), The Collected Letters, Essays, and Journalism of George Orwell. Harcourt Brace and World, New York (1968).

Sandburg, C., Abraham Lincoln: The War Years. Harcourt Brace, New York (1936).

The Great Screen Clowns and the Development of World Cinema

Stuart Keen

Upton Pyne, Exeter

'The Great Screen Clowns' came under review at The International Conference on the Psychology of Humour and Laughter[1]. Only five 'screen clowns' are generally considered nowadays to have survived, despite all the attempts by commercial re-issue hacks and television to re-edit them, speed up projection, and introduce 'new methods of presentation' – which means the addition of tasteless sound effects and facetious and condescending commentaries. But, if only one had access to at least one copy of every film ever made since 1896, it would be seen that upwards of one hundred of the world's most brilliant clowns, comics or actors excelling in comedy have contributed to world cinema audiences, even for periods eclipsing in popularity the so-called 'great' ones.

Undoubtedly the comics have contributed greatly to the development of the cinema, from as far back as 1894, in America, when it was discovered that the filming of a man sneezing produced gales of laughter when shown on a screen. The first 'cinemas' in America, Britain, France and elsewhere were converted booths or dis-used shops; smelly and ill-ventilated and not considered suitable places for respectable people to be seen entering. The programmes lasted about forty minutes and each separate film ran no more than seven minutes. But small 'purpose-built' cinemas soon took over and grew into giant 'electric palaces'. These dated from about 1910 and the programmes grew longer, consisting of the 'Feature' or 'Big Film', the 'Topical Budget' or 'News Reel' and, of course, the additional one- or two-reel comedy (from 15 to 30 mins) which was considered by exhibitors to be essential: any programme without them was unthinkable.

At this period Max Linder (France) was very popular. His films were slightly more subtle than the American slapstick examples, and I think Chaplin, whose first films were a failure and nearly diverted him back to the stage, derived inspiration from Linder. Chaplin was cajoled by Chester Conklin into persevering in the new medium until he tumbled by accident or despair into Fatty Arbuckle's trousers, Charlie Avery's coat, the brown Derby hat belonging to Arbuckle's father-in-law, some crepe hair and a pair of scissors, the bamboo cane – then, he immediately felt 'right' as the Universal Tramp. Mack Sennett many years later said in his biography: 'I wonder if in all the history of the world, giving the kings and captains and heroes and celebrated women their full due – I wonder if there was ever a single person so beloved and so well-known to millions of people everywhere as that baggy-pants tramp invented by accident one rainy day in Edendale'.

Mack Sennett (originally a boiler maker by trade) created out of seemingly nothing a whole school of comedy and clowning, turning out at least two films each week up to around 1923 when this extremely lucrative market began to die as a result of exhibitors deciding to introduce the double-feature programme. Sennett's first films were plotless but gradually introduced and developed stories and characters. By 1924 the films of Keaton (a Sennett pupil), for example SHERLOCK JUNIOR, had a degree of sophistication via editing and trick photography, which from the point of view of advancing world film art, had a polish equal to none in the world.

Of course the real role played by the great screen clowns in the development of world cinema lay in their vast popularity and their ability thereby to attract audiences to the cinema, especially during the years of the Great War by helping to relieve pain with laughter. Many of the best editors in film-making learned their craft from the early comedies where timing was essential – the kind of timing which the audience is unaware of, though one should say in passing that one particular actress – Mabel Normand – was so skilled as a comedienne that her films hardly needed editing. The end of the silent era (around 1929) also silenced forever those marvellous lunatics of Sennett's menagerie, and hundreds of reels have vanished forever. Some of the best of his 'stable' were carried through into the talkie era: Buster

Keaton, Harold Lloyd, W.C. Fields and Chaplin, but of these only Fields and Chaplin were successful with the new technique. Despite all the mutilations, however, the silent comedians are still less dated than those who adapted to dialogue, with the exception of the Marx Brothers around whom an extraordinary cult developed. They came onto the scene around 1929 with films heavily loaded with dialogue just as they had spoken it in the Vaudeville world of theatre.

'Humour is a funny thing' says the advertisement – meaning 'funny peculiar' because no scientific study of the subject can deny that it is a very personal matter, and, since I have mentioned the Marx Brothers, possibly an acquired taste also. I recently sat behind a man and a woman during the following short scene:

> Groucho (to irate Margaret Dumont): 'allright we'll talk business – you see that
> man over there eating spaghetti?'

> Margaret D: 'No!'

> Groucho: 'Well, you see the spaghetti, don't you? Now behind that spaghetti
> is none other than Herman Gottleib, Director of the New York Opera –
> do you follow me?'

> Margaret D: 'Yes!'

> Groucho: 'Well stop following me, or I'll have you arrested!'

All this of course accompanied visually by Groucho's leer and raised eyebrows etcetera. This dialogue and scene belongs to the mid-thirties. I myself was in fits; the man in front was almost yelling to be relieved from the pain of his sides; the woman's face was stone cold and she must have loathed us both for enjoying ourselves so much. It is the same with Laurel and Hardy, two of the greatest screen clowns of all time – children love them; adults, who can appreciate their skill in trying not to be funny but to conceal their discomfort from the audience, love them also; but the 'sophisticated' think them 'just silly'. I think Keaton can command the largest modern audience because although he is another variation of the little man against adversity (Harry Langdon and Chaplin are others), his comedy is absolutely simple and straight, in fact 'pure', and his films are well photographed and very smoothly directed. Chaplin does not seem to be in the ascendancy again in England. Again, perhaps sophisticated audiences and teenage groups, though enjoying the comic sequences, cannot appreciate the depth of Chaplin's characterizations and I think his pathos is so cruel in its effectiveness (the final scene in CITY LIGHTS is of the most profound) that they shy off. And, of course, the few Chaplin films shown on television come off badly and ought to be kept for the cinemas, for large audiences. This rule applies in my view to all comedy films originally made for cinemas, so that their effectiveness can at least be partly judged within this context and bearing in mind also that the pre-twenties two-reelers were reckoned, at the time, to have a life of no more than four years around the world.

FOOTNOTE

1. Stuart Keen lectured on two evenings during the Conference and his illustrative film
material included:

        Charlie Chaplin – City Lights
        Buster Keaton   – Sherlock Junior
        Harold Lloyd   – From Hand to Mouth
        Laurel & Hardy – Big Business
        Monty Banks   – Chasing Choo-Choos

The Art of Revue: Further Emphases for the Psychology of Humour

Michael O'Mahony, Robert Palmer and Jennifer King

University of Bristol

WHAT IS A REVUE?: DEFINING THE EXPERIMENTAL SITUATION

A 'revue' is defined by the Pocket Oxford Dictionary (Le Mesurier & McIntosh, 1946) as 'a loosely constructed play or series of scenes or spectacles satirizing current events'. Chambers Twentieth Century Dictionary (Geddie, 1964) gives a vaguer definition: 'a loosely constructed theatrical show, more or less topical and musical'; this allows a broader variety of items and is nearer the truth for revues today.

Early revues (e.g., Farjeon, 1940) were a pleasant mixture of mildly satirical sketches and music but it was not until 'Beyond The Fringe' (Bennett et al., 1961) that the satire became more biting and political figures and the establishment were targets for ridicule. At this time satire became popular with the media and the university revue companies, which spawned 'The Fringe', received a boost. Such companies became the powerhouses for future successful revues like 'Monty Python's Flying Circus'.

Revue varies a great deal depending on the author, director and company involved. The particular style of revue considered here was developed by the first author for the Bristol University Revue Company. It is a mixture of the mainstream of satirical revue and a more aggressive style of cabaret entertainment developed in Bristol nightclubs. The latter style is played to an audience resembling those of the working men's clubs in the North of England. Such an audience is free to talk and drink, should they not wish to view the cabaret, and they have no hesitation in doing so, should they not find the cabaret of sufficient interest. This necessitates greater aggression and pace in the performance compared to that required by a less rowdy, captive theatre audience.

From a psychologist's point of view, a revue is a situation in which a stimulus, the revue, is presented to an audience to elicit a maximum response of laughter and applause. Whether or not laughter and applause are the best indicators of humour appreciation, they are the only indicators readily available and it is reasonable to assume that they have a high correlation with humour appreciation; certainly they appear to correlate highly with ticket sales. The situation is manipulated by the actors and director to maximize audience response and, unlike serious drama, there is constant feedback given during the performance.

The current discussion examines some of the variables, not all of which derive from the script, which are manipulated to maximize audience response. As psychologists, the authors find themselves making observations of the effects of such variables. Naturally, these observations are not made in controlled experimental conditions but they may perhaps be seen as having the status of data collected 'in the field' and as such, may be a stimulus for more controlled experimental investigation. Furthermore, many of the variables discussed, especially those dealing with the presentation of humour stimuli, are largely neglected by humour theorists.

THE REVUE PERFORMANCE: PERFECTING THE STIMULUS

Where and When: Occurrence of the Stimulus

A review is generally a late-night event. At the Edinburgh Festival, the showplace for British university revue groups, revues are approximately one-hour long and are timed to start around 11 pm or midnight, so that theatre-goers can go to a revue, having seen a play earlier in the evening. In this way, a revue will provide a light-hearted ending to the evening and, because of its popularity, provide much-needed finance for theatrical companies.

Get On. Get Off. And Quickly!: Intermittent Nature of the Stimulus and
Temporal Considerations

The type of revue, discussed here, is a collection of sketches and musical pieces separated
by blackouts. Once, such blackouts enabled scenery and costumes to be changed and often they
would last as long as fifteen seconds or so. However, the current style of revue only allows
the blackout to last as long as the audience is applauding; as soon as the laughter dies down,
the lights go on for the next sketch. This means that the blackout becomes merely a signal
to the audience for laughter; as such it helps to maximize audience response. Considerable
rehearsal time has to be devoted to getting actors on and off the stage during the blackout
and efficiency in this area gives 'pace' and 'polish' to the show. The considerable speed of
the show imposes the minimum of scenery (a couple of chairs with a white backdrop upon which
coloured lights or slides can be projected) and minimal costume change (generally a few props
such as hats, pistols, clerical collars etc.). These scant requirements lend economic
advantages to a revue.

Fillers: Stimuli Providing a High Joke Frequency

Besides the sketches and musical items, a revue will often have 'quickies' or 'fillers'.
These are short two- or three-line sketches originally employed to fill the time during
scenery changes but which can be employed to add pace to the show and bombard the audience with a
variety of brief joke stimuli and again maximize audience response. A rapid succession of
fillers makes a useful backbone for a revue or cabaret because the high frequency of jokes
commands attention. Incidentally, because of their relative simplicity, fillers can also be
used as excellent teaching exercises in drama.

Listen to Their Laughter: Audience Feedback

A revue with the fast pace discussed above allows any failed jokes to be 'forgotten' quickly
because the show will have moved on to the next item, before adequate time has passed for
consideration of the failure. The pace also provides the actors with a high frequency of
stimuli with which to manipulate audience response. Should audience response fall off it can
be restored by speeding up the performance (more jokes per second) and 'bigger' acting
(louder speech, exaggerated movements). Throughout the revue actors are constantly varying
their performance according to the readily available audience feedback.

Using feedback, an actor can become 'seasoned' by experimenting with the variables involved
in acting out a joke. Such skills as optimum timing, facial and vocal expression and bodily
stance have a great effect on the reaction to a given joke; these skills are largely
neglected by humour theorists. A humorous script is merely a tool; only when spoken by an
experienced actor, using all his skills of expression and timing, will it become a really
potent humour stimulus. The correct use of the blank look, the 'double take', the optimum
pause can transform an apparently unamusing script into the funny sketch it was intended to
be. The joke itself is only part of the humour stimulus, the skills in the acting out of the
joke probably account for about half of the humour; for this reason close cooperation is
required between the revue writer, actor and director who may often be one and the same person.
It is a shame that the techniques used by actors and directors are still considered to be
part of an art rather than a skill whose acquisition is open to experimental investigation.

Quickfire Comedy: Rapid Presentation of Stimuli

A fast pace in a show appears to maximize audience responses; when there are long pauses
(10-30 secs) between sketches the audience appears to 'cool off' and is not so responsive to
the humour. It could be that speed itself is humorous and it could also be that the close
temporal proximity of the jokes has some effect. In an unpublished study conducted by the
first author (O'Mahony & Brown, 1976), it was found that a series of cartoons received higher
humour ratings when viewed with other cartoons interposed than with neutral pictures interposed, indicating an effect due to temporal proximity of cartoons. This effect could be a
'carryover' or 'cumulation' of humour from prior cartoons caused by, say, a slow decay function
of the humorous response to the cartoons. It could also be due to an 'arousal' effect due
to the need to attend to the interposed cartoons more than neutral pictures. Godkewitsch's
(1976) point is taken, however, that 'arousal' is an ill-defined concept in humour theory.
Whatever the mechanism may be for the speed effect, speed certainly appears to increase
audience response.

The use of speed is essential to the design of a revue. Sketches and fillers follow in rapid
succession to maximize any speed or arousal/cumulation effects. The same appears to be true
of jokes within a sketch or song. Consider the following excerpt from a piece entitled 'The

Anatomy of the English Joke' (O'Mahony, 1969). Try saying the jokes as rapidly as possible
without even pausing for breath:

> What happens when you cross a rat with a rhinocerous?
> I don't know. What happens when you cross a rat with a rhinocerous?
> You get bigger holes in your skirting boards!
>
> What is it that a man does standing up, a woman does sitting down and
> a dog does on three legs?
> I don't know. What is it that a man does standing up, a woman does
> sitting down and a dog does on three legs?
> Shake hands!
>
> Who said 'I've got the time if you've got the inclination'?
> I don't know. Who said 'I've got the time if you've got the inclination'?
> Big Ben to the Leaning Tower of Pisa!
>
> What do you call a man who doesn't use contraceptives?
> I don't know. What do you call a man who doesn't use contraceptives?
> Daddy!

Now, these jokes are old and generally well known, and do not elicit much laughter when told
separately. But if they are all told rapidly and in quick succession they will always elicit
considerable audience laughter, effectively demonstrating the effects of speed and arousal
cumulation. Furthermore, if the jokes are told sufficiently rapidly, the audience will remain
silent until the final joke and will then laugh when given the appropriate signal; in this
case the signal is the song's chorus, between sketches it is a blackout.

Brevity Is....: Adaptation or Habituation Effects

A golden rule for writers of revue is the adage: 'brevity is the soul of wit'. An author
may be able to provide enough jokes to last ten minutes on one particular theme, but no matter
how brilliant the jokes, the audience will tire of the theme after about three minutes. Thus
the revue writer must adopt the discipline of the copywriter and cut a script down to the
bare minimum.

It is important to note that the audience response does not decline to humour per se but only
to humour on a given theme. As soon as the theme is changed the humour response increases
again. Thus it appears that the humorous response can selectively adapt or habituate to
stimuli concerned with a given subject content.

Set it to Music: An Alternative Stimulus Presentation Procedure

Musical items are often included in a revue merely to provide variety. However, a sketch
given in musical form tends to elicit more laughter than if spoken. The same is true of
rhyme; a joke or humorous story appears funnier if told in rhyme than if in prose. Limericks
are a good example of the rhyming joke while Alan Melville's sketch 'Old Girls' (Melville &
Zwar, 1949) is an excellent example of the rhyming monologue. Perhaps the extra skill involved
in generating humour within the restrictions defined by a song (e.g., rhyme) adds to its
enjoyment. If an experienced revue writer finds that his sketch does not appear sufficiently
humorous, he can make it funnier by setting it to music.

IN THE AUDITORIUM: ENVIRONMENT OF THE SUBJECTS

To elicit maximum audience response from the revue stimuli, there are certain environmental
conditions important for that audience.

A Full House is a Good House: The Packing Variable

For a given show and a given number of audience members, it appears that an audience will
laugh louder and longer when they pack a small theatre than when they half fill a large
auditorium. Chapman (1976) has discussed social facilitation of laughter for children and
has noted that even invasion of body space promotes laughter. Certainly, a packed audience
appears to laugh more readily even when uncomfortably crowded. It could be hypothesized that
a group cohesiveness (Pollio & Edgerly, 1976) is built up by the intimacy of packing, so

facilitating laughter. Of course packing can be an interactive process; the large audience can inspire the actor to give a better performance and their subsequent larger reaction can inspire him more. Whatever the precise mechanism, it can be worth giving away tickets, if necessary, to make sure that the theatre is full.

Good Audiences, Bad Audiences: Group Differences

Audiences differ from night to night; one night a joke is heartily applauded, the next it is ignored. Performance variables may well be the cause of this variation and a good director will experiment with sections of revue in which the audience reaction is not up to expectation.

Certainly, audiences will vary depending on how well they know the comedian or actor. When a famous comedian walks on the stage there is often laughter among the initial applause, before he has even started his act. The announcement that the comedian will appear sets the scene as one that will involve laughter and the mere appearance of the comedian can act as a signal for laughter, just like the blackout between sketches. If, during a revue, one particular actor has established himself as a comedian, his entrance on stage will often be greeted by laughter.

No Gels!: Attention and Light Adaptation

Generally lighting technicians will bathe the stage in a soft light using coloured gelatin filters over the spotlights. For revue, no filters are used, providing the brightest stage lighting possible. It appears to draw the audience's attention to the stage and increases their response as well as performing the useful function of light-adapting the audience so that they cannot see the actors moving on and off during the blackouts.

Overtures: Warm Up Effects

There has been discussion of warm up effects in humour (e.g. Giles and Oxford, 1970) and certainly it appears that music played in the auditorium before the show affects the response of the audience to the initial part of the revue. Cheerful jazz or rock 'n' roll (e.g., Twelfth Street Rag by Pee Wee Hunt or Yakety Sax by Boots Randolph) appears to give a preferable warm up to gentle or sad music (e.g., Greensleeves) or aggressive music (e.g., Honky Tonk Women, by The Rolling Stones). If a director is rash enough to perform a revue in a discotheque (O'Mahony, 1976) the succession of aggressive 'rock' records played before the show will mean that actors must match the mood of the music by using noisy aggressive sketches and fillers.

USEFUL PLOYS FOR REVUE WRITERS: SOME INFORMAL CATEGORIES OF REVUE HUMOUR

It is not our intention in this paper to examine the causes of humour responses to revue nor is it our intention to list the fundamental types of humour used by revue writers. Any verbal categorization of humour will depend in turn on linguistic categories and may have little to do with fundamental types of humour. However, an informal categorization can be made of some of the elements of humour that appear to be involved. Such a categorization has no fundamental validity; it is merely a checklist of useful ploys for revue writers. It is hoped, however, that it may be of some interest to psychologists interested in humour typology.

United Nations and Sexual Encounters: Satire

The most common form of humour associated with revue is satire. Satirical revue has been used to make both political and social comment and it is still a popular form of entertainment.

Because politicians change more rapidly than the unwritten rules and conventions of society, political satire needs more constant revision and updating than social satire. For an example of political satire, let us consider the following verses from 'The United Nations Drinking Song' (O'Mahony, 1976), in which various national leaders introduce themselves in song:

  I'm Gerald Ford and stupid,
  Jimmy says I've had my day.
  I can't control the Mafia,
  Nor the CIA.

My name is Mr. Callaghan,
Harold's spiritual heir.
I'm fatherly and smiling,
As if Ulster wasn't there.

Vote for Mr. Brezhnev,
All Russians vote for me.
Or else they go to a luny bin,
Run by the KGB.

My name is Idi Amin,
A chieftain loud and strong.
If ever you come to Uganda,
You won't be living long.

I'm good Queen Juliana,
From poverty I'm freed.
I used to ride a bicycle,
'Til my husband met Lockheed.

My name is Dr. Vorster,
Soweto's getting tight.
But South Africa's a paradise,
As long as you are White.

Such verses elicit more reaction if they are topical and thus need constant revision just
about every week; at the time of writing the verses were topical but the authors anticipate
that by the time of publication they will be out of date and some of the leaders may be
leaders no longer.

Social situations afford a longer lasting satire. 'Fancy Meeting You' (O'Mahony, 1969) is a
sketch which explores the situation in which a boy asks a girl for a date but the girl does
not want a date. Being English, she follows the unwritten rules of this situation and instead
of telling him outright that she does not wish to date him, she merely makes excuses for each
night that he suggests. Being English he will take the hint and give up without ever having
to be told that she does not like him. But what if he does not take the hint; consider the
following excerpt:

    Boy: I say! Hello. Fancy meeting you.

    Girl: (Not pleased to see him) Oh. Hello.

    Boy: Did you enjoy our smashing evening at the British Butterfly Collectors'
            Convention at the Royal Festival Hall?

    Girl: Er .... yes .... thank you very much.

    Boy: We must do it again sometime.

    Girl: Yes I'd love to .... well .... must dash.

    Boy: But you're in a bus queue.

    Girl: So I am. Oh well. I've just remembered I've got to go.
            'Bye .... see you.

    Boy: Yes .... see you .... (Girl begins to leave) .... When?

    Girl: When? .... oh er .... sometime next month or something. Give me a
            ring sometime.

    Boy: You're not on the phone. Besides, I might not bump into you again
            or you might be booked up like last time. How about tomorrow?

    Girl: I'm washing my hair.

    Boy: After that?

    Girl: Drying my hair.

Boy: Let's say Tuesday.

Girl: Tuesday .... um .... oh yes, I'm going out Tuesday.

Boy: Where?

Girl: Where? .... er .... to the theatre.

Boy: What are you going to see? I could meet you there.

Girl: Oh no .... it's a private performance .... at my Uncle's castle.

Boy: Could I come?

Girl: No. You wouldn't like it. It's in Greek.

Boy: How about Wednesday?

Girl: No, can't make it. It's my brother's birthday.

Boy: You haven't got a brother.

Girl: Oh, silly me .... my cousin's birthday. He's like a brother to me.

Boy: Thursday then.

Girl: I don't think so (consulting diary). Oh yes, that's it.
           (Obviously lying). That's the night of my Extra Mural Chemistry lesson.

Boy: Friday?

Girl: Oh Lord .... (thumbing through diary in panic, trying to manufacture
           an excuse). Er .... the moon is in its first quarter. Couldn't
           possibly. The .... er .... gravitational pull gives me a headache.

Boy: Saturday?

Girl: Working late at the office.

Boy: Sunday?

Girl: Working late.

Boy: Monday?

Girl: Working late.

Boy: Honestly. You've used the same excuse three times.

Girl: Well, I can't think of any others.

Boy: Really! Sometimes I think you don't want me to take you out in the
           evenings .... can't really think why we got married!

Note that the humour is provided by the situation, unlike the United Nation's Drinking Song
where the words provide more of the humour. The twist at the end is a surprise to signal the
end of the sketch and generate laughter during the blackout.

The Twist in the Tail: Redefinition of the Situation

The twist in the tail of a revue sketch is a fairly common 'punchline', while fillers depend
almost exclusively on this form of humour. Essentially, the surprise caused by a redefinition
of the situation elicits humour. The fact that the boy and girl were not merely casual
acquaintances but were actually married affords a whole new interpretation of the situation
and, as such, elicits laughter. Another example of the 'twist' or 'surprise' is the following
filler:

Army recruitment officer gives a talk to potential recruits:

> Join the army and see the world. Visit strange exciting exotic places;
> meet strange exotic, exciting people. And shoot them!

A refinement of the twist is the situation where the audience cannot understand what the actor is doing; the twist-line suddenly explains the situation redefining it as 'sense' not 'nonsense'. For example:

Vicar sings from a hymn book

> 'Leon, Leon'.

He looks perturbed, realises his mistake, turns the book upside down and sings

> 'Noel, Noel'.

Another example:

First actor (haughtily): Cling! ..... (pause)
                          Cling!
          (irritably): Cling!

Enter butler answering his call: You clang sir?

An alternative refinement is the twist which gives a measure of relief from possible embarrassment. Here the audience is led into believing that the punchline may be taboo in some way; the audience finds it humorous when, on redefinition of the situation as nontaboo, they discover their mistake. For example:

Two vicars are discovered on a park bench with their newspapers, they are doing their respective crossword puzzles.

First vicar (agitated):   Tut tut, oh! tut tut.

Second vicar: Is er .... anything the matter, vicar?

First vicar: Oh dear, yes. It's this crossword puzzle.
                         Most troubling, most embarrassing.

Second vicar: Well, let me help.

First vicar: It's the second clue down. A four letter word,
                         ends in UNT and the clue is 'essentially feminine'.

Second vicar: UNT, UNT, Mmm! 'Essentially feminine', you say.
                         Oh yes, I know. That'll be 'aunt'.

First vicar: 'Aunt' - oh yes, yes I see. Mmm .... 'aunt'.
                         (Pause). Er, you don't have a rubber I could
                         borrow, do you?

American readers, who may be mystified by the joke, note that a 'rubber' is an 'eraser' and not what they thought.

To heighten the situational comedy, the actors played vicars to whom such taboo words are popularly thought to be especially worrying.

That was no Lady, that was my Car: Two Definitions of the Situation

The taboo situation can be altered slightly so that the audience knows there is no taboo but one of the actors does not. This supplies a device that has been used many times in pantomime and farce, namely the situation where two actors converse but the audience knows that they are both talking about different topics.

Probably one of the oldest examples is the misunderstanding that occurs when one actor is talking about his car, while the other believes he is talking about his wife. Such phrases as: 'She goes like a bomb', 'my father loves to get his hands on her', 'he was in and out of her within seconds', 'she's got plenty of room for all our tools', or more bizarre: 'we used that black paint to seal her bottom', 'if you push her too hard she develops a rattle'.

'I've just had her sprayed racing-green', have been the stuff of farce and are typical of this genre.

Everybody Groan: Puns

Puns have long been popular as humour stimuli. Many fillers rely on the quick pun. For example:

    Announcer: Here is a brief traffic announcement:
                   The M4 roadworks .... so that'll be nice!

or, consider a further example:

    Announcer: Israel will spend twenty million pounds on defence.
                   De fence will run round de borders of Israel, de
                   Golan Heights and de Sinai desert.

A long succession of puns on a given theme may be made the basis of a whole sketch. The following verse uses puns on the names of artists. It relates the words used by an artist to seduce a young girl and describes his subsequent progress in this venture:

    You'll Gainsborough much if you Dali with me
    Henry Moore than you'd normally see
    With no Constable near
    I'll pay you well dear
    Give you Monet and Buffet for tea

    His Stubbs at love were not deep
    He'd Van Cough or Van Duck but not reap
    He'd Turner in a melee
    Slap her Boticelli
    And then fall soundly asleep

A similar verse describes the progress of an Indian doctor and uses puns on India:

    Now, at Kama Sutra we'll play
    Kiss, Kiss, Kashmir all day
    And when I get near you
    I'll Goa to steer you
    And we'll Everest in the day

    Himalay down and I'll vow
    To accurately show you how
    A Punjab in the alley
    No Delhi no dally
    All over, Ceylon for now

    Ceylon was used in the absence of a suitable pun on Sri Lanka.

The Hook Line: Mere Repetition as a Humour Stimulus

The establishment of a catch phrase like 'A good idea son' (Max Bygraves in 'Educating Archie') or 'You dirty rotten swine, you!' (Bluebottle, by Peter Sellers in 'The Goon Show') is a gift indeed for writers of weekly comedy shows. Mere recognition of the phrase, which is not in itself funny, appears to act as a signal for laughter. Similarly, mere repetition of a hook-line in a song or sketch can provide humour on a shorter time-scale than the weekly catch phrase. The following excerpt from a song for children illustrates the point. The song concerns a forty-million-year-old fossil, the Pantolambdabathmodon, which all geologists will immediately know to be a paleocene amblypod.

    While walking on the mountains upon a rainy day
    A thing came up and kicked me and said 'Sir, will you play?
    You see I am so lonely because I am so odd
    I'm a pantolambdabathmodonpaleoceneamblypod'

    I went to a pub just yesterday and tried to get a beer
    They said they wouldn't serve me because I was so queer
    'The museum's the place for you, my lad', they all said with a nod
    'For a pantolambdabathmodonpaleoceneamblypod'

    I went to the tailor's yesterday for a coat to fit my size
    The man said 'You don't fool me, you're a psychologist in disguise'
    'Have you got a coat for me, one that is fairly mod?
    For a pantolambdabathmodonpaleoceneamblypod'

The song builds up expectation for the hook-line until the final verse:

    I went down to the museum 'cos I was feeling low
    If only I had a girlfriend I would love her so
    And then at last I saw her, we were like two peas in a pod
    Another pantolambdabathmodonpaleoceneamblypod

A Definite No-No: Changing a Variable of Everyday Behaviour

The changing of a situational variable and logically following its consequences can often be
a source of humour for revue sketches. Replacing all letters 's' at the beginning of a word
by 'f', under the pretext that the script was written in the seventeenth century, or by 'th',
under the pretext that it is in Spanish, can afford some amusement, as the audience spot the
various distortions that result from the change. Another possibility is to reverse time,
that is run a story backwards. A 'western' played this way (O'Mahony, 1971) involved a scene
where a dead cowboy rose from the ground, pulled an arrow from his stomach, threw it to an
Indian who threaded it into his bow and rode off backwards. Given the initial idea, the
sketch becomes merely an exploration of a selection of situations where the changed variable
has a recognisable effect.

An example of a more verbal variable change is provided by an excerpt from the sketch 'A
Definite No-No' (O'Mahony, 1976) in which a girl always repeats herself, saying every word
not once but twice. This exasperates a man who is talking to her, and he tries to catch her
out. The sketch becomes an exploration of the occasions on which words or syllables are
normally repeated.

    Man: You know. There's something a bit odd about you.

    Girl: Yes? Yes?

    Man: You always say everything twice.

    Girl: Me? Me?

    Man: There. You did it again.

    Girl: Oh - Oh.

    Man: Playing a game eh. Well. I know your sort. I'm not going to have
             you joking around with me. I'll stop you.

    Girl: Now now!

    Man: I'll catch you out.

    Girl: Silly silly.

    Man: I will. I'll trick you.

    Girl: Ha ha.

    Man: Alright then. What's your name?

    Girl: Mimi.

    Man: Your mother's name?

    Girl: Dee dee.

    Man: Father's name?

    Girl: Papa.

    Man: When did you last eat?

    Girl: 10.10 .

Man: Supper?

Girl: Din din.

Man: What's your favourite show?

Girl: Gigi.

Man: Favourite singer?

Girl: Lulu.

Man: Can you dance?

Girl: Cha-cha.

Man: Is that all?

Girl: Can-can, go-go.

Man: Name a bird.

Girl: Dodo.

Man: That's extinct.

Girl: Cuckoo.

And so it continues until the man acknowledges defeat, and as a crowning humiliation repeats himself too.

Winnie the Sexpot: Mixing Categories

The types of humour discussed here are a few of the major categories, which are a useful guide for the revue writer. Naturally, other categorizations are possible and generally more than one element will be present in the sketch. In the following excerpt from 'You'll Be Shocked' (O'Mahony, 1971), sexual exploitation by the Sunday newspapers is satirized while puns and misinterpretations are used to reveal 'Winnie the Pooh' as a classic of pornography:

Newspaperman: You'll be shocked!

Girl: You'll be amazed!

Newspaperman: It is our duty to reveal to you this scandal in detail.

Girl: In intimate detail.

Newspaperman: In very intimate detail! This terrible piece of pornography,
                Winnie the Pooh, will shock you. Just listen to the overtones
                of Oedipal incest.

Girl: God bless Mummy, I know that's right.
                And wasn't it fun in the bath tonight.

Newspaperman: Infantile sexual adventures.

Girl: When Anne and I go out for a walk
                We hold each other's hand and talk
                Of all the things we mean to do
                When Anne and I are forty-two
                And when we've thought about a thing
                Like bowling hoops and bicycling
                Or falling down on Anne's balloon
                We do it in the afternoon.

Newspaperman: And there's homosexuality.

Girl: I want a soldier to come and play with me.
                I want a soldier who plays the drum.
                Daddy's going to get one as soon as he can come.

Newspaperman:	And there's also lesbianism.
Girl:	Elizabeth Anne said softly 'Oh' 'Thank you Jennifer. Now I know'.
Newspaperman:	There is also an unhealthy dwelling upon love making.
Girl:	And God bless Mummy and make her.
Newspaperman:	Yes, you'll be shocked!
Girl:	You'll be shocked!
Newspaperman:	You'll be shocked at the unnatural preoccupation with sexual anatomy.
Girl:	Mine has a hood, and I lie in bed. And pull the hood right over my head.
Newspaperman:	Shocking descriptions of cruel sadism.
Girl:	Nurse took pins from her mouth and said Now then darling it's time for bed.
Newspaperman:	There's even more. Fur fetishes!
Girl:	For I'd have fur boots and a brown fur wrap And brown fur knickers and a big fur cap With brown furry-down right up to my head I'd sleep all winter in a big fur bed.

The sketch continues to 'expose' Winnie the Pooh, finishing with a final flourish:- group sex.

Newspaperman:	You'll be shocked at the gang bang orgy held by Winnie the Pooh, Piglet, Rabbit and Baby Roo - thinly disguised as a stick race.
Girl:	'I can see mine' cried Roo 'can you see yours piglet?' 'Can you see yours Pooh?' 'I can see yours Piglet' said Pooh suddenly. 'Mine's a sort of greyish one' said Piglet not daring to lean too far over in case he fell. 'Yes that's what I can see. It's coming over on to my side'. Rabbit leant over further than ever looking for his and Roo wriggled up and down calling out and Piglet got very excited. 'It's coming' said Pooh. 'Are you sure it's mine?' squeaked Piglet excitedly. 'Yes because it's grey. A big grey one'.
Newspaperman:	Yes, you'll be shocked as we report Winnie the Pooh in detail.
Girl:	In intimate detail.
Newspaperman:	You'll be shocked!

Interestingly enough, the use of an innocent looking girl to read the lines from Winnie the Pooh appears to elicit a greater audience response, in spite of the resulting illogicality of some of her lines. The more innocent the girl, the funnier the sketch. Perhaps the contrast between the innocence and the lines spoken assists the humour or perhaps it merely prevents the sketch obviously transgressing the bounds of so-called good taste.

Every revue artist will have his own typology for humour and the preceding scheme may be seen only as suggesting a few broad categories, which the present authors find useful. One may, for instance, include the recognition of stereotypes or famous characters as eliciting humour or one may include such humour under the present scheme's loose heading of satire. One may distinguish between sketches involving actors or other devices such as a series of slides projected on a screen with musical accompaniment. Revue can include anything and it is this which makes it such an adaptable medium.

FINALE: CONCLUSION

Revue is a dramatic form which is popular with the British both on television and in the professional theatre. However, revue is also being written and performed by nonprofessionals, especially in colleges and universities and this means that it will be a constantly changing form of entertainment which, for better or for worse, reflects the social conditions of the day. Revue is also a fairly controlled form of dramatic presentation with plenty of opportunities for measuring audience response and as such could be a useful tool for humour research under performance conditions. Certainly, noncasual observation, over a decade of revue presentation, has resulted in certain rules of thumb for maximizing audience response and such rules are susceptible to controlled experimental investigation. Moreover, these observations must be explained by any general theory of humour. Why do jokes appear funnier if told rapidly, if recited or sung in rhyme or if phrased with an optimally timed pause before the punchline? How much does a blackout between sketches, the appearance of a well-known comedian or the speaking of a hook-line or catch phrase merely signal laughter? Why is a joke funnier if it is topical; is it merely novelty? Revue may be a tool for humour research but it may also provide some theoretical challenges.

REFERENCES

See Bibliography for publications on humour, laughter and comedy

Bennett, A., Cook, P., Miller, J. & Moore, D., Beyond the Fringe. Samuel French, London (1961).

Farjeon, H., Herbert Farjeon's Little Revue. Samuel French, London (1940).

Geddie, W., Chamber's Twentieth Century Dictionary. Chambers, Edinburgh (1964).

Le Mesurier, H.G. & McIntosh, E., The Pocket Oxford Dictionary of Current English (4th Edition, Revised). Clarendon Press, Oxford (1946).

Melville, A. & Zwar, C., A La Carte. Samuel French, London (1949).

O'Mahony, M., Bristol Cream, Revue at Viewforth Centre. Edinburgh Festival (unpublished) (1969).

O'Mahony, M., Bristol Vintage, Revue at Viewforth Centre. Edinburgh Festival (unpublished) (1971).

O'Mahony, M., Whispering Bells, Revue at Raquel's Discotheque. Bristol (unpublished) (1976).

APPROACHES TO THE
STUDY OF HUMOUR

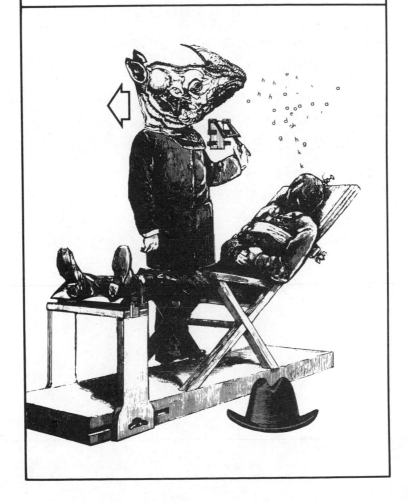

Psychological Approaches to the Study of Humour[1]

Mary K. Rothbart

University of Oregon

During the last ten years, there has been a tremendous increase in the psychological exploration of laughter and humour. Work has been carried out at several different levels of analysis: development of general theory, analysis of humour materials, study of individual and group responses to humour presentations, and applications of humour to real-life settings. This paper will attempt to review some current approaches to theory and research in humour and laughter as practised by psychologists and by our colleagues in related disciplines.

Since the scope of this symposium and its overview was necessarily very broad, the reader is encouraged to explore symposia on specific topics for more detailed information about current work in laughter and humour. The present review will be primarily concerned with arousal and cognitive processing approaches to theory and research, although other current areas of humour research and applications will be briefly described.

AROUSAL THEORY AND RESEARCH

The approach followed by most recent general theories of laughter and humour is based on the concept of arousal. Contemporary arousal analyses of humour and laughter owe a great debt to Berlyne (1960, 1972) who attempted to describe how momentary fluctuations in arousal, that is, excitement or activation, may lead to pleasure.

In Berlyne's general theory (1960, 1967), he identified three types of arousal fluctuation as leading to general feelings of pleasure: (1) conditions under which high arousal is reduced; (2) conditions under which there is a moderate rise and drop in arousal (the 'arousal jag'); and (3) conditions in which there is a moderate increase in arousal. In Berlyne's view, moderate boosts in arousal may lead to pleasure, while still higher arousal levels are presumed to activate an aversion reaction, leading at first to inhibition of pleasant feelings and at still higher levels to a negative reaction. Berlyne's model predicts an inverted-U relation between arousal level and pleasure, suggesting that at moderate levels of arousal, pleasure will be higher than at either low or high levels of arousal, and that at very high levels of arousal, negative affect will be experienced.

In his earliest formulations about humour, Berlyne (1960) developed the 'arousal jag' model for describing fluctuations of arousal level occurring during humour. In the arousal jag, according to Berlyne, 'slight and transitory jumps in arousal become pleasurable as a consequence of the drop in arousal that quickly terminate them' (1960, p199). In this view, humour is a relief phenomenon, occurring when an increase in excitation or tension has been dissipated. Sources of arousal, in Berlyne's view included sexual, aggressive, or anxiety-inducing subject matter, as well as collative variables including novelty, complexity, and incongruity.

Since his general theory proposes two other possibilities for arousal fluctuations leading to pleasure, Berlyne later (1972) questioned whether the arousal boost or decreases in arousal from high arousal levels might operate in the experience of humour in addition to the arousal jag. He concluded that a smile may result from 'any kind of pleasure, whether it comes from the arousal boost or from arousal reduction. On the other hand, laughter... seems restricted to situations in which a period or a moment of aversively high arousal is followed by sudden and pronounced arousal reduction... In short, our speculation is that humour and laughter do not work through pure arousal boosts. They appear to require arousal jags or arousal boost-jags.' (Berlyne, 1972, pp58-59). Here, Berlyne argues that both the arousal jag and the sudden decrease from high levels of arousal lead to humour; the arousal boost does not lead to humour.

Rothbart (1973) modified Berlyne's position to argue that arousal increases of any size will be accompanied by pleasurable affect when they are associated with the subject's judgment that the situation is a 'safe' or non-threatening one. Rothbart also suggested that experience of high intensity stimulation may lead to immediate avoidance. Under these conditions, the person does not remain in a situation long enough to make a possible 'safety' judgment. Shultz' (1976) description of arousal-relief in young children's laughter is consistent with Rothbart's model, and Sroufe and Waters' (1976) analysis of smiling and laughter is also consistent with the model. Apter and Smith's theory (this volume), presented in the present symposium, is also an arousal theory, although a good deal of new terminology is introduced in its explication. Apter and Smith propose that there are two optimal levels of arousal; one of them low (when the organism is pursuing problem solving or 'work' activities) and one of them high (when the organism is seeking excitement). Humour is a high arousal activity occurring only when the individual is seeking excitement; a change in state from excitement-seeking to problem-solving may result in shifts of affect from positive to negative.

Numerous researchers have also taken an arousal approach to the laboratory investigation of laughter and humour. Increased humour levels have been related to sexual arousal of subjects, (e.g., Lamb, 1968; Strickland, 1959), arousal of anger or hostility in subjects (e.g., Dworkin and Efran, 1967; Strickland, 1959) and arousal of anxiety in laboratory subjects (Shurcliff, 1968).

Some of the most persuasive recent research relating humour to arousal has used psychophysiological methods (e.g., Chapman, 1976; Godkewitsch, 1976; Langevin & Day, 1972). Langevin and Day (1972) found a positive relation between humour ratings, galvanic skin response amplitude and recovery time, maximum heart rate response and mean change in heart rate. Godkewitsch (1976) divided written jokes into two parts: joke bodies and punchlines, so that physiological arousal changes could be recorded for each section. If Berlyne's original 'arousal jag' were operating in this humour situation (increases in arousal accompanied by reduction), increased arousal should be observed during processing of the joke body and decreased arousal during or immediately after processing the punchline. Both heart rate and skin conductance measures indicated, however, that the punchline actually increased arousal, and arousal induced by the punchline was positively related to ratings of joke funniness; that is, with higher arousal levels, jokes were experienced by subjects as being funnier.

Chapman's (1976) work, employing electromyographic measures (EMG), showed that EMG measures rose regularly for his subjects during telling of a joke, while they did not for a dull passage of financial news and the beating of a metronome. In all three of these psychophysiological studies, no evidence of an aversive effect of high levels of arousal was found; however, it is also unlikely that subjects were encountering extremely high levels of arousal in the laboratory. To date, most experimental work is congruent with the existence of a linearly positive relation between arousal and humour, that is, an 'arousal boost' rather than an 'arousal jag.'

An interesting application of arousal theory to individual differences research is suggested by the presentation of Svebak in this symposium. His results (this volume) indicate that individuals showing respiratory patterns associated with high levels of tension show greater laughter than individuals without the high tension patterns. Additional work in this area with multiple physiological measures would be of definite interest.

Arousal-safety theories (Rothbart, 1973; Shultz, 1976; Sroufe & Waters, 1976) suggest that in addition to conditions of heightened arousal a safety judgment is required for laughter to take place. Rothbart (1973, 1976) and, I think, Apter and Smith in the present symposium, would argue that an arousal-safety principle applies to the perception of humour as well, if we consider that the tension involved in searching for a solution may be released when the 'meaning' of a joke is discovered. Understanding of the joke would be seen as a safety signal.

Safety judgments in humour appear to be influenced by the following factors:

(1) Safety may be signalled when arousal is induced in a familiar context, for example, in the presence of a familiar person or persons. Lewis and Brookes (1974) in a study of stranger anxiety, found that an infant's reaction to the approach of a strange adult, a strange child, the mother, or self (in a mirror) was related to both distance of the stimulus person from the child and the particular stimulus person involved. The mother and the self evoked a strong positive reaction, while the strange adult evoked a negative reaction. The strange child evoked a reaction at a level between the self and mother and the adult stranger. It should be noted that Gale, Spratt, Chapman and Smallbone (1975) have independently established with adult subjects that distance of an approaching person is negatively related to physiological

(EEG) arousal level; that is, the closer the person approaches to a laboratory
subject, the higher the level of physiological arousal in a laboratory subject. In
a study by Murphy and Pollio (1973) groups made up of mutual friends and strangers
listened to recordings of a nonhostile humorist (Bill Cosby) or a hostile humorist
(Don Rickles). While both comedians were enjoyed more in the groups of friends, there
was less movement, laughing, and smiling when groups of strangers listened to hostile
humour than when they listened to nonhostile humour.

(2) Safety may occur through sudden relief from anxiety cues. Shurcliff (1968) varied
level of anxiety in three groups of college students by assigning them one of three
tasks: subjects in a low-anxiety group were told they would be asked to pick up a
quite docile rat, and hold it for five seconds. Subjects in a moderate-anxiety group
were asked to take a small sample of blood from a white rat, and told this would be
an easy task. Subjects in a high-anxiety group were asked to take two cubic
centimetres of blood from a rat that might be expected to bite through their glove or
escape. When the students began the task, they discovered the rat to be only a toy.
Subjects were then asked to rate the situation for humour, anxiety and surprisingness.
Humour ratings increased with the anxiety group; subjects in the high anxiety group
found the trick most funny. There was also a significant correlation between self-
rated anxiety and humour, and between surprisingness and humour ratings.
Surprisingness and anxiety ratings were not significantly related to each other.

(3) Safety may occur in situations involving 'fantasy assimilation' (McGhee, 1972b), that
is, situations in which a person recognizes that an event could not really have
happened, or in a context that is labelled 'just for fun,' for example, by the social
cues surrounding the presentation of humour stimuli (Emerson, 1969; Giles, Bourhis,
Gadfield, Davies & Davies, 1976; McGhee & Johnson, 1975), the identification of
particular persons as comics, clowns, or comedians, or the identification of films,
plays, and novels as comedies.

(4) Context effects may result in 'non-safety' judgments for particular kinds of humour
stimuli. Singer, Gollob and Levine (1967) set up inhibitions about the expression
of aggression in half their college student subjects by having them study Goya
etchings on the horror of brutality and aggression; the other half of their subjects
viewed Goya works with nonaggressive subject matter. Subjects then rated twelve
cartoons, four of which were on nonsense themes, four of which involved moderate
interpersonal aggression, and four high interpersonal aggression. Inhibition of
aggressiveness had the effect of interfering with appreciation of aggressive, but not
neutral cartoons.

(5) Social-psychological studies on derogation humour are also congruent with a 'safety'
mechanism (Gutman & Priest, 1969; La Fave, 1972; La Fave, Haddad & Maesen, 1976;
Zillmann & Bryant, 1974; Zillmann & Cantor, 1972). When the object of aggressive
humour is the self, a person close to the self, or a person with whom one identifies,
it is unlikely that aggressive wit directed against one of these persons will be seen
as 'safe'. Studies of derogation humour may be helpful in determining to what extent
'safety' is an all-or-nothing judgment. It is possible that degrees of safety may be
represented in derogation humour, having effects ranging from slight inhibition of
humour appreciation to total inhibition of humour appreciation and a negative reaction
to the joke.

Arousal studies using humour situations have not been limited to tests of hypotheses about
humour; other arousal-related hypotheses have been tested using humour stimuli. For example,
Chapman (1976) used research on children's laughter to test Zajonc's (1965) social facilitation
hypothesis. He tested whether the 'mere presence' of another person increases a subject's
arousal level and thereby increases the subject's dominant response in the situation, in this
case, laughing. A humour situation involving children provided an experimental situation
free from evaluation apprehension, a confounding factor in previous social facilitation
studies with adult subjects. Children in Chapman's study heard humorous material through
earphones either (a) with a non-listening companion, (b) with a companion listening to the
same material, or (c) alone. Children with a listening companion laughed and smiled more
than solitary children. The difference between conditions (a) and (c) was used to argue for
the arousing effects of the 'mere presence' of another person.

Other arousal-related hypotheses have been tested using humour situations: Godkewitsch
(1976) tested Thayer's (1970) hypothesis that self-reported arousal reflects 'general
activation' more than do individual psychophysiological measures by correlating humour ratings
of jokes with self-reported feelings of arousal: the self-report measure predicted humour
ratings as well as did a multiple correlation of five physiological indices of arousal in a
parallel experiment.

Social psychologists (Baron & Ball, 1974; Berkowitz, 1970; Dworkin & Efran, 1974; Landy & Mettee, 1969; Singer, 1968) have also tested the relation between the experience of humour (especially aggressive humour) and possible relief of laboratory-induced hostility or anger arousal. Freud's 'catharsis' hypothesis predicts that aggressive impulses may be alleviated by behavioural expression of aggression. The majority of studies in this area have assumed, with Freud (1905), that appreciation of hostile humour allows the release of repressed aggressive impulses or tendencies, in appreciation of 'tendency wit.' According to Freud's theory, enjoyment of hostile humour should be particularly effective in decreasing later aggressive tendencies of a subject.

Taken strictly, Freud's theory requires that hostile humour must decrease aggressive drive, and that measurement of conscious mood is not an adequate measure for aggressive drive, which may be unconscious. The strict interpretation of Freud's theory has received support from Leak (1974), who found that hostile humour decreased the extent to which the experimenter was disliked more than nonhostile humour. Freud's theory was not supported by Berkowitz (1970). Berkowitz angered women subjects and then presented a four-minute tape-recording of either a hostile comedian (Don Rickles) or a nonhostile comedian (George Carlin). Later, when allowed to aggress against the person who had angered them, the women who heard the hostile comedian were more aggressive in their ratings of the person than women who heard the nonhostile comedian.

A more general theory, however, has received some support. This approach accepts subjects' verbal reports of their feelings as data and utilizes a more general arousal concept, predicting that experience of any type of humour will decrease arousal levels as reflected in mood reports or aggressive response.

In these studies, both hostile and nonhostile humour is presented to angered subjects. The effects of the humour has been to: (a) lower subjects' reported feelings of aggressiveness (Dworkin & Efran, 1967; Singer, 1968), and (b) reduce the degree to which the aggressor was disliked (Landy & Mettee, 1969). Baron and Ball (1974) have also reported that giving nonhostile cartoons to angered subjects decreases the duration of shocks later administered by the subjects, in comparison with shocks administered by subjects given pictures to look at. Baron and Ball's (1974) findings parallel those of Dworkin and Efran (1967), who reported that angered subject groups showed decreased feelings of aggressiveness and anxiety after being given hostile or nonhostile cartoons, with no difference between effects of the two kinds of humour, while control subjects who heard music or documentaries showed no decrease of aggressive or anxious feelings. Berkowitz' (1970) results may at first glance seem counter to results in this area, but since Berkowitz' study had no nonhumour condition, we do not know what effects humour per se might have had on decreasing subjects' aggressive responses. Leak's (1974) study also did not have a nonhumour control group. At present, results on the more general adaptation of Freud's theory suggest that appreciation of humour of any variety may serve to decrease expressed anger arousal of subjects.

COGNITIVE PROCESSING THEORIES AND RESEARCH

A second approach to theory in the area of laughter and humour has been the development of models to describe the cognitive processing involved in the appreciation of humour stimuli. This position has been developed by Suls (1972) and by Shultz in a series of researches (Shultz, 1972; Shultz, 1974; Shultz & Horibe, 1974). In addition, McGhee (1974a) has explored the contributions of feelings of mastery to the humour experience.

As in general arousal theory, Berlyne (1960, 1971, 1972, 1973) has been a major contributor to cognitive analyses of humour materials, having related cognitive aspects of humour to the arousal fluctuations and hence, the pleasure, we experience. While some arousal theorists have attempted to explain only children's laughter and/or smiling in arousal terms (Shultz, 1976; Sroufe & Waters, 1976), Berlyne (1973) and later, Rothbart and Pien (Rothbart, 1973; Rothbart & Pien, this volume) have attempted to analyze humour materials as well as laughter-provoking situations within an arousal framework.

Berlyne (1971) has identified three general characteristics of stimuli leading to arousal. The first refers to psychophysical properties, for example, size, shape, frequency, and duration of the stimulus independent of the observer; according to Godkewitsch (1976), they presumably play a relatively minor role in enjoyment of humour. The second characteristic refers to ecological properties, and these are properties associated with the physiology or the past experience of the subject which have either a beneficial or noxious consequence for the subject.

A third set of characteristics identified by Berlyne as having arousal value are what he called collative properties of stimuli, involving a relation between stimulus properties and the experience of the subject. In Berlyne's terms, 'collative' refers 'to the fact that, in order to decide how novel, surprising, complex, and so on, a pattern is, one must compare or collate information from two or more sources' (1971, p69). Collative properties include novelty or surprise, complexity, incongruity, redundancy, and uncertainty.

Recent theorists of cognitive processing have attempted, I believe, to include Berlyne's collative properties, with the exception of redundancy and complexity factors, within the term 'incongruity.' They have also stressed the idea that for humour to occur, at least for older children and adults, resolution of perceived incongruity is necessary. Shultz defines incongruity as 'a conflict between what is expected and what actually occurs in jokes,' while resolution is 'a second, more subtle aspect of jokes which renders incongruity meaningful or appropriate by resolving or explaining it.' (1976, p13).

Suls' (1972) two stages in the cognitive processing of jokes are described as follows: 'In the first stage, the perceiver finds his expectations about the text disconfirmed by the ending of the joke or, in the case of a cartoon, his expectations about the picture disconfirmed by the caption... In the second stage, the perceiver engages in a form of problem solving to find a cognitive rule which makes the punchline follow from the main part of the joke and reconciles the incongruous parts.' A cognitive rule is defined by Suls as 'a logical proposition, or a fact of experience.' (Suls, 1972, p82).

Rothbart and Pien argue elsewhere in this conference book that there are problems with a simple incongruity-resolution analysis: resolutions of jokes often add new incongruities, while an incongruity may not be made wholly meaningful by the 'resolution' or may be left entirely unresolved. Given these problems, Suls' definition of resolution as finding a cognitive rule making the incongruity follow from the rest of the joke would be preferable to Shultz' requirement of meaningfulness, in that it would allow for partial resolution of an incongruity. At the same time, Suls' (1972) identification of an incongruity with the punchline only is an over-simplification of the way jokes work. For example, in the joke: 'What is grey, has four legs, and a trunk?' 'A mouse on vacation,' there is incongruity or surprise in the joke body before we reach the punchline. We do not expect a riddle to have an easy, obvious answer, while for this riddle, 'an elephant' is the obvious answer. The punchline adds surprise, but we have already been surprised by the riddle question itself.

At the present stage of research on incongruity and resolution in humour, precise definitions of both incongruity and resolution will be necessary in order for progress to occur. At the present time, even distinguishing resolution from incongruity is difficult. The very identification of an incongruity, for example, noting that a cartoon figure's hat is much smaller than most hats, requires that we identify the dimension along which the stimulus differs. Is this a case of incongruity resolution or of sheer incongruity? Shultz (1976) has suggested that we adopt Charlesworth's (1969) distinction between 'novelty' and 'surprise' in our definitions of incongruity. In Charlesworth's view surprise occurs when our expectations are disconfirmed; novelty occurs when we do not have a specific expectancy about an event, either because it occurs without warning or because we have not associated the event with its usual preceding stimuli. Pien (personal communication, 1976) argues that we may define instances of both surprise and novelty as cases of incongruity, but that more search for a resolution will be likely to occur in the case of a surprising stimulus than in the case of a novel stimulus.

There is at present disagreement concerning whether perception of incongruity alone is sufficient for humour in older children and adults. Shultz (1976) and Suls (1972) feel that it is not, while Rothbart (1976) argues that incongruity perceived in a safe or joking context is sufficient for humour to be experienced. In the experimental area, some of the most ingenious studies on laughter have been done testing the hypothesis that sheer incongruity leads to enjoyment. Nerhardt (1970) had college student subjects judge a series of weights, with some of the weights diverging widely from those expected in the experiment. He found greater laughter for weights diverging in both the very light and very heavy directions than for weights representative of the central tendency in the experiment. Deckers and Kizer (1975) used the method of constant stimuli and varied the incongruity between an expected weight and a weight actually presented. They found that laughter and smiling were greater as incongruity increased between the expected and presented weights. Laughter and smiling were also greater the more presentations of stimuli before the incongruous stimulus was presented. Although these experiments referred to smiling and laughter as expressions of humour, it is unfortunate that they did not ask for humour ratings from their subjects. Shurcliff's (1968) study suggests that a surprising situation may be seen as humorous by subjects as well as resulting in their laughter.

Evidence for the effects of incongruity on humour has also been presented by Kreitler and Kreitler (1970), Rothbart (1976) and Shultz (1976) for young children. In addition, McGhee and Johnson (1975) have reported appreciation of incongruity humour in third and fifth grade children. Shultz (Shultz, 1972; Shultz & Horibe, 1974) has also found that eleven- and twelve-year-old children prefer resolution removed jokes and cartoons (i.e., sheer incongruity) over forms without incongruity, indicating that older children also appreciate incongruity humour.

In connection with resolution aspects of humour, Shultz has proposed a developmental theory of the humour process. On the basis of research with cartoons, jokes, and riddles (Shultz, 1972; Shultz, 1974; Shultz & Horibe, 1974) he has concluded that there are two distinct stages in the development of humour. The first, lasting until the age of six to seven years, is characterized by an appreciation of incongruity only. After the age of six to seven, resolution components are necessary for humour to be appreciated. However, Pien and Rothbart (in press; this volume) have collected data indicating that four- and five-year-olds also appreciate humour resolution, and have suggested that even infants may appreciate resolution aspects of humour.

McGhee (1974a) has suggested that the resolution-aspect of humour combined with additional assimilation involved in understanding jokes constitutes a mastery effect leading to pleasure in the experience of humour. In McGhee's view this mastery effect is essential to the humour process, especially in children's humour. In connection with McGhee's analysis, it should be mentioned that the very identification of an incongruity, as in identifying the cartoon figure's small hat mentioned above, may involve cognitive effort from the subject. We may therefore talk about mastery effects even in jokes or cartoons without resolution aspects.

COMBINING AROUSAL AND COGNITIVE PROCESSING APPROACHES TO THE STUDY OF HUMOUR

The reader will have noted that arousal and cognitive processing approaches do not represent competing theories of humour; instead they represent analyses of humour at two different and quite compatible levels of abstraction. Arousal theory is a general theory attempting to account for both laughter and humour. In Berlyne's view (1960) arousal theory may also be used to analyze exploration, curiosity, and aesthetics. Within arousal theory, identification of incongruity is seen as one of many factors influencing an increase in arousal; tendency factors such as sexual and aggressive content of humorous materials may also increase arousal level. Although Berlyne identifies incongruity as a factor increasing arousal, his requirement of an 'arousal jag' in order for humour to occur may require some resolution of incongruity in order for humour to occur. In terms of Berlyne's theory the effect of resolution of incongruity would be to suddenly decrease arousal leading to the experience of humour. In Rothbart's view, incongruity alone, experienced in a safe and/or playful situation would also satisfy the conditions of arousal with safety and could result in humour.

Any incongruity-resolution analysis of humour is problematic in that, given current formulations, we cannot distinguish the process of humour appreciation from the process of problem-solving. In analyzing our own reactions to solving problems, we know that reaching a problem solution, especially solving a difficult problem, often results in feelings of pleasure and excitement; we may even smile and laugh in response to solving the problem (Harter, Shultz & Blum, 1971). However, it is extremely doubtful whether we would be willing to call this pleasure a humour experience.

One dimension differentiating humour from problem-solving in the case of 'sheer incongruity' humour involves cues identifying a situation as being 'in fun' rather than a situation requiring serious problem-solving. Three studies of children's humour involving the appreciation of pure incongruity (Kreitler & Kreitler, 1970; McGhee & Johnson, 1975; Rothbart, 1976) have indicated that providing fantasy cues (McGhee & Johnson, 1975; Rothbart, 1976) or identifying the situation as a non problem-solving one through the subjects' attitude of criticism, mockery, or wonder toward incongruities (Kreitler & Kreitler, 1970) leads to relative facilitation of humour.

In the incongruity-resolution situation, on the other hand, a problem-solving approach is clearly required in order for us to fully understand a joke. Here, the identification of the situation as a joking, playful, or non-serious one is probably also important. In our analysis of jokes that do not fit a strict incongruity-resolution paradigm (Rothbart & Pien, this volume), we have found that jokes often involve only partial resolution with remaining incongruity that cannot be resolved, as in the riddle: 'Why did the cookie cry?' 'Because his mother had been a wafer so long.' Achieving even partial resolution of this joke requires anthropomorphizing the cookie so as to allow it to cry: the punchline adds an additional impossible incongruity of the cookie having a mother. These additional unresolved incongruity elements may further signal to us that we are not engaging in the usual kind of problem-solving; the 'willing suspension of disbelief' is required for us even partially to resolve the riddle, and it is likely that the remaining unresolved incongruity contributes to our enjoyment of the joke. McGhee's (1972b) term 'fantasy assimilation' aptly describes the process involved in these types of jokes.

Problems of Measurement

If there is some agreement, as indicated above, concerning a general theoretical approach to the study of humour, there has been much less agreement concerning the proper measurement of humour. Since it is possible to achieve agreement in the definition of laughter, it would have been ideal to be able to use laughter as a direct index of humour. There is general agreement with Darwin (1872) that the sound of laughter involves, 'a deep inspiration followed by short, interrupted, spasmodic contractions of the chest... During laughter the mouth is opened more or less widely with the corners drawn much backwards, as well as a little upwards; and the upper lip is somewhat raised' (1872, p200).

In addition to behavioural observations of laughter, Pollio, Mers & Lucchesi (1972) have introduced measures of amplitude and duration in the study of group laughter. Mair and Kirkland in this symposium also report on a new method of measuring laughter, the laryngograph, which allows identification of laughter patterns as distinct from other conversational vocalization.

We also know, however, that laughter may be induced by many conditions, the perception of humorous stimuli being only one of these, and that we sometimes are amused when we do not laugh. Therefore, as La Fave et al (1976) have argued, humour is neither a necessary nor sufficient condition for laughter. The relation between laughter, smiling, and the perception of humour continues to trouble us, and much more work on this problem remains to be done.

Two kinds of measures have been traditionally used in the study of humour: first, humour or 'funniness' ratings are analyzed, where subjects are asked to indicate on a numbered scale how funny the humour stimulus appears to them. A second measure, usually analyzed to compare with humour ratings, has been the 'mirth response'. As originally developed by Zigler, Levine and Gould (1966) and adapted by other researchers (e.g., Shultz, 1972; Leventhal & Mace, 1970), the mirth measurement index has involved direct observation of the subject, leading to a weighted measure of positive affect. The scale ranges from 0 to 4: 0 = negative response (e.g., grimace), 1 = no response, 2 = inhibited smile, 3 = full smile, and 4 = audible laughter. Adaptations of this measure have eliminated a negative response and scored no response as zero; laughter as 3 (Rothbart, 1976). These measurements are reliable, and in studies with children consistent positive correlations have been found between mirth indices and humour ratings, (e.g., Pien & Rothbart, 1976; Shultz, 1972). However, Chapman (1976) has argued that the mirth index, 'is a crude and insensitive measuring technique, based tacitly upon a number of untested and implausible premises and paying no heed to crucial problems of quantification' (1976, p156).

The mirth index does represent a crude ordinal scale; it is based on the intuitive observation that laughter appears to be a more intense reaction to humour stimuli than smiling. The mirth index fails to take into account individual differences in response to humour; while some individuals may characteristically laugh when they are amused, others may smile, and still others may show no facial sign of humour appreciation even though they are enjoying the humour situation.

In one of the few methodological studies in the area of laughter and humour, Branch, Fine and Jones (1973) investigated the relation between humour ratings of college students and frequency and duration measures for both smiling and laughter as coded from videotapes. Branch et al's findings are difficult to interpret: smiling scores were generally better predictors of an individual's humour ratings than laughter scores, while laughter scores were the better predictor of ordinal rankings of humour stimuli by the group. Unfortunately, the experimenters did not use composite mirth scores in their study, a comparison that would have been most useful in deciding whether the mirth index is an appropriate measure of humour. More research is definitely needed on this problem.

Two recent innovations in the measurement of laughter, mentioned above, have been amplitude and duration measures of laughter (Branch et al, 1973; Pollio, Mers & Lucchesi, 1972). Although these measures have been applauded (Chapman, 1976) as being innovative indices of humour, one of the same criticisms applying to the mirth index also applies to amplitude measures: how do we know that louder laughter indicates greater amusement than quieter laughter? The measure is chosen for its intuitive appeal and supported by significant correlations between amplitude scores and group humour ratings. While duration seems to provide an excellent ratio scale for our analyses, how do we know whether a two-second laugh psychologically constitutes twice as great a humour response as a one-second laugh?

At present, it seems wise for researchers to supplement any mirth measure with a humour rating, although this procedure becomes very difficult when subjects are young children, and impossible when subjects are pre-verbal children and other primates. Pien and Rothbart (this volume) discuss some of the many problems associated with carrying out humour research with young children, given this difficulty. Clearly more methodological research is greatly needed interrelating behavioural, attitudinal, and psychophysiological measures of humour. The use of laughter and smiling scores as a sole index of humour is highly questionable; as adjuncts to humour ratings, observed smiling and laughter provide excellent supporting data.

FOOTNOTE

[1]The author wishes to express appreciation for the extremely helpful comments and criticisms of Diana Pien and Myron Rothbart on earlier versions of this chapter.

REFERENCES

See Bibliography for publications on humour, laughter and comedy

Berlyne, D.E., Arousal and reinforcement. In: D. Levine (Ed.), Nebraska Symposium on Motivation. University of Nebraska Press, Lincoln (1967).

Berlyne, D.E., Aesthetics and Psychobiology. Appleton-Century-Crofts, New York (1971).

Branch, A.Y., Fine, G.A. & Jones, J.M., Laughter, smiling, and rating scales: An analysis of responses to tape recorded humor. Proceedings of the 81st Annual Convention of the American Psychological Association, Montreal, Canada, 8, 189-190 (1973).

Charlesworth, W.R., The role of surprise in cognitive development. In: D. Elkind & J.H. Flavell, (Eds.), Studies in Cognitive Development. Oxford University Press, New York (1969).

Gale, A., Spratt, G., Chapman, A.J. & Smallbone, A., EEG correlates of eye contact and interpersonal distance. Biological Psychology, 3, 237-245 (1975).

Lewis, M. & Brookes, J., Self, other, and fear: Infants' reactions to people. In: M. Lewis & L.A. Rosenblam (Eds.), The Origins of Fear. Wiley, New York (1974).

Thayer, R.E., Activation states as assessed by verbal report and four psychophysiological variables. Psychophysiology, 7, 86-94 (1970).

Zajonc, R.B., Social facilitation. Science, 149, 269-274 (1965).

Humour and the Theory of Psychological Reversals

Michael J. Apter* and K.C.P. Smith**

*University College, Cardiff, **Bristol

INTRODUCTION: REVERSAL THEORY

The theory of psychological reversals put forward by Smith and Apter (1975) is an attempt to provide insight into many kinds of non-rational behaviour by interpreting such behaviour as resulting from the action of psychological processes which display bistability rather than homeostasis. A bistable system has two rather than one preferred state. When there is a switch from one preferred state to the alternative, this is referred to in the theory as a reversal.

The theory is therefore in a sense a cybernetic theory, but it is also a phenomenological theory in that it is particularly concerned with certain subjective characteristics of the individual's cognitions and also especially with the way in which he interprets his own behaviour. The dimensions on which attention has so far been primarily concentrated in the theory, and in terms of which the preferred bistable states are defined, are essentially phenomenological rather than behavioural dimensions, and are mainly motivational.

This does not mean that behaviour is ignored in the theory but rather that the theory attempts to explain behaviour in terms of phenomenological processes which are themselves believed to operate in accordance with certain cybernetic principles. In these terms explanations have been provided for certain aspects of various kinds of non-rational experience and behaviour, including crime, sport, the arts, ritual and religion as well as various psychopathological processes.

The theory therefore was not devised specifically to deal with humour, but humour can also be included in the list above. A number of concepts have been developed in the theory, but only those necessary to discuss humour will be introduced here – namely the telic-paratelic bistability (which is one of a number of bistabilities discussed in the theory) and the concept of cognitive synergy. These are both central concepts in the theory and have been used in the attempt to explain aspects of various kinds of behaviour.

The theory asserts that at any time an individual will tend to be either in a telic or a paratelic state: that is, this is a bistable dimension. When the individual is in a telic state he strives for goals which phenomenologically are seen by him as essential to him and imposed on him, either by the requirements of his own body (e.g., hunger drive) or by the requirements of society (e.g., to pass an examination). When the individual is in a paratelic state he behaves because he enjoys the behaviour in itself and, where goals are involved, these are seen by him as being freely chosen or adopted by him and in some sense inessential (e.g., climbing, to reach the top of a mountain). In other words, in the telic state behaviour is chosen to achieve goals, in the paratelic state goals are chosen (where they are chosen at all) to provide a raison d'être for the behaviour.

A further distinction between these two states, or systems, is that in the telic system the preferred level of arousal is low and in the paratelic system it is high. So in the telic system a high state of arousal has a negative affective tone ('anxiety') and a low state of arousal has a positive affective tone ('relaxation'); in the paratelic system, conversely, a high state of arousal has a positive affective tone ('excitement') and a low state of arousal has a negative affective tone ('boredom'). The relationship between arousal and affective tone is therefore, it is supposed, something like that shown in Fig. 1. This motivational aspect of the theory constitutes a departure from all other motivational theories in psychology in that it does not postulate one preferred level (e.g., of drive, arousal, tension, information input) but rather argues that there are two.

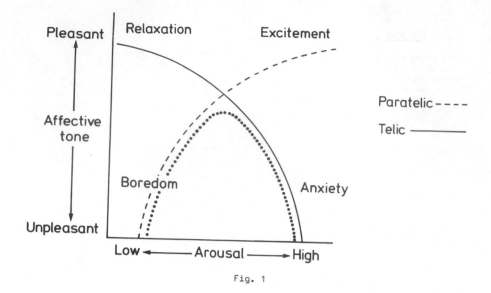

Fig. 1

However, arousal and affective tone are not entirely independent because a sudden increase in arousal is threatening and this may cause a reversal to the telic state (if the individual is not already in it). This is because escape from threat is an example of a telic situation: hence the inverted-U curve so often found in experiments relating arousal and affective tone and shown with dots in Figure 1.

So, in order to reach the upper right quadrant of the graph (labelled 'excitement'), other aspects of the situation must counterbalance the tendency to reverse to the telic state. Much of our culture may be seen as providing ways of arousing the individual while maintaining the paratelic state. For example, in sport the conventional setting and atmosphere and the strict rules by which the game is governed provide sufficient security for the uncertainty, surprise and risk within the game itself to result in pleasant rather than unpleasant arousal. Humour, it will be argued, constitutes another method used by human beings in order to achieve the enjoyment of arousal. Consistent with this, a positive relation between arousal and felt humour has been found in recent physiological research (e.g., Godkewitsch, 1976a).

The other concept which needs to be introduced is that of synergy. By a synergy, in the theory, is meant the bringing together of two cognitive opposites so as to enhance each other's phenomenological qualities. This effect, it is supposed, is of the same kind as contrast effects in perception: for example, the complementary colours red and green placed next to each other, or shown immediately after each other, enhance each other's vividness. In reversal theory the concern is more with such effects at the apperceptive rather than strictly perceptual level. For example, someone rich in a poor context, or someone poor in a rich context: the rich person will seem richer and the poor person poorer. A further assertion in the theory is that synergies as such produce feelings of pleasure in the paratelic state and displeasure in the telic state.

There are various kinds of cognitive synergies; humorous situations, it will be argued, always involve a particular kind of synergy called an 'identity synergy': here the opposites are seen as being two aspects of the same situation so that opposition and identity are perceived concurrently. An example would be a man dressed and behaving like a woman: maleness and femaleness are expressed simultaneously through one identity.

THE HUMOUR PROCESS

From the point of view of the theory, felt humour occurs in the presence of three conditions: the individual must be in a paratelic state, an identity synergy must occur, and there must be something unexpected about the synergy. Together, these conditions are both necessary and sufficient to bring about that particular enjoyment of high arousal which can be referred to as, and which has the special phenomenological qualities of, felt humour. The high arousal in humour, of course, is transient in comparison with some other situations, for example, in sport, where it is often more long-lasting.

What happens in humour, we believe, is this: the unexpectedness causes an increase in arousal, the identity synergy induces reversal to the paratelic state if the individual is not already in it, and maintenance of it if the individual is, and the conjunction of increased arousal and the paratelic state is felt as pleasant as long as it lasts. The synergy itself is also felt as pleasant in the paratelic state and may also play some part in increasing arousal quite apart from the unexpectedness. This is all summarized in Fig. 2 in which connecting lines which join and continue together (e.g., increased arousal and paratelic outputs joining before entering the box labelled 'pleasure') represent conjunctive conditions and separate lines represent disjunctive conditions.

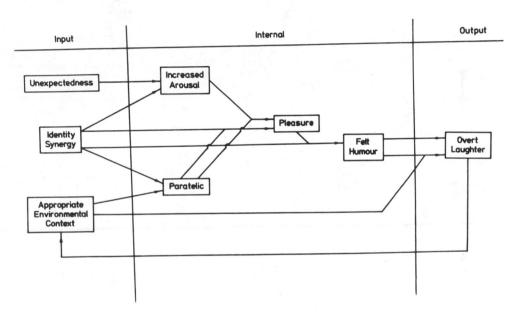

Fig. 2

Figure 2 also refers to the effects of the environmental context. This context may help to define the situation as paratelic, for example, the fact of being in a theatre, or of watching a television screen may identify the situation in its widest context as a non-threatening one. Furthermore, if we suppose that there is a threshold above which the strength of felt humour results in overt laughter, and if an individual in a social situation reaches this threshold and laughs, then this laughter becomes, for the others, part of the environmental context. That is to say, overt laughter may become a cue which defines the situation to others within earshot as a paratelic one and therefore increases their chances of themselves being in a paratelic state and perceiving the situation as humorous. This process, together with a social facilitation effect which, we may suppose, will bring about a lowering of the threshold for overt laughter, should induce laughter in more and more people in the social group. In turn, this defines the situation increasingly strongly as paratelic for the whole group, including those not yet laughing. In other words, a positive feedback situation is set up which, provided the source of stimulation continues, should eventually result in felt humour and laughter in the group as a whole (cf. Foot & Chapman, 1976, on the social functions of laughter).

IDENTITY SYNERGIES

How does an identity synergy itself induce the paratelic state, quite apart from the environmental context? The answer is that it not only fails to make sense but clearly, by its very structure, cannot be made to make sense unless its playfulness is recognized. It does not make sense because opposition and identity are mutually exclusive: making them occur together in such a way that they are not mutually exclusive is therefore something which is cognitively playful and not threatening, especially when one of the opposites is clearly pretending to be the other, or appears to be the other, and when the opposites are exaggerated (a point which will be returned to below). Put another way, an identity synergy represents an escape, or at least a playful escape, from logic. In particular it represents an escape from the law of non-contradiction which states that A cannot be both B and not-B. The identity synergy is a particularly strong form of contradiction since 'not-B' is not just something different from B but (which is not encompassed in traditional or modern symbolic logic), something which is its opposite. In the example of humour given a little earlier, A is both a man (B) and, by pretence, a woman (not-B) and here not-B is the opposite of B. To give another example: 'Don't panic' said in a panicky voice (a frequently used phrase of the character Corporal Jones in the series 'Dad's Army' on BBC television). Here the message (A) says two opposite things at the same time: 'Panic' (B) and 'Don't panic' (not-B). The first is the real message, the second the ostensible message.

There are a large number of opposites which can be, and often are, unified into identity synergies for the purpose of humour: for example, sacred-profane, superior-inferior, poor-rich, White-Negro, and intelligent-stupid.

One set of opposites in particular appears to be found widely in humour, and this is the set of opposites to the concept 'man'. There are four of these: 'animal', 'child', 'woman', and 'machine'. That is, one meaning of man is 'the opposite of animal', another is 'the opposite of child', and so on. Perhaps these are so ubiquitous in humour because the concept 'man' is central to our understanding of ourselves and, if some semanticists like Ogden (1967) are to be believed, understanding the meaning of a word may depend on recognizing its opposite. So humour is often created by bringing some opposite to 'man' and 'man' into an identity synergy either by 'man' pretending (or appearing) to be the opposite or vice-versa. Let us look at some examples:

    man as animal: pantomime horse
    animal as man: Mickey Mouse and other similar cartoons
    man as child: circus clown
    child as man: Peanuts strip cartoon
    man as woman: pantomime dame
    woman as man: aggressively masculine women in situation comedy
    man as machine: slapstick in silent films
    machine as man: puppets, ventriloquist's dolls

Identity synergies which are unexpected will always, according to the theory, cause some degree of felt humour, but this may only be a minimal amount. The felt humour may be amplified, we would suggest, in the following three ways:

(1) Exaggeration

The contrast of the cognitive opposites is made as clear as possible: thus, we would expect a very masculine individual wearing feminine clothes to look funnier than a not very masculine individual wearing only slightly feminine clothes. As well as increasing the effect of the synergy through contrast, such exaggeration may also help to define the situation as a paratelic one since it emphasizes its 'make-believe' and playful qualities.

(2) Multiple Identity Synergies

Children appear to enjoy single identity synergies. For adults, however, more than one synergy in the situation appears to make it funnier. Identity synergies can be combined in various ways:

    (a) Unrelated identity synergies may just get added to each other. For example, take the character of Basil Fawlty in the BBC television series 'Fawlty Towers'. His character may be said to display the following identity synergies: coward/bully, obsequious/sneering, competent/incompetent, inferior/superior, among others. Other characters who interact with him, and other aspects of the situations developed in the plot, display other identity synergies.

(b) Two symmetrically opposite identity synergies may be combined. For example, the comedians Morecambe and Wise: Morecambe is a 'wise guy' pretending to be foolish, Wise is a foolish man pretending to be clever, that is, 'wise'.

(c) One of the terms in the identity synergy may itself be split into a further identity synergy. For example, when Morecambe slaps Wise's cheek (which he does frequently), this is a gesture which is both friendly and an attack. However, sometimes he slaps so hard that he hurts his own hand and grimaces with the pain: here the attack-half of the original identity synergy is itself split into two opposing terms which make a new identity synergy. The two new opposites are: aggression against another and aggression against oneself.

(d) The same stimulus situation may involve different synergies in different aspects of the situation. To give a simple example: saying of someone that he is 'as thick as two short planks'. On the one hand, this is a man/object identity synergy; on the other, the phrase appears to be meaningful and precise but is as meaningless and imprecise as the phrase 'as long as a piece of string'. That is, the second synergy involves the opposites meaningful/ meaningless.

(3) Tension

Felt humour is increased if one of the cognitive opposites is one which is normally highly arousing, that is, which in the telic state causes unpleasant high arousal or anxiety. This unpleasant arousal is then converted into pleasant arousal in the paratelic state. Hence the use of sex, cruelty, death and other arousal-producing situations in humour (and indeed in other forms of entertainment like thriller novels and horror films).

CONCLUSIONS

There is not space here to carry out detailed analyses of the way in which identity synergies are used by particular professional comedians or in particular comedy plays, television series, etcetera, nor to show how the theory relates to particular kinds of humour like punning, slapstick, verbal wit, irony and tickling. Such analyses have already been made by us and it is hoped to publish them at a later stage.

It is probably most useful to conclude by making clear the difference of this theory from several other popular theories of humour. Firstly, the theory is obviously different from theories utilizing the concept of optimal arousal, such as that of Berlyne (1960), in that it does not postulate one single optimal level (homeostasis) but two preferred levels (bistability). The theory does however, like Berlyne's, make central use of the concept of arousal.

The theory is also the opposite of theories using the concept of relief. It is the arousal itself, it is claimed in reversal theory, which is pleasant, felt as humour, and leads to laughter, not the subsequent relief from the arousal. This is consistent with recent physiological evidence due to Godkewitsch (1976a) that felt humour is related to the amount of arousal induced by the punchlines of jokes rather than reduced by them. However, the theory does bear some resemblance to the recent theory of Rothbart (1973, 1976) which uses the concept of relief as well as other concepts. This resemblance is due to the fact that, like Rothbart, reversal theory suggests that arousal within safety is one of the necessary characteristics of felt humour: as we have seen, according to reversal theory, perceived safety helps to induce the operation of the paratelic system, the arousal-producing stimuli then being interpreted in a non-threatening way.

Finally, on the cognitive side the theory is a form of incongruity theory, but it asserts that not any form of incongruity will do. Rather, it identifies a particular kind of incongruity – namely that involved in what we have called identity synergies and especially multiple identity synergies – and argues that it is these which elicit felt humour and laughter under the appropriate circumstances.

REFERENCES

See Bibliography for publications on humour, laughter and comedy

Ogden, C.K., Opposition: A Linguistic and Psychological Analysis. Indiana University Press, Bloomington, (Originally published in 1932) (1967).

Smith, K.C.P. & Apter, M.J., A Theory of Psychological Reversals. Picton Press, Chippenham, Wiltshire (1975).

Some Characteristics of Resting Respiration as Predictors of Laughter

Sven Sveback

University of Bergen, Norway

The physiological correlates of humour appreciation have been observed, not as antecedent conditions predisposing to enjoyment, but rather as part of the actual humorous experience itself. Reviews of this literature may be found in Langevin and Day (1972) and in Stern, Farr and Ray (1975). When studies of the physiological correlates of humour appreciation are taken together, they indicate that there is a general biological basis of enjoyment. The energy mobilization during such mental states has been demonstrated in observations of the endocrine glands (adreno-medullary), the autonomic nervous system, and muscular activity. Berlyne (1972) has indicated that pleasure can depend on either of two mechanisms activated by changes in arousal: one is related to a moderate rise in arousal ('arousal boost'); the other is a combination of a rise in arousal with a succeeding drop ('arousal jag'). The physiological correlates of humour appreciation seem to fit well into the Berlyne hypothesis. Nevertheless, one should keep in mind that energy mobilization (activation) is a typical correlate of virtually any change in stimulus conditions and in most emotional states (see, for example, Frankenhaeuser, 1975; Lang, Rice & Sternbach, 1972).

The classic formulation of Freud (1905) postulated that the pleasure derived from a positive response to humorous material is the result of gratification of unconscious motivations that would remain repressed under ordinary circumstances. In this sense humour effects a reduction of situationally aroused tension. Consequently, a person who is not (ego-) involved in an actual comical situation will not be receptive to humour. Persons displaying signs of increased tension (involvement) in an introductory resting period should therefore be the most prone to laughter in a subsequent entertainment period.

In a previous report (Svebak, 1975a) the variability of tonus in abdominal muscles of females during laughter proved to be positively correlated with magnitude of laughter, while no such correlation was observed in males. In the present report the resting respiratory patterns (abdominal and thoracic body circumference changes during inhalation-exhalation) of the males and females referred to above are investigated as predictors of amount of laughter in a subsequent entertainment period.

On the basis of an extensive survey of studies in respiration and personality published by Christiansen (1972), three particular kinds of respiratory patterns were selected for quantification: (1) the pattern of 'sighing', (2) the 'respiratory plateaus', i.e. a period of inactivity sometimes occurring between one exhalation and the succeeding inhalation, and (3) the so-called 'paradoxical respiration' where the thoracic and abdominal body circumferences are oppositional for at least one respiratory cycle (inhalation-exhalation period). According to Christiansen (1972) the sighing pattern is typically observed in anxiety states (most frequently seen in states of anxiety neurosis). The sighing pattern might thus indicate a state of anxious tension provoked by the actual experimental situation (none of the subjects belonged to any psychiatric population), and that this situationally aroused resting tension (if present in some of the subjects prior to the entertainment programme) might be released by a relatively high frequency of subsequent laughter responses. As for the pattern of respiratory plateaus, this has been associated with some kind of socio-emotional remoteness (most typically observed in schizoid states, cf. Christiansen, 1972). If this pattern is observed in some of the subjects during the period prior to entertainment, it might indicate a mental 'defense' against becoming involved in entertainment. Alternatively, this kind of respiratory pattern might simply signal a very low metabolic rate (causing reduced need for oxygen-intake etcetera). In such a state of low physiological arousal one would predict low frequencies of laughter too.

Finally, the disorganized action of respiratory muscles indicated by the 'paradoxical respiration' pattern is most frequently seen in schizophrenic states (cf. Christiansen, 1972). If it is observed in some of the non-hospitalized subjects pariticipating in this experiment, one might suggest that it is related to the same lack of situational involvement as that probably underlying the respiratory plateaus.

METHOD

Twenty-five subjects (thirteen women, twelve men) were recruited from students in introductory university courses. They were all volunteers, and they were told that the purpose of the experiment was to make observations on individual differences in responses to entertainment material.

All recordings were made on the Beckman Type R Dynograph Recorder. Two channels described the abdominal and thoracic respiratory patterns respectively (couplers 9875B). Alteration of body circumference caused by respiratory-muscle activity was measured by means of Hg-gauges made of silicone tubing filled with mercury and having a platinum wire inserted into each end of the silicone tube. The thoracic gauge was fastened as close to the armpits as possible, and the abdominal gauge was fastened half-way between the lowest point on the rib-bones and the highest point on the hip-bones (sitting position). A more detailed description of the technique is found in Svebak (1975a).

Great care was taken by the experimenter to assume a playful manner in order to promote a humorous social ambience. The subject was placed in front of a TV apparatus. Before starting the play-back of an entertainment programme, there was a five-minute interval for the scoring of resting respiratory patterns. The experimenter then informed the subject about the nature of the programme ('candid-camera', cf. Svebak, 1974c). During the play-back, the experimenter sat in a chair six feet to the left of the subject, and operated a hidden switch to trace laughter-responses from the subject.

A plateau was scored when the inhalation-exhalation cycle was arrested for ten seconds or more. Paradoxical respiration was scored when the inversion surpassed the mean resting amplitude (calculated as the mean amplitude during the last minute of the resting period as a percentage fraction of the mean smallest circumference during this period) for the thoracic and abdominal patterns respectively. It was essential that the inversion be prolonged throughout the mean duration of one cycle in the resting period or more. The score of 'sighing' was obtained when the amplitude suddenly increased by more than three times its mean resting range and made a sharp inhalation-exhalation transposition. If the criterion of sighing was reached by one channel only, it was still scored as a sigh. It was essential that a blind scoring procedure be established for the assessment of respiratory patterns and laughter responses.

In Fig. 1 one example is given of each of the three respiratory patterns scored according to the operational criteria described above.

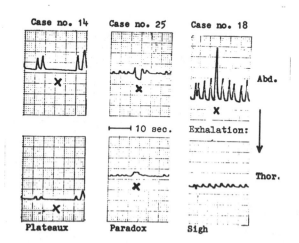

Fig. 1. Examples of respiratory patterns scored as 'respiratory plateaus', 'paradoxical respiration', and 'sighing' respectively

RESULTS

For each subject two scores on laughter were calculated: (1) the total number of laughter-responses (group mean: 98, s.d.: 32); and (2) the mean duration of the five longest laughter-responses (group mean: 4.4 sec; s.d.: 1.3 seconds). A mean Z-score of the two variables was calculated for all subjects. Those obtaining positive Z-scores (N=12) were classed as the 'high' laughter group, and those obtaining negative Z-scores were classed as the 'low' laughter group (N= 13). There was no sex difference in magnitude of laughter responses.

The subjects were also classed into two groups on the basis of each category of respiratory patterns, i.e. those showing at least one instance of the patterns of sighing, respiratory plateaus, and paradoxical respiration respectively, and those where no score was obtained on each of the three categories. In Table 1 the distribution of subjects with and without these patterns in the high and low laughter groups are presented.

TABLE 1   The number of subjects in two groups (high and low scores on laughter) showing respiratory patterns of sighing, respiratory plateaus, and paradoxical respiration in a five-minute period prior to entertainment

Laughter-response	Sigh	Plateaus	Paradox
High (N=12)	10	3	0
Low (N=13)	3	2	6

The nonparametric Simple Chi-Square Test (cf. Bruning & Kintz, 1968) was applied for analysis of discriminative trends in the distribution of respiratory patterns. The occurrence of sighing in the high laughter group was significantly higher than in the low laughter group (x^2=4.84; df=1; p < 0.03). No significant group difference in the distribution of respiratory plateaus and paradoxical respiration was observed. In the introduction (see above) it was suggested that these categories of respiratory patterns are related to the same motivational trend (lack of situational involvement). A composite score on 'remoteness' patterns was therefore calculated (eight in the low laughter and three in the high laughter group), and a nearly 5% level of significance was obtained for the higher occurrence of this composite pattern of the low laughter group (x^2=3.24; df=1; p < 0.07).

DISCUSSION

In order to provide a fair opportunity for these respiratory patterns to occur, the resting period prior to the entertainment programme was arbitrarily set at five minutes. A reduction to four minutes was also tested, and no reduction in level of significance was observed for the composite remoteness scores. In the case of sighing, however, the Chi-square value dropped to the 5% level of significance. It is assumed that an extension of the resting period (where the subject was left alone) would run counter to the intended establishment of a humorous ambience (induced during the introductory period of technical arrangements) prior to the entertainment programme, the subject then tending, instead, to regress gradually into a mood of ennui.

To the extent that sighing is a valid indicator of situationally aroused tension, one may well conclude that the Freudian hypothesis on laughter as a releaser of tension gained some support. In spite of the fact that the composite remoteness criterion was slightly discriminatory when related to the high and low laughter groups, the plateaus scores were not at all discriminatory when tested alone. It is, of course, possible that the remoteness patterns are not equally sensitive to motivational characteristics in non-hospitalized persons.

The validity of the respiratory patterns as indicators of varying levels of bodily activation (energy mobilization) should be tested in follow-up studies in comparison with scores on other physiological indicators of activation (e.g., heart rate, galvanic skin resistance, etcetera). The practical joke style typical of the 'candid-camera' material applied here should then be supplemented by other styles of humour in order to test the reliability with which predictions carry over into other types of humour as well.

One is sometimes met with the objection that respiration is partly a voluntary performance and that therefore observations relating to autonomic nervous system activity should be preferred as indicators of activation. In addition, the scoring of respiratory parameters is definitely more complex than the scoring of autonomic parameters like Galvanic Skin Resistance and Heart Rate. In my view the partly voluntary control of respiration makes respiratory parameters superior to those derived from purely autonomic activity when relations between personality and somatic activity are studied.

I would emphasize, in conclusion, that there are methodological problems at two different levels connected with this approach to research on humour. First, we have the question of how far such respiratory patterns are valid indicators of the current state of mind (nervous tension and lack of situational involvement). Second, there is the question of the degree of sensitivity of these indicators in experimental situations of this type, i.e. where research into validity is conducted with non-psychiatric subjects. It is necessary to be particularly cautious in the drawing of conclusions based on the remoteness patterns, in view of the fact that these have been most frequently observed in schizoid and schizophrenic patients.

REFERENCES

See Bibliography for publications on humour, laughter and comedy

Bruning, J.L. & Kintz, B.L., Computational Handbook of Statistics. Scott & Foresman, Glenview (1969).

Christiansen, B., Thus Speaks the Body. Arno Press, New York (1972).

Frankenhaeuser, M., Sympathetic-adrenomedullary activity, behaviour and the psychosocial environment. In: P.H. Venables & M.J. Christie (Eds.), Research in Psychophysiology. Wiley, London (1975).

Lang, P.J., Rice, D.G. & Sternbach, R.A., The psychophysiology of emotion. In: N.S. Greenfield & R.A. Sternbach (Eds.), Handbook of Psychophysiology. Holt, Rinehart & Winston, London (1972).

Stern, R.M., Farr, J.H. & Ray, W.J., Pleasure. In: P.H. Venables & M.J. Christie (Eds.), Research in Psychophysiology. Wiley, London (1975).

Mirth Measurement: A New Technique

Michael Mair[1] and John Kirkland[2]

University of London Institute of Education

The approach to the study of mirth described here is part of an investigation both of movement and of sound patterns generated by participants in interaction. Let us first explain about some of the data collected including a description of how these were taken, and then go on to explore their significance in a broader context.

METHOD

At present our equipment can deliver four types of measurement. Briefly these include: basal intonation contour; voice onset and offset; total speech pressure wave; and, finally, manual frame-by-frame plotting of face movements.

The first three are acoustic variables. These are delivered by use of the laryngograph[3], tape-recorder, and ultra-violet pen-corder. The laryngograph monitors each opening and closure of the vocal folds by measuring impedance change between disc-electrodes placed on each side of the thyroid cartilage. This signal is electrically converted to a graphic plot showing fundamental frequency (Hz). Paper speed is 10 cm per second. Thus the acoustic equipment delivers speech pressure wave, the original signal, and the conversion. These traces are displayed simultaneously (see Fourcin, 1974; Fourcin & Abberton, 1971).

Figure 1 shows fundamental frequency traces from two mirthful episodes. The visual record is obtained by monitoring a single point on the face (medial canthus of an eye or tip of nose) as it changes its position between successive single frames on a video-corder. The equipment used is a Sanyo (Model 1100 SL) which delivers stable single frames. These frames are numbered by including a digital clock during recording. The time interval between frames is chosen as 0.1 second, because inertia of the head makes notable changes of direction impossible within a shorter time period. Additionally, critical fusion frequency is around this speed and makes perception of faster changes unlikely. For a single frame the selected face-point can be established by noting co-ordinates (x,y) in two-dimensional space. By following this point across successive frames we include time (t). These data are represented as x/t; y/t; and x/y.

To eliminate parallax errors when obtaining face-point co-ordinates a transparent grid is first applied to the front of the video monitor. The film is then viewed through a pinhole mounted at a fixed but convenient distance from the monitor (in our case 1m). This pin-hole is a retina immobiliser. One alternative would be to incorporate grid and cross-wires into the input video signal but this is expensive.

Subjects were chosen who already knew one another. Our discussion is based on data taken from three subjects. Two mirrors arranged to form a convex-angled V were placed on a table between seated interactants who could still maintain eye contact. This device enabled us to film simultaneously two subjects with a single video-camera. Two laryngograph electrodes, each the size of a two-pence piece, were attached. An ordinary microphone was used as well. It enabled later location of critical tape sections. Thus each subject's acoustic signals were fed into twin-tracks of a single tape-recorder. Selected portions of audio-tapes were transcribed by the ultra-violet pen-corder.

Subjects were kept naive about the purposes of the study. Their sole instructions were that they should 'chat'.

DATA

We are considering mirth from the aspects of fundamental frequency, rhythmicity, supra-glottal modification, movement, and synchrony. For completeness, we have also included other physiologic eruptions, speech, and a miscellaneous category comprising such events as 'hums', 'moans', etcetera. The categories are demarcated for convenience although in real communication they merge. However, if we consider them exhaustively from each aspect we may see whether they survive in any sense. We shall conclude 'mirth' in this way.

Example 1

The acoustic variables are shown in Figure 1, and the head movement in Figure 2. These data were obtained from an exchange between interactants, demarcated from the surrounding conversation by silence, and separate from it in topic as well. This exchange consists of a question: Male voice: 'Great fun breaking up polystyrene glasses isn't it?' and an answer: Female voice: 'Yeah, make a very great mess can't you?' The male laugh occurred over the word 'glasses', and the female laugh preceded her utterance and occurred synchronously with the male laugh. The Figures show:

1. Fundamental frequency (C): the male laugh occurred over the word 'glasses'. In all, his utterance consisted of two 'S' shaped falls, linked by a slow rise. The laugh disturbed, but did not destroy, the shape of the slow rise, which continued as a trajectory through it. The female laugh also has pitch, which was high, as was the commencement of her utterance.

2. Rhythmicity: the male laugh turned the word 'glasses' into a stutter. The female laugh also consisted of more than one pulse.

3. Supra-glottal modification: the male laugh disturbed the articulation of the word 'glasses'. The female laugh was not accompanied by an attempt at articulation.

4. Non-articular movement: our technique delivers a record of gross head movement only. In Figure 2 we see that the male went into a relatively immobile head position from frame 9 to 17. His escape from immobility occurred at about frame 18, which was close to the onset of the laugh, and he returned to relative immobility at frame 36. The female entered the episode in a condition of relative immobility. Her movement also coincided with her laugh, and returned to relative immobility.

5. Synchrony: this refers to the extent to which they moved together during the laugh. They initiated the laugh movement within 0.4 second of each other. The laugh vocalisation was more closely synchronised.

Example 2

This is a record of a solo female whose laugh occurred in an interaction involving three people (not shown). It was sparked off when the experimenter attempted to join the conversation. It consisted of a laugh, followed by the comment 'Hm, bring you into the conversation', followed by an unclassifiable vocalization. Figures 1 and 2 show:

1. Fundamental frequency (C): the pulses followed a falling contour which was continued into the beginning of the utterance.

2. Rhythmicity: the laugh had a three pulse, two pulse, three pulse sequence.

3. Supra-glottal modification: the laugh was free from supra-glottal modification.

4. Non-articular movement: there was an abrupt onset of movement at the vocalized part of the laugh, and the subsequent movement is represented in Figure 2 by large loops which become a more detailed shape when she is speaking (frame 28). Rapid movement is resumed over the final syllable, when she also looks down.

5. Synchrony: not applicable.

DISCUSSION

Our examples are evidently too few to prove any interpretation. However, we do not intend to deny ourselves this opportunity to put forward a theory, albeit speculative, which links some features of these examples, and places them in the wider context of some observations on speech. Let us list the features of mirth from our examples.

1. Fundamental frequency: this is related to the contour of the utterance in which the mirth is embedded.

2. Rhythmicity: mirth's rhythms are simple and pulse-like.

3. Supra-glottal modification: articulation is either disturbed (the stutter), or absent.

4. Non-articular movement: mirth involves gross body movement with abrupt onset.

5. Synchrony: the onset of the movement was near synchronous for the interactional example.

How do these features compare with the same categories manifesting during speech?

1. Fundamental frequency: the relationship between fundamental frequency and perceived intonation is complex, but close. Certainly, the auditory effect of the laryngograph output is very similar to the perceived intonation of speech. Fundamental frequency as measured by the laryngograph is a monitoring of motor activity in the muscles regulating the vocal folds. The question why mirth should participate in the frequency shape of the utterance cannot be approached separate of the question why speech should have a fundamental frequency shape at all. Observation of the fundamental frequency contour for numerous utterances demonstrates smooth shapes, which continue across pauses and silences to be continued where they would have got to if the pauses had not occurred. We propose the term 'trajectory' to express the slower wholeness of intonation tune over utterances (there is also a finer embroidery corresponding to segmentation). It is the shapes themselves that suggest they be considered as trajectories.

2. Rhythmicity: the complex rhythms of speech have attracted much study. At this point, it is sufficient to note the contrast between them and the simple rhythmic vocalization of mirth.

3. Supra-glottal modification: this is the articulatory component of speech. Again, at this point it is sufficient to note that it is very detailed, and its study has an enormous literature.

4. Non-articular movement: this also is very detailed, and there are many approaches to its study (e.g., Ekman, 1969). We have noted that it is going with speech, and this realization follows the work of Condon and Ogsten (1967) with Kendon (1972). It is in contrast to the gross movement of mirth.

5. Synchrony: the question of synchronous movement between participants in interaction is also being explored by us; we have many examples of it. Again, we follow the work of Condon and Ogston (1967).

It is the fate of students of human communication to have to demarcate aspects of it for study, while being aware that in the process of communicating, all these aspects interlock. Perhaps a conference on humour can be the place to present a theory which might arouse mirth in another context?

We suggest that when studying communication - when trying to make sense of it - we are in fact studying the process by which sense is made; that when people are communicating, they are trying to make sense to each other. Trying to make sense of the process itself differs from the sorts of sense that people habitually try and make only in subject, and setting. We propose to call the unit of sense the 'model'. There are numerous other concepts with which this can be aligned, for example, the 'word group' (O'Connor & Arnold, 1974), the 'sentence' (Goldman Eisler, 1972, after Wundt), the 'tone group' (Kendon, 1972), the 'act' (Thom, 1975). Each seeks to delineate a unit of speech which is both an information unit, and a physically demarcatable stretch of speech.

Part of the problem is that for such a model (a realization of a state of affairs) to be communicated, nothing need actually be said. A wink can do it, or a chuckle. Even a silence can 'be so loud so as to drown out the scuffle of feet' (Birdwhistell, 1971). Such a silence clearly communicated a state of affairs or, as we prefer to call it, a model. That such as these can 'click' a model into existence points to two features of models. They are to a greater or lesser extent implicit, and they are shared - people are immersed in them, rather than exchanging them like counters. Of course, in formal situations (like this), the passage seems more one-way. But even here we share much more than my individual utterance contributes. We call these models 'interactional', to stress that in colloquial conversation, the model is a joint production, and evolves by the collaboration of the participants.

M. Mair & J. Kirkland

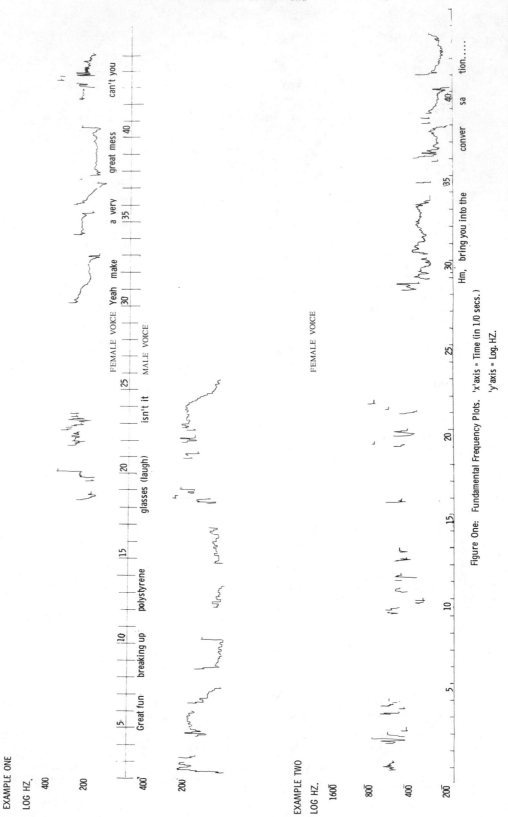

Figure One: Fundamental Frequency Plots.   'x'axis = Time (in 1/0 secs.)
'y'axis = Log. HZ.

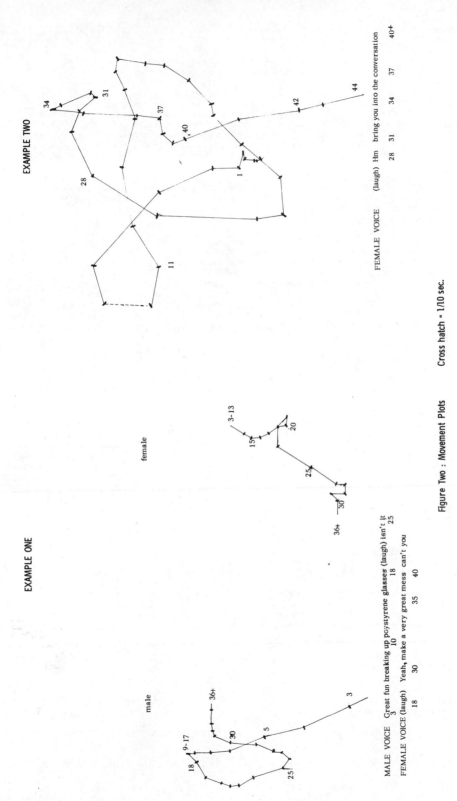

Figure Two : Movement Plots   Cross hatch = 1/10 sec.

The study of colloquial conversation performed by this technique might give verification to this view. Again, we make our list:

1. Intonation contour: this is far from random. O'Connor and Arnold (1974) suggest that there are but ten common tunes in colloquial English. The nucleus of the utterance coincides with accent and pitch change, and is always semantically important. Thom (1975) has a predatory theory of language, in which it is seen as virtual action, and grammar as being the same as the syntax of action. His archetypal morphologies (verb types, such as capture, emit, almost) look uncommonly like some common intonation contours. In colloquial chat, we complete each other's utterances, continue each other's contours. Together we make the model. It is as if the intonation contour is always just appropriate to where the model has got to in its elaboration.

2. Rhythmicity: if we consider contour as trajectory in this way, then we might suggest that it is the shape of the trajectory which divides up time into rhythm. Rhythm is not perfectly metrical, yet it is predictable. This view might contribute to the thoughts on rhythm offered by authors such as Abercrombie (1969) and Allen (1973).

3. Supra-glottal modification: Condon and Ogston (1967) have claimed that micro-movements go with speech to a detail as fine as the phoneme. Lieberman (1972) notes that for phonemes to be perceived sequentially would be beyond the discriminatory capacity of the ear. Ivimey (in press) points out the dramatic short cuts taken in articulation during spontaneous speech, and our studies confirm this (for example, 'sort of' becomes 'stv', or less). Micro-movements do certainly occur to a detail equal to the actual change points in articulation and Kendon (1972) has suggested that it is as if speech and the movements that immediately accompany it are under the same controlling mechanism. But intonation change can occur with this detail as well. So:

4. Non-articular movement, and 5. Synchronous movement cannot be approached theoretically separate from all the other categories above. Furthermore the 'controlling mechanism' which effects synchronous movement might best be considered supra-individual.

The comparison of speech with mirth shows up what mirth lacks. Complex rhythms are replaced by simple spasmodic rhythm, articulation (supra-glottal modification) is disturbed or abandoned. Detailed body movement becomes gross body movement. Frequency contour is at first maintained but even this is lost in extreme cases. The interactants are in a state of uncontrol (Douglas, 1975), on the floor, helpless, pouring secretions from eyes and mucous membranes (vagus nerve), sometimes incontinent. Only the synchrony of onset is preserved. It is catastrophic, and the way that the punchline of a joke can do this to the rest of the model preceding it is reminiscent of the way a Necker cube abruptly flips from one interpretation to another (as Gestalt theorists suggest). Our interactants must recover. Why we should seek out this experience is a weighty question indeed, but it seems that mirth may survive as a demonstrable pattern of behaviour.

FOOTNOTES

[1] Support by a grant from the Social Science Research Council is acknowledged.

[2] Now at Education Department, Massey University, Palmerston North, New Zealand.

[3] The laryngograph was devised in the Phonetics Department, University College, London. It is available from Laryngograph Ltd., 24 Highclere Drive, Hemel Hempstead, Herts., HP3 8BY.

REFERENCES

See Bibliography for publications on humour, laughter and comedy

Abercrombie, D., Voice qualities. In: N.N. Markel (Ed.), Psycholinguistics. Dorsey Press, Homewood, Illinois (1969).

Allen, C.D., Segmental timing and control in speech production. Journal of Phonetics, 1, 219-237 (1973).

Birdwhistell, R.L., Essays on Body-Motion Communication. Penguin, Harmondsworth (1971).

Condon, W.S. & Ogston, W.D., A segmentation of behavior. Journal of Psychiatric Research, 5, 221-235 (1967).

Ekman, P., The repertoire of non-verbal behaviour: categories, origins, usage, and coding. Semiotica, 1, 449-498 (1969).

Fourcin, A.J., Laryngographic examination of vocal-fold vibration. In: B. Wyke (Ed.), Ventilatory and Phonatory Control Systems. Oxford University Press, London (1974).

Fourcin, A.J. & Abberton, E., First applications of a new laryngograph. Medical and Biological Illustration, 2, 172-182 (1971).

Goldman Eisler, F., Pauses, clauses and sentences. Language and Speech, 15 (1972).

Ivimey, G.P., The perception of speech: An information processing approach. Teacher of the Deaf, in press.

Kendon, A., Some relationships between body motion and speech. In: A.W. Siegman & B. Pope Eds.), Studies in Dyadic Communication. Proceedings of a Research Conference on the Interview. Pergamon, New York (1972).

Lieberman, A.M., Perception of the speech code. In: E. David & P. Denes (Eds.), Human Communication, a Unified View. McGraw-Hill, New York (1972).

O'Connor, J.D. & Arnold, G.F., Intonation of Colloquial English. Longman, London (1974).

Thom, R., Structural Stability and Morphogenesis. (Translated D.H. Fowler). Benjamin, Massachusetts (1975).

The Logic of Humour and the Humour in Logic

John Paulos

Temple University, Philadelphia

Philosophers, psychologists, writers, and even some humorists have attempted to come to an understanding of humour. What remains controversial and problematical is the psychology of humour. Does it spring from a feeling of hostility, a sense of superiority, a releasing of repressed energy (Freud, 1905), a playful attitude, a swelling of pure joy? What seems fairly uncontroversial or unproblematical is the logic of humour. Most theorists agree, once allowance is made for different phrasings and emphasis, that a necessary ingredient for humour is that two incongruous ways of viewing something (a person, a sentence, a situation, etcetera) be juxtaposed. Different theorists have emphasized different incongruities: expectation versus surprise, mechanical versus spiritual (Bergson, 1911), superiority versus incompetence, propriety versus vulgarity. For our purposes then we will understand humour to result from incongruous juxtapositions in the appropriate emotional climate. We shall not bother about the appropriate emotional climate; we shall, however, try to indicate how some notions from logic provide formal analogues for certain kinds of incongruities. We shall also mention aspects of logic which are themselves humorous. Like most work on humour, however, this paper is not humorous (unless the mere attempt to analyze humour strikes one as humorous).

The logic of our first sort of joke can be explained in terms of a notion from model theory[1]. Jokes of this sort result when a sentence has two or more different interpretations or models. The classic burlesque joke is an example. 'What goes in hard and dry and comes out soft and wet?' 'Well, let's see, uh...' 'Chewing gum!' In other words 'chewing gum' plays the role of a nonstandard (incongruous, unexpected) model[2] of the defining sentences. Needless to say in most jokes of this type the sentence is usually implicit and the two different frames of reference or models are also usually only indirectly suggested. For example, there is the story of the young man who registered his requirements at a computer dating-centre. He wanted someone who enjoyed water sports, liked company, formal attire, and was very short. The computer sent him a penguin.

A joke of this sort in logic might be a non-standard model of Peano's axioms or Poincare's model of a non-Euclidean geometry[3]. The emotional climate for humour mentioned in the first paragraph is not quite right here, but there is a sort of intellectual smile at least associated with recognizing a structure with infinite elements as a model of Peano's axioms or a circle with 'curved' lines as a model for a non-Euclidean geometry.

The notion of the logical level of a statement is a very important one in logic. A statement can be an object language statement of the formal system, a meta-level statement about the formal system, or even a meta-meta level statement about meta-level statements. Something like the notion of a meta-level, call it a vantage point, a sense of perspective or whatever, is needed to appreciate humour. Dogmatists, idealogues, people with one-track minds are notoriously humourless (though often unintentionally funny). For example in order to see a joke of the kind we have just discussed, one has to be able to step back and recognize the incongruity between two different ways of interpreting a sentence (two different models). This psychic stepping back and recognition of incongruity is a sort of meta-level operation.

There is a common type of joke which depends entirely on an interplay between levels. Examples are 'commentary' jokes where a comedian comments (usually unfavourably) on his own jokes thereby eliciting a laugh at this new meta-joke. Sometimes the same statement can be interpreted differently on the two levels, the meta-level statement or comment often only being indicated by a code word or phrase. A Godel numbering[4] is a joke of this sort since statements about number can be interpreted on the meta-level.

Closely related to the above level jokes are three other common types of jokes involving some form of self-reference: (i) modal paradoxes; (ii) Russell jokes; (iii) iterated

level jokes. This classification is quite arbitrary and should not be taken too strictly.
Modal paradoxes result when the content of a statement is incongruous with its form or mode
of expression. Examples are paperweights with 'Think Ahead' squeezed on them or billboards
advertising 'Want to learn how to read? Call 632-0641 for further information.' Russell
jokes are simply jokes whose logical underpinning is some form of Russell's paradox
concerning the class of all classes not containing themselves as members. Two examples of
Russell jokes are: (a) Groucho Marx's classic quip that he would never join any club that
would accept him as a member and (b) the neurotic's worrying about not having any worries.
A standard example of an iterated level joke is the following. A philosopher is asked 'Why
do philosophers ask so many questions?' and responds 'Why shouldn't philosophers ask so many
questions?' Another is a tow-truck towing a tow-truck.

The last kind of humour we shall consider results from the purposeful confusion of the logic
(grammar) of one term or phrase for that of another. Wittgenstein once said that a serious
work in philosophy (read logic) could be written which consisted entirely of jokes of this
kind. The work of Lewis Carroll comes close to proving Wittgenstein's remark. Whether he
is talking of storing up wasted time for future use, of the supposed difference between saying
something and meaning something (Humpty-Dumpty), or about the peculiarities of naming,
Carroll's humour depends largely on the wilful misapplication of logical and grammatical facts
and principles or, in some cases, on too literal an adherence to these facts and principles.
A short excerpt from Woody Allen provides a more recent example of the same type of humour.
'The first ink blots, it was learned, were crude, constructed to eleven feet in diameter and
fooled nobody. However, with the discovery of the concept of smaller size by a Swiss physicist,
who proved that an object of a particular size could be reduced in size simply by "making it
smaller", the fake ink blot came into its own. It remained in its own until 1934 when Franklin
Roosevelt removed it from its own and placed it in someone else's.' Another example concerns
the little boy who says to his little girl friend 'Are you the opposite sex or am I?'

A more logical (philosophical) example of the same sort of humour (though not treated
humorously) is Wittgenstein's concern that one does not talk about having a pain in one's
shoe even though one may have a pain in one's foot and the foot is in the shoe. The
grammatical similarities between 'going on to Chicago' and 'going on to infinity' or between
'a vicious murderer' and 'an alleged murderer' provide further examples. Anyone familiar
with the 'linguistic turn' in philosophy will realize that the work of many modern philosophers
and logicians (Ryle, Austin, etcetera) is full of such humour.

We stated in the beginning that humour results from incongruity (in the appropriate emotional
climate) and we have sketched three sorts of incongruity suggested by logic: nonstandard
models, level and type confusions, and misleading grammatical forms. There are other logical
principles which give rise to humour - exaggeration and reductio ad absurdum, part-whole and
relational reversals[5], intensional modalities[6], etcetera - but our limited aims have been
achieved: there is often a logical basis to humour and there is sometimes a humorous aspect
to logic.

Did you hear the one about the logician who...

FOOTNOTES

1. Model theory is that branch of mathematical logic which deals with the connection between
   a sentence and interpretations or models in which the sentence is true. Most sentences
   are true in more than one model or interpretation. The intended interpretation is called
   the standard model of the sentence, the others the nonstandard models.

2. More accurately, it is the whole scenario suggested by chewing gum, and not just chewing
   gum, which is the nonstandard model.

3. Peano's axioms are a set of sentences whose standard model is the positive integers under
   addition and multiplication. The axioms (surprisingly, maybe) also have nonstandard
   models. A similar situation holds for Poincare's model.

4. A Godel numbering is an assignment of a number to each formal expression in a formal
   language. Statements about numbers in the formal system can then be interpreted as
   meta-statements about formal expressions on the meta-level.

5. Relational reversals, $R(x,y)$ in place of $R(y,x)$, are often humorous. A bus tattooed on the
   side of a greyhound is an example of such a relational reversal.

6. Modal logic, which deals with the connection between truth and modalities such as belief,
   intention, obligation, etcetera, provides us with a basis for many types of jokes.

From Joseph Grimaldi to Charlie Cairoli: A Semiotic Approach to Humour

Paul Bouissac

Victoria College, University of Toronto

The circus still ranks very high among the institutions which provide a setting for displays of humour. Clowns are indeed popular performers in our culture. (Reference is made here to actual circus clowns, not to literary, artistic or cinematographic uses of clowns as visual themes or characters). Clown performances, and their impact on their audiences, are readily observable. Any clown act is a strictly patterned sequence of behaviour and does not vary significantly from one performance to another. It can be precisely described and recorded.

Clown acts are generally viewed as being nonsensical, but it is obvious that the actions the clowns perform, the objects they manipulate and the dialogues in which they engage themselves, are in some respects relevant to the contextual culture, if only because, in order to be successful, clowns have to modify some elements of their acts according to the country in which they perform. This applies, of course, to the spoken parts, but also to culturally bound nonverbal elements such as gestures, costumes and accessories. In addition, clowns, even the most successful ones, occasionally experience failures (i.e., parts of actions designed to be humorous fail to trigger the expected response from the audience). Therefore it is patent that clown acts are at one and the same time nonsensical and non-contingential. This nonsensical behaviour is not a succession of erratic occurrences, but is patterned by rules.

As expressed in its title the methodological approach of this paper is not psychological but semiotic, that is, it relies on the methods of a discipline which is currently taking shape in the no man's land between psychology, sociology and anthropology and is concerned not only with signalling behaviour in man and animals and the symbolic processes it presupposes but also with the sign systems comprising any culture (cf. Sebeok, 1975a,b). As semiotics already includes several directions or schools of thought I should state that the approach outlined in this paper is influenced by the French structuralist strain and that, accordingly, its biases are: first, to give priority to the elicitation of symbolic systems able to account for particular instances rather than to focus on the individual responses of the persons involved in those instances and, secondly, to consider the level of experience and the level of intellection as somewhat incompatible; that is, either you laugh or you understand what is going on. In contrast with the hermeneutic approach, I would even contend that someone who would have never laughed would benefit from a privileged position for understanding laughter.

The main consequence of this general approach for the study of humour and laughter is that it focuses not on laughter but on the systemic operations correlated with laughter. This should bring forth some precise correlations between specific semiotic operations and differentiated categories of laughter and shed some light on the ever puzzling phenomenon to which we refer as humour in our culture and which is all the more elusive as it is familiar. Practically in my research on circus clowns I take laughter as an indicator enabling one to sort certain situations and operations which in turn are being analyzed in and for themselves.

Therefore, a semiotic approach to the study of clown humour will consist of (1) identifying the signs, and systems of signs, which they 'borrow' from their contextual culture, and (2) eliciting the rules through which they transform and combine these signs. The ultimate goal of such an approach is to uncover the set of constraints which determine all the constructions observed (i.e., a grammar accounting for the creativity of clown humour), and to understand the socio-cultural and psychological significance of the so-called nonsensical displays. The hypothesis which underlies this research is that humour, at least as observed in the setting of clown acts, is a meta-semiotic operation that manipulates, so to speak, meaning as an object of thought from the outside of 'sensicality'.

It is surprising that in the study of humour circus clowns have been given so little attention whereas their raison d'être is precisely to elicit laughter. Indeed, they can survive only as long as they produce humorous actions and objects. In fact, they create complex sequences of gags bound together in a scenario whose importance should not be overlooked as it provides more than a mere pretext or background for the gags. I have shown in my book that such scenarios are consistent and refer to the constitutive rules of their contextual culture in a way which I will attempt now to illustrate by two limited examples (Bouissac, in press).

There is no doubt that the famous nineteenth-century clown, Joseph Grimaldi, was making people laugh as he was called 'the Michael Angelo of buffoonery'. He was particularly known for his jokes of construction (Disher, 1968). Among the few which were recorded is the construction of the attire of a fierce Hussard with various objects. The construction is described as follows: 'His hat: a lady's muff — a watchpocket pinned to the side of it — a table brush stuck out of the crown — his cords and tassels are contrived with a bell rope. His boots: a pair of coal-scuttles (handles like spurs) — the sword — a poker.' There also exists a print showing another version of the same construction which can help to visualize the description which I just gave. The legend reads: Grimaldi, Bold Dragon in the Popular Pantomime of the Red Dwarf.

The second example comes from one of the greatest clowns of our time, Charlie Cairoli, who has been performing at the Blackpool Tower Circus for the last thirty-seven years. As most clowns he has a small workshop in which he constructs all sorts of artifacts designed to play their humorous part in a given scenario. Of course, these artifacts are instantly discarded if they fail to trigger the expected laughter. Mr. Cairoli was kind enough to lend me one of them for the occasion of this Conference. It consists of a toilet seat that has been stringed as if it were a lyre. It is used in the following context: As a comment on a gesture by Charlie Cairoli the orchestra plays the tune 'When the Saints Go Marching In' and at the same time one of his partners appears dressed in a white gown and playing this instrument.

Let us now try to analyze these two examples and to interpret them in the light of our hypothesis. In the case of Grimaldi's 'joke of construction' we note that all the objects selected for the construction belong to the same paradigm and are not picked up at random. With respect to the contextual culture all these objects are indeed women's attributes, that is, ladies' garments and objects belonging to the home, more particularly to the fireplace, the hearth. In my opinion the unexpectedness of the use of these objects cannot account alone for the laughter which was triggered. There is a definite relationship of mutual exclusion between a warrior's attributes and a woman's attributes and it is this crucial relationship which is in focus in this joke of construction. This view seems to be confirmed by another joke by Grimaldi in which he was pretending to be a boxer but used loaves of bread instead of boxing gloves. This construction shows the same relationship as above but on a reduced scale. The point of these jokes is not the surprise they cause but the way in which they operate on semantic or cognitive categories.

Cairoli's example is even more striking in this respect. The gag I have presented belongs to a rich paradigm in the circus tradition. This instrument however is to my knowledge unique. It is a perfect example of creativity but in the sense that a grammatical rule can generate new sentences. Actually we can set forth a formal rule which enables one to describe adequately some other instances which I will now list:

(1) A clown announces that a violin recital will be performed by a famous virtuoso. Another clown, wearing a formal tailcoat over his outfit, enters the ring carrying a violin case. He bows ceremoniously to the audience, opens the case and extracts from it first a napkin, which he ties around his neck, then a bottle of cheap wine. He drinks noisily from the bottle, wipes his mouth, and puts the bottle and the napkin back in the case. He bows again to the audience — and is driven out of the ring by the outraged ringmaster.

(2) Same initial situation as in (1) except that the clown enters with a violin. As he starts playing, an explosion occurs in the violin. It falls apart and its contents spill out: strings of thick red sausages. Same conclusion as in (1).

(3) Same beginning as in (2), except that a horn is attached to the neck of the violin. Instead of playing the violin, the clown blows the horn. Same conclusion.

My hypothesis is that these four instances are four versions of the same operation which consists of relating in the form of an equation two categories of sounds that are strictly disjoined in our culture, although they may be situated on a continuous scale or distributed differently from the point of view of acoustics: they are sounds associated with nutrition (ingestion, digestion, and excretion) and sounds belonging to the category of music. These operations are performed through the use of rhetorical devices such as metaphors or metonymies. Cairoli's construction actualizes the same operation in an extreme form: celestial music vs excretion noises[1].

Sounds		
Nature	Culture	
	Normative Differentiation	

continuous scale of various acoustic properties	undesirable in social setting:
	
	sounds produced by the nutritional processes:
	
	   — ingestion
	   — digestion
	   — excretion
	
	(from moderately undesirable to highly undesirable sounds)
		desirable in social setting:
		
		musical sounds
		
		Strings: lyre
		        harp
		        violin
		
		Winds: honking horn
		
		(from highly sophisticated to 'primitive' sounds)

Finally, one can at least formulate a problem in view of these data and their tentative interpretation. It seems that the statements produced by the existence of these jokes of construction are meta-semiotic, that is, their objects are those rules which govern the semanticity of our cultural environment and the normality of our social behaviour (Bouissac, 1976). They refer in their own way to those learned distinctions between sex-roles and to those learned differentiations between sounds which are otherwise acoustically neutral or indifferentiable. If this is true and if these aspects are in fact crucial for such jokes then the question is why does a meta-semiotic activity elicit laughter?

In conclusion, it seems to me that concepts such as unexpectedness and incongruity that are central to much current research on humour and laughter are in fact misleading because they emphasize the irrational aspects of jokes. They take the attention of the researcher away from the actual semantic or semiotic operations that are performed and for some reasons cause laughter. As it has been obvious in this paper, my hypothesis is that on the contrary jokes are highly rational and systematic operations. Of course the reason why such semiotic operations trigger laughter remains to be solved, but at least this approach may help to define a target for further research.

FOOTNOTE

1. In a Russian puppet show which toured Western Europe in 1972, a satirical performance of a piece of modern music was concluded by one of the musicians pulling the chain of a toilet and producing the familiar noise of water falling in the toilet bowl.

REFERENCES

Bouissac, P., Circus and Culture, A Semiotic Approach. Indiana University Press, Bloomington, (in press).

Bouissac, P., Semiotics and spectacles: the circus, institution and representations. In: T.A. Sebeok (Ed.), A Profusion of Signs. Indiana University Press, Bloomington (1976).

Disher, M.W., Clowns and Pantomimes. Bengamin Blom, London (1968). (First published 1925).

Sebeok, T.A., The semiotic web: a chronicle of prejudices. Bulletin of Library Semiotics, 2, December (1975a).

Sebeok, T.A., The Tell-Tale Sign: A Survey of Semiotics. Peter de Ridder Press, Lisse, Netherlands (1975b).

ACKNOWLEDGEMENT

This paper reports part of a research project on the semiotics of circus clowns supported by the Guggenheim Foundation (1973/74).

Comic Mythos and Children's Literature - Or, Out of the Fryeing Pan and into the Pyre

Samuel Schuman

Cornell College, Iowa

The study of literature, as perhaps my title hints, sometimes creates strange intellectual bedfellows. There are times, however, when the very strangeness of comparison, like some metaphysical conceit, reveals something new about the objects compared. In what follows I will quickly note a few striking similarities between a pattern found in comedy by a group of Jungian 'myth critics' and three classics of children's literature: 'The Wizard of Oz', by L. Frank Baum; and 'Jack and the Beanstalk' and 'Hansel and Gretel', both collected by the brothers Grimm.

The mythic pattern of comedy is perhaps most convincingly and fully articulated by Northrop Frye (1948/1949). Frye suggests that New Comedy has dominated Western comic literature since Aristophanes, and that all New Comedies share certain characteristics. The comedy reproduces the pattern of a fertility rite (itself an echo of seasonal sterility and growth): 'the ritual of death and revival'. It begins in a world of personal, social, and natural disorder and sterility. Frequently the 'normal' pattern of family relationships is distorted (often by the prevention of a 'right' mating by a sexually jealous 'senex'). This opening world is the 'wasteland'. From the barrenness of this wasted landscape, the comedy moves to a new and magical terrain, a setting of natural wildness and beauty, a 'green world ... of fairies, dreams, disembodied souls, and pastoral lovers' (p88). This green world works a rejuvenative magic on the comic protagonists (usually young lovers), who then return, properly coupled, to the initial setting, but now 'in the general atmosphere of reconciation'. While this process of renewal is at first a personal one, it is 'an individual release which is also a social reconciliation (producing) a renewed sense of social integration'. The fisher king is healed, the wasteland is fertile again, Spring returns in its annual mystery. Thus the action of the comedy begins in a world represented as a normal world, moves into the green world, goes into a metamorphosis there in which the comic resolution is achieved, and returns to the normal world.

While Frye, and other critics of his persuasion such as C.L. Barber, generally focus their attention upon the workings of this regenerative pattern in Shakespearean 'adult' comedy, it is not difficult to see the same basic movements in children's literature. 'The Wizard of Oz' thus begins in drought-stricken Kansas:

> 'When Dorothy stood in the doorway and looked around, she could see nothing but
> the great gray prairie on every side. Not a tree nor a house broke the broad
> sweep of flat country that reached the edge of the sky in all directions. The
> sun had baked the plowed land into a gray mass, with little cracks running through
> it. Even the grass was not green, for the sun had burned the tops of the long
> blades until they were the same gray color to be seen everywhere'. (L. Frank Baum,
> 'The Wizard of Oz', Indianapolis, 1899, p12).

How far is Dorothy's Kansas from T.S. Eliot's more famous modern wasteland?

> 'A heap of broken images, where the sun beats,
> And the dead tree gives no shelter, the cricket no relief
> And the dry stone no sound of water'. (T.S. Eliot, 'The Wasteland', 1922, p11).

The infertility of the land is echoed in an unsatisfactory family relationship. Uncle Henry and Aunt Em are too concerned about the troubles down on the farm to give Dorothy the love and care she needs. From this wasteland, the chief comic protagonist (and her dog, Toto) are miraculously transported to a new world — the Land of Oz, which is quite obviously not the Kansas prairie. The translators of 'The Wizard of Oz' from book to movie caught perfectly the mythic flavour of this geographic shift: in the film version of the work, instantly upon Dorothy's arrival in Oz, the image shifts from black-and-white to colour.

In keeping with Frye's archetypical comic pattern, Oz is a land of magic. In fact, Baum foreshadows Frye's vocabulary by centering his 'green world' around - what else - the Emerald City! Frye (1966), incidentally, has observed that:

> 'In the comic vision the mineral world is a city, or one building or temple,
> or one stone, normally a glowing precious stone...'

Within the green world of Oz, evil (in the form of two wicked witches) is exorcised, hypocrisy and sham (in the form of one humbug wizard) is discovered and chastized, and good (Dorothy herself, Munchkins, Glinda, etcetera) liberated. Indeed, thanks to the transformational magic of Oz, several partial personalities are made whole: the Tin Woodman gets his heart; the Scarecrow, his brain; the cowardly Lion, his courage. (Shades of curing or making whole the ritual god? Dare we compare the quest of the Scarecrow, Lion and Woodman to Jessie Weston's 'achieved quest... (in which) the wounded king at last was healed'? Is the Tin Woodman the fisher king?) The novel, of course, concludes in perfect New Comedy form. Dorothy returns to Kansas, but through her return, Kansas and its inhabitants seem changed. The land is less hostile, the family is reconciled. The greenness of Oz has renewed the fertility of the 'normal' world.

'Hansel and Gretel', as the tale appears in the Grimms' collection, also adheres strikingly to Frye's mythic, Jungian, New Comedy pattern. The tale begins in sterility and familial disharmony - the children are to be abandoned by a hateful step-mother as a solution to the problem of starvation. Hansel and Gretel are left in the woods where, predictably, they encounter the world of magic. Interestingly, the tale seems to replicate the mother-figure in increasingly stylized and increasingly evil reflections. If the step-mother is some sort of simplified symbolic version of all that is hateful or feared in mothers - particularly stealing the affection of the father away from the children to the point of literal abandonment the evil witch of the story seems to move this distorted image one step farther into the fantasy world. She feeds the children, and houses them, but these typical parental actions parody the maternal care they resemble. The witch is actually nurturing Hansel and Gretel not as a consequence of affection but as a livestock crop: she plans to eat them.

In any event, the children transcend and conquer the threat of the forest, and return to the initial home environment of the tale altered and able to help alter that disharmonious homestead. Since they return with heaps of jewels pilfered from the witch's cottage, they should be able to mitigate the poverty which caused their plight in the first place. Further, things have changed at home while hero and heroine were in the forest: one children's edition of the story concludes thus:

> 'They began to run and rushed inside, where they threw their arms around their
> father's neck. The man had not had a single happy moment since he deserted
> his children in the wood, and in the meantime his wife had died.' ('Grimm's Fairy
> Tales'. Tr., Lucas et al. New York, 1945, p340).

This same basic pattern is also found in 'Jack and the Beanstalk', a mythic tale found in several cultures, including American Indian cultures. As we know the story, it conforms rather closely to the sterility - magic - renewal form. Like the other children's works we have been considering, Jack's story begins with the double discords of sterility and disharmony. The initial actions of the tale (those having to do with the sale of the family cow for the magic beans) are motivated, as were the beginnings of 'Hansel and Gretel', by the pangs of hunger. Again, as seems to be typically the case, the fury of Jack's mother arising from his precipitous venture into speculative capitalism represents a context of family strife, a break in the natural and normal loving relationship between parent and child. Jack, who is without a father, is compensated by what must be one of the world's most obvious and dramatic symbols of paternal vigour, the embarrassingly Freudian beanstalk. Jack ascends this green and natural entryway into the world of magic, where, like the other infant protagonists we have considered, he encounters both threat and salvation. The threat, of course, is the cannibalistic giant, and the salvation lies with the hen which lays golden eggs and the magical harp (pragmatism and art). Jack returns to his home, bearing the saving hen and harp. He chops down the beanstalk, killing the giant, and thus eliminates at one stroke two rather grotesque reminders of the differences between little boys and big men. Needless to say, he and his mother live happily ever after. This game - find the mythic pattern and see how the tales fit - has a rather intoxicating allure and can be played almost indefinitely. We might well turn our attention similarly to other children's classics, written or folkloric (the epics of Goldilocks or Cinderella, for instance) and find them equally New Comical.

That there is a pattern, and that it is a meaningful one cannot, I believe, be doubted. The
three works we have briefly considered - and several others which we might have considered -
all begin with that most obvious consequence of seasonal or earthly sterility, the lack of
food. (We are defining 'sterility', rather broadly, as 'the inability to produce'). Dorothy,
Jack, and Hansel and Gretel are all hungry when their stories begin. They are also all, in
varying degrees, the victims of pseudo-parental neglect or ill-treatment. But note that in
none of the three cases are the full complement of 'natural' parents present: we have,
instead, an aunt and uncle, a father and step-mother, and a widowed mother. Again, if we
slightly broaden Frye's notion of sexual disruption, we observe that each tale begins with
a distorted and unhappy family situation, one with undue stress upon a child/parent
relationship. All the works move from this situation - unsatisfactory for both body and
soul - into a world of nature, of magic, of threat and of salvation. The youthful
protagonists of the tales re-emerge from this green world into the regular, civilized
landscape, which is thus restored as both loving and productive.

The similarity between Frye's archetypical comic pattern and these popular children's stories
does not (at least automatically) lead to the silly or debunking conclusions one could expect.
It would be quite easy to parody Frye using this material, or to suggest that what we have
here is little more than a cautionary amusing coincidence. To me, at least, the parallels
are too neat and too suggestive to be discarded this lightly.

To approach the question from a different perspective, is it not possible that it is
precisely to children's literature that we might turn for confirmation of Frye's theories?
If, as Professor Wylie Sypher (1956) suggests, 'the comic gesture reaches down toward the
unconscious', if, at the heart of literary comedy is an important and basic seasonal ritual
answering some equally basic and profound human need, then perhaps it is most clear in works
of the most basic sort. Children are notorious - or admirable, depending upon one's point
of view - for confronting the basic issues of life and death in a manner less disguised and
sublimated than we adults. Any child old enough to enjoy 'The Wizard of Oz', 'Jack and the
Beanstalk', or 'Hansel and Gretel' is certainly old enough to have noticed Winter and Spring,
hunger and satisfaction, anger and domestic harmony. Indeed, it is perhaps in its ability to
confront such primordial issues within the limiting framework of art (in effect, to face
life-and-death issues in a non-life-and-death arena) that comedy is linked to humour (to
paraphrase Apter and Smith's work, in this volume, art as a key to paratelicism). Bergson
(1911) noted that two of the three defining characteristics of comedy were 'social
significance' and 'absence of feeling'. Certainly it has been commonly theorized that
humour is a mechanism by which we react, explosively, to deep and even terrible issues when
those issues have at least partially lost the sting of reality - cartoon characters suffer
horribly, but their suffering is funny because it doesn't really hurt. Such theories appear
frequently in papers presented at this conference, and have historical precedent in the
works of Baudelaire, Freud, Jekels, Bentley and others.

An additional direction for further research in the relationship between the sorts of
comedies we have been discussing here and humour and laughter is suggested by the 'incongruity'
generated by the disparity between literary characters obviously imperfect in morals and/or
intelligence (and our expectations for such flawed figures) and the 'happy ending' of
comedies.

Humour, then, and comedy, are human ways of dealing with a universe which often seems
impenetrably tragic. The New Comic pattern of regeneration and restoration within a magical
green world as a curative for a jangling and sterile civilization seems to be a model from
which are derived a number of children's classics. Perhaps, then, one legitimate means of
rediscovering some of the magic of humour, of children, and of the literary experience is no
more complex than heeding some good advice from 'The Wizard of Oz': 'follow the yellow
brick road'.

REFERENCES

See Bibliography for publications on humour, laughter and comedy

Approaches to the Study of Humour: Discussion

Anthony Gale

University of Wales Institute of Science and Technology

We were faced here with a very mixed bag of theoretical, quasi-literary, anthropological, logical and methodological contributions, raising issues which range across the subject matter of many of the other sessions. We were presented with a general theory of individual and general behaviour, of which humour is considered as a special case, with a physiological study of individual differences relating to the probability of overt expression of mirth, with a study of exact method of mirth expression and with a preliminary analysis of the formal logic of mirth-eliciting propositions. We had an analysis of clowning, which it claimed, is not nonsensical, but meaningful in terms of its cultural context. Here the analysis focused largely on nonverbal behaviours, at a somewhat more general level than the detailed analysis offered for timing and frequency of mirth, but obviously sharing certain methodological problems. We concluded with an analysis of a particularly speculative and intangible theory of the basis of children's literature.

May I begin with Apter and Smith's presentation, to which I shall devote most of this discussion, because I am already familiar with this developing model of human behaviour. The first thing in favour of this theory is its claim to attempt to explain what the authors call non-rational behaviours. If indeed it achieves this ambition in explaining behaviours which other theories fail to explain, then of course it will gain considerable force. Of course, in the time allowed for presentation we could not expect a detailed account of a general theory. Nevertheless, a number of issues arise which the authors may wish to comment upon. The first is the distinction between rational and non-rational. I would challenge Apter and Smith's ready adoption of this vernacular terminology, without further explanation. Can they provide us with a check-list of behaviours which we can readily check off as rational and non-rational? Even so, I think we need to have a presentation of their account of rational behaviours, so that we can compare and contrast these two universes of description and explanation. Certainly many general theories of behaviour classify most of our behaviour as irrational in origin; Freud presents the best example of this. We may ask also whether engaging in rational behaviour, that is studying symbolic logic or devoting a lifetime of scholarship to the solution of theoretical mathematical problems, is rational?

This brings us to a consideration of the criteria upon which any general theory in psychology is to be judged as useful or not. I refer in particular to the relatively straightforward and logico-positivistic guidelines set down by Hall and Lindzey in their classic 'Theories of Personality' (1970). Boiled down to a simple list the requirements are: (1) statement of the basic assumptions; (2) rules for inter-relating the basic assumptions; (3) internal consistency; (4) empirical rules; and (5) comprehensiveness. These characteristics are essential for achieving explicitness and lack of ambiguity. We saw in the conference session the dangers of a theory couched in molar terms. At least six people in the session claimed that Apter and Smith's theory was similar to their own and accounts for hitherto not-understood behaviour. Now Apter and Smith do present us with their basic assumptions, but I am rather worried about the rest. My problem is that I find it difficult to see, as with all other theories of personality, how prediction can be set up ante hoc rather than post hoc. The proof of Apter and Smith's pudding must of course be in the eating, and we await further empirical evidence supporting the theory. Nevertheless, there are some difficulties which may make empirical prediction difficult. I suspect, for example, that the notion of bistability, which is a keystone of the theory, may also prove to be a tripping stone. The problem with theories which have bipolar, bistable, or opposite-state propositions as fundamental propositions is that such theories can never lose on prediction and are in principle unfalsifiable. Use of opposites, generally speaking, enables the theorist to account for anything, and in logical terms reduces to a built-in formal internal inconsistency, which as any student of logic knows, may be used to prove anything. Throughout the theory, because of the bistable characteristic, there is a danger that what cannot be explained in terms of one pole or state will be explained in terms of the other. That is why very strict and formal empirical rules are essential. Many of Apter and Smith's paratelic phenomena are what Allport would call functionally autonomous drives. But Apter and Smith relate this group of behaviours, as does Berlyne, to a general basic drive or twin-drive state of arousal. The issue not discussed is whether arousal reduction or increase is in fact itself a basic drive and therefore in my understanding, telic in nature. The difficulty arises of course over the notion of motivation and over the apparent discrepancy between subjective access to telic and paratelic motivators. Incidentally, I believe Apter and Smith have erred in relation to the inverted-U. The ordinate is normally labelled 'performance' and not 'affective tone', since affective tone would now be considered to be curvilinear rather than linear in scale. This raises the problem of Apter and Smith's triple world or three universes of discourse, since their theory refers at one and the same time, to subjective, behavioural and physiological events. Perhaps any general theory is obliged to do this, because that is the way things are. However, it constitutes an immediate rejection of an informal but useful property of theory, and that is parsimony. Again it demands of the authors a series of rules for establishing the relationships between these universes of discourse, not only in terms of parallel sets of events, presumably sharing a common time scale, but also in terms of antecedent and consequent events. Apter and Smith are, I think, in danger of arguing themselves into the Cartesian cul-de-sac.

What I like about the theory is its rejection of the notion of consistency as a basic datum of psychology, a misleading concept which has been espoused by so many theorists in psychopathology and social psychology in particular. Again, although it does raise difficulties, the concept of arousal as a central source of motivation, raises the promise of operationalization in physiological form, that is, in terms of central and peripheral measures of arousal and activation.

The paper by Svebak links up with that of Apter and Smith in the suggestion that there may be individual differences in physiological responsiveness, which in turn will relate to predisposition to laughter and/or humour appreciation. To some of you, these notions may appear to be far-fetched. But some of the most exciting work in psychophysiology is that concerning longitudinal studies of children at-risk and the prediction of later abnormalities in social and cognitive behaviours on the basis of psychophysiological indicators, such as infant patterns in the half recovery time of the skin conductance orienting response. Very recent and unpublished work by Venables and his associates shows that skin conductance patterns recorded within the first year of life predict levels of creative play and social observation behaviours when the child is three years of age or older (Venables, 1976). As a psychophysiologist, I must question Svebak's dependence upon this very difficult measure of respiration, which is under both voluntary and involuntary control, requires a face mask for measurement of volume rather than rate (and therefore makes observation of laughter difficult) and which is more likely than other measurements to be confounded by subject awareness of rate and the possibility of intra-experimental unwanted feedback. Certainly, respiration is not a frequent measure in the psychophysiological literature, where of course skin conductance and heart-rate are by far the most popular of the peripheral indices of activation or arousal. Since Svebak's theoretical commitment is to the role of defence mechanisms, a measure not under voluntary control might be preferable, though in laughter research such a measure might be just the right thing. Some of us might consider respiration to be a confounded variable in this study since its determination of laughter scores might be merely the reflection of trivial anatomical rather than psychological factors, which determine the limits of both respiration and laughter.

At present, psychophysiological measurement, in spite of its undoubted advantages in the context of group behaviour, is relatively coarse in measurement compared with the more detailed analysis of vocalization and micromovements provided by Mair and Kirkland. A combination of these measures is clearly desirable, although the point must come when the investment of time, effort and ingenuity in the development of hardware must be set against the empirical and theoretical pay-off. There have been many occasions in psychology when obsession with what I have elsewhere called 'meccanophilia' (Gale, 1973), serves to obscure the central issues. In certain fields of enquiry, sophistication in measurement has outpaced the existing theoretical framework and tends to generate morasses of uninterpretable data; complex measurement is no substitute for clear thinking. We must await with anticipation for the demonstration from Mair and Kirkland, that their measures, as well as their undoubted reliability, have also some validity for humour and laughter research. Their emphasis on interaction must, of course, create complications for measurement since not only individual patterns must be measured but also synchrony, sequential development and interactional dynamics.

Paulos' paper provides us with a formal basis for the analysis of mirth-eliciting stimuli. I should like to see here a formal logic set out, in which these ideas are developed and whose theorems may allow the generation of jokeful propositions or statements. This model raises the interesting question of which rule or rules are general enough to encompass all instances of mirth-eliciting stimuli. Are Paulos' classes only special cases or can they stand at a higher explanatory level? Certainly, they do provide us with a taxonomy and I look forward to hearing more. The similarity between Apter and Smith's examples and Paulos' logical examples is indeed striking. Clearly there is some sound basis here for inter-disciplinary collaboration. The emphasis here is, of course, upon the cognitive aspects of humorous material. However, the most exciting prospect which it raises is that psychological theorizing about humour might be parasitical upon the mathematicians' and logicians' developments relating to the formal logical models presented by Paulos. Certainly, we would benefit from the rigour of logic, which compares favourably with the rigor mortis of contemporary psychology. A difficulty of course is whether Paulos' taxonomy is the basis of humour appreciation per se or is a meta-language for describing the logic of humorous material. Might I refer Paulos to the work of the fellow mathematician Stephen Leacock and particularly to his essay on 'Boarding House Geometry'.

With Bouissac's paper we see the necessity for linking our understanding of humour to its socio-cultural context. His source of data is behaviour which is purposefully humorous and it is remarkable, as he points out, that the Circus has not been the subject of psychological study. It seems to me that an analysis of the formal characteristics of those artifacts used successfully to elicit mirth may prove useful. Bouissac's analysis of Grimaldi's artifacts is that they represent familiar domestic objects in incongruous context or in totally unpredictable use. He emphasizes in particular the surrealist nature of many of these artifacts. However, it remains to be demonstrated that (1) people would laugh at these if they did not expect to laugh, that is, if they were not at the circus and (2) they have the cultural significance which Bouissac suggests. One of the difficulties of theories of this molar level is that it is difficult to determine the grounds on which Bouissac's interpret-ations can be shown to be true or false.

What Bouissac emphasizes as central to clowning may be merely a traditional framework determined by chance factors and which creates the context within which the clown himself as an individual is appreciated. I suspect that the differences between successful clowns may be much greater than the similarities. It is always tempting to suggest that symbols are symbolic of something. But the demonstration of the truth or falsehood of such claims is notoriously difficult.

As in the case of Apter and Smith's presentation we have only had a tantalizing sample of the theory, so we look forward to the book which Bouissac promised us.

Schuman's paper is subject to criticisms similar to those which I have levelled at Bouissac's presentation. The suggestion here is that children's stories contain archetypal themes and that this says something about the nature of comedy (though to be frank I do not see much comedy in some of the tales to which Schuman refers). Schuman claims that children have a nose for the truth and that this means that popular children's stories are popular because they contain eternal verities. This is, of course, fallacious reasoning. Horses have four legs; but this does not imply that all four-legged animals are horses. Also Schuman forgets that children do not write stories, they are written by adults, and often funny adults at that. Again, it may well be that stories are popular because they are popular and not because of some deep and intensely significant subconscious reason. It must be admitted that the mores of most children's stories would be quite unacceptable in what we call civilized society. This perhaps is a necessary condition shared by some forms of humour, but that does not make children's stories and humour identical.

With a little effort then, we see that the papers presented here can be related. What we have is a good sample of the essential ingredients required for laughter and humour research: (1) a general theory which embraces among other things, humorous behaviours and humour appreciation, and incorporating predictions relating to individual differences; (2) a technique for relating individual differences in physiological response to subsequent mirth behaviour; (3) a technique for exact measurement of mirth vocalizations in terms of frequency and rhythm; (4) a logical basis for a taxonomy of mirth-eliciting propositions; (5) a basis for the analysis of gesture and other nonverbal behaviours in a situation and in a profession set up specifically for the purpose of eliciting mirth; and finally (6) a reminder that people other than psychologists have something useful to say about humour, but perhaps in a language, which for the present at least, exceeds the conceptual simplicity of psychological language.

REFERENCES

Gale, A., The psychophysiology of individual differences: Studies of extraversion and the EEG. In: P. Kline (Ed.), New Approaches in Psychological Measurement. Wiley, London (1973).

Hall, C.S. & Lindzey, G., Theories of Personality. (Second Edition). Wiley, New York (1970).

Venables, P., Personal Communication (1976).

HUMOUR AS
A FORM OF THERAPY

Humour as a form of Therapy: Introduction to Symposium

Jacob Levine

Veterans Administration Hospital, West Haven, Connecticut (And, Yale University)

People may rightly wonder about the need for a symposium on humour as therapy since everyone knows how therapeutic humour can be, especially when spirits are low or tensions high. I suppose the reaction of most people who hear that behavioural scientists are now occupying themselves with investigating one more wholesome aspect of humour and thereby further despoiling the joy of laughter, will be to shrug their shoulders, shake their heads, wondering why we bother. E.B. White, that great American humourist and essayist expressed it most vividly, 'Humor can be dissected, as a frog can, but the thing dies in the process and the innards are discouraging to any but the pure scientific mind'. His friend and fellow humourist Robert Benchley, was more scornful, 'There seems to be no lengths to which humorless people will not go to analyze humor'. The painful truth is that when we apply our scientific minds to trying to explain humour, we become terribly serious - even solemn - and very boring. I guess it is difficult to be both interesting and cheerful in theorizing about humour. It reminds me of what a scholar once said to Samuel Johnson, 'You are a philosopher, Dr. Johnson. I have tried, too, in my time to be a philosopher, but I don't know how, cheerfulness was always breaking in'.

We are fortunate that the participants in this Symposium are not handicapped by an absence of cheerfulness in their theorizing about humour as therapy. They can talk about humour cheerfully, yes even homorously, and still have something important to say. Our intent in this symposium is to discuss how humour contributed to the well-being and growth of man. We shall explore together the various ways that a sense of humour helps us cope with life and its problems. We plan to discuss how, by adopting a humorous attitude, we feel more capable of mastering our fears and tolerating our distress. To be 'in humour' is liberating and turns pain into pleasure. As usual, Freud expressed it well, 'Like jokes and the comic, humor has something liberating about it; but it also has something of grandeur and elevation, which is lacking in the other ways of obtaining pleasure from intellectual activity. The grandeur in it clearly lies in the triumph of narcissism, the victorious assertion of the ego's invulnerability. The ego refuses to be distressed by the provocations of reality, to let itself be compelled to suffer. It insists that it cannot be affected by the traumas of the external world; it shows, in fact, that such traumas are no more occasions for it to gain pleasure. This last feature is a quite essential element of humor'.

The theme that to be 'in humour' is to assume an orientation of invulnerability and mastery over whatever fate has in store did not originate with Freud, but has been expressed in many ways going at least as far back as Aristotle. Aristotle conceived of humour as being due to the 'sudden feeling of triumph which comes with the sudden perception of a superiority in us by the comparison with inferiority of others or our own former inferiority'. It was restated by Hobbes in 1651 in his definition of laughter: 'a sudden glory arising from some conception of some eminency in ourselves, by comparison with the infirmity of others, or with our own formerly'. These views of humour have most often been classified under theories of humour emphasizing superiority over others, but they fail to recognize the latter part of the statements which points up the mastery of one's own infirmities. From the psychoanalytic view, the psychogenesis of humour encompasses the growing pleasure in the ego's power and mastery of activitist functions formerly not possible. More recently, Kris expressed the psychoanalytic view most simply, 'What was feared yesterday is fatal to appear funny when seen today'.

The humorous attitude is then a state of mind. In that state, man re-asserts his invulnerability and refuses to submit to threat or fear. Again, Freud put it best, 'Humour is not resigned; it is rebellious. It signifies not only the triumph of the ego but also of the pleasure principle, which is able here to assert itself against the unkindness of the real circumstances'. These last two features - the rejection of the claims of reality and putting through of the pleasure principle - bring humour near to the regressive or reactionary processes which engage our attention so extensively in psychopathology. Its fending off

of the possibility of suffering places it among the great series of methods which the human
mind has constructed in order to evade the compulsions to suffer – a series which includes
intoxication, self-absorption and ecstacy'.

Psychoanalytically, humour is thus one of a number of psychological processes which are
functionally adaptive modes of withdrawal from reality into the world of the imagination.
The ability to withdraw voluntarily from reality is an eagerly pursued mental state and may
take many forms: play, literature, sports, alcohol, drugs, sleep, yoga, movies, television,
and humour. Psychodynamically, neuroses to psychoses are recognized as similar regressive
detachments from reality, but they are pathological, and are not voluntary or adaptive. They
are maladaptive attempts to cope with conflict and anxiety, and do not function for ego
gratification or pleasure. They are essentially psychologically defensive flights from
painful reality.

The purpose of this brief excursion into psychoanalytic humour theory is to provide a
theoretical basis for the view that humour can be both a source of pleasure and a form of
therapy. Humour is innately pleasurable but we learn that humour and laughter can relieve
anxiety and reassert the ego's mastery. This learning is integral to the process of
maturation, the evidence is sketchy but the growing research interest in the development of
smiling, laughing and humour promises to provide us with a deepening understanding of the process.
It is truly hard to imagine how the complex behaviour pattern of humour in the form of a joke
or cartoon would develop from the elemental affective connective smile.

In a television interview on April 19, 1959, the great Zen Master Suzuki was discussing Zen
Buddhism. He described how Zen Buddhism began. It was during a lecture by Buddha when he
held out a bouquet of flowers which had been handed to him. None of the pupils sitting
before Buddha understood what Buddha meant by his holding out the flowers with his
outstretched arms – except one old monk. This monk looked up at Buddha and smiled. Buddha
smiled back. And that is how Zen Buddhism began. The story may not help very much in the
understanding of Zen Buddhism, but it beautifully illustrates the meaningfulness of the simple
smile, and the mutual understanding that can occur between two people with but a smile. The
story points up the interpersonal character of the smile with the immediacy and depth of
communication which it can achieve. This form of communication is one point of the fable in
that the smile is a gateway to intimate communication, contrasted with language which, as
Koestler, so rightly noted, actually restricts communication. The smile is truly the first
emotional and communicative contact between two people.

By now a number of investigators have observed that, shortly after birth, the young infant
begins to smile. These first smiles appear to be autochthonous in the sense that they are
responses to pleasant internal states. Very shortly thereafter, however, the infant begins
to smile and laugh at external objects, particularly the familiar face of the mother. These
responses are the initial expressions of pleasure and awareness of another person. They
usher in the entire developmental process of interpersonal interaction and socialization.
From them evolves the ever-expanding range of affective communication processes. It may
well be that the earliest smiles of the newborn infant, say of one week, are merely automatic
expressions of internal states. But it is not much later that the infant's smiles are
communications of pleasure at the appearance of the familiar face of the doting mother. In
her little poem, 'Infant Prodigy', Margaret Fishback expressed the sentiments of all mothers,
'At six weeks baby grinned a grin that spread from mouth to eyes to chin, and Doc, the
smarty, had the brass to tell me it was only gas'.

Sentiment aside, we know that the earliest smiles and laughs are innate responses to pleasant
sensations both internal and external. However, we also know that these innate responses to
pleasant rhythmic tactile and auditory stimulation become associated with social expressions
of pleasure. Thus, Sroufe and Wunsch (1972) have found that, by the third and fourth
trimester of life, visual and social stimuli have become the primary stimuli for laughter.
These authors also noted that infants' laughter quickly becomes responsive to simple
incongruities in social situations. For example, an infant learns to laugh at the sight of
his mother sucking on his bottle or when she plays the peek-a-boo game.

Edith Jacobson (1946) has noted how laughter, the more intense twin of smiling, occurs most
primitively in two phases. The initial phase of 'thrill' involves 'anxious tension mixed
with quickly increasing pleasure which dissolves the fears'. Though partly derived from
motor pleasure, the major emotional pleasure component of this phase is associated with
memories of previous similar experiences of laughter or associated with motor movements such
as tossing in the air or the sudden re-appearance of mother in peek-a-boo. The second phase,
the final discharge, comes as a surprising climax which is experienced as a sudden relief
with intense pleasurable convulsive motor discharge in laughter. What is particularly
striking in this early developmental period is how learning becomes involved with these innate
pleasurable responses to become increasingly social processes. Thus, the developmental
changes in smiling and laughing in early infancy reflect the rapidity with which these
emotional responses become important elements in the interactions between the infant and his

social environment. In summary, we suggest the conceptualization of two components in
the development of the humour process. The first component is the innate pleasure in mastery.
The second is the learned 'whistling in the dark' or 'laughing it off' phenomenon, in which
we use humour to restore those familiar feelings of mastery when we are made anxious or are
threatened.

Humour, which evolves from these early smiling and laughing situations, has generally been
regarded as epiphenomenal in child development. Humour has always been viewed as an
incidental and relatively trivial activity in human affairs. True, the smiling and laughing
infant is a most appealing object of delight and affection, just as an adult with a 'good
sense of humour' is seen as having an attractive personality. Despite the growing interest
in humour, little concern about how and if humour contributes to the developmental process
has been manifested up to this point.

Oddly enough, the best evidence which demonstrates the importance of humour as expressed by
smiling and laughing is given by clinical observations of their absence. When young infants
fail to smile or laugh in appropriate situations, it is fairly evident that these infants are
not experiencing the situation as pleasurable but rather as distressing or frightening.
Sroufe and Wunsch (1972) noted this fact when they observed that infants who were distressed
cried in response to stimuli normally evoking laughter. Wolff (1969) also reported that
distressed infants, when tickled, cried instead of laughed. A number of clinical studies by
Bowlby (1965), Mahler (1961), Provence and Ritvo (1961) have dealt with the fact that
institutionalized infants and infants lacking mothering failed ever to smile or laugh. They
relapsed into a state of unresponsiveness and helplessness, and rarely interacted with anyone
except by crying. One wonders what the long-term effects are of these early depressed states
where the infants cannot learn to use smiling or laughing as so-called 'social releasers' to
evoke positive responses in others. Restrictions in the use of smiling and laughing as the
primordial roots of humour and affective communication during these critical periods of child
development may well have significant effects upon emotional development. One can assume
that these early experiences of exchanging pleasurable contacts with others are the basic
determinants of what ultimately becomes a sense of humour — or the lack of one. Clearly
longitudinal studies of the development of humour and of laughing, and smiling are sorely
needed.

It is indeed a giant step from the innate elemental reactions of infants to pleasing
stimulation to a fully developed sense of humour in adults. The developmental steps between
the two phases are relatively unexplored. But in this paper, I propose to present a
formulation of the development of humour drawn from diverse sources which, if it does not
add much to our understanding of the evolution of humour, at least will call attention to the
problem.

Investigations of Edward Zigler, our students, and myself, along with a rapidly increasing
number of studies by others, point to humour as an intrinsic and essential component of the
normal growth process. It is not epiphenomenal; it is a critical segment of the growing
repertoire of evolving behaviour patterns available to the child. As a process of adaptation,
humour provides the individual with the opportunity to re-experience the gratifications of
cognitive and interpersonal mastery. The child learns that humour, like play, is a source
of pleasure at each stage of development by momentarily re-experiencing the mastery of
functions and relations of earlier stages. By the time adulthood is attained, the sources
of these states of mastery become myriad, the forms and techniques of the humour become so
subtle that it is impossible to recognize their archaic antecedents. As Berlyne and others
have suggested, humour has close affinities with other psychological processes like play,
curiosity, exploratory behaviour, and art, in their unique ways of relating to the environment
in a pleasure-giving manner. The motivational bases for these different behaviour processes
appear to be the same. What differentiates one from the other are the structural properties
of the techniques. Whether in reality or in fantasy, and whether under stress or relaxation,
humour reasserts one's mastery over the environment. In fact, humour flourishes best when
fertilized by newly mastered anxieties as many sages have long observed.

What is unique about humour is the way in which it expresses pleasure in momentary achievement,
in the sense of cognitive or interpersonal mastery. This appears to be the common path
which goes back to early infancy. Piaget (1950, 1951) for example, commented that the first
experience of cognitive success by the infant was expressed by a smile. He also noted that
whenever there is a developmental change in a child's cognitive functions which he has
mastered, he laughs as he re-experiences this new achievement. Piaget maintained that
smiling and laughing always accompany a child's cognitive masteries from early infancy
onward.

Based on Piaget's concepts of assimilation and accommodation in cognitive development,
Shultz and Zigler (1970) demonstrated that infants between eight and eighteen weeks smiled
and vocalized maximally when they could successfully assimilate visual stimuli. In our own
research studies, we have applied this notion of effectance motivation as presented by White

(1959) to the investigation of humour development. We confirmed the hypothesis that an important determinant of children's humour responses is the degree to which the humour requires them to use their cognitive abilities maximally. We presented cartoons to children between the ages of eight and thirteen and recorded their mirth responses, preferences, and degree of comprehension. We found that as children grew older, they enjoyed and laughed at cartoons which were increasingly difficult to understand. Cartoons which were too easy did not present a cognitive challenge and were least appreciated.

Empirical data from different areas provide meaningful support for the antithesis between humour as a gratifying state of effectance and anxiety as a painful state of helplessness. The clinical findings of the helpless state of infants who lack warm mothering and who also never smile or laugh reflect this antithesis. Recent experimental studies of learned helplessness in animals and humans have demonstrated that when an individual's responses cannot control painful events or reinforcers, his behaviour is characterized by depression and passivity. These individuals have serious difficulty not only in reacting adaptively, but in learning. In the face of their state of helplessness, they view all of their inter-actions as ineffective. Thus, their view of the environment is one of anticipated pain and incapability to master the environment. Just as humour has frequently been viewed as a faith in one's mastery of fate, learned helplessness is a state characterized by resignation to fate. Based upon a number of animal studies, by investigators like Seligman, Hiroto and others. Seligman, has suggested that learned helplessness may provide a model for reactive depression in man. Animal studies have demonstrated that the way to prevent this state of learned helplessness in animals is by prior mastery and learning. Analogously, Seligman recommends that therapy for reactive depression in man is to help the patient feel that he is an effective human being and to believe that his responses can produce the gratification that he desires. In a recent study, Harter, Shultz, and Blum (1971) found that normal children manifest their gratification derived from a sense of cognitive competence by smiling but Harter (1972) could find no such smiling behaviour in retarded children.

Other empirical findings tend to support the view that humour is a mode of reasserting one's mastery. Lefcourt et al (1972) for example, found that individuals who have a cognitive view of themselves as being in control or masters of their own fate, so-called 'internals', smiled and laughed more at humour than did so-called 'externals' who conceived of themselves as incapable of controlling external events.

On the basis of the hypothesized antithesis between humour and anxiety, we can appreciate how humour is frequently used to dispel anxiety. By secondary reinforcement humour becomes a learned motive to experience mastery in the face of anxiety. It is a 'whistling in the dark' phenomenon. Man has learned to laugh and joke in order to feel effective and through humour he will try to recapture previous feelings of mastery when he is threatened. Humour helps man to rise above his present state of pain. How else can we explain gallows humour as in the joke about the man who is about to be shot by a firing squad. When asked if he would like a last cigarette, he refuses with 'No thanks, I'm trying to give up smoking'; or the many instances found in recorded history, where ritual laughter was the prescribed form of behaviour when individuals were put to death. Victoroff (1969), the French sociologist, noted that aged parents in Sardinia were expected to laugh when immolated by their own children. In Phoenicia, parents were also expected to laugh when their children were immolated. Victoroff reported that in India individuals were expected to laugh heartily when mounting their ritual pyre. Clearly the laughter represents the mastery of the fear of death, and gallows humour performs a similar function.

A striking example of how laughter and humour serve as assurances that everything is alright is reported as an incidental finding in the interpersonal research studies of Stanley Milgram (1963, 1965). In these experiments, individuals who were forced to give what they thought were extremely painful shocks to others suddenly burst out laughing in the face of their great stress. These uncontrolled outbursts of laughter are perhaps extreme examples of the 'whistling in the dark' phenomenon. Serving to reassure oneself that it is not serious and everything will be alright.

A proper delineation of the course of humour development from the viewpoint of our pleasure-in-mastery formulation requires some demonstration that it reflects the normal growth process. We need to show that the progressive development of humour corresponds to the timetable of maturation and reflects a sequence of increasing effectiveness in intellectual and social functioning. Unfortunately, we have only suggestive evidence at the present time to support the validity of our formulations.

Investigations of the relationship of humour to cognitive development has recently attracted the interest of behavioural scientists with Piaget's conceptualization of stages in cognitive development as the major framework. Piaget's interest was clearly not in humour but in cognitive growth. Yet, as I indicated before, he often noted the incidental finding that laughter and smiling accompanies cognitive success in infants.

In a recent doctoral thesis, Park (1971) applied Piaget's stages of cognitive development in children to a categorization of children's riddles at different ages. She viewed the changes in riddles used by children of different ages as manifestations of the cognitive patterns associated with Piaget's developmental periods, namely, pre-operational, concrete, and formal operational. Although all age groups used all types of riddles, each age group tended to emphasize one type over the others. For example, kindergarteners emphasized riddles of causal relations, whereas second graders preferred those of logical relations. It was not until seventh or eighth grade that riddles of psychological relations predominated. At the same time, riddle content reflected cognitive developmental periods of the children.

In several studies, McGhee (e.g., 1971a) has compared the relation of humour comprehension and appreciation of five-, seven-, and nine-year-old boys with the degree of their acquisition of operational thinking in Piagetian terms. His general findings are that, as one would expect, children who are more developed cognitively are better able to understand most types of humour. However, this correlation between cognitive development and humour comprehension does not necessarily mean a corresponding increase in appreciation of such humour.

In our own research studies, we have used the hypothesis of effectance motivation as a necessary condition for the enjoyment of humour. We have established that children's humour responses are greatest when they have to use their cognitive abilities the most. For example, in one study by Zigler, Levine and Gould, we found that the humour most appreciated and which evoked the most laughter in second-, third-, fourth-, and fifth-graders is that which makes the greatest cognitive demand and is at the upper limit of the child's ability to comprehend. It is the humour which lies at the growing edge of the capacities that they enjoy the most.

It is when children are just beginning to master language that their jokes involve playing with words. In her clinical observations of humour of children at various ages, Wolfenstein (1954) has described how the devices of joking vary with age. She has associated what children at different ages require for satisfactory joking with particular critical problems and conflicts of children at those different ages. For example, between the ages of six and eleven, children are intensely preoccupied with smartness and dumbness. It is at this time that they most enjoy moron jokes and riddles which are simply humorous puzzles. At the age of four, children find the shifting of names from boy to girl a good joke which can readily be traced to three-year-olds calling a boy a girl and vice versa. A good dirty joke for children of four or five is to tease someone with 'You're a doody' or 'You make peepee on the floor'. For adolescents who have more or less fully developed cognitively, anecdotes replace riddles and comic mimicry.

Wolfenstein has described in some detail what she considers to be the developmental phases of joking and the use of the joke facade. According to her, the child must find ways to gratify his impulses while disclaiming responsibility for them. He does this by an increasing indirection of expression. He will attribute the performance of naughty deeds to other children rather than to himself and ultimately to an entirely fictitious character. Frequently, even authority figures are made responsible for the deeds. As an illustration, she describes a sequence of dirty jokes of children aged between four and eleven to demonstrate the increasing complication of the joke facade. She uses excretory activities as the theme since this is what children are largely preoccupied with in their dirty jokes. 'For a four-year-old, it is a good dirty joke to shout at someone: "Hello, Doody!" or with slightly more subtle mockery: "Hello, Mr. Doody!"' That the child finds this funny shows that he already has some misgiving about saying it. But in moments of weakened inhibition or strengthened impulse, which easily occur in his unstable inner economy, he can enjoy such a breakthrough of the forbidden without requiring any elaborate facade. However, there is already some indirectness in this seemingly blunt attack. Instead of precipitating his excreta on the victim, the child has substituted a verbal expression. He has embarked on the first stage of the development which will eventuate in the more complicated forms of wit'. Thus, up to four, it is the actual act which is a joke.

It is clear from naturalistic observations that children learn to laugh and joke about all areas of functioning over which they have just achieved mastery. These include body functions, language and verbal fluency, motor skills, and finally, interpersonal interactions. Children's jokes about excreta, plays on words, riddles, puns, clowning and pratfalls, all reflect these steps in development.

Perhaps the best illustration of how humour reaffirms an adult's as well as a child's new-found ability to overcome infirmity and fear is to be found in the person of the circus clown. Children have great fun laughing at his grotesque features and dress, his apparent clumsiness, and the silly tricks he plays on his partners. In his self-debasement and his pitfalls, the circus clown dramatically, but in humour, expresses the concerns and achievements of children over their physical inadequacy. Thus, they laugh at the clown as they laugh at the physically deformed and handicapped. The grotesque comic antics of the circus clown evokes great laughter in children because it is 'in humour'. This means that the audience accepts the pretence of the clown that he is clumsy and grotesque. The children share in this pretence, recognizing that the clown is really skilful and really master of his actions. They 'know' he will not be hurt by his pratfalls. The pretence in the clowning condenses both the early clumsiness of the young child who has not yet learned to master his body movements and the observing children's relatively recent mastery of these actions.

A recent episode in the new television show 'The Electric Company' beautifully illustrates how hilarious it is for children who have just mastered counting to see an adult fail in the task of counting to four. In this sequence, the marvellous clown, Bill Cosby, masterfully makes a fool of himself by repeatedly counting only three children, overlooking a fourth child behind him. The children scream with glee that there are four children and he only counted three.

We know far too little about the social aspects of humour development. Yet, the issue of mastery or effectance, as White prefers to call it, is no different in the psychosocial sphere than it is in the cognitive. Erikson's theory of the sequence of phases of psychosocial development may be as applicable to humour development as Piaget's cognitive stages are.

Socialization in terms of self-control and proper social conduct is well documented by the developmental changes which occur in the expression of aggression through humour as the child matures. One of the first things we learn about humour is that it is a way of enjoying things, activities, and thoughts which are otherwise forbidden. We learn to circumvent prohibitions of conduct by being humorous. Thus, young children will violate social prohibitions by exposing themselves, making fun of other children's immaturities, or telling jokes about other children's social indiscretions. The aggression in the humour of young children is direct and open. Poking fun, teasing, taunting, and even physical attacks are all forms of aggression in children's humour. But, as they grow, and increased internalization of social controls occurs, the humour of children becomes less direct, and the children dissociate themselves increasingly from the aggressive impulses in the humour. The jokes become more impersonal and aggression is more indirect. From open teasing and poking fun, the humour is transformed into anecdotes and the subtleties of witty or satirical remarks. In this fashion, the expression of aggression in humour reflects the maturing mastery of one's own impulses.

Thus, as Freud pointed out, the development of humour is characterized by the increasing use of indirect expressions of aggression shifting from motoric to verbal attack. The latter he has called 'tendentious' humour. The indirect expression of aggression in humour is achieved by what Freud labelled the 'joke-work' or 'joke facade'. The construction of a joke which children must learn involves techniques like absurdity, incongruity, puns, and plays on words which in themselves give pleasure by providing a cognitive challenge to resolve. But, Freud's great insight was to recognize that this joke facade, although in itself gratifying, serves as a distraction from the underlying aggressive or sexual theme. As Freud put it, 'I hope I have now also shown that the absurdity-techniques of jokes are a source of pleasure'.

Not unlike his use of alcohol, psychedelic drugs, and states of ecstasy, man has pursued laughter and humour to enjoy the moments of pleasure through self-glorification and feelings of effectance. As with drugs and alcohol, he has learned that humour and laughter may be used not only for momentary pleasure but also to overcome anxious and painful moments. Skinner has, in fact, developed a world view based upon those basic behavioural processes by which organisms learn to repeat those activities which reduce painful or potentially dangerous stimuli. But this is not meant by any means to depreciate the importance of the pursuit of humour for its own sake and for the pleasure it gives.

The paradox of humour is the extraordinary diversity of purposes it serves. In fact some are diametrically opposite to one another. We may laugh in scorn and derision or in sympathy and affection. We may tell a joke to convey hostility or to share intimacy. Humour both exposes hypocrisy, and hides unpleasant truth. If you laugh without restraint, you are considered to be either mad or mentally healthy. We may laugh to allay anxiety, like 'whistling in the dark', or our laughter may express the opposite, relief from anxiety. A joke is 'one man's meat but another man's poison', or as William Hazlitt put it, 'sport to one but death to another'. Viewed one way, humour is regarded as a trifling, destructive, and degrading force to morality, religion and art; viewed another, it is a liberating and socially constructive force by exposing sham and hypocrisy. It is, therefore, little wonder that some of our greatest philosophers from Plato and Aristotle have regarded humour as a destructive force to be avoided by civilized man who never laughs because it is too base an emotion. It defies authority and debases morality. Many theories of humour view it as originating from self-glorification at others' expense, often by exposing their infirmities and defects. We now find the same conflicting views of humour as it is used in psychotherapy.

In his paper emphasizing the destructive effects that humour can have in psychotherapy, Kubie (1971), one of the most eminent American psychoanalysts, listed at least sixteen ways in which humour can be destructive to the therapeutic process. There certainly are many other ways in which humour can be used destructively besides those mentioned by Kubie, and they must all be acknowledged. One must also agree with Kubie's recognition of the great power of humour, but that power can be used constructively as well as destructively in therapy as in all human affairs.

My disagreement with Kubie and with those who view humour as destructive to therapy can be simply stated. If the psychotherapist's use of humour is destructive to the therapeutic process in any way, including those listed by Kubie, he is acting incompetently. The therapist is using humour, not to facilitate therapy, but to serve his own interests or needs. Clearly, if the therapist engages in an activity for the purpose of satisfying some need or interest of his own and ignores those of the patient or the therapy, it must be destructive to the therapeutic process. Kubie, like all those who see humour as a trivial and harmful distraction from any activity that is serious and important, failed to see that humour, properly used, can facilitate the awareness of profound insights. Within the context of the transference the therapist can take in his telling of a joke a tolerant and supportive stance toward the patient. He can thereby help the patient to assume a humorous attitude towards his guilty secrets and thereby find them more tolerable. Because humour is ego enhancing, by fostering a sense of mastery, it facilitates the acknowledgment of painful insights with reduced anxiety. Thus, the pith of an analytic idea is acceptable via humour and thereby useful to the therapeutic process.

An example here, taken from a therapeutic session, illustrates how humour can be helpful in facilitating therapeutic process. A forty-year-old female patient constantly complained about her unfaithful and inconsiderate husband. The marriage was a failure since she disliked her husband, found sex with him disgusting, and generally considered his behaviour contemptable. The therapist felt moved to comment that she still chose to live with him and did not consider divorce. The patient responded that she was afraid that she would not be able to replace him and as bad as he was she felt that loneliness would be worse. The therapist remarked that he could understand her fears of loneliness but felt that there was another aspect of her preference for remaining married which was suggested by the story of the man who worked in the circus cleaning up after the animals and giving enemas to constipated elephants. An old friend of his observing the menial type of work that he was doing offered to help him get another job. To which he replied, 'What, and give up show biz?' The patient at first was indignant about this analogy but then began to laugh about it. She was able to come to grips with some of her covert motives in her complaints about her husband. She came to recognize that despite these constant complaints her marriage had some redeeming features and did satisfy some of her needs, not the least of which was the opportunity to complain and to blame others for her unsatisfied needs.

These ambivalences towards the use of humour are not limited to psychotherapy but are pervasive and occur wherever people take themselves and their endeavours too seriously. Ten years ago I wrote an article on humour in play and sports for a book in which I pointed out that present day sports are now serious competitive enterprises devoid of joyfulness (Levine, 1967). Playfulness and fun are eliminated and joking is seen as an unpleasant distraction which is destructive to the game. Because of its irreverent attitude, humour makes light of these solemn sports events. Winning the game is a serious business which permits no levity or diversion. In that paper, I recalled the story of a dedicated golfer who was just about to make a putt at the eighteenth hole in a closely contested match when he stopped suddenly, took off his hat and stood respectfully while a funeral cortège passed slowly by on the road nearby. After it had passed, he carefully and skilfully sank a twenty-foot putt and won the match. His defeated opponent, though disappointed, congratulated him, and remarked, 'You must have had iron nerve not to let that funeral procession fluster you into missing that putt': 'It wasn't easy', admitted the winner, 'on Saturday we would have been married twenty-five years'.

Recently in a review by John Leonard, the chief cultural correspondent of the New York Times, of a book on sports, Leonard quoted the author, Michael Novack, as saying that 'sports are far more serious than dramatic arts'. Sports are identified with 'the struggles of the human spirit to prevail'. He proposed sports as a 'civil religion' full of 'sacred time' and 'sacred space' which is 'an essential salvific religion in our present madness'. Leonard concluded his review with the statement, 'Anybody who describes the football season as a "guelling ascesis" needs a remedial giggle'.

The endowment of psychotherapy and sports, which are basically rooted in child play, with religious solemnity and meaning, dramatizes our need to take ourselves and everything we do too seriously for critical examination. It seems that whenever we do not wish to examine an activity critically, we endow it with solemn ritual, and thereby do not have to look too closely at the reasons for doing it. Humour is too irreverent to permit such self-destruction. In sports, motives other than play rob the game of the fun and laughter.

To be able to assume a humorous attitude requires not only a freedom from reality but a freedom to laugh at one's self. It has often been maintained that a sense of humour depends almost entirely upon the ability to laugh at one's self, not to take one's self so seriously that one cannot take a joke at one's own expense. Some of our modern writers have deplored the fact that America has lost its sense of humour because it takes itself so seriously that it cannot laugh at itself or poke fun at its foibles. In our country with its one-liners, wisecracks, gags, and glib comebacks, our humour seems to suffer from superficiality and an unwillingness to acknowledge weakness or to tolerate being laughed at. And so, if we are too serious about ourselves and take our successes and accomplishments to be so important that failures are shameful, then our sports become merely extensions of our real life and not recreations.

The rejection of humour in any activity reflects an unwillingness to take a chance and expose oneself to the laughter of others. In American culture we seem to have a definite need to be appreciated and accepted and sports very often serve as the vehicle. (Saint Peter, from his heavenly perch, once saw a priest playing golf on the Sabbath. Irate, he reported this sinful act to the Lord. 'I'll fix him', said the Lord, and on the next hole the priest made a four-hundred-yard hole in one. 'Is that how you fix him?' asked Saint Peter, aghast. 'Yes', replied the Lord. 'Whom is he going to be able to tell?'

For this present symposium on therapy, the distinction should be made between humour itself as therapy in contradistinction to the uses we make of humour not only to help therapy but to allay fear, express hostility, expose sham and to facilitate social relations. It is often hard for us to remember that humour, like sex, is pleasurable without serving any other purpose. Humour itself is therapeutic because of the way it gives pleasure, and I subscribe to the psychoanalytic view that humour is the most acceptable way of enjoying something that is forbidden. However, when the intent is to use humour for communicative purpose as in psychotherapy, pleasure gain is secondary. In these situations, we assume a humorous attitude which gives us the freedom to be playful and make light of matters that normally may be distressing or even frightening to us. Denying and rising above the fears and limitations of real-life gives us the gratifying feeling of mastery and superiority.

James Thurber, quoting Lord Boothby stated, 'Humor is the only solvent of terror and tension'. To be able to be 'in humour' is clearly of itself a therapeutic experience for it both gratifies unexpressable wishes and creates a sense of mastery. Aristotle, long ago, said it well: humour is a 'sudden feeling of triumph which comes with the sudden perception of a superiority in us by the comparison with the inferiority of others or of our own former inferiority'. It was restated by Hobbes in 1651 in his definition of laughter, 'a sudden glory arising from some conception of some eminency in ourselves, by comparison with the inferiority of others, or with ours formerly'. In 'Back to Mother Sebah', G.B. Shaw had the serpent laugh to which Adam (brightening) responded, 'that noise takes away fear'. One of our American humourists, Donald Ogden Stewart, put it more concretely, 'My comic hero would be a man who overcame death not by religion, but by humor, and who would laugh at the electric chair as he walked to it'. From a therapeutic viewpoint then, humour enables us to face our worst fears, whether they originate from internal or external sources.

Being 'in humour' frees us not only from feelings of helplessness and fear but from reality. As Freud put it, the opposite of humour is not being serious but reality. In this respect humour is like all forms of art. The state of unreality which the humorous attitude creates is not unique to it, but is the essence of all artistic experiences. The humour illusion is but one form of the aesthetic illusion. As Alexander expressed it, 'Illusion is the essence of the work of art'. According to Freud too, all art is based on illusion for 'art constitutes a region half-way between reality which frustrates wishes and the wish-fulfilling world of the imagination — a region in which, as it were, primitive man's strivings for omnipotence are still in full force'.

Unless cognitive failure or emotional distress prevent it, immersion in the humour illusion can readily occur, although not everyone is able to do it. But once individuals are 'in humour', they freely share in the regressive imaginative play, without guilt or feelings of responsibility for the defiance of reason or propriety. But the immersion in the humour illusion is not total, for the make-believe is not total renunciation or reality: when we view a painting or a play, we do not, for the moment, believe that what we are seeing is total reality. We know that what we are viewing is an abstraction and representation of reality. As Coleridge put it, art 'is the willing suspension of disbelief'.

Aristotle viewed art as a cathartic experience, a 'purging of the soul'. The laughter of humour is that expression of catharsis. In that sense also, humour is therapeutic. But art, and humour too, are therapeutic not only because they are cathartic. They also improve the quality of life.

From the psychoanalytic view of art, the humour illusion, as one form of the aesthetic illusion, is a source of double pleasure: (1) the cathartic effects of the artistic fantasy created by the joke or the cartoon which invites the participant to share in the release of forbidden thoughts and wishes without guilt or responsibility; and (2) the playful release from the constraints of reality by the various techniques of the joke-work such as play on words, absurdity, condensations, double entendre, displacement.

By the adoption of the humorous attitude, we are free to do outrageous things and think outrageous thoughts, and enjoy them without guilt. As Harry Hershfield, the American humorist, put it, 'a conscience cannot prevent sin, it only prevents you from enjoying it'. In humour we can both commit sin and enjoy it. Hershfield was famous for his enormous fund of jokes and when he was asked to tell his favourite joke, he told this one: 'The president of a lodge was telling the members a very funny story, so funny that they all broke into great laughter. All but one. He didn't laugh or even crack a smile. They asked him, "Don't you think it's a funny story?" "Yes", he said, "but I'm not a member of the lodge"'.

By the adoption of the humorous attitude we have the licence to do outrageous things and think outrageous thoughts. To be 'in humour' gives us freedom from rational and moral inhibitions, and for the moment we have the licence to say and act without regard for logic, proper conduct, and even offensiveness. The degrees of freedom are set only by the social context. We can act and talk silly, poke fun at the mighty, be profane, and play at sex. Only the altered states brought on by psychosis, alcohol and drugs gives us similar licence.

These characteristics of humour are well illustrated in the ritual clowning behaviour of many societies throughout the world. In a study of the ritual clowns of some of our American indians which was published some years back (Levine, 1961), I found that under the cloak of clowning and joking in some of their ritual ceremonies, the clown can invite his people to participate in activities normally subject to the strongest taboos. Among tribes like the Hopi, who are reserved and very proper, participants in the ritual clowning are free to violate nearly every social taboo, even incest. By the assumption of the humorous attitude, the clown and his participants throw off reality restraints and can act out the most childish and vulgar behaviours without undue consequences. Following psychoanalytic thinking, I hypothesized that these institutionalized forms of humour not only gratify archaic urges but also serve as a therapeutic way of permitting the regulated release of many socially unacceptable impulses. In a subsequent study, I tried to show that the institutionalized humour of the joking relationship among many cultures provides external controls for the sexual and aggressive urges that are most likely to seek expression in the violation of important social taboos. By formalized joking behaviour, nearly every culture provides individuals and groups acceptable outlets for the expression of forbidden wishes and thoughts. But it is only by the assumption of the humorous attitude that such licences are permitted. Otherwise the aggression in ridicule and poking fun, if not masked, would be taken seriously and lead to serious consequences, even suicide.

Freud (1928) expressed it well, 'in every epoch of history those who have had something to say but could not say it without peril have eagerly assumed a fool's cap. The audience at whom their forbidden speech was aimed tolerated it more easily if they could at the same time laugh and flatter themselves with the reflection that the unwelcome words were clearly nonsensical'.

A father scolded his young son, 'I'm ashamed of you, Robert, I saw you kick your little friend while you were playing together. Why did you do that?' 'Oh, I was tired of playing with him and wanted him to go home'. 'Why didn't you ask him to go home?', asked the father. 'Why, Daddy', cried the boy, 'that wouldn't have been polite'.

When the humour illusion is not present, many anthropological examples have been given of the extreme reactions of shame and disgrace suffered by individuals who are publicly laughed at. A dramatic example of how the use of humour for regulating interpersonal relations by institutionalization is shown among the Greenland Eskimos where important quarrels are resolved by a duel with laughter. Each contestant armed only with a drum which he uses as an accompaniment, recites humorous insult and obscene jokes ridiculing the opponent. The duelist who wins the most laughter from the audience is the victor. The loser is profoundly humiliated, often going into exile.

How the joke facade serves to permit the release of aggression without guilt is illustrated by the story of a British anthropologist who was visiting an isolated African tribe. The members tried to impress him with how much they had learned from the civilized white men. They told him, 'You know, we are a just people, and we closely follow British legal procedures here. We learned all about it from reports we read from British trials'. To demonstrate, he was taken to witness an ongoing trial. He was amazed to see how carefully and exactly all the form of a British Court had been reproduced. Judge and lawyers were dressed in black robes and wigs and with great formality disputed the case. The anthropologist was very impressed but was puzzled by one thing; at regular intervals a man, dressed only in a loin cloth, ran through the audience and touched each woman's bare breasts. He finally asked his informant about this. The man explained, 'We always read in the accounts of your trials "a titter ran through the audience"'. This joke obviously disparages the African tribesmen who despite their efforts to emulate civilized society reveal themselves as still savages. Their childish misinterpretations of one word brings home that they remain uncivilized in their preoccupation with sexuality. By a play on the single word the point is made that the tribe sees no incongruity in the mixing of sex with formal legal procedures. It makes a mockery of the trial with the meaningless mimicking of all the details. Much more can be said about the implications of this joke but I merely wish to illustrate the extraordinary communicative power of a joke based on just one word.

In telling a joke, we invite others to be 'in humour' or, as Freud put it, humour 'is an invitation to common aggression and common regression'. A pact is made between the participants to suspend for the moment the ordinary rules of conduct, logic and speech. The sharing of the laughter establishes an intimacy in interpersonal relations and facilitates communication. It is interesting, a fact every experienced comedian knows, how once some affiliation is created among a group how easy it becomes to evoke laughter. On the other hand, in a group of strangers it is very difficult to get them to be 'in humour' and the humour must be that much cleverer. Actually, humour creates a group or a community; even a smile can communicate more than a long discourse.

The social usefulness of humour has previously been noted as providing a safety valve to control the expression of sexual and aggressive urges. But this hardly exhausts the many other therapeutic and constructive social effects of humour. With that great Spanish classic Don Quixote, Cerrvantes was able to laugh out of existence the ridiculous posturing and hypocrisy of mediaeval chivalry. Thomas Nast, in 1871, with just a few cartoons single-handedly brought about the downfall of the notorious but very powerful Tweed political ring in New York. During the blitz in World War Two the morale of Great Britain was greatly strengthened by the sudden eruption of joking at this time of great peril. There is nothing a people shares so completely as laughter. And in the sharing of laughter, people become unified and lose their fear. As Worcester put it, 'The intellectual, critical spirit that attacks pretense and acts as the watchdog of society is the comic spirit'.

I would like to close my remarks by suggesting that of the many therapeutic uses of humour, the classroom is one of the places where it might be most helpful. Take enormous success of the children's television programme 'Sesame Street'. Children have been taught to read, and to count, and to use concepts, in the context of funny and ridiculous situations. Learning can be fun. I wonder if more significant learning could be achieved with humour if the children actively participated in the activity instead of sitting passively watching TV. The learning would occur not so much because the humour kept the children passively attentive but as active participants in cognitive and social achievements. Learning with humour has still to be fully explored.

REFERENCES

See Bibliography for publications on humour, laughter and comedy

Bowlby, J., Grief and mourning in infancy and early childhood. In: G.E. Daniels (Ed.), New Perspectives in Psychoanalysis. Grune and Stratton, New York (1965).

Erikson, E.H., Childhood and Society. (Revised Edition). Norton, New York (1964).

Harlow, H.F., Mice, monkeys, men and motives. Psychological Review, 60, 23-32 (1953).

Harter, S., Smiling and mastery in retarded children. Unpublished manuscript, Yale University (1972).

Hiroto, D.S., Learned helplessness and external control of reinforcement. Unpublished manuscript, University of Portland (1971).

Hobbes, T., Humane Nature. In: W. Molesworth (Ed.), The English Works of Thomas Hobbes. Volume 4, John Bohn, London (1840). (Originally published, 1651).

Lefcourt, H.M., Sordoni, C. & Sordoni, C., Locus of control, field dependence and the expression of humor. Unpublished manuscript, University of Waterloo (1972).

Levine, J., The Joking relationship. Unpublished manuscript.

Mahler, M.S., On sadness and grief in infancy and childhood: loss and restoration of the symbiotic love object. In: The Psychoanalytic Study of The Child. Volume 16, International Universities Press, New York (1961).

Milgram, S., Behavioral study of obedience. Journal of Abnormal and Social Psychology, 67, 371-378 (1963).

Milgram, S., Some conditions of obedience and disobedience to authority. Human Relations, 18, 57-76 (1965).

Park, R.R., An investigation of riddles of children, ages five - fourteen, using Piaget-derived definitions. Unpublished doctoral dissertation, Columbia University (1971).

Piaget, J., Psychology of Intelligence in The Child. Routledge and Kegan Paul (1950).

Piaget, J., Play, Dreams and Imitation In Childhood. Norton, New York (1951).

Provence, S. & Ritvo, S., Effects of deprivation on institutionalized infants: Disturbances in development of relationship to inanimate objects. In: The Psychoanalytic Study of The Child. Volume 16, International Universities Press, New York (1961).

Putnam, M.C., Rank, B. & Kaplan, S., Notes on John I: A case of primal depression in an infant. In: The Psychoanalytic Study of The Child. Volume 6, International Universities Press, New York (1951).

Seligman, M.E.P., Depression and learned helplessness. Unpublished manuscript, University of Pennsylvania (1971).

Seligman, M.E.P., Maier, S.F. & Geer, J.H., Alleviation of learned helplessness in the dog. Journal of Abnormal Psychology, 73, 256-262 (1968).

Skinner, B.F., Beyond Freedom and Dignity. Knopf, New York (1971).

Spitz, R.A. & Wolf, K.M., Anaclitic depression: an inquiry into the genesis of psychiatric conditions in early childhood. II. In: The Psychoanalytic Study of the Child. Volume 2, International Universities Press, New York (1946).

Spitz, R.A. & Wolf, K.M., The origin of the smiling response. In: D.C. McClelland (Ed.), Studies in Motivation. Appleton-Century-Crofts, New York (1955).

White, R.W., Motivation reconsidered: the concept of competence. Psychological Review, 66, 297-333 (1959).

Wolff, P.H., The natural history of crying and other vocalizations in early infancy. In: B.M. Foss (Ed.), Determinants of Infant Behaviour. Volume 4, Methuen, London (1969).

The Essential Ambiguity of, and in, Humour

Aaron Hershkowitz

Yeshiva University, New York

Humour is a desirable, enjoyable state. Hardly anyone questions its usefulness in that intensive relationship called therapy. It creates a relaxed atmosphere; it encourages communication - particularly on sensitive matters; it may provide an impetus for insight. This is hardly the case when the state of ambiguity is considered. In a therapeutic relationship, where what is needed is clear, direct, unifying information, it may be argued that ambiguity is neither desirable nor enjoyable.

The thesis of this paper is that ambiguities of a certain sort - to be described shortly - are intimately, even essentially, related to humour. As such, they may play an important part in therapy. It will be argued that humour is a way of presenting ambiguities which are acceptable, even sought for, and which may serve to make the patient tolerate a world that is not always an 'either-or' world. It may enable him to imagine, and even act out, ambivalences (a form of ambiguity), in a relatively safe, non-threatening way. Moreover, for some patients it can be salutary in that it can permit them to entertain contradictory views without having to make disavowals; without appearing irrational; without feeling guilty.

As a starting point for an analysis we shall use the data of immediate, direct experience (for basic phenomenological method see Gurwitsch, 1964; Spiegelberg, 1960; Straus, 1966). It is particularly helpful to seize a phenomenon which is available to everyone in an ostensive, unquestioned way. Humour, it would seem, is that experience par excellance. Everyone can appreciate a joke - more or less. Everyone can create a joke - for better or worse. A joke can serve as an ideal specimen, an 'experimentum crucis' around which all discussion could focus and revolve. Humour is made to order for a phenomenological analysis. And yet, it is with a great deal of trepidation that one should venture into this area. Every teller of a joke is something of an expert. Every laugher at a joke is something of a connoisseur. The obvious is never simple. In fact, the more obvious, the more complex ultimately. The mundane in our life is never self-revealing. The 'taken for granted' invariably leads to the unexpected. It is all very discouraging, but there may be something hopeful about. The very nature of our predicament may provide a basis for understanding.

Every experience is composed of three mutually inter-related levels: figure, ground, horizon. As a case in point, the joke proper stands, sui generis, as a figural unit. On the ground level, there is the context - the relationship between the presented things and happenings (in the joke) and the people and events outside the joke (i.e., the participants). Finally, there is the over-arching horizon enveloping both joke and context. All levels contribute to that positive, affective experience called humour. These nesting layers of experience are structured by inner and outer boundaries which are clear, but never completely rigid. When there is a disturbance or deformation to these limits, originally distinct and disparate regions may become ambiguous (by contrast or overlap). Humour, we shall argue, is both a cause and a consequence of such boundary shifts; it leads to, and is the result of, ambiguities in experience. In what follows, an effort will be made to concretely describe the nature of the boundary disturbance, the kind of ambiguities, and the affects and after-effects of ambiguity.

Before this is done, a few remarks must be made to clarify these terms in a direct experiential way. Some perceptual examples, though not inherently humorous, may help. A coin is seen spinning rapidly on its axis at right angles to the line of vision. At some point, quite momentarily, it is possible to see both sides (head and tail). Except for the immediate beginning and the near end, the perception is not blurred, indeterminate or amorphous. There is a stabilized 'doubleness' co-present: it refers to the same object, in the same place, at virtually the same time. Like the proverbial sides of a question, the two sides are both there. Another example. If a tautly stretched elastic band (separating two regions) is plucked, 'vibrations' cause an overlap or doubling of boundaries. What has been part of one region (inside) is now part of another (outside). Or, stated differently, one boundary has now become two; two distinctive areas have now become one region.

It should be evident that we are speaking of a special kind of ambiguity and a specific type of disturbance[1]. Here, the ambiguity is brief, stable, and clear. It allows for a perception of 'two disparate things at once'. On a logical level, the conjunction 'and' replaces 'or' in a proposition. There are other experiences of this sort. Ambivalence, under certain conditions, is an affective ambiguous state. Paradoxes and oxymorons are logical ambiguities; puns are ambiguities of meaning.

As for the changes in the boundary conditions, these are sharp, sudden reversible incursions in the experiential stream. They may be experienced, variously, as a sudden thrust, an opening, a crack, a point, or a nub. Though they are disruptive in one sense, they are constructive in the sense that they lead to a temporary stability. The examples of the spinning coin and the moving band are useful. If the 'vibrations' are good (i.e., they are not too wild and erratic) they establish an overlap of two different regions. If the 'spin' is right (i.e., the orientation and rotation is optimum) it offers a unitary view of alternative and incompatible aspects. We now turn to a description of these acceptable ambiguities. Such an analysis, while it does not pretend at originality or novelty, may provide some insights into the state of humour.

HORIZON: PARADOXES OF PLAY

There is general agreement that a prime condition for humour is a playful orientation to the world. Under the right circumstances, this horizonal level, with its ambiance, can spread humour across the entire landscape. Without it, even the funniest event can fall flat. How can we describe this orientation? Susanna Millar, based on her study of animals and children concludes:

> 'Play is paradoxical behavior. Exploring what is familiar, practicing what has already been mastered, friendly aggression, sex without coition, ... pretence not intended to deceive.'

One can agree with this statement without adopting a behavioural or developmental bias. From a phenomenological point of view, play is a mode of being-in-the-world that is equally, perhaps more, accessible to adults. On the one hand, it is ordinarily contrasted to the world of work, with its 'nothing-but' or 'either-or' character. On the other hand, it is quite distinct from fantasy, with its 'anything-goes' or 'nothing-matters' orientation[2]. These states, at the extremes, are clear and there is no need to go into details. For our purposes it is necessary to point out the boundary conditions (and the disturbances) which serve to make play a stabilized ambiguous region.

Play is a world in which reality and fantasy join and overlap; where seriousness and triviality converge; where spontaneity and constraint meet. At the outer edges of play lies hard, opaque reality, with its practicality and determinateness. At the other extreme is amorphous, transparent fantasy, with its indulgence and license. Play is that overlapping zone between them. Without that buffer, one would be like the man in the Chinese legend who 'dreamt he was a butterfly and then awoke... only to wonder anxiously whether he was not now a butterfly dreaming he was a man'. When stresses at either extreme are insuperable, a rebound into the zone of play can occur. Anything out of the ordinary can breach the limits. Gallows humour and humour of the grotesque are examples of this.

Though play is not always humorous, it is evident that it provides a home for such a state. This can be made clearer by considering three prototypic actors who occupy the play world. The athlete is one whose play is reality directed. He pits his strength, endurance and prowess against the boundaries of reality. The artist is one whose play is fantasy inspired. He matches his imagination, sensibility and technique against the veil of fantasy. The clown is the quintessential player; he is a bit of both. He is a player of players in a world of play.

What are the forces which make this paradoxical world so attractive? Three inter-related factors are worth noting. One, is the relaxation that comes from intense involvement with the other extremes. Relief, diversion, amusement, entertainment, are all affective components of play. Two, is the exuberance that comes from the realization that one can, however momentarily, live in the best of both worlds. Like having one's cake and eating it. Finally, there is the sheer delight that comes from coming to terms with ambiguity itself — on ambiguous terms. To skip, flip, slip, trip from one world to the next with a minimum of effort and a maximum of impunity.

The humour inherent in play is contagious. Everything it touches becomes ambiguous. It is spontaneous; it cannot be artificially induced. Since it has no figural integrity, it cannot be transplanted or recreated. Any change (time, place, people) dissipates the mood.

And, what is funny is impossible to communicate. Finally, there is a mutual dependent (and ambiguous) relationship between humour and play. One can be the cause and consequence of the other.

GROUND: AMBIVALENCES OF PARTICIPATION

The playful orientation may be a condition for humour, but it is rather unfocused and general. One can also approach humour as a participational event - between speaker-listener, actors-observers. There are three inherent dualities in this context. Again we shall describe the boundaries (and the disturbances) which lead to acceptable and enjoyable ambiguities. Ordinarily, it should be remembered, the limits involved are highly charged, polarized, and clear. First, there are the characters and things in the joke (fictively) and the people and events outside the joke (non-fictively). In humour, the direct and the indirect can mix; the representational and the real can overlap. This aesthetic illusion (Kris, 1952) provides an ambiguity of position: being inside and outside. Such a state can allow one to be daring in a safe way; to feel anxiety and fear while secure; in short, to dance without paying the piper. Second, there is the separateness of the self and the other. Any rapid and momentary vacillation between these ordinarily separate agents; any short-circuiting of polarities, can be a basis for humour. One can go toward and away; push and pull; resist and comply. One can be friendly while disliking; show strength in weakness, and vice-versa. Third, is the duality of the self as actor and the self as reflector. In humour there is a coming together of agent and instrument. There is an oscillation between passivity and activity. Here, it is possible to 'catch' oneself in the act; to 'play' with oneself; to 'sneak' a glimpse in the mirror; to 'manipulate' one's shadow. This temporary 'doubleness' can be fundamental for the comic.

It is superfluous to dwell on the affective charges of this level. It is rich in inversions, ambivalences, and identifications. Intense, irregular or chronic disruptions may be threatening and traumatic. But, if the breach is sudden, brief, and reversible (and, if it should also happen in the play zone) then it can be humorous. Humour of this sort, with its ambiguity of fusion and separateness, cannot be an unalloyed experience. Since it often involves others, such ambiguities cannot be symmetrical or regular. To use the prevailing term, it is tendentious (Freud, 1905). It encourages identification at the expense of disjunction. Ethnicity, dialect, topicality, impersonations are prime materials for participatory humour. Jesting, bantering, 'sounding' are probes in the limits of the other. Here, there can be faddism and fashion; self-depreciation or boasting; asides and ad-libs. If the ambiguity is acceptable, then the 'give and take' and the 'double talk' can be funny. It can also be instructive and informative. Matching the point of a joke across participational boundaries is the humorous equivalent of the parable.

FIGURE: REVERSALS OF PREMISES

The horizonal level is important in colouring humour and the ground can have a decisive effect upon it. But these are actually extrinsic to the figure itself. So much has been written about this focal event that it needs no elaboration. (cf. Berlyne, 1968; Goldstein & McGhee, 1972). Here, we shall briefly describe those premises of those short, simple, unitary presentations (for example, jokes) which, when disturbed and reversed, lead to ambiguities.

First is the 'taken for granted' premise of plot direction. No matter what the twists and turns, there is a necessary connection between beginning and end. If someone is hanging a gun on the wall in the first act, then there will surely be a shooting in the third act. (Burke, 1969). When the push from the starting point is taken over by the pull of the end point, a highly charged, suspenseful duality is created. Is one coming or going? Is the glass half-empty or half-full? At the critical juncture does one take path A or B? A slight momentary jarring allows one to see both alternatives. More than this, the likely, or best choice, may turn out to be the worst. Second, is the tacit assumption that there is one meaning that best fits a given presentation (expressed as a word, gesture, etcetera). Even when alternatives or changes occur, they replace, more or less permanently, the old meaning. In humour, however, there is a reversal, and the two meanings can be co-present... each can be, in its own way, 'better' or 'worse.' Finally, there is the implicit expectation that primary agents be characterized by simple (often extreme and idealized) polarities. If there is a hero, there must be a villain; a wise man needs a fool for a foil; a 'goat' calls for a 'bully.' Transformations of character usually come about slowly, logically, and in a manner consistent with a context. In humour, not only are there quick, sudden reversals ('the worm turns') but both aspects are accepted - for the same or different people.

For all such reversals, it should be noted that after the breach (the punchline) hindsight reveals that both sides were there all the time, waiting to be exposed like the sides of a spinning coin. And, we do not feel cheated or disappointed at this 'turn of events.' Indeed, we welcome it because it may afford us an added ambiguity to play with. Humour on this level can survive context transplantation and endless thematic variations. It can be anthologized and categorized. It can be honed and tuned to match setting and mood. Though technique is important (the time and delivery of reversals) it is easily communicable.

CONCLUSION

To the description of ambiguities within each level, one must add that there are interaction effects across boundary levels. A complete analysis of such reverberating cycles cannot be adequate. It may be that nothing really new or original can be contributed in principle. Humour is directly experienced and understood; all explanations are gratuitous. It may be equally correct to put it this way. If humour, to be appreciated and created, needs a modicum of ambiguity, then the understanding and explanation of it may require a similar dosage, Perhaps a metaphor is the best way to express it: humour can be an implosion of play; it can be a groundquake of participation; it can be an explosion of premises.

After the comic dust has settled, theorists, the demolition and bomb squad experts, try to reconstruct the event. The myriads of ways in which boundaries can be disrupted and the variety of levels on which this can occur, gives ample room for any theory. For surprise and relief, superiority and aggression, incongruity and re-structuring, theorists can choose their own jokes and generate evidence. There is something correct and valid about all theories. And yet, there's this crack in the boundary. If that indeed be the case, if they are all true, then it is equally clear that they are all wrong. Which reminds me of a joke: A couple consulted a psychologist about their marriage. Listening to the husband's version, he nodded in agreement. 'You're right. Absolutely right!' When the wife gave her side, he vigorously assented. 'Of course, you're right. Certainly, you're right!' His assistant took him to task. 'How could you tell the husband he's right, then turn around and tell the wife that she's right?' The psychologist thought a while. 'You know something. You're right too!'

FOOTNOTES

1. Wiener (1958) has treated ambiguity as a probability of perception or as an uncertainty of response. Ambiguity as a personality variable was introduced by Frenkel-Brunswik (1948). Psychological boundaries and regions, and disturbances, are discussed, in different contexts, by Lewin (1935) and by Rokeach (1960).

2. For a background to the notion of 'worlds' that we live in see Schutz (1962) and Berger and Luckmann (1966).

REFERENCES

See Bibliography for publications on humour, laughter and comedy

Berger, P.L. & Luckmann, T., The Social Construction of Reality. Doubleday, New York (1966).

Burke, K., A Grammar of Motives. University of California Press, Berkley (1969).

Frenkel-Brunswik, E., A study of prejudice in children. Human Relations, 1, 295-306 (1948).

Gurwitsch, A., The Field of Consciousness. Duquesne University Press, Pitts (1964).

Lewin, K., A Dynamic Theory of Personality, Selected Papers. McGraw-Hill, New York (1935).

Rokeach, M., The Open and Closed Mind. Basic Books, New York (1960).

Schutz, A., On multiple realities. In: Collected Papers, Vol. 1, Martin Nijhoff, The Hague (1962).

Spiegelberg, H., The Phenomenological Movement. Martin Nijhoff, The Hague (1960).

Straus, E., Phenomenological Psychology. Basic Books, New York (1966).

Wiener, M., Certainty of judgment as a variable in conformity behavior. Journal of Social Psychology, 48, 257-263 (1958).

Millar, S., The Psychology of Play. Penguin Books, Harmondsworth (1968).

The Sense of Humour: Actualizer of Persons and Theories

Walter E. O'Connell

Houston, Texas

CHRONIC UNDIFFERENTIATED DYSHUMORIA

'There is no point in the struggle to survive unless we can become aware of the fundamental ecstatic component in almost every kind of activity. Nearly every "task": can be performed in the spirit of dancing, playing a guitar, or working out a game of chess... At first, the notion seems absurd, for the bus driver, like all of us, is under immense social pressure to "get there." But when you get there, "there" is "here", and if you can't live completely "here", what is the point of going "there"?' (Watts, 1970, p1).

We psychologists trained around the middle of the twentieth century grew up for the most part to be mechanical academicians. Our active imaginations withered on the vine from disuse atrophy. The average psychologist of those days diagnosed patients according to descriptive nomenclature, assisted clients to adjust to 'reality', and pursued pure knowledge solely through the canons of experimental design. Very few of us ever verbalized heretical questions about the ultimate validities of descriptive diagnoses, theories and techniques of therapy, and premises of research designs as the only road to truth. Our subtle but intense efforts to control patients, data, reality, and monopolize truth made us appropriate objects of humour, yet we were unable to perceive ourselves in a vitalizing humorous light. Perhaps this ego-syntonic dyshumoria partially explains our lack of impact in the real world of everyday constrictions, miseries, and joys. Decades later, my guiding fiction now is that only when we teach students of psychology the sense of their innate personal worth and inherent belonging will they be able to exist joyously within an inherently paradoxical world in which each man is the creator and creation of his own self-training, for better or for worse. My Moral: The truths of personal actualization are created within before they can be discovered and analyzed from without.

Freud's Definition

In my explorations Freud's (1928) clinical examples of humour were highlighted. Here the humour producer and/or appreciator is a person who can, under severe objective stress, make a sudden perceptual switch from incipient painful affects to a state reflective of the triumph of the ego and the pleasure principle. It is impossible faithfully to follow Freud further since he incongruously considered humour to be the epitome of maturity as well as the pathological denial of reality. Freud's picture of the humorist as one with a benign superego added to the confusion at a time when the superego was routinely regarded as prohibitive in nature. In addition Freud's descriptive and abstract thinking on the humorist did not take account of the variables influencing life-style change. Freud pictured the humorist as one who had 'hypercathexis of the superego.' He thereby isolated movement-oriented behavioural concepts from abstract theory. Freud made a distinction between the active producer of humour who saw himself or others in a humorous light. The former I designated Type B, the humour of the self, the most 'encouragenic'. Regarding others in a humorous vein was called Type A, a risky venture because the absence of an equal relationship might trigger a hostile response to intended humour (O'Connell, 1976).

Another of Freud's observations was that humour was a reaction to incipient negative (painful) affects. Successful humour circumvented and prevented these negative unpleasant states and eventuated in pleasure for the humour creators and those observers of a like psychic disposition. The precipitator of humour, whether self or other-directed, in Freud's structure and approach was the superego's perception that all is 'child's play': the very thing to jest about under severe stress. Humour therefore depended upon the presence of gentle empathy and love toward oneself (Type B) and toward others (Type A), rather than the influence of an angry autocratic superego.

O'Connell's Contribution

> ...A smile is itself a sign of wisdom — so thought the Greek fathers. Indeed
> Origen.... goes so far as to say that the truly wise man is like a child that
> smiles and plays by the bier of its parents... (O'Connell, 1975).

This paper presents tentative theoretical sketches, at most distilled from clinical and
research experiences. The curious reader who wants to know why I believe I became addicted
to the study of humour and where this pilgrimage of over a quarter century has taken me is
referred to other sources (O'Connell, 1975, 1976). Since I have ruminated and researched
for a quarter century upon Freud's clinical examples, I will forthwith present my own views.
For the moment, man is to be imagined as a creative creature capable of infinite inner
expansion through such learned (but seldom taught) reactions as an art of humour. First of
all, one may 'intend' wit or humour and entirely miss the mark. Or what starts to be humour
may eventuate in wit, a response of feeling oneself the victim of a hostile put-down. This
crucial point has been overlooked because wit and humour were approached in earlier times as
if they were encapsulated entities, rather than merely convenient constructs to identify
certain processes within a framework of communications. Because wit and humour grow out of
communication between dyads, intended Type A humour may end-up as anything but humour in the
eyes of the dyadic other. The extent of such interactional subtleties can be seen in the
behaviour of a lady in one of my therapy groups. Whenever she relates her litany of panics
and protestations, she demands that other members follow her lead with suitable verbal and
nonverbal signs of reflected pain and discouragement. Eventually she reaches a point where
she makes a sudden switch and regards her frustrations as humorous and experiences personal
enhancement. Yet if anyone gives signs of 'all-this-is-child's-play' before she does, her
response is one of shock at the 'hostility' of the other. Needless to say, she has not yet
viewed her initiating ploys of hopeless-helplessness in a humorous light.

Intended Type B humour cannot be judged to be 'humour' until after the fact. The criteria
of humour is thereby centred upon a subsequent expansion of worth and significance and not
upon the immediate outer smiles, laughter and tears of the participants. In other words,
the reactions of wit and humour are to be judged by effects upon the constriction or expansion
of self-esteem (SE) and social interest (SI) of those involved. Such criteria do not solve
the measurement problems, but they do point to a fruitful direction for exploration. As an
example, take the prisoner story cited by Freud. The punchline of the lad about to be hanged
on a Monday, 'This is a good beginning to the week,' could have been reacted to in many ways.
The prisoner could have focused on discouraging irony and constricted his SE and SI, feeling
worthless and isolated. He would then follow with the movements of injured worth and
isolation, the opposite of encouragenic actions. True Type B humour would reflect the
workings of humanistic identification of the natural high (O'Connell, 1975): encouragement
(expansion of SE and SI). Likewise with observers, the same discouragenic or encouragenic
atmosphere would emerge, determined by the self-created attitudes and perceptions of persons
involved. One may attempt to produce an encouragenic humorous atmosphere, but message sent
may not be message received. The purpose or goal of the sending and receiving persons is
vital and is completely overlooked in a mechanistic theory of humour production and
appreciation.

THE MAN FOR ALL PARADOXES

> ...The tensions between the sacred and the profane, and the taboos enforcing them,
> are transcended through a momentary recapture of that state in which such
> categories do not exist...the mystery that cannot be contained and ordered by man...
> (Hyers, 1969, pp213-214).

Increased energy from the reconciliation of opposites has long been a contention of Jungian
psychology. The inner dialogue between the conscious state and emerging archetypes creates
the Transcendent function, a positive growth state akin to the natural high. Dynamic
psychology in general would also hold that repressing energies released from ceasing to
centre on one pole of a paradox (for example, masculine-feminine, good-bad) would result in
a greater accumulation of conscious psychic energies.

In my case energy lacks meaning unless directionality or purpose of expression is specified.
Hyers (1973) mentions a tremendous energy release in religious ceremonies where symbols of
aloof gods and deflating humans move throughout rituals without upsetting or deflating each
other. Similar energy was created and directed toward life's tasks in Death and Dying
'labs' in which death is acted upon in the midst of life. Participants reported intense
and enlivening perceptions and renewed vigour following an encouragement 'lab' which
included paradoxical death and dying exercises. The most striking example of renewed energy
directed toward social interest developed in such encouragement 'labs' in which a psychodrama
of death was experienced (O'Connell, in press). The simultaneous presentation of the

dying-living paradox (or more accurately the rapid fluctuation between these polar extremes) stimulated energy growth within and between participants. Until then, I had never seen four groups of persons crying, yet paradoxically attending to others and not using emotions to create distance or gain special services. After a year, these participants still communicate with each other and wonder why this particular session was worlds apart from the usual encounter group experience.

The authentic humorist is one who leaves no pole of a paradox for long. His sudden inner paradoxical switches from pole to pole provide the inner catharsis that result in a sudden smile. Type B humour, using the 'God's eye view' or the innate sense of detachment, is primarily an inner mechanism giving relief from attachments which might lose for the humorist the control of his inner strength, self-esteem (SE) and social interest (SI). Type A and B humour, as Freud implied, is of growth-value to the spectator only if he has empathic similarity (or social interest) with the humorist. Thomas More's humour on his gallows (O'Connell, 1975, 1976), still greatly admired by much of the Western world, did nothing for the social interest of his detractors who saw only crazy self-deception in his smiling greetings of death.

Such psychoanalytic experts on humour as Grotjahn (1956) connect the humorist with the mourning of external object-loss, but they are less cognizant of the switch to the other pole of the paradox, the self-containing God-within stance of Meister Eckhart, Carl Jung, or Teilhard de Chardin (1969). The world is full of paradoxes and opposites which need to be reconciled within the humorist's psyche. Only a sampling of these is noted in the polemics of masculine-feminine, sacred-profane, inner-outer, past-present, youth-age, life-death, conscious-unconscious. Such extremes are consistently (albeit temporally) united in the sudden perceptual switches of the consciousness of the humorist. Three paradoxes lightly labelled as 'St. Augustine's', the 'tragicomic', and the 'existential' paradoxes will serve as illustrations (O'Connell, 1976).

One pole of St. Augustine's paradox is that my death does not matter; the swing to the other pole is marked by the belief that what I am now doing is of universal importance. Polemics cannot contribute to enhancement of self-esteem and universal belonging unless they are admitted and integrated in quick succession into consciousness. My death (and mini-deaths of disappointing endings) can only be tolerated in light of my faith in the evolutionary process on equal footing with all vibrant matter (Teilhard de Chardin, 1969). Others will repeat what I am doing, even though human life tasks bid me to add my unique movements. Twentieth century scientism is critical of such 'philosophy' as totally archaic and regressive; yet a creative-growth world view has psychological survival value in stimulating positive loving actions in the here and now.

The humorist has self-generated experience focusing upon the dual poles of the existential paradox. The negative pole, that of innate 'finitude' - decay, dirt and death, concentrated upon for excessive periods creates depressive states of worthlessness and isolation. The opposite extreme, the God-like capacity for self-enhancing imagination and meaning, can trigger paranoia if fixated by selective 'arrangement' on narcissistic isolation. These 'grandiose' cognitions, untempered by reactive perceptual swings, call forth external blame on others for one's unacknowledged imperfections. To dwell at either extreme is constrictive. The skill of the humorist is to call forth both extremes in rapid succession. To Jungians, this skilful manoeuvre is the reconciliation of opposites; to Hyers (1973), it is the simultaneous evoking of a paradox; to O'Connell, who cannot imagine divergent ideation simultaneously presented in consciousness, the technique is that of a rapid perceptual swing of inner dialectics.

Acceptance of tragicomic paradox often heralds the birth of Type B humour. The budding humorist, looking at his past, unites (or re-solves) these paradoxical poles. One tragicomic extreme is that of chronic self-devaluation caused by invidious comparisons, negative nonsense, and diminished self-esteem. The other extreme is chronic demands for unconditional love from others. In a negative state, one cannot or will not esteem himself, yet often demands that others do so automatically. The psychic spark between the poles is sometimes referred to in clinical jargon as the Transcendent function, decrease in defensive negative nonsense, liberated archaic energy, or what have you. All such concepts refer to a non-rational and as yet unscientific zest for living.

The sudden cognitive-perceptual switches of the humorist are rapid vacillations between the poles of a paradox, both of which have been incorporated into the humorist's life-style. Here he differs vastly from the average person who aims to totally incorporate one pole into his ideal, although even this normal person seems to fall far short of reaching his unipolar ideal. In contrast, the humorist can see himself as strong and weak, masculine and feminine, saint and sinner, rather than identify with one pole and repress the other. Such a refusal to self-exclude any facet of the human is both cause and effect of a profound sense of social interest. Both poles of human paradoxes are admitted to consciousness in quick succession. In terms of the paradoxes mentioned previously, the temporal transformation is often from

the worthless side of life (for example, the depressive stance) to a responsible and
expansive dimension. The humorist retains the capability of being either dysphoric or
euphoric, for example. The change from the former to the latter is more readily noted as
the hallmark of the humorist. Yet it is equally apparent that the change can proceed from
the euphoric to dysphoric quality, although such moves are not seen as humorous. The quick
pulsation from constricted to courageous (active social interest) is what stimulates the
humorous response. The equal awareness of both poles generates the energic increase noted
earlier. If humour-oriented research can show a valid increase in psychic energy, deployed
along the channels of SE and SI, the most outstanding human energy shortage will be solved -
with a smile of welfare rather than another explosion of warfare.

A HUMORIST'S CREED: THE ALCHEMY OF THE ULTIMATE GAME

...The God of creation, whose work we are permitted to call a game...both full of
meaning and yet bound by no dictate of necessity. This tremendous outpouring,
a happening in which the human mingles with the divine, has been called by me a
game - and in this I have followed some of the most illustrious of Christian
mystics - because there is...nothing here of compulsion or calculation... (Rahner,
1967, p46).

Humour is the utmost delicate movement of the whole body in the game-of-games (Ehrmann, 1971).
Such serious play is the pastime and vocation of the constantly actualizing human being. The
main reason for Being is the expansion of self-esteem and social interest, called at times
humanistic identification or the natural high (O'Connell, 1976b). The humorist knows that
persons, in their own creativity, can continuously constrict self-knowledge and growth
experiences in a 'three-ring-circus' of life simultaneously. The three-rings of the
Existential Circus are the inner-(I), inter-(II), and transpersonal (III) dimensions
(O'Connell, 1975, 1976). Constriction fulminates with invidious comparisons and isolation
which are in the service of the Hell of inadequate identification, learned early and readily
in life. Constricting 'mortal sins' decrease a person's worth and belonging on all three
levels. Feelings of worth and significance are entirely under the control of the humorist,
simply because he accepts the premise that SE and SI are the only two variables he can
completely control in life.

Level I, the Inner, is a pure morass of demanding and blaming, accompanying the constriction
of SE and SI. Knowledge of the inner workings of constriction represents an initial
development of the humorous self-attitude. The humorist must be able to notice incipient
demands for perfection and circumvent symptoms of constriction with a devastating smile,
before he is transformed into a static entity of mechanical normal adjustment, marked by
petty peeves and petulances.

The humorist accepts his connectedness to others - and to the whole wiggling expanding
Universe (Teilhard de Chardin, 1969). At Level II, he practices the overt steps of
Encouragement (O'Connell, 1975) in hopes that others may come to know how to move away from
constrictive discouragement, and realize their dormant God-like powers of expansive creativity.
Active and passive competition and hyperdependency can utterly destroy encouragenic feedback,
so the humorist alerts his fellows to give him immediate feedback when they note the weeds
of self-discouragement choking his fruits of interpersonal joy. The humorist never
underestimates the process of discouragement as manifested in the useless goals of life of
others. Much feedback from others may be inspired by their needs for special service, power
struggles, revenge and displays of disabilities. The humorist, to remain so, must ask for
and listen to feedback about his behaviours, but never abdicates his responsibility for
personal change. In the universe of the humorist, all contribute; all are responsible;
no one is to blame.

Level III, each person's search for his loving God, is an embarrassment to institutionalized
religion and traditional science, both of whom prescribe their rituals and trappings for
discerning reliable truths. The humorist, never unaware of the 'holiness' of SE and SI, is
likewise alerted to the ephemeral and contingent basis of external sources of worth
(O'Connell, 1976b). To base one's esteem upon influence (or power) from others is to
sabotage one's true strength. Esteem given today can be summarily withdrawn tomorrow. Only
Gods securely anchored within and giving purpose to life by needing human hands to carry out
evolutionary goals can be accepted by the real humorist.

The 'normal' human often turns to drugs and violence to assuage his hurt when constricted
persons and goals fail to guarantee instant and constant ecstasy. The road of the humorist,
the true pilgrim, is toward developing the joyous delusion that he has rediscovered the lost
euphorias of childhood with the certainty that no matter what inanities the rational post-
reformation world may visit upon him, he has access to the source of innate worth and inherent
belonging. In the words of Hesse (see Serrano, 1968, p19), 'In their old age, some men have

the gift of once again experiencing the paradisiacal state of their childhood.' He may never be discouraged unless he chooses to be. The humorist then transforms paradoxes into energy — re-solving and re-solving — and centres the vibrations into movements of innate worth and inherent belonging. Not because he so chooses, the humorist will always be an elite element of life. Given the choice of euphoric optimism or dysphoric pessimism — both beyond ultimate proof — the bulk of mankind will favour the latter. Institutions of religion and learning seem to require an inert, apathetic humanoid base upon which to build unwittingly their edifices for degradation of the human spirit — and thereby to bury humour forever. This is why the humorist, the ultimate athlete of the game-of-games, is his own coach, referee and audience (Ehrmann, 1971).

The art of humour — total and flexible concern with both poles of a paradox — provides the person with the rewarding experience of 'flow', the total awareness and heightened involvement with activity, basic to fun (Furlong, 1976). The true humorist views life as an evolutionary game in which there is no necessity or compulsion to play. He can play at whatever tempo he cares to function: without blame, demands, or competition. These sacred ploys lead to a flowing expansion of SE and SI, and therefore are intrinsically rewarding. Paradoxically the humorist is also skilled at constricting his humanistic identification and can so move if he wants to avoid-dance on the useless side of life. Knowing one can play as well as he desires is a rule of the ultimate game of life. As he realizes that the non-compulsive sport is rewarding for himself and mankind, the humorist creates and experiences 'flow'. Now add to this happy scheme a Teilhardian directionality: the energy of the Universe is increased through loving actions (in meditation and interpersonal movements) and we have a universal dance with a perennially happy beat. Natural highs, 'flows', humour, humanistic identification — all in all — symbolize inner state of the merry-grave man (Rahner, 1967) who glides with every paradox in a finite world which all too often uses its will-power in the service of unhappiness. Conversely, creativity in the expansion of SE and SI, the energy potential inherent in the acceptance of a paradoxically playful seriousness, is the playground for the serious game of games.

REFERENCES

See Bibliography for publications on humour, laughter and comedy

Ehrmann, J., Game, Play, Literature. Beacon, Boston (1971).

O'Connell, W., The 'Friends of Adler' Phenomenon. Journal of Individual Psychology, 32, 5-18 (1976b).

O'Connell, W.E., Action Therapy and Adlerian Theory. Alfred Adler Institute, Chicago (1975).

O'Connell, W.E., The Death Lab as a Catalyst for Natural Highs. Omega (in press).

Rahner, H., Man at Play. Herder & Herder, New York (1967).

Serrano, M., C.G. Jung and Hermann Hesse: A Record of Two Friendships. Schoken, New York (1968).

Teilhard de Chardin, P., Building the Earth. Avon, New York (1969).

Watts, A., Alan Watts Journal, 1, 1 (1970).

The Use of Jokes in Psychotherapy

Saul A. Grossman

Mever-Manhattan Psychiatric Center, New York

The presence of humour in everyday life makes it an area of interest per se. It has been pointed out that humour and the ability to laugh is a distinguishing characteristic of the human race (Grotjahn, 1958). It was Freud (1905) in his monumental work, 'Wit and Its Relation to the Unconscious,' who brought the attention of the world to the relationship between the comic and personality. He indicated that humour was a basic mechanism of defense, just as neuroses and psychoses are defenses. The essential difference, as he saw it, was that humour alone was not pathological. There have been many studies since Freud that have dealt with the type of humour people prefer and its relation to specific problems they may have, or to personality dynamics. Zwerling (1955), in a clinical paper, observed that 'A favorite joke may provide direct insight into an area of conflict otherwise obscure'. He thus concluded that the favourite joke serves to reveal anxiety related to central conflict in the personality. My own work has experimentally and clinically demonstrated that both general personality factors and problems of personal significance find their means of expression overtly through jokes. Indeed a patient's favourite joke has been found sometimes to reveal hidden dynamics behind anxiety that is attributed to other causes. Other authors, among them Redlich and Levine (1955), have indicated that jokes offer insight very much like dreams, early memories, or responses to a projective test, with the advantage of being more concise and direct.

The joke is often used to express forbidden pleasure-seeking fantasies, thus bypassing the censure of the super-ego. It is evident that because of the nature of our society and its moral values, the sex joke would be the most common form of humour. Under the guide of the comic, society permits the individual to say almost anything. This might be best exemplified by the jester. The jester, under the umbrella of the comic, was able to say almost anything to the king even though it was unpopular or unacceptable or forbidden to others. The same holds true for current-day comedians, satirists, and cartoonists. We may thus conclude that humour makes it more permissible to speak of forbidden topics.

The disguise of a joke must go far enough to avoid guilt, but it must not go far enough to lose gratification of the impulse. If the disguise of the impulse is not successful, there will not be pleasure as a result of the joke, but instead guilt or embarrassment, because of the true nature of the impulse being recognized. Indeed, the absence of laughter to a joke is a signal that the joke has offended or not been understood, or the joke may have hit an area of conflict. Humour is relatively easy to understand and, except for idiosyncratic jokes (jokes of schizophrenic patients or culturally determined jokes), the failure to understand a joke is usually a response to the danger of an unacceptable impulse breaking through into consciousness. The joke may refer to an area that has not yet been mastered or it may be that the subject identifies with the person laughed at. In such a case discomfort is felt instead of pleasure.

The joke in psychotherapy is a multifaceted tool that may be used by both patient and therapist. Unlike the dream, it is at the disposal of both members of the treatment dyad; as well as any member of a group or family. It is unusual for a therapist to tell his patients his own dreams, but it is not at all unusual or out of place to use jokes as interpretive devices. If we speak of the dream as the 'royal road' to the unconscious, the joke may be termed as a less traditional road, possibly a private path to be used by both patient and therapist for personal communication, a much less threatening road to travel. In many instances we have found a patient more readily able to tell his favourite joke than to remember dreams. This may, to some extent, be due to the patient's concept that to tell a dream is to reveal himself, but to tell a joke is not nearly as threatening since the telling of jokes has been part of his everyday life since childhood, largely connected with pleasant situations. On the other hand, the reporting of dreams in psychotherapy is seen as strictly a psychoanalytic manoeuvre to get a person to reveal his most inner secrets.

Among intellectual patients, it has been noted by Theodore Reik that jokes are used to hide problems or conflicts. It may be said that when a joke is made, a problem is hidden and the joke is a defense against facing the problem.

In the following instance, the therapist used a joke as an interpretive device. The patient was a very intelligent, well-educated thirty-year-old man, who had been unable to achieve his professional goal of becoming an attorney because of a very severe obsessive character disorder. He was always able to rationalize and intellectualize any and all interpretations. He found fault with the behaviour of others but always had 'logical' reasons for his own behaviour. In short, he was his own worst enemy. He spent most of his time ruminating and obsessing about his situation and came up with plans to solve his problem by ritualistic behaviour that led nowhere. In short, he used his intellect to avoid insight. After failing his bar exams he proceeded to ruminate about a new system that would make it possible for him to pass the bar next time without any further real effort; or he ruminated as to whether he wanted to be a lawyer in the first place. The therapist had to cut through the rumination and came up with the following joke. A dog was playing along a railroad-track and a train came by and cut off a piece of his tail. The dog was very upset by the situation and sat down on the track and contemplated what life would be like with a shorter tail; how would it be to live without a tail like he had all his life? As he was sitting and ruminating an express train came along and killed the dog.

The patient responded to this joke by saying, 'You mean I am wasting all my life thinking about things rather than doing anything'. I said, 'Yes'. He then said, 'I am going to write this joke down and try to refer to it in different situations'. But he immediately went on to obsessing about how people treat him. I said, 'You are sitting on the track again'. Then, next session, he reported that he had spent a great deal of time thinking of ways to avoid rumination and do things. I again used the punchline. 'You are sitting on the track again'. For the first time in four years of therapy the man allowed himself to cry. He was very upset and said, 'Knowing this is something I have been trying to avoid seeing about myself all my life'. A new phase of therapy was able to start. Here the joke was used as an interpretive device in less threatening fashion, to a point where it could be understood by the patient and utilized in a creative way.

A young man active in the Jewish Defense League was quite fearful of the Black activists, and his own aggressive feelings. He was paranoid and expressed fear of attack by Black activist groups. He told the following joke: What is another way of saying prune juice? - Black Power. I asked him what he felt about the Black movement. He laughed and associated it to bowel movement. We were able to trace this to his fear of loss at faecal control and his anal-aggressive feelings.

The following joke was told by a twenty-four-year-old male school teacher whose presenting complaint was overwhelming anxiety and depression. He spoke of having an adequate social life. At the time of his first visit he was having a relationship with a woman, and they were living together. He was a physical education instructor and very much concerned with physical fitness, exercising a great deal. He was also very conscious of his short stature. In addition, there was an inordinate fear of physical illness and that he might die of an incurable disease.

The young man told the following joke. There were two men hiking in a desert and it was very hot. They approached an oasis that had a spring-fed lake that seemed cool and inviting. On one side of the lake there was a group of people picnicking. The two friends chose a secluded area and proceeded to get undressed to get into the water for a swim. Suddenly one of the men was bitten on the penis by a rattle-snake. They both were very upset and did not know what to do. The man who was bitten begged his friend to do something to help him. The friend said, 'I don't know what to do but I will go right across the lake and find out, from the people there, if anyone can be of help'. He put on his trousers and ran quickly to the other side of the lake and spoke to the people there, telling them that his friend had been bitten by a snake. What is the best way to apply first-aid and what should he do? He was told by the people that the best way to treat this emergency, was to take a sharp knife and cut across where the fangs had penetrated and suck the poison out and then take his friend to a hospital. Without this first-aid his friend could possibly die. He went back to his friend on the other side of the lake. His friend asked, 'What did they tell you? What can you do for me'? His friend responded, 'You are going to die!'

The above joke alerted the therapist to a problem that the patient had not mentioned when he came into therapy. He was not consciously aware of homosexual conflict. It was much later in therapy that this young man became aware of, and reported that he found himself sexually attracted to the boys on the basket-ball team he coached. Because he had these feelings he thought he might become an active homosexual. His great fear was that he might not be able to control his behaviour and might seduce or rape a child in the school. Here the existence of a problem area was communicated through a joke while the patient was not yet consciously

aware of the cause of his anxiety. Another aspect of the joke revealed the feeling that he
would die of the poison within him. It also indicated that he could not depend on, or trust
the therapist once the therapist knew the nature of his problem. The therapist would let
him 'die' rather than help in the difficult situation he found himself. During therapy
sessions the patient would block, say things he thought the therapist would like to hear.
Talking about his fears or inner feelings was very difficult. It was only after he felt
confident that he would not be rejected and developed some self-esteem, that he was able to
trust the therapist and bring to awareness what was so anxiety-provoking. It must be noted
that because of the patient's poor ego-organization, the therapist, although he knew from
the joke of the patient's homosexual problems, did not bring up the topic but waited until
the patient brought up his homosexual thoughts. Instead we worked on his difficulty in
dealing with closeness and poor self-concept.

Another joke that alerted the therapist to a specific problem area and the prognosis for the
patient in treatment, is the following, told by a paranoid twenty-three-year-old male patient
who had delusions of persecution and of being followed by the F.B.I. This man comes to a
doctor, complaining that his voice was too deep and his penis too long. He tells the doctor
that his wife complains of the way he sounds and that he would like to be able to speak in a
softer and higher-pitched voice. The doctor examines him and tells him that he can help him
by cutting off several inches from his penis. The man agreed and the operation is a success.
Soon after the operation he returns to the surgeon, and speaking in a well-modulated voice
tells him that although his voice is everything he wanted it to be, still his wife was not
happy. She would like him to have his long penis again. The doctor replies, in a very deep
voice, 'that would be a very difficult operation'. This patient was very difficult to motivate
to become involved in therapy. His constant fear was that, in curing him, the doctor would
take something away from him. This individual left therapy after a short period of time with
the feeling that he would rather keep his problem than change.

The therapist is very much like the jester but he must always keep in mind not to use the
joke as a harmful or aggressive instrument. Comments about jokes or punchlines, like all
interpretations, have to be very carefully timed so that they are made at the most opportune
moment in treatment. It is essential that the therapist should not misuse the joke as a
hostile, aggressive weapon, or as a one-upmanship manoeuvre over the patient. Although the
joke or witticism is a release mechanism offering sudden and subtle release of repressed
energies, usually aggressive or sexual when used by the patient, in the hands of a therapist,
humour should be a mature means of communication which does not seek to overwhelm or threaten
the patient. Rather, it should make the patient aware of the understanding that the
therapist has for his feelings. Jokes are a light touch that may be valuable for approaching
a patient in a nonthreatening fashion when some of the more traditional means are not
adequate or appropriate.

It is essential to point out the limitations of the use of jokes. The joke is no more the
'magic pill' than any other therapeutic technique in our armamentarium. The favourite joke
is not always directly connected with a patient's problem: on many occasions it may merely
be a joke that was heard and repeated with success. The reward of laughter might be enough
to make this a joke that the patient might repeat on all occasions. The reward is what
makes the joke a favourite and not its personal meaning.

It may also be that some jokes that are reported as favourites are more a function of social
learning and may reflect problems of cultural groups, not specifically those of the individual
who repeats them. This does not, however, preclude the possibility that the social problem
is not a troublesome one of the patient. In addition, some people's problems may be so
complex that many kinds of jokes reflect some aspect of their personality.

The Place of Humour in Adult Psychotherapy

Barbara Killinger

York University, Ontario

The ability to find humour in almost any situation has 'therapist survival value', especially when one is involved in intensive therapy with disturbed patients. One's sense of humour often serves to keep problems in perspective, or provides a different focus during some of the discouraging or depressing low points. The form of humour most typically used in the therapeutic setting is not the prepared joke, but instead the spontaneous creation of a situation-specific amusing event. To clarify, a personal example from my own experience describes a patient in hospital for her third suicide attempt, having lost all will to live. The first ray of hope appeared when she began to use her own humour in response to mine. At first it was very sarcastic and self-depreciating, but gradually she developed a twinkle in her eyes, and as she regained her will to live, her use of humour became more positive; she began to laugh at herself, see humour in the ward situation, and tease me. One particular day stands out in memory. The Gestalt chair technique was being used to try to get her to confront her voices and hallucinations, and talk to them. In a very scarey moment, she suddenly shot her chair back against the wall, and started to withdraw visibly. In response to my challenge that she was giving up, she sat forward and shouted 'No, I won't. I won't', and came back to reality. She expressed her feelings of closeness, and began to talk about her voices and hallucinations openly, describing them vividly for the first time. The subject of peanut butter sandwiches had come up at the beginning of the interview, and I reintroduced the subject and presented to her the imagery of her voices struggling vainly to talk to her through a mouth full of peanut butter. This broke us up completely, and the office resounded with laughter. She told me later that that image saved her many times from avoiding the voices; she became less fearful of them, and gradually they ceased to be a problem for her.

A review of the literature on humour begun around this time revealed that although humour is widely acknowledged to be useful and facilitative to the therapeutic process, there is almost no empirical data specifically on how humour is used in psychotherapy. The few studies on humour and psychotherapy, although often imaginative and interesting, are largely anecdotal, lack methodological rigour, or fail to provide any theoretical base.

Two papers strongly influenced the decision to do a dissertation on the use of humour in psychotherapy. Kubie's (1971) paper warned that therapist humour can be potentially destructive to the therapeutic relationship and process, especially in the early stages of therapy. He further suggested that beginning therapists are not likely to use humour effectively, and that even experienced therapists should use humour with caution. The other paper was an unpublished dissertation by Kaneko (1971) who developed a research model for examining the role of humour in psychotherapy. This model later served in the development of the methodology of the present thesis.

This present study is an exploration of the use of verbal humour in the early and later phases of therapy. The frequency and category of humour used by the therapist is under investigation, as well as the intent and the immediate outcome of the humour. The study proposes to clarify whether the use of humour by the therapist is a facilitative skill, or one which serves destructive tendencies such as inhibiting or blocking therapeutic process.

Beginning and more experienced therapists from the Counselling Centres of York University, Toronto, and the University of Waterloo, Waterloo, received permission to tape-record the therapy interviews of two clients each of whom was willing to participate in this blind study during therapy. Based on a mean of six therapy sessions as the average number of interviews at the Centre, two early fifty-minute therapy sessions were chosen from the second, third or fourth interviews, and two later sessions from the sixth, seventh or eighth sessions, depending on the availability of tapes. A total of eleven therapists with twenty-two clients in four interviews each resulted in approximately eighty-five hours of tapes to be processed. Client problem areas were of the less severe, adjustment type faced by a college population, and therapist orientation was client-centered, behavioural, or eclectic in approach.

Humour was identified by incidents where laughter behaviour occurred, or a verbal report of amusement was made by either participant in direct response to a therapist remark, and humour took the form of one or more of the seven categories of humour adapted from Landis and Ross (1933): (1) Exaggeration or Simplification; (2) Incongruity; (3) Unexpectedness or Surprise; (4) Revelation or Truth; (5) Superiority or Ridicule; (6) Repression or Release; and (7) Word Play.

A second category of non-laughter humour was devised by the author because the above behavioural definition, modelled after Kaneko's study, excluded many very clever, unusual, amusing and humorous incidents where no laughter accompanied such statements. Non-laughter humour was identified as occurring when one or more of the seven categories of humour was used by the therapist in the form of a figure of speech or some clever phrasing of words which was judged as humorous by the criteria of originality, emphasis or economy suggested by Koestler's (1974) judgment of whether humour is good, bad or indifferent: (1) The therapist's statement provides the essential element of surprise which cuts across our expectations by its use of originality, uniqueness or cleverness; or (2) It has tension-accumulating effects through various techniques of suggestive emphasis, such as exaggeration, simplification, repetition, or an implosive piling-on; or (3) It has implicit hints instead of explicit statements which call for extrapolation, interpolation and transposition, and allow one to play with the words or thoughts. This criterion served to assess the qualitative differences in therapist statements which are cleverly stated expressions of thought from those which also contain some form of humour expression as well. A qualitative rating scale of (1), (2) and (3) was used to assess the relative strength of the imagery to hold one's attention or thoughts and whether it was original in thought, strong in emphasis, or cleverly brief. Each level was specifically defined, and only those statements meeting the criteria of a (2) or (3) rating were retained as non-laughter humour. In addition, three nonhumorous therapist statements were chosen from each third of the fifty-minute interview as a baseline control measure.

The author edited out all names and identifiers from the eighty-five tapes collected, coded each tape, and established a random listening order. Three sets of judges were used in the processing of these tapes. The first set identified and framed the humour incidents as well as control segments, and the second and third set of judges, both blind to the exact nature of the study, judged the framed incidents on the therapist's intent and the immediate outcome of the therapist's statement respectively.

The first set of raters consisted of two raters who listened independently to half of the tapes, and a third rater who listened independently to all of the tapes. These raters were trained to recognize reliably when a humour incident occurred, record whether laughter or nonlaughter humour, record frequency as well as category of humour used, assign a rating to the nonlaughter humorous statements, and also frame each incident. Framing procedures for each humour incident included recording one therapist and client statement footage just prior to the therapist's humour or control statement, the therapist's statement itself, followed by the footage for three complete client-therapist-client statements. The usual frame therefore consisted of a Therapist-Client exchange, Therapist Statement, followed by a Client-Therapist-Client exchange. Extensions in framing were made only if the subject of the interaction before the therapist's statement was not clear from the initial therapist-client exchange. Incomplete statements did not count for framing purposes, and single word responses; simple agreement or disagreement; short clarification necessitated by a hearing or misunderstanding difficulty; or a short, incomplete thought or idea were not considered as statements. All identified frames were then coded, randomized and transcribed onto a master tape.

The therapist's intent in the use of humour was evaluated by the second set of two independent judges who rated each humour incident according to the direction of the communication (other-directed versus self-focused), therapist's manner of delivery (non-defensive versus defensive), and content (relevant versus irrelevant). Judgments were made on the therapist's humour or control statement and the preceeding therapist-client exchange. It was hypothsized that therapist humour more often than not would be other-directed, nondefensive, and relate in content to the topic of the interaction before the humour statement.

Of principal concern in determining whether humour is facilitative was the immediate outcome of the humour from the client's frame-of-reference. Judgments were made on the therapist's humour or control statement and the following client-therapist-client exchange. The third set of two independent judges using a seven-point scale evaluated the outcome of the interaction immediately after the humour incident or the control statement on the basis of the content of the client's statements, and the attitude of the client towards the therapist. It was hypothesized that therapist humour would result more often than not in further client exploration of the topic and a positive client attitude towards the therapist.

Interjudge reliability was established by a percentage agreement method (80%) for the first
and second set of raters. An interjudge discrepancy method was used for the third set of
outcome judges, with the number of agreements within one reaching 85%. The study also
examined any differences in facilitativeness of humour as used by experienced and inexperienced
therapists, as well as their humorous and randomly-selected nonhumorous interventions.

Since statistics and humour are somewhat incongruous bedfellows, I would like to forego the
incomplete data analysis, and instead conclude with a resumé of the 'hurdles' encountered in
implementing this research design:

(1)   The therapist's anxiety around asking client permission to use interview tapes
      was met by giving the therapists the choice of asking sometime during the second
      interview, or leaving it to the seventh or eighth interview when they were certain
      that a client would complete eight sessions and qualify for the study. The
      therapists' 'comfort level' was the focus here as it was felt that this was
      important in affecting the ease with which they made their requests.

(2)   The 'protective mother syndrome' is the phrase chosen to best describe the
      procrastination which took place when any inquiries were made as to when completed
      tapes would be handed in. Such resistance seemed somewhat puzzling coming from
      seemingly willing and co-operative therapists who had kindly agreed to participate.

(3)   Never again would this author promise to delete all names and identifiers from
      therapy interviews. This is a very arduous, difficult job technically and very
      time-consuming as some clients mention the names of numerous friends, their
      friend's friends, room-mates, or relatives. The use of raters from outside the
      setting, and only deleting the client's name are better solutions to this ethical
      issue.

(4)   The overwhelming task of listening to seemingly endless hours of interviews by the
      first set of judges trained to identify the use of humour was complicated by the
      difficulty of suspending their own frames-of-reference as to what was amusing or
      clever in favour of the study's strict criteria. These raters also were cautioned
      against 'tripping', a term coined by this author to describe a process of second-
      guessing what the therapist had in mind or what the client was probably thinking,
      instead of judging strictly from the verbal content.

(5)   The decisions of the second set of 'intent' judges were fairly clear-cut, except
      for the quality of delivery category where they had to decide whether the therapist
      was being nondefensive or defensive. Here the voice quality, along with the verbal
      content, was the key factor in deciding for example whether the therapist was
      teasing, joking, or being sarcastic or ridiculing. However, since the judges knew
      only that the study somehow related to humour, these terms could not be used
      specifically to describe negative or positive aspects of the therapist's intent.
      Instead terms such as 'gentle, light, easy-going, soft' as opposed to 'pointed,
      harsh, abrupt, sharp' were used to describe voice quality accompanying verbalizations.

(6)   The third set of 'immediate outcome' judges had a far more difficult task in that
      content and attitude each were measured on seven-point scales, with gradations
      from −3 to +3 specifically defined. For example, on the negative side of the content
      scale (−3) indicated an obvious shift or an irrelevant topic, (−2) topic was of
      tangential relevance, (−1) slightly off-topic, while 0 was reserved for occasions
      when little was said by the client. On the positive side, (+1) indicated a simple
      affirmation, confirmation, disagreement or question, (+2) topic remained the same
      but more open and detailed, and (+3) therapist's statement definitely contributed
      to further client exploration. Scoring was determined from a client-therapist-
      client exchange, always from the client's frame-of-reference.

Because using humour is often a risk-taking venture, what happened at times was that the
therapist would make a point with humour and then if he felt he had gone too far, would
come in with a 'recovery' statement based on the client's immediate response. A decision was
therefore made that when judging whether the topic of the interaction remained the same or
changed after the therapist's statement, the first client statement only would be used to
decide whether the rating would fall on the negative or positive side of the scale. However,
the exact score on the content scale would be determined by weighting the first client
statement double compared to the second statement. A ruling was also made that for content,
if the second therapist statement introduced a new topic for discussion and the second client
statement was a direct response to that, only the first client statement would be considered.
Similar attitude scales and weighting procedures were used in assessing overall client

attitude towards the therapist. This example perhaps gives some indication of the decision-making processes necessitated by the complexities involved in process-type research where therapist-client interaction is under evaluation.

Although the rating procedures are complete, the statistical analysis has not been done. From a preliminary assessment of the data, however, it would appear that therapists do indeed use humour which is most often other-directed, nondefensive and related in topic to the ongoing interaction. An assessment of the outcome measures further reveals that the use of humour seems in most instances to stimulate positive client discussion of the topic, and positive client feelings towards the therapist predominate.

<u>REFERENCES</u>

See Bibliography for publications on humour, laughter and comedy

Kaneko, S., The role of humor in psychotherapy. Unpublished Manuscript, Smith College
    School for Social Work (1971).

Humour, Irony and Self-Detachment

David Cohen

Bedford College, University of London

The psychology of irony is not one of the most developed areas of psychology. There are, to begin with, problems of definition such as where one draws the line between irony and sarcasm; and it may be that there is much less of a distinction in psychological than in literary terms. The purpose of this paper is not to present results but rather to suggest that irony deserves some psychological attention.

In his book on jokes, Freud (1960) suggested that jokes allowed us to express thoughts and feelings that would otherwise be censored. In a joke, such taboo thoughts could slip through into consciousness. Freud was concerned with aggressive, sarcastic jokes as well as smutty ones as is clear from examples he quotes of a certain Herr N who said of one acquaintance: 'Yes, vanity is one of his four Achilles' heels'. And of another: 'I drove with him tête à bête'. Freud argued that Herr N would never have allowed himself to express the naked, hostile thoughts behind these jokes but that, spiced with humour, they could become conscious and, also, socially acceptable.

Bergson (1911), another early student of laughter, saw laughter as being nearly all 'laughing at;' a theory that leaves much scope for irony. Bergson believed that society encourages us to laugh at those whose behaviour is strange, threatening or unacceptable. Since it is unpleasant to be laughed at, laughter could be used as a tool for modelling behaviour. And irony is an especially skilful way of doing that. If a person is foolish or open enough to reveal that his real ambition is to write a prize winning novel or become Prime Minister, he lays himself open to much ironic laughter. Irony can help perhaps bring one back to reality.

These brief remarks suggest certain questions that may be useful. Is making aggression acceptable one of the main functions of irony and sarcasm? What sorts of situation provoke irony? Are there people who rely either on irony or on sarcasm as a style of behaviour? And, if so, what kinds of people are they? What constructive use can one make of less cutting ironies in, for example, trying to alter someone's behaviour. Moreover, the study of irony raises the questions of when and how children learn to use this skill. Young children do not like to be laughed at and seem capable of fearing irony and sarcasm. How does this fear develop?

Usually it is as little fun for adults as for children to be laughed at and, also, usually, it is fun to make other people laugh. But there is a third sort of situation which is to make other people laugh at oneself. I crack an excellent joke at my own expense. To be able to see oneself with a little irony is generally considered to be an excellent quality.

Few psychologists have seen anything of primary importance in the ability to see oneself with irony, but Frankl (1946) has long championed the ability to laugh at oneself as a major human attribute. Frankl developed a therapeutic technique called paradoxical intention which relied on — and, indeed, developed — this ability to see oneself with irony. The basics of the technique can be simply enough illustrated from one case. Frankl had a patient once, a young doctor who trembled each time a superior walked into the operating theatre. Frankl instructed him that the next time this happened he was to do his best to tremble as much and as loudly as possible so that he could show what a good trembler he was. Frankl claims that by exaggerating the phobia one cures it for 'the wind is taken out of the sails of the phobia' and he approvingly quotes Allport (1950) who wrote that 'the neurotic who learns to laugh at himself may be on the way to self-management, perhaps to cure.' That may mean, of course, that only certain neurotics learn to laugh at themselves. Frankl claims that paradoxical intention works because it uses the specifically human capacity for self-detachment inherent in a sense of humour. And this ability is for Frankl 'among the basic human capacities.'

157

Laughing at oneself may not always be a sign of psychic health: it may be a strategy that allows one to avoid confronting certain problems. But, leaving that aside, self-irony would seem to be a form of humour that is psychologically rich and that would repay study. How do we learn to make such self-detached jokes? Does everyone master this skill? What kinds of cognitive stages do children have to go through before they can develop such self-detached humour? These are all interesting questions.

REFERENCES

See Bibliography for publications on humour, laughter and comedy

Allport, G.W., The Individual and His Religion. Macmillan, New York (1950).

Frankl, V.E., The Doctor and The Soul. Souvenir Press (1969).

The Use and Abuse of Humour in the World of the Family: Current Trends in America

Melanie Allen

California State University

This paper explored the use of humour in the family as both a constructive coping mechanism and a device for damage to the operation of the family system. Particular emphasis was given to the current zeitgeist in America and the adaptation of humour to family style and structure in the seventies. Observations were based on the author's personal experience, on clinical and research data, and on family humour as currently presented in the mass media. A clear delineation was made between the self-actualizing or self-transcendant qualities of humour as opposed to strategies involving the use of humour as a put-down to one's self or other family members. The significance of the mass media, in particular, television, as a modelling agent of attitude toward the family was explored. The data presented were placed in a framework of contemporary personality and humour theory.

Humour in Psychotherapy

Harold Greenwald

United States International University, San Diego, California

One of my great pleasures is observing the absurdity of this world. There are very few things
as absurd, in my opinion, as this Conference. We sit around and grimly talk about humour.
So, if you don't mind, I'm really a very profound person but for the benefit of illustrating
what I have to talk about I'm going to try to do it as humorously as I can. I'm very
concerned about psychologists becoming interested in humour. It is almost as bad as the fact
that the Church has become interested in sex. They will begin to take the pleasure out of
that. I'm reminded of a story. I don't like telling stories ordinarily, and I know this
will be completely revealing about my personal problems, as our distinguished colleague just
reminded us, but the story is about the man who had a lot of trouble with his memory and so
he went to a psychologist who specialized in helping people remember things and he taught
him association: how you associate something already well-known with something not so well-
known. Well, it worked quite well and then one day, proud of his new-found ability, the young
man was walking in London, in Trafalgar Square when he spotted a familiar face. He walked
up to the man and said, 'I know you. I met you in Cardiff in 1971. At that time you were
wearing a blue suit, a yellow shirt, and a green tie.' (He was a quietly dressed man). 'And
you were with a young lady in a gold lamé sun suit.' He continued, 'I know you very well,
don't tell me, your name is Fred Tompkins.' The fellow stared at him in amazement and said,
'What's the matter with you? Are you crazy? I'm your brother Jake.'

I personally had a lot of difficulty with this whole problem of humour but would like to
discuss humour and reality. I don't think humour is distinct from reality. I think there
is nothing as funny as reality if we look at it properly. You know the women's liberation
movement is very strong in the United States and one of my daughter-in-law's friends, a very
strong liberationist, decided that instead of buying her daughter dolls and house things, as
they usually buy for young girls, she bought her a football. The little girl was delighted
with the football, put it in the carriage, covered it with a blanket and fed it a bottle.

Now, how do I use humour? I'm in the process of revising all the notions I've been proceeding
on as far as psychotherapy is concerned as a result of a study I have been carrying on for the
last five years. I've been doing something which is even less respectable than my previous
study on prostitution (Greenwald, 1958), and that is I am studying happy people. Now we know
that psychologists are not concerned about happy people; that's boring, so I'm told. But I
found something fascinating. You know, the happy ones experienced as many traumas,
difficulties, and problems as the most neurotic, psychotic patients. But they're happy! Now,
you could say they're crazy; if so, that's some of the divine madness I hope we can all
share. So my goal now in therapy is not necessarily to wipe out the traumas of the past but
to see how we can use them for our own enhancement, for our enjoyment, for our pleasure. A
bone is never as strong as where it was broken and healed, and many of the differences between
the unhappy, neurotic persons and the happy ones is how they choose to deal with their
problems. Therefore my entire approach to therapy described in an excellent book, called
Direct Decision Therapy (Greenwald, 1973), of which I happen to be the author, is to deal
with these very decisions, the choices we make. (I'm doing an in-depth study, not a
statistical study, because statistical studies tell us less and less about fewer and fewer
things). As one of the happy people I interviewed said, when I asked her how she managed to
be happy: 'Well, at a certain point in my life, I decided I could laugh or I could cry. I
chose to laugh.'

So what I try to do is help but not force the people I work with; they can cry if they want
to. It's their choice; but if they want to laugh at some of their problems, we try to help
them see that if you're stuck with a lemon, it's a good idea to make lemonade. How does one
do that? One of the things that I try to do in my whole attitude, my whole approach, is to
lessen the gap between myself and the patient. Psychotherapy is a very dangerous art,
particularly for the therapist because most therapists do develop a kind of megalomania in

which they think that they know so much more than the person that they are working with rather
than recognizing that the person they are working with is the best possible consultant they can
have. He is the one that can help us much more than anything else that we can do. Therefore
in working with them I try to lessen that gap and I am fortunate in that I can tell a lot of
jokes about myself. For example, I should add that before I embarked on this, I tried a
whole variety of approaches, including encounter groups. That's where psychopaths teach
obsessive compulsives to behave like schizophrenics. Because of my humorous approach I had
a great deal of difficulty getting through the psychoanalytic institute that I attended. In
those days I believed in psychoanalysis; I still do and I think that it was the therapy of
choice for people born in Vienna in the year 1880. Since then I'm not so sure. But when I
was going through the psychoanalytic institute they told me that I had serious problems of
oral sadism, because of my humour, and I had never bitten anybody at that time. You know about
the various psychosexual stages of development. If you don't, I can best illustrate it by
something one of my students wrote while I was teaching at Pratt Institute in Brooklyn, New
York. When I asked him what he had got most out of the course in psychology I had given, he
said it was the theory of psychosexual development. 'First is the oral stage, when the child
is interested in the products that go into his mouth, and then there's the anal stage when
he's interested in the waste products, and then comes the phallic stage when he's interested
in the gentile area.' The funny thing is, he wasn't Jewish, he was a genital.

One of the major problems I find, is that so many of our patients are still busy complaining
about their mothers. They have very little cause to do so compared with my mother. Freud
in one of his papers about humour speaks about how the humorous person is able to take the
most drastic circumstances and turn it into something funny, and therefore into a victory.
My mother is able to take the most magnificent victory and turn it into total disaster, and
she is entitled to ethnically. Let me give you some examples. It was very cold in the
winters in New York and she was getting older, and so we used to send her to Florida. She
greeted each suggestion of going off to Florida like, 'They're sending me off to Florida for
the whole winter,' as if she were being banished. Or the time on her 80th birthday when her
three sons got together and bought her a mink coat, and as she opened the box, for a moment
she forgot herself and a happy smile spread over her face but she made a quick recovery. She
said, 'A mink coat they buy me, and I haven't got what to wear to the supermarket.'

So I'm happy to share with the people I work with some of the stories about my mother,
including that my mother is improving. Only recently she called up and I was talking to her
on the phone and my wife was on the extension, and I was speaking very loudly because my
mother doesn't hear very well, or doesn't pay too much attention, and my wife said, 'Why are
you yelling at your mother?' I figured in any conflict between my wife and myself I must win,
because as far as my mother's concerned, and this is after thirty-nine years of marriage, my
wife is still 'she'. My mother says, 'Does she have anything for dinner for you?' I look
as if I'm starving but it doesn't matter. So I asked my mother, 'Ma, am I yelling at you?'
She used it magnificently. She answered, 'When do I ever see you, you should yell at me?'
So I'm happy to share some of these things, and when my mother had her 90th birthday
recently, she was always known as poor sick Lilly in our family, and that just happened a
few months ago. She was able to drink her three sons under the table and go dancing on
until two o'clock in the morning. So there may be some very important protective device
in this ability. In fact, only recently she demonstrated it wonderfully. She said, 'I went
to the cemetery to see Pappa'. My father is dead, and I thought this was going to be another
hearts and flowers tale. She said to him, 'Pappa, I'm coming, pappa, I'm coming, but I'm
not in a hurry'.

So you see one of the major functions of humour, why I think that it's a distinct human
ability, is that all of us as human beings suffer from the knowledge that we are about to
die and humour is one of the few aspects, one of the few ways of dealing with that knowledge.
That's why there are so many jokes about death.

Another important advantage in the use of humour in psychotherapy is reflecting. The kind
of reflection that I have found the client-centred or non-directive therapists do is rather
boring; you know, where they play the echo thing. The patient says something, the therapist
repeats it, or client as they say. So that's a little difficult. I find it more fun to act
out reflection. A patient I used to have was like me. Whenever anything fantastic
and wonderful happened in her life she would come in deeply depressed. She had been
complaining all session, for session after session, about a course she was taking — she was
a teacher. It was very necessary that she passed that course or she would be fired. She
kept saying 'I am going to fail.' Finally at the last moment she called me up and said,
'You know what he did? He gave me an A+.' That's the best possible grade one could receive,
and so when she came the next day I was prepared. She came in her depressed costume. She
had a special costume, all in black you know, and no make-up and I was sitting in the corner
and when she walked in I sighed deeply, and she started to talk, and I sighed some more.
And she said, 'Life is terrible, life is awful' and I said, 'Yes, I know.' She continued
some more to complain and I sighed some more, and finally I said, 'Well, maybe I could help
you, but what's the use, you're only going to die.' This is something she had always said

to me. We continued that way, and I was beginning to enjoy it, because I rarely get depressed and I realized, you know, it's a lot of fun as I try to teach my depressed patients, 'If that's all you've got, enjoy it.' Suddenly she looked at me and said, 'You know, Dr. Greenwald, my last analyst whenever she didn't feel well, she would cancel the session.' I said, 'I suppose I could have. What difference would it make?' Suddenly she said, 'You son-of-a-bitch,' you see, suddenly she had a positive transference, she said, 'You son-of-a-bitch, you're acting the way I do. How do you put up with me?' From then on the session went on much better. Many therapists frequently believe that depression is anger turned inwards and try to get the person to release his anger so he becomes undepressed. I don't find that that's the only thing. I think the thing that works there is that anger and depression are incompatible emotions. But anger isn't the only emotion that's incompatible with depression. Laughter is also incompatible with depression and for me a helluva lot more fun, because since I believe in decisions, one of the decisions I made (Greenwald, 1973) a long time ago was that therapy should be fun for me because how else can I set an example for the people with whom I work. One of the most valuable things we can do is to model, to set an example for the people we work with. When I started, I could not do that, because at school, both at the analytic institute and the university where I took my doctorate, they gave us a lot of very elaborate theory about how you have to uncover the unconscious, and you have to follow the libido, you know where it gets stuck up there and you unstick it, and all that kind of stuff. But how the hell do you do it? You don't know how to speak to people. So where do you start learning from? Watching movies, and in the movie the therapist usually acts like the dedicated co-sufferer. So I would sit there and suffer with my patients, and every time I felt like telling a joke, because some of the things they said were just hilarious, and commenting on that I would strictly hold myself, because I didn't want to be an oral sadist. Eventually, I had one man who had been a wonderful analytically trained patient. He had gone to an orthodox analyst before he came to see me. He was a very proper gentleman, a broker on Wall Street (the 'city' in England) and he always wore his dark suit, white shirt, narrow tie, black shoes, well-shined. He would come in and he would carefully lie down on the couch and say, 'I had the following dreams: one, two, three. These are my associations, one, two, three. They relate to my present life, one, two, three'. But nothing happened and I didn't know how to break through this, until one day he was complaining about his wife and her inordinate sexual demands upon him. (You see, whenever I see an audience getting a little restless, I introduce sex, to get their interest back.) So he was telling me about his wife. One of the fascinating changes that has taken place in the twenty-five years that I have been doing therapy is that twenty-five years ago it was very customary for men to complain that their wives didn't want to have sex because they were too tired. Today it's the opposite. I constantly get women complaining that their husbands don't want to have sex or men complaining about their wives. As one said, 'I thought she was a bird, she turned out to be a vulture, always demanding.' Always complaining, you know, his wife was always complaining, and finally in desperation to break through the complete system he had, I said, 'You know, if you're having so much trouble with your wife, I've met your wife, she's very attractive, next time bring her in, I'll be glad to help you out.' It's the first time I ever saw anybody get off the couch horizontally. Levitation! He turned to me and in a furious voice said, 'Dr. Greenwald, someday you'll go too far.' After that we had a more human interchange and eventually he even came in a sports shirt which was for him a tremendous breakthrough.

One of my approaches and one of my decisions is to erase the difference between work and play, to make work play; and when I find that any work I'm doing is not play, I'm going to quit it and do something else. I don't know though, what made me decide to come 5,000 miles to swelter in this heat? I guess I'm not perfect yet. One of the things I try to help people do, is to see the absurdity in so much that goes on in the nature of work. Take in our own field, that's where you have to start. One of the misfortunes of becoming fairly well-known as a therapist is that most of the people that come to you are other therapists. It's like taking in each other's laundry. Frequently my patients have serious problems with their supervisors who tell them all kinds of impossible things, so I've given them a few simple rules for survival in that situation. 'When a supervisor tells you something ridiculous, don't argue. You've got to lose.' Instead, I suggest they say something like, 'I never would have thought of that.' Because they never would have. Or 'wow, that's really something,' like when you look at an ugly baby, what do you say? You can't say 'that's an ugly baby', you say, as I said recently when I saw my friend's ugly baby (she had her mother's old nose before she had the operation) I looked at that baby and I said, 'That's a baby!'

About three years ago I had the opportunity of working with a top executive in one of our multi-national corporations and he was telling me about how driven he was and how hard his work was and I asked him to describe his boss' office. He said that it was filled with all kinds of charts. I asked, 'What do those charts mean?' He said, 'I don't know, they look important.' I said, 'Don't you see what the hell he's doing? He's playing 'big business.' These guys aren't serious, they're playing the same games they did as little children, just play it, you don't have to be serious about it. If you know how to play it.' We saw some very good examples of people playing the professor game, right here. You know, with their

footnotes and the serious things. They did it very well, very impressive. I wish I could
do it sometime.

One important warning is that I did discover that I cannot use humour with some patients I
don't really like, because then it can become destructive. Then it turns from irony, then
it turns from understanding, to a remembrance of the old days as a child when humour was
used to attack the child, as it so frequently was used. For so many children that is more
traumatic than being beaten. So, I can't use humour unless I like the person concerned, and
because I like my friend Saul Grossman so much I thought I would help him out a little bit
with his continuing self-therapy. He said that the favourite jokes tell you something about
the person's personality and his problem. He then told us three jokes. One was about a
dog whose tail was cut, the other was a fellow who was bitten on the penis, the third was
about a fellow whose penis was too long. Now let me explain. This is cultural, because in
his religion you get an operation when you're eight days old which causes you problems for
the rest of your life. They don't know, you might want to blow the religion. May be 'blow'
is bad terminology in this context. One of the hallmarks (talking about irony) of the
highly intelligent person, and I've met them all over the world, I've found myself in
immediate communication, immediately feeling quite at home, this is my kind of person and
usually they are people capable of great irony. When I was in Spain, I met some of the
professors and they made remarks about Franco and the pig and things like that. I knew that
I was amongst friends and it was done with humour, with wit, with irony. In fact, the
leaders of our profession, the ones that I have heard and read have all had this fantastic
ability for humour. Freud, his collection of jokes and wit and humour is so good that I
recently recommended it to one of my patients who is a comedian. He came back and said,
'You know that Freud, he tells some good stories, but he don't know how to tell them right.'
Alfred Adler, who I had the opportunity to hear was extremely humorous. Skinner, coming
from a completely different orientation, if any of you ever heard Fred Skinner discuss the
pigeon bomb, it's a very funny story, or Frankl, who was mentioned here before, is very funny.
Albert Ellis, from a completely different point of view, is also very funny.

One other thing about humour, if more of our psychiatrists had a sense of humour, they
wouldn't have to use so many pills because there is nothing more tension-relieving, nothing
that helps more to relieve anxiety than humour, much more than many of these pills, without
doping the patients up. I think above all, as I've already indicated, my view of the world
is that it's absurd. In the Charlie Chaplin movie 'City Lights,' you see a picture; if you
looked at it from one angle it is deep and dark tragedy, but just by slightly moving it, by
looking at the absurdity of that situation, you are able to join in the relief of laughter.
If we can just do that - if we could help the people around us see that! Can you imagine
if Hitler was able to laugh at himself? There wouldn't have been a Hitler. We have a few
politicians who could use some of that in the United States; you know there's one fellow
bumps his head all the time and a few other clowns.

I once had the opportunity to speak on the application of psychotherapy to the problems of
the world. One of my suggestions was to look at some of the things going on in the world
and to realize there is an organization of men that dress up in fancy uniform and go around
training young, very young men, to pierce the bodies of other men. You know what that
organization is? They're the armed forces of the world and they're so busy trying to prove
themselves so masculine, so powerful, with this thing, not understanding the implications of
what they're doing. Humour is a fantastic weapon, let's treasure it and not overuse it.

REFERENCES

Greenwald, H., The Call Girl - A Social and Psychoanalytic Study. Ballantine Books, New York
     (1958).

Greenwald, H., Direct Decision Therapy. Edits, San Diego (1973).

CROSS-CULTURAL HUMOUR

Cross Cultural Research: Humour Here and There

Jeffrey H. Goldstein

Temple University, Philadelphia

The search for general principles of humour has occurred largely in the English-speaking world. In his 1954 review of humour and laughter, Flugel was able to discuss under the heading of 'national differences' only a handful of studies on the humour of non-English-speaking peoples – nearly all of them Westerners.

There is not only a tendency among behavioural researchers to generalize from the college student population to nonstudents, but perhaps more importantly, from Western culture to others. This ethnocentric bias is present in a good deal of research, but in the case of humour it may be particularly detrimental to theory development. Psychologists and sociologists display a tendency to assume that the topics of their inquiry are universalistic principles of behaviour; an assumption which is, in certain instances, tenable even though it may remain untested. There are any number of psychological experiments which, when repeated in countries other than their country of origin, are found to hold cross-nationally (e.g., Goldstein, Rosnow, Raday, Silverman & Gaskell, 1975; Mantell, 1971; Shaw, Briscoe & Garcia-Esteve, 1968; Sommer, 1968). On the other hand, there is perhaps an equal number of studies which have failed to replicate across cultures or countries (e.g., Kelley et al, 1970; McGinnies & Ward, 1974; Sanada & Norbeck, 1975). Of course, the vast majority of studies are never repeated and so it becomes impossible to know their delimiting national or cultural conditions.

One might best make the assumption of cultural universality when dealing with the most fundamental sorts of behaviour. Physiological processes, for example, are quite likely to be trans-cultural, as are basic perceptual-cognitive principles, and certain structural features of social interaction. As one deals with less biological and more social aspects of psychological functioning, however, the assumption of cultural universalism becomes less tenable. It is, of course, necessary to distinguish between process and content when dealing with cross-cultural generality. With respect to humour, one would be more likely to find trans-cultural differences when studying the particular content of humorous materials, than when examining the underlying cognitive or physiological processes involved in humour and laughter (see the paper by Shultz, this volume). As shall be shown, the few studies which have examined humour cross-culturally have rarely made any such distinction between form and substance.

For the sake of convenience, research on cultural and national differences in humour has been divided into three categories. The first deals with what may be considered true cross-cultural or cross-national comparisons. Here the researcher has built culture (or country) into the research design so that logical and statistical comparisons could be made across cultures. The second group of studies, called cross-national replications, consists of studies which have been replicated by a second party in a country other than that in which the original study was conducted. The third category, nonWestern intracultural research, consists of observational, correlational and, occasionally, experimental studies conducted primarily with non-English-speaking peoples. Most of the studies in this group are anthropological accounts of joking among African tribal communities, although occasional reference will be made to accounts of joking in other cultures.

TRUE CROSS-CULTURAL AND CROSS-NATIONAL COMPARISONS

While the studies reviewed under this heading will consist of cross-cultural comparisons of humour, I will also include studies conducted cross-nationally, though still within a single, usually Western, culture. To exclude cross-national studies would reduce this category to very few cases. Indeed, even with the inclusion of cross-national studies, and even counting secondary references to cross-cultural humour research available to the author, there are no more than a dozen efforts to compare the humour of different societies. Table 1 presents a summary of cross-cultural and cross-national humour research.

TABLE 1   Cross-Cultural and Cross-National Humour Studies

AUTHOR (DATE)	COUNTRIES OR CULTURES STUDIED	TYPE(S) OF HUMOUR STUDIED	DEPENDENT VARIABLE(S)
Brant (1972)	183 nonWestern societies	Cross-sex joking relationships	Joking relationships in different kinship systems
Castell & Goldstein (1976)	Belgium Hong Kong U.S.A.	Funniest joke; Situations evoking laughter	Content analysis of jokes & situations
Egnar (1932)	England France Germany U.S.A.	Cartoons, jokes from magazines	Content of humour
Eysenck (1944)	Canada England France Germany U.S.A.	Three studies. Jokes, cartoons	Rating scale. Guess nationality of jokes. Rankings
Goldstein, Silverman & Anderson (1976)	Japan Senegal U.S.A.	Jokes varying in hostility and familiarity	Rating scale
Handelman & Kapferer (1972)	Israel Zambia	Setting-specific & category-routinized joking	Nature, setting of joking
Heim (1936)	England France Germany U.S.A.	Thirty-two jokes from four countries	Rating scale
Kimmins (1928)	England U.S.A.	Children's jokes and stories	Content analysis of themes
La Fave, McCarthy & Haddad (1973)	Canada U.S.A.	Pro- & anti- U.S. and Canada jokes	Rating scale
Shultz (1976)	NonWestern cultures	Riddles in folk- lore	Structural analysis
Smith & Vinacke (1951)	Caucasian, Chinese and Japanese Hawaiians	Jokes from different subcultures; Jokes to be completed	Content analysis of themes; Rating scales

Perhaps the major conclusion one can draw from cross-cultural research on humour is that so very little of it has been done. Of the studies in Table 1 only five are true cross-cultural studies (Brant, 1972; Castell & Goldstein, this volume; Goldstein, Silverman & Anderson, 1976; Handelman & Kapferer, 1972; Shultz, this volume). The remainder consists largely of comparisons made within a single country of subjects of different national origin, or of comparisons between countries which share a common culture.

Rather than review each of the studies separately, let us begin by noting that the majority of them fail to find significant differences between national or cultural groups. There are, of course, occasional differences reported, such as the finding by Kimmins (1928) that young children in England tell more jokes about clergymen while American children tend to joke more about classroom incidents, or the finding by Castell and Goldstein that Belgian students tend to tell jokes about Dutchmen while Americans tell jokes about Poles. From a theoretical point of view, such differences tend to be relatively trivial. As Eysenck concludes in his 1944 paper: 'The various studies on the existence of national differences in "sense of humor" reported in this paper all serve to emphasize the point that the agreement found between different nationals is far more striking than are the differences. In fact, no indisputably national differences were discovered in the appreciation of humor, in judgments of the origin of humorous items, or in the analysis of humorous papers from diverse countries' (pp52-53).

This conclusion should come as no surprise. On what basis might one expect the humour of Englishmen, Americans, Canadians, Frenchmen and Germans to differ? There are at least two requirements for a prediction of cross-cultural or cross-national differences in humour: one is a theory in which particular differences in socialization, experience or world-view underlies the appreciation of humour, and the second is a recognition of the difference between process and content in humour.

No one to my knowledge has proposed any but a universal theory of humour dynamics. Those theories, for example, which explain humour on the basis of superiority or surprise assume that superiority or surprise underlie humour among all peoples. This is true even while acknowledging that the particular events which lead to surprise or a feeling of superiority may well differ from one group of people to another. Any such theory, by virtue of assuming universality of structure, function or dynamic, becomes less inviting for cross-cultural test. If all one can hope to do is replicate results in a number of cultures, it hardly seems worth the effort. On the other hand, as we learn more about the development of humour and laughter in children, as theories increasingly specify the cognitive, social and experiential determinants of humour, then cross-cultural tests become more meaningful and theoretically more important, for we are no longer dealing with mere replication, but with cultural differences which may well be crucial to a complete theory of the phenomenon.

There are occasions when cultural differences, not of dynamics, but of content might be predicted from theory. For example, La Fave, McCarthy and Haddad (1973) predicted that Americans would evaluate pro- and anti-American jokes differently than Canadians. The predicted differences in humour evaluations between Canadians and Americans were assumed to be due to what might be called surface variables (in this case, the subjects' positive and negative reference groups), while both groups presumably appreciated particular jokes for the same dynamic reasons. In this example, we have a theoretically-predicted national difference in content preferences, but not in the dynamic properties of humour, per se.

Much of my own research on humour over the past several years has been concerned with content differences in humour appreciation (e.g., Goldstein, 1970; Goldstein, Suls & Anthony, 1972; Goldstein, 1976). The hypothesis is that different content matter of jokes and cartoons is appreciated more or less depending upon the cognitive and experiential set of the respondent. This does not imply that the dynamics of humour – the humour process – differs from one person or group of people to the next. The underlying processes of humour are assumed to be constant across people and hence across cultures. The theory states that familiarity or salience is a process variable involved in the enjoyment of certain kinds of humorous material; that people enjoy, because they are able to cognitively integrate, jokes which deal with familiar or salient themes. This would lead to the prediction, for example, that jokes which deal with marital infidelity would be appreciated more by people in monogamous cultures than by those in cultures which practise polygamy.

In one cross-cultural study (Goldstein, Silverman & Anderson, 1976), college and high-school students in Japan, Senegal and the United States rated jokes (presented in the appropriate language) which varied in two ways. Some jokes dealt with familiar subject matter, while others dealt with unfamiliar themes; and secondly, some of the jokes were hostile in nature while others were nonhostile. We expected to find that, regardless of culture, those jokes with familiar themes would be perceived as more humorous than those with unfamiliar themes. Thus, familiarity was examined as a process variable assumed to operate transculturally. The implication of this is that a particular joke might be seen as funny in Japan (where its theme was familiar) but unfunny in the U.S. or West Africa (where its theme was unfamiliar). We also anticipated more favourable ratings for hostile jokes from American students than from the others, reasoning that aggression and violence are more prevalent, salient and familiar to Americans. Both these hypotheses were supported.

A question which can be raised about such research is whether or not it demonstrates a 'cross-cultural difference' in humour. The answer - like all good scientific answers - is yes and no. The data indicate that, for a particular joke, there were cultural differences. But for a particular kind of joke (that is, familiar versus unfamiliar; hostile versus nonhostile) there were no cultural differences. In other words, there were no cultural differences in process variables, but there were differences in content variables.

The same may be said of most other cross-cultural or cross-national studies. A question which must be kept in mind is whether content differences are at all capable of telling us anything about humour from a theoretical point of view. At the conclusion of their study of Caucasian, Chinese and Japanese Hawaiians, for example, Smith and Vinacke (1951) forthrightly acknowledge: 'We do not feel that it is possible at the present time to interpret meaningfully the results of this research'. Their difficulty lies primarily in the failure to distinguish between content and process variables.

If cross-cultural research is to become more meaningful than it has generally been, differences will have to be predicted from some theoretical base. Such was the case in an early study by Brant, originally conducted in 1942 and published some thirty years later. While not specifically concerned with the dynamics of humour per se, he was interested in the existence of joking as a social phenomenon. Brant hypothesized that joking relationships would be most likely to exist between people who might potentially be engaged in a sexual relationship. He divided 183 societies into four categories: sororate (potential sexual relationship between a man and his wife's sister), levirate (between a man and his brother's wife), maternal cross-cousin (a man and his mother's brother's daughter), and paternal cross-cousin (a man and his father's sister's daughter). He then examined the existence of joking relationships in each type of society. The findings indicate a moderately strong relationship between marital category and joking. This can be interpreted as indicating that joking relationships are most apt to occur in situations where stress is present in the relationship.

Anthropological studies on humour, such as that by Brant, generally focus on the social situations in which joking is likely to be present. While I have elsewhere discussed one such study at length (Goldstein, 1975), let me reiterate a summary of the research by Handelman and Kapferer (1972). This study is of interest to researchers for several reasons. First, it provides a general procedure for studying humour and joking in vivo. Second, it examines the circumstances under which joking is likely to arise. Third, it is concerned with the termination of joking activity once it is underway.

After a brief theoretical introduction, Handelman and Kapferer present a number of joking exchanges among Israeli and Zambian workers. The following interaction occurred in a small Israeli workshop:

1. Chai saunters past the workshop sink, stops at Yaacov's worktable and peers at Yaacov's work....
2. Yaacov continues to work...then he raises his head and utters to the room: 'Chai is fat.'
3. Chai quickly ripostes: 'I'm not fat, I'm pregnant.'
4. Rena, the shop supervisor, smiles and asks: 'Oh? When will the baby arrive?' Chai replies: 'In four months time.' Shimon...says loudly: 'Congratulations...' At this point all the participants are laughing.
5. Zahava now interjects quickly and loudly: 'Pregant? Fooey. He just drinks too much water.'
6. The interchange ends abruptly and Chai returns to his worktable. (p486).

Handelman and Kapferer's analysis of this brief joking sequence concerns the relationships between participants, changes in the relationships during and as a result of the interchange, and some attempt to determine the underlying structural dynamics involved. Their research raises a number of questions which should be of value to behavioural researchers. Foremost among them is the structuralist interpretation provided by Handelman and Kapferer, which suggests that there are rules or 'frames' which guide the joking interaction, and that these frames are transcultural.   This theme is elaborated upon in Handelman's 1976 paper, which foll·ws. In an extended version of this paper, two kinds of joking activity are distinguished. In one form, called setting-specific, joking arises out of the immediate setting and the individuals present, while in category-routinized joking, there is a culturally recognized licence to joke between particular categories of people. The example given above is setting-specific, while the kind of joking examined by Brant is category-routinized.

CROSS-NATIONAL REPLICATIONS

Under this heading will be included studies which were replicated in a country other than that in which an initial study was conducted. If we restrict this category to psychological research on humour and laughter, the category reduces to one member of which I am aware[1], and that is the study initially conducted by Nerhardt (1970), which was replicated by Deckers and Kizer (1974, 1975). Nerhardt conducted his research with Swedish students at the University of Uppsala. He adapted a familiar psychophysical task to the study of laughter by varying the last weight in a graded series of lifted weights and recording the amount of smiling and laughter elicited by weights of varying discrepancy from the series. He reports that laughter increased as the last weight varied from the subjects' expectations. This study was replicated in the United States by Deckers and Kizer. They too found that students laughed and smiled most when lifted weights were most discrepant from a previous series of weights.

If we consider as cross-national replications studies conducted in the United States and then in Canada (or vice versa), this category increases in size. But such a refinement in the category seems unwarranted. Not only are the two cultures remarkably similar but a good deal of 'contamination' exists by virtue of the large number of American students enrolled at Canadian universities and the large number of Canadians attending American universities. Thus, for example, tests of Berlyne's model of humour (1960, 1972) conducted in Canada and the U.S. (Godkewitsch, 1972; Goldstein, Harman, McGhee & Karasik, 1975; Schwartz, 1972) hardly qualify as cross-national replications.

If we were to include anecdotal observations on the humour of different peoples in this category, its size would expand considerably. There are literally scores of informal accounts of the humorous preferences of various peoples, such as Macrae's 'National humour: Scottish, English, Irish, Welsh, Cockney, American'; Daninos' 'Le tour du monde du rire' (1952), and Bergson's informal remarks on humour in different countries (1911). But such observations can be misleading. Of course the methodology of such research is open to question; most often it is unknown. One should also bear in mind the fact that there is humour produced within any country for mass consumption and humour produced for an intellectual elite. As Feinberg (1971) writes:

> ...the cultural proletariat of one country often has more in common with the cultural
> proletariat of another country than it does with its own intelligentsia. The
> bourgeoisie shares the same tastes, regardless of national borders. In satire and
> humor this taste reveals a clear preference for the obvious and physical, and a
> distaste for the subtle and the intellectual. American comic strips are popular
> all over Asia, but Thurber and E.B. White are read only by a few aesthetes scattered
> throughout the Orient. Critics may say that they are discussing a nation's humor,
> but it almost always proves to be only one selected part of that humor that they are
> discussing. At its lowest level - slapstick, physical deformity or mental
> deficiency, embarrassment - humor seems to be pretty much the same in all cultures.
> (p4)

While Feinberg may somewhat overstate the case, it is well to ask how representative is the humour of any country which is utilized for the purposes of national comparison. Until a country's 'humour population' can be identified, it is risky to compare the humour of one country with that of another in the hopes of drawing conclusions either about humour or about nations. On the other hand, the replication of psychological research cross-nationally is often a judicious procedure and in the case of humour and laughter research may be beneficial, not only in strengthening one's confidence in the generality of a finding (as the Deckers and Kizer studies do), but in refining theory as well. Research on children's humour in particular may profit from cross-cultural replication, if sufficiently conceptualized (see McGhee, 1972a).

INTRACULTURAL RESEARCH

Of all the varieties of cross-cultural and cross-national research on humour and related topics, the preponderance of studies are intracultural researches in nonWestern societies. We may consider them in a paper on cross-cultural aspects of humour because often the researcher implicitly compares such humour with his or her own, usually Western, culture and the consumers of such research are generally Westerners who implicitly make such cultural comparisons.

The vast majority of humour studies on nonWestern peoples was conducted by anthropologists and folklorists beginning with Radcliffe-Brown's observations on joking relationships in the nineteen-forties (1940, 1949). To this day anthropologists concern themselves with joking relationships, though their interest in humour has broadened considerably within the last ten years. Many of the recent anthropological studies of various facets of humour are able to provide suggestive hypotheses about the social dynamics of humour and even about the psychological processes involved in humour and laughter. While it is not my intention to provide an exhaustive review of this literature, a representative sampling of studies is presented in Table 2.

Structuralism has been with anthropology considerably longer than it has psychology, and as a result there are several studies on structural aspects of riddles and joking (e.g., Haring, 1974; Harries, 1971; Sein & Dundes, 1964). (See also Handelman & Kapferer, 1972; Handelman, this volume; Shultz, this volume). Of particular interest to psychologists are the papers in this symposium by Handelman and by Shultz, and a paper by Ellie Kongas Maranda (1971). Maranda discusses riddles in African societies, their social functions and their structural characteristics. She notes that 'The primary function of riddles is to question at least certain kinds of established order....Riddles make a point of playing with conceptual borderlines and crossing them for the intellectual pleasure of showing that things are not quite as they appear' (p53). She also notes that riddles, like other folk arts, are handed down from one generation to another but that they are not repeated word for word. From this she infers that the speaker employs, à la Chomsky, certain transformational rules which enable him to pose riddles which are structurally similar to those previously heard, but unique in their own wording. She specifies the types of transformation which can be

found in riddles (such as 'specification,' 'generalization,' 'inversion,' and 'reversal';
See Maranda, (p55) and means by which such linguistic data may be computer-analyzed.

TABLE 2   Selected Intracultural Studies

AUTHOR (DATE)	COUNTRY OR CULTURE	HUMOUR STUDIED	FOCUS OF STUDY
Basgoz (1965)	Turkey	Riddles	Functions
Benavent-Oltra (1969)	Spain	Humour tests	Children's reactions
Blyth (1959)	Japan	Jokes, poems, drama, novels	Anecdotal; History
Chapman et al (1977)	Wales	Anti-Welsh or -English jokes	Disposition theory
Easton (1970)	American Indian	Stories	Anecdotal
Feinberg (1971)	Ceylon, China, India, Japan	Jokes, poems, drama, novels	Anecdotal; History
Handelman (1976)	Ik of Uganda	Joking	Meta-communication
Hansen (1976)	U.S.A.	Exaggeration in literature	Types of exaggeration
Haring (1974)	Africa	Riddles	Definition; Functions
Harries (1971)	Africa	Riddles	Definition; Structure
Hes & Levine (1962)	Israel	Oral humour	Conflict
Hyers (1973)	Asia	Humour in Zen	Humour as world-view
Jones & Liverpool (1976)	Trinidad	Calypso humour	Social functions
Kleivan (1975)	Greenland	Jokes about Greenlanders and Danes	Social functions
Kreitler & Kreitler (1970)	Israel	Cartoons	Cognitive strategies in humour perception
Levine (1961)	American Indian	Ritual clowning	Psychic functions
Maranda (1971)	Africa, Finland	Riddles	Structural analysis
Obrdlik (1942)	Czechoslovakia	Jokes	Functions of during Nazi occupation
Oring (1967)	Israel	'Chizbat humour'	Paradoxical jokes; Functions
Schneider (1967)	Africa	Folk tales	Functions; Relation to values
Sein & Dundes (1962)	Burma	Riddles	Functions
Weller et al (1976)	Israel	Jokes	Social functions
Zug (1967)	Asia	Zen Koan	Functions

Many of the ideas proposed by Maranda and other field researchers (e.g., Hyers, 1973; Levine, 1961) are difficult to test experimentally. But they are worth the attention of psychologists. Certainly a complete theory of humour will require the kind of precise definitions which anthropologists have attempted to provide for riddles and joking relationships; a specification of the conditions and situations under which joking will arise, and under which it will be terminated; and a clear distinction between trans-cultural processes and culture-bound surface manifestations of humour.

THE PRESENT CONTRIBUTIONS

The papers in this symposium represent an interesting and diverse group. There are contributions by those in anthropology, English literature, developmental and social psychology. As wide a range of methods and approaches is taken.

Don Handelman presented us with a fascinating interpretation of the functions of joking among the Ik, the 'mountain people' of Northern Uganda. Employing information provided in ethnological accounts of the Ik, most notably by Colin Turnbull, Handelman, after first presenting a meta-communication theory of play and ritual, discussed in his extended paper the functions which humour serves for these people whose way of life was so abruptly disrupted. Psychologists will be familiar with the meta-communications of which Handelman speaks from their knowledge of Bateson et al's theory of schizophrenia (1956) and from Fry's book, 'Sweet madness' (1963). Handelman expands upon the notion of meta-communication by exploring its implications for social systems in ritual and play.

Two reports in these proceedings represent different methodological approaches to the cross-cultural study of humour. Thomas Shultz continues his studies of the structural-linguistic bases of humour (see Shultz & Horibe, 1974) by examining lexical and phonological characteristics of humour in nonWestern cultures. Castell and Goldstein explore cultural differences in social situations which give rise to joking. In both cases, culture may be viewed as an independent variable. And, as in so much social anthropological research, there is found to be as much heterogeneity within, as between cultures. Shultz raises an important issue when he notes that the extent of cultural variation in humour depends very much on the level of analysis undertaken.

Examining the humour of a particular culture, but at different times in history, Arlen Hansen discusses the American tradition of exaggeration, as exemplified most particularly in the humour of the South and SouthWest following the Civil War, but still present in much contemporary literature. Hansen distinguishes two types of exaggeration: epitomization and transformation, differentiated by their use of language and by their ultimate ends.

FOOTNOTE

[1] I am aware of one unpublished replication of Goldstein (1970) conducted in Canada, but for reasons specified in the following paragraph have chosen not to discuss it in this paper.

REFERENCES

See Bibliography for publications on humour, laughter and comedy

Bateson, G., Jackson, D., Haley, J. & Weakland, J., Toward a theory of schizophrenia. Behavioral Science, 1, 251-264 (1956).

Benavent Oltra, J.A., Estudios sobre la risa y la hilaridad en la infancia y la juventud. Psicometria e Investigacion Psicologica, 16, 208-235 (Madrid) (1970).

Daninos, P., Le Tour du Monde du Rire. Hachette, Paris (1952).

Egnar, F., Humor und Witz unter strukturpsychologischem Standpunkt. Cited in Flugel (1954).

Goldstein, J.H., Recent trends in the psychological study of humor and laughter. Paper presented at American Psychological Association symposium, 'Wit and humor: Its proper place in psychology.' Chicago, September (1975).

Goldstein, J.H., Rosnow, R.L., Raday, T., Silverman, I. & Gaskell, G.D., Punitiveness in response to films varying in content: A cross-national field study of aggression. European Journal of Social Psychology, 5, 149-165 (1975).

Goldstein, J.H., Silverman, A.F. & Anderson, P.K., A cross-cultural investigation of humour: appreciation of jokes varying in familiarity and hostility. Paper presented at XXIst International Congress of Psychology. Paris, July (1976).

Kelley, H.H., Shure, G., Deutsch, M., Faucheux, C., Lanzetta, J., Moscovici, S., Nuttin, J.M. Jr., Rabbie, J. & Thibaut, J.W., A comparative experimental study of negotiation behavior. Journal of Personality and Social Psychology, 16, 411-438 (1970).

Mantell, D.M., The potential for violence in Germany. Journal of Social Issues, 27, 101-112 (1971).

McGinnies, E. & Ward, C.D., Persuasibility as a function of source credibility and locus of control: Five cross-cultural experiments. Journal of Personality, 42, 360-371 (1974).

Sanada, T. & Norbeck, E., Prophecy continues to fail: A Japanese sect. Journal of Cross-Cultural Psychology, 6, 331-345 (1975).

Shaw, M.E., Briscoe, M. & Garcia-Esteve, J., A cross-cultural study of attribution of responsibility. International Journal of Psychology, 3, 51-60 (1968).

Sommer, R., Intimacy ratings in five countries. International Journal of Psychology, 3, 109-114 (1968).

A Cross-Cultural Study of the Structure of Humour

Thomas R. Shultz

McGill University, Montreal, Canada

One of the enduring issues in humour research has been the structure of humour and its relation to cognitive processing. It is often assumed that jokes, regardless of their particular content, share some underlying structure and that a person's cognitive processes must somehow match this structure in order for him to appreciate a joke. Recent analyses of the structure of humour have specified two structural features: incongruity and resolution (Shultz, 1976; Suls, 1972). The concept of 'incongruity' reflects the idea that the joke contains something which is surprising, unusual, or misexpected. The concept of 'resolution' further specifies that the joke contains information which serves to resolve, explain, or make sense of the incongruity.

The incongruity and resolution theory has generated a fair amount of empirical research on various aspects of the comprehension and appreciation of humour (Jones, 1970; Shultz, 1972, 1974a, 1974b, 1976; Shultz & Horibe, 1974; Shultz & Scott, 1974). Until now, this body of research has been restricted to English speaking, North American samples. In this sense, it constitutes a cognitive-structural account of the humour existing in a particular cultural-linguistic context. Although it is generally assumed that humour is prevalent in all cultural groups, possible cultural variations in the cognitive-structural features of humour have not been systematically studied. This question can be viewed as part of the general problem of the relation between culture and thinking, an issue which has generated a wide range of opinions. There are those who have proposed that the basic functions of thought are common to all of humanity (Boas, 1911; Cole, Gay, Glick & Sharp, 1971; Horton, 1967a, 1967b; Levi-Strauss, 1966) as well as those who have postulated substantial differences in culturally-imposed thought structures (Frake, 1968; Wallace, 1962).

The focus of the present research was to investigate cultural variations in the structural features of humour. English translations of verbal humour were collected from the folklore literature of cultures vastly different from that of Western technological society. These instances of humour were subjected to a structural analysis similar to that performed on Western humorous materials (e.g., Jones, 1970; Shultz, 1976; Suls, 1972). The analyses are discussed under four different headings: Chinese jokes, riddles from nonliterate cultures, Japanese riddles, and folk-tales.

CHINESE JOKES

The only substantial collection of nonWestern jokes the author was able to find was from China (Giles, 1925). Of these 242 jokes, 210 were found to possess a structure of incongruity and resolution; 6 did not appear to have this structure; and 20 others remained inscrutable. Understanding the substance of a joke was, of course, a prerequisite for determining whether it fitted within the theoretical model. There were striking similarities between the resolutions employed in the Chinese jokes and those employed in Western jokes (cf. Shultz & Horibe, 1974). A number were resolved on the basis of either lexical or phonological ambiguity. For example, one joke resolved on the basis of phonological ambiguity concerned a Buddhist priest, a Taoist priest, and a man with a beard who were crossing the Yangtsze together when a bad squall suddenly came on. The two priests threw their prayer book overboard and called on their Gods to save them. The other man, not having any religious articles, pulled a hair out of his beard and threw that into the river. When the priests asked him why he did that, he answered, 'I thought it was time to drop my mao'. The author explains that the words for 'hair' and 'anchor' are both expressed by the same sound, 'mao' (Giles, 1925). In terms of the theory, the incongruity in this joke is that the man reacts to the storm by throwing a hair of his beard into the river. The resolution is based on the phonological ambiguity of the words for 'hair' and 'anchor'.

Resolutions by means other than linguistic ambiguity were common among the Chinese jokes as
they are among Western jokes. An example is a joke about a father and a son who were chopping
firewood together. When the father accidentally wounded the son's fingers with the hatchet,
the son cried, 'You old pimp, are you blind?' The grandson, who was standing by, hearing his
grandfather cursed in this very disrespectful way, turned to his father and said, 'You son of
a bitch! Do you curse your own father?' (Giles, 1925). The incongruity in this joke is that
the grandson, despite his intention to protest the disrespect shown by his father to his
grandfather, in fact curses his father and his grandmother, thereby showing even more
disrespect than he was protesting. The precise form of the resolution depends on how much
knowledge is attributed to the grandson. Either he inadvertently insults his elders in his
anger over his father's action or he intentionally insults them under the guise of criticizing
his father's disrespect.

RIDDLES FROM NONLITERATE CULTURES

The riddle is a form of humour which is found in many cultures, particularly those with a
high level of institutional interrogation (Roberts & Forman, 1971). Children between about
seven years and adolescence seem to be the most typical users of riddles; adults apparently
prefer more complex forms such as tales and anecdotes (Hart, 1964). Riddles may be somewhat
better suited to children because they are relatively easy to tell and remember. Sutton-Smith
(1975) asked American children to relate their favourite jokes and found that the younger
children tended to contribute riddles while the older ones told jokes. The particular context
for riddling varies somewhat from culture to culture but wakes, harvest times, courtships,
and puberty initiation ceremonies are often cited as occasions for riddling (Hart, 1964).
Riddle games and contests are also quite common and, in many cultures, riddling is restricted
to the evening hours (Hart, 1964). It is sometimes held that, if riddles are asked in the
daytime (during working hours), they may be answered by evil spirits or otherwise bring bad
luck (Hart, 1964).

An important structural analysis of the riddle was undertaken by Georges and Dundes (1963).
Utilizing Taylor's (1951) extensive collection of traditional English riddles, they defined
three principal riddle types: literal, metaphorical, and oppositional. In the literal
riddle, the referent or answer is identical to the topic of the descriptive elements in the
question: 'Got somet'in yeller inside an' green outside. (Pumpkin.)' (Taylor, 1951). In
the literal riddle, the question is given a straightforward, rational answer. There is no
incongruity and, consequently, no need for resolution. In contrast, the answer to a
metaphorical riddle is incongruous or surprising. This is because the referent is different
than the topic of the descriptive elements: 'Two rows of white horses on a red hill.
(Teeth.)' (Taylor, 1951). The resolution is provided by the metaphorical relation between the
referent and the descriptive elements. In an oppositional riddle, the incongruity is contained
within the question itself and the answer or referent provides the resolution. The question
expresses an opposition between at least one pair of descriptive elements: 'What turns and
never moves? (A road.)' (Taylor, 1951). Oppositional riddles are almost always metaphorical
or have some combination of metaphorical and literal descriptions (Georges & Dundes, 1963).

Collections of riddles from six nonliterate cultures (two Asian, two African, and two American)
were analyzed and classified as literal, metaphorical, or oppositional[1]. An example of a
literal riddle is taken from the Makua: 'What thing flourishes in the dry season? (The
nfangwi tree, which blossoms only in the dry season.)' (Harries, 1942-43). An example of a
metaphorical riddle is from Burma: 'A cup of milk spilled over the whole countryside. (The
moon.)' (Sein & Dundes, 1964). And an example of an oppositional riddle is from the Bisayans:
'Always taking shelter but forever wet. (Tongue.)' (Hart, 1964). All riddles of the
metaphorical and oppositional types were considered to possess a structure of incongruity and
resolution while literal riddles were not considered to have this structure. The numbers of
riddles of each type are presented in Table 1 for each of the six cultures.

The results of the classification indicate that the vast majority of the riddles in each
culture were characterized by the incongruity and resolution structure. The only notable
exceptions were the literal riddles found in the Bisayan, Burmese, Nyanja, Makua, and Ten'a
cultures. Although literal riddles were in the minority in each of these cultures, they
existed in sufficient numbers to constitute a substantial exception and were also present in
Taylor's (1951) sample of English riddles. Their presence may perhaps be explained in terms
of Rapp's (1949) interesting theory of the phylogenesis of humour. He viewed the riddle as
a direct descendant of the 'duel of mental skill' in which pairs of primitive people would
stage an intense nonphysical competition. While the winner of such a duel might well have
laughed at the climactic outcome, Rapp claimed that it was only much later in history that
the verbal exchanges per se became humorous. Literal riddles could be considered as vestiges
from these primitive wit duels. If so, it should be possible to demonstrate that they are
gradually being replaced by the funnier metaphorical and oppositional riddles. This seems

TABLE 1 Classification of Riddles by Type

	Literal	Metaphorical	Oppositional
Bisayan (Filipino)	19	54	28
Burmese	5	13	5
Nyanja (Eastern Bantu)	10	102	11
Makua (Bantu)	13	104	18
Amuzgo (Mexican)	0	32	13
Ten'a (Yukon)	27	73	2

to be true in Western culture as the author has been unable to locate a single literal riddle in any current English publications of riddles for children. Recent studies in which American children have been asked to relate their favourite riddles also suggest that literal riddles are relatively primitive. Park (1971) and Sutton-Smith (1975) both found that literal riddles (or what they called 'preriddles') were common among very young children but were extremely rare among older children. It would be interesting to determine if these findings could be extended to nonWestern cultures and to test the hypothesis that, where literal riddles exist, they are less funny than metaphorical and oppositional riddles.

JAPANESE RIDDLES

Japanese riddles are discussed separately because it was found that many of them do not fit the structural scheme of Georges and Dundes. Three different forms of Japanese riddles have been identified: kangaemono, nazo, and children's nazo. Polivanov (translated from Russian by Preston) described the kangaemono (kangae = 'think', mono = 'object') as a question consisting of two sentences with a consistently occurring antithesis (Preston, 1948). Of the seven kangaemono collected by Preston (1948), two appeared to be metaphorical, four oppositional, and one was difficult to understand. Both of the metaphorical kangaemono and three of the four oppositional kangaemono were resolved by phonological ambiguity. An example of the latter is the following: 'Everybody likes pie but everyone dislikes a certain pie. What (what kind of) pie is it? (Worry.) (Note - the wordplay involves pai "pie" as a constituent sequence of sinpai worry.)' (Patterson, 1948).

Polivanov described the nazo (riddle) as a question-and-answer formally united into a whole which includes three sentences: (1) the question, 'What can such-and-such be compared with?', (2) the answer, 'It may be compared with such-and-such.', and (3) the explanation of the comparison (Patterson, 1948). Although the nazo does not at all fit the scheme of Georges and Dundes, it surely can be understood in terms of incongruity and resolution. The first two sentences constitute an incongruous comparison which is resolved by the third sentence. Many of their resolutions are based on the types of linguistic ambiguity common to Western riddles (cf. Shultz, 1974a). Of the 189 nazo contained in two published collections (Preston, 1948; Starr, 1910-12), 133 were resolved on the basis of lexical ambiguity, 32 on the basis of phonological ambiguity, 2 on the basis of a combination of lexical and phonological ambiguities, and 21 were resolved by nonlinguistic means (the remaining nazo was difficult to interpret). An example of the last category is the following: 'What can you compare a bride from the aristocracy with? With a hundred yen banknote. That's because neither the one nor the other is obtained by the poor man.' (Preston, 1948).

The structure of the children's nazo is quite different from that of the nazo proper (Starr, 1910-12). Children's nazo consist of two parts rather than three. The first part describes an unknown object which is to be guessed; the second part is the answer to the riddle. Although they are considered rather inferior to true nazo, they appear to be quite similar to Western riddles and thus can be analyzed according to the Georges and Dundes system. Of the thirteen children's nazo collected by Starr, four were metaphorical, five were oppositional, and four were difficult to understand. One of the metaphorical type was resolved by a lexical ambiguity and one of the oppositional type was resolved by phonological ambiguity. The remainder were resolved by nonlinguistic means. An example of this last category is the following: 'Having six feet, it walks with four. What is that? (Man on horseback.)' (Starr, 1910-12).

FOLK-TALES

Folk-tales are somewhat more complicated than riddles or simple jokes. They are considerably longer and thus more difficult to remember. Recitation of folk-tales is often quite dramatic being supplemented with expressive gestures, mimicry, and other devices. Rather than searching through the vast literature on folk-tales, it was decided to analyze a fairly representative set of fourteen humorous tales which were collected by Bowman (1939). These tales are from a variety of cultures; most of them are archetypal in the sense that different versions of the same story can be found in other cultures. The main point of each of the fourteen tales was found to have a definite structure of incongruity and resolution. Two examples follow. A fairly common type of humorous tale is that in which one character outwits the others by pitting them against each other. 'In an African story, for example, the rabbit challenges first the hippopotamus and then the elephant to a tug of war. He arranges that they pull against each other, each thinking, of course, that his opponent is the rabbit. The huge beasts pull and strain, baffled at the "rabbit's" strength, until they are exhausted, whereupon the crafty rabbit goes to each separately and claims the victory, which the stupid and unsuspecting pachyderms are forced to concede.' (Bowman, 1939). In this tale it is, of course, incongruous that the hippopotamus and the elephant are defeated in a tug of war by the much smaller rabbit. The resolution is that the rabbit has cleverly arranged for the two larger animals to unknowingly pull against each other.

'Tales of the hare-and-tortoise type, in which the slower animal wins the race, are common, although the victory is achieved more often by trickery than by perseverance. In a Bondei story the tortoise and the falcon compete for the hand of the chief's daughter. The tortoise, knowing that he has no chance to win unless he resorts to trickery, consults the hare, who evolves a plan. In accordance with this, the tortoise enlists the cooperation of a number of his tortoise friends, all of whom look alike to the falcon. One of them hides at each resting place along the route. The race begins and the falcon reaches the first resting place confident that he has left his competitor far behind, only to find that the "tortoise" is already there. This is repeated at each stop and again at the finish line in the village, where the tortoise himself is hiding. When the falcon comes flying into the village, crying that he has beaten the tortoise, the latter emerges out of hiding, claims the victory, and wins the hand of the chief's daughter. In an Ikon version the frog races with the bushbuck and wins by stationing other frogs along the route. In a Benga tale the tortoise defeats the antelope by the same kind of plot, and a similar version is told by the Wakweli.' (Bowman, 1939). In these tales it is incongruous for the slower animal to win a race over the faster one; the resolution is that the slower animal only appears to win through the trick of stationing his relatives along the route.

DISCUSSION

An answer to the question of cultural variation in humour depends very much on the level at which humour is analyzed. On the most abstract level, it seems to be the case that all cultures possess humour in some form (cf. Bowman, 1939). At least there are no reports of a culture in which instances of humour are absent. On the most concrete level, it is equally obvious that different cultures joke about different things. The Chinese jokes were generally concerned with problems in social relationships. In contrast, humour in the Bisayan, Burmese, Nyanja, Makua, Amuzgo, and Ten'a cultures was more often focused on aspects of the immediate physical environment. As Freud (1960) pointed out, Western humour deals principally with the twin preoccupations of sex and aggression (cf. Goldstein, Suls & Anthony, 1972).

Intermediate levels of analysis must be explored to answer questions of cultural variation in the structure of humour. There is a great deal of cultural variation in specific structural and stylistic techniques. Roberts and Forman (1971) found that certain forms of humour, such as the riddle, are prevalent in some cultures but nonexistent in others. In the present study, it was noted that lexical and phonological ambiguities were commonly used to resolve incongruities in the literate cultures but were rare in the nonliterate cultures sampled. Similarly, syntactic ambiguity is employed as a resolution device in a small number of Western jokes and riddles (Shultz, 1974a; Shultz & Horibe, 1974) but was not observed in any of the present nonWestern samples. Certain stylistic forms, such as the tripartite Japanese nazo, also appeared to be culturally idiosyncratic.

At a more basic level, however, there was a striking commonality across cultures in the use of incongruity and resolution. This structure was found in the vast majority of the jokes, riddles, and humorous tales of every culture sampled. As such, the results of the present study offer considerable support for the 'psychic-unity' hypothesis proposed many years ago by Boas (1911). This is the idea that the most basic structures of mind are common to all of humanity. But why should the structure of incongruity and resolution be a universal feature of humour? This is not too mysterious when one considers the incongruity and resolution structure in terms of its relation to pleasure and arousal. It has been hypothesized that the cognitive experience of incongruity and resolution has physiological correlates in terms of momentary fluctuations in arousal (Berlyne, 1972; Shultz, 1976). It may be that the discovery of the incongruity in a joke arouses the listener and the construction of a resolution returns the arousal to its baseline level. The pleasure-giving potential of arousal induction and reduction in man and animals has been well documented in experimental psychology (Berlyne, 1967). Since this sequence is compressed into an extremely short time interval in most jokes, the pleasure associated with humour could be expected to be quite intense.

ACKNOWLEDGEMENT

This research was supported in part by a grant from the Faculty of Graduate Studies and Research, McGill University.

FOOTNOTE

1. The 101 Bisayan riddles were selected from Hart's (1964) extensive collection of 909. Hart's riddles were arranged in nineteen content groups, listed alphabetically within each group. Every ninth riddle in Hart's collection was selected for the present study. The entire collections of riddles from the Burmese (Sein & Dundes, 1964), Nyanja (Grey, 1949), Makua (Harries, 1942-43), Amuzgo (Scott, 1963), and Ten'a (Jette, 1913) sources were analyzed.

REFERENCES

See Bibliography for publications on humour, laughter and comedy

Berlyne, D.E., Arousal and reinforcement. In: D. Levine (Ed.), Nebraska Symposium on Motivation. University of Nebraska Press, Lincoln (1967).

Boas, F., The Mind of Primitive Man. Macmillan, New York (1911).

Cole, M., Gay, J., Glick, J.A. & Sharp, D.W., The Cultural Context of Learning and Thinking: An Exploration in Experimental Anthropology. Basic Books, New York (1971).

Frake, C.O., The ethnographic study of cognitive systems. In: R.A. Manners & D. Kaplan (Eds.), Theory in Anthropology. Aldine, Chicago (1968).

Giles, H.A., Quips from a Chinese Jest Book. Kelly & Walsh, Shanghai (1925).

Horton, R., African traditional thought and Western science: part I: from tradition to science. Africa, 37, 50 (1967a).

Horton, R., African traditional thought and Western science: part II: the closed and open predicaments. Africa, 37, 155 (1967b).

Jones, J.M., Cognitive factors in the appreciation of humor: a theoretical and experimental analysis. Unpublished doctoral dissertation, Yale University (1970).

Levi-Strauss, C., The Savage Mind. University of Chicago Press, Chicago (1966).

Park, R.F., An investigation of riddles of children aged five - fourteen using Piaget derived definitions. Unpublished doctoral dissertation, Columbia University (1971).

Wallace, A.F.C., Culture and cognition. Science, 135, 351 (1962).

Magnificent Liars: Exaggeration in American Humour

Arlen J. Hansen

University of the Pacific, California

'The grotesque exaggeration and broad irony with which the life is described
are conjecturably the truest colors that could have been used, for all existence
there (in Nevada) must have looked like an extravagant joke....'
W.D. Howells, review of Mark Twain's 'Roughing It' (Atlantic Monthly, 1872,
June, p754).

In 1864 Dr. Thomas Low Nichols, an American in voluntary exile in England, published his
reflections upon life in the United States, 'Forty Years of American Life, 1821-1861.' In a
chapter titled 'Peculiarities and Eccentricities' Nichols informs his British audience that
'American humour consists largely of exaggeration, and of strange and quaint expressions'
(p67, 1937 Edition). Although preoccupied with the 'quaint expressions', Nichols briefly
comments on the American fondness for humorous exaggeration: 'Americans', he notes, 'have
a passion for making improvements on everything' (p68). He then illustrates his point by
alluding to 'the story of a land so rich that a squash vine, in its rapid growth, overtook
and smothered a drove of pigs'. Nichols is correct in suggesting that there is a clear
tradition in America of the 'improving' exaggeration, but his squash vine illustration points
to a different tradition of American exaggeration, one which Nichols and most other
commentators have overlooked. This essay attempts a brief and embryonic distinction between
the two traditions.

Mody C. Boatright (1949) has observed that 'the folk liar does not depend upon mere
exaggeration... (which) is in itself neither folkish nor funny'. The magnificent liars who
populate American humour - whether the raucous backwoodsman or the frenzied urbanite - lie,
dream, or fantasize apparently at will, but they are not merely exaggerators. As characters
they may be said to fall into two classes: the 'epitomizers' and the 'transformers'. The
exaggerations of the epitomizer serve to capture and define some essential quality of his
life. The epitomizer uses language to articulate in a metaphoric way who he is and what his
life is like. Language is his means of suggesting the real quality of his existence. The
transformer's exaggerations serve to 'make improvements' and to generate an alternative,
preferred sense of himself or his lot in life. The transformer uses language to remake his
reality, to heighten, intensify, or otherwise to alter the quality and style of his life.

The tradition of the transformer, whose lies 'improve' his life, has been widely discussed.
Constance Rourke (1931) points to this tradition in her influential study, 'American Humor:
A Study of the National Character'. Rourke sees humorous exaggeration as a psychological
defense mechanism:

'He (the backwoodsman, like the Yankee) assumed
in gross form the faults with which he was
charged. He was considered uncouth, and he
swaggered the more roughly. He was called a
bragger and a liar: he gently retouched his
exploits.' (p46).

Hansen (1974) has noted elsewhere that when W.C. Fields as Cuthbert J. Twilley calls the
libidinous Flower Belle (Mae West) 'my little chickadee', it is not a matter of stretching
the truth. It is not the truth at all. Mae West is neither his, little, nor - by any
stretch of the imagination - a chickadee. But neither does Fields' epithet suggest that
he is wildly or irresponsibly hallucinating; rather, it reveals his way of touching up his
real situation: by renaming it. Consistent with all his other well-intentioned and habitual
transformations, Fields is determined to perceive the brazen Miss West as his little
chickadee, despite all mitigating evidence. A similar tendency, to transform reality belongs
to James Thurber's 'Walter Mitty', whose secret, day-dream life enables him to overlook and

tolerate the monotony, trivia, and unpleasantness of his daily existence. Joseph Baldwin's
Ovid Bolus, an incomparable liar from the 'flush times' of 1835-37 in the old Southwest, is
a similar transformer, lying 'because the truth was too small for him'. To a large degree
Bolus lies - as do Fields, Mitty, and Jim Baker and Simon Wheeler in Mark Twain's stories -
'from the delight of invention and the charm of fictitious narrative'. By virtue of his
lies, the world of Ovid Bolus and others 'was not the hard, work-day world the groundlings
live in: he moved in a sphere of poetry: he lived amidst the ideal and romantic'. One
thinks today of Woody Allen who desperately tries to represent himself as Humphrey Bogart;
he succeeds, however, only in hilarious self-delusion. These men, then, are the transformers,
whose imaginations creatively attempt to fulfil their hunger for things that are not. James
Russell Lowell was one of the first of the established, 'genteel' critics of the mid-nineteenth
century to recognize the genius that lay behind this kind of transforming lie. Referring to
the technique that other critics belittled as inartistic exaggeration, Lowell observed that
it 'is more fitly to be called intensity and picturesqueness, symptoms of the imaginative
faculty in full health'.

The other type of exaggerator - the epitomizer - is seldom distinguished from his kinsman,
the transformer. The epitomizer conceives of himself and his circumstances as being virtually
indescribable. So extreme or surreal seems his lot to him that it defies ordinary
description. When T.B. Thorpe's 'big bear' of Arkansas says 'I'll give you an idea of a bear
hunt', he admittedly is attempting to epitomize what it is like to hunt in the lush Arkansas
canebrake. In the Preface to the 1854 collection ('The Hive of the Bee Hunter') which
contains this tall tale, Thorpe writes: 'There are growing up, in these primitive wilds,
men, whose daily life and conversation, when detailed, form exaggerations; but whose historie
are, after all, only the natural developments of the mighty associations which surround them'
It takes hyperbolic language, Thorpe suggests, to express even the commonplace in the mighty
'primitive wilds'. In the same way Nichols' story of the rapidly growing squash vine reveals
the teller's desire to suggest the awesome, if not ineffable, fertility and richness of the
land. The tall tale encapsulates as well the speaker's pride in being connected with such
land. The story functions, then, as a suggestive and metaphoric epitome.

As a rule, the epitomizer of the nineteenth century was engaged in the act of self-definition.
Daniel Hoffman sees in 'Yankee self-assertion...the impulse of self-definition through
symbolic action'. As a corollary one might suggest that the self-definition of the
frontiersman usually involves tall talk, symbolic language. One such tall talker was
Congressman David Crockett - or, more likely, 'Colonel Davy Crockett', the persona created by
Matthew St. Clair Cooke who was the likely compiler of the 1833 collection of Crockett
stories which initiated the Davy Crockett legend. Voicing the feelings of the frontiersman,
Crockett proclaims:

    'I'm that same David Crockett, fresh from the backwoods, half-horse, half-
    alligator, a little touched with the snapping-turtle; can wade the Mississippi,
    leap the Ohio, ride upon a streak of lightning, and slip without a scratch down
    a honey locust....' (quoted in Boatright, 1949).

This hyperbolic boast, like Odysseus' and Beowulf's before it, allows the speaker to define
himself by figuring and proclaiming his character as tough and strong, not to be lightly
reckoned with. Epitomizing his character as such, Crockett speaks for all frontiersmen and
captures the essential nature of the pioneer - as the pioneer sees it, that is. In a speech
ostensibly (but not really) delivered before Congress, Colonel Crockett describes his
technique as 'summing up', i.e., epitomizing:

    'The gentleman from Massachusetts talks of summing up the merits of the
    question, but I'll sum up my own. In one word I'm a screamer, and have got
    the roughest racking horse, the prettiest sister, the surest rifle, and the
    ugliest dog in the district.... I can run faster, dive deeper, stay under
    longer, and come out drier, than any chap this side of the Big Swamp
    (Atlantic Ocean?)' (quoted in Boatright, 1949).

Merely surviving in the wilderness of Western Kentucky and Tennessee in the 1820's must
have promoted a great deal of self-assurance. It is hardly surprising that the frontiersman
felt god-like and arrogantly or playfully proud of his resourcefulness, power, and
accomplishments. Having endured the dangers and met the challenges of the wilderness, he
was capable, it must have seemed to him, of nearly anything. This pride and feeling of
indomitable power is readily detected in Crockett's fantastic trope of diving down deeper,
staying under longer, and coming out drier than anyone else.

The use of exaggerated language to epitomize personal and regional traits decreased as the
regional identities became fixed and popularized. Once Crockett and others had defined the
essential sensations of frontier life, there was less need for repeatedly epitomizing them.
But the humour of the exaggerated epitome did not disappear: it shifted subjects and
became more universal and less local. It came to express general human qualities - not

simply regional characteristics. Mark Twain, for example, incorporated into one of his most
popular lectures (and into 'Roughing It') a tall story epitomizing human meanness and the
pettiness of profiteering. His yarn involves a man hired to blast rock for a mining company.
While tamping down the blasting powder in a hole drilled four feet into a rock, the man's
crowbar struck a spark and caused the powder to explode, launching him and his bar into the
air and completely out of sight.

> 'Presently he came in sight again looking no bigger than a bee; and he came
> further and further and further till he was as big as a dog, and further and
> further and further till he was as big as a boy, and he came further and further
> till he assumed the full size and shape of a man, and he came down and fell
> right into the same old spot and went to tamping again'. (Lorch, 1968).

Clemens then notes that the company docked his wages for the loss of fifteen minutes' work.

America's greatest folksinger, Woody Guthrie, created similar tall tales in his 'Talking
Blues' songs. Whether epitomizing human greed, as in 'Talking Mean Blues', or the importance
of civil liberty in 'Talking Constitution', Guthrie follows in Crockett's and Thorpe's
footsteps. Guthrie's 'Talking Hard Luck Blues' is filled with exaggerations that epitomize
the foolishness and the power of the American male ego when it compels one to try to prove
to women its worth and prowess. Guthrie's speaker exerts Herculean effort to impress one
particular woman:

> 'I shook hands with 97 of her kinfolks and her blood relatives,
> And I done the same with 86 people who were just her friends, and her neighbors....
> I kissed 73 babies and I put dry pants on 34 of them....
> I chopped and I weeded 48 rows of short cotton,
> Thirteen acres of bad corn;
> I cut the sticker weeds out of eleven back yards,
> All on account a-cause I wanted to show her that I was a man that liked to work....'

These exaggerations accumulate to express how hopelessly captivated a man can be — captivated
both by a woman and his own ego. As the song ends, Guthrie's speaker adopts a tone that
indicates that he knows full well that he is being foolishly, if irresistably, driven by his
own ego:

> 'I'm just sitting here now trying to study
> up on what else I can do to show that
> woman that I still ain't afraid of hard
> work'. ('Woody Guthrie Sings Folk Songs', Vol.2, Folkways Records, Album FA 2484).

Thorpe, Crockett, Clemens, and Guthrie — not to mention Philip Roth's Alexander Portnoy or
the characters in Joseph Heller's 'Catch-22' or Lenny Bruce's striking portrayals — make
creative use of language merely to suggest the quality of their (or their personae's)
lives. Rather than touching up or improving upon their lives — as do the exaggerations of
Fields and Mitty (the transformers), the exaggerations of the epitomizers serve as a means
of expressing what otherwise would be inexpressible.

Both the epitomizers and the transformers rely on language, rather than action, as their
basic medium. It is primarily their talk, not their conduct, that is funny. In the one
instance, that of the transformer, the talk is humorous perhaps because it is obviously an
alteration of the actual state of affairs. In the other, the epitomizer's talk is humorous
because — while its literal level of meaning is so exaggerated as to inspire disbelief — its
metaphoric properties are richly suggestive and expressive, and usually very much to the
point. Beyond their shared reliance on language, these two traditions can be seen as
natural opposites. The transformer uses language to realize as far as possible his desired
fantasy; the epitomizer uses language to express his indescribable — perhaps fantastic —
reality.

REFERENCES

See Bibliography for publications on humour, laughter and comedy

Baldwin, J.G., The Flush Times of Alabama and Mississippi. Sagamore Press, New York,
    (Twentieth Century Series) (1957).

Hoffman, D., Form and Fable in American Fiction. Norton, New York (1965).

Lorch, F.W., Trouble begins at Eight: Mark Twain's Lecture Tours. Iowa State University
    Press (1968).
Nichols, T.L. Forty Years of American Life, 1821-1861. New York (Reprint of London, 1864
    Edition) (1937).

Play and Ritual: Complementary Frames of Meta-Communication[1]

Don Handelman

The Hebrew University of Jerusalem, Israel

The relationship of play to social order remains obscure, with play usually relegated to a peripheral location in the ordering of adult social life. In part, this dismissal of play is the result of the prominence of one of its most popular criteria: its 'unserious' property, in contrast to the 'serious' character of other social activity. This has permitted anthropology to treat play as a secondary derivation in a functional equation: when play appears it is as a substitute which oils the gears and bearings of serious social phenomena (Kennedy, 1970; Radcliffe-Brown, 1940). Such attitudes to adult play in traditional societies have enabled us to avoid thinking about play as a systemic mode of meta-communication, and therefore as central to social life.

In a speculative and schematic manner, this paper argues that in more simply organized societies one elementary contrast is not so much between the domain of play and that of serious life, but instead between play and another domain, that of ritual, which also exhibits systemic features of meta-communication. In this regard ritual and play complement one another in the kinds of messages they communicate to the social order. Both are consistent and integral features of the cosmological equation that conceives of society, not only as a social order, but also as a moral one.

THE DOMAIN OF PLAY

The general rubric 'play' subsumes a wide variety of expressive behaviour which ranges from the highly organized and strictly bounded in time and space to fleeting excursions into the domain of play. Such activities include at least the following: rule-bound play (Miller, 1973), make-believe play (Goffman, 1974; Miller, 1973), joking relationships (Kennedy, 1970), joking activity (Handelman & Kapferer, 1972), jokes (Douglas, 1968), pranks, mimicry, and forms of role-play (Handelman, 1975). Underlying these apparently disparate activities are certain common assumptions.

Play is a way of organizing activity, and not a particular set of activities (Miller, 1973). This organization is predicated upon a reduction in available types of roles and relationships, and the introduction of symbolic types and relationships which posit the social limits and cognitive relevance of the play activity (Grathoff, 1970). In play, symbolic types enable the means-ends relationship to be altered, such that ends do not determine means, and means are provided with a relative degree of autonomy (Miller, 1973). In turn, within the possibilities and limitations afforded by symbolic types, players are enabled to alter their usual coordination of acts through repetition, exaggeration, novel combinations, and a high degree of freedom.

Taking on symbolic types of 'player', and of a particular type of player, permits actors to 'forget' their social selves, particularly in more comprehensive forms of play. Unlike life in the ordinary social order, the reality of play is not negotiable: the self (which takes the role of the other) need not mediate between ego and others in order to define a common definition of the situation. Since all are 'players', they all hold to the same definition of the play reality, within an unambiguous system of symbols. Thus a player need not express a social self different from that of other players, the social self is superfluous (Csikszentmihalyi & Bennett, 1971), and within the strictures of symbolic types players perceive one another as full, discrete human beings. Whether we deal with comprehensive or fleeting play forms, the above assumptions are necessary to perceive play as a different order of reality, in form, content, and its logic of composition.

THE FRAME OF PLAY AND META-COMMUNICATION

If the logic of composition of the domain of play is different from that of the ordinary social order, then passage from the latter to the former requires a radical transformation in cognition and perception, akin perhaps to what Norbeck (1973) terms transcendence. Play activity is 'framed' differently from the activity of ordinary life. For Bateson (1972) this frame is cognitive: it delimits a set of messages which directs the perceptions of participants. The premises of the frame instruct participants to use a different sort of thinking in interpreting what occurs within it. Thus the frame is defined as a logical type of cognition by its enclosed messages, which share common premises of mutual relevance. Goffman (1974) develops a parallel idea of 'frame', relating its capacity to separate logical types of reality to its 'organizational premises'.

Unsurprisingly, passage between the logical types of ordinary reality and that of play hinges on a paradox which summates the logical incongruity of their coexistence. Bateson (1972) describes the paradox of play as follows: '...(a) that the messages or signals exchanged in play are in a certain sense untrue or not meant; and (b) that that which is denoted by these signals is nonexistent' (p183). We should discover an analogous paradox of passage from the reality of ordinary life to that of ritual. But if the logical types of ordinary life and play are separated by paradox, there must exist a level of communication which over-rides those levels of communication which are inextricably bound to the logic of composition of one or another reality, and which cannot serve as bridges of cognition and perception between realities. This level of communication is the meta-communicative, in which 'the subject of discourse is the relationship between the speakers' (p178).

Now a frame is itself meta-communicative, since 'Any message which either explicitly or implicitly defines a frame, ipso facto gives the receiver instructions or aids in his attempt to understand the messages included within the frame' (p188). Conversely, the messages within the frame define the frame itself. But there are two kinds of meta-communication in play which concern us here. The first, the message 'this is play' (Bateson, 1956) arises in ordinary life, and erects the reality of the play domain. This meta-communication bridges the separate logical types while over-riding the paradox which the meta-message itself has created. But meta-communication is multi-directional. The meta-message which establishes this bridge, and thus comments on the place of play in ordinary life, also opens the way for a second kind of meta-communication.

These are the meta-messages which arise in the play domain and in turn comment on the nature of ordinary life. That such meta-messages are communicated through play to the social order places certain restrictions on their reception and effect. Yet, within a unity of experience that embraces ritual, ordinary life and play, such meta-messages may be one of the most important correlates of play (Handelman, 1975, 1976). Again, a parallel will be drawn with the meta-messages of ritual. Transformations to the world of play and the logic of its composition are not restricted to comprehensive forms of play but should be generally consistent with this kind of transposition, as for example, in the joking relationship (Kennedy, 1970) and in the joke (Douglas, 1968). While the play-upon-form of the joke communicates the meta-message 'this is play', its particular logic of transposition and composition constitute a meta-message which arises in play, but which comments upon the arbitrary ordering of ordinary reality, and its usually submerged or shadowed themes (Douglas, 1968).

That play communicates about the arbitrariness and subjectivism of ordinary experience leads to a final attribute. Huizinga (1970) writes that: 'Play lies outside the antithesis of wisdom and folly .... truth and falsehood, good and evil .... it has no moral function. The valuations of vice and virtue do not apply here' (p85). Csikszentmihalyi and Bennett (1971) note that play is a social system without deviance; while Huizinga considers play to be a world of temporary limited perfection. This suggests that the domain of play is amoral.

Neither moral nor immoral realms of experience can exist independently, or without deviance, and neither is arbitrary or subjective. Instead it is their systemic objectivization which permits the rendering of the 'moral community' in social terms; and which in turn strengthens this community by differentiating between responsible members and deviants (Erikson, 1966). While the moral realm communicates about 'what should be', in contrast to the immoral which communicates about 'what is', the amoral realm, arbitrarily, communicates about 'what can be'. Subjectively, play (the amoral realm) pleases players by permitting them a masked individuality (playing at symbolic types, identical definition of the situation, loss of self) which enables mass participation without collective responsibility.

The domain of play exists in counterpoint to that of ritual. But it is the resolution of their respective contributions which provides the social order with a distinctive blend of morality/amorality (that is, immorality). In ordinary life this has been identified as the ongoing struggle between societal conformity and individual creativity (Miller, 1973).

RITUAL AND PLAY

Ritual and play are similar domains of experience in their logic of composition; complementary, yet mutually exclusive in contrast to their relationships to the social order, which they both influence. What are their similarities?

The Ritual Frame

Previously I argued that play is 'framed' behaviour. Writing of ritual Douglas (1966) states: '... a ritual provides a frame. The marked off time or place alerts a special kind of expectancy, just as the oft-repeated "Once upon a time" creates a mood receptive to fantastic tales....' (p63). Douglas continues: 'So ritual ... changes perception because it changes the selective principles'(p64). The logic of composition of ritual delineates a distinct set of related premises which is meta-communicative: like play it aids participants to interpret what occurs within the frame, according to premises which are defined by the frame, and which in turn define it.

Given these premises, the ritual frame reduces the social types that are relevant, and provides symbolic models of relationship and of conceptions of humanity through which its reality is communicated to participants. As in more comprehensive forms of play, typificatory schemes (Grathoff, 1970) keyed to the frame establish the relevance of symbolic types, and the order of their appearance. Like play, the mundane means-ends relationship no longer holds, and ritual action is often extended and involuted to hold participants within a transcendent experience.

As in the passage to play, that from ordinary reality to ritual is predicated upon a paradox of experience: in the sense that a paradox cannot be resolved only in terms of its own referents of perception, in other words, those that delineate the mundane social order. Hence the recourse to metaphors like that of 'transcendence' (Norbeck, 1973). Instead these passages are resolved through symboling alternative domains of reality, predicated upon premises which bypass the paradox. But if the bypass to play is predicated upon a premise of 'make-believe', that to ritual is predicated upon a premise of 'let us believe', thus controlling the kinds of meta-communication each can sustain. From the perspective of the ordinary social order, human beings recognize the 'inauthenticity' of one and the 'truth' of the other.

The Liminal in Ritual and Play

Following Van Gennep, Turner (1974) has analyzed ritual as a set of phases of passage from one culturally-defined state to another, of which the 'liminal' phase is of interest here. He defines 'liminality' as: '... any condition outside or on the peripheries of everyday life. It is often a sacred condition or can readily become one' (p47). Liminality exists apart from 'structure', which is roughly equivalent to the 'ordinary social order'. 'Structure' represents the social order as an organization of 'jural, political and economic positions, offices, statuses, and roles, in which the individual is only ambiguously grasped behind the social persona'; and which is '... differentiated, culturally structured, segmented, and often hierarchical...' (Turner, 1969, p177).

During the liminal phase of ritual, behaviour and symbolism are temporarily freed from mundane norms and values; social relationships are simplified; myth and ritual activity are elaborated; and there is a general withdrawal from regular modes of social action. In other words, liminality is marked by a reduction of social types and by an introduction of symbolic types. This is particularly striking in those rites termed 'rituals of status reversal' (Turner, 1969; see also Gluckman, 1963; Norbeck, 1973). Their liminal phases are marked by violations of the normal rules of etiquette, propriety, and morality. Frequently the hierarchy of mundane structural relationships is upended so that the structurally inferior become equal or superior. The social selves of the participants are 'masked': they become anonymous beings, levelled and stripped of their social insignia. Like the 'players' in play, those in ritual define the one situation in the same way. Their social selves become superfluous; and they are free to see one another as concrete idiosyncratic human beings.

Collective participation in the liminal phase of ritual engenders sentiments of 'communitas'. Liminality is a domain of perception which encompasses equally well the individual in solitude and the collectivity in concert. But communitas is a social modality struck in the image of: '... the direct, immediate, and total confrontation of human identities which tends to make those experiencing it think of mankind as a homogeneous, unstructured, and free community' (Turner, 1974, p169). Such collective sentiments are remarkably similar to sentiments reportedly experienced within comprehensive forms of play, and in more fleeting forms of play. As ritual is a liminal phenomenon, so is play.

Given their similarities, play and ritual should complement one another experientially, in preparing persons for the transfer to a liminal domain of experience. Thus the experience of ritual should prepare one for play, and that of play for ritual. Turner (1974) notes that: 'Communitas in ritual can only be evoked easily when there are many occasions outside the ritual on which communitas has been achieved' (p56; see also Handelman, 1976).

Meta-communication in Ritual and Play

Like the play frame, that of ritual communicates a meta-message; while the messages communicated within the ritual frame are also meta-communicative, in that they comment on the ordinary social order. Were this not so, the communicative content of ritual activity would have social relevance only for the ritual domain. Ritual participants are expected to value these experiences within the mundane social order. This is why Turner (1969) can argue that every society must experience the periodic revitalization of communitas-like sentiments. If the meta-communication 'this is ritual' opens an experiential bridge between ordinary social order and the ritual domain, then meta-communications which arise in the ritual domain comment in turn about the nature of the social order. Thus Turner (1974) suggests that communitas is the 'critique' of structure.

Therefore play and ritual transmit two kinds of meta-messages, both of which are vital to the social order. The first is the direct experience of a communitas-like state; and the second is what the liminal has to say about the structural, not only by contrast, but directed pointedly at the social order.

Ritual and play may be the major liminal experiences of persons in traditional society. They have more in common with one another than either has with the social order. Analogous, yet not identical, they are socially separate, although elements of either may be lodged in the other. What is it, then, that specifies their distinctiveness? Turner (1969) suggests that the state of communitas within the ritual frame is sacred because it dissolves norms that control the fabric of social order, while accompanied by experiences of great potency. But play too is pregnant with potential, and is predicated upon such dissolutions; yet it is not sacred.

Perhaps their distinctiveness should be sought in the kinds of meta-messages these frames communicate to participants. Rapaport (1971) argues that sanctity is a 'meta-statement' which bounds the premises, propositions and promises located within the ritual frame. 'Sanctity', he states, 'is the quality of unquestionable truthfulness imputed by the faithful to unverifiable propositions. Sanctity thus is not ultimately a property of physical or metaphysical objects, but of discourse about such objects ... to sanctify statements is to certify them' (p69). Thus the meta-communication of the ritual frame itself, 'this is ritual', is conjoined by the meta-communications, 'all messages included within this frame are sanctified' and 'all messages included within this frame are true'. Therefore the messages within the ritual frame are imbued with moral worth, while the frame itself is woven of messages of morality.

Even in the liminal phase of rituals of reversal, when social norms are often mocked and berated through play, the messages of sanctity and morality are not subverted, for they are encapsulated within the ritual frame. Play messages of potential chaos only pass through to the ordinary social world after they are sieved through the ritual frame of morality, and are shorn of their potential for disorder. The transgressions of play-within-ritual do not draw upon all potential re-orderings of the social world which man can excerpt from the finite realm of his experience. Instead, such re-arrangements are sculpted and adumbrated to highlight messages which maintain values and norms within the ordinary social order (Bricker, 1973). The ritual frame controls the potential of creation in play precisely because it is sanctified and imbued with morality.

The 'carrying capacity' of ritual meta-messages has a particularly high amplitude due to their sanctification, but also because of their audience. The collectivity of participants in ritual activity receives meta-messages which are statements about the nature of their relationships with one another. But often this collectivity, morally depicted within ritual, also forms a 'community', or an important segment of a community which is articulated with a socio-political unit in the ordinary social order. It is such social units which are limned as moral entities within the ritual frame, and are then returned to the mundane world as moral communities whose memberships continue to be affected by their experience.

The ultimate value is to act in terms of 'communitas' values even while enacting structural roles (Turner, 1969). It is in this sense that ritual meta-communications can define a moral community which, within the mundane world, will retain something of this sediment. With such 'responsibility' toward the organization of the social order, ritual, although imbued with creative capacity, must have this potential tempered and controlled to adumbrate and reinforce the meta-messages of morality within ordinary life.

As a meta-message of the ritual frame communicates, 'all messages within this frame are true, not only within but also without', so the frame of play communicates a meta-message, 'all messages within this frame are false in some sense, and are false without'. Thus Bateson's (1972) expansion of the message 'this is play' reads: 'These actions, in which we now engage, do not denote what would be denoted by those actions which these actions denote' (p180).

Play doubts the social order, while ritual integrates it. Ritual may doubt the social order before re-integrating it, but play suggests that either the social order is false or the domain of play is false. Where ritual validates the social order, play questions this validity. Play is amoral, not immoral, because it seeks rather to deny accepted values and norms than to deviate from them. Only the social order itself is immoral, for it simultaneously affirms and doubts its own validity.

If ritual is the most stable liminal domain, then play is the most plastic. Because play is fraught with the potential for randomized creativity, the validity of its meta-communications must be weak. It is defined as 'unserious', 'untrue', 'pretend', 'make-believe', 'unreal', and so forth, precisely because it is a fount of unorder against which the social order must be buffered. By definition it cannot be permitted to define a moral community, since, unlike ritual, the directions of its transformative capacity are uncharted.

By the same token, the play frame itself is weaker, less resilient, than the ritual frame so that play participants can be returned with comparative ease from 'fantasy' to the reality of the social order. Although ritual communitas may be institutionalized as a moral cum social community (Turner, 1968), play is not instituted as the rationale of community. The more play is institutionalized as an event, the more it is permitted only sporadic or periodic expression. Huizinga's (1970) 'play-community' signifies only that individual participants carry over into ordinary reality some of the flavour of messages communicated within play.

But these attributes of play make it a particularly suitable context for the communication of messages which cannot be transmitted with ease in ritual or ordinary life. Numerous commentators note that expression in jest, in 'fun', in humour, or in play need not be accorded the same degree of serious evaluation as other actions. This is another way of stating that in play the means-ends relationship is altered, so that the ends which are ordinarily denoted by such means are not denoted by those actions which denote those means. In contrast to ritual messages, those of play are stripped of their capacity to be received in the mode in which they were transmitted. This is a prime function of the paradox of play.

Meta-messages of play doubt the validity of the social order, not as it should be constituted according to ritual meta-messages, but as it is constituted in the here and now. This sense of untelescoped 'present' (an aspect of the amoral) makes the messages of play such acute commentaries on ongoing social life. In addition, play suggests how aspects of social order can be constituted in hypothetical configurations of meaning. But, because of their dangerously creative potential, such messages cannot be received as transmitted. Although messages of play can express hypothetical states, they can hardly change arrangements within the social order. But, this comparative faintness in reception permits play a very wide range of commentary on the social order.

In this there is no denigration of 'expression', for to express is to communicate, perhaps to share. Yet this is a shadow image of the similarity of sentiment evoked within the ritual frame, which can be translated into social action to affect the social order. If the symbolic types of the ritual domain should appear in the social world (viz prophets, incarnations, and so forth) they are imbued with vigour to influence the arrangements of ordinary reality. But the symbolic types of the play domain, should they escape, are rendered impotent: the sad clown, the happy-go-lucky joker, the pitiful fool, the irresponsible lunatic, and so forth.

Nonetheless, because play meta-messages are stripped of their instrumental potency, the range of meta-communication in play is greater than that of ritual; and play is free to comment on the social order, as it is fleetingly constituted. This ritual cannot do. Ritual is bound by the sanctity of its frame to scrutinize the meta-messages it transmits, while the amorality of play permits a freer and more immediately salient transmission.

Ritual and play are shadow images of one another in the kinds of messages they transmit to the social order. They are analogous states of cognition and perception, whose messages are complementary for the resolution of the ongoing, immoral, deviant, domain of ordinary reality. As alternate channels of meta-communication they invest social reality with the stability of hope and predictivity and with the insubstantiality of the possible.

COMMUNICATION AND CHANGE

In this rudimentary formulation traditional society is treated as a system of communication predicated upon two major domains of information-transmission (ritual, play) and one major domain of reception (social order). Thus, binary oppositions of the form 'real:unreal', play:non-play, sacred:secular, seem incomplete. Instead, social order is seen as the resolution of the complementary opposition, ritual:play.

TABLE 1   Characteristics of Ritual and Play

	Ritual	Play
analogous	1. reduction of social types	1. reduction of social types
	2. symbolic types	2. symbolic types
	3. alteration of means-ends	3. alteration of means-ends
	4. all definitions of situation the same	4. all definitions of situation the same
	5. superfluity of social self	5. superfluity of social self
	6. framed domain	6. framed domain
	7. meta-message of liminality	7. meta-message of liminality
	8. meta-messages about ordering of social reality	8. meta-messages about ordering of social reality
complementary	9. complex passage to ritual	9. easy passage to play
	10. resilient frame	10. weak frame
	11. defines moral community	11. accentuates plasticity of ideation
	12. meta-messages of sanctity/morality/truth	12. meta-messages of doubt/amorality/falsity
	13. expressive for social order	13. expressive of social order
	14. narrower range/band of commentary	14. wider range/band of commentary
	15. comments on totality of structures in time and space	15. comments on immediate on-going fragments of social reality

alternating channels of communication

If play has the communicative capacity I have ascribed to it in a social order, that is the resolution of the 'morally ideal' and the 'amorally possible', then ritual and play are not only opposed, but complement one another. Like mirror images the organization of their frames are quite analogous, the features within these frames are highly similar, but those of each are reversed in the other. As their opposition is complementary, so their intersection provides the social order with a lengthy series of structural dilemmas (viz morality/ amorality, harmony/disharmony, order/disorder, integration/opposition, faith/pretence, status/power, etcetera), the resolutions of which replicate and generate social forms which inform society with a unity of experience.

Such a formulation assumes that the social order strikes notes of equilibrium among the messages of ritual and play, which are continuously expressed in social life. Thus, a question which only will be broached here: how do societies differ in the kinds of resolution of ritual and play that they acquire, and what are the apparent effects of such resolutions on forms of social order?

But the above assumption raises another question: if a simple society undergoes drastic social change, including the virtual disintegration of the ritual domain, then what are the consequences for the social order of the continuing presence of the domain of play? My hunch is that play can survive the disintegration of the ritual domain. As the meta-communications of ritual atrophy and fall silent, and as the fabric of social relationship unravels, the commentaries of play increase in significance as media of communication about the state of the social order.

The weaker frame of play, the comparative ease of transition to this liminal domain, its plasticity, and the manifold ways in which it is moulded to fit the contours of social form, make play a highly adaptable and resilient medium of communication to express ongoing local conditions (Handelman, 1975, 1976). Put simply, as a meta-communicative channel play has a higher survival value than does ritual. But, unlike ritual, play messages cannot define the moral community, its values as a collectivity, and their ideal relationship to behaviour.

Predicated on premises of amorality, doubt, and falsity, with a voluminous capacity to comment on the immediate, play is tailored more precisely to express the contours of public anomie and personal alienation, than it is to express the lengthy durations of collective integration and harmony that are the provinces of ritual. In the absence of ritual, attempts to transmit meta-messages akin to those of ritual through the play channel are stripped of their sanctity morality and truth, and are rendered 'unserious', faint, and ineffectual.

FOOTNOTES

1. I am indebted to Victor Turner and Shlomo Deshen for their comments during the preparation of this paper.

2. In an unabridged version of this paper (presented to the Conference) I demonstrate these points using Turnbull's (1973) description of the Ik of Uganda.

REFERENCES

See Bibliography for publications on humour, laughter and comedy

Bateson, G., The message 'this is play'. In: B. Schaffner (Ed.), Group Processes. Josiah Macy Foundation, New York (1956).

Bateson, G., A theory of play and fantasy. In: G. Bateson (Ed.), Steps to an Ecology of Mind. Ballantine, New York (1972).

Csikszentmihalyi, M. & Bennett, S., An exploratory model of play. American Anthropology, 73, 45-58 (1971).

Douglas, M., Purity and Danger. Routledge & Kegan Paul, London (1966).

Erikson, K.T., Wayward Puritans. Wiley, New York (1966).

Gluckman, M., Rituals of rebellion in South-East Africa. In: M. Gluckman (Ed.), Order and Rebellion in Tribal Africa. Free Press, New York (1963).

Goffman, E., Frame Analysis. Harper Colophon, New York (1974).

Grathoff, R.H., The Structure of Social Inconsistencies: a Contribution to a Unified Theory of Play, Game and Social Action. Nijhoff, The Hague (1970).

Handelman, D., Expressive interaction and social structure: play and an emergent game form in an Israeli social setting. In: A. Kendon, R. Harris & M.R. Key (Eds.), Organization of Behavior in Face-to-Face Interaction. Mouton, The Hague (1975).

Handelman, D., Re-thinking 'banana time': symbolic integration in a work setting. Urban Life, 4, 433-448 (1976).

Huizinga, J., Homo Ludens. Paladin, London (1970).

Kennedy, J.G., Bonds of laughter among the Tarahumara Indians: toward a rethinking of
     joking relationship theory. In: W. Goldschmidt & H. Hoijer (Eds.), The Social
     Anthropology of Latin America. University of California Press, Los Angeles (1970).

Miller, S., Ends, means, and galumphing: some leitmotifs of play. American Anthropology,
     75, 87–98 (1973).

Norbeck, E., Religion and human play. Paper read to the Ninth ICAES, Chicago (1973).

Rapaport, R.A., Ritual, sanctity, and cybernetics. American Anthropology, 73, 59–76 (1971).

Turnbull, C.M., The Mountain People. Cape, London (1973).

Turner, V., The Ritual Process. Aldine, Chicago (1969).

Turner, V., Dramas, Fields, and Metaphors. Cornell University Press, Ithaca (1974).

Social Occasions for Joking: A Cross-Cultural Study

Patricia J. Castell and Jeffrey H. Goldstein

Temple University, Philadelphia

Humour is most often studied in the experimental laboratory and within a single culture. The only attempt to study humour in vivo on a cross-cultural level has been reported by Handelman and Kapferer (1972). These anthropologists identified two types of joking situation: setting-specific and category-routinized. Among the distinctions made between these two joking situations is that in setting-specific joking, humour arises out of the immediate setting in a more or less spontaneous fashion, whereas with category-routinized joking there is a socially accepted licence to joke between members of various classes of individual. The Handelman and Kapferer study was conducted in a small workshop in Israel and in a factory in Zambia, and in each setting both types of joking were observed, though the frequency with which each type occurred was not reported.

Category-routinized joking was examined in a study by Goldstein and Kernis in 1976. That study was an attempt to determine, in a limited context, characteristics of the audience toward which jokes were directed. Letters written to the advice column, 'Dear Abby,' were divided by two judges into those in which Abby's responses were witty and those in which her responses were serious. These two groups of letters - those with serious and those with humorous responses - were then judged with respect to the age and sex of the letter writer, the writer's marital status, what and who the letter was about. These data were then analyzed by Chi-squares. While no main effects were obtained on any of the variables, there were a number of interesting interaction effects. When letter writers were divided at the median into older and younger males and females, it was found that younger males were given joking replies more than younger females, but that older males were never given joking replies, whereas older females received joking replies nearly one-third of the time. This finding suggests that joking may be age and sex linked. Joking responses were also found to be a function of the topic of the letter which interacted with the sex of the letter writer. When females wrote about themselves or about their relatives, they often received humorous replies, as opposed to males who wrote about the same topics. On the other hand, when males wrote about their neighbours or friends, they more often received joking replies than females who wrote about the same topics.

The present study involves an examination of the situations which produce laughter among college students in Belgium, Hong Kong and the United States. Our interest was two-fold. First, we wanted to examine the content of humour most often enjoyed by individuals in these three locations. In previous cross-cultural research, Goldstein, Silverman and Anderson (1976) found that American students appreciated aggressive humour more than nonaggressive humour, whereas students in Senegal, West Africa, and Tokyo, Japan, appreciated nonaggressive more than aggressive humour. In that research, however, students were provided with a list of preselected jokes, and so conclusions cannot be drawn about the content of spontaneously produced or appreciated humour in the three cultures. The present study requested students to write the joke which they found to be most humorous, with no restrictions placed on the content of jokes. It was hypothesized, based on the earlier Goldstein et al study, that Americans would write considerably more aggressive jokes as their most favourite than would Belgian or Chinese students.

The second focus of the study was on the social settings in which laughter occurred. We asked students to write about the last time they made someone laugh. They were requested to write down what it was that they did or said which made someone laugh; who was present at the time; whether their behaviour was intentionally designed to promote laughter; where they were and what they were doing at the time; and other relevant information about the joking occasion.

Since this part of the research was considered largely exploratory, we had few specific hypotheses. We did expect to find cross-cultural differences in the type of event which evoked laughter, but we did not anticipate significant cultural differences in the social settings in which laughter occurred. We believed that joking would be more frequent among same-sex groups than in opposite- or mixed-sex groups; that jokes would most often be told among peers; and that a sizeable number of humorous situations would not involve intentional joking at all, but would involve slips of the tongue, pratfalls, double entendres and mimicry.

We also wished to examine sex differences both within and between cultures. We reasoned that females would be less likely to joke intentionally in the presence of males than would males in the presence of females. Also we anticipated that females, when they did joke in the presence of males, would be more likely to tell incongruous jokes than they would sexual and aggressive jokes, whereas males would not show any appreciable differences in the kind of jokes which they would tell in the presence of males or females. Underlying these sex-difference hypotheses is the implicit assumption that joking is in some ways 'masculine'; that males have more licence to joke than females. We therefore predicted that the presence of females would not inhibit the frequency or content of male joking, but that the presence of males would influence the nature of female joking.

In general the present research aimed to examine patterns of joking situations both within and between cultures and sexes. We wished to examine both the frequency of different types of joking activity and the intentionality of different kinds of joking as a function of the social and physical setting. The ultimate purpose of the research is to arrive at a theory which is capable of predicting attempts at humour, and we shall have more to say about this matter later.

PROCEDURE

Male and female students at universities in Louvin, Belgium, Hong Kong, and Philadelphia, were given a three-page questionnaire. The questionnaire, which was presented either in English (in Hong Kong and Philadelphia) or Flemish (Louvin), contained three questions, each on a separate page. Question 1 read: 'What is the funniest joke that you remember?....' Question 2 read: 'Please write a paragraph describing what made the joke funny to you....' And Question 3 asked: 'When was the last time that you made someone else laugh? Was it intentional? .. Please describe the circumstances and what you said or did which caused others to laugh.' Following these questions, the student's age and sex were recorded. In all, sixty Belgian, ninety-seven Chinese and thirty-two American students completed the questionnaire.

Coding schemes were devised for each question. Although there are scores of permutations and combinations of these variables which could be examined, the results reported here represent initial analyses of the data. A more complete report of this and related research is in preparation.

RESULTS

The results which will be presented involve Question 1 (analysis of favourite jokes) and Question 3 (social setting for joking).

Analysis of Favourite Jokes

Our primary interest with respect to Question 1 was whether there would be cross-cultural differences in content. Responses were divided into aggressive, sexual and neutral/incongruous and analyzed by means of a 3 x 3 Chi-square. As predicted, there were more aggressive jokes written by Americans than by Chinese or Belgian students ($\chi^2 = 12.9$; df = 4; p < .05). Americans also reported more sexual jokes than others. In Table 1 it can be seen that over half the jokes reported by Belgian and Chinese students were neutral in content, while only one-fourth of the jokes reported by Americans were neutral. The same pattern of results was obtained when the content of jokes in response to Question 3 were analyzed.

TABLE 1   Content of Favourite Jokes

Joke Content	COUNTRY		
	Belgium (55)	Hong Kong (97)	USA (22)
Aggressive	31%	25%	46%
Sexual	13%	8%	27%
Neutral	56%	67%	27%

Note (for Table 1): Not all subjects recorded jokes in response to
question 1. Hence, N is 174 rather than 189.

The Occasion for Joking: Intentionality

One of our predictions was simply that a good amount of laughter would occur in response to
actions rather than being initiated intentionally. Nearly forty per cent of all incidents
reported involved unintentional laugh-producing behaviour. Intentionality was found to
interact with country and with the sex of the subject. A three-factor Chi-square was
computed on intentional and unintentional joking by sex of subject by country (see Table 2).
The analysis yielded three significant effects. A country by intentionality interaction
($x^2 = 6.4$; $p < .05$), which indicated that more of the laughter evoked by Chinese students
was unintentional (47%) than was the case with Belgian (32%) or American (23%) students.
There was also a sex of subject by intentionality interaction ($x^2 = 4.0$; $p < .05$), which
indicated that females evoked laughter unintentionally (47%) more often than males (31%).
Finally, a country by sex by intentionality interaction ($x^2 = 29.8$; df = 2; $p < .01$)
suggested that females were most likely to evoke laughter unintentionally among Chinese
students and least likely among Belgian students.

What we must consider is not simply whether males or females joke unintentionally more often,
but whether such behaviour is differentially influenced by the social setting.

TABLE 2   Intentional and Unintentional Joking

	Belgium		Hong Kong		USA	
	Males	Females	Males	Females	Males	Females
	(46)	(7)	(29)	(54)	(18)	(12)
Intentional	65%	86%	62%	48%	89%	58%
Unintentional	35%	14%	38%	52%	11%	42%

The Social Situation and Joking: Effects of Sex

We earlier reasoned that intentional joking by males and females would be differentially
influenced by the sex of others present at the time. Of particular interest was the
assumption that intentional joking was primarily a masculine trait. While the frequencies
in Table 3 are not sufficiently great to permit detailed analysis, we can see that in the
Chinese sample, most of the instances in which females elicited laughter from males were
unintentional (74%). In all three countries, males were more likely to joke intentionally
in the presence of females than were females in the presence of males.

TABLE 3   Joking by Social Setting (Frequencies)

	Belgium		Hong Kong		USA	
SOCIAL SETTING:	Males	Females	Males	Females	Males	Females
Same Sex Present						
Intentional	16	4	7	11	9	1
Unintentional	7	0	1	8	1	2
Opposite Sex Present						
Intentional	6	1	8	5	4	1
Unintentional	4	0	7	14	1	2

Note: n's are reduced because not all subjects provided information which could
be coded for each variable.

We noted too that in no case did a female actually relate a 'joke' which had been previously
heard from another party. Males reported passing on jokes in twelve per cent of the cases.
This lends further credence to joking as 'masculine'.

We proposed that male joking would not vary whether the audience was male or female, whereas
female joking would be different if the audience consisted of males than if it consisted
solely of females. This was found to be the case. Although the frequencies are small, in
no instance did a female intentionally tell an aggressive or sexual joke in the presence of
the opposite sex, although they did tell such jokes in the presence of other females. On

the other hand, males told sexual and aggressive jokes about as often in the presence of females (5 of 15 incidents) as they did in the presence of males (9 of 30 incidents).

The unintentional mistakes of females were often the cause of laughter by males (16 of 23, or 70%, of cross-sex incidents) while females rarely laughed at unintentional male mistakes (12 of 30, or 40%, of cross-sex incidents: $x^2 = 3.5$; df = 1; p <.07).

While those findings support a 'joking-as-masculine' hypothesis, they are also open to alternative interpretations. It may be that females are simply more sensitive to the social situation than males, and therefore modify their behaviour according to the sex of those present. It is also possible that the data reflect status differences between males and females. If, in the three countries studied, females have lower status than males, they might initiate fewer intentional jokes. This latter interpretation is consistent with Handelman and Kapferer's notion of the need for a licence to joke.

The Physical Setting

The physical setting had little influence on the frequency or content of joking, although it was found that there was a difference in the proportion of intentional and unintentional joking in different locations ($x^2 = 13.4$; df = 3; p <.01). As can be seen from Table 4, most joking in public places (e.g., restaurants, bars, etcetera) was intentional, whereas joking at school and at home tended to be unintentional, and consisted primarily of verbal double entendres and behavioural mistakes and blunders.

If we examine the type of event which provoked laughter in different settings, we find that the most frequent laugh-producing event is some verbal statement, followed in frequency by a mistake (e.g., mistaken identity, breach of etiquette), followed by an attempt to cause laughter behaviourally, through mimicry or facial expression. The frequency of these events, however, is a function of intent. Behavioural mistakes were the most frequent unintentional laughter-inducing events while verbal statements (puns, repeating jokes heard from others) were the most frequent intentional events causing laughter.

TABLE 4   Joking by Physical Setting

	P H Y S I C A L L O C A T I O N			
	Home, Dormitory (25)	Restaurant, Bar, Cafe (34)	At school, In class (37)	Other (8)
Intentional	52%	82%	41%	50%
Unintentional	48%	18%	59%	50%

The Time of Most Recent Joking

Subjects were requested to write the date and time of the most recent joking incident. These data were coded along a five-point continuum from (1) less than three hours ago, to (5) more than seven days ago. A 2 x 3 analysis of variance (unweighted means solution) was computed on these data, the factors being sex of subject and country. Only one effect was significant, the main effect for country (F = 3.7; df = 2, 125; p <.05). Chinese students reported that the most recent joking incident occurred less recently ($\overline{X} = 3.00$) than American ($\overline{X} = 2.57$) or Belgian ($\overline{X} = 2.15$) students.

Modal Situations for Intentional Joking

If we examine the most frequent social and physical setting for intentional joking we find overall that an incongruous verbal statement is made in the presence of one or two members of the same sex as the jokester and that such an event is most likely to occur at school. The only variations in modes for the six groups of subjects were relatively minor. Males in the USA were more likely to do than say something incongruous; American females were likely to tell an aggressive rather than an incongruous joke; and Chinese females were more likely to make a verbally incongruous statement in a restaurant or cafeteria than at school.

DISCUSSION

While this research is largely exploratory in nature it does permit us to draw several tentative conclusions and to suggest a number of hypotheses which emerge from the data. First, as in previous research, we found that there is a greater tendency for Americans than for others to appreciate aggressive humour. This is true of favourite jokes as well as of joking which is spontaneously initiated. We have previously explained these results as indicating one of two possible phenomena. Either the greater familiarity of violence to Americans leads them to joke aggressively or the joking may be a means of coping with the violence so prevalent in major American cities (see Goldstein, Suls & Anthony, 1972; Goldstein, Silverman & Anderson, 1976). We do not believe that the tendency toward aggressive joking represents a tendency toward violent behaviour among the American subjects (see Goldstein, 1975, p52-59).

The results of this research also lend support to the notion that joking may generally be considered a masculine activity. Males more than females in all three cultures initiate joking, laugh at the unintentional mistakes of females, and joke about as often in the presence of males and females. Females, on the other hand, seem much more sensitive to the social setting. While they tell aggressive and sexual jokes to other females, they do not do so when males are present. Females often reported that they had no favourite jokes or could not remember any jokes or joking incidents in response to our questions. Males rarely had this difficulty. While others have also proposed that joking may be masculine (cf. McGhee, 1976b; Leventhal & Cupchik, 1976), we must stress that, as we have indicated, there are other ways in which these data may be interpreted.

With respect to cultural differences, what few differences we obtained were generally attributable to the Chinese sample. For example, while Americans told more aggressive and sexual jokes in response to Question 1, Chinese students told the least sexual and aggressive jokes. On most items, American and Belgian students tended to behave alike while, when discrepancies were found, they could be attributed to the Hong Kong students.

Of course, we can thus question whether the research reported here is truly cross-cultural, and, if so, what are the cultures involved. It could be argued that college students, regardless of nationality, constitute one vast cross-national but unitary culture. In this sense, our three groups of students may represent a single culture. Our results belie this notion, however. While college students undoubtedly share a number of values and experiences, there is no denying the fact that they also enjoy unique values and experiences attributable to national culture. Since we have earlier implied that studies conducted simultaneously in North America and Western Europe are not truly cross-cultural (see Goldstein, this volume), then we should consider our Belgian and American students to represent two sub-groups of a single 'Western' culture. Less strong is the case that Chinese students have more in common with American and Belgian students than they do with Chinese nonstudents. In this sense, the Chinese students may constitute an 'Eastern' culture. We should, of course, recognize that cultural differences in our study will be minimized because college students in general may have common cognitions which they do not share with their nonstudent countrymen.

ACKNOWLEDGEMENT

We are deeply indebted to Professor Jozef Nuttin, Jr., of the University of Louvin, and Reverend E. Kvan of the University of Hong Kong, without whose cooperation and assistance this research could not have been done.

REFERENCES

See Bibliography for publications on humour, laughter and comedy

Goldstein, J.H., Aggression and Crimes of Violence. Oxford University Press, New York (1975).

Goldstein, J.H. & Kernis, M., Category-routinized joking: An analysis of letters to 'Dear Abby'. Unpublished manuscript, Temple University (1976).

Goldstein, J.H., Silverman, A.F. & Anderson, P.K., A cross-cultural investigation of humour: Appreciation of jokes varying in familiarity and hostility. Paper presented at XXIst International Congress of Psychology, Paris (1976).

CHILDREN'S HUMOUR

Children's Humour: A Review of Current Research Trends

Paul E. McGhee

Fels Research Institute, Yellow Springs, Ohio

INTRODUCTION

The children's humour symposium included six papers, focusing on varying social, cognitive, affective, and methodological issues, This chapter places these studies in perspective by reviewing recent theoretical and empirical developments and drawing attention to methodological problems common to any attempt to study the developmental aspects of humour. Since three review articles dealing with children's laughter or humour have been published in the past five years (McGhee, 1971b, 1974a; Rothbart, 1973), primary attention will be given here to new developments in the field.

THEORETICAL ADVANCES

Three new or revised theoretical models have been advanced in the past year (McGhee, this volume; Shultz, 1976; Sroufe & Waters, 1976). Shultz (1972, 1974a; Shultz & Horibe, 1974) has distinguished between two stages in the development of humour appreciation: (1) humour in pure, unresolved incongruity, and (2) humour in resolved incongruity. The former stage lasts until approximately six years of age, and then is replaced by the latter, which is maintained through adulthood. Considerable support for this two-stage model has been provided in Shultz's studies, but it is important to note that this support stems almost exclusively from humour based on verbal jokes or riddles. There is now evidence that this transition into appreciation of resolvable incongruity merely reflects the fact that children below the age of six or so do not understand these verbal forms of humour. Shultz and Pilon (1973), for example, found that it was only after six years of age that children began to detect linguistic ambiguity. Similarly, McGhee (1974b) and Prentice and Fathman (1975) found that first graders were unable to distinguish between joking and nonjoking versions of riddles based on linguistic ambiguity. In the first paper presented in the symposium, Pien and Rothbart tested Shultz's model by using cartoons which do not require comprehension of linguistic ambiguity. They manipulated the presence of incongruity and resolution information, and found that even preschool children are capable of appreciating resolvable incongruities. The timing of the onset of appreciation of resolution information in incongruity humour, then, remains unclear.

Shultz (1976) has most recently proposed that appreciation of humour in pure incongruity begins at about eighteen months, corresponding to the beginnings of symbolic play. However, several more primitive forms of humour are also suggested to exist prior to the development of symbolic capacities. One form of humour in infancy is 'characterized principally in terms of pleasure in cognitive mastery.' Shultz draws here from Piaget's (1962) view that infants derive pleasure from the successful assimilation of discrepant stimulus events (i.e., where some accommodation is required). McCall and McGhee (in press) reviewed infant research along these lines and concluded that this pleasure is likely to be maximized when some optimal moderate amount of discrepancy is processed by the infant. Other forms of humour in the first year are found in connection with certain games, such as peek-a-boo, the tickling game, and chasing games. The laughter and smiling which accompany these activities are considered to constitute early forms of humour because they share the biphasic sequence of arousal increase (presumably based on uncertainty) followed by arousal decrease which is hypothesized to occur in the identification and resolution of incongruities among older children and adults.

McGhee (this volume) disagrees with Shultz's (1976) contention that infants are capable of experiencing humour in the first year. He has argued that the experience of humour requires the capacity for assimilating events in a fantasy or make-believe sense. This does not occur until some time in the second year. McGhee's position is in agreement with Shultz's view that smiling or laughing following the effortful assimilation of a discrepant event indicates that this process is pleasurable, but this pleasure cannot automatically be equated with humour. The effortful processing of discrepant information may contribute to the funniness of jokes or cartoons (McGhee, 1976a), but this activity is also intrinsically pleasurable in its own right. Studies of problem solving in young children (e.g., Harter, 1974; Kagan, 1971) support this view, demonstrating increased probability of smiling following problem solution, and following the solution of more difficult problems. In McGhee's view, the fact that the cognitive mastery of new information (and certain games, such as peek-a-boo) shares the biphasic arousal fluctuations assumed to be operative in humour has no implications for whether the former must be classified as humour.

Sroufe and Waters (1976) have also emphasized the importance of arousal fluctuations present in infant smiling and laughing. In contrast to Shultz (1976), however, they do not consider it necessary to bring the concept of humour to bear on these reactions in order to explain them. They argue that something akin to Berlyne's (1960, 1972) 'arousal jag' is required to produce both smiling and laughter in the infant. That is, there must be a tension increase followed by a sudden recovery or drop in tension. 'In comparison with smiling, laughter ... requires a greater and typically more rapid build up of tension.' Sroufe and Waters emphasize, however, that the early tension increase which results from encountering an incongruous event is very similar for both positive and negative forms of affect. When any new or discrepant stimulus is first encountered, there is an initial orienting and appraisal process. Physiological records of arousal do not differ until after this appraisal has occurred. If the event is evaluated as safe or unthreatening, smiling or laughter will occur. If the child is insecure or interprets the event as a threat, crying or some other form of negative affect will occur (see Sroufe, Waters & Matas, 1974). The important point for our present concerns is that 'the initial orienting, appraisal, and tension production is not affectively charged and that affect is determined by context as well as by stimulus discrepancy' (Sroufe & Waters, 1976).

EMPIRICAL ADVANCES

Cognitive Aspects of Humour

In addition to the recent studies providing support for Shultz's two-stage model (Shultz, 1974a; Shultz & Bloom, 1974; Shultz & Horibe, 1974; Shultz & Pilon, 1973), two recent studies have further tested the 'cognitive congruency principle' initially described by Zigler, Levine, and Gould (1966a). According to this principle, appreciation of the humour in jokes or cartoons should be greatest when the humour stimuli are 'in keeping with the complexity of the child's cognitive apparatus.' Maximal humour appreciation should be associated with some optimal moderate amount of cognitive challenge to comprehension. Zigler, Levine, and Gould (1967) and McGhee (1971a) made unsatisfactory attempts to test this view. In the former study, amount of cognitive challenge was defined in terms of comprehension scores obtained for the humour stimuli used. No attempt was made to assess either the cognitive resources of the subjects tested, or the cognitive demand features of the particular humour stimuli used. Moreover, it does not necessarily follow that greater amounts of cognitive effort precede high rather than low comprehension scores. In the latter study, these deficiencies were overcome by using humour stimuli whose comprehension depended on the acquisition of concrete operational thinking. However, it was still not possible to specify in advance relative differences in amount of cognitive effort required by different children to understand the humour depicted. The second symposium paper, presented by Chris Athey, was aimed at a further analysis of the relationship between difficulty level of the humour stimulus, comprehension, and appreciation, and it shares many of the difficulties of these two earlier studies.

McGhee (1976a) appears to have provided a satisfactory test of the cognitive congruency principle by using jokes whose comprehension depends on the acquisition of specific measurable concepts or abilities. More importantly, an independent basis was achieved for predicting in advance how much effort should be required for comprehension. Using jokes based on the violation of conservation and class inclusion concepts, appreciation (based on funniness ratings) was greatest soon after these concepts were acquired. Reduced levels of appreciation were shown both by children who had not yet acquired these concepts and by children who had mastered them several years previously. Thus, appreciation was greatest when comprehension should have been most challenging to existing cognitive skills.

Schaier and Cicirelli (1976) presented conservation jokes similar to those used by McGhee (1976a) to ninety-six elderly men and women. Within an age range of fifty to eighty years, they found that comprehension of the jokes used decreased with age, while appreciation increased with age. This is the opposite direction of findings usually obtained for children. They interpreted these findings as being consistent with the cognitive congruency principle. Presumably, the jokes placed a greater demand on the intellectual capacities of the older individuals, and this made them funnier.

Two studies exploring the child's moral development have shed further light on the relationship between cognitive development and children's humour. Zillmann and Bryant (1975) found that among adults, humour is maximized when retaliatory acts equitably compensate for some provocation. Over- and under-retaliation were found to lead to reduced levels of appreciation. In other words, humour tends to be maximized when our intuitive sense of justice is satisfied. This view was tested by obtaining groups of children at two different levels of moral functioning, as described by Piaget (1932): expiatory and equitable retribution. While children in the former stage tend to see more extreme levels of punishment as more just, children in the latter see just punishment as that which 'fits' (is equitable to) the misdeed. When presented with a fairy-tale containing equitable, over-, or under-retaliation to a provocation, children at the less mature expiatory moral level showed greater appreciation in the over-retaliation condition, while those at the more mature moral level showed maximal appreciation when retaliation was equitable. At both moral levels, then, humour was most appreciated when retaliation was viewed as adequate and just.

Piaget (1932) also described a transition from a heteronomous to an autonomous level of moral functioning at the age of six or seven years. In the former stage, it is the more objective quantitative aspects of an event that determine how naughty or wrong it is perceived to be. Children at this stage are very egocentric and unaware of the intentions of a potential aggressor. For the autonomous child, damaging or harmful events are considered naughty or wrong only if they are considered to be intentional. McGhee (1974c) presented pairs of humorous stories containing either high or low levels of damaging outcomes inflicted either intentionally or accidentally, to children at these two moral levels. He found that heteronomous children found more damaging outcomes funnier than less damaging ones (apart from their accidental or intentional nature) while autonomous children found accidental outcomes funnier apart from the level of damage depicted. Heteronomous children also explained their choices in terms of the greater amount of damage, while autonomous children explained their choices in terms of the accidental nature of the damaging event. These findings contrast with the findings of Zillmann and Bryant (1975) for children at the expiatory level, in that the morally less mature heteronomous children judged the same types of events judged to be morally wrong to also be funnier (when placed in a humorous context). The more advanced autonomous children, on the other hand, like Zillmann and Bryant's more advanced children judged events considered morally wrong to be less funny. Thus, the impact of the progression into higher levels of cognitive-moral functioning appears to contribute to developmental changes in the child's humour appreciation in a more complicated fashion than previously thought. These findings do help account for the frequently observed 'cruelty' in much of young children's laughter and humour, but additional research along these lines is clearly needed. It might be fruitful to extend Kohlberg's (1969) model of moral development to humour studies of the type reported here.

Personality Variables

The study of personality and other individual difference variables associated with children's humour responsiveness remains at a virtual standstill. Brodzinsky (1975) took a step toward filling this void by relating children's information processing styles to their comprehension and appreciation of humour stimuli varying in difficulty level and degree of affective salience. Testing six- to eleven-year-olds, he found that reflective children (at two of the three age levels) showed better comprehension than impulsives of the cartoons used, but impulsives showed more smiling and laughter. While appreciation is undoubtedly influenced to some extent by such factors as degree of comprehension or the ease with which that comprehension is achieved, as noted previously, these findings suggest that we must also consider various individual difference variables which serve to determine appreciation given that the cartoon or joke is understood. It is important to note that in Brodzinsky's study, impulsives did not differ from reflective children in their intellectual evaluation of the funniness of the cartoons seen.

LaChance (1972) asked fifth-graders to write down as many jokes or humorous events as they could, and found that those who listed more also had higher scores on a measure of self-concept. Children with low self-concepts in the area of peer relationships reported more instances of hostility in their humour items. Waterman (1973) presented film segments from 'Laugh-in' to seven- to twelve-year-old 'normal' boys, and to nine- to eleven-year-old boys considered to have either behaviour problems or withdrawal symptoms. Normal children were more likely to show the full range of smiling and laughter responses than either of the other two groups. Withdrawn children, however, were most likely to use smiling to express their humour, while children with behaviour problems were most likely to demonstrate laughing. Finally, Gidynsky (1972) used a group of preadolescent boys and found that children who were highly anxious about peer rejection, along with those who were, in fact, frequently rejected by their peers (based on sociometric ratings), rated all types of humour presented as being funnier than did less anxious and less rejected children. These data might be interpreted as supporting Wolfenstein's (1954) view that children use humour as a means of coping with stress.

Social Influences

The study of social influences on different aspects of humour appears to be the most rapidly developing area of humour research at this time. In the area of children's humour, this can be primarily linked to the efforts of Chapman and his associates. The extent of reversal of previous research trends may be seen in the fact that all of the studies of the social aspects of humour cited in McGhee's (1971b) initial literature review were completed in the nineteen-thirties. In the first study to re-open this research area, Leventhal and Mace (1970) used children in grades one to five to determine the effect of conditions designed to facilitate laughter upon both the subsequent laughter and ratings of funniness of slapstick films. In one of their studies, children were encouraged to either laugh a lot at the film, or to not laugh at all – that is, to suppress laughter. The most important finding in this study concerned sex differences in responsiveness under these conditions. Both boys and girls laughed more in the facilitation condition, but the sexes differed in their intellectual evaluations of the funniness of the film. Girls also rated the film as funnier in the facilitation condition (consistent with their laughter), while boys gave higher funniness ratings in the inhibition condition. Thus, overt expressions of mirth and intellectual judgments seemed to be more independent among boys than among girls.

A second part of the study by Leventhal and Mace (1970) explored the same question, using the presence or absence of canned laughter rather than instructions to laugh or not laugh. Again, both sexes tended to show more laughter in the canned laughter condition, but only girls showed a corresponding effect for funniness ratings; boys judged the film less funny under the canned laughter condition. Thus, it appears that girls show a greater reliance upon feedback from their own expressive behaviour than do boys in making judgments about funniness.

Chapman and his associates have also found important sex differences in their work, although they have not been primarily concerned with factors influencing the consistency between affective and intellectual measures of appreciation. This work (Chapman, 1973b, 1975b; Chapman & Wright, 1976) is reviewed in detail by Chapman (1976) and is also mentioned elsewhere in this book. Some of Chapman's work involves the use of adult samples; these studies are closely integrated with his work with children, but will not be reviewed here. In most cases, Chapman presented tape-recorded materials to children over headphones. Variables manipulated included whether the child heard the material alone or in the presence of a companion (who was assumed to be listening to either the same or different material), the presence or absence of a confederate who showed one of several levels of laughter or looking at another confederate, distance between children, and degree of social intimacy within pairs of children.

This programme of research has yielded the following findings: (1) children whose companion was assumed to be listening to the same material (coaction condition) showed greater amounts of laughter and smiling than children with a nonlistening companion (audience condition). Children in the audience condition in turn showed more laughter than children in an alone condition. The latter finding was interpreted as suggesting that the 'mere presence' of another child is sufficient to facilitate laughter. While laughter in a companion may enhance the child's laughter, it is not necessary for the facilitatory effect to occur; (2) children in an alone condition showed less smiling and laughter than children with either a listening or nonlistening companion; (3) the presence of a companion is associated with increased laughter, regardless of whether the companion is listening to the same or different material. This (and other findings) was interpreted as supporting the view that it is the 'sharing of the social situation' which facilitates the child's laughter, not the sharing of the humour stimulus. Waterman (1973) interpreted her data in a similar fashion; (4) girls showed more smiling and looking at their companion than did boys. This was interpreted as an indication that girls tend to be more interested than boys in sharing the social situation; (5) increased smiling and laughter by a coacting confederate produced increased smiling, laughter and looking (at the confederate) in test subjects. Increased looking alone by the confederate, however, produced only increased smiling and looking – not increased laughter; (6) even an unresponsive child companion enhances laughter (although this inhibits laughter among adult subjects – Osborne & Chapman, this volume); (7) as pairs of confederates look at each other less, test subjects' smiling and laughter increased; (8) a second confederate does not increase laughter beyond that resulting from presence of a single confederate; (9) smiling, laughter and eye-contact are increased by sitting closer together; (10) increased social intimacy (as manipulated by seating arrangement and gaze pattern) is associated with increased smiling and laughter.

Foot and Chapman (1976) replicated some of the above findings, but not others. Again, both boys and girls showed more laughter and smiling when watching films in the presence of a companion than when alone. This held both when the partners were of the same and opposite sex. Boys, however, showed equal amounts of smiling and laughter regardless of whether they were with a boy or girl, while girls laughed and smiled more when with a boy than when with a girl. Distance between children while watching the films, and between children and the experimenter, was not related to amount of smiling, laughter, or looking behaviour. The discrepancy between these and Chapman's earlier findings is probably due to the difference in mode of presentation of humour materials, since eye-contact between children should be minimized during pictorial presentations.

These studies have provided substantial gains in our understanding of the social aspects of children's humour, and point out the complexity of social forms of influence on the humour process. Those of us interested in other aspects of children's humour must be aware of these potential social influences in planning future studies and interpreting data. Inconsistency of findings regarding more cognitive aspects of humour, for example, may simply reflect different social circumstances present in the testing situation.

Creative Aspects of Humour

The development of the creative aspects of humour continues to attract little attention among humour researchers. This is surprising, since it is likely that the earliest forms of humour are self-generated. On the other hand, a number of unique methodological problems make it considerably more difficult to study children's ability to create humour. Most importantly, humour is typically created in nonstressful conditions and among friends. Asking a child to produce humorous captions or cartoon completions in a laboratory setting may produce a form of test anxiety, which might, in turn, interfere with performance. Wallach and Kogan (1965) have noted the importance of avoiding the instilling of a task or test orientation in subjects when testing for creativity in general.

It is equally important to note that one cannot always tell whether a child has just spontaneously gained some new humorous insight, or whether s/he is merely parroting some humorous response heard previously. Wolfenstein (1954) first drew attention to the fact that children laugh at jokes and tell jokes themselves before they actually understand the basis for humour in the joke. When asked to produce a funny answer or event, the child may give the investigator some kind of response simply because s/he was asked to do so. In most cases, some perceptually prominent feature of the stimulus event will be alluded to, without any real conviction that this feature somehow makes the event funny.

Perhaps the most difficult problem facing investigators attempting to study children's ability to create humour lies in the determination of the nature of the joking relationship actually created by the child. Investigators must be careful to avoid 'adultomorphizing' here: that is, the more advanced cognitive capacities of the adult investigator may lead him/her to perceive a more complicated humour relationship than that intended by the child. For example, it seems safe to assume that a five-year-old child has no awareness at all of the abstract features that an adult might identify in the child's joke. With adult samples, this difficulty can be avoided simply by asking the individual to explain the point or nature of the joke (although it is often difficult for even adults to do this). The young child's limited verbal facilities, however, make it difficult to accept any verbal explanation as an index of the level of understanding achieved.

The limited work which has been completed along these lines has focused on characteristics of the child who is creative in general. For example, children who do well on tests of creativity are better at creating their own humour (as well as understanding and appreciating the humour of others), are more likely to have a generally playful attitude, attach greater importance to having a 'good sense of humour,' are considered by both peers and teachers to have a better sense of humour, have a greater curiosity about new ideas or events, are more willing to risk a 'crazy idea,' and demonstrate more frequent daydreaming and make-believe play during the early preschool years (Getzels & Jackson, 1962; Gidynsky, 1972; Hauck & Thomas, 1972; Lieberman, 1965, 1967; Singer, 1973; Singer & Rummo, 1973; Torrance, 1962; Wallach & Kogan, 1965; Weisberg & Springer, 1961). Throughout these studies (and in studies of adults), a close link is repeatedly noted between humour, playfulness, and creativity.

Only one attempt has been made to study age differences in children's ability to create a joking relationship. McGhee (1974b) found that the ability to produce 'double meaning' answers to riddle questions increased progressively between grades one to six. The infrequent success of first-graders in this study was not surprising, in that it has already been noted that it is only by age six or so that children become capable of understanding the linguistic ambiguities which comprise double meaning jokes.

A common approach to studying children's humour involves simply asking children to tell their favourite jokes. The paper presented by Jennings Bryant in this symposium adopted this approach. Assuming that the kinds of jokes children tell at any given developmental level reflect underlying cognitive capacities and 'current concerns' (Klinger, 1971), this approach may be useful in determining the types of humour stimuli which might be presented to children at different ages in order to study their ability to achieve new humorous insights.

Humour as a Facilitator of Children's Learning

If humour is agreed to be a pleasurable experience, it follows that stimuli associated with humour should have enhanced reward value. This suggests that humour might be useful as a means of facilitating learning in children. The producers of 'Sesame Street' would appear to be operating under this assumption, since humorous incongruities are commonly used in an effort to attract the child's attention and teach basic concepts. Unfortunately, few attempts have been made to test humour's usefulness along these lines. Curran (1972) and Neumann (1972) found no significant differences in retention of class material as a function of whether or not cartoons were used as an aid to learning. Children in the Curran study showed comparable levels of interest in the two conditions, as did males in the Neumann study. Females, however, preferred classes where cartoons were included in the instruction. An especially interesting finding was obtained by Hauck and Thomas (1972), who demonstrated that humour facilitates incidental learning, but not intentional learning.

One study using adults may have important implications for the role of humour in children's learning. Smith, Ascough, Ettinger, and Nelson (1971) administered either a nonhumorous or humorous (one-third of the test items) course examination to college students differing in level of test anxiety. If humour does serve to release tension and anxiety, as suggested by the findings of Dworkin and Efran (1967) and Singer (1968), then highly anxious subjects should show better test performance when humour is introduced into the testing situation. (It has long been demonstrated that high test anxiety interferes with test performance. See Sarason, 1960). As expected, highly anxious subjects scored better in the humorous than in the nonhumorous condition. The performance of moderately anxious individuals, however, was poorer in the humour condition. Several of the latter individuals subsequently indicated that they found the humour in the test distracting.

The relationship between humour and the learning process deserves further attention. The entertainment potential of humorous events is readily apparent, but it is equally apparent that entertainment conditions do not necessarily provide the optimal conditions for learning and remembering. It may be that humour is ideal for getting and maintaining the child's attention, but the frequent inclusion of humour may lead the child to seek out such instances, resulting in relative inattention to nonhumorous episodes. More importantly, such a tuning in on the more entertaining humorous features in a learning situation may lead the child to lose the point of intended lesson in the process of 'having a good time.' The distraction effect described above may prove to be of central importance in this regard. It may also be that the inclusion of humour in a classroom lesson or other learning situation creates a playful mood or set which is incompatible with learning. That is, it may create a set to 'fantasy assimilate' (see McGhee, 1972b) any new material which might be introduced. Since the accommodative processes required for cognitive change (learning) do not occur when events are fantasy assimilated, the inclusion of humour might be expected to interfere with learning rather than facilitate it.

Behavioural Antecedents of Humour Responsiveness

Two types of questions about the development of children's humour require a longitudinal approach. First, what is the relationship between early maternal or child behaviour and subsequent humour responsiveness? Secondly, how stable are laughter, verbal and behavioural attempts to create humour, etcetera as the child develops toward adulthood? To my knowledge, no data have yet been obtained regarding the latter question. I have recently obtained data relevant to the former, however, using the Fels longitudinal sample. Some of these findings were reported in McGhee (1976b), but most remain unpublished.

McGhee (1976b) related detailed observations of prior maternal and child behaviour available in the permanent Fels' files to several different aspects of the child's humour responsiveness at seven to eleven years of age. This included separate ratings of (1) amount of laughter, (2) frequency of behavioural attempts to initiate humour, and (3) frequency of verbal attempts to initiate humour. All three ratings were obtained on the basis of activity in a nonstructured play situation.

The most surprising finding in this study indicated that early maternal behaviour bore very little relationship to the child's subsequent humour responsiveness. It is especially interesting to note that the extent to which the mother initiated joking or other forms of humour interaction toward the child was not significantly related to any of the three humour measures obtained on their offspring between seven and eleven years. This suggests that a simple parent modelling explanation is not adequate to account for individual differences in humour responsiveness. It may be, however, that modelling influences are important, but they are provided by either the father or other siblings or peers.

The most consistent antecedents of the three measures of the child's humour (the pattern of prediction was generally similar for all three) were found in the child's own previous behaviour. High levels of humour responsiveness in middle childhood were anteceded (from three years of age to the child's present age) by: (1) high levels of physical and verbal aggressiveness, (2) dominance over peers, (3) frequent imitation of peers, (4) extreme restlessness (males only), (5) frequent engagement in social play (males only), (6) lack of effort toward mastery of fine motor skills, but increased effort toward mastery of gross motor skills, (7) increased instrumental help-seeking and recognition-seeking (relative to achievement tasks) from adults, and (8) more frequent speech and a higher quality of language. These findings suggest that it is the child who is highly assertive (aggressive, dominating, and generally active - both physically and socially) toward peers, but who is also very sensitive to (perhaps even dependent on) adults and their reactions, who is most likely to show frequent laughter and/or try to make others laugh during the middle childhood years. In general, the strength of these predictions was significantly greater for girls than for boys. Measures of social play, effort at mastery of fine motor skills and intellectual activities, restlessness, and amount of speech predicted more strongly for boys.

METHODOLOGICAL ISSUES

Comparison of the studies reviewed here with studies reviewed earlier by McGhee (1971b, 1974a) and Rothbart (1973) suggest that we are progressing at an accelerating rate in our understanding of the development of children's humour. Our level of conceptualization of many research issues is steadily advancing, and we are continuing to extend our research efforts into new areas. However, a number of basic methodological problems continue to plague investigators of children's humour. For the most part, these are measurement problems, and we must confront them more seriously than we have to this point if we are to make satisfactory progress in our understanding of children's humour.

Measuring Appreciation

The development of valid and reliable measures of humour appreciation continues to be a source of concern among many humour researchers. One problem lies in the fact that affective (that is, degree of smiling-laughter shown) and intellectual (ratings of a funniness scale given by the child) measures of appreciation frequently do not correlate significantly with each other. Most often, this correlation is positive, but low (e.g., .30 to .40). The factors which influence the strength of this relationship are not yet clear, although it does appear that overt expressions of smiling and laughter are more readily influenced by changes in the social environment than are judgments of funniness. The work of Chapman and of Leventhal and their associates further suggest that sex differences may exist in the operation of such influences. In any case, it now appears likely that these two types of measures are measuring different aspects of appreciation. It follows that progress in advancing our understanding of the nature and determinants of humour appreciation will be slow until investigators uniformly include both measures as dependent variables and report the correlation obtained between them. This will provide a data base from which hypotheses may be drawn and tested regarding factors which influence the relationship between affective and intellectual measures of appreciation. It would also permit a cataloguing of the types of experimental manipulations to which each measure is sensitive.

Investigators using overt expressions of affect as an index of appreciation have typically assumed that smiling and laughter lie along a single continuum, conceptualizing laughter simply as a more intense form of smile. This assumption deserves more critical examination. Chapman's (1976) work, for example, suggests that smiling and laughter may be differentially sensitive to different experimental manipulations. It may be,then, that separate measures of smiling and laughing should be obtained. Similarly, consideration should be given to the usefulness of measures of latency and duration of laughter, as suggested by Chapman (1976) and Pollio, Mers and Lucchesi (1972).

In most cases, a three- or four-point scale has been used to determine the 'degree' of smiling-laughing shown. This scale appears to have become popular because it is easy to obtain high reliabilities among raters using the scale. Since the bottom of the scale is defined as 'no reaction at all,' this leaves one level of smiling and one level of laughter in a three-point scale. If the single-continuum approach continues to be used, attention should be given to the development of a scale which increases the number of levels of smiling and laughing distinguished. Age and sex differences in the number of such levels should also be investigated. Finally, it may be profitable to use duration and latency measures in conjunction with the rating obtained on such a smiling-laughter scale.

Giles and Oxford (1970a) emphasized the importance of distinguishing between humorous and nonhumorous forms of laughter. No systematic attempt has been made to distinguish between these two forms of laughter, although Chapman (1976) has noted that in his studies of the social aspects of humour it was often easy to distinguish between mirthful and nonmirthful forms of laughter. All of us who have tested children (or adults) in humour studies have been convinced that children sometimes produce 'artificial' laughter when presented a cartoon or joke: that is, the laughter occurs simply because a joke has been presented, even though the child gives no evidence of understanding the meaning of the humour depicted. Development of a means of operationally distinguishing between humorous and nonhumorous laughter would be of immense value to humour researchers, in that it would permit data analyses to focus only on cases of 'genuine' appreciation. It may be that this kind of distinction will prove possible only if additional forms of behaviour (e.g., eye-contact, response latency, postural changes, etc.) are taken into consideration.

Individual differences in children's pattern of affective expression have also been given insufficient attention in previous research on children's humour. A child's 'resting state' of affect has considerable influence on the mean score obtained for a given series of cartoons or jokes: that is, some children enter the testing situation with a smile on their face and maintain it throughout the experimental session. Others have a very neutral level of baseline responsiveness - or perhaps even a frown. The question here is whether we should consider the child's baseline level of responsiveness in rating the response shown. Does a full grin with teeth showing have the same meaning for both types of children? We have scored such reactions equivalently in the past, but this practice clearly needs critical examination by future investigators of children's humour.

Measures of appreciation based on rating scales completed by the child also have their problems. Typically, children have been asked to rate the funniness of a cartoon or joke using a five- to seven-point funniness scale ranging from 'not funny at all' to 'very funny,' 'hilarious,' etcetera. While this approach seems satisfactory for older children as progressively younger children are used the validity of any results based on such a scale becomes increasingly questionable. No studies of age differences in children's ability to use this scale have been completed, although most researchers have not attempted to use such a scale with children below five years of age.

In the case of preschool children, the safest approach may be to simply obtain a dichotomous judgment from the child. That is, the child should be asked whether or not the cartoon or joke is funny. Equally promising, however, is the paired comparison approach described in this symposium by Pien and Rothbart, and used previously by McGhee and Grodzitsky (1973). Instead of indicating how funny a given cartoon is, the child is presented two cartoons and is asked which one is funnier.

Measuring Comprehension

There is little agreement among humour researchers regarding the importance of determining the extent to which the recipient of a cartoon or joke understands the humour represented. It seems commonly agreed that if the recipient does not understand the point of a joke, any accompanying laughter can hardly be considered as an index of appreciation. In studies using adults, jokes can be selected through pretest which have clearly specifiable elements which must be identified before the joke can be said to be understood. In most cases, adults can be asked to explain the joke in order to assure that they have identified these key elements. Children, on the other hand, cannot be expected to translate their perceptions of humour into verbal explanations as readily as adults. As progressively younger children are tested, it becomes increasingly difficult to rely on such explanations as an index of whether or not the child understood the humour depicted. Given the difficulty even adults have in analyzing and explaining humour, it is questionable whether either a child's or adult's explanation really reflects the level of understanding of the material achieved. Along these lines, Françoise Bariaud has suggested in this symposium that explanations are probably not explanatory of the deep meanings of the humour to the recipient.

These difficulties suggest that nonverbal means of determining comprehension should be developed. The already discussed approach of presenting the child pairs of stimuli may be valuable in this regard. That is, key elements which produce humour might be included in one version, but not the other. If the child consistently chooses the version containing those elements as funnier, then s/he has clearly understood the humour at some level. On the other hand, it might be argued that the child is simply discriminating the unusual from the more common event, and that this has little implication for how well the humour based on the unusual or incongruous event is understood.

One investigator asked children to change a cartoon or joke so that it would not be funny any more. The central issue here is whether the child can pinpoint the key stimulus elements which carry the humour. If these key elements can be withdrawn (without changing the cartoon or joke completely), substituting nonhumorous elements in their place, the child must be considered to understand the joke at some basic level. Similarly, if a child can consistently choose the funniest of three alternate joke endings or cartoon completions or captions, some evidence of comprehension has been provided. As children become capable of understanding increasingly abstract and satirical forms of humour, these approaches become questionable indices of the child's understanding of the subtler meanings that compose humour. They may be of value, however, in studies using cases of simple perceptual incongruities as bases for humour.

For at least certain types of humour, then, there appears to be no substitute for asking the child for information regarding why s/he thinks the cartoon or joke is funny. Such explanations can clearly indicate when the child does understand the humour depicted, but do not necessarily indicate that the humour is not understood. Since appreciation data are of little value without some evidence that the humour has been understood, procedures need to be developed which maximize the probability of demonstrating comprehension when comprehension has, in fact, occurred. One valuable suggestion along these lines was advanced during discussions after the formal presentation of papers in this Symposium. Since verbal explanations offer the best evidence of the nature and depth of a child's understanding of a joke or cartoon, why not provide some training at analyzing and describing the humour one sees? A series of stimuli might be presented to the child, with another child or adult model explaining in the child's presence why s/he thinks they are funny. This would tune the child in on what to look for, and how to describe it. The child might then be given practice at such analyses before being presented the experimental stimuli.

The difficulty with this approach is that the model might lead the child to tune in on dimensions of the humour stimulus that would not have been noticed otherwise. One could avoid channelling the child into a particular type of explanation, however, by providing a broad range of levels of meaningful explanations. This would make the child (with the cognitive capabilities for understanding the full range of explanations provided by the model) aware that there are several ways of describing what is going on in the humour stimulus; in explaining experimental stimuli later, s/he can simply choose the level of explanation s/he thinks provides the best reason for why the cartoon or joke is funny. Investigations of alternate research strategies in this area should be most fruitful.

To this point, investigators who have attempted to measure humour comprehension have typically conceptualized comprehension in terms of discrete units along a single scale. For any given cartoon or joke, a child might show no comprehension at all, partial comprehension, or full comprehension. Thus, it has not been uncommon for four- or five-point scales to be used. These scale values are based on progressively closer approximations to adult opinions regarding the full meaning of the joke. The fact that most studies show increased comprehension with increasing age reflects the fact that children tend to perceive the joke like adults perceive it as they get older. The merits of, and exclusive reliance on, this approach are worth questioning. We should be giving more attention to qualitative differences in the way children understand humour as they develop. This might begin by searching for age-related stages in the types of explanations children give for funniness. Alice Sheppard's paper in this symposium constitutes an important step in this direction.

While the obtaining of some type of information from the child as a means of determining comprehension seems essential, it is important to note that there is now some basis for arguing that the actual process of obtaining such comprehension information may interfere with the appreciation of the humour identified. In an unpublished study, I presented cartoons and jokes at two levels of difficulty to children in grades two, five and eight. Half of the children were asked to explain why they thought the cartoons and jokes were funny, while the remaining half were shown the stimuli without being asked to give an explanation. A significant interaction effect indicated that for simple humour stimuli, amount of smiling-laughter did not vary as a function of explanation condition. For more complex stimuli, however, children who gave explanations gave reduced levels of smiling and laughter relative to children who did not give explanations. Thus, the obligation to analyze and explain humour is most likely to interfere with appreciation when the humour stimulus is sufficiently complex to challenge the child's thought capacities. Consistent with these findings, Reutener and Kazak (1976) found that college students who had just engaged in a taxing cognitive task perceived complex cartoons to be less humorous than students who had just engaged in an easy task. This effect was not obtained, however, for simple cartoons.

Similarly, Rothbart (1976) presented a series of visual incongruities to five- to six-year-olds and either simply described the incongruity or both described and explained it. She found that explaining the incongruity served to reduce both the child's laughter and ratings of funniness. She concluded that a problem-solving orientation detracts from appreciation. Kreitler and Kreitler (1970) have obtained data consistent with this view.

The best solution to this dilemma may be to present all of the stimuli used twice. On the first presentation, funniness ratings and measures of affect might be obtained (assuming

that a request for a funniness rating does not produce a comparable interference effect).
Explanatory information can then be provided during the second presentation of the stimuli.
Attention should be given to the possibility, however, that the examination process required
to explain a joke may itself lead to new insights (that is, new levels of comprehension)
which were not present at the time appreciation data were obtained. This would provide
misleading evidence regarding the relationship between comprehension and appreciation.

Experimenter Effects

Little attention has been given to experimenter effects in studies of humour. If affective
measures of appreciation prove to be easily influenced by changes in the social environment,
the behaviour of the experimenter may play an important role in determining subjects'
responsiveness. Foot and Chapman (1976), for example, found significant differences in
amount of smiling and laughter of seven-year-olds at short cartoon films as a function of
which of two experimenters was present. Comparison of results across studies will remain
difficult until experimenter effects are thoroughly studied.

Awareness of Being Observed

Chapman (1976) found that if children were told that they would be observed through a one-
way mirror, laughter was diminished, although smiling and eye-contact increased. It seems
likely that the feeling that one is being watched is present to varying degrees in different
humour studies. A standard laboratory environment might be especially conducive to producing
such an awareness in children, thereby inhibiting laughter. Of course, the behaviour of the
experimenter, as suggested above, might play the key role in generating such an awareness.
In any case, it would appear that humour investigators might profitably take precautions
against giving children the impression in humour studies that they are being observed or
evaluated.

REFERENCES

See Bibliography for publications on humour, laughter and comedy

Curran, F.W., A developmental study of cartoon humor appreciation and its use in facilitating
     learning. Unpublished doctoral dissertation, Catholic University of America (1972).

Getzels, J. & Jackson, P.W., Creativity and Intelligence. Wiley, New York (1962).

Gidynsky, C.G., Associative shift, peer rejection and humor response in children: an
     exploratory study. Unpublished doctoral dissertation, Columbia University (1972).

Harter, S., Pleasure derived from cognitive challenge and mastery. Child Development, 45,
     661–669 (1974).

Kagan, J., Change and Continuity in Infancy. Wiley, New York (1971).

Klinger, E., Structure and Functions of Fantasy. Wiley, New York (1971).

Kohlberg, L., Stage in The Development of Moral Thought and Action. Holt, Rinehart & Winston,
     New York (1969).

LaChance, A.I., A study of the correlation between humor and self concept in fifth grade
     boys and girls. Unpublished doctoral dissertation, University of Maryland (1972).

Lieberman, J.N., The relationship between playfulness and divergent thinking at the
     kindergarten level. Journal of Genetic Psychology, 107, 219–224 (1965).

Lieberman, J.N., A developmental analysis of playfulness as a clue to cognitive style. The
     Journal of Creative Behavior, 1, 391–397 (1967).

McCall, R.B. & McGhee, P.E., The discrepancy hypothesis of attention and affect in infants.
     In: I.C. Uzgiris & F. Weizmann (Eds.), The Structuring of Experience. Plenum, New York,
     in press.

Neumann, L.E., Humor in classroom instruction: a comparative study of cartoon humor in high
     school biology instruction. Unpublished doctoral dissertation, St. Louis University
     (1972).

Piaget, J., The Moral Judgment of The Child. Kegan Paul, London (1932).

Piaget, J., Play, Dreams, and Imitation in Childhood. Norton, New York (1962).

Sarason, I.G., Empirical findings and theoretical problems in the use of anxiety scales. Psychological Bulletin, 57, 403–415 (1960).

Shultz, T.R. & Bloom, L., Concrete operational thought and the appreciation of verbal jokes. Unpublished paper cited by Shultz (1976).

Shultz, T.R. & Pilon, R., Development of the ability to detect linguistic ambiguity. Child Development, 44, 728–733 (1973).

Singer, D.L. & Rummo, J., Ideational creativity and behavioral style in kindergarten-age children. Developmental Psychology, 8, 154–161 (1973).

Singer, J.L., The Child's World of Make-Believe: Experimental Studies of Imaginative Play. Academic Press, New York (1973).

Sroufe, L.A., Waters, E. & Matas, L., Contextual determinants of infant affective response. In: M. Lewis & L. Rosenblum (Eds.), The Origins of Fear. Wiley, New York (1974).

Torrance, E.P., Guiding Creative Talent. Prentice-Hall, Englewood Cliffs N.J. (1962).

Wallach, M.A. & Kogan, N., Modes of Thinking in Young Children: A Study of The Creativity-Intelligence Distinction. Holt, Rinehart & Winston, New York (1965).

Waterman, J., Dependent variables in children's humor research. Paper presented at meeting of the Society for Research in Child Development, Philadelphia (1973).

Weissberg, P.S. & Springer, K.J., Environmental factors in creative function. Archives of General Psychiatry, 5, 64–74 (1961).

Zillmann, D. & Bryant, J., Viewer's moral sanction of retribution in the appreciation of dramatic presentations. Journal of Experimental Social Psychology, 11, 572–582 (1975).

Measuring Effects of Incongruity and Resolution in Children's Humour

Diana Pien and Mary K. Rothbart

University of Oregon

One major issue in children's humour research concerns the nature of differences between children's and adults' humour appreciation. Two important components of adults' humour appreciation are the identification of a surprising or unexpected event, that is, incongruity, and the resolution or explanation of that incongruity (e.g., Suls, 1972; Shultz, 1972, 1974a). Arousal theorists propose that the same arousal processes may be responsible for humour in both adults and children where the perception of incongruity in a safe or playful situation and the perception of incongruities with resolution both lead to humour (e.g., Rothbart, 1976). In contrast, Shultz (1972, 1974a) proposes that the development of humour appreciation is characterized by two distinct stages: up until the age of seven or eight, children appreciate a surprising or unexpected event (an incongruity) and find it humorous, while beginning at the age of seven or eight, and continuing throughout adulthood, humour involving incongruity is appreciated only when the incongruity has been resolved or made meaningful in some way. In performing his research, Shultz created resolution-removed versions of original jokes by presenting children with an incongruity while deleting information necessary for its resolution. For example, in the original riddle: 'Why did the cookie cry?' 'Because its mother had been a wafer so long,' resolution was removed by creating the version: 'Why did the cookie cry?' 'Because its mother was a wafer.' Six-year-olds did not give the original versions of such jokes any higher ratings than the resolution-removed versions of the jokes, while eight-year-old and older children rated the original versions as funnier than the versions with incongruity alone. Comparable results were found by Shultz in research with jokes (Shultz & Horibe, 1974) and with cartoons (Shultz, 1972).

An alternative explanation of Shultz' results is possible, however. Younger children in Shultz' experiments on jokes and riddles (Shultz & Horibe, 1974; Shultz, 1974a) were not able to provide resolutions for over seventy-five per cent of the experimental jokes and riddles, and it is possible that younger children's difficulties in understanding Shultz' humour materials may have been responsible for their failure to differentiate between original and resolution-removed forms of humour. In attempting to clarify the nature of humour appreciation by four- and five-year-old children, we encountered a number of serious methodological problems which are relevant to adults' as well as children's humour research. These problems involve the following three areas: type of humour materials; measurement of humour appreciation; and context effects. In this paper we would like to share the problems and some of our attempted solutions.

First, it was necessary to consider what types of humour materials would be appropriate in difficulty level for four- to five-year-old children. Jokes and riddles often require detection of linguistic ambiguities, and Shultz and Pilon (1973) have demonstrated that children six-years-old and younger do not appear to have developed the skills to detect linguistic ambiguities. Although phonological skills appear to develop earlier, a young child may not yet know one or both of the double meanings of words used in a joke; for example, the child may be unaware of the meaning of wafer as a type of cookie, even though s/he knows the meaning of 'away for.' Furthermore, even the simplest phonological ambiguities may not be appropriate for young children if the speed of processing both meanings is slow and disrupts the timing of the joke.

In early stages of our research we attempted to use very simple 'knock-knock' jokes of the variety: 'Knock knock.' 'Who's there?' 'Lettuce.' 'Lettuce who?' 'Lettuce in, it's cold outside!' While the phonological ambiguities were simple, children failed to understand the jokes because of lack of familiarity with the 'knock-knock' joke format. All of the four- and five-year-olds were bewildered by the question and answer format, and none of them understood the jokes. Use of other types of jokes and riddles such as 'What has one horn and gives milk?' 'A milk truck.' also presented difficulties. In addition to not knowing what milk trucks are, many children had forgotten the beginning of the joke by the time they

heard the punchline. To eliminate these memory and vocabulary problems, we finally used
sequential cartoons involving chiefly visual incongruity, and found that four- and five-year-
olds seemed to appreciate this type of humour material without receiving additional training.

An additional problem in finding appropriate stimulus materials to study effects of resolution
on humour appreciation concerned the creation of resolution-removed forms of humour materials.
If a researcher does not retain the same incongruity for both original and resolution-removed
forms, the incongruity-alone condition may present a different level of incongruity than the
original version. For example, in the illustration for Shultz' (1972) study of cartoons, the
original cartoon showing a cow with an 'Out-of-order' sign and a girl walking angrily away
with an empty pail was changed in the resolution-removed version to only a picture of the cow
with the 'Out-of-order' sign. In this example, the original cartoon presumably contains more
elements of incongruity than the incongruity alone (resolution-removed) version; the girl's
angry expression and empty pail in the presence of a cow add two additional elements of
incongruity to the original version. If the original version of the cartoon is preferred by
a subject, we do not know whether it is due to appreciation of resolution aspects or to
appreciation of additional incongruities present.

Young children's lack of vocabulary may also mean that incongruity forms will be more incongruous
for them than for older children. In the cookie-crying joke, for example, the resolution-
removed form is 'Why did the cookie cry?' 'Because its mother was a wafer.' If 'wafer' is a
nonsense word to a young child, the joke may contain more incongruity for young children than
the incongruity perceived by older children when they fail to find a joking answer to the
riddle.

The problem of creating resolution-removed versions is even more difficult if adult subjects
are used. In many complex cartoons and jokes, the resolution introduces new incongruities so
that deletion of the resolution necessarily eliminates some of the original incongruous
elements (see Rothbart & Pien, this volume). Deletion of the resolution, however, may also
add new incongruity by violating the joke or cartoon format resulting in an absurd joke or
cartoon. When we were creating resolution-removed forms of children's cartoons, several
adults remarked that these forms were funnier than the original versions because the
resolution-removed versions were so absurd and nonsensical. Thus, removal of resolution can
either increase and/or decrease the amount of incongruity present.

A second difficult problem area in any humour study with children concerns measurement of
humour appreciation in young children. The standard method in studying children's appreciation
of incongruity and resolution has been to give one group of children the original version of
a cartoon, while a second group is shown the resolution-removed version. Each child is asked
to rate the funniness of the cartoon on a five-point scale. There are several difficulties
in this use of this method. First, for any particular joke we do not know how much of the
humour response is based on incongruity aspects of the joke and how much on resolution
aspects. Most of the humour may in fact be due to the incongruity component, with resolution
adding very little. If this is the case, we require a very sensitive measure to detect a
difference between the two forms and a rating scale may not be sensitive enough. With young
children we have even further difficulties in using a rating scale. Are four-year-old
children capable of giving reliable judgments of humour on a five-point scale? We are not
sure that this is the case; additional research on the question would be extremely helpful.

There are also wide individual differences in subjects' reactions to humour materials. A
paired-comparison method allowing the same subject to compare the two forms of humour
materials, original and resolution-removed, rather than statistically comparing responses of
two different groups of subjects to different forms of materials again offers a more sensitive
measure of preference. In the paired-comparison procedure both the original and resolution-
removed versions are presented and the child is asked to pick which version is funnier.

In our final study of young children's use of resolution in humour (Pien & Rothbart, in press),
we used the more sensitive paired-comparison technique in an attempt to control for (a)
individual differences in reactions to humour materials, (b) differences in relative
contribution of incongruity and resolution components to humour, and (c) problems in using
a rating method with young children. We also attempted to compare the paired-comparison
technique with the single-cartoon rating procedure in our test of whether young children
could appreciate resolution information in simple sequential cartoons.

Children aged four- and five-years were each given seven paired comparison choices of
sequential cartoons such as the following. A boy sits in a chair reading a book, which he
is holding upside-down. An adult tells him, 'you're holding the book upside-down.' Two
ending frames were offered the child for this cartoon. In one, the original, the child
stands on his head in the chair while continuing to read the book; in the incongruity-alone
version, the child stands on his head but is no longer reading the book. The book is in the
picture on the arm of the chair. Children were asked which of the two frames made the cartoon

funnier for them. In some cartoons, the children were asked to choose a beginning frame that made the cartoon funnier; in others, the child chose the funnier ending frame. The choice frames were independently presented to a group of children the same age as our subjects, and were found to be equally funny when viewed alone. The results of our paired comparison study indicated that both four- and five-year-olds preferred the original version to the incongruity-alone version significantly more often and showed more laughing and smiling to the original version.

At the same time, children were asked to rate a set of six single cartoons, half of which were original cartoons and half incongruity-alone versions. Children were asked whether they thought the cartoon was funny or not funny; if they thought the cartoon was funny, they were asked whether it was a little funny, or a lot. The child's responses allowed us to score their reactions on a three-point scale. As in Shultz' study, children showed no preference for the original cartoons using the single presentation method, either in rating scores or in smiling and laughter responses.

We would like to suggest that a paired comparison technique may be the technique of choice in studying humour preferences in young children. Infant research on visual preferences has found similar results to the present study (Saayman, Ames & Moffitt, 1964); infants may not show a preference for visual stimuli when they are presented singly, but do show a preference when they are presented simultaneously.

An unexpected finding of this study was a strong trend for more correct choices when the paired comparison task followed rather than preceded the single cartoon task. This trend suggests that context effects are very important. Presenting additional humour material before the experimental material may help insure that children view the materials as humorous and not serious tasks. Furthermore, observations of children's affect reactions during the experiment provided a way of assessing their attitude toward the task. In our study we recorded children's affect reactions on each trial and found differential smiling and laughing to the two forms only in the paired-comparison procedure. These data suggest that real humour judgments are involved in our experiment. In addition, even if young children were not making authentic humour judgments, they are clearly demonstrating that they are capable of using resolution information.

We have a great deal to learn about developmental changes and continuity in humour appreciation. We hope that the considerations described above will be useful to other researchers in this area.

REFERENCES

See Bibliography for publications on humour, laughter and comedy

Berlyne, D.E. & Frommer, F.D., Some determinants of the incidence and content of children's questions. Child Development, 37, 177-189 (1966).

Saayman, J., Ames, C.W. & Moffitt, A., Response to novelty as an indication of visual discrimination in the human infant. Journal of Experimental Child Psychology, 1, 189-198 (1964).

Shultz, T.R. & Pilon, R., Development of the ability to detect linguistic ambiguity. Child Development, 44, 728-733 (1973).

Humour in Children Related to Piaget's Theory of Intellectual Development

Chris Athey

The Froebel Educational Institute, London

If a symbol could be invented to stand for humour, it might be a glass slipper. A glass slipper is suitably fragile and every theoretical foot can fit into it to a certain extent. The most ubiquitous explanation of humour in the literature, if taken over centuries, appears to be that of comic incongruity. Comic incongruity describes the cognitive and affective state of the person who is amused. The expression of that state can range from a loud laugh right through to a feeling of slight amusement. Comic incongruity, or 'bisociation' (Koestler, 1964), is experienced when there is a certain juxtaposition of categories which do not really belong together. For instance, in one of Koestler's examples, Jewish homespun philosophy and an important concept of psychoanalysis are comically juxtaposed. A friend, on being told that the Jewish boy had an Oedipus complex, replies: 'Oedipus, Schmoedipus, what does it matter as long as he's a good boy and loves his mother'.

There are certain objections to this theory (Medawar, 1967, 1969). One is that the theory does not yet explain in a satisfactory way the fundamental differences between incongruity which disturbs (Berlyne, 1960), incongruity which surprises (Charlesworth, 1969), or incongruity which simply engenders the focused attention which accompanies any kind of 'effort after meaning' (Bartlett, 1958). Hebb (1961), Bateson (1969), Kris (1962) and Bronowski (1967) have recently joined the ranks of those who have attempted to explain the difference between incongruity which disturbs and incongruity which amuses. It is suggested here that research on the relationship between perceived incongruity and types, or degrees of affect, can be advanced by employing aspects of Piaget's theory.

Within Piaget's theory of intellectual development, the continuum of affective states, from slight disturbance, through focused attention, to playful and humorous states, describes the route taken by children when they are learning in general. Within Piaget's theory 'affect' is intrinsic to all cognitive functioning. The process of accommodation to new knowledge is typically accompanied by a certain degree of struggle. Intelligent adaptation, where accommodation and assimilation are said to be in a state of equilibrium, is typified by focused attention. Playfulness and humorousness are experienced at the assimilatory pole of functioning (Piaget, 1962). This is the position where knowledge has become so stable that it can be used simply for fun. Freud (1955), Huizinga (1949) and Piaget (1962) all appear to agree on the relationship between assimilatory functioning and playfulness. As long ago as the 1920's, Karl Buhler (1928) described humour as 'functioning for the sake of pleasure'. In order to perceive, or create, a comic incongruity, a child needs to have acquired at least two stable categories or classes, or some kind of stable order. Chukovsky (1966) describes the first intentional joke made by his two-year-old granddaughter. The child had learned that dogs bark and cats miaow. Her first joke was: 'doggie miaows' ('oggy miaow).

Piaget has only discussed humour in relation to very young children (Piaget, 1962). His descriptions of stage characteristics, however, particularly as they are presented in 'The Early Growth of Logic' (Inhelder and Piaget, 1964), can be employed usefully in research on humour. Stage characteristics can be used for describing, before testing, the structural characteristics of humour stimuli. The same criteria can then be used to ascertain different levels of comprehension in children of different ages. Information gained from studies of this type could help to illuminate a central issue in child development. In cognitive development in general there is the ever-present problem of what constitutes a 'match' or 'mismatch' between the logical complexity of stimuli and the stage of cognitive complexity in the child.

My pilot study produced two hundred examples of funny stories, events, jokes and riddles. Sixty-four children of five, seven and nine years of age were tape-recorded, talking about things they found funny. When the complexity levels of the examples were worked out in relation to chronological age, it was found that only 0.9 per cent of the examples classified as concrete-operational were given by the children under six years of age. Only 8 per cent of the pre-operational examples were given by children over six. In other words, 91 per cent of the examples matched the level of humour complexity that had been predicted within Piaget's stage theory. On the assumption that sense is a necessary condition for the appreciation of non-sense, three questions were asked in relation to each example: (i) What is the nature of the congruence? (ii) What is the nature of the incongruence? (iii) What stage level of thinking is indicated? Ninety per cent of the five-year-old examples consisted of comic incongruity to do with movement, established images, the use of objects and the location of objects. Instances of this early level of comic incongruity are as follows: (a) Animals walking sideways (movement incongruity); (b) Singing a song on one note (auditory image incongruity); (c) A man smelt like rubbish (olfactory image incongruity); (d) Someone sat on a cello instead of a chair (incongruity of use or location); (e) The cook put newly cooked food in the dustbin (incongruity of location). The pilot study indicated that schemes or congruities of movement, image, use and place had been sufficiently well assimilated by five years of age for incongruities based on those categories to be perceived as comic. Six items at this level of incongruence were chosen for the pre-operational level of a humour test. These included a lamb flying with a propeller in its mouth, a dog skipping, an animal upside-down and a fish in a tea-pot. The main purpose of the test was to see whether humour comprehension followed the same developmental route in children as other areas of cognitive development.

Concrete-operational thinking, according to Piaget, is typified by the ability to classify and to order objects and events into series. Classification and ordering are said to be truly present when the child shows that he can hold in mind part-whole relationships, and when he has the flexibility of functioning to shift backwards and forwards between the two (Inhelder & Piaget, 1964). A typical test item in logical development is to ask children whether there are more white, brown or wooden beads, the two colours being the sub-sets of the whole of the wooden set. The largest number of humour examples from the seven-year-old group consisted of riddling puns. These seem to require similar cognitive structure as that required in the logic test.

The meaning given to the word 'pun' varies in the literature. Different interpretations can be linked with different stage levels of cognition. Freud (1905) states 'A pun is a bad play on words, since it plays on the word not as a word but as a sound'. This describes the very earliest form of punning found in five-year-olds where a loose sound similarity is linked with two meanings: A man said 'This is a red rose', a boy replied 'What a gonky nose'. The pun is not so much the lowest form of wit, but one of the earliest forms of wit. Berlyne (1960) states that the pun derives multiplicity of interpretations from multiplicity of meaning. This describes a much later stage level of cognition. A nine-year-old asked: 'What international disaster would it cause if a housewife dropped the Christmas plates? The downfall of turkey, the destruction of china and the overthrow of grease'. The congruity in this case involves the knowledge of the names of three countries and three Christmas events with the same sounding names. The triple pun bounces from one set of meanings to the other. This level of complexity coincides with research on logical thinking where typical nine-year-olds can hold on to three criteria simultaneously (Inhelder & Piaget, 1964). It is interesting to note that built into the understanding of this triple pun are typical early pre-operational concerns of 'falling', 'breaking', and 'spilling'. Piaget (1962) states that earlier modes of thought, plus their affective components, persist in existing schemata. The level of understanding required for the appreciation of puns at the early junior school level resembles that required in tests of logic. In the riddle, attention is directed to one meaning of the pun, but the answer is given within the other meaning. 'How can you make time fly?' directs attention to the passing of time. 'Throw it out of the window' shifts the listener to the movement meaning of 'flies'. Funniness is not experienced before the two meanings are known sufficiently well for one meaning to be substituted rapidly for the other.

Certain punning riddles, in subsequent tests were laughed at by five-year-olds. The hypothesis stated that they would not laugh because they would not understand the substitution of one meaning for another. However, when the children's explanations were analyzed, they were found to be at a typical pre-operational level. The following riddle, for instance, had been given the test status of an early concrete-operational level of complexity: 'Why is an author a strange kind of animal? Because his tale comes out of his head'. There were a hundred and ninety-four cases where there was a laugh but the explanation did not fit the hypothesized complexity level. However, a hundred and forty of the explanations did match the pre-operational level. In relation to the examples just given the incongruity was based on something in the wrong place.

A similar cognitive structure and flexibility of functioning is required for the appreciation of non-punning riddles: 'How do you know if you're buying eggs without chickens in them? Buy duck eggs!' The form of the riddle makes the listener focus on some aspect of a sub-set of eggs, that is, chickens' eggs; the answer bounces the listener over to the other sub-set, that is, ducks' eggs. A large number of the jokes put forward by the seven- and nine-year-olds had a seriation structure. 'What is the definition of a skeleton? A strip-tease that's gone too far!' Here the comic incongruity is based on going beyond the limits of the series, in this case the order of undressing. The punning riddle, the non-punning riddle, and the seriation riddle all resemble logical thinking at the concrete-operational level. There is, in all cases, the ability to arrange events within classes and within orders. There is also flexibility of cognitive functioning within these classes and orders.

After two pilot studies, thirty items were analyzed and a humour scale was constructed. The test items were classified into five levels of increasing logical complexity. The test was given to three groups of twenty-four children (mean ages, 9:4, 7:4 and 5:5). Scores were attached to three levels of comprehension and three levels of mirth. The three levels of comprehension were as follows: (i) The highest level was the level postulated in the prior analysis of the items. (ii) The middle level was where separate aspects of the stimulus were perceived but not linked together (syncretism). (iii) The lowest level was where an irrelevant aspect of the situation was perceived, or, where there was no response. Mirth scores were given to the laugh, the smile, and no laugh or smile.

The humour scale was tested by scalogram analysis. This yielded a co-efficient of reproducibility of 0.87. This level of measurement indicates that the humour test does constitute a scale (Peel, 1959) measuring simultaneously: (a) the logical variable contained in the thirty humour items and (b) the psychological variable of comprehension contained in the children's responses. The most difficult items to analyze were those designed to tap a level of cognitive complexity more complex than that described as early concrete-operations. Piaget's descriptions of formal-operations are difficult to use in the analysis of test items. However, Inhelder and Piaget (1961) point out that the serial ordering of asymmetrical transitive relations, acquired during the concrete-operational stage, leads to the later ability to group events into a single sequence of implication. A group of cartoons was found which could only be understood at the postulated level if there was the cognitive ability to connect up a set of discrete events into a ludic cause and effect relationship. One item depicted a porter, happily and effortlessly, carrying a large case on his shoulder. He weighed it, saw how heavy it was and walked off bent double by his burden.

Analysis of Variance, followed by t-tests, was applied to comprehension and mirth scores (see Table 1).

TABLE 1 Mean comprehension and mirth scores at three category levels and three mean ages

Mean Age	N	Pre-operational Category		Concrete-operational Category		Early Formal-operational Category	
		Comp.	Mirth	Comp.	Mirth	Comp.	Mirth
9:4	24	17.95	11.5	15.83	15.6	14.79	10.62
7:4	24	17.54	11.45	14.16	12.95	11.62	7.08
5:5	24	16.45	13.20	10.37	11.66	8.0	6.7

Results showed (i) there was an increase in comprehension with increase in age ($F=74$; $p < 0.001$); (ii) there was a difference between the pre-operational and the concrete-operational levels of the tests ($t=8.0$; $df=70$; $p < 0.001$), and between the concrete-operational and early formal-operational level ($t=3.2$; $df=70$; $p < 0.01$). These results gave some empirical support to the prior grouping of the humour stimuli, in terms of difficulty level, but only in relation to three stages and not the postulated five.

The mirth of the five-year-old children peaked at the pre-operational level of complexity when compared with the concrete-operational level ($t=2.5$; $df=46$; $p < 0.02$ and > 0.01). The mirth of the seven-year-olds peaked at the concrete-operational level of complexity ($t=2.7$; $df=46$; $p < 0.01$), but they laughed significantly more at the pre-operational level than they did at the early formal-operational level. The nine-year-old group also peaked at the middle level of complexity, but they laughed at the most difficult items significantly more than the two younger groups.

Spearman's rank-order correlation coefficient was applied to English Picture Vocabulary Test Scores and humour comprehension scores at each of the three ages. A highly significant association was found in each case.

When comprehension and mirth scores were analyzed in a 3 × 3 matrix, it was found that 28 per cent of the total scores consisted of the laugh accompanied by the highest level of comprehension. Twenty-one per cent of the scores consisted of the lowest level of comprehension and mirth. As stated earlier, in the one hundred and ninety-four cases where there was a laugh at a middle level of comprehension, the children's explanations matched a lower category level.

The results can be simplified by saying that there is very little mirth in relation to either a 'tired old' comprehension or in relation to a 'too new' comprehension. In Piaget's terminology: either too much assimilation has taken place, to the point of perseveration, or, not enough assimilation has taken place for there to be a playful and humorous response. It would appear that the speed and flexibility of perception, required for a humorous response, does not take place when the complexity of the stimulus makes accommodatory demands on the subject. No difference was found, in comprehension or mirth, between boys and girls. This finding was predicted as, within Piaget's theory, there would be no reason to postulate differences. All the results of this study indicate that humour comprehension and mirth responses in children can be predicted with a high degree of accuracy by utilizing the structural and functional aspects of Piaget's theory of intellectual development (Athey, 1970).

REFERENCES

See Bibliography for publications on humour, laughter and comedy

Athey, C., Humour in Children Related to Piaget's Theory of Intellectual Development.
    Unpublished Master of Education Thesis, University of Leicester (1970).

Bartlett, F.C., Thinking. Allen & Unwin, London (1958).

Bronowski, J., The Identity of Man. Penguin Books, Harmondsworth (1967).

Buhler, K., Displeasure and pleasure in relation to activity. In: M.L. Reymer (Ed.),
    Feelings and Emotions: The Wittenberg Symposium. Clark University Press, Massachusettes
    (1928).

Charlsworth, W.R., The role of surprise in cognitive development. Studies in Cognitive
    Development, 257–311 (1969).

Chukovsky, K., From Two to Five. University of California Press (1966).

Freud, S., Beyond the Pleasure Principle. Standard edition of complete psychological works,
    Vol. 18. Hogarth, London (1955).

Hebb, D.O., Organization of Behaviour. Science Editions, New York (1961).

Huizinga, J., Homo-Ludens: A Study of the Play Elements in Culture. Routledge & Kegan Paul,
    London (1949).

Inhelder, B. & Piaget, J., The Early Growth Logic in the Child. Routledge & Kegan Paul,
    London (1964).

Medawar, P.B., Scientific Method. The Listener, (12th October) (1967).

Medawar, P.B., The Art of the Soluble. Penguin Books, Harmondsworth (1969).

Peel, E.A., Experimental examination of some of Piaget's schemata concerning children's
    perception and thinking, and a discussion of their educational significance. British
    Journal of Educational Psychology, 29, 89–103 (1959).

Piaget, J., Play, Dreams and Imitation in Childhood. Routledge & Kegan Paul, London (1962).

Birth Order and Humour Responsiveness in Young Children

Antony J. Chapman and Linda J. M. Speck

University of Wales Institute of Science and Technology

'Birth order' effects (psychological correlates of ordinal position amongst siblings) have been researched for more than a century. In literally hundreds of studies, first-born children have been compared with later-born children: behavioural and personality differences have then been discussed in terms of the contrasting psychological environments provided for first-borns and later-borns.

Various features distinguishing these environments have been spotlighted in theoretical analyses. Firstly, in physiological terms, a first-born child has the benefits of a richer uterine environment, although later pregnancies and deliveries are usually easier for the mother; secondly, parents may be more anxious about their first child and perhaps more indulgent and protective towards him or her, but they may be relatively inconsistent in their child-rearing practices because of their inexperience and, later on, the attention they devote to their first-born child may be substantially reduced with the arrival of more children; thirdly, the 'dethronement' of a first-born following the birth of a sibling may lead the child to seek again the monopoly of parental attention and affection that he or she once experienced; and, fourthly, later-borns always have at least one sibling with whom to interact. Other factors may be important too. For example, a first-born is sometimes an only child and perhaps thereby more adult oriented and/or self-centred. Finally, amongst other explanations of birth order effects which have been put forward are those based upon economics and changing financial circumstances concomitant with the growth in size of an individual family.

The empirical data available do not offer overwhelming support for any one theory, or partial theory; nor do they permit us to discount entirely any theory so far advanced. There are in the psychological literature studies on children and adults relating birth order to attitudes, educational attainment, delinquency, alcoholism, anxiety, dependence, conformity, vocational choice, psychiatric disorders, and other factors. A number of review articles have appeared in recent years (e.g., Adams, 1972; Schooler, 1972; Warren, 1966; Zajonc & Markus, 1975), and there has been a marked increase in attention paid to the methodological inadequacies of birth order research. In a sceptical review, Schooler suggested that many of the birth order relationships which did exist before the mid-sixties have diminished because of changing population trends. Nevertheless, more than three hundred birth order papers were published in the five years prior to his review (cf. Vockell, Felker & Miley, 1973) and the deluge continues unabated.

As social psychologists working with children, our special interest in birth order centres on what until recently was reported as a comparatively robust finding: namely that first-borns tend to be more affiliative. Although this relationship is reported in a number of studies (e.g., Dember, 1964; Koenig, 1969; Nowicki, 1971), the findings as a whole are not conclusive. In fact, there is some evidence that later-borns, not first-borns, are more affiliative (Baker & O'Brien, 1969), and a recent theoretical paper by Zajonc and Markus (1975) would predict that the difference would be in this direction. They argue that later-borns should have greater affiliative skills because, as young children, they have a greater variety of affiliative targets, in the form of older brothers and sisters. Also, a recent study can be interpreted as offering empirical support for this argument (Miller & Maruyama, 1976); it reports that later-borns are more popular than their first-born peers in school.

The recent work on affiliation was largely inspired by Schachter's (1959) classic monograph in which he formulated the hypothesis that, when anxious, first-borns (being particularly vulnerable to stress) become more affiliative, whereas later-borns do not. Subsequent studies in which subjects have been placed under stress provide a somewhat confusing picture.

In men particularly, the relationship seems to depend on the nature of the stress and the degree of anxiety or fear invoked.

An open question is whether stress is a prerequisite for the manifestation of birth order effects in affiliative behaviours. It is our view that, for the major part, the theoretical and empirical analyses of the relationship between birth order and affiliation can be integrated in a single statement. We offer it in a tentative fashion: later-borns tend to be more socially responsive than first-borns except under anxiety-invoking conditions when first-borns become more affiliative. Our study is designed as a preliminary investigation of this hypothesis.

McGhee (1973) has published the only previous humour study on birth order effects. Interpreting overt reactions to humour (laughter and smiling) as affiliative responses, as do we, he obtained support for Schachter's original hypothesis. In an anxiety-provoking situation, he found that later-borns appreciate humour more when they are alone than when in a group, and that there is a tendency towards the converse for first-borns. The subjects of his study were students; they were presented with single-frame cartoons; an experimenter was present throughout; and a confederate was present in the group situation to help rate behavioural reactions. On each of these major methodological details, our study differs from McGhee's, but our prime aim was to determine whether an equivalent pattern of results would emerge when subjects were observed under circumstances in which anxiety was gradually dissipated.

Our mobile-laboratory is ideal for studying children precisely because in this setting they can quickly be made to feel uninhibited and relaxed. In this experiment, we took the laboratory to a local Infants school and we observed, without their knowledge, forty boys and forty girls. They were aged $6\frac{3}{4}$ to $7\frac{1}{2}$ years, and family size was not significantly different for first-borns (2.6 children) and later-borns (2.7 children): in only five instances were the first-borns also 'only' children. In the absence of the experimenters, the children watched a cartoon titled 'Woody Woodpecker in Woody's Clip Joint', lasting 5 minutes 42 seconds. Ten first-borns and ten later-borns were tested in a solitary condition, and the remaining sixty children were tested in groups of three, keeping separate first-borns and later-borns, and boys and girls. All sessions were video-tape-recorded and, in the group situations, data were obtained only for the children who were centrally-seated in the triads. The dependent behaviours were durations of laughter and smiling (for operational definitions, see Chapman, 1976), taken at one-minute intervals. Ratings of funniness were solicited at the end of test sessions: subjects were asked whether they thought the film was "not very funny", "quite funny" or "very funny".

In one major respect, this study was different from any of our others: the children were not given any exposure to the laboratory prior to testing. The intention here was that children should be slightly tense on being confronted with the novelty of the situation, and it was then expected that they would become relaxed during the film: this is invariably the sequence of events in our standard 'warm-up' sessions.

In general terms, it was expected that first-borns would laugh and smile more in the early part of sessions and that the differences between first-borns and later-borns would diminish with time into the film.

TABLE 1   Mean Laughter and Smiling Scores (in seconds)
            for Subjects in Triads

	First Minute	Second Minute	Third Minute	Fourth Minute	Fifth Minute	Final 42 Seconds
LAUGHTER						
First-borns	5.1	1.9	1.4	1.0	2.0	2.5
Later-borns	1.7	1.8	1.7	1.2	1.9	0.9
SMILING						
First-borns	8.3	2.1	1.1	1.0	0.7	3.2
Later-borns	2.3	2.2	1.2	1.3	1.4	2.0

The results were in line with this expectation. For sessions as a whole (and consistent with previous findings), first-borns in groups laughed more than did later-borns ($F=4.56$; $df=1,16$; $p<.05$) and they smiled more ($F=11.82$; $df=1,16$; $p<.01$); but the significant differences were actually confined to just the first minute of the film (when anxiety is presumed to have been at its highest), and at this time they were highly pronounced ($p<.001$). We found no sex effects nor interaction effects in our analyses of variance.

Funniness ratings were uniformly high for all twenty solitary children and all twenty subjects in the triadic group conditions (that is, the twenty children who sat centrally in the groups of three): the high ratings are no doubt attributable to demand characteristics inherent in the brief post-film questionning period.

McGhee in his 'individual' condition found that later-borns showed greater humour appreciation than did first-borns. In our study, there was no such difference. Both first-borns and later-borns when on their own laughed and smiled minimally, there being in grand total from the twenty alone children, zero seconds of laughter and sixteen seconds of smiling. There were major methodological differences between the two studies which together might account for this difference. Arguably, the most salient is that no experimenter or confederate was present with any of our subjects (cf. Chapman, 1976, for discussion of social facilitation effects). If an experimenter had been present, the scores of alone children would certainly have been boosted.

In summary, we have worked from the assumption that children are initially apprehensive when they first enter our mobile-laboratory and that their anxiety diminishes with time; perhaps it is rapidly attenuated because they are shown a humorous cartoon film. Our principal finding is that first-born children in particular seem to make use of the humour in interacting with companions, and this is presumably to relieve their anxiety.

Again, we have demonstrated that laughter and smiling are not necessarily related in any clear-cut fashion to the funniness of humour. In the case of children (and no doubt adults as well — see Osborne & Chapman, in this volume), the amount of laughing that occurs is dependent very much on social aspects of the 'humour situation' in which they find themselves. How much laughter occurs after the presentation of humour is a complex function of many interacting factors. The humour itself and the way it is presented constitutes but one set of factors. Social factors seem to be just as important.

REFERENCES

See Bibliography for publications on humour, laughter and comedy

Adams, B.N., Birth order: a critical review. Sociometry, 35, 411-439 (1972).

Baker, F. & O'Brien, G.M., Birth order and fraternity affiliation. Journal of Social Psychology, 78, 41-43 (1969).

Dember, W.N., Birth order and need affiliation. Journal of Abnormal & Social Psychology, 68, 555-557 (1964).

Koenig, F., Definitions of self and ordinal position of birth. Journal of Social Psychology, 78, 287-288 (1969).

Miller, N. & Maruyama, G., Ordinal position and peer popularity. Journal of Personality and Social Psychology, 33, 123-131 (1976).

Nowicki, S., Ordinal position, approval motivation, and interpersonal attraction. Journal of Consulting & Clinical Psychology, 36, 265-267 (1971).

Schachter, S., The Psychology of Affiliation: Experimental Studies of the Sources of Gregariousness. Stanford, University Press (1959).

Schooler, C., Birth order effects: Not here, not now! Psychological Review, 78, 161-175 (1972).

Vockell, E.L., Felker, D.W. & Miley, C.H., Birth order literature 1967-1971: Bibliography and index. Journal of Individual Psychology, 29, 39-53 (1973).

Warren, J.R., Birth order and social behavior. Psychological Bulletin, 65, 38-49 (1966).

Zajonc, R.B. & Markus, G.B., Birth order and intellectual development. Psychological Review, 82, 74-88 (1975).

ACKNOWLEDGEMENT

We are extremely grateful to Miss M. George and the Staff at Springwood County Infants School for their warm hospitality during this research.

A Developmental Analysis of Children's Favourite Jokes

Jennings Bryant and Timothy P. Meyer

University of Massachusetts

In order to evaluate humorous material that is most appealing to children at various stages of development, favourite jokes were solicited from one-hundred-and-twenty 5-6, 7-8, and 9-10 year-old boys and girls. These humorous communications were examined by a panel of judges on numerous dimensions which have been demonstrated to be relevant components of the kinds of humour appreciated by adults. Each judged response was treated by regression analysis with age and sex as the independent or predictor variables; canonical regression analysis was also performed to identify varying combinations of predictor and criterion variables. It was anticipated that this approach would permit some determination of the time of onset of various components of so-called mature humour and allow a comparison of the relative frequency of occurrence and importance of these several attributes at different ages.

A large number of the features which were assumed to occur rather frequently in the humour of adults apparently are not particularly important for describing children's humour. The judges determined that only one joke employed the provocation-retaliation format which is so common to the humour of adults; moreover, the judges perceived no ridicule, satire, insult, or sexual reference in any of the children's jokes, and only trivial amounts of violence, defiance, or references to scatological or moral judgmental elements were found. On the other hand, the following features occurred rather frequently across age and sex categories and were subjected to further analysis: exaggeration, incongruity, surprise, absurdity, slapstick, verbal humour, visual humour, abstraction, bodily function, movement, logical elements, fantasy orientation, cognitive complexity, intellectual sophistication, personal experience and creativity.

Sex of the participant was not a significant predictor, either alone or in combination with other predictors, on any of the measures employed in the regression analysis. Age of the participant was a significant predictor in five of the joke variables analyzed: verbal humour, visual humour, logical elements, intellectual sophistication, and language sophistication. The older children's sense of humour is decidedly more verbally-based than that of the younger children. Additionally, the humour of older children compared to younger children is defined by an increased portion of logical elements and higher levels of intellectual and language sophistication.

The canonical regression analyses employed revealed three independent and statistically significant canonical variates (predictors/criteria combinations). The first combination revealed degree of abstraction and cognitive complexity as related to the level of intellectual sophistication of the joke. As might be expected, higher levels of abstraction and cognitive complexity were related to higher levels of intellectual sophistication. The second combination included degree of slapstick, fantasy orientation, and perceived personal experience with the joke content as predictors of visual humour. The more slapstick, the greater the fantasy orientation, and the more the evidence of personal experience, the greater the reliance on elements of visual humour in the joke. The third combination showed age and intellectual sophistication related to logical elements, cognitive complexity, and incongruity. The relationship was such that greater proportions of logical elements, cognitive complexity and incongruity were predicted by increasing age, with older children's jokes reflecting higher levels of intellectual sophistication.

Two additional findings not specifically related to the content of the jokes were also noteworthy. Regarding the nature of the protagonists, the youngest children showed a strong preference for animal-protagonists, whereas the oldest females displayed an even stronger preference for no protagonist, tending to opt instead for more abstract riddles without characters. Regarding the format of the humorous communications, females (especially the older girls) utilized the riddle format extensively, whereas males tended to rely on joke or funny story formats. Both of these findings merit further consideration.

Developmental Levels in Explanations of Humour From Childhood to Late Adolescence

Alice Sheppard

California State University, Fresno

Much humour presented in television, comic strips, and jokes serves both child and adult audiences. In attempting to understand the factors underlying this broad range of appeal, the question arises as to whether children and adults are really laughing at the same things, or, instead, if different levels of meaning and appreciation exist. Furthermore, as children get older, do they simply gain an ability to view more things as funny, or does the structure of humour itself change? In what ways does the humour of adolescence differ from that of childhood?

Traditional research on children's humour has demonstrated the role of comprehension or cognitive factors in children's humour (e.g., McGhee, 1971a; Shultz, 1972; Zigler, Levine & Gould, 1967). However, in addition to simply 'getting the joke', there is evidence that the child's attitude toward the humorous object is important. For example, Kreitler and Kreitler (1970) demonstrated that young children who expressed an attitude of criticism, wonder, or mockery to a set of incongruous drawings displayed proportionately greater smiling and laughing. The cognitive framework to which an individual assimilates a humorous event thus appears to be a major aspect of humour appreciation.

The present work proposes a continuous transition from childhood to adolescence in the meaning of humour by assuming that such changes reflect the cognitive restructuring of experience. That is, with increasing development one finds not merely a linear increase in understanding, but qualitative advances in the ability to relate humorous events to personal experience and to seek a generality of meaning in humour. In order to demonstrate the validity of this approach, at least two issues are raised. First, do individuals adopt different attitudes toward explaining humour and, secondly, are such responses related to age?

The basic procedure involved asking individuals why an event was funny and then categorizing the responses into levels; an approach which assumes that responses can be distinguished reliably by level. Moreover, the levels are presumed to reflect developmental changes in the meaning of humour, analogous to levels schemes used in psychological studies of moral development (Kohlberg, 1963, 1968), personality growth (Loevinger, 1966; Loevinger & Wessler, 1970), the ego-ideal (Van den Daele, 1968), and intellectual changes during college (Perry, 1970). All of these approaches assume that changes in cognitive structuring of ideas and values are central to an understanding of personality and intellectual growth. Such an approach seems similarly applicable to humour research.

The humour levels scheme proposed in the present study included six levels, roughly paralleling the Kohlberg and Loevinger stages. The major levels were described as: (1) idiosyncratic; (2) partial explanation; (3) normative; (4) relational; (5) extra-contextual; and (6) philosophical. It was expected that children would progress from simple assertion and identification of elements, toward an increasing understanding of the relationship to their own experience, recognition of the interplay of multiple aspects of a situation, and, finally, an attempt to use humour to comprehend and accept the nature of their world. The levels were defined as follows:

Level 1	Idiosyncratic	Response is by assertion of personal attitude or feeling. No attempt to explain the humour.
Level 2	Partial	Description of major element involved in humour without indication of incongruity.
Level 3A	Normative	Generalization or statement which implies rule or convention and its violation.
	3B Expectation	Reference to unusualness or improbability of event.

Level 4	Relational	Concern for inner motives related to situation, relations between events, and multiple aspects of the situation.
Level 5	Extra-contextual	Context beyond situation implied in notion of parody, take-off, irony, or satire. Distinction between appearance and reality noted. Humour revealed as contingent upon subtle aspects of events.
Level 6	Philosophical	Humour as the ability to see what is ridiculous in the nature of things. Generalized outlook drawn from humour example.

STUDY 1

The first study was conducted with college students in an effort to determine the feasibility of distinguishing responses on the basis of 'levels'. A set of photographs was selected, photographs being chosen as a medium closer to real life and consistent with Freud's (1960) notion that 'a joke is made, the comic is found'. Also consistent with Freud's descriptions, comic of person and of situation were distinguished, though further subdivided into realistic versus obviously contrived situations, such as double exposures. A set of twenty photographs was used, consisting of males, females, situations, and contrived settings. They were shown to forty students individually, an equal number of males and females, at a small Liberal Arts College. They rated each photograph on a seven-point scale from 'not funny' to 'very funny' and then explained why they thought each one was funny.

In order to evaluate the 'levels' responses, it should first be mentioned that subjects did not find the set overwhelmingly funny, and that no photograph type reached the midpoint of the funniness scale. Nevertheless, students rated realistic situational photographs funniest, followed by humorous persons, male and female. While statistical analyses showed strong effects attributable to photograph type, a weak interaction emerged from the fact that men displayed a heightened preference for situational over person humour. In the analysis of humour justifications into levels, responses were obtained at all levels and were distributed as follows: Idiosyncratic (2.7%); Partial explanation (15.7%); Normative (29.5%); Relational (30.2%); Extra-contextual (19.8%); Philosophical (2.2%). Moreover, it was found that the type of photograph presented influenced the types of explanations given: that is, higher-level descriptions were given for situational humour than for persons. As these were also rated funnier, there may be a general relationship between degree of appreciation and humour level, although it is also possible that situational humour is simply more complex, thereby encouraging subjects to provide more detailed descriptions.

STUDY 2

The concept of a 'levels' score requires either an a priori basis for characterizing one level as 'higher' than another, or a general relationship to chronological age. To test an age re_ationship, a second study was designed assessing children's humour responses by the levels scheme. Children were chosen at three ages, eight, twelve, and sixteen years, thus approximating to Piaget's descriptions of concrete, transitional, and formal operational thinking.

As a partial control for the influence of stimulus factors on the type of humour explanations given, both cartoons and photographs were used. Moreover, three thematic types were included within each set: aggression, incompetence, and incongruity. 'Aggression' was defined as the tendentious use of hostility, violence, and threat: 'incompetence' as themes portraying individuals as inept, bungling, or unable to comprehend a situation; and 'incongruity' as the juxtaposition of incompatible elements in a context lacking deep significance.

The subjects included twenty-four children each from grades two, six and ten in an elementary school and adjacent high school in a small Midwestern town. The number of boys and girls at each age was equal; all subjects were tested individually. After rating each stimulus on a five-point funniness scale, the child was asked to explain the joke in each one, or tell why some other child might find it funny if he or she did not. The examiner observed the child's initial reaction to each stimulus and recorded it on a mirth response scale for smiling and laughing.

In terms of total scores, children found the photographs funnier than the cartoons. Age differences, moreover, revealed a decline in mean ratings of funniness from 3.91 (age 8), 3.31 (age 12) to 2.80 (age 16), although the mirth response score showed no significant changes. (These findings underscore the problems of developmental research when different measures not only give different results, but lead to such conclusions as that the child progressively loses his or her sense of humour with age!)

Use of the levels scheme showed reasonably high agreement between raters (85.4%), while a new level was added as a result of the study. This was a transitional level where the student indicated that something was funny by relating it to his or her own experience - a phenomenon which did not appear before adolescence. Unlike the previous study, no 'philosophical' explanations were found at these ages. Percentage responses for the subjects at each age were as follows:

	8 years	12 years	16 years
Idiosyncratic	0.5	0.8	1.4
Partial explanation	18.0	10.6	10.4
Normative	68.4	68.8	65.9
Relational	12.9	18.8	17.1
Personal experience	0.2	0.8	3.2
Extra-contextual	0	0.2	1.7
Philosophical	0	0	0

This reveals a relationship between humour levels and age, especially in the decrease in partial explanations by the age of twelve, the increase in relational ones at twelve, and the addition of personal experience and extra-contextual responses at the age of sixteen. These results do not seem as dramatic as was anticipated, but nonetheless show clear results in the predicted direction.

When cartoons and photographs are examined separately, differences emerge in the types of explanations used. In general, photographs seemed to elicit somewhat higher-level responses than did cartoons, with relational and extra-contextual responses found more frequently, while partial explanations, in contrast, were more characteristic of cartoon responses. This implies that the cartoon is viewed as a self-contained structure, analyzed with a search for the incongruous element or elements within its boundaries, while the photograph is often seen as funny because of its multiple aspects and relation to general principles of conduct and social meaning.

DISCUSSION AND CONCLUSIONS

Humour explanations appear to be of three major types: (1) pre-explanatory, where no real reason is given; (2) statements of rule, where recognition of incongruity or unexpectedness is regarded as a sufficient explanation; and (3) generalized-universal, where an attempt is made to relate a given event to other experiences and to discover metaphorical truths. Our findings reveal that over 60% of the responses from three age groups were statements of rule, while developmental shifts emerged in the decline of pre-explanatory responses (levels 1 and 2) after the age of eight, in the appearance of generalized responses (levels 4/5, 5) at the age of sixteen, and of a few philosophical explanations in college. Thus, broadly stated, the humour of adolescence differs from the child's in its ability to incorporate self-reference, to apply a metaphorical interpretation to events, and to discover social truths in humour or satire.

The humour researcher has long been plagued by the many types and definitions of humour. However, for much of the humour of real life it seems useful to posit humour as an attitude which one may variously choose to adopt. Freud (1928) assumed that humour, which he distinguished from other forms of the comic, was basically a mental attitude used to alleviate suffering, deny reality, and to reduce the external world to mere child's play. While his definition of its uses appears overly pessimistic, he does contribute by emphasizing its relation to unique mental attitudes. Viewing humour as a type of perception, the anthropologist Mary Douglas (1968), has described the humorist as a minor mystic or 'one of those people who pass beyond the bounds of reason and society and give glimpses of a truth which escapes through the mesh of structured concepts' (p373).

In conclusion, the attempt to discover how the child develops the ability to use humour is a goal with implications for mental health, education, and the study of cognitive development. The present work has begun to explore the ways in which the humour of adolescence contrasts with that of childhood, while it is anticipated that further research along these lines will help to clarify both the emergence of individual differences in world views at adolescence and their relation to other personality and cognitive structures.

FOOTNOTE

I gratefully acknowledge the assistance of Barbara Duncan, Betty Haynes, Bob Hung, Derek Hybels, Elisa Klein, and Sharon Porteous. The cooperation of Vassar College and the Portage Public Schools, Portage, Michigan, was greatly appreciated.

REFERENCES

See Bibliography for publications on humour, laughter and comedy

Kohlberg, L., The development of children's orientations toward a moral order: I. Sequence in the development of moral thought. Vita Humana, 6, 11 (1963).

Kohlberg, L., Stage and sequence: the cognitive-developmental approach to socialization. In: D. Goslin (Ed.), Handbook of Socialization Theory and Research. Rand-McNally, Chicago (1968).

Loevinger, J., The meaning and measurement of ego development. American Psychologist, 21, 195 (1966).

Loevinger, J. & Wessler, R., Measuring Ego Development. Jossey-Bass, San Francisco (1970).

Perry, W.G., Forms of Intellectual and Ethical Development in the College Years. Holt, Rinehart and Winston, New York (1970).

Van den Daele, L., A developmental study of the ego-ideal. Genetic Psychology Monographs, 78, 191 (1968).

Comprehension and Emotional Adhesion in the Genetics of Humour

Françoise Bariaud

Laboratoire de Psychobiologie de l'enfant, Paris

To study humour means that, from the start, one accepts remaining enclosed within a paradox: focussing on an undefined object; endeavouring to grasp it while it is essentially mobile; dissecting it while analysis kills it; imprisoning it in an experimental frame while it can only really exist without any constraint. We are conscious of the risks and limitations of such a venture and we present our work as a mere exploration which raises more questions about the genetics of humour than it provides answers.

The evolutive outlook should enable us to discover the moment when humour appears in the course of development, its premises and the conditions it requires to exist, and lastly perhaps how it is to be differentiated from the comical. Our work is centred upon the encounter of the receiver and the humour message (graphic message); in this context, the creator, regretfully, remains confined solely to his presence in what he transmits.

One cannot, a priori, exhaustively define what it is that makes the quality of a message 'humorous', but incongruity appears as a primordial element. However, incongruity per se will not give rise to a smile or to the feeling that there is something funny. To achieve this, it has to carry a meaning which, in our opinion, involves the reversal (or at least the questioning) of social or existential values.

As to the response, the most productive theory (offered by Shultz) is that of a two-part process in understanding: firstly the grasping of the incongruity, then the search for and discovery of the meaning (resolution) which carries the author's intent. But it may readily happen that this intent is understood without being considered funny; in such an instance we cannot speak of a humour response, because the humour response implies an emotional adhesion to the recognized meaning of the incongruity; that is to say acceptance of the discovered sense, an emotional participation with the author's intention. This is finally expressed by the judgment 'it is funny!' even more than by the smile which in an experimental situation is a very fragile indicator.

This theoretical model, which relates only to the cognitive mechanisms of response, involves the idea of a relatively complex decoding of the message, the message (often but not always) containing in itself elements of resolution. Already the question may be raised concerning the possibility of generalizing this model to all forms of humour; particularly to the kind of humour that is grasped all at once (in some cartoons, for instance), where the elements of resolution are external to the message, where incongruity and meaning seem blended and which, in the end, one is usually unable to 'explain'. Really the most difficult thing for the subject is to answer the question 'why is this funny?'. The explanations we obtain may help us to understand better in what manner the subject has perceived the message, how he has organized its various elements and which are those he has ascribed as funny; but, in most cases, they give but a mere glimpse of the deep meaning of humour.

The proposals we are about to present here originate in interviews with children aged five, seven and nine, following the principles of Piaget's clinical method. The material was composed of cartoons without any captions, showing funny things that 'do not exist' (for natural or social reasons). This seems to be the category of messages which best permits an exploration of an essential aspect of humour and the reaction it induces, namely, the twofold play on reality and fantasy. Keeping that question in mind we have chosen to limit ourselves to a few points: recognizing (or not) the incongruity, assigning a meaning to it, and the points of view which arise.

IDENTIFICATION OF INCONGRUITY

Necessity of previously constituted cognitive schemata

It is obvious that in order to grasp the anomaly of an object (a being or even a behaviour) the child must possess the mental schema corresponding to the usual appearance of the object and be able to identify it in spite of its oddness. It must be noted that the object's strangeness does not impinge on it heavily enough to make it lose its identity and become completely 'fantastic'. With young children (five years old) the researcher should always be able to distinguish the cases where incongruity is not perceived because of a cognitive gap (and this is banal) from those cases where incongruity is not perceived for other reasons, more difficult to discern.

Instances where the incongruity is not grasped, even when the child possesses the necessary cognitive skill

The humour response implies that, firstly, one places oneself simultaneously on two levels: reality and fantasy. The norms of reality merely serve as a reference. And one must be able to ignore them to accept the existence of the incongruous on the level of play and of unreality. Also, it is probably the fact of being situated on this other plane that makes even the most agonizing humour bearable.

But some humour responses seem impossible to illicit because of what one might call the child's 'realism'; sometimes it is as though the schema of the usual object and the concrete experience the child has of it were so powerful as to prevent the grasping of the incongruity. This can be seen in the reactions of the youngest children in the context of incongruities which are not, cognitively, too complex for them but which nevertheless they fail to perceive.

'– it's not funny, it's a bike, like mine (– same as yours, you're sure?) – yes, I've got another one, one day I'll show it to you' (five-year-old).

'– it's not funny, I saw bikes like that when I was in Corsica (– yes, but how does one ride it?) – you put one foot here and one there, one there and one there (– four feet?) – yes, that's to put your feet on and then you pedal (– hmm, but how many feet do people have?) – hey? (– how many feet do you have?) – two (– so, how does one manage here?) – well, you just pedal!' (five-year-old).

A similar difficulty to break away from the concrete seems contained in the categorical rejection of the incongruity when presented to some children who then stress 'materialistic' arguments: '– no, you can't put a man there and another there because the saddle is too small' (five-year-old).

Instances where incongruity is grasped but not accepted and destroyed

The responses we have just mentioned consist of superimposing reality and its norms on that which is incongruous. This may also occur in a more complex form, particularly in children of about seven and up to the age of nine: after a tenuous grasping of the anomaly they reject it because 'it cannot be'. For the incongruities which require the children to work out a construction, putting together and relating the contradictory components in the drawing, we observe flat refusals to do so:

'(– is this funny or not?) – no, because here you see the horse and here are footprints (– whose prints?) – I suppose they cannot be the horse's prints, he can't have hoofs and feet (– hmm, still, if one follows them, look) – or else the horse follows his master's prints (– but they can't be the horse's prints?) – no, it's round with a little tip (– hmm, is it funny if he leaves prints like that?) – no' (nine-year-old).

For more obvious incongruities the non-acceptance takes another form. The reaction then consists, after perception of the anomaly, of making it legitimate by resorting to causes which belong to the realm of the usual and the possible: '– it's a broken bike, it's not funny' (seven-year-old). The incongruity is considered, but immediately destroyed as the child introduces an element which enables him to make it congruous, borrowing from reality. It may well be that this latter mechanism is in evolutive filiation with resolution. By no means, however, may they be assimilated to each other as their effects are radically opposed. The only relationship with resolution that this mechanism has is that it also begins by a search for the 'why' of the oddness. However, if the resolution process also consists of looking for a reason and assigning it to the incongruity, it functions in a quite different way. In our opinion, resolution is in full accordance with fantasy, and the incongruous character of the message remains whole. The resolution implies, after the perception and acceptance of the incongruity, that there is restoration of a certain congruency, by integration into the context of values reversed from the normal. Yet the response we have observed results in annihilating or at least in reducing the anomaly.

The mention of a plausible explanation is sometimes preceded by an expression of surprise or explicit interrogations:

'– that! two men meeting, one takes his hat off and the other one is taking his off; this one, why isn't his head hung up like the other one? Hey, why? (– I don't know) – is it broken? (– he took it off) – ah, he took his head off! how does he do it? he cuts it off? (– is it funny or isn't it?) – it's funny but how does he take it off? (– you think one can?) – well no, he cuts it off, he cut himself, he can really, he takes a great big knife or scissors' (five-year-old).

This example shows how such a justification of the unbelievable is not necessarily accompanied by the non-appreciation ('it isn't funny'). The judgment varies in accordance with the emotional content of the evocations (here sadistic) and the individual characteristics of personality.

Lastly, it may be noted that among the 'explanations' some must be differentiated and placed on another level because they are of a playful quality: reference to fancy-dress, for instance, or mention of false appearances, which always go with positive feeling and begins to play on the ambiguity of reality and fantasy.

    '– there's a man who wants to say hello to the... like that, and it was a dummy, so he too wants to say hello then his head goes off, there's no hand, one can see it's a dummy' (nine-year-old).

<u>GRASPING OF THE INCONGRUITY AND EMOTIONAL ADHESION TO ITS MEANING</u>

The modalities of realism which we have just examined involve the non-understanding of the workings of the joke and therefore can not lead us to the humour reaction. If this reaction is to appear, it means that the receiver is able to shift from the norms of reality and consider the possibility of questioning them. This allows not only the grasping of the incongruity, but also its acceptance as originating something funny.

    '– of course I know a horse's prints are not like that, that's why it's funny!' (nine-year-old).
    '(– can you tell me what's funny here?) – it's the prints (– yes, why are the prints funny?) – because it's the horse that makes the prints and they are a man's prints (– hmm, are you sure that it is the horse who makes them?) – yes' (nine-year-old).

The same capacity for disconnecting from reality is expressed when the experimenter offers the possible existence of incongruous objects:

'(- one could make scissors like that,
couldn't one?) - yes, but just for fun!'
(nine-year-old).

'- people could make scissors like that for
a joke but they wouldn't put them in a shop
window' (nine-year-old).

Thus, in the realm of humoristic play and fantasy, the recognized 'impossible' exists and
functions. The mere statement of its nonconformity is not enough, if one stops at this:
'- this bike is odd but I don't think it funny' (five-year-old). But the incongruous is
funny in and by its imaginary existence:

'- it's funny this bike because when someone sits down he can go this side or this
side, or then if there's someone who wants to ride with someone else, one's going
to go there and the other there, but it's going to get broken' (nine-year-old).

Here the incongruity functions; it works so as to make fun of characters who are only
suggested through the use made of the object. The child, as an onlooker, is amused by the
misfortunes he imagines may assail them:

'- if they want to make a turn, on this bike, they'll crash' (nine-year-old);

'- they'll never be able to start' (nine-year-old);   '- they'll fall down'
(seven-year-old);

'- they're going to get their feet mixed up' (nine-year-old).

Thus, humour presumes that for a given time reality is granted to the anomaly. However, it
also presumes one more step. It seems, in fact, that within the framework of this kind of
recognition of the incongruous in the imaginary two viewpoints may be differentiated; for
us, only the second of these corresponds to the humour response. The first point of view is
that of the onlooker; as seen above it leads the subject to smile at the victims of the
oddness. Such a smile, we think, is more closely related to the comical, as it concerns that
person who, failing to follow the norm, is then open to due loss of value. The second
viewpoint, which truly characterizes the humour reaction, is that of a creator in the sense
that one does not merely grant the incongruity an existence but moreover justifies it. Such
a resolution may not necessarily be the result of a search or of a discursive strategy, we
even think it may escape consciousness insofar as it sometimes remains impossible to explain
('- me, when it's funny, I laugh, but I can't say why it's funny!' (five-year-old). It
seems that the receiver has a justification for the existence of the incongruity. So, for
instance, he could give reasons for the examples we use: confusion of identities (the
horse), rigidity of people or bodily dismemberment (the greeting), uselessness of social
objects (the bike)... All these mean questioning, or even making fun of the usual ways of
thinking (superiority of man over animal, usefulness of man-made objects...). At the same
time, this seriously reveals a certain outlook on another aspect of reality: one that would
be a source of anxiety, were it not clad in humour. To react with humour the receiver
himself must share this other outlook on the world. This is how we think we can understand
the complicity which arises, in humour, between the receiver and the creator.

And so, in the end, the initial reality takes on a new meaning, thanks to humour...

Children's Humour: Discussion

Derek S. Wright

School of Education, University of Leicester

The papers in this symposium are all emprical studies of particular problems in the
development of humour in children. As is inevitable, I suppose, when the topic is
developmental, the ubiquitous spirit of Piaget was present throughout, though his theory was
more proximately mediated through the work of Shultz and McGhee. One way or another, most
of the symposiasts were concerned to show how the growth of humour slots into Piaget's
developmental framework. Consistent with this, the kind of humour studied is that which,
following Shultz and others, can be analyzed into a two-element process, the perception of
incongruity and the perception of the resolution of this incongruity; that is, the
perception of congruity in the incongruity. I therefore think it is useful in approaching
these papers to remind ourselves of certain important features of Piaget's theory, in
particular those concerned with the change from preoperational thinking to operational.

The preoperational child, as shown for instance in the famous conservation experiments, is
perceptually centred. His judgment is determined by the one relationship which is currently
commanding his attention. He is quite capable of perceiving other relationships present in
the task, but when he does notice them he 'forgets' what he has just seen and makes a fresh
and usually different judgment in the light of the relationship he is now centred upon. The
concrete operational child, on the other hand, is able to take account of two or more
relationships in his judgment. Now it is crucial to Piaget's structural theory that the
two relationships are taken account of simultaneously. The child is able to vary two
relationships in a compensatory fashion at the same time, and this implies a certain freedom
from perceptual domination. He does not consciously infer from one relationship to another.
There is no conscious deduction going on, though he may later be able to read out such
deduction if required. Because his cognitive structures can now process and integrate two
or more bits of information at the same time and in a systematic way, the conservation of
the object is self-evidently and directly given to him in his awareness of it. Indeed it is
so obvious he may be puzzled why he is being questioned on the topic at all.

Now a continuing problem with Piaget's theory is to define the kind of response in the child
which can be taken as an index of the existence of structures of the kind described. There
are two possibilities. Since in the conservation task there is a correct response which
implies the relating of two relationships, we can either take the child's instant and
correct judgment as our index, or take his subsequent rationalization of that judgment in
terms of inference. There is a good case for arguing that the former is the better index.

In the area of humour, as analyzed by Shultz, we have two relationships, one of incongruity
and one of resolution or congruity. There is moreover a 'correct' response, namely 'seeing
the joke', whether it is felt as funny or not, and this event is a sudden occurrence
implying the simultaneous awareness of the two relationships. If the joke is funny, the
involuntary amusement response is of course the best index that the joke has been seen.
Shultz' original claim was that young children can see the incongruity relationship but not
its resolution. We might say they were perceptually centred on incongruity. Only
operational children can see the resolution relationship. In their excellent experiments,
Pien and Rothbart have clearly shown that under certain circumstances young children can
also perceive the resolution. They conclude that the method they used to do this, that of
paired comparison, must therefore be a better measure of humour development than the
technique used by Shultz. But the paired comparison technique is one in which the child's
attention is drawn to the two relationships present sequentially. I therefore want to
question whether it is a technique which can satisfactorily show that a child can process
both relationships simultaneously and thereby in the full sense 'see the joke'.

The incongruity-resolution model has obvious utility in the analysis of certain kinds of
humour; equally obviously it is by itself inadequate. In various guises the same model

has been used to explain such diverse phenomena as attitude change, curiosity and the
development of moral reasoning. The conditions under which the model predicts the amusement
response still need to be fully specified. Chris Athey's valuable study shows that the
degree of complexity in humour enjoyed by the child follows closely his/her stage of
cognitive development as defined by Piaget. Her more interesting finding is that there is
some kind of optimal level of complexity for the child in producing the amusement response.
If the joke strains comprehension, or is too easily understood, amusement is less. She
links this, following Piaget, to playfulness, in which assimilation predominates over
accommodation. That is to say, maximum amusement is associated with the playful expression
of some newly attained cognitive mastery which has not yet become so automatic as to be no
longer a source of pleasure.

This perspective can be applied to some of the more intriguing findings in Françoise
Bariaud's paper. Her approach is more authentically Piagetian since she used his method of
clinical interrogation. She attempted to trace the development of the child's response to
incongruity. Under certain conditions she found that the child's response was one of
rejection of the incongruity or of 'scientifically' explaining it away. In Athey's sense
this could be either because it was too easy or too difficult. But as Bariaud points out,
there is more to it. The child must accept, entertain and preserve the incongruity if s/he
is to find the situation amusing. She talks of the need for emotional adhesion to fantasy.
In doing so she is moving away from the explanatory categories which Piaget has to offer.

The paper by Alice Sheppard deals more directly with humour in adolescence. She draws
attention to the fact that humour is related to what might be called the adolescent's
philosophical world view and to his developing self-objectivity. This emphasizes the fact
that humour is embedded in wider and more general cognitive activity as the child approaches
adulthood. Similarly, Chapman and Speck remind us of the need to take account of both
individual differences and of the social situation in understanding children's humour
responses.

Before leaving Piaget, however, there is a point raised by the papers of Athey, Bariaud and
Sheppard which is perhaps worth making. All three deal, not just with the child's amusement
response, but also with his understanding of a joke, his explanation of why it is funny.
None has recourse to a principle inherent in Piaget's theory which one might have thought
relevant, his principle of conscious realisation. This states that a degree of cognitive
complexity appears at the self-reflective level after its appearance, so to speak, in
action. There is a time-lag between them. What this might suggest is that a child will
only be able adequately to explain a joke after it has ceased to be optimally amusing for
him. At least it helps to explain why the jokes used in humour research on children are
received in polite silence by adults; we are all too boringly familiar with the mechanism
behind them.

Another curious feature of jokes, brought out by Bryant's developmental study of children's
favourite jokes, is the difficulty in remembering them. His general finding that the main
elements in jokes are the same at all ages is perhaps not surprising, though worth documenting.
To my mind, however, the fact that his subjects found it difficult to remember their
'favourite joke' and in the main remembered 'old' ones, tells us something important about
humour that needs more investigation. Intuitively it seems that the jokes found most funny
at the time are most easily forgotten. It is the stale ones, which we have already taken
much social mileage out of, which we remember. I am of course excluding those whose
self-appointed social role requires them to have a good memory for jokes.

Finally I want to take up and emphasize a point touched on by Bryant. As this symposium
bears witness, there is a strong tendency to assimilate the development of humour in children
to Piaget's cognitive theory. This is of course a reasonable preliminary step. It is an
open question, however, to what extent this serves merely to confirm Piagetian theory and to
what extent it enlightens us about humour. Certainly it would be nice if the study of humour
forced some measure of accommodation upon Piaget's conceptual scheme. Doctrines which assert
that humour is a form of play and therefore in some sense an aside from the serious business
of intelligent adaptation must be strongly questioned. Laughter, amusement, delight in wit
or the absurd, indeed the pervasive attitude of playfulness, these may well be of profound
importance for sane and intelligent adaptation in life.

Alice Sheppard quoted Mary Douglas as describing the humorist as a 'minor mystic'. That
seems to me a very important remark. The humour response is an 'altered state of
consciousness', one in which potentially at least an expanded and more balanced perspective
is brought to a situation. In this sense it is properly described as a minor version of the
mystical experience. The need for that perspective, not least in the area of research into
humour, hardly needs to be asserted.

ETHNIC HUMOUR

Ethnic Humour: From Paradoxes Towards Principles

Lawrence La Fave

University of Windsor

Is humour a serious subject? Many think otherwise. For instance, an article, 'Killing Laughter,' was recently published by 'Time' (a weekly fiction and weakly non-fiction magazine). Time London Correspondent Christopher Byron (1976, p58) based his piece of one hackmanship on that very International Conference on Humour and Laughter which provides many pages for this book. The Time article concurred with Robert Benchley: 'There seems to be no lengths to which humorless people will not go to analyze humor.' The piece treated our humour conference as a joke — prejudging that any theory of humour is a humorous theory. In fact, the Time story was itself a 'joke' — based upon the common formula for generating amusement, the logical blunder of confounding object language with meta-language. Had the Time correspondent attended the interesting paper by mathematical logician, John Paulos (this volume), 'The logic of humour and the humour in logic,' he might have avoided the nonsequitur of jumping to the conclusion that the study of humour is necessarily humorous.

The present chapter therefore need offer no apologies to Logic for taking the study of humour in general, and ethnic humour in particular, seriously. Contrary to Time, this chapter believes few if any subjects more worthy of serious study than humour — particularly ethnic humour. Why? Today, modern technology threatens to fashion history's pages in radioactive dust. Then truly would all men be cremated equal. I have expressed my concern in a distinguished scientific journal (Playboy, June, 1971, p60):

> 'Will you still find me attractive,
> After I'm radioactive,
> After we've tasted victory in World War Three?
> Will you still find me attractive,
> After I'm radioactive,
> After the world consists of just you and me?'

Of course the social Darwinists and Hitlerites (to whom I say 'Amin') might welcome nuclear war, observing: 'Genetic devolution we shall then replace, as we carve out of ashes a superior race.' But I cannot really say Amin to that! I believe we should do what we can to reduce man's inhumanity to man and spare Spaceship Earth from the early fate of a Hellish Crematorium. How? Arthur Koestler (1968) brings wisdom to bear on the subject. Much, perhaps most, of man's inhumanity to man, Koestler reasons, has been in the name of good intentions. 'Onward Christian soldiers marching as to war with the cross of Jesus going on before. And so I cut off thy head in the name of Christian Brotherhood.' A scientific understanding of ethnic humour could do much to provide pedagogic tools for reducing prejudice and discrimination against ethnic groups, for reducing ethnocentrism and those tensions and misperceptions which cause war. With such important goals we need not take much time out to listen to Time out to ridicule us. To the contrary, we must recognize the smug ethnocentrism of Time as part of the problem. We must ask ourselves why such communication media in affluent capitalist societies feel threatened by challenges to the conventional 'wisdom' about ethnic humour. So this chapter's task is to advance scientific understanding of ethnic humour. But how?

A first step proven useful in science and mathematics focuses on certain paradoxes central to the field of study. The next step depends upon metatheoretical tools from the philosophy and history of science to resolve these paradoxes. Application of useful methodology conjoined with empirical study of ethnic humour would then hopefully lead to a useful substantive theory of humour. Such scientific knowledge could be applied to reduce ethnic prejudice, discrimination, and the likelihood of war.

HUMOROUS PARADOXES

This chapter will first parade eight humorous paradoxes especially relevant to ethnic humour.

Paradox 1:   The Whole ≠ the Sum of Its Parts

This paradox, which surfaces whenever levels of analysis are confounded, has already thrice
revealed itself. The heading for the present section of this chapter is one example; it
deliberately exploits an ambiguity with respect to levels of abstraction by its use of the
phrase 'Humorous Paradoxes.' On one level (the level this chapter usually intends)
'Humorous Paradoxes' refers to paradoxes of humour — meaning that puzzles are encountered
when we study humour. At another level the phrase means that the paradoxes are themselves
amusing.

A second illustration resides in the title of this very book — 'It's a Funny Thing, Humour.'
That title amuses because it holds three meanings. The word 'funny' can, as the title of
Anthony Buffery's paper in this volume suggests, mean 'Funny Ha Ha or Funny Peculiar.'
Suppose the meaning 'Funny Peculiar' is dispensed with by substituting the partial synonym
'humorous' for 'funny.' The title now becomes 'It's a humorous thing, humour.' Even that
title is not without humour — suggesting two levels of analysis. At a lower level it
indicates humour; at a higher, the humour of humour. In an analogous manner we could refer
to the comedian's comedian, the maid's maid, the criminal's criminal, ad infinitum. A child
psychologist does not usually refer to a psychologist who hasn't yet reached puberty.

A third example of Paradox 1 is exhibited in our discussions of the Time hatchet-piece
sneered at above. The Time piece was concocted on the gratuitous assumption that a theory
of humour is necessarily a humorous theory. Similarly, media people who have interviewed us
have sometimes been disappointed to learn that our humour research is not humorous research —
as if our primary purpose should have been to entertain the subjects rather than test the
hypotheses. Some people, and some humour researchers, believe that a good humour researcher
must also be a good comedian. Yet none of us expect our tailors to be the best-dressed men
in town. None of us insist that our physicians be the healthiest. No one argued that, since
Einstein could not play centrefield as well as one of Marilyn Monroe's former husbands,
Einstein knew less about the physics of baseball than did Joe Dimaggio. What renders Bernard
Shaw's epigram, 'Those who can, do; those who can't, teach,' amusing? Is it a feeling of
superiority to the teacher due to confounding object and metalanguages? And was the wit who
added, 'And those who can't teach, teach teachers,' amusing because of confusion of the
metalanguage with the metametalanguage? Logical necessity does not demand of a good humour
researcher that he be a good comedian; nor conversely. And I contemplate (but will save for
some future occasion) at least half-a-dozen reasons why one could be proficient at one while
inexpert at the other.

Suppose a humour researcher is being interviewed by a brash sadistic media person. The
interviewer's strategy will be to entice the humour researcher into playing the role of a
comedian. Either the researcher will prove a good comic or bad. If bad, the interviewer can
do a metajoke — transforming the student of humour into a humorous student. So the student
of humour himself becomes the joke — at whom, rather than with whom, the audience laughs.
Suppose our humour researcher proves a good comic. Then the interviewer again succeeds in
entertaining his audience. Our humour researcher wins a battle and loses the war; allowing
himself to get sidetracked into entertaining (rather than educating) he converts his means
to his end. Yet our humour researcher could have entertained while staying within his
pedagogic role, had he amused to illustrate theoretic points — rather than committimg
himself to being a funny person.

When I am orally interviewed, the interviewer typically begins by aggressing with 'Tell me
a joke!' My inclination is to respond 'You've got a great show!' More likely I retort with:

Paradox 2:   There's No Such Thing as a Joke

Nor am I joking when I say this. In fact, it would be impossible for me to make a joke about
jokes since there are no jokes. Permit me to illustrate the point with a joke: One Jewish
clothing store salesman whispers to another: 'Turn on the green light. The man vants a
green suit.' The point of that joke is that it nicely illustrates the point that there are
no jokes. The Gestalt psychologists were right; stimuli do not have absolute stimulating
value. Therefore a joke as humorous stimulus nonexists. Later, when discussing incongruity
humour theory, we shall return to the nonexistence of jokes (not joking about the subject
this time) and what might be done to redefine jokes into existence.

Paradox 3:   No One Has a Sense of Humour

Of course whether anyone holds a sense of humour depends upon the phrase's definition. Our argument bases itself upon the common definition of a sense of humour as ability to be amused at one's own expense. From that definition it follows that no one possesses such a virtuous trait; no one in the history of the human race has ever been amused at his own expense. Why then does almost everyone believe that some people do own a sense of humour thus defined? We have given our answers on previous occasions (La Fave, Haddad & Maesen, 1976; La Fave & Mannell, 1976a). We find sense of humour possession to be a myopic illusion for at least nine reasons which are relevant to ethnic humour and immigrant groups.

Paradox 4:   An Extreme Insult is Less Insulting Than a Mild Insult

This paradox helps explain why you always hurt the one you love. One of the nine reasons for Paradox 3 is this irony of irony: that an extreme insult (under specifiable conditions) is more likely taken as a 'left-handed insult' or compliment in disguise than is a mild insult. Hence the myopic illusion is created that the recipient is amused at a joke at his own expense; rather, he cognitively restructures the remark nonliterally as a compliment.

Paradox 5:   Don't Take Sides in Family Quarrels or Both Sides Will Turn on You

This paradox throws some cold water on the arguments of those who oppose bystander apathy. Of course in many instances the consequences of bystander apathy are anti-humane. This paradox provides, however, an important reason why the road to Hell is often paved with good intentions.

> A Lone Stranger rides into town. Just as he prepares to dismount, he overhears a quarrel between a husband and wife. After listening in for a few moments, the Lone Stranger, a behaviouristic learning theorist, emits a verbal report: 'Sir, I have been listening to your family quarrel these past few minutes and it has become clear that you are correct; the lady is mistaken.' Now the Lone Stranger, having punished the wife, anticipates eliciting a negative verbal report from her. However, having positively reinforced the husband, the Lone Stranger anticipates eliciting a positive verbal report from him. Counter to the Lone Stranger's anticipation, nonetheless, the husband reports: 'Mind your own business, Lone Stranger! This is a family quarrel!' And so, as the sun sets rapidly in the West, the Lone Stranger gallops out of town with the sheriff's posse in hot pursuit and we hear the cry: 'The Lone Stranger sides again!'

Paradox 6:   There's Comedy in Tragedy and Tragedy in Comedy

A good tragic playwright will throw in some comic relief else too much tension builds up and the audience may find its own comic relief by judging tragic incongruities hilarious. Conversely, a good comic will build tension by creating an apparently fearful or embarrassing situation. Then suddenly he will pull a serious-to-playful switch. The resultant amusement and laughter will exceed what they would have been had he not created the unpleasant situation first; the amusement being greater the greater the increment in happiness per unit time. Charlie Chaplin seems to exemplify the comic genius of tragedy in comedy and Max Eastman's (1936) playful-pain humour theory finds some relevance here.

Paradox 7:   The Wise Fool

The mediaeval jester said things which made the King laugh his head off. If these same remarks were made by anyone else, the King would have cut his head off. Why was the court fool both permitted to and capable of uttering devastating words of wisdom?

Paradox 8:   We Witness Here the Involuntary Nonconformist – His Heart in the Right Place But His Foot in His Mouth, Victim of a Habit Learned Wisely But Too Well

The butt of the joke as described by Henri Bergson (1911) often committed a faux pas because he encrusted the mechanical upon the living – responding automatically when he should have been acting in a living, vitalistic way. Since such a butt usually wished to conform to the social norm, but only nonconformed maladroitly, the question raises itself as to what prompted such involuntary nonconformity. 'Subadditive fusion', a subtype of Paradox 1, offers an answer. Here the whole, in a sense, equals less than the sum of its parts. That the whole can equal less than the sum of its parts first revealed itself to me courtesy of student feedback. I had hoped a test question would elicit the answer that the whole equals more than the sum of its parts. Instead a student responded: 'The whole equals some of its parts.'

PARADOXES OF ETHNIC HUMOUR

Now that we've breezed through the humorous paradoxes, let's run through again - at a more
leisurely pace. This trip will reveal more specifically how these paradoxes relate to ethnic
humour. And our slower pace should allow us more time to use our metatheoretical magnifying
glass to expose the flaws which provide the paradoxes of ethnic humour. By 'metatheory' is
intended the methodology of science - and by methodology is not meant technique (cf. La Fave,
1971). Nor will we be much concerned here with research or statistical inference metatheories.
Rather, our primary interest is in the methodology of scientific theory construction, the
logical base - the axiomatic, philosophical foundations. The kinds of metatheoretical questions
we would raise are those typically encountered in the philosophy and history of science.
What are the methodological criteria by which we ought to evaluate scientific theory? How may
application of such criteria advance our understanding of ethnic humour? One important
metatheoretical criterion for evaluating any scientific theory is of course the precision of
that theory - not only with respect to the tightness of its syntactic structure; also, the
precision of its technical terms. Of course before such terms can be precise they must be
defined.

So an effort will be made to define technical terms. In doing so it is realized that a
hallowed tradition of psychology, and most so-called social sciences, will be violated. One
usually survives as a theorist in these oceans of ignorance precisely to the degree one can
refuse to be precise, while perhaps creating the illusion of being so. Chameleons live long
in these troubled waters. As Fodor (1966) wrote of the terminology of such neobehaviouristic
mediation 'theories' as Osgood and Berlyne's, 'Everytime you look the pea is under a different
shell.'

A theory which does not condescend to define most of its technical terms is of course
nonfalsifiable (and falsifiability is another closely related metatheoretical criterion for
evaluating scientific theory). Such imprecise theories have enabled many naked emperors to
strut around in 'sciences' such as psychology - hiding their embarrassments behind the fig
leaves provided by their verbal smoke screens. An imprecise theory leads to nonfalsifiability
by becoming logically inconsistent. And an easy proof in mathematical logic finds that, for
every theorem or hypothesis deducible from a self-contradictory theory, the negation of that
hypothesis also follows (cf. Copi, 1954, pp55-56). Such a theory, by predicting everything,
predicts nothing; it excludes no alternatives and thereby is empty of extensional information.
Hence consistency is another essential and closely related metatheoretical criterion in
evaluating scientific theory. A first task for us, then, is to define our technical terms,
and a good place to start is at the beginning. Consider then the terminology in the title
of this chapter. These terms are (1) ethnic humour, (2) paradox, and (3) principle.

Ethnic humour will be defined here as any communication which amuses and makes reference to
a particular subculture or to a representative of that subculture. The above definition
itself may prove amusing in that its imprecision renders it a parody of what a scientific
definition ought be. In defence of my apparent failure to practice what I preach, hear my
excuses. The present chapter makes no pretence of developing an adequate scientific theory
of ethnic humour. The more modest goal of the above 'definition' is to help rope off the
arena of the present chapter's concern. If at some future date I should attempt a theory of
ethnic humour, I would need to sharpen up that definition. However, that event is unlikely.
What I am groping towards is a general theory of humour, which would encompass ethnic humour.
However, as philosophers of science such as Quine (1961, pp20-46) and Norwood Hanson (1969,
pp84-93) seem aware, it is only necessary that the theory as a whole be falsifiable - not its
parts or subsystems. The above definition of ethnic humour is also apparently inconsistent
with my treatment of humour in previous publications as a mental experience - i.e., an
organismic phenomenon, rather than on the stimulus side as in the present definition. To
resolve the contradiction perhaps I should only refer to the mental experience as amusement,
rather than humour.

A paradox will be defined for present purpose as an incongruity involving an apparently logical
or physical impossibility. Paradoxes 5 and 8 above seem to involve physical impossibility
and the remaining six logical impossibility (i.e., contradiction).

A scientific (i.e., substantive or theoretical) principle may be defined as a general fact.
A fact is a proposition. For instance, 'Ken Dodd' is not a fact because it is a name, not a
proposition. However, 'Ken Dodd exists' is a proposition. Any proposition may be expressed
as a declarative sentence. What distinguishes declaratives from other types of sentences
(such as imperatives and interrogatives) is that declaratives have truth value (i.e., are
capable of being true or false or having some probability). However, a fact is not just any
proposition but a proposition which is true. Further, a fact is not just any kind of true
proposition but a synthetic (i.e., empirical or substantive) truth rather than an analytic
truth (such as a tautology). 'Ken Dodd is a comedian' is a fact because it is a true
synthetic proposition. However, 'Ken Dodd is a comedian' fails to qualify as a scientific
principle because it is a specific, rather than general, fact.

A scientific theory obviously cannot be constructed from specific facts because a potentially infinite number of them would need to be memorized by scientists with only finite storage capacity computers. The metatheoretical principle of parsimony would thus be quite severely violated. A better candidate for qualification as a scientific principle would be such a general fact as, 'all men are mortal.' By conjoining such rules of inference as modus ponens and universal instantiation, many specific facts could be derived from it (and therefore need not be committed to memory).

Two other and closely intertwined metatheoretical criteria for evaluating a scientific theory are comprehensiveness and contributiveness. By comprehensiveness is intended the generality of the theory – how many specific facts it can successfully embrace. Ceteris paribus, the more comprehensive of two theories is superior. But comprehensiveness is only a virtue when certain other specifiable metatheoretic criteria are achieved equally well by the more general theory. We have seen that a theory can be too comprehensive because it is self-contradictory, predicting, in a sense, twice as much as it ought to. Compare, for instance, two recent theoretical approaches which seem quite relevant to ethnic humour – one by Zillmann and Cantor (1976), another by our group (La Fave, Haddad & Maesen, 1976). The Zillmann and Cantor claim is that their disposition theory is more comprehensive than our approach. And of course they are right. But they are right for the wrong reasons. They are right because nowhere do they define their highly ambiguous key word 'disposition' (whose ambiguity shall be specified later). For this and other reasons to be indicated later, their so-called disposition theory is self-contradictory; thus nonfalsifiable and overly 'comprehensive.'

The metatheoretical criterion of 'contributiveness' is easy to confuse with comprehensiveness. Yet the distinction is important here; the contributiveness criterion offers many fruitful suggestions for the evolution of ethnic humour theory. The distinction between comprehensiveness and contributiveness can perhaps be aided by a metaphor. Imagine two islands: one island, A, and a slightly smaller island, B. Let each island represent a humour theory and the area of each island its comprehensiveness. Since the two islands do not touch, they cover completely different territories; and because A is larger, it is the more comprehensive. What would be very desirable in this case would be to build a bridge between the two theories, enabling a more comprehensive theory, C, which would include theories A and B, plus the area of the bridge itself. Now the area of the bridge is very small relative to the area of either island. Thus building that bridge added few new facts. The great value of that bridge is its contributiveness, not its comprehensiveness per se.

Incidentally, the Time fiction piece referred to earlier, which mocked our use of technical jargon at the International Conference, seemed totally naive as to why such jargon is often needed. Not only can such terms provide needed precision, consistency, and falsifiability but, most importantly, contributiveness also. If we are to attain a scientific understanding of ethnic humour, we must build conceptual bridges. First, we must not isolate ethnic humour from other areas of humour but seek as many fruitful connections as possible. For instance, the number of papers in this book relevant to ethnic humour other than the ethnic humour symposium papers themselves is so numerous it would be a simpler task to list the papers irrelevant. Finding any papers in the symposium on cross-cultural research chaired by Goldstein, for example, that are not relevant is difficult. That the assignment of papers to the Ethnic Humour symposium was somewhat arbitrary is reflected in the fact that some papers not assigned to the Ethnic Humour symposium seem even more relevant than some which are. Thus, two papers in that symposium, one by Mannell, the other by La Fave, Mannell & Guilmette, neither employed nor were about ethnic groups. I believe, however, those papers especially relevant to certain theoretical developments needed in the ethnic humour area, and tie in well theoretically with other papers in that symposium.

Second, a scientific understanding of ethnic humour requires building intra-disciplinary bridges between humour in general (and ethnic humour in particular) and psychology's other areas. It is encouraging therefore to see Nerhardt (1970) borrowing from psychophysics, McGhee (1971a) from the developmental psychology of Piaget, others from physiological psychology, social psychology, perception, clinical psychology, and other intradisciplinary areas. The rapid and healthy growth of humour research in psychology is largely due to the imaginative willingness of humour researchers to break through conventional boundaries within psychology.

Third, maximal progress in ethnic humour demands that psychology does not arrogantly seal itself off from other disciplines, scientific and humanistic. Ethnic humour could profit immensely from brilliant work in philosophy, mathematical logic, linguistics, sociology, cultural anthropology, literature and other disciplines. Its approach must be interdisciplinary. For instance, the psychology of humour incorporated its most basic ideas from such philosophers as Plato, Hobbes, Spencer, Bergson, and many others. Cultural anthropologists such as Radcliffe-Brown (1940) teach us of the cultural universality of the joking relationship. In fact, this International Conference itself, by bringing together scholars from more than a dozen nations, unselfconsciously offers cross-cultural comparisons so central to cultural anthropology. Sociologists Zijderveld (1968) and Martineau (1972) have much to tell about social functions of humour. Work in neurology (e.g., Stearns, 1972) informs us of relations between laughter and amusement and work in physiology helps provide 'operational' definitions of humour. Literary figures such as Swift and Eastman (1936) also offer much of value.

In fact, much of the basis for the success of the convention upon which this book bases itself is found in its intradisciplinary and interdisciplinary nature. Humour researchers and theorists were not merely present from various areas of psychology; also from anthropology, sociology, political science, literature, biology, psychiatry, mathematical logic, and other disciplines. Without such intradisciplinary and interdisciplinary bridges, the would-be humour theorist is like the proverbial blind man in the dark cellar groping for the black cat that isn't there. There is not a single intradisciplinary or interdisciplinary area referred to above that our own approach to ethnic humour is not indebted to. For instance, our construct of Identification Classes grew out of the reference-group construct — which was very fruitful in suggesting interdisciplinary bridges between psychology and the social sciences. However, an interdisciplinary approach need extend itself yet further than have reference-group theorists. The construct reference group soon took on chameleon-like qualities — sometimes meaning 'identification,' sometimes 'comparison,' sometimes 'socialization,' etcetera. The great virtue of the reference-group construct, its wide-ranging quality, was bought at a high price — imprecision, inconsistency, nonfalsifiability. But the contributiveness quality of that construct is well worth preserving.

Attempts to clarify what need be saved drove us into the study of philosophy of science, mathematical logic, and linguistics. No coincidence then if most of the nine ways the emerging mathematical model of Identification Classes claims to improve upon the reference-group construct (La Fave, Haddad & Marshall, 1974; La Fave, Haddad & Maesen, 1976, p66) sound more like the kinds of distinctions one would expect to find in a philosophy of science rather than social-psychological journal. It is thus also no coincidence if the Identification Classes (ICs) construct claims relevance for many other areas besides humour, ethnic or otherwise. Although the ICs term emerged from humour research (particularly the hypothesis on switching levels of generality in La Fave, 1961), the fact it apparently holds implications for many other areas suggests the interdisciplinary process need not be one-way; ethnic humour theory profits much from the study of other areas, yet its relation to them can prove symbiotic.

What Zillmann and Cantor (1976) claim as indicative of the superiority of their disposition theory over an ICs based vicarious superiority humour approach really exhibits their theory's weakness, not its strength. Not merely does use of the highly ambiguous, undefined term 'disposition' reduce their 'theory' to imprecision, inconsistency, and nonfalsifiability, it also imposes severe constraints upon the interdisciplinary capacity and, therefore, upon the contributiveness of their approach. For the vague word 'disposition' has no social referent, unlike the term 'Identification Classes,' which specifies the social categories denoted. (Fortunately, however, humour researchers Zillmann and Cantor are several standard deviations superior to theorists Zillmann and Cantor. Consequently, their sound intuitions, as not infrequently happens in the history of science, have enabled them to make creative, constructive contributions to the advancement of our understanding of humour in general and ethnic humour in particular). The great virtue of the contributiveness metatheoretical criterion we have been discussing raises yet another metatheoretical issue. And that metatheoretical issue returns us, full circle, to Paradox 1. To advance our scientific understanding of ethnic humour, what should our ontological commitment be on the holism-atomism issue?

Paradox 1:   The Holism-Atomism Controversy and the Concept of Levels of Analysis

The 'levels of analysis' construct refers to the fact that each science has its basic building blocks which may be molecular relative to sciences above them and molar relative to sciences below. Cells, building blocks of biology, are subsystems of individual organisms, and it is the mental experiences and behaviours of these individual organisms which are the basic building blocks of psychology. However, individuals are subsystems of groups, and the intersubjectivity of group members and group behaviour are basic building blocks of the social sciences.

One philosophical school of thought believes that a unity of the sciences can be parsimoniously achieved by a reduction of each higher science to a lower one. George Homans, for instance, believes that sociology is reducible to the psychology of individual behaviour. His friend, B.F. Skinner, agrees — then adds that psychology itself is reducible to physics (perhaps being in such a hurry to climb down the ladder as to skip over the steps of biology and chemistry along the way). Others, however, would first reduce psychology to neurophysiology, then neurophysiology to biochemistry, then biochemistry (passing perhaps through inorganic chemistry) to atomic physics — which in turn reduces to nuclear physics, and then to sub-nuclear physics. Atom smashers are almost invariably reductionists — believing their field is the frontier of all science and that they deserve the largest government research grants. And the history of science clearly reveals that reductionist approaches have led to great scientific advances. At the other extreme is the philosophical doctrine of 'universal

interactionism.' This antiscientific view generates the holistic mystic — who argues that,
since everything is related to everything else, you can't analyze without failing to see the
forest from the trees.

A more moderate view than either of the two above rejects universal interactionism, confessing
it expedient to isolate a system at an appropriate level and analyze it; the error introduced
by assuming it a closed system lies within tolerable limits for the scientific purposes at
hand. However, this view also rejects atomistic reductionism, maintaining that 'emergent
products' exist irreducible to a lower level of analysis.

Perhaps the above discussion seems like pedantic armchair philosophizing. To the contrary,
this section hopes to exhibit that few distinctions if any could prove more useful in
advancing humour theory, and that the last metatheoretical position above is the most
appropriate one for advancing understanding of ethnic humour. The points which need be made
here appear to be the following: (1) To avoid the logical blunders resulting from Paradox 1,
levels of analysis must not be confounded. (2) To see the woods from the trees, glance at
the levels most immediately above to crosscheck findings against valid, emergent ones
obtained at those higher levels. (3) To 'operationalize' definitions and enhance validity,
results at higher levels should be crosschecked with those obtained at lower.

Functions of Ethnic Humour. Surely one of the most important questions about ethnic humour
(both at a theoretical and practical level) is 'What functions does ethnic humour serve?'
If attempts to answer this question are to climb off the ground, the following additional
questions demand answers: How can we delimit the meaning of the ambiguous word 'function'?
How can we ensure a parsimonious and comprehensive typology of functions at a given level of
analysis? At what 'level of analysis' does the function under consideration, whether latent
(and sometimes counterintuitive) or manifest, emerge? How do these functions relate across
the various levels of analysis? The word 'function' shall not employ itself here in the
mathematical sense; rather in the evolutionary biological sense of 'consequence for
survival' (for the individual organism or its group or species, depending on the level of
analysis). Each level of analysis would indicate a different type of function. We are a
long way from being able to satisfy an ideal typology for classifying functions of ethnic
humour. In relating functions to levels, let's start at the individual psychological level
of analysis and proceed, in either direction, up or down.

At least three basic conditions seem needed to generate amusement; a (1) sudden (2)
happiness increment must be a consequence of (3) an epistemic (i.e., 'perceived') incongruity.
If so, one function of ethnic humour may be to increase the happiness of vicarious victors.
It also seems clear, nonetheless, that vicarious butts of ethnic humour may suffer happiness
decrement. This decrement in happiness may represent a manifest function of ethnic humour
for the victims (as when the victim's self-esteem is lowered upon hearing such humour at their
own expense). However, the latent function of happiness decrement could be served even if
the victim, having not heard the communication, was thereby incapable of being directly
offended. In such instance constant use of ethnic humour at the expense of his group led to
discrimination against that group, lowering his standard of living and decreasing his
happiness.

The consequences of such individual psychological functions of ethnic humour also reflect
themselves at a macrosociological or political science level. Suppose a nation decides that,
besides assessing its nation's health by the Gross National Product, it would employ a
noneconomic, immaterial measure — its Quality of Life. Imagine also that it defines Quality
of Life by the happiness of its members. That nation might then investigate how ethnic humour
could increase, rather than decrease, the nation's happiness and, therefore, Quality of Life.
Within the nation, would immigrants and minority groups also rendered cosmopolitan by virtue
of their marginal status between cultures be amused more often relative to their standard of
living and thereby have a higher Quality of Life than WASPs?

A physiological level of analysis might ask what functions ethnic humour serves. Is ethnic
humour likely to result in laughter? If so, could too much laughter physiologically damage
the organism as Fry (paper in this volume) suggests? If so, an overdose of ethnic humour
could conceivably serve the macrosociological function of destroying an entire civilization.
(Although the Time article blasphemed earlier seems to be killing itself laughing at Fry's
theory). Levels above the individual psychological level might be viewed as intragroup,
intergroup, and macrosociological levels, in ascending order. Above, happiness increment was
treated as a necessary condition of amusement at the individual psychological level.

Research by ourselves (La Fave, 1961; La Fave, 1972a) and others demonstrating how vicarious
superiority via reference groups and ICs could enhance amusement for the individual was
applied to intragroup and intergroup levels by Martineau (1972). But Martineau did not
merely apply such theory to higher levels of analysis. He recognized emergent social
functions at these higher levels not existing at the individual psychological level. For
instance, humour (including ethnic humour) can not at the individual psychological level be

employed as a means of achieving intragroup solidarity, or intragroup conflict, or controlling
the group. Yet all these social functions, and more, emerge at the intragroup level. These
social functions, as Martineau saw, could also be recognized at the intergroup level. Ethnic
humour (for instance, disparaging the outgroup) might generate conflict between groups (as
it simultaneously raises morale within the group that initiated the disparaging ethnic humour).
Or ethnic humour at the expense of one's own group may reduce intragroup morale while also
reducing conflict between groups. For instance, an immigrant ethnic group, by employing
ethnic humour at the expense of its own members, may provide heat for the melting pot - helping
acculturate immigrants to the dominant society (La Fave & Mannell, 1976a).

Thus ethnic humour may perform the politically conservative social control function (Bergson,
1911) of helping maintain the pecking order both within and between groups or social classes.
The joking relationship (Radcliffe-Brown, 1940; Zijderveld, 1968) seems typically to perform
this conservative function. (See also the paper by Burnand, this volume). On the contrary,
ethnic humour might be employed against the dominant group (e.g., anti-WASP humour) to
expose naked emperors and reduce their prestige (and, therefore their power). Resultant
demoralization among the 'top dogs' could also disorganize them and, by reducing their bark
to a whimper, decrease their power and permute the status hierarchy. Such ethnic humour may
also increase the ingroup morale of the downtrodden, providing them with the spiritual strength
to fight the system. For instance, the Black American comedian Dick Gregory entitled his
autobiography 'nigger'. dedicating it to his dead mother: 'Dear Momma - wherever you are, if
ever you hear the word "nigger" again, remember they are advertising my book.' In this way
Gregory probably helped defuse the power of the word 'nigger' to hurt the Negro.

Consider a few examples of the kind of ethnic humour which could serve such functions during
the days of pervasive racial segregation in the Southern USA.

1. A White woman is exiting from a passenger train while a Negro porter watches from
    the platform below. She slips! The porter starts to catch her, then suddenly
    changes his mind, letting her fall.

2. A passenger train is crowded with Whites. However, there is one car which carries
    only one passenger, a Black man.

3. Black comedian Dick Gregory's book, 'From the Back of the Bus', shows a photo
    of him in resplendent relaxation as the only passenger in the back of the bus.

Where 1 above may seem pointless to a honkie, prejudice's victims can empathize and sympathize
with the porter. They know that if he touches a white women he may get lynched. So 1, like
2 and 3, finds racial discrimination backfiring on the dominant group. The disadvantaged race
is amused because it 'perceives' the incongruity in each story, and feels vicarious superiority
when whitey becomes butt.

The 'Big Red Joke Book' by Benton and Loomes (1976), and of course writers like Swift,
Molière, Bernard Shaw, and Black USA comedian Dick Gregory are in the tradition of employing
ethnic humour in the service of powerless groups. In the same radical spirit is the highly
spirited paper by Husband in this ethnic humour symposium. Husband pulls no punches in
telling us what functions he thinks ethnic humour serves in a racist society such as Britain.
At the individual psychological level he believes such humour helps the Bigot maintain his
prejudice, rather than panglossing over its anti-humane functions as Martin Grotjahn's
tension-reduction and Gordon W. Allport's if-only-the-Bigot-had-a-sense-of-humour approaches
do. Consistent with Husband's reaction to Allport, we (La Fave & Mannell, 1976a) have argued
that the implicit definitions the powers that be give to such terms as 'joke' and 'sense of
humour' as such as to provide them with ethnocentric rationalizations which, at the individual
psychological level, maintain their smugly high self-esteem and, at higher levels, help
maintain the status quo. Similarly, Husband argues that the function of ethnic humour at a
macrosociological level is to help Britain remain a racist society. And all this Britons do,
Husband maintains, under the smug assumption that their's is a tolerant society. We are
reminded of Swift's 'A Modest Proposal' in which the British gentlemen, to solve the twin
problems of an overpopulated and underfed Irish population, are instructed to kindly assist
these miserables by treating their babies as gourmet delicacies.

However, though my heart is with Husband, and with Vidmar and Rokeach (1974) too, I fear that
the situational comedies invoking ethnic humour which they deplore serve both conservative
and radicalizing functions and merely correlational data such as Vidmar and Rokeach present
is not capable of the unambiguous interpretations they give it. The argument that ethnic
humour invariably harms the ethnic group could result in some dysfunctional, antihumane
results leading to legislation and court decisions against the use of ethnic humour. In the
USA such attempts are already in progress (cf. La Fave & Mannell, 1976a, 1976b; Winick,
1976). Ethnic humour prohibition could conceivably lead to ethnic humour bootlegging. But
the relevant point here is that Husband's paper suggests functions of ethnic humour at more
than one level of analysis. An illustration of using ethnic humour to serve the 'radical'

function of reducing racial prejudice and discrimination by educating the bigoted group to
its own myopic ethnocentrism is offered by comedian Dick Gregory (1964) again in his
autobiography, 'nigger'. Gregory suggests that during his childhood in a Black ghetto in
St. Louis, his middle-class school teacher rejected his homework because it was soiled.
Gregory wondered how he could get her to understand why it was soiled. He was one of six
children, and his deserted mother had to work as a maid taking care of White folks' children,
to the 'neglect' of her own. Winters in St. Louis could be quite severe and there was no
fire in the furnace so Dick had to do his homework under the covers with a flashlight.
After doing so he fell asleep and one of the other kids must have peed on it. A related use
of ethnic humour is to radicalize the powerless group by unmasking the Establishment's
authority, employing humour to panic the Establishment into physical brutality (Zijderveld,
1968, p311).

In still another sense ethnic humour serves an unmasking function; by revealing a society's
preoccupations (Berger, this volume), such humour represents a disguised attitude and/or
belief measure. Such a projective test of attitudes was recognized by Winick (1976, p126),
Wolff, Smith & Murray (1934), and Zijderveld (1968, p308). Our own original interest in
humour research was to find a badly needed disguised way of measuring ego-involving attitudes
(as non-disguised ways are likely to prove invalid). Our vicarious superiority humour
experiments (La Fave, Haddad & Maesen, 1976) were designed as disguised measures of subjects'
attitudes and other experiments in this tradition can also be so interpreted. Two of the
papers by our group in the present ethnic humour symposium (Mutuma et al, and Issar et al)
were especially designed to serve as 'disguised belief measures' by tapping subjective
incongruity, as will be discussed later. Changing fashions in ethnic humour therefore
reflect social change in belief and attitude (value) social norms, and changes in the social
stratification of the ethnic groups involved, as well (of course) as changes in the attitudes
and beliefs of individual societal members.

Ethnic humour can also serve such social functions as releasing tension, reducing boredom,
helping group members discover sexual partners, and enabling the joker to escape responsibility
for his remarks (Ullian, 1976, p129). Ethnic humour could also affect the flow of social
conversation (La Gaipa, this volume). Other functions of ethnic humour are suggested by
Kane et al (this volume), and Winick (1976). When we return to the Wise Fool, we shall also
discuss some social functions his humour (ethnic and otherwise) apparently serves.

Functions of ethnic humour have been treated under Paradox 1 because, as the whole unequals
the sum of its parts, levels of analysis must be separated when dealing with such functions.
What is functional at one level of analysis may prove dysfunctional at another. To illustrate,
members of an ethnic group may be amused at the involuntary anticonformity behaviour of a
member. Their resultant laughter could serve as a negative social sanction for the object of
ridicule, motivating him to 'get back in line' and conform to that social norm. The
consequence may prove functional for the group's survival, but dysfunctional for him –
resulting in loss of face and unhappiness. In an extreme case he may commit suicide.

Determinants of Ethnic Humour. The treatment of functions of ethnic humour above views
ethnic humour or its absence as an independent variable. Consider now ethnic humour or its
absence as the dependent variable. As we continue to grapple with Paradox 1, the need
reveals itself, in contemplating consequences for ethnic humour, to separate levels of
analysis. It also seems desirable to consider ethnic humour as dependent upon the Quality of
Life. A nation with a higher Quality of Life index might be predicted to create and employ
a different mix of ethnic humour from that typical in lower Quality of Life nations. Was the
ethnic humour which typified Nazi Germany more sadistic and more often at the expense of a
scapegoat ethnic group than in contemporary West or East Germany?

Closely related is the influence of attitudes and beliefs in generating ethnic humour. If a
society's basic belief and value norms were known, could the types of ethnic humour prevailing
in that society be predicted? Attitudes and beliefs are here considered determinants of
ethnic humour at the (1) individual psychological level of analysis. However, in defining
in this ethnic humour symposium a value social norm as the intersection (overlap) of the
individual attitude norms, Mutuma et al and Issar et al are functioning at (2), the intragroup level (as Issar et al also do in the process of defining a belief social norm).
However, those two papers, by talking of the different cultures (i.e., different social
norms) of their different populations, are also functioning at (3), the intergroup level of
analysis.

The Bourhis et al experiment in this ethnic humour symposium also talks at all three of
those levels in much the same way; though that experiment seems more closely related to our
work on vicarious superiority humour theory (La Fave, 1972a; La Fave, Haddad & Maesen, 1976)
and to the interesting theoretical implications at higher levels, briefly mentioned earlier,
by Martineau (1972) and the Husband paper in this ethnic humour symposium. The Bourhis et
al 'salience' independent variable sounds much like our attitude switching construct (La
Fave, Haddad & Marshall, 1974, first tested in 1961) and perhaps also the salience notion of

Goldstein, Suls & Anthony, 1972). Yet the Bourhis et al experiment introduces new dependent measures and represents very much the kind of ethnic-humour experimentation most needed. An interesting technical feature of that experiment is the use of 'accents.' Such use typically increases the amusement value of ethnic humour because the accent is epistemically incongruous to the other group, which consequently feels superior.

The excellent paper in this ethnic humour symposium by Husband, referred to earlier, relates to all three of the above levels and to (4), the macrosociological level as well. Albeit its main concentration, as with researches of its type generally, seems to be on the relationships between levels (1) and (4) - i.e., the individual in the larger society.

The ethnic humour symposium papers by Mutuma et al and Issar et al centrally concern themselves at the individual psychological level of analysis, with the implications of epistemic (i.e., 'perceived') incongruity for ethnic humour, rather than with the influence of vicarious superiority. However, the remaining two papers in this symposium (by Mannell, and by La Fave et al) try to build conceptual bridges between vicarious superiority and epistemic incongruity humour theory (and, by implication) ethnic humour theory. These last two papers relate to level of analysis (1) and, less explicitly (2) and (3) above.

The papers by Mutuma et al and Issar et al illustrate the holistic, antireductionistic thesis involved in Paradox 1 - that emergent properties at higher levels render them irreducible to lower levels. Hence the social sciences are not reducible to second-hand psychology (Freud and Skinner and other reductionists notwithstanding). For instance, the above two papers find useful the definition of a social norm (sociological level) as the intersection of the individual (psychological level) norms (where the number of individual norms is at least two). Immediately following from such a definition is Irreducibility Theorem 1: The social norm is a subset of each individual norm for each member of the society on the social issue in question. However, the subset (or inclusion) mathematical relation is antisymmetric. Therefore, each individual norm will only be a subset of the social norm in that very rare case in which all the individual norms implicated are equal to each other. Irreducibility Theorem 2: The numerosity or 'size' of the social norm is able, within specifiable upper and lower limits, to vary 'inversely' with the numerosity of the mean psychological or individual norm. (The lower limit is the numerosity of the unit set, i.e., 1, and the upper limit is the numerosity of the least numerous psychological norm involved in defining the social norm). This definition, conjoined with other reasonable empirical assumptions and definitions, gives paradoxical Theorem 3: Social change can occur without nonconformity. This last paradoxical deduction bridges social statics and social dynamics: 'Social Change without Nonconformity: A Connecting Link between Functional and Historical (or Evolutionary) Approaches to Sociological Theory' (La Fave, 1963, 1965). (For further theoretical implications of this approach see La Fave, 1969a & b, 1971).

The situational comedies so popular on TV these days nicely illustrate ethnic humour as an emergent product. It is not an easy task to persuade your like-minded friend as to why a given situational comedy he did not see amused you. You cannot simply repeat one liners from these sit-coms out of context to him; they will not typically contain within themselves the ambiguity or other noticeable incongruities needed to amuse. Instead, you need reconstruct the essential components of the entire situation, and commanding his attention long enough to do so will require no little skill. Even slapstick comedy is typically situational; just as in Nerhardt's (1970) experiment, no weight (regardless of how heavy or light) was capable of being judged a joke by itself. The weight needed to be highly discrepant from a previously established range (situational context) of weights before it could amuse.

Mintz's paper (this volume) discusses determinants of (ethnic) humour at a macrosociological level - especially with reference to the importance of topicality (Zeitgeist). He paints the useful metaphor of the aerial photograph which exhibits beautiful patterns from the air that disappear at ground level.

Prerost (this volume) discusses such determinants of (ethnic) humour appreciation as 'social' and 'spatial densities'. Would the ethnic humorist better amuse his audience by packing them in a small auditorium than by scattering them through a large one? Could, as some professional comedians believe, a 'killjoy' sitting near the stage socially inhibit the comedian's amusement impact on his audience? The social conformity experiments on humour appreciation are obviously relevant here, some of which we have referred to previously (La Fave, Haddad & Maesen, 1976, p81).

Taylor (this volume) suggests a theoretical approach involving a communication model within a sociological framework. He indicates several determinants of (ethnic) humour. One of these, 'the creator's perception of the audience', seems at the psychological level. Another, the medium of the message, appears physical (although, if technically augmented, would require material culture, the macrosociological level of analysis). Another determinant involves structural differentiation - which could also move into intragroup (e.g., group status hierarchy) and intergroup (e.g., social class theory) levels.

The teasing or joking relationship (Burnand, this volume) raises questions concerning the social determinants of such (ethnic) humour. A classic paper by Radcliffe-Brown (1940) suggests such social determinants as status symmetrical and asymmetrical joking relationships, and formal versus informal. These joking relationships may also be verbal or nonverbal.

Before we say goodbye to the subject of the social determinants of ethnic humour, we must ask whether these social determinants only exhibit themselves in interpersonal relations. A tragic mistake assumes they do. When William James wrote that all psychology is social psychology, he did not utter a gross exaggeration but a profound truth. With John Donne we can assert that no man is an island. Is man lonely only when alone? David Riesman recognized The Lonely Crowd. We must also recognize The Unlonely Loner. But perhaps man is the most lonely animal of all. For, in some ways, ignorance is bliss. Man alone among the animal kingdom is cursed to know that as he lives today he must die tomorrow. Now alongside the Wise Fool we must add the Foolish Wiseguy. 'Where ignorance is bliss 'tis folly to be wise.' Human tasted of the apple of knowledge and was booted from the Garden of Eden. And human was kicked out because human was human, because human had evolved the biologic capacity for conceptual functioning - for being symbol-minded. Thus humans have developed as no other animals have (McGhee's phylogenetic article in this volume notwithstanding) the capacity to escape stimulus boundness - to jump over the associationistic psychologist's principle of contiguity (whether spatial or temporal). And as human escaped stimulus boundness he became lonely in crowds and escaped loneliness when alone.

What Sherif's (1936) classic autokinetic experiment demonstrated which few psychologists understand is that the group member internalizes the group culture as his own. And once he has, he is an individual no more; he has been permanently and (short of brain damage) irretrievably, socialized. He may pompously proclaim his free will. He may enhance his self-esteem by thinking he is 'doing his thing.' But the group's culture is pulling his strings. However, his DNA is helping (i.e., interacting with) his culture to pull those strings. In fact, the culture wouldn't be there to do any pulling if his DNA had not earlier started pushing.

It seems ironic that psychologists of radical empirical persuasion, with their treatment of learning as the prime mover, have not understood socialization. Yet such is the case. Consider Berlyne (1972), for instance. Berlyne observes that (humorous) laughter 'can occur in a solitary individual, so that it seems doubtful that its prime significance is a social one' (p51). Foot and Chapman (1976, p187) adroitly point out a non sequitur in such reasoning with an appropriate analogy: 'because buses can be driven around the city streets empty their primary purpose is not to ferry passengers around.' Berlyne's statement represents a double blunder; even if amused laughter could only occur in a solitary individual, that fact would not justify the conclusion that such laughter's primary function is not a social one. It is a common prejudice that a person who engages in amused laughter to himself is psychotic (in the sense of out of touch with social reality). To the contrary, amused laughter to himself can represent the most social phenomenon imaginable - if he is laughing at that which his society taught him is supposed to amuse.

Earlier, in discussing metatheory, logical consistency was indicated to be a sine qua non of an adequate scientific theory. Yet logical inconsistency, we have seen (such as confusing levels of analysis), is often employed to generate 'jokes'; and the Paulos paper (this volume) especially emphasizes the importance of such inconsistency in generating amusement. As we mainly agree with him in our discussion of incongruity humour theory (to be discussed later), are we ourselves then not consistently inconsistent?

No! An adequate scientific theory of humour would need to be consistent at the metalinguistic level though it talks about and uses inconsistency at the object language level as so-called joke formulae.

Paradox 2: There's No Such Thing as a Joke

To render the above more directly relevant to ethnic humour we may rephrase it as: Paradox 2: There's No Such Thing as Ethnic Humour. Why then are we wasting so much space writing about a nonexistent 'object'? An obvious answer is that in doing so we are in the mainstream of the history of psychology. We are defining joke and ethnic humour in the usual way when we argue that they don't exist. That is, each is being defined as a stimulus. The word stimulus has a long and undistinguished career in the history of psychology. Almost all psychological theorists use the term but few bother to define it, for a very good reason: They don't dare! I will not attempt an adequate definition here but will argue that any respect for the word's history demands it be given at least the following three necessary properties: It is a (1) physical event which is (2) here (3) now.

The papers in this ethnic humour symposium by Mutuma et al and Issar et al present experiments especially dedicated to the proposition that jokes and ethnic humour (if each

is defined as a stimulus) nonexist. We have presented further arguments for their nonexistence previously (La Fave, Haddad & Maesen, 1976, pp83-88; La Fave & Mannell, 1976a;
1976b). It only needs be reiterated now that many powerful figures in our society have
vested interests in defending the ethnocentric myth that jokes qua humorous stimuli exist,
and employ this myth to sustain prejudice and discrimination against certain ethnic groups.

Paradox 3:   No One Has a Sense of Humour

This paradox only holds when one defines sense of humour as 'ability to be amused at one's
own expense' (where the word 'own' in this definition is employed in the 'spiritual' sense
common to such social psychologists as symbolic interactionists). There seems no need to
discuss the reasons for the myopic illusion that a sense of humour, thus defined, exists - as
we have presented these elsewhere. The La Fave and Mannell (1976a) article specifically
relates nine such reasons to ethnic humour theory. However, there exist at least two other
common definitions of the phrase 'sense of humour' and, by both of these, sense of humour
does exist. One of these definitions is the same as that given above, except the word 'own'
in the definition is defined 'physically' (more like the layman's usage), rather than in the
'spiritual self or ego' sense employed by many social psychologists. Consider the ethnic
group member who, preferring the dominant society to his own ethnic group, is therefore amused
at that ethnic group's expense. By the self or 'spiritual' concept of 'own,' that amused
party does not thereby demonstrate possession of a sense of humour; a larger part of his ego
merely feels vicarious superiority amusement for triumphing over a smaller aspect. However,
by the physical sense of 'own,' the above example does succeed in demonstrating sense-of-humour
possession.

This second definition of sense of humour is also very relevant to ethnic humour; it suggests
that the cultural pluralism of the ethnic group member may provide him with a superior sense of
humour to that of the ethnocentric, unicultural WASP. How? The cosmopolite who has
internalized a plurality of cultures is provided thereby with the potential gift of being
able to detach himself from one of his cultures and look at it with the distant perspective
of another of his internalized cultures. Such a marginal man (as sociologists Robert Park
and George Simmel observed) can play the role of a stranger. He is equipped with the
potential to get 'outside' himself to 'laugh at himself.' That is, one part of him is able
to look with detached amusement at the expense of another part. In this manner irritations,
frustrations and embarrassments generated by objective stress can be transformed into
pleasurable amusement; liabilities into assets and insults compliments. A sense of humour
enables its bearer to rise above the occasion and 'perceive' the otherwise unpleasant event
with amusement.

A third definition of sense of humour concerns frequency of amusement; a person holds a
sense of humour if and only if he is amused an above average amount of time. The experimental
results in the Issar et al paper seem to provide suggestive evidence for the superior sense
of humour of bilingual East Indians to native Canadians. Tsang (1976) found a hint that
Hong Kong Chinese living in Canada are more frequently amused than native Canadian Caucasians.

The immigrant or marginal man, having been socialized to a plurality of cultures, may resolve
whatever conflicts his cosmopolitan multiperspective generates by a creative synthesis of the
relevant aspects of these cultures or a resolution of cognitive inconsistencies. Creative
genius throughout human history seems to have been produced in disproportionate amounts by
this type of cosmopolitan marginal man - reflecting creative ethnicity. It is surely no
coincidence that, despite their relatively small numbers, the Jews have displayed both a
sense of humour and creative genius in amounts disproportionately large.

Paradox 4:   An Extreme Insult Is Less Insulting (and More Amusing) Than a Mild Insult

This paradox is offered in our irony of irony experiment (La Fave et al) in this ethnic
humour symposium. The extreme insult often represents anticonformity to the norms of an
ethnic group's culture. Thus this experiment has theoretical connecting links with those
in this ethnic humour symposium by Mutuma et al and Issar et al. Further, an extreme insult
may generate amusement by enabling a serious-to-playful transformation. That is, the
communication is judged opposite to its literal meaning. Therefore, consistent with Mannell's
paper in this ethnic humour symposium, a viable vicarious superiority humour theory ought to
allow for nonliteral interpretations.

Paradox 5:   Don't Take Sides in Family Quarrels or Both Sides Will Turn on You

This paradox can be resolved by our attitude switching (not to be confounded with attitude
change) construct; and an hypothesis based on attitude switching was substantiated relevant
to ethnic humour in the La Fave 1961 humour experiment. (See also La Fave, 1972a; La Fave,
Haddad & Marshall, 1974; La Fave, Haddad & Maesen, 1976). It, like Paradox 4 before it,
represents a reason for the myopic illusion that men are capable of amusement at their own

expense (by the first definition of sense of humour discussed under Paradox 3 above). In
the Lone Stranger illustration earlier the husband always holds a positive attitude with
respect to whatever Identification Class he consciously believes himself a member of and a
negative attitude regarding whatever IC he consciously believes himself a nonmember of which
is compared with his membership IC. Let's refer to these two ICs as A and A^C respectively.
Now suppose he tentatively forgets about A and A^C and his mind turns to B and B^C, such that
A is properly included within B. That is, he consciously now believes himself a member of
B and a nonmember of B^C. Once again he achieves cognitive consistency by holding a positive
attitude with respect to his subjective membership IC, B, and a negative attitude with
respect to his subjective nonmembership IC, B^C. But his 'irrationality' is that he dislikes
at the first moment the person he has assigned to IC A^C, but likes that same person later
when he assigns that person to B. That is, his attitude with respect to that person switched
(not changed) when he generalized regarding his own conscious membership IC.

The fact that this phenomenon is better conceptualized as attitude switching than attitude
change becomes clearer if now we proceed down the latter of generality from B to A. Then
his conscious attitude with respect to the person who is believed a member of both B and A^C
(the husband's wife in the Lone Stranger illustration) will switch back from positive to
negative. In the Lone Stranger example the husband's paradoxical verbal behaviour suddenly
makes sense when we recognize the phenomenon of attitude switching. When quarrelling with
his wife, he believed her a member of a disliked nonmembership IC, A^C. However, when an
outsider entered the family quarrel, the husband generalized with respect to the membership
IC of which he was consciously aware, so that his wife became a member of the same IC as
himself, B, ('our family') and the Lone Stranger a member of a disliked nonmembership IC, B^C,
nonfamily. In a similar manner Einstein (Merton, 1957, p288) observed at the Sorbonne: 'If
my theory of relativity is proven successful, Germany will claim me as a German and France
will declare that I am a citizen of the world. Should my theory prove untrue, France will
say I am a German and Germany will declare that I am a Jew.'

When the Bourhis et al paper in this ethnic humour symposium talks about 'salience,' it
implicitly assumed attitude switching phenomena, as does Goldstein (1976). Zillmann and
Cantor (1976) are in a similar vein when they write of transitory dominance. But they add
(pp103-104) that our Identification Classes model (like that of reference group) can only
handle affiliations relatively stable over time. For this and other reasons, they claim,
the ICs model is far less comprehensive than their 'disposition theory of humour and mirth.'
Of course they are right. They are correct because they never bother to define their highly
ambiguous key word, 'disposition.' Therefore, (for reasons indicated under our metatheoretical discussion earlier) their 'theory' is imprecise, nonfalsifiable, and logically
inconsistent. To the contrary, our key term 'Identification Classes' is defined with such
relative precision as to enable ICs to become a mathematical model. Counter to their claim
that no essential difference exists between the ICs and reference-group construct, we list
nine essential ways in which the ICs model improves upon that of reference group. The best
statement of the first eight of these improvements is presented in La Fave, Haddad and
Marshall (1974). The ninth improvement, the fact that each IC intertwines both an attitude
and a belief (to be defined later) is presented in La Fave, Haddad and Maesen (1976).
Zillmann and Cantor (1976, p98) maintain, to the contrary, no essential difference between
the ICs and reference group construct as used by Sherif. The essential point is that the ICs
model, by allowing for attitude and belief switching phenomena, is able to handle transitory
dominance, salience, transcendance, differentiation, and related phenomena (such as
attribution theory as discussed by Suls and Miller, 1976). It can do so by generating new
(and often transitory) ICs through use of such mathematical operations as union, intersection,
complementation, Cartesian products, and by tying these to such mathematical relations as
membership, proper inclusion, various embeddings, etcetera. For instance, suppose our subject
believes himself a member of the Catholic class. Then, he can employ the unary operator,
complementation, to generate a new class, non-Catholic (of which he will think himself a
nonmember). Suppose he also considers himself a Democrat. The binary operator, intersection,
now generates for him the new class, Catholic-Democrats. This Catholic-Democrats IC may be
transitory for him in the sense that he uses it seldom, perhaps when listening to a 'joke'
which talks about both Catholics and Democrats. He may store only a few thousand relatively
permanent ICs in his memory system. But the normal adult has the linguistic competence to
generate an almost infinite number of new (rather transitory ICs) as the situations 'demand.'

To begin to comprehend the full significance of attitude- and belief-switching phenomena, it
is necessary to return for a moment to metatheory. Consistent with the approach of the
linguist and mathematical logician Noam Chomsky, any nontrivial scientific theory must be
generative. That is, it must not only be sufficiently comprehensive in predicting the known
facts; it must also predict facts yet undiscovered. In other words, a nontrivial scientific
theory is rational, rather than empirical; it races way out in front of the facts already
collected. It even goes beyond the number of facts that ever can be collected; for such a
theory generates an infinite number of hypotheses. Any theory which predicts an unidimensional
continuum is nontrivial in the above sense, as an unidimensional continuum is equivalent to
an infinite set of real numbers.

For instance, our statement of vicarious superiority humour theory (La Fave, Haddad & Maesen, 1976, p66) is nontrivial in this sense; it predicts a continuum (albeit the predictions are insufficiently explicated with respect to the relative weights of attitude regarding ICs and attitudes re behaviour). Here again Zillmann and Cantor (1976, p100) have grotesquely distorted our position by claiming it offers only two (rather than an infinite number) of predictions. At no time have we ever taken a position contrary to our present one.

Paradox 6:   There's Comedy in Tragedy and Tragedy in Comedy

An immigrant continues to conform to certain of his ethnic group norms in nonconformance to those of his new culture. These nonconformances may be perceived as incongruous from the perspective of an ethnocentric provincial of the host country. Feeling superior to the immigrant, the ethnocentric sees him as a comic character. From the immigrant's perspective, his inappropriate behaviour may be tragic. Sometimes, however, nonconformity to a culture occurs inadvertently even when one is thoroughly familiar with its norms. Such a strange result is the subject of Paradox 8. But first, let us return to the Wise Fool.

Paradox 7:   The Wise Fool and the Royal Buffoon

Two interesting papers by Healey (this volume) talk about the Wise Fool. What social functions did the Wise Fool serve which enabled one of such lowly status to get away with ridiculing an absolute monarch? Berger (1976, p114) believes that the fool can tell the truth (i.e., utter words of wisdom) because he is not taken seriously. Zijderveld's (1968, pp306-307) comments on the mediaeval institution of the royal buffoon and the joking relationship. The royal buffoon, he observes:

> '...was allowed and even expected to expose the princely ruler to antics and jokes. Here we have an example of an institutionalized form of joking with someone in a superior social position. As Wertheim observes, "counterpoint was used here as a well-devised design by those in power to reduce the protest to futility." The social sublimation of protest and conflict by means of joking, therefore, is not just a relief from the social frustration of those who are dominated, but may also be a technique manipulated by the powerful in order to keep protest and conflict within certain limits and to provide society at the same time with a possible outlet. Joking in this case functions as a safety valve, installed on society by those in power....Brecht's statement, "one should not fight dictators, one should ridicule them", therefore holds true only in those societies in which the powerful leaders are still not yet acquainted with the possibilities of a manipulatory use of joking.'

Sometimes an ethnic wins acceptance into a group from the dominant society whose leader then patronizes him - permitting him to play the Wise Fool and allow the leaders to look both tolerant and a good sport in the process. However, such a tactic could also backfire for the absolute monarch - by exposing his weaknesses, his charisma, his prestige power may reduce. Yet the absolute monarch perhaps tolerates the Wise Fool for at least two other reasons: (1) Entertainment. Bored with his yes-men and secure in his power, incongruous insults by a powerless (nonthreatening) fool amuse - like being kicked by a child. (2) Educational. The absolute monarch may realize that his yes-men distort communication in a positive direction as it travels up the status hierarchy to him. He needs the Wise Fool to help him keep in touch with realities to fathom court intrigues and thus remain in power.

Paradox 8:   The Involuntary Nonconformist

We have discussed this humorous paradox previously (La Fave, Haddad & Maesen, 1976, p88) and related it to Bergson's (1911) humour theory, and to our own approach (La Fave & Teeley, 1967; La Fave, 1972b; Mannell & Duthie, 1975). Its relevance to ethnic humour is that an immigrant or other ethnic group member may have so thoroughly habituated his conformance to particular norms of his ethnic culture that, even though he wishes to nonconform to his ethnic culture in deference to the dominant culture, his nervous system trips him up - prompting him to commit the faux pas of involuntarily nonconforming to the dominant culture - amusing observers from the dominant (and perhaps from his ethnic) society.

TOWARDS SCIENTIFIC PRINCIPLES OF HUMOUR

Attempts to cope with the above eight paradoxes have provided a less unclear idea of where we do not want to go. First, as for Paradox 1, the discussion in this section shall focus primarily upon development of principles of humour at the individual psychological level of analysis. Attempts to add emergent, social principles at higher levels have been discussed under Paradox 1 above. Second, at the psychological level to be emphasized here, to attempt to develop ethnic humour (as opposed to simply humour) principles appears unwise; earlier it was argued that a theory of humour, rather than a theory of ethnic humour, should probably

be the goal — as a theory of humour will enable understanding ethnic humour anyway. A
fortiori, a theory of ethnic humour, emphasizing social levels of analysis, should be avoided
at the individual psychological level.   Third, some necessary conditions or principles of an
individual psychological theory of humour would seem to involve a (1) sudden (2) happiness
increment as a consequence of (3) an epistemic (i.e., 'perceived') incongruity. Fourth,
relevant technical terms within these principles should be defined and related one to another.
One of these three necessary conditions of amusement, suddenness, will attract little
attention here. Suddenness seems a necessary condition for an amusing mental experience
because it is needed to insure that the happiness increment slope is steep enough per unit
time to generate amusement, rather than some milder, pleasant experience.

The term 'happiness increment' apparently involves such constructs as vicarious superiority,
change in level of arousal, enhanced self-esteem, resolution, sense of mastery, and reduction
of 'perceived' threat. How do we relate such terms one to another under the umbrella construct,
happiness increment? What relationship exists between subjective (epistemic) incongruity
and objective incongruity? How does the serious-playful distinction pertain to incongruity?
How do the types of incongruity involve terms under happiness increment?

Perhaps the three main lines of humour research at the individual psychological level have
involved arousal (or tension), superiority, and incongruity. Three important technical terms
in general psychology are drive, attitude, and belief. Drive is perhaps the essential
independent variable in arousal humour research, attitude in superiority humour research, and
belief in incongruity humour research. The proper start then would define these three
psychological terms, distinguish them from closely related terms, and tie them to humour
theory.

Definitions of Terms

The psychological literature has completely confounded the terms attitude and belief; and,
until these terms are less inadequately defined, it is difficult to conceive how much
scientific progress can transpire. Sometimes an attitude is defined as having only one
component, an 'evaluative'; sometimes a second component, 'cognitive', is added, and sometimes
even a third, 'motivational' (with 'behavioural' often being erroneously used interchangeably
with 'motivational'). It is customary also to confuse completely attitudes with beliefs.
Works by Fishbein and Ajzen (1975) and Rokeach (1973) at least have the merit of recognizing
that it is useful to treat attitudes and beliefs as different. However, both these writers,
despite a number of good empirical insights, are thoroughly confused and illogical. But for
real illogical slapstick, the article by Kelman (1974) entitled 'Attitudes are Alive and
Well and Gainfully Employed in the Sphere of Action' is must reading. The magical term
attitude, as used by Kelman, is able to perform all kinds of tricks. It can sometimes hold
one component, sometimes two, at others three. Still at other times it transforms into a
belief.

The term attitude, as employed here, has two components — an evaluative and a cognitive.
Any belief also has a cognitive component. However, there exists a crucial distinction
between attitude and belief. Any belief is a proposition which has a truth value. That is,
any belief can be expressed as a declarative sentence. A belief is an hypothesis and,
therefore, can be mistaken in either of the two basic ways suggested by Type 1 and Type 2
errors in statistical inference; one can believe something true which is false or something
false which is true. To the contrary, no attitude can be mistaken. Nor can any attitude
be correct. That is, an attitude is never expressible as a declarative sentence. Consider
the following:

    (1) Reg believes that Hortense is a whore.
    (2) Reg dislikes whores.

Thus (1) is a belief statement and (2) is an attitude statement. The belief in (1) is
properly embedded within its belief statement. Thus Reg's belief is 'Hortense is a whore.'
Similarly, the attitude in (2) is properly embedded within the attitude statement. The
attitude Reg holds in this case is 'dislikes whores,' with 'dislikes' being the evaluative
component of the attitude and 'whores' the cognitive. Note that Reg's attitude in (2) is
not a declarative sentence. In fact, it is not even a sentence. However, any attitude
statement is expressible as a declarative sentence. It is a true declarative sentence if
and only if Reg does dislike whores; otherwise false. Consider now the attitude statement:

    (3) Fred dislikes whores.

If we did not distinguish between an attitude and an attitude statement, and called the
attitude statement an attitude, then (2) and (3), being unequal, would not express the same
attitude. The construct attitude then could hardly be a central term for psychology if no
two people could hold the same attitude. That (2) $\neq$ (3) is true both extensionally — (2)
could be true when (3) is false, or conversely, and intensionally — the two statements have
different meanings because their subjects denote different persons.

Similarly, if we did not distinguish a belief from a belief statement, no two persons could hold the same belief. We could then not develop any attitude or belief social norms and would lack the terms needed for a scientific social psychology. Any belief statement is expressible as a declarative sentence which properly embeds a declarative sentence. Thus one type of mistaken belief is when the embedded declarative is true and the embedding sentence false in the sense that the subject holds the opposite belief from the embedded one. For instance, 'Hortense is a whore' is true but 'Reg believes that Hortense is not a whore' is also true. The other type of mistaken belief occurs when the belief statement is true but the belief it embeds is false. Hence, 'Reg believes that Hortense is a whore' is true but 'Hortense is a whore' is false.

The term 'knowledge,' as used here, indicates a correct belief. Therefore any bit of knowledge is expressible as a true declarative sentence such that knowledge is a type of belief. Some social psychologists, such as Muzafer Sherif, like to conceive of an attitude as also containing a motivational component. But that is only true of some attitudes — not all — and therefore cannot be part of our definition of the term attitude. Thus an intentional attitude has three components and is always expressible as an imperative sentence. For instance, 'I must finish this chapter in time for the deadline!' An imperative sentence holds no truth value; rather, its extension (denotative meaning) is neither true nor false but a behaviour. However, a motive itself is not a behaviour but a mental experience. The intension (connotative meaning) of a motive is its cognitive component and directional (i.e., evaluative) component.

However, a motive is very different from a drive (a distinction typically overlooked by tension reduction humour theorists and their kin). A drive simply refers to physiological arousal and has no cognitive component. A motive, to the contrary, has a cognitive component but no arousal component. For instance, I may be motivated to finish this chapter by the deadline but fail to do so because I am not aroused enough and, consequently, too damned lazy. On the opposite end of the arousal dimension, I may be motivated to finish this chapter by the deadline but not do so because my arousal level is so high that I panic and my performance degenerates into trembling.

Of the above five terms just defined, drive, attitude, and belief are the key ones — not only because they are each most central to one of the three main areas of psychological humour research; also, we have seen that attitude and belief are terms which subsume those of motive and knowledge respectively. It is clear then why Zillmann and Cantor's (1976) so-called disposition theory of humour and mirth cannot be called a theory at all. By their failure to define the highly ambiguous word 'disposition,' we never know when they are using it in the sense of drive, or belief, or attitude (whether motivational or not).

A common device of the behaviouristic psychologist is to hide his naive realism epistemology by confounding knowledge with belief (i.e., ignoring the possibility that a belief is mistaken). Essentially the same mistake is found in the work of objective incongruity humour theorists who treat the incongruity as out there in the stimulus material and ignore, in the process, one or both types of mistaken beliefs. That is, one can not only fail to 'perceive' an incongruity that is there, but can also 'perceive' an incongruity not there. A necessary ingredient for an amusing mental experience is epistemic or subjective, not objective, incongruity per se.

Failure to understand the essential distinction between an attitude and a belief has enticed social psychologists into an illicit romance with technical terms which blur this crucial distinction — such as 'opinion,' 'judgment,' and 'expectation.' If I ask, 'What is your opinion as to who will win Tuesday's election?', I am asking for your belief. However, should I enquire, 'What is your opinion of allowing Dick Nixon to run for political office; should they let him do it?', I am trying to get the evaluative component of your attitude. (Notice that the two senses of opinion above can each be replaced by either judgment or expectation).

We have found the Identification Classes model very useful in our work on vicarious superiority humour theory. And we have defined an IC as an interlocked attitude-belief system (La Fave, Haddad & Maesen, 1976, pp66-67). However, we argued above that the central independent variable in vicarious superiority humour research is attitude. So how did the belief sneak into an IC? Consider two British subjects, one of whom hates the Irish Republican Army and the other of whom loves it. Now tell them the following alleged joke: 'Did you hear about the IRA member who was instructed to blow up a bus? But his lips got stuck to the exhaust pipe!' Vicarious superiority humour theory predicts that the above 'joke' will tend to be more amusing to the subject who hates the IRA than to he who loves it. However, the belief component of the IC is the same for both subjects; i.e., both subjects believe the victim in the 'joke' is a member of the IRA. The independent variable therefore is not the belief component of the IC but the attitude component — for one subject the IRA is a positive IC; for the other it is negative.

The conjunctions of propositions (4) and (5) below represent one of Reg's ICs:

    (4) Reg believes himself handsome.
    (5) Reg likes handsomeness.

In the above IC, (4) of course expresses Reg's belief and (5) his attitude. But now we find ourselves in a dilemma. For reasons indicated elsewhere (La Fave, 1971) only a mentalistic psychology can become scientific. However, the key kinds of mathematical relations needed in a mentalistic psychology, expressed by such verbs as believes and likes, are emasculated with respect to deductive power. Thus, the binary relation likes has the properties of being nonreflexive, nonsymmetric, and nontransitive. Urgently needed to build a scientific mentalistic psychology, therefore, are new rules of inference which provide needed deductive power. Steven Shew of the Mathematics Department at Arizona State University and I believe we have found one such new rule (La Fave & Shew, 1973). Statement (4) above can be derived from the first formula in this new rule and statement (5) from the second - permitting the deduction, 'Reg likes what Reg believes to be the handsome aspect of Reg.' Thus the new rule permits a derivation which interlocks a belief and an attitude to generate an IC.

Returning for a moment to a higher level of analysis, we have defined a social norm as the intersection of the individual, psychological norms in question. There are two basic types of social norms - belief social norms and value (or attitude) social norms. Both are considered in the paper by Issar et al in this ethnic humour symposium. That paper, and the one by Mutuma et al in this symposium, also need four additional terms: conformity, nonconformity, anticonformity, and nonanticonfirmity. All four of these terms refer to behaviour - where behaviour is defined as a class of responses.

Conformity represents any behaviour within the set representing the intersection of the psychological norms in question. Nonconformity is any behaviour within the universe of discourse which is in the complementary set to the intersection. That is, conformity behaviour falls inside any relevant psychological norm whereas nonconformity behaviour falls outside at least one of these individual norms. Anticonformity, however, falls outside every one of the relevant psychological norms. Nonanticonformity behaviour falls within the union of the relevant psychological norms. Since nonanticonformity is in the complementary set to anticonformity, anticonformity is in the complementary set to the union.

Imagine a three-man society in which A feels the driving speed ought be within the closed interval from 50 to 70 miles per hour. B, however, is ethnically committed to the position that the speed should be not under 45 nor over 60. C maintains that the lower limit ought be 50 and the upper 80. As the intersection in the above example is from 50 to 60 mph, so the social norm is that infinite set of real numbers within the closed interval of 50 to 60. Any driving behaviour not under 50 nor over 60 mph therefore conforms to the social norm, for driving speed. Since this norm represents the consensus as to how fast driving ought to be (rather than how fast it is likely to be), so it is an attitude (or value) social norm. Further, it is a motivational attitude social norm (being expressible by the imperative sentence 'Drive within the limits of 50 to 60 miles per hour!'). Any driving speed greater than 60 or less than 50 in the above illustration represents nonconformity behaviour. Any driving speed less than 45 or greater than 80 represents anticonformity behaviour. Any driving speed not less than 45 and not greater than 80 represents nonanticonformity behaviour.

Now suppose person A's psychological norm above is not with respect to how fast a motorist ought to drive; rather, that a motorist is likely (i.e., greater than 50% subjective probability for A) to drive not under 50 nor over 70. Suppose B and C also have the same ranges as above, only as belief, rather than motivational attitude, psychological norms. Then the set of speeds from 50 to 60 represents the belief social norm for driving speed of this three-person society.

The Psychology of Humour: Towards a General Theory

If belief, as suggested earlier, is the central independent variable for epistemic incongruity humour theory, then why do experiments on social-normative incongruity theory by Mutuma et al and Issar et al in this ethnic humour symposium employ some attitude social norms as independent variables? We have here an example of Paradox 1 - which can be resolved by carefully distinguishing between levels of analysis. Suppose in the above belief-social-norm driving example our three gentlemen observe a good law-abiding Christian racing along at 85 mph. Then, if the perceptions of each of these three gentlemen are accurate, they will each believe the good Christian has anticonformed to their norm; hence, they will be 'surprised.' Their hypothesis has been disconfirmed. They did not believe he would do what they believe he did. (Note there are two 'believes' in the above sentence; the relevant belief is underlined). Take, however, the attitude social norm driving example above. Now, as he races along at 85 mph, our three accurate observers are displeased; the driver is acting immorally for them by anticonforming to their attitude social norm. That is, they believe he is doing what they feel he ought not do. That the underlined belief in both examples above is a genuine belief (as defined earlier) is indicated in that it has a truth value and that truth value could be false. For instance, perhaps the driver was only going 60 but mass hysteria prompted their collective delusion (mistaken belief) that he anti-conformed.

We have previously suggested some connecting links between the epistemic or social-normative incongruity humour theory such as above, and vicarious superiority humour theory (La Fave, Haddad & Maesen, 1976). However, we reported no social-normative incongruity humour experiments at that time that used items designed to amuse. Two experimental papers in this ethnic humour symposium (Mutuma et al and Issar et al) do present such research. In addition the experimental papers in this ethnic humour symposium by Mannell and La Fave et al attempt to establish connecting links between epistemic incongruity and vicarious superiority (or enhanced self-esteem) humour theory.

These last two papers suggest that any vicarious superiority humour theory must distinguish derogation from pseudo-derogation, between compliment and pseudo-compliment. An inadequacy of theories along such a line as Zillmann and Cantor's (1976) is that 'theory's' failure to distinguish between literally and non-literally intended statements and related phenomena. Mannell's experiment, attempting to carefully control for such variables, finds evidence contrary to the retaliatory equity theory of Zillmann and Bryant (1974). La Fave, Haddad and Maesen (1976, pp77-78) had suggested why no good evidence existed previously for such retaliatory equity humour theory, including the inadequate experimental controls in the Zillmann and Bryant experiment and others by the Zillmann group. However, Zillmann and Cantor (1976) try to incorporate the retaliatory equity theory as a part of their disposition theory. Their wish to incorporate it, nonetheless, seems ambivalent; their chapter contradicts itself on whether their disposition theory includes retaliatory equity humour theory or not; their general statements of disposition theory at the end of their chapter make no mention of retaliatory equity assumptions.

Our own vicarious superiority model (La Fave, Haddad & Maesen, 1976) seeks to avoid the two above apparent mistakes by the Zillmann group. First, our model also can deal with degree of retaliation, but predicts a monotonically increasing amount of amusement from over- to underretaliation (counter to the Zillmann and Bryant nonmonotonic, curvilinear model). The facts seem in better support of, or at least less embarrassing to, our model. However, we probably stated our case a little too strongly when we suggested a linear model (p78). A better guesstimate would seem to continue to argue that the velocity increases from over- to underretaliation; however, instead of being linear (i.e., of zero acceleration) is negatively accelerated. In differential calculus terms this would mean that our theoretical curve would have a positive first derivative and a negative second derivative. Our model also avoids the error of literally interpreting every so-called humorous communication. It circumvents this mistake by being epistemic - by talking not about who is the butt, but who the subject believes to be the butt, etcetera (La Fave, Haddad & Maesen, 1976, p66).

One problem for well-intended critics such as Husband (paper in this symposium) and Vidmar and Rokeach (1974), is that their criticism of particular TV situation comedies as serving an anti-humane function should not be based on too literal an interpretation of what is happening. These critics are aware that some viewers will 'perceive' these sit-coms as employing irony or satire; but they may underestimate the ability of the audience to do that.

Mannell's paper in this symposium attempts not merely to distinguish the playful-serious dimension which the subject of irony suggests, but to argue that such a dimension is orthogonal to McGhee's fantasy-reality dimension. On intuitive grounds we think Mannell's theoretical approach likely to help disclose new facts. However, such terms as 'playful' and 'reality' are highly ambiguous. TAASP (The Anthropological Association for the Study of Play) has not succeeded in agreeing on a meaning for play (Stevens, 1976, p139) and philosophers have debated the meaning of reality for millennia. Before Mannell's promissory note can get cashed in at more than nominal value, it will be necessary for terms such as 'playful' and 'reality' to receive some useful precising definitions.

The arguments above suggest a close tie between the resolution to Paradoxes 4 (irony of irony) and 6 (tragic-comic conjunction). Mannell's 'distinctions' might unite with vicarious superiority and epistemic incongruity to generate such hypotheses as: (1) It is amusing when something tragic happens to an enemy in an incongruous way (especially under fantasy conditions). (2) It is amusing when something pseudo-tragic (e.g., pseudo insult as in La Fave et al paper in this symposium) happens to a nonnegative character in a playful way. Zillmann and Cantor (1976, p99) credit to us the position 'that the enhancement of positive identification classes (i.e., vicarious superiority) is an autonomous factor in humour appreciation and, as such, a sufficient condition to induce a humour response.' But we have never taken such a silly position as that vicarious superiority is a sufficient condition for amusement. Of course we could defend such a position, if we left the phrase vicarious superiority as completely undefined as they leave their key term disposition. However, we define vicarious superiority in terms of our mathematical model of ICs. Counter to Zillmann and Cantor's accusation, it is our position here, and has been (e.g., La Fave, Haddad & Maesen, 1976) that, rather than being sufficient, at least two other necessary conditions besides vicarious superiority exist – suddenness and epistemic incongruity. Further, vicarious superiority is not even one of these three necessary conditions. Rather we treat vicarious superiority as only a subtype under happiness increment.

Zillmann and Cantor's view of our vicarious superiority humour theory may be parsimoniously summarized: what's good in our approach is not new; what is new is not good. They only attribute one essentially new idea to us. Their position (p99) is 'that enjoyment does not amount to humour unless someone or something is somehow disparaged or victimized.' They accuse us (pp98–99) of arguing the novel position that one could be altruistically amused at the success of some other person or class in which no one is disparaged. They argue that no such thing could amuse. We plead guilty to allowing for altruistic amusement, and will give an example. Circa 1960, I attended a seminar at Northwestern University conducted by the psychologist, Donald T. Campbell. He introduced to social psychologist Jack Sawyer and a few others of us a social scientist colleague, Harold Guetzkow, as follows: 'Dr. Guetzkow is a professor in half-a-dozen Departments here.' That was a slight exaggeration; I believe Guetzkow was in three Departments at that time. But Campbell's statement amused us. Why? (1) We 'perceived' an incongruity – to be a professor in six Departments. (2) We positively identified with Guetzkow, so that his victory (being a professor in several Departments at a leading University) was vicariously enjoyed as our victory. But, and this is crucial, there was no butt! Yes! Zillmann and Cantor, there are communications which amuse while possessing hero-persons sans butts. Such 'jokes' also apparently contradict the humour theory of Arthur Koestler (1964) who, before Zillmann and Cantor, argued that such items (involving sympathy) might be experienced as aesthetic but not amusing.

The former quote from Zillmann and Cantor (1976, p99) even goes so far as to apparently state that there can be no amusement without disparagement. The counter-factuality of that assertion is so obvious as to seem absurd. McGhee, for instance, has a useful notion of 'mastery' which he applies to the humour area; and certainly many puzzles are humorous to children who achieve the resolution incongruity which humour theorist Thomas Shultz talks about without such puzzles needing disparage anyone. Of course one could be amused because of mastery over others – in which case superiority would seem to get itself involved. Or one could feel a sense of amused mastery in solving a riddle for the first time. Perhaps it would stretch the meaning of superiority a bit to suggest that 'present me' feels superior to 'past me'.

It appears then that McGhee's mastery notion may explain some happiness increments involved in amusing experiences which do not demand a feeling of superiority. Another construct which seems useful and perhaps falls under happiness increment but not totally under vicarious superiority involves Rothbart's (1976) notion of 'threat' – which is used to advantage in the Issar et al and Mutuma et al papers. The construct also seems to hold implications at higher levels of analysis than that of individual psychology. Thus, so-called dirty 'jokes' may amuse few in a Puritanical era but amuse a much higher proportion when the society has had the kind of sexual revolution which has occurred in non-Latin North America in the past decade or two. These 'jokes' (Freud notwithstanding) apparently now amuse more because they threaten less.

A consensus among humour theorists seems to be developing that incongruity is a necessary ingredient in a recipe for humour at the psychological level. But is this incongruity subjective (i.e., epistemic) or objective? Is it a logical incongruity, linguistic, social, or physical, or (as balance cognitive consistency theories might maintain) psychological? At a higher level of analysis: is the incongruity culturally relative or culturally absolute? And, speaking of levels, Pien and Rothbart (this volume) ask the incisive question: At what level of explanation does the incongruity occur? What, they also enquire, is meant by the ambiguous word resolution in the context resolution of an incongruity? The problem they pinpoint is that resolution of one incongruity may generate another unresolved incongruity. Resolution, we contend, would enable humour appreciation when it apparently provides the sudden happiness increment to accompany the epistemic incongruity. (Such an emphasis also seems indebted to Gestalt psychology).

We believe the problems regarding types of incongruity cannot be dismissed simply by calling them different names for the same type; there are important differences between these types. However, we need acknowledge only one type at the level of analysis at which we are working. That one type is epistemic (i.e., subjective or psychological) incongruity. In arguing thus we are not assuming the atomistic reductionist position resisted earlier! For instance, we do not maintain that social normative incongruity is reducible to nothing but psychological incongruity, just as a social norm for us, as we showed earlier, is not reducible to nothing but psychological norms. In fact, the papers in this ethnic humour sympsium by Mutuma et al and Issar et al shuttle between psychological and social incongruity levels of analysis without, hopefully, getting lost in the shuttle. Social incongruity belongs to sociology; psychological incongruity to psychology; and the relation between them to social psychology.

The paper by Brodzinsky (this volume) speaks of several types of linguistic ambiguities or incongruities. But scientific linguistics is at the social science, not psychological, level of analysis. Linguistic norms are social norms. For instance, linguistic norms involve belief social norms since they make it possible for us to predict how members of a linguistic community will speak (in terms of phonological, semantic, and syntactic rules). What Bradshaw (this volume) calls punchline features seem to be linguistic belief norms. Yet linguistic norms also involve value or attitude norms; they inform us how members of that linguistic community feel they ought to speak. The field most directly relevant for our present level of analysis, however, is not the social science of linguistics, but psycholinguistics. And at this level we are interested in epistemic incongruity. Similarly, physical incongruity is not our present level of analysis. Physical incongruity is objective incongruity. We do not deny the existence of such incongruities. Some might even say that entropy is incongruous and negentropy is congruous, and our universe is headed towards maximum objective incongruity. Yet our relevant level is psychophysics, not physics. And in such psychophysical experiments as Nerhardt's (1970), we are concerned with subjective incongruity.

The paper by mathematical logician Paulos deals solely with logical incongruities. He discusses mainly three basic types. But a necessary (though not sufficient) condition for any of these three types to be amusing is that an incongruity be 'perceived'. For instance, all three of his types involve ambiguity. In his Model Theory type, to illustrate, there are a plural number of interpretations possible of a given sentence. That is, the sentence must be ambiguous. Thus: 'Confucious say: "Woman who fly upside down have crack up,"' has two models. However, to be amused, it is not enough to be able to see a plurality of models or interpretations; one must also see these different interpretations simultaneously (Kaplan & Kris, 1947). That is why (relevant to McGhee's phylogenetic paper in this volume) humour is almost exclusively, if not exclusively, human. Because only a human quite fully escapes stimulus boundness and therefore 'sees' simultaneous ambiguity to much extent. And only a human escapes the 'principle' of contiguity quite completely because only he/she has the kind of DNA which enables humans to be extensively symbol-minded, and to substitute this 'second signal system' for the objects and relations they denote.

Consider reversible figure-ground relationships which Gestalt psychologists wisely emphasize and can be handled as belief switching within our ICs model. It can be amusing to see Napoleon followed by the trees, the beautiful young lady then the ugly old hag, etcetera. But a stimulus bound animal could not be amused. Limited to the perceptual level of cognition, he would not possess, once the beautiful young lady disappeared, enough 'marbles' to remind him of her as he scrutinized the ugly old hag. It is even humanly impossible to perceive both the young lady and old hag simultaneously. But a conceptual-functioning animal, employing a more abstract type of cognition in addition to perception, can conceive of them both simultaneously and by the incongruity be amused.

A second type of logical incongruity for Paulos returns us to Paradox 1. This type involves confounding levels of analysis or abstraction so as to generate the type of 'jokes' discussed early in this chapter. The illogic here mistreats the membership relation as reflexive. Mathematical logician Bertrand Russell pointed out this type of illogic around the turn of the century. For instance, there is a certain barber in the village who shaves everyone who does not shave himself. Does he shave himself? If it is true that he shaves himself, then it is false that he shaves himself since he only shaves those who do not shave themselves. Yet if he does not shave himself then he does shave himself since he shaves anyone who does not shave himself. Some humans find such examples amusing. Yet they can only be amused if simultaneously aware of the ambiguity with respect to levels of abstraction. Once again, epistemic incongruity must get itself involved if amusement is to occur. Nevertheless, such a necessary condition as epistemic incongruity is not sufficient. For instance, discoveries of such paradoxes brought about a crisis in mathematical logic and set theory around the turn of the century. Russell pointed out these paradoxes to the outstanding 19th century mathematician Frege. Frege was certainly intelligent enough to experience epistemic incongruity. But he was apparently too threatened à la Rothbart to enjoy this paradox and be amused. Russell informs us that, in despair, Frege gave up his life work in such mathematics.

We have had some minor success in programming a computer to write 'jokes' based on confounding levels of abstraction. One of its abortions is:

1. Secretaries are abundant.
2. That woman is a secretary.
3. Therefore, that woman is abundant.

The third type of logical incongruity Paulos emphasizes involves misleading grammatical forms. For instance, waitresses have sometimes found it mildly amusing when I have said to them: 'I'll have coffee with cream or vice versa.' Adding the 'or vice versa' suggests that the binary operation of conjunction is noncummutative (when it is really commutative).

(The waitress does not usually know the technical terms but she does notice the incongruity).

We deliberately programmed the following poorly formed formula into the computer: x is between y. That is, we intentionally mistreated the ternary relation between as if it were binary. The computer responded with the following 'joke': Reg is between Hortense. But the computer did not find that 'joke' amusing; only we did; only we could experience epistemic incongruity.

Does not our modest computer work suggest not merely the existence of jokes but also of joke formulae? For instance, we plug an algorithm such as a joke formula into the computer and, by such rules of inference as universal instantiation, it can theoretically cough up a different joke each time it substitutes from its memory system a different set of values for the set of variables. From work on computers and by Paulos, and by incongruity humour theorists like Shultz and Suls, it seems there must really exist such an animal as a joke after all. Surely there is something here worth preserving! I agree we ought to preserve something akin to that which we now call a joke. Our reason for denying the existence of jokes has been because of their standard definition as humorous stimuli. As we mentioned earlier, a stimulus is a (1) physical event (2) here (3) now. But then no humorous stimuli nor jokes exist; nothing amusing satisfies those three properties! Thus, the same so-called joke can be written with different handwriting styles, in different sizes, different colours, etcetera. It can also be presented in a different sensory modality, such as spoken instead of written. Also, it frequently can be given in a different language. Such a 'phenomenon' is obviously too abstract and relational to be a stimulus by any reasonable definition of stimulus.

Yet if we redefine joke counter to the usual meaning of humorous stimulus, we are guilty of violating a pedagogic metatheoretic principle of science by misusing a technical term to exploit negative transfer and cause communication problems between scientists. We also denied the existence of jokes to help de-ethnocentrize humour theory, so cultural relativity could be incorporated. However, without changing our theoretical position, let us change the definition of joke (despite the negative transfer!) to help capture what is valuable in the approaches of incongruity theorists such as Shultz.

Those kinds of incongruity theorists would seem to focus on 'cultural universals.' We have never wished to deny cultural universals (being fans of Noam Chomsky). But we had wished to call the attention of incongruity humour theorists to cultural relatives which appeared to be getting insufficient attention. So, there are both cultural relatives and cultural universals! In fact, were there no cultural universals, psychological and social sciences would be impossible in principle! Then critics of social psychology such as Kenneth Gergen (1973), and of sociology such as C. Wright Mills (1961), would be perfectly correct in their empiricistic pessimism that there are no social laws (and cannot be!) that are cross-cultural or cross-historical. But, happily, they are wrong!

The question then is what relationship exists at the psychological level between cultural universals and cultural relatives? The relationship is essentially that between 'form' and 'content,' 'syntax' and 'semantics,' 'abstract' and 'concrete.'

The Gestalt psychologists recognized the distinction by pointing out that you could play the same song (form) with two mutually exclusive sets of notes by transposing octaves or keys; or two different songs by permuting the same set of notes. Chomsky recognizes the need for such a distinction by finding the normal human child inherits via his DNA a universal grammar (abstract syntax). This universal grammar is said to enable the child to learn the particular grammar of his linguistic community (less abstract syntax) by the age of six (and to learn some more concrete semantic vocabulary from that community as well). Thomas Shultz appears sensitized to such issues (as his paper regarding cultural universals in this volume perhaps suggests) as do his (1976) Chomskyan distinctions between semantic and syntactic ambiguities, and then between different types of syntactic ambiguities in turn. An example of interrelating such incongruity research to vicarious superiority humour research is perhaps illustrated by briefly mentioning one of our pilot studies. Subjects were asked to supply the correct punctuation for syntactically ambiguous sentences such as the following: 'woman without her man would be lost.' We predicted a Women's Libber would punctuate such sentences as: (1) Woman, without her, man would be lost! However, that a Men's Libber would provide punctuation closer to the following: (2) Woman without her man, would be lost! Although our hypothesis was substantiated, the trend was too little above chance to provide any confidence in it. But this pilot study was inadequately controlled on a number of counts. For instance, we knew the sex of each subject, but not the sexual preference.

The new definition of a joke needed to capture the quintessence of the above would be culturally universal in the sense that a homo sapiens of any culture or historical period who found the item epistemically incongruous and whose happiness was raised suddenly enough by it would invariably find it amusing. Jokes, thus defined, would not be tied to any specific language. If the joke employed language to express itself, the joke would consist

of what many mathematical logicians would call propositions, rather than sentences. By
this definition two humans who spoke different languages could decode into the same
propositions and thus appreciate the same joke. At a more abstract level, our joke formulae
would consist of propositional formulae, rather than sentential formulae. We would also
have metajokes (as does Paulos), such as jokes about jokes; and perhaps even metametajokes
(which might enjoy their greatest popularity among mathematicians).

So, at this level we are only basically concerned with one type of incongruity - psychological.
Now the main intellectual fashion in social psychology in the 1960's involved cognitive
consistency theories. These theories emphasize that cognitive inconsistency is a motivating
state of psychological disharmony and tension - that the organism attempts to restore psychic
equilibration by restoring balance, reducing dissonance, resolving incongruity, etcetera.
But cognitive inconsistency is partially synonymous with epistemic incongruity. We wonder,
then, what light cognitive consistency theories may shed on the psychology of humour.
Consider the balance approach of the father of cognitive consistency theory, Fritz Heider.
Since an amusing experience requires a happiness increment, and restoring balance is a
happiness increment, so any attempt to apply such cognitive consistency theories to the
psychology of humour must apparently assume that only reduction in cognitive inconsistency
can amuse. Thus, such theories would be tension reduction theories of humour.

However, Gutman (1968), Goldstein (1976) and La Fave, Haddad and Maesen (1976) have suggested
that balance theory can be related to what we would refer to as vicarious superiority humour
theory. All those writers also find some problems with cognitive consistency theories.
Consider a triangular love affair with Reginald at one end, Hortense at another, and
Ferdinand the third. Imagine further that the society is monogamous and the following
relations hold:

1. Reginald loves Hortense.
2. Reg's best friend is Ferdinand.
3. Hortense is running around with Ferdinand.

From Reg's perspective there is a + on the line between himself and Hortense, and a + on the
line running from Reg to Ferdinand. Since an even number of negatives is a state of balance,
if the remaining line is a +, Reg should be in a state of heavenly bliss. But there exist
both logical and psychological (i.e., empirical) problems involving the remaining line.
Since Hortense and Ferdinand are running around together, we could assign the line a + (for
the fact they are associating). Since we have zero negatives then, Reg should be delighted.
But would we expect Reg to be contented if, in a monogamous society, his beloved Hortense is
is running around with his best friend Ferdinand? Balance Theory in this instance seems
empirically wrong!

Above we interpreted the third line objectively; Hortense and Ferdinand really are running
around together. But suppose we interpreted that line epistemically (or subjectively). In
this instance our triangle would interrelate two attitudes with a belief. Assume Reg
mistakenly believes Hortense is not running around with Ferdinand. Then the third line
provides a - on this interpretation. Since one - is a state of imbalance, Reg should be
unhappy with the situation - again empirically countering intuitions. Or the third line
co'ld be labelled + to indicate that Hortense and Ferdinand love each other (an arrangement,
despite its balanced state, which Reg might not be too enchanted with). Or a + on the third
line might denote Reg's belief that Hortense and Ferdinand love each other (again a balanced
state which would be unlikely to render Reg happy). Or a + on the third line could indicate
Reg's love for the fact that Hortense and Ferdinand are running around together. Therefore,
we have at least five mathematically nonequivalent relations which the sign on the third line
could indicate.

We see, then, that such cognitive consistency theories are highly ambiguous and often empirically wrong (when they can be pinned down to predicting anything). Serious application of
mathematical logic in order to carefully define technical terms is urgent if such theories
are to scientifically progress. Nonetheless, Heider's interesting idea that an even number
of negatives is a state of balance is apparently useful in humour theory. Not only can such
theory relate to vicarious superiority humour theory, as suggested above, but to epistemic
incongruity humour theory also. For instance, it sometimes seems useful to conceive of a
balanced state based on two negatives as incongruously amusing. (Although incongruity here
could not mean cognitive inconsistency, since two negatives is cognitive consistency, whereas
no negatives, though a balanced state, is unamusing. Two negatives seems to lead to the
amusing formula for kiss of death phenomena. For instance, in an effort to maximize his
power in a Psychology Department, the psychologist might deliberately cultivate personal
obnoxiousness. Then, whenever he wishes a colleague to carry out his orders, if the colleague
resists, he can always threaten to compliment him publicly. Of course a potentially infinite
number of 'jokes' can be constructed on this kiss-of-death formula.

One of the ambiguities in cognitive consistency theories mentioned above also found in
reference group theory confounds subjective with objective. The Copi (1961) logic text

nicely distinguishes between subjective, conventional, and objective. For us the subjective belongs to mentalistic psychology; the conventional is shared subjective, our definition of a social norm. Such intersubjectivity belongs to sociology. The objective meaning for us is metaphysical. Our ICs model improves on reference-group theory by disambiguating and concerning itself only with the subjective (La Fave, Haddad & Marshall, 1974).

One of the criticisms of balance theory which Goldstein (1976, p107) correctly offers is that ethnic humour at the expense of one's own group can amuse counter to what balance theory would seem to suggest. For balance theory, a negative remark about oneself would apparently provide only one (which should be a state of imbalance and thus unamusing). In the ICs model of vicarious superiority humour theory, however, such humour can be accounted for (provided the subject holds a negative attitude with respect to the class which he is a member of). (Chapman & Gadfield, 1976, p142, apparently fail to understand the ICs model's ability to predict such phenomena. In fact, the problem cited by Chapman and Gadfield is also handled by the Haddad and La Fave experiment: La Fave, Haddad & Maesen, 1976). Recall, however, that the ICs model employs subjective, not objective, membership, in defining ICs. Therefore, the ICs model also has a second way to account for this amusement-at-own-ethnic-group's-expense phenomenon; one may 'psychotically' refuse to assign himself to a class he is objectively a member of; for example, a Negro who denies his racial membership even though a blue-black.

CONCLUSION

This chapter has argued that a scientific understanding of ethnic humour requires development of a general theory of humour. Further, such a humour theory ought to be highly intradisciplinary and interdisciplinary. A useful strategy would seem to begin with major paradoxes for humour theory and, aided by metatheoretical principles and empirical insights, move towards a resolution of these paradoxes and, in the process, towards a theory of humour. The main criterion for judging the success of this chapter is the extent to which it has persuaded you that we are a long way from our goal of a scientific understanding of ethnic humour.

REFERENCES

See Bibliography for publications on humour, laughter and comedy

Benton, G. & Loomes, G., Big Red Joke Book. Pluto Press, London (1976).

Copi, I.M., Symbolic Logic. Macmillan, New York (1954).

Copi, I.M., Introduction to Logic. Macmillan, New York (1961).

Fishbein, M. & Ajzen, I., Belief, Attitude, Intention, and Behavior: An Introduction to Theory and Research. Addison-Wesley, Reading, Massachusettes (1975).

Fodor, J.A., More about mediators: a reply to Berlyne and Osgood. Journal of Verbal Learning and Verbal Behavior, 5, 412-415 (1966).

Gergen, K.J., Social psychology as history. Journal of Personality and Social Psychology, 26, 309-320 (1973).

Gregory, D., nigger. Dutton, New York (1964).

Gutman, J., The effects of justice, balance, and hostility on mirth. Unpublished doctoral dissertation, University of Southern California, (1968).

Hanson, N.R., Scientific laws are many-splendored things. In:L.I. Krimerman (Ed.), The Nature and Scope of Social Science: A Critical Anthology. Appleton-Century-Crofts, New York (1969).

Kaplan, A. & Kris, E., Esthetic ambiguity. Philosophy and Phenomenological Research, 8, 415-435 (1947).

Kelman, H.C., Attitudes are alive and well and gainfully employed in the sphere of action. American Psychologist, 29, 310-324 (1974).

Koestler, A., The Ghost in the Machine. Macmillan, New York (1968).

La Fave, L., Humor judgments as a function of reference groups: an experimental study. Unpublished doctoral dissertation, University of Oklahoma (1961).

La Fave, L., Social change without nonconformity: a connecting link between functional and historical approaches to sociological theory. Paper presented before the American Association for the Advancement of Science, Cleveland (1963).

La Fave, L., Social change without nonconformity. Department of Sociology University of Wisconsin—Milwaukee, Milwaukee, microfiche, Clearinghouse for Sociological Literature, 65–68 (1965).

La Fave, L., The holism—atomism controversy: Gestalt psychology confronts the revised law of inverse variation. Psychological Reports, 24, 699–704 (1969a).

La Fave, L., Reply to Copi's critique. Psychological Reports, 25, 318 (1969b).

La Fave, L., Psychological methodology: should it differ from that of natural science? Canadian Psychologist, 12, 513–525 (1971).

La Fave, L., Implications of subadditive fusions for complex motor skills. In: I.D. Williams & L.M. Wankel (Eds.), Proceedings of the Fourth Canadian Psycho—Motor Learning and Sport Psychology Symposium. University of Waterloo (1972b).

La Fave, L. & Shew, S., A new rule of inference for an epistemic logic applied to cognitive psychology. Psychological Reports, 33, 31–38 (1973).

La Fave, L. & Teeley, P., Involuntary nonconformity as a function of habit lag. Perceptual and Motor Skills, 24, 227–234 (1967).

Mannell, R.C. & Duthie, J.H., Habit lag: when automatization is dysfunctional. The Journal of Psychology, 89, 73–80 (1975).

Merton, R.K., Social Theory and Social Structure (Revised Edition). Free Press, Glencoe, Illinois (1957).

Mills, C.W., The Sociological Imagination. Grove Press, New York (1961).

Quine, W.V.O., From a Logical Point of View. Harper & Row, New York (1961).

Rokeach, M., The Nature of Human Values. Free Press, New York (1973).

Sherif, M., The Psychology of Social Norms. Harper & Row, New York (1936).

Stevens, P., Expressive aspects of play. In: D.F. Lancy & B.A. Tindall (Eds.), The Anthropological Study of Play: Problems and Prospects. Leisure Press, New York (1976).

Tsang, S.Y.W., Amusement, tastefulness and playfulness judgements as functions of number of social normative incongruity dimensions. Unpublished Master's thesis, University of Windsor (1976).

Vidmar, N. & Rokeach, M., Archie Bunker's bigotry: a study in selective perception and exposure. Journal of Communication, 24, 36–47 (1974).

Context and Ethnic Humour in Intergroup Relations

Richard Y. Bourhis,* Nicholas J. Gadfield,**
Howard Giles* and Henri Tajfel*

*University of Bristol
**University of Wales Institute of Science and Technology

This study investigates the role of three variables influencing the perception and appreciation
of ethnic humour in intergroup relations. The three variables are: (1) the butt of the
humour - anti-ingroup or anti-outgroup butt; (2) the source of the humour - ingroup or
outgroup source; and (3) the context of the intergroup humour situation - salient intergroup
context or nonsalient intergroup context. These variables are discussed in turn.

It has been argued by humour theorists such as Zillmann and Cantor (1976) that hostile or
derogatory jokes are least appreciated when they attack oneself or group members with whom
one identifies and likes. Such derogatory jokes are most appreciated when they attack group
members with whom one does not identify, or whom one does not like. Support for these notions
in intergroup contexts has come from empirical studies which show that people react more
favourably to anti-outgroup humour than they do to anti-ingroup humour. This research has
been conducted with groups such as political parties (Priest & Abrahams, 1970), religious
groups (La Fave, 1972) and the sexes (Chapman & Gadfield, 1976). Support for the above notion
has not always been so clear in the inter-ethnic group area (e.g., Barron, 1950; La Fave,
Haddad & Maesen, 1976; La Fave, McCarthy & Haddad, 1973; Middleton, 1959). Nevertheless,
recent advances in Disposition Theory (Zillmann & Cantor, 1976) seem to account for many of
the discrepancies appearing in the literature. Overall then, there is some agreement that
an ethnic ingroup will use anti-outgroup humour, not only to express hostility against the
outgroup (e.g., Burma, 1950; Obrdlik, 1942; Arnez & Anthony, 1968) but also as Martineau
(1972) has suggested, to strengthen the morale and solidarity of the ingroup, and to undermine
the morale of the outgroup (see also Stephenson, 1951). It is interesting to note from the
standpoint of Tajfel's (1974) general theory of intergroup behaviour, similar predictions can
be made about the role of anti-outgroup humour in intergroup situations. For Tajfel, anti-
outgroup humour can, through outgroup devaluation and denigration, be a creative and potent
way of asserting ingroup pride and distinctiveness from a dominant outgroup. It is as a
result of the strength gained from positive distinctiveness that Tajfel sees ingroup members
mobilizing to challenge the superior position of an outgroup.

Much of the research on inter-ethnic group humour has originated from Canada and the USA.
Our study was designed to examine an ethnic group's reaction to ingroup and outgroup humour
in a specific European setting, namely in Wales. The Welsh situation in Britain is
interesting because it is an example of an ethnic minority group that is redefining and
re-negotiating its relationship with the outgroup, in this case the English. Since Wales was
conquered and incorporated into the English political system in the sixteenth century (cf.
Corrado, 1976), the status given to Welshmen and their national language in Britain has been
that of a subordinate or second-class group. Until fairly recently many Welshmen felt that
the only way of succeeding and becoming 'respectable' was by acting as though they were
'Englishmen'. Many Welshmen did this by shedding their Welsh language, assuming English
accents, anglicizing their names or moving to England. But over the last decade in Wales
there has been amongst many Welshmen an awareness that such strategies of 'passing' in terms
of linguistic and cultural assimilation to the English, were no longer acceptable or legitimate.
For many Welshmen the low status imposed on the Welsh language and culture was seen as unfair
and oppressive. Alternative views of the Welsh language, culture and nation were sought.
As a first step towards a more positive redefinition of Welshness a number of Welshmen
regained their pride in being able to speak Welsh while others who had lost their national
language began to learn Welsh again as a symbol of their allegiance to Welsh national and
cultural values (Bourhis & Giles, 1976; Bourhis, Giles & Tajfel, 1973). For many years the
Welsh Language Society has been taking strong social action to improve the status of Welsh
in Wales, while the National Party of Wales is beginning to flourish. Thus far the focus
of this redefinition has been the Welsh Language and culture, but there is evidence of growing

267

militancy with respect to Welsh grievances on the economic, social and political fronts. Given such an overview of the Welsh situation, highlighting intergroup tension, it seems probable that in this cultural context also anti-outgroup humour against the English would be more favourably reacted to by Welshmen, than anti-ingroup humour directed at Welshmen themselves.

Little empirical work has been done in Europe on the source of ethnic group humour. Given the context of intergroup relations in Wales, and given the rising feelings of solidarity amongst Welshmen, it might be expected that humour emitted by an ingroup source would be more favourably perceived by Welshmen, than humour emitted by an outgroup source such as the English. This could be the case particularly in view of the fact that research by Bourhis et al (1973) has shown that, in Wales, Welshmen react more favourably to Welsh – than to English-sounding speakers.

Another variable investigated in this study was the salience of the intergroup relation situation for the subjects or the context of the intergroup humour situation. When tension is heightened between groups, Doise and Sinclair (1973) have suggested that inter-group differences will be accentuated, while intra-group differences will be attenuated (see also Tajfel, 1959, 1972). Indeed Lemaine (1974) suggested that when intergroup categorization is made explicit and salient for group members, there will follow 'a search for a difference, for otherness, by the creation and accentuation of heterogeneity'. Empirical support for such a process comes from a study conducted in Wales by Christian, Gadfield, Giles and Taylor (1976) using the Multidimensional Scaling Technique. They found that Welsh subjects who were required to write an essay about the past history of conflict between England and Wales (salient intergroup context) tended, after the essay, to ally themselves closer to fellow Welshmen and made themselves more distant from Englishmen than Welsh subjects who had written an essay on a neutral topic (nonsalient intergroup context). It could be argued then, that Welshmen would appreciate anti-outgroup humour more, but anti-ingroup humour less, under conditions of salient intergroup categorization than in neutral conditions. Some support for the first prediction comes from Singer's observation (in Berlyne, 1969) that a group of Blacks told an increasing number of hostile anti-White jokes as interracial tension increased over the years in the USA.

Previous work on ethnic humour focused mainly upon reactions of a group to humour where the butt of the joke is either a member of the ethnic ingroup or the ethnic outgroup. This study attempts to investigate more closely the dynamics of humour in a Welsh-English context by also examining the roles of the source of humour and the social context of the intergroup humour situation (the salience of the intergroup conflict for the subjects).

Eighty fifteen-year-old secondary school students attending a comprehensive school in Wales participated in this experiment. All were Welsh-born and described themselves as being 'very Welsh' although none reported being fluent in the Welsh language. The subjects matched for sex, were randomly assigned to one of eight experimental conditions. A 2 x 2 x 2 factorial design was used in this study with: two levels of butt of joke (ingroup vs. outgroup), source of humour (ingroup vs. outgroup) and salience of intergroup context (salient vs. neutral). In the post-experimental self-ratings, all the subjects rated themselves to be very Welsh and reported having strong Welsh accents in their English as well as being quite dissatisfied with the lack of autonomy granted to Wales by Westminster.

A male experimenter from French Canada ('irrelevant' outgroup member) conducted the experiment during school time and attended each experimental group separately. After a standard introduction and suitable instructions, subjects were asked to write a ten-minute essay on two randomly assigned topics. This was the salience of the intergroup context manipulation. In the 'neutral' context condition, half the subjects wrote an essay on pollution and ecology. In the 'salient intergroup categorization context' the other half of the subjects wrote an essay on the ways in which the Welsh way of life had suffered through English supremacy in Wales over the last hundred years. On the basis of the study by Christian et al on a similar local population, it was anticipated that writing an essay on the ways in which Welsh life had suffered through English domination would make intergroup conflict between the subjects and the English more vivid and salient. Those who wrote an essay on how the English had destroyed the Welsh way of life focused upon ethnic relations, and all subjects strongly endorsed the idea proposed in the essay title. All subjects in the neutral condition agreed with the proposition of the essay, and topic of Welsh-English relations never emerged in these essays.

After the essay the subjects were given a second set of instructions to the effect that the experimenter was also interested in humour and wished to have their reactions to some jokes he had been collecting in different parts of Britain. The experimenter told the subjects that he had tape-recorded interviews with many people in the street about their impressions of humour and had asked them to tell him some jokes. Subjects were told that they would hear one of these interviewees on tape and would be required to evaluate his jokes. The source

of the humour manipulation was as follows: half the subjects heard a speaker on tape that
was categorized as a member of the ingroup from his distinctive Welsh accent (Giles &
Powesland, 1975) and from the fact that the interview had been conducted in Wales. The
other half of the subjects heard exactly the same interview, but this time, the speaker
assumed a Standard English accent (Received Pronunciation, RP) and was therefore categorized
as a member of the English outgroup. Reference was also made on tape that the interview had
been conducted in an English city.

The same bidialectal speaker was used for both interviews. The stimulus speaker's guise had
been independently assessed as a valid representation of the two accents concerned in two
previous studies (Bourhis et al., 1973; Bourhis & Giles, 1976). He assumed both accents
realistically across the two recordings as in the matched-guise technique developed by
Lambert (1967) and as refined by Giles and Bourhis (1977). At the instant the speaker was
about to tell his ethnic jokes a great deal of traffic noise and interference was heard on
the tape. Because of this the experimenter turned off the tape saying that the recording
from then on was of poor quality and so the interviewee's jokes had been transcribed for the
subjects. The jokes were presented visually because of the problems involved in relating
a joke in different speech styles while keeping exactly the same humorous tone.

The same three ethnic jokes were used for all the conditions, they were typed out for the
subjects and all three were disparaging and derogatory. Subjects actually read four jokes,
the first of which was a practice joke to familiarize subjects with the procedure and rating
scales. All jokes were approximately of the same length, between fifty and eighty words.
The butt of the humour manipulation was as follows: for half the subjects the three jokes
were all anti-English (anti-outgroup); for the other half of the subjects the three jokes
were all anti-Welsh (anti-ingroup). The three jokes were not disparaging towards any
specific stereotyped Welsh or English characteristics. The jokes were chosen such that it
was realistic to relate them with the butt of the humour being either the ingroup or the
outgroup. The subjects were required to rate how they felt towards the three jokes on
seven-point rating-scales printed after each joke on the questionnaire. The students were
required to rate how funny, clever, original, hostile, and enjoyable each joke seemed to
them. After the experiment per se, the subjects were debriefed and a short discussion on
ethnic humour was initiated in the classroom with the students.

The subjects' ratings for the three stimulus jokes were collapsed for each of the five
scales and 2 x 2 x 2 ANOVAs were applied to each trait. The results for the three jokes
were collapsed since the same evaluative trends had emerged for each when they were analyzed
separately (see Chapman & Gadfield, 1976). Significant effects did emerge between the
experimental conditions. The subjects' ratings of the first practice joke were also
subjected to five separate 2 x 2 x 2 ANOVAs corresponding to each dependent measure, and
no differences emerged between any of the experimental conditions in the subjects' reactions
on any scale. A main effect was found for the 'butt' manipulation on four of the scales.
Anti-English jokes were considered more funny ($F = 8.79$; $p < .01$), more clever ($F = 7.31$;
$p < .01$), more original ($F = 6.08$; $p < .01$) and more enjoyable ($F = 7.31$; $p < .01$) than anti-
Welsh jokes. In addition, a source of humour by salience of intergroup context interaction
emerged on both the scales of originality ($F = 4.39$; $p < .01$) and enjoyability ($F = 7.31$;
$p < .01$). On these scales it was found that the Welsh speaker's jokes were rated more
favourably than those of the English speaker in the neutral context condition. When the
intergroup categorization was made salient (salient intergroup context), opposite results
were found: the English speaker's jokes were found more original and enjoyable than those
of the Welsh speaker. A three-way interaction effect was also found on the scales of
funniness ($F = 7.61$; $p < .01$) and cleverness ($F = 4.09$; $p < .05$) but not on the other three
scales. This three-way interaction can be stated as follows. Anti-Welsh humour which was
rated less favourably than anti-English humour was not susceptible to any influence from
the other two variables. Difference tests between these means, showed that anti-Welsh
humour was equally disliked under all the conditions. The results were different with
regard to anti-English jokes: the anti-outgroup humour was perceived to be more funny and
clever when the source was Welsh in the neutral condition only. In the salient intergroup
categorization condition anti-outgroup humour was perceived to be more funny and clever when
the source was the English speaker.

These results can be summarized as follows. Welsh subjects did not appreciate anti-Welsh
humour under any of the experimental situations. This result is consistent with findings of
Chapman, Smith and Foot (1976, 1977) that 4- to 6-year-old Welsh children laugh more at
English-butt humour than at Welsh-butt humour.

However in the present study the Welsh subjects reacted very positively to anti-outgroup
humour, but in a complex manner. When the intergroup context was made salient for the
subjects, they reacted more favourably when the source of the anti-outgroup humour was
English rather than Welsh. Alternatively, when the intergroup context was not made salient,
Welshmen reacted to anti-outgroup humour more favourably when the source was Welsh rather

than English. Why was the Welshmen's anti-outgroup humour not favourably perceived by ingroup members in the salient intergroup context condition? It may well be that under such circumstances, blatant anti-outgroup humour may have been considered too obvious and transparent a way of attacking the outgroup, and as such may have been an ineffective way of boosting ingroup morale, pride and distinctiveness. Priest (1972) has suggested that 'humour is only an indirect method of communicating hostility, and is useful in polite relationships where the communicator does not wish to risk too open a conflict with members of outside groups'. In such a situation the protagonist could, if challenged, excuse his apparent hostility by claiming that all that was said was meant purely in jest. In addition Priest argues that 'as the level of hostility between groups increases, there should be a tendency to switch from humorous ridicule to more direct forms of hostile expression'. Under these conditions the situation may also be perceived as being too serious to joke about and the excuse of 'just trying to be funny' will no longer be effective or sufficient. These then may have been the processes that were triggered in our manipulation of the saliency of the intergroup context conditions in this experiment.

The fact that anti-English humour was reacted to more favourably when the source of the humour was English rather than Welsh in the salient intergroup context condition may, as Martineau (1972) suggested, be particularly pleasing to ingroup members since it may give them the impression that the outgroup is in a state of confusion or demoralization. For example, this type of humour could be perceived as a sign that the outgroup (English) may be aware that their higher status position is illegitimate and unfair or that the outgroup is ready to accept the ingroup's (Welshmen's) new definition of the intergroup hierarchy. This study has shown that the variables of source of ethnic humour and the social context of the intergroup humour situation, as they interact, deserve further empirical attention in other inter-ethnic group contexts.

In this study the nature of the hostile humour directed against the outgroup was of a general derogatory nature and could easily have been transformed to attack almost any social or ethnic group. This is not to say that all anti-group humour in times of increased intergroup tension (salient context) would be unfavourably perceived by the ingroup. It may be that such situations lead to a qualitative change in the nature of the hostile humour deemed to be most effective in such circumstances. Indeed, the ingroup may use more subtle humour to (a) attack dimensions of ethnic identity which are particularly salient and specific to the outgroup and/or (b) to highlight characteristics of the outgroup which are most vulnerable and sensitive to attack. And so anti-outgroup humour may have been very favourably rated by the ingroup if the Welsh speaker had told sensitive jokes about the English monarchy or a recent English 'disaster' after a rugby union match against a good Welsh side.

We have evidence then, that for a group redefining its ethnic identity in a more positive direction as are the Welsh, hostile anti-ingroup humour is not favourably evaluated under any condition. It may be that such anti-ingroup humour may be perceived as too threatening for the Welsh at a time when positive identity is still being redefined and re-negotiated within Wales itself.

In this experiment we also have some evidence to show that when the intergroup context is not salient, Welshmen react to anti-outgroup humour most favourably when the source is Welsh (rather than English). Using Tajfel's notions as an explanatory framework, one may consider such humour from the ingroup as a creative and potent way of asserting ingroup pride and distinctiveness from the dominant outgroup. In this way, anti-outgroup humour may function to provide the ingroup with more courage and determination to challenge the outgroup on other behavioural levels as well. Indeed, in intergroup situations where direct forms of action are not possible such as that described by Obrdlik (1942) in Czechoslovakia during the Nazi occupation, anti-outgroup humour by the subordinate group may be the only form of behaviour available to symbolize resistance, uplift morale and re-establish positive ingroup distinctiveness.

Further empirical studies may allow one to chart developmentally the types and purposes of humour ingroup-outgroup members direct at each other in situations of social change where the intergroup power structure is being redefined. One may also be able to assess or even predict the degree of tension and type of relationship existing between two groups by analyzing the type of humour they direct at each other. Surely more progress can be made in the understanding of the social role of ethnic humour if one also approaches the field from the standpoint of some more general theories of intergroup behaviour. Conversely ethnic humour appears to be an ideal tool for the study of some of the more subtle, pernicious and sensitive aspects of intergroup behaviour.

REFERENCES

See Bibliography for publications on humour, laughter and comedy

Bourhis, R.Y. & Giles, H., The language of cooperation in Wales: a field study. Language and Sciences, in press (1976).

Bourhis, R.Y., Giles, H. & Tajfel, H., Language as a determinant of Welsh identity. European Journal of Social Psychology, 3, 447–460 (1973).

Chapman, A.J., Smith, J.R. & Foot, H.C., Ethnic humour in children. Paper presented at the Annual Conference of the British Psychological Society, Social Psychology Section, York, September (1976).

Christian, J., Gadfield, N.J., Giles, H. & Taylor, D.N., The multidimensional and dynamic nature of ethnic identity. Mimeo: University of Bristol (1976).

Corrado, R., Welsh nationalism: an empirical evaluation. Ethnicity, in press (1976).

Doise, W. & Sinclair, A., The categorization process in intergroup relations. European Journal of Social Psychology, 3, 145–157 (1973).

Giles, H. & Bourhis, R.Y., Methodological issues in dialect perception: some social psychological perspectives. Anthropological Linguistics, in press (1977).

Giles, H. & Powesland, P.F., Speech Style and Social Evaluation. Academic Press, London (1975).

Lambert, W.E., The social psychology of bilingualism. Journal of Social Issues, 23, 91–109 (1967).

Lemaine, G., Social differentiation and social originality. European Journal of Social Psychology, 4, 17–52 (1974).

Tajfel, H., Quantitative judgment in social perception. British Journal of Psychology, 50, 16–29 (1959).

Tajfel, H., La categorization sociale. In: S. Moscovici (Ed.), Introduction à la psychologie sociale. Larousse, Paris (1972).

Tajfel, H., Social identity and intergroup behaviour. Social Sciences Information, 13, 65–93 (1974).

The Mass Media and the Functions of Ethnic Humour in a Racist Society

Charles Husband

School of Social Work, University of Leicester

The impetus behind this paper lies in an event some five years ago when I was attending a 'modestly select' conference on Race Relations in Britain. One of the participants included in his contribution a racial joke, directed at the number of Asians in Bradford, and was rebuked by another participant on the grounds that this element of his statement was more an example of the problem under discussion than a contribution to its solution. This brought down upon the critic a retaliatory broadside from many of the 'experts' there who cast doubts upon her intellect, and with paternalistic euphemism mourned the pettiness of her critique. Despite some emotive, but Jonah-like support which was treated with all the seriousness that the emergence of folie à deux apparently warranted, the consensus clearly ruled out of order any challenge to the benign or indeed cathartic function of racial humour.

In retrospect, I believe I was surprised at the perspective on the function of humour implicit in this consensus, but more than that I was shocked at the vehemence with which it was declaimed. Over the subsequent five years, on every occasion when I have spoken to groups on the topic of race relations in Britain, I have raised racial humour as an issue; and, in particular, I have discussed the likely impact of such television series as 'Till Death Us Do Part'. At conferences of academics, school teachers, college lecturers and more heterogeneous gatherings, I have found the dominant response to be entirely consistent with the consensus of that first conference. Though I did not afford them the opportunity to ratify my conclusion, it seemed that the majority of these more than twenty audiences would have endorsed Grotjahn's (1957) statement that:-

> Everything done with laughter helps us to be human. Laughter is a way of human communication which is essentially and exclusively human. It can be used to express an unending variety of emotions. It is based on guilt-free release of aggression and any release makes us perhaps a little better and more capable of understanding one another, ourselves and life. What is learned with laughter is learned well. Laughter gives freedom and freedom gives laughter. He who understands the comic begins to understand humanity and the struggle for freedom and happiness.

Yet Grotjahn, in following Freud's analysis of wit and humour in a naive and decontextualized way (cf. Moscovici, 1972; Tajfel, 1972) produces spurious support for the belief that humour is entirely benign: in his phrase, 'any release makes us perhaps a little better'. This is, however, a widely held assumption voiced in folk wisdom; for example, 'it's not so bad if you can laugh about it' or, 'if we can laugh together we can live together' - and in social science - for example,

> But we venture to assert that humour is probably an important variable in relation to prejudice.... The Judgment is impressionistic. Yet if the syndrome of the prejudiced personality is correctly defined in Chapter 25, we can easily believe that humour is a missing ingredient; also that it is a present ingredient in the syndrome of tolerance ... (G.W. Allport, 'The Nature of Prejudice', p409).

What I wish to suggest is that this assumption takes on a particular significance in Britain where it exists in symbiotic association with another widely held belief: namely that Britain is a tolerant society. The belief in Britain as a safe haven for refugees is lodged deep in the mythological interstices of the British educational system; and more visibly in popular consensus. Indeed, in May 1976, the Home Secretary invoked '... Britain's historic role as providing refuge for the poor and repressed ...' (Guardian, 25 May 1976) in an attempt to counter the fetid anti-Asian immigrant sentiments of Enoch Powell. Yet in doing so he joined a long and eminent line of British parliamentarians who have invoked our national tolerance whilst supporting discriminatory immigration policies. Indeed, our national concern for tolerant intergroup relations has not infrequently been used to justify

the restriction of immigrants on the grounds that they would endanger harmonious community
relations. A classic example occurred following the pogrom of 'Crystal Night' in 1938 in
Nazi Germany when the British government responded with plans to admit some 'selected' adults
and a limited number of children for training: prior to re-emigration to the colonies. This
parsimony was occasioned by the belief that to do more would lead to a 'definite anti-Jewish
movement in the country', (Krausz, 1971). Surely an ironic concern that even Jewish humour
would find hard to absorb.
The true nature of tolerance such as this is illustrated by King (1976) who succinctly points
out that:

> It remains that the fundamental question underlying all discussions of tolerance
> is really to do with the legitimacy of the advantage which tolerators may enjoy.
> If we look about us, wherever we are, we may readily perceive not merely unequal
> advantage, but unjustifiably unequal advantage. And if any form of promotion of
> tolerance is confounded with the promotion of avoidable inequity, then we are
> confronted with a calamity wrapped up in a mistake.

British tolerance in the 1960's and 1970's in passing discriminatory legislation against
Black immigration in order to sustain good community relations in Britain and the erection of
an effete and toothless Race Relations Board to guarantee racial equity, are classic examples
of the promotion of tolerance confounded by an unwillingness to challenge existing inequity,
or a desire to sustain it (cf. Dummett & Dummett, 1969; Foot, 1965; Humphry & Ward, 1974;
Husband, 1975a; Moore & Wallace, 1975).

An examination of the deed, rather than the word, regarding British tolerance, exposes the
truly mythical nature of this national conceit. But it must be remembered that it is the
myth which has consensual validation; and the ubiquity of the belief in British tolerance
allows for its symbiotic existence with the equally prevalent acceptance of humour as benign.
Thus, it seems probable that through this interaction ready acceptance of racial humour has
become 'a characteristic feature' of British 'tolerance': a highly stable and idealogical
entity.

This, of itself, would have a significant implication for an understanding of the functioning
of humour in Britain in its own right, but it becomes much more salient when we consider that
not only is British tolerance largely mythical; but that rather Britain is de facto a racist
society. Contained within its language and culture, Britain possesses a fundamental deposit
of racist assumptions, nuances and beliefs (cf. Dummett, 1973; Hartmann & Husband, 1974;
Husband, 1975b; Jordan, 1969: Searle, 1972; Walvin, 1971). Indeed, British Government
policy and popular discriminatory behaviour in wide areas of inter-racial contact re-affirm
through behavioural expression the racism of British society (cf. Bridges, 1975; Dummett &
Dummett, 1969; Humphry, 1972; Moore, 1975; Sivanandan, 1976; Smith, 1976).

It is against this background of Britain as a racist society in which the dominant White
population is still of the opinion that Britain is a White and tolerant society that we must
examine the function of racial humour; and for our particular purposes, television series
wherein racial humour plays a central part.

And it is the centrality of this 'definition of the situation' of Britain as a tolerant
society wherein racial humour is benign and legitimate that I wish to stress. Though I
shall be referring to the work of Vidmar and Rokeach, and of Surlin in identifying ethnocentrism and dogmatism as determinants of audience response to racial humour, I wish to argue
that a definition of the situation, in which ethnic humour is seen as benign and unquestionably
legitimate, is a superordinate construct determining both (a) the availability of such series,
and (b) the response even of those low in ethnocentrism and dogmatism.

This argument finds complementary support in the findings of Hartmann and Husband's (1974)
study of the role of the media in shaping the White response to Black immigration into
Britain. It was found that the emergence of a dominant and near ubiquitous definition of the
situation, of Britain as a liberal society with a critical immigration problem, served to
limit the significance of individual affective attitudes towards Black people. Through the
prevalence of this definition of the situation the behavioural range represented by 'tolerance'
and 'prejudice' was narrowed; so that even the 'tolerant' operated from within a perspective
where discriminatory behaviour was already legitimated and apparently inevitable. So too, the
ready acceptance of the benign function of humour within a 'tolerant' society blunts the
critical sensitivity of even the 'liberal' audience of racial humour. Thus studies of
intergroup humour where 'attitude' represents the level of independent variable employed may
well generate results which are partial, and which mask the alternative reality to be found
at a different level of analysis.

The success of 'Till Death Us Do Part' in 1966 set the scene for its re-appearance on an
infrequent basis over the next nine years. Perhaps more than anything else its success in

terms of audience size, 16 million in 1972 (BBC, 1975), guaranteed its future and laid the way for other derivative 'racial' series: such as 'Curry and Chips', wherein Spike Milligan played an obviously blacked-up Pakistani-Irishman; 'Love Thy Neighbour', which introduced verbal rivalry between a White man and wife, and their Black, West Indian neighbours: and 'It Ain't Half Hot Mum', where stereotyped images of 1940's India provided the background for a military situation comedy. With the possible exception of perhaps 'Love Thy Neighbour' there was a noticeable absence of the Black aggressively satirical comedy described by Arnez and Anthony (1968).

What was perhaps a crucial aspect of the commercial viability of 'Till Death Us Do Part', and surely a significant catalyst to the emergence of the derivative variants which followed it, was that from the outset the socialist, ex-working class author/script writer of the series, Johnny Speight, clearly stated the purpose of the series to be an attack upon prejudice — a view which was supported then, and has been sustained since, by the BBC who were the authority broadcasting the series. This legitimating ethos has been echoed in support of both the American and German variants of 'Till Death Us Do Part' by those responsible for their production.

Research data available on the American programme 'All in the Family' has consistently cast doubt upon this positive function of racial/racist humour in that series. Vidmar and Rokeach (1974) hypothesised that selective perception would be found in that prejudiced viewers would be favourably disposed toward Archie Bunker and his views; and that selective exposure would be demonstrated in that more ethnocentric individuals would be more likely to view the programme. Their data supported the first hypothesis, and provided partial support for the second. Surlin (1974), and Tate and Surlin (1975) have shown data consistent with Vidmar and Rokeach's first hypothesis in demonstrating a positive relationship between high dogmatism and agreement with Archie Bunker. In Germany, the educational function of Alf Tetzlaff's anti-semitic and anti-Social Democrat invective; he, for example, referred to Chancellor Willy Brandt as 'that slum kid from Lubeck', clearly boomeranged. In a WDR sample poll of viewers taken after the Tetzlaff programmes, which included references to Brandt's illegitimate birth and an attack on Rosa Luxemburg, 1679 viewers approved of the programme and 3 were critical. Wolfgang Menge, author of the Tetzlaff scripts said, 'In the first eight programmes we would never have dreamt that Alfred with his reactionary criticisms would get so much popular applause' (Terry, 1974).

Clearly, the therapeutic intent of authors and producers and their faith in the power of humour are not sufficient to guarantee the positive social consequence they intend. Perhaps had they been aware of the work of La Fave (1973) and others (e.g., La Fave, 1961; La Fave, 1972; La Fave, Haddad & Marshall, 1970; La Fave, McCarthy & Haddad, 1973; Priest, 1966; Priest & Abrahams, 1970) on the significance of identification classes in determining the response to humour they might have been more circumspect. As long ago as 1946, Burma concluded that racial humour '... definitely can be related to racial competition and conflict and the social and cultural patterns which have arisen from them'. As Vidmar and Rokeach (1974) and others had found in North America, what you find in such comedy series is a function of what you bring to them.

It is thus appropriate to look again at Britain in the late 1960's and early 1970's and note that this was a period of marked racial awareness and conflict. Increasingly over the period there has been real inter-ethnic competition for scarce resources in housing, employment and education (cf. Moore, 1975; Rex & Moore, 1967; Sivanandan, 1976). In keeping with his statement that politicians try 'to provide people with words and ideas which will fit their predicament better than the words and ideas which they are using at the moment' (Seymour-Ure, 1974), Enoch Powell, the poet laureate of the prejudiced, orchestrated the sentiments of the period in a manner which made very salient the White Briton's awareness of his ethnicity; and implicitly his Whiteness. As we have already noted above, Government policy and popular behaviour made apparent the existence of this intergroup conflict. It was in this context that 'Till Death Us Do Part', 'Curry and Chips', and 'Love Thy Neighbour' were broadcast. In 1975, the BBC Audience Research Department published a summary of research they had carried out on the audience response to the 'Till Death Us Do Part' series, which ran from 13 September to 25 October 1972. I am grateful to the BBC for letting me refer to the Report ('Till Death Us Do Part, As Anti-Prejudice Propaganda'. BBC, March, 1973) from which their Summary ('Reports on Some ad hoc Research Studies'. Annual Review of Audience Research, Vol. 1, 1975, pp26-35) was drawn. Having said that I shall be sufficiently ungrateful to discuss their Summary as an example of the inherent limitations of arguments derived from an implicit acceptance of British 'tolerance' and the positive power of humour.

When looking at the extent of agreement with Alf Garnett, the Summary states that:

C. Husband

As far as Alf is concerned, the greatest amount of support came for the statement 'Although his views are too extreme most of the time, some of the things he says are true'. Even half of the non-viewers gave Alf Garnett this qualified approval, whereas one half of the regular viewers of the series went further and claimed that he is 'Right more often than he's wrong'.

The relevant figures from the Report show in fact, just how great was the variation between 'regular viewers' and non-viewers.

TABLE 1   Audience Opinions of Alf Garnett

		Regular Viewers %	Occasional Viewers %	Non-Viewers %
'Although his views are too extreme most of the time, some of the things he says are true'	Agree	84	74	50
	Disagree	10	15	24
	No opinion	6	11	26
		100	100	100
'Right more often than he's wrong'	Agree	45	25	13
	Disagree	46	60	59
	No opinion	9	15	28
		100	100	100

Vidmar and Rokeach's selective exposure and perception were embarrassingly apparent in this audience. To qualify the possible implications of these data the Summary continued by saying:

However, the great majority of both groups apparently recognised him as something of a cipher, a harmless buffoon, agreeing with one or more of the three statements. 'So extreme as to be just a joke'. 'Unimportant and insignificant', or 'Misguided but harmless'.

Again the relevant data in the Report are interesting, since they indicate the weight to be given to the phrase 'the great majority of both groups' could only be justified by summing over all three statements.

TABLE 2   Audience Opinions of Alf Garnett

		Regular Viewers %	Occasional Viewers %	Non-Viewers %
'So extreme in his view that he's just a joke'	Agree	62	63	58
	Disagree	33	27	15
	No opinion	5	10	27
		100	100	100
'Unimportant and insignificant'	Agree	42	56	58
	Disagree	50	31	22
	No opinion	8	13	20
		100	100	100
'Misguided but harmless'	Agree	65	55	39
	Disagree	26	28	33
	No opinion	9	17	28
		100	100	100

The importance of this 'great majority' becomes apparent in the next paragraph of the Summary where it is argued that, 'it would seem undeniable that if a person regards Garnett as "harmless and unimportant", this must take precedence over the fact that he also believes him to be "right on occasions".' Certainly, this argument would appear to be consistent with

Surlin's (1974) hypothesis of congruence between liking of source and statement. However, I
have argued elsewhere (Husband, 1975a) that the learning potential of racial humour may lie
in the rehearsal of the assumption underlying the joke; and hence it may be possible to
regard Garnett in toto as extreme whilst still finding the humour funny. An interpretation
completely contrary to the BBC Summary can be developed; namely, that these data indicate a
classic instance where learning can take place in a situation where defences are down (cf.
Krugman, 1965). Since Garnett is a harmless buffoon then the audience need feel no
embarrassment. And, given the legitimacy of racial humour, they may suspend moral monitoring
and in this way they are able to reject the man and accept his views; but it is his views
which are the problem. Garnett is not talking in an attitudinal vacuum; his views are
consistent with a long cultural tradition of racism (cf. references above) and therefore they
exist in a cultural environment where they have at least 'illegitimate' consensual support.
Thus, if the programme is classed as entertainment, and harmless entertainment in particular,
then the viewer is able to rehearse these beliefs in a situation where they are freed from
moral sanction and need of validation (cf. Emerson, 1969).

'Till Death Us Do Part' was, after all, screened at a time when the White audience's positive
identification class as British was very salient. Thus, the racial humour of 'Till Death Us
Do Part' which was based very much on the inferiority and exclusion of Blacks was an opportunity
to rehearse those assumptions locked in our culture and then so currently salient to the
White population's concerns.

A re-analysis of the BBC Report from within the assumptive framework of Vidmar and Rokeach,
rather than that of Speight and the BBC, produces a powerful case for the deleterious potential
of the series based on selective exposure to it and selective perception of the programme
content.

The BBC Summary states that:

> The regular viewers of the series were, not surprisingly, much more 'pro' (Garnett)
> than were the non-viewers of the series;

and that:

> some of the large number who tended to regard Alf Garnett as 'on the whole
> reasonable most of the time' may, it seems, have had their prejudices confirmed;
> though the evidence suggests that very few of them went further and adopted his
> more extreme views.

The implication being that it is acceptable to merely reinforce existing prejudice.

It seems impossible that as a society we could contemplate such a notion, without the
submerging of our extensive racism beneath the myth of our national tolerance. Only by
denying the extent of prejudice can we sustain the belief in the cathartic, anti-prejudice
function of such racial humour: otherwise the realities of selective exposure and selective
perception are too pressing. In an ironic way the presence of such humour on national network
television may assist in sustaining the mythology of our national tolerance, since racial
jokes are 'characteristic of a tolerant society'.

Clearly, despite the espoused manifest function of such programmes as 'Till Death Us Do Part',
given the prior conditions in contemporary Britain the latent function is likely to be to
exacerbate racial feeling, not ease it.

REFERENCES

See Bibliography for publications on humour, laughter and comedy

Allport, G.W., The Nature of Prejudice. Anchor Books, Garden City, New York (1968).

Bridges, L., The Ministry of Internal Security: British Urban Social Policy 1968-74. Race
      and Class, 16, 375 (1975).

British Broadcasting Corporation, 'Till Death Us Do Part' As Anti-Prejudice Propaganda (1973).

British Broadcasting Corporation, 'Till Death Us Do Part' as anti-prejudice propaganda.
      Annual Review of Audience Research, Volume 1 (1975).

Dummett, A., A Portrait of English Racism. Penguin Books, Harmondsworth (1973).

Dummett, M. & Dummett, A., The Role of Government in Britain's Racial Crisis. In: L. Donnelly
      (Ed.), Justice First. Sheed & Ward, London (1969).

Foot, P., Immigration and Race in British Politics. Penguin Books, Harmondsworth (1965).

Hartmann, P. & Husband, C., Racism and the Mass Media. Davis-Poynter, London (1974).

Humphry, D., Police Power and Black People. Panther Books, London (1972).

Humphry , D. & Ward, M., Passports and Politics. Penguin Books, Harmondsworth (1974).

Husband, C., Racism in Society and the Mass Media: A Critical Interaction. In: C. Husband
     (Ed.), White Media and Black Britain. Arrow Books, London (1975a).

Husband, C., (Ed.), White Media and Black Britain. Arrow Books, London (1975b).

Jordan, W.D., White Over Black. Penguin Books, Harmonsworth (1969).

King, P., Toleration. George Allen and Unwin Ltd., London (1976).

Krausz, E., Ethnic Minorities in Britain. MacGibbon and Kee, London (1971).

Krugman, H.E., The impact of television advertising: learning without involvement. Public
     Opinion Quarterly, 29, 349 (1965).

Moore, R., Racism and Black Resistance in Britain. Pluto Press, London (1975).

Moore, R. & Wallace, T., Immigration Control. Martin Robertson, London (1975).

Moscovici, S., Society and Theory in Social Psychology. In: J. Israel & H. Tajfel (Eds.),
     The Context of Social Psychology. Academic Press, London (1972).

Rex, J. & Moore, R., Race, Community and Conflict. O.U.P./I.R.R., London (1967).

Searle, C., The Forsaken Lover. Penguin Books, Harmondsworth (1973).

Seymour-Ure, C., The Political Impact of the Mass Media. Constable, London (1974).

Smith, D.J., The Facts of Racial Disadvantage. P.E.P., London (1976).

Sivanandan, A., Race, class and the state: the Black experience in Britain. Race and Class,
     17, 347 (1976).

Surlin, S.H., Bigotry on air and in life: The Archie Bunker Case. Public Telecommunications
     Review, 2, 34 (1974).

Tajfel, H., Experiments in a vacuum. In: J. Israel & H. Tajfel (Eds.), The Context of Social
     Psychology. Academic Press, London (1972).

Tate, E.D. & Surlin, S.H., Agreement with Opinionated Television Characters. Paper given to
     International Communication Association, Intercultural Communications Division,
     Chicago, Illinois, April (1975).

Terry, A., Personal communication.

Vidmar, N. & Rokeach, M., Archie Bunker's bigotry: A study in selective perception and
     exposure. The Journal of Communication, 24, 36 (1974).

Walvin, J., The Black Presence. Orbach and Chambers, London (1971).

Vicarious Superiority, Injustice, and Aggression in Humour: The Role of the Playful 'Judgmental Set'

Roger C. Mannell

Acadia University, Canada

Complex social conventions have evolved in many cultures to regulate the actual expression and enjoyment of various forms of violence and interpersonal aggression. Since it appears necessary to the stability and well-being of a social system to regulate the violent and aggressive actions of its members, these phenomena have received considerable attention from social scientists (see Scherer, Abeles, and Fischer, 1975). It is generally assumed that the members of most Western cultures acquire, through the socialization process, inhibitions and negative attitudes toward both the expression and enjoyment of interpersonal aggression.

How is the enjoyment of aggression and injustice as frequently depicted symbolically in art, literature, and of particular interest here, in humour affected by these attitudes? Research which has begun to examine the question has typically used 'squelch' humour in which the humour communication can be viewed as a mini-drama in which several characters, often members of ethnic groups, act out and exchange verbal and physical aggression. Vicarious superiority research has been successful in predicting humour appreciation when the theme 'interpersonal aggression' is depicted in the humour communication where the observer positively or negatively identifies with the protagonists (La Fave, 1972; La Fave, Haddad & Maesen, 1976). Emphasis has been on 'who aggresses toward whom,' with the view that the aggression depicted is symbolic of the victory or superiority attained by one protagonist over another. Several recent models (Gutman & Priest, 1969; Zillmann & Bryant, 1974), concerned with an observer's attitudes toward social injustice and aggression as they affect humour appreciation, assume that an observer's notions of social justice and inhibitions regarding aggression will mediate his humour appreciation as if the aggression and injustice depicted in the fantasy of the humour was perceived as an actual event and taken seriously.

Despite experimental support for these models, certain unique qualities of humour and other forms of fantasy would be missed if the above was assumed always to be the case. Cartoons and 'jokes' are found highly amusing and enjoyable by many persons, even when depicting situations or events which would normally disgust, sadden, or outrage. While writers (cf. Flugel, 1954; Keith-Spiegal, 1972) have viewed the humour experience as dependent on the observer adopting a 'frame of mind' such that the humorous communication is interpreted as fantasy, unreal, nonserious, or play, no systematic attempt has been made to define these 'mental sets,' their role in the humour experience and the conditions in which they operate.

While McGhee (1974c) has argued that the interpretation of an event as fantasy (not really occurring) will lead observers to find greater aggression and injustice increasingly amusing, the present author (Mannell & La Fave, 1976) has argued that the interpretation of a communication as fantasy is not a sufficient condition to guarantee that an observer's internalized attitudes toward aggression and injustice will not act to reduce his humour appreciation. The observer may approach something he defines as fantasy with one of two mental sets. The term 'serious judgmental set' will be used to refer to those instances when an observer's attitudes toward interpersonal aggression and its justification are 'active' or perceived 'relevant' and used as a 'standard of comparison' for acceptable behaviour. 'Playful judgmental set' will refer to a temporary 'suspension' of the observer's attitudes, concerning depicted behaviours normally defined as socially unacceptable or unjust, as a 'standard of comparison.'

We interpret a theatre play as fantasy yet we may react to the injustice, violence and interpersonal aggression exhibited by the characters either as extremely amusing (playful judgmental set) or extremely saddening (serious judgmental set). A typical reaction to a Picasso painting depicting the mutilation of quasi-human figures, while defined as fantasy, is not one of amusement but horror or sadness. Why, then, do we find amusing certain cartoons showing equally exaggerated depictions of human figures undergoing disfigurement (e.g., the disembodiment of characters in children's animated cartoons)? This question can be answered by asking what conditions determine whether a serious versus playful judgmental set is adopted.

Humorous communications (cartoons) were developed and always defined for the subjects as fantasy and the subjects' perceptions of these materials as serious or playful were manipulated. It was predicted that a playful judgmental set would negate the tendency for unjustified aggression to reduce amusement ratings, while a serious set would tend to produce amusement ratings consistent with the predictions made by the Gutman and Priest (1969) or Zillmann and Bryant (1974) models. Not only could the conflicting predictions of these models be tested but their lack of predictability in cases where subjects were not encouraged to respond to the humour seriously could be demonstrated. To test the central hypothesis that the observer's judgmental set will influence his judgments of a humour communication, two sets of factors, one internal and one external to the humour communication were examined (cartoon fidelity, art and literature evaluation task).

METHOD

Degree of aggressive retaliation was manipulated by developing cartoons which depicted two characters, a victor (delivers a punchline plus performs one of three degrees of physical aggression toward a second character, the victim) and a victim (the butt of the punchline and recipient of one of the degrees of aggression). The victor's punchline was the same and the initial behaviour of the victim appeared equally obnoxious and deserving of retaliation in all versions. The severity of the retaliatory physical damage done to the victim by the victor was varied in the last panel of each of the three cartoons developed. The three degrees of retaliation were: (1) 'under' (victor does not go far enough to get even), (2) 'fair' (victor returned the same aggressive behaviour and did an equivalent amount of damage as the victim), and (3) 'over' (victor goes too far and is more aggressive than victim and creates more physical damage).

Cartoon fidelity was manipulated by developing two versions of each retaliation version of each cartoon. The protagonists were depicted as either human (high fidelity) or as animals acting like humans (low fidelity). Also the damage done to the victim was as severe in both high and low fidelity versions but in former case it was portrayed more 'realistically' (blood where suitable, actual bodily reactions to aggression), whereas with the low fidelity versions the damage was portrayed in a bloodless manner and in ways in which human or animal body tissue could not react (body parts shattering like glass). The cartoons went through a series, of pre-tests to ensure the required manipulations were achieved.

Two sets of literature and art items were chosen depicting hostile or benign themes. Three thematically hostile literary passages and five pictorial art items described humans in conflict, causing each other damage. The benign literary passages and pictorial art items were selected to be devoid of human conflict and suffering. Subjects judged all items on Likert and semantic differential scales as well as rating the cartoons for amusement on nine-point scales.

One hundred and eighty Acadia University undergraduates served as subjects. The materials were administered to the subjects in groups ranging from twelve to thirty-two in number. The materials for all experimental treatments were administered in each session and the experimenter was unaware of which materials a subject received. Subjects were led to believe they were volunteering to participate in a study of aesthetics. They were told that they would be judging several types of art which included literary passages, pictorial art, and cartoon-humour. Subjects were assured that no special training in art was required and that their judgments were anonymous. Subjects received the materials in booklet form.

Degree of retaliation (under, fair, over) and three combinations of benign or hostile art and literary items and low or high fidelity cartoons were the independent variables.

The second independent variable involved three of four possible combinations of art and literature items and cartoon fidelity used to create playful (benign art and literature-low fidelity cartoons) and serious (hostile art and literature-low fidelity cartoons; benign art and literature-high fidelity cartoons) judgmental sets. The three combinations allowed the role of cartoon fidelity and the art and literature evaluation task in creating a serious judgmental set to be examined. Each subject saw only three of nine cartoon-retaliation version combinations (three cartoons X three levels of retaliation) and all were either low or high fidelity. A latin square design was utilized (Winer, 1971, Plan 9).

RESULTS AND CONCLUSIONS

The usefulness of the playful versus serious judgmental set distinction was strongly supported. Two techniques were used to lead subjects to adopt a serious set - the judgment of hostile art and literature items and high fidelity cartoons. Subjects rating low fidelity cartoons and who were exposed to hostile art and literature items judged under (4.45) and fair (3.75) versions marginally significantly different (p < .056) and fair and over retaliation significantly different in amusement (p < .05). This decrease in amusement from under to over retaliation versions was not found among subjects who were exposed to benign art and literature items. For subjects exposed to the benign art and literature items and low fidelity cartoons the slight but insignificant (p > .05) increase in amusement from under (4.25), fair (4.3) to over (4.5) retaliation supports the hypothesis that subjects adopting a playful judgmental set would not judge less amusing those cartoons depicting greater injustice and interpersonal aggression as would be found for subjects adopting a serious judgmental set.

The second technique used to create a serious set was suggested by the frequent use of the 'cartoon technique' by comic strip cartoonists and producers of animated children's cartoons. A quote from Walt Disney (Flugel, 1954) regarding the ability of 'cruel' and 'sadistic' happenings to evoke laughter when made 'tolerable by the cartoon technique' summarizes the essential idea behind the manipulation.

The subjects exposed to benign art and literature items but high fidelity cartoons judged over (3.35) significantly less amusing (p < .01) than fair (4.52), while under retaliation (4.53) was not judged significantly less amusing than fair (p > .05). The expectation that increasing the 'humanness' of the cartoon characters and the 'realism' of the damage inflicted on the victim would activate the observer's negative attitudes toward aggression and injustice and consequently reduce humour appreciation of those versions was not completely supported. It is unlikely that increasing the humanness of the characters did lead the subjects to take the cartoons seriously, since high character realism was common to the under, fair, and over high fidelity versions. Only the high fidelity depiction of the extreme aggression and damage to the victim in the over retaliation version appears to have accomplished the playful to serious judgmental set switch.

The different aggressive actions and injustices played out in the drama of the cartoons did not differentially effect humour appreciation when subjects were not switched into a serious judgmental set. This finding is clearly in contradiction of the Gutman and Priest (1969) and Zillmann and Bryant (1974) predictions. Therefore there is support for the notion that humour researchers by structuring the experimental situation, forcing subjects to adopt a serious judgmental set, have purposely or inadvertently eliminated the playful element in the appreciation of humour. Eastman's (1936) suggestion that a 'playatory' rather than a laboratory is needed for the experimental study of humour would seem to be a valuable one.

Several recent models offer predictions concerning the relationship between the degree of aggression and injustice depicted and humour appreciation. Zillmann and Bryant predict a curvilinear relationship between humour appreciation and degree of injustice with under and over less amusing than fair retaliation while arguing that Gutman and Priest predict a linear decrease in humour appreciation from under to over retaliation. Since amusement decreased from under to over retaliation when subjects adopted a serious set the Gutman and Priest prediction is supported while the Zillmann and Bryant hypothesis is not. Coupled with the technical criticisms made by La Fave, Haddad and Maesen (1976) which suggest that support for the retaliatory equity model may be due to experimental artifacts resulting from the nature of the technique used to manipulate the degrees of retaliatory equity, there is evidence to question the model's usefulness in humour theory.

While two types of cues were utilized to activate a serious judgmental set in the present experiment, many conditions may cause our attitudes toward aggression and injustice to intrude into the playful contemplation of humour. Socialization into one's culture through the family, educational system, popular literature, cinema etcetera, alert us that certain symbolic, fantasy forms are to be taken seriously, being intended to engage our notions of justice and morality in an attempt to explore the 'human condition.'

While certain forms of humour may require for their full appreciation the 'activation' of negative attitudes toward social injustice (for example, satire), the success of a great deal of humour clearly requires the suspension of these attitudes. Through social learning individuals may come automatically to adopt a playful judgmental set when they encounter a communication which is judged a 'joke' or cartoon.

REFERENCES

See Bibliography for publications on humour, laughter and comedy

Scherer, K.R., Abeles, R.P. & Fischer, C.S., Human Aggression and Conflict. Prentice-Hall, Englewood Cliffs, New Jersey (1975).

Winer, B.J., Statistical Principles in Experimental Design (2nd Edition). McGraw, New York (1971).

Ethnic Humour is No Joke

Hwenje Mutuma, Lawrence La Fave,
Roger Mannell and Ann Marie Guilmette

University of Windsor, Canada

The almost complete lack of systematic crosscultural research on incongruity humour is surprising in the light of the persistent fascination with incongruity humour by educated men over the centuries. The Gestalt psychologists emphasize that certain structures, particular relations between elements of a perceived pattern, can prove disharmonious or disturbing. Gestalt psychology thereby provides a theoretical base for incongruity humour theory — that man imposes structure upon an unstructured situation such that sense or meaningfulness is perceived in the nonsensical or incongruous. The achievement of such closure appears, under appropriate circumstances, to be a pleasant, amusing mental experience.

A number of earlier incongruity theories had been posited, going back at least to Aristotle. Gerard (1759) described the objects of humour as uncommon mixtures of relations and the contrariety in things. Beattie (1776) held that laughter emanated as a consequence of two or more inconsistent or unsuitable circumstances put together in a united complex. A noted incongruity humour theorist, Kant (1790), described laughter as 'an affection arising from the sudden transformation of a strained expectation into nothing'. For Spencer (1860), laughter resulted when 'the conscious is unawares transferred from great things to small — only when there is a descending incongruity'. According to Spencer then, not all incongruities cause laughter — only incongruities descending, in a sense, from the sublime to the ridiculous. Bergson (1911) saw humour as a result of 'something mechanical encrusted on the living'. He elaborated that a situation is invariably comic when it belongs simultaneously to two altogether independent series of events and is capable of being interpreted in two entirely different meanings simultaneously.

Among more recent and research-oriented writers, Bryne (1961) defines incongruity as 'a state of contradiction, disharmony or inconsistency'. Shultz (1972) demonstrated experimentally that an appreciation of cartoon humour is determined by an ability to notice an incongruity in the cartoon and then resolve or explain the incongruity. Suls' (1972) model is similar to that of Shultz. He argues that two major operations occur in the cognitive processing of verbal jokes — comprehension and appreciation. McGhee (1972b) and Berlyne (1972) also seem to regard the quintessentials as involving resolution of a perceived incongruity. Other relevant incongruity humour researchers include Nerhardt (1970) and Rothbart (1973) — who treat expectancy violation as central to the humour experience. Zijderveld (1968), concentrating on the social functions of humour, suggests that jokes belonging to one particular institution could very well prove nonjokes in another social institution endorsing some other culture.

The present experiment finds its theoretical base by combining such views as Nerhardt's and Zijderveld's and Rothbart's. Multidimensional anticonformity to value social norms is hypothesized, under appropriate circumstances, to become amusing. Thus, our theoretical base involves the cultural relativity of humour; whatever amuses in one society may not in another. For instance, what might be humorous in American and Canadian societies may not in African or Chinese, and conversely. 'One man's joke is another man's insult'. It is our thesis that jokes, defined in the conventional way as humorous stimuli, hold no points or inherent incongruities which transcend cultural boundaries.

The Tchambuli tribe, according to Mead (1950), would seem to help clarify the point. She found that in Tchambuli society women are more aggressive than men. In our society, on the contrary, it was expected (at least until recently) that men ought to be more aggressive and dominate women. Thus a 'joke' whose point is based on the culturally-relative incongruity of women dominating men could have been incongruously amusing in our society but not among the Tchambuli, we would postdict.

Nerhardt (1970) and Deckers and Kizer (1974) also seem indirectly to provide evidence (in their experiments which measure discrepancy of weights from an expected range established by a series of weights previously lifted) for the cultural relativity of humour. Their results indicate that the most laughter and presumably humour is generated by the most discrepant weights. However, neither these authors nor anyone else conceives of the weights which generated amusement as jokes. These experiments then appear to provide evidence for the cultural relativity of incongruity; one's background of weight lifting and other past experiences will typically be culturally relative.

The view that an incongruity (violation of expectancy – whether of the physical environment or social) must be nonthreatening and nonserious for a humorous mental experience is the central issue in our model. This model suggests that the so-called 'joke' does not have absolute stimulating value, but may be culturally relative – stressing that, in the case of 'social normative' violations of expectations, what is a violation of social convention for one culture, ethnic, or social group may be nonanticonformity to the norms of yet a different group. Incongruity has typically been defined as a violation of expectancies. The present paper then is centrally concerned with the cultural relativity of those expectancies called social norms. This paper also hopes to help clarify the conditions under which anticonforming behaviour may be not only judged incongruous but also amusing.

Three hypotheses were tested: (1) the subject will more often judge a picture-story amusing when it violates at least three value social norms of the culture he prefers than when the picture-story nonanticonforms to all his value social norms; (2) and (3) these are the same as Hypothesis 1, mutatis mutandis. Hypothesis 2 substitutes 'a joke' for 'amusing' and Hypothesis 3 substitutes 'strange' for 'amusing'.

METHOD

The subjects were drawn from two populations. One sample of forty-four subjects consisted of Caucasian Canadian Senior Citizens living in Windsor, Ontario quite ignorant of Black African culture and who preferred Canadian culture. The other sample of forty-four subjects consisted of Black African university or college students also living in Windsor and believed to prefer Black African culture. A post-judgmental questionnaire was used to insure that Black African subjects prefer Black African culture and Caucasian Canadians prefer Canadian.

Subjects were tested anonymously. To help insure subjects that they were really being tested anonymously, five or more (from the same population) were tested at a time. The stimulus materials for any subject consisted of a booklet containing three sets of the same ten picture-story items. Any set of ten items was dichotomized into two permutations of five items each: that is, there were five picture-stories each nonanticonforming in all respects to Black African value norms and each anticonforming to Canadian norms in at least three dimensions. The other permutation consisted of five picture-stories nonanticonforming to all Canadian value norms, and each such item was social-normatively incongruous with respect to at least three Black African value norms. In addition to the two-valued organismic independent variable of 'population', and the two-valued stimulus repeated-measures independent variable of 'permutation', a third two-valued independent variable was also employed, which was a stimulus variable.

Subjects were randomly assigned to one of two treatments. One treatment consisted of only picture-stories in which the protagonists were Black Africans in a Black African setting. The other treatment booklet contained solely picture-stories with Caucasians in a Canadian setting. Thus a 2 x 2 x 2 factorial design was employed with repeated measures on one factor.

Why were at least three dimensions of incongruity needed in the present experiment when Nerhardt (1970) and Deckers and Kizer (1974) needed only one? Apparently because their weights only violated nonthreatening belief norms while our experiment violated ego-involving value (that is, attitude) social norms. (The distinction between two types of social normative expectancies used here is from La Fave, Haddad and Maesen, 1976). Violations of three or more value social norms should often prove so ridiculous to the subject that he cannot decode the communication literally and thus finds the story an amusing joke rather than a real threat. The reason for amusement at anticonformance to the subject's own ethical values is because the multidimensionality of the incongruity has belief-switched that subject in a serious-to-playful transformation.

Each subject was tested by an experimenter who is a member of that subject's own race and had been socialized into that subject's culture. Such a procedure seems preferable to that of systematically varying experimenters across the two subject populations; this latter technique would apparently more probably damage rapport and invalidate results when the experimenter were of the opposite race to the subject.

Each subject received a large envelope with his first set of instructions pasted on the outside. Within each of the large envelopes were four smaller envelopes. The first of these four contained an amusement instruction-scoring sheet with directions and a set of ten picture-stories. This set of ten such items was randomly numbered with each subject receiving the set in a different random order. The second smaller envelope within the larger one consisted of a joke instruction-scoring sheet with instructions and the identical set of ten picture-stories, albeit in a different random order. The third smaller envelope consisted of a strange instruction-scoring sheet with instructions and again the identical set of ten picture-stories, yet in still a different random order. All three sets of picture-stories in one large treatment envelope consisted of Black African protagonists in a Black African cultural setting. All three sets of items in the other large treatment envelope consisted of only Caucasians in a Canadian cultural setting. Thus this race-setting two-valued treatment variable is the only basic difference between the materials in the two sets of treatment envelopes. (However, no hypotheses are based in the present study on this treatment independent variable). The fourth smaller envelope within a given larger envelope consisted merely of a brief questionnaire requesting which culture he preferred, how long he lived in that society, his age, sex, and educational level.

The instructions to subjects are those given, in the order indicated above, on the four instruction sheets and questionnaire. The experimenter read the instructions on top of the large envelope aloud to the subjects, and instructed them thereby on how to proceed with the four smaller envelopes they would find inside. With respect to the three dependent measures employed (that is, amusement, joke, and strange) subjects were instructed to rate both amusement and strangeness for each picture-story on a five-point scale which ranged from 'very amusing' to 'not at all amusing' or from 'very strange' to 'not at all strange'. On the joke measurement the subjects were to check either of two boxes provided on the answer sheet as to whether they thought each picture-story was a joke or nonjoke.

RESULTS

The first hypothesis was tested employing a sign-test as follows: a given item for a given hypothesis was predicted by the formula: $(A - \bar{A}) > (a - \bar{a})$ where "A" is the proportion of subjects who reported that story either very amusing or amusing and whose value norms were multidimensionally anticonformed to in that picture-story. "a" is the proportion of subjects who reported that story either very amusing or amusing and whose value norms were all nonanticonformed to in that same story. "$\bar{A}$" is the mean proportion of subjects either reporting themselves very amused or amused across the ten picture-stories from the sample whose value norms were multidimensionally anticonformed to in that same picture-story. "$\bar{a}$" is the mean proportion of subjects either reporting themselves very amused or amused across the ten picture-stories from the sample whose value norms were all nonanticonformed to on that same picture-story.

The other two hypotheses were also tested in exactly the same way as Hypothesis 1 — with the following changes: substitute 'joke' for wherever 'very amusing' or 'amusing' occurs above for Hypothesis 2. For Hypothesis 3 substitute 'very strange' or 'strange' for wherever 'very amusing' or 'amusing' occurs above.

The probability of each picture story being predicted correctly for a given dependent measure is one-half. The probability of all ten such stories being predicted correctly for a given hypothesis is one-half to the power nine (one degree of freedom, 10 - 1 = 9, having been lost through the use of means). All ten items were predicted in the correct direction by the formula presented above on all three dependent variables. Hence each hypothesis is significant at $p < .002$.

CONCLUSION

Since all three hypotheses were strongly substantiated, the cultural relativity of multi-dimensional social normative value incongruity humour seems evident. Experiments now in progress hope to establish whether fewer than three dimensions of value normative anticonformity suffice to generate incongruity humour, and whether the minimum number of required dimensions anticonformed to depends upon if the norms violated represent ego-involving values or non-ego-involving beliefs.

H. Mutuma, L. La Fave, R. Mannell & A. M. Guilmette

REFERENCES

See Bibliography for publications on humour, laughter and comedy

Gerard, A., An Essay On Taste. Anchor, London (1759).

Kant, I., Kritik der Urteilskraft. Lagarde, Berlin (1790).

Mead, M., Sex and Temperament In Three Primitive Societies. Mentor Books, New York (1950).

Ethnic Humour as a Function of Social-Normative Incongruity and Ego-Involvement

Naresh Issar, Sarah Yee Wah Tsang, Lawrence La Fave,
Ann Guilmette and Khetar Issar

University of Windsor, Canada

The experiment by Mutuma, La Fave, Mannell and Guilmette (this volume) suggests that tridimensional social-normative anticonformity is sufficient to generate substantial amusement. However, that experiment could not also tell us whether three dimensions were necessary. Perhaps only unidimensional anticonformity was needed to generate amusement. After all, Nerhardt (1970) and Deckers and Kizer (1974, 1975) apparently found unidimensional anticonformity to a norm established by the experimenter could generate a significant amount of amusement. However, Mutuma et al thought they needed three anticonformity dimensions to generate significant amusement because otherwise subjects would be threatened and feel hostile, rather than amused. Yet with three dimensions, it was reasoned with the help of Rothbart's (1973) theory, that the subjects would transform from a serious to playful mood and no longer be threatened and thus become capable of amusement. Our reasoning was that neither Nerhardt nor Deckers and Kizer needed more than one dimension of anticonformity to generate amusement because they were dealing with nonthreatening beliefs rather than threatening attitudes. Therefore, their subjects would not be ego-involved (that is, threatened).

If such reasoning is correct, then anticonformity to unidimensional belief social norms should be amusing while unidimensional anticonformity to attitude social norms should not. However, such a prediction would only hold for those beliefs which are non-ego-involving and those attitudes which are ego-involving. Although non-ego-involving attitudes and ego-involving beliefs also exist, we reasoned that, as a rule, attitudes are more ego-involving than are beliefs. In this sense the central two-valued independent variable considered here is whether or not ego-involvement is present, rather than whether the item unidimensionally anticonforms to an attitude or belief per se.

The distinction between an 'attitude' and a 'belief social norm' involves essentially the difference between what is felt ought to be the case and what is the case. For instance, suppose a cow is being permitted to eat potato chips in a grocery store. If Canadian society feels that allowing the cow to do so is immoral while East Indians do not agree that permitting such behaviour is unethical, then such an item unidimensionally anticonforms to a Canadian attitude social norm but nonanticonforms to an East Indian attitude social norm. However, should such behaviour by a cow be considered improbable by Canadian society but not improbable by East Indian society, then the cow's action unidimensionally anticonforms to a Canadian belief social norm but unidimensionally nonanticonforms to an East Indian belief social norm.

The present experiment involves a 3 x 2 x 2 factorial design with repeated measures on the last two factors. Sixty-two subjects were selected from three populations: (1) twenty Caucasian Canadian high school students from the rural area of Kingsville, Ontario, Canada; (2) twenty-three East Indians tested in English; and (3) nineteen East Indians tested in Hindi. (Both sets of East Indians were tested in New Delhi, India). The second and third independent variables are two-valued repeated-measures. One variable is permutation. In one permutation of eight items, each item always anticonforms to an unidimensional East Indian social norm while nonanticonforming to a unidimensional Canadian social norm. The other permutation anticonforms to an unidimensional Canadian social norm while nonanticonforming to a unidimensional East Indian social norm. The remaining independent variable concerns whether or not threatening ego-involvement is present. Eight of the sixteen items each unidimensionally anticonform to one culture's attitude social norm but not to the other culture's, while the remaining eight items each unidimensionally anticonform to one culture's belief social norm but not to the other culture's. Thus the set of sixteen items was partitioned into four types of items consisting of four items each.

Three dependent measures were used - judgements of (1) amusement, (2) hostility, and (3) surprisingness. Each hypothesis was tested three times: by comparing the Caucasian

Canadians with (1) the East Indians in the English language treatment, with (2) the East Indians in the Hindi language treatment, and with (3) the two sets of Indians combined.

Each of the three hypotheses predicts a three-way interaction. Hypothesis 1 predicts that anticonformity to a nonthreatening unidimensional belief social norm would be more amusing than anticonformity to a threatening unidimensional attitude social norm or nonanticonformity to either attitude or belief social norms. Hypothesis 1 was only tentatively substantiated on the Indian Hindi-Canadian comparison as only eleven 1/2 items were predicted correctly and four 1/2 incorrectly (p < .10). However, more relevant is the Indian English-Canadian comparison (since no language translation problems are involved). On that comparison fifteen items were predicted correctly (p < .0005). The third test combining the two sets of Indians found thirteen items predicted correctly (p < .02). From these three tests (especially the one that involves no confounding with translation problems) we conclude that Hypothesis 1 is clearly substantiated.

Hypothesis 2 is much like Hypothesis 1 except 'surprising' judgments are substituted for 'amusing' judgments. Hypothesis 2 in effect predicts that items which unidimensionally anticonform to belief social norms are the most surprising. This hypothesis was strongly substantiated for all three tests.

Hypothesis 3 predicts in effect that, of the four types of items, only those which unidimensionally anticonform to attitude social norms generate above average hostility judgments. Hypothesis 3 was substantiated at p < .02 on each of the three tests (thirteen items scoring in the predicted direction on each test).

Notice that these hypotheses suggest a negative correlation between amusement and hostility judgments for non-ego-involved unidimensional anticonformity, but a positive correlation between these two dependent measures for nonanticonformity. Such predictable reversals of the signs of the correlations between amusement and hostility are analogous to those found by La Fave, Mannell and Guilmette (this volume). The analogy is especially appropriate since an extreme insult in their 'irony of irony' experiment is typically equivalent to anticonformity.

A subsequent experiment involving Chinese subjects (Tsang et al, in preparation) seeks to determine the necessary number of dimensions of attitude social-normative anticonformity to generate amusement by rendering a serious-to-playful judgmental set transformation. We hope by distinguishing between deep and surface semantics à la Noam Chomsky to untangle the technical problems involved there, and to find that tridimensional attitude social-normative anticonformity is judged both more amusing and more playful than either zero, one, or two dimensional attitude social-normative anticonformity, and perhaps in better taste. In this respect we hope eventually to establish both the necessary and sufficient number of dimensions for social-normative incongruity as it relates to ethnic humour.

REFERENCES

See Bibliography for publications on humour, laughter and comedy

An Irony of Irony: The Left-Handed Insult in Intragroup Humour

Lawrence La Fave, Roger Mannell, and Ann Marie Guilmette

University of Windsor, Canada

La Fave and colleagues (La Fave, 1971, 1972; La Fave, Haddad & Maesen, 1976) have suggested that one of the reasons for the illusion that some men hold a sense of humour (in the sense of ability to be amused at one's own expense) involves an extreme insult. The irony of irony is that this extreme insult is judged less insulting than a mild insult.

If experimental evidence could be provided for such an irony of irony, we would seem to have a major connecting link between several types of humour theories - superiority, incongruity, Eastman's (1936) playful pain theory, and others. In addition, negative evidence would thereby be provided concerning the comprehensiveness of certain superiority humour theories (e.g., Hobbes, 1651, 1968; Wolff, Smith & Murray, 1934; Zillmann & Cantor, 1976) and the related retaliatory equity theory of Zillmann and Bryant (1974).

We have tried to develop a vicarious superiority humour theory with an extension cord extending from it which plugs into incongruity humour theory. Our most general statement of this vicarious superiority humour theory (La Fave et al, 1976, p66) is as an epistemic proposition with reference to key terms. For instance, what matters in our theory is not whether a given item objectively is a joke but whether the judge believes it to be a joke; not whether a protagonist is really insulted but whether the judge believes the protagonist to be insulted, etcetera. Thus our theory can accommodate such ironies of irony as pseudo insults and pseudo compliments, thereby permitting the serious-playful distinction discussed by Mannell and La Fave (1976).

The extension cord into incongruity humour theory referred to above is not into objective incongruity but into subjective (i.e., epistemic) incongruity. Thus an irony is incongruous for us only if the irony is believed (or perceived). Of course, beliefs can be mistaken in either of the two ways corresponding to the two types of errors in hypothesis testing. For instance, one can believe an incongruous irony was intended when it was not or one can believe it was not intended when it was. Also an extreme pseudo insult usually literally anticonforms to a social norm. Hence, in the experiment to be discussed, extreme insults often function in ways similar to social normative perceived incongruity.

Three two-valued independent variables and three dependent variables were employed in the present pilot experiment. The three independent variables concerned: (1) whether the insult was extreme or mild; (2) whether the insult was realistic or unrealistic; and (3) whether the insulter and insultee were friends or enemies. The three dependent variables involved: (1) insulting; (2) kidding (i.e., playful); and (3) amusing judgments.

Hypothesis 1 predicts that the subjects who receive the treatment in which the 'victim' in the story is extremely insulted in the unrealistic, friendly condition will judge the victim to feel less insulted than will the subjects who receive the treatment in which the victim in the story is mildly insulted in the realistic, enemy condition.

But why should such an irony of irony occur? Hypothesis 2 helps provide a theoretical explanation for Hypothesis 1: Hypothesis 2 predicts that the reason the extreme insult under the unrealistic, friendly condition will ironically be judged the lesser insulting is because the subjects will judge the 'insulter' delivered a pseudo insult (i.e., was not serious or was kidding or in a playful mood). Therefore the insult cannot be taken literally and, perhaps, was even a compliment in disguise - indicating the insulter's assumption that the 'insultee' was a good sport who could 'take a joke'.

But what then has all this to do with humour theory? An answer is provided by Hypothesis 3: The unrealistic, extreme insult by a friend condition will be more amusing to the subjects than the realistic, mild insult by an enemy.

What patterns would be expected for each subject on each item? The disjunction of two patterns should occur with greater than chance probability. In other words, the disjunction of the remaining six logically-possible three-tuple patterns will occur with below-chance probability. These two patterns are: (1) amusing, noninsulting, and kidding; and (2) unamusing, insulting and not kidding (i.e., serious). Hypothesis 4 thus in effect predicts a significant nonparametric multiple correlation between the three dependent measures.

The present pilot experiment employed the two treatments discussed above: Treatment A: subjects in this treatment received several stories. Three of these were 'dummy stories' to disguise the intent of the experiment and were always in the second, fourth, and sixth ordinal positions. The remaining four 'experimental stories' depicted a 'victim' receiving an (1) unrealistic, (2) extreme insult, (3) by a friend. Treatment B differed from A in that the experimental stories depicted a victim receiving a (1) realistic, (2) mild insult, (3) by an enemy.

An independent groups design was used; each of the two groups being randomly drawn from the same population of students at a public high school in Windsor, Ontario. A total of eighty-eight students were tested. Three who failed to complete the scales were discarded. Of the remaining eighty-five subjects, thirty-nine received Treatment A and forty-six Treatment B.

Because only two treatments were employed in an independent-groups design, this would appear to be a single-factorial design with a two-valued independent variable. However, it is really an incomplete design since there were 8 (i.e., 2 x 2 x 2) possible treatments. If these eight possible treatments are visualized as the eight corners of a cube, then the two treatments actually employed are the end-points of a three-dimensional diagonal through this cube.

All possible treatments were used in a pretest. However, since the present hypotheses could be tested with only two treatments, and the other cells used in the pretest did not suggest any new problems, the other cells were conveniently excluded here. (However, we intend to do a follow-up experiment employing all eight treatments).

Subjects were instructed that they were judges in an experiment on person perception. The subjects, tested in classes of five or more to insure anonymity, were asked to rate each of the seven stories on a five-point scale in two ways: first, how amusing the story is to the rater and, second, how amusing the rater believes the story would be to the person in the story who receives the literal insult. Next the subjects received the same set of seven stories again (in different random orders) and were asked to rate them in the same two ways on a five-point scale, but with respect to the dependent measure of degree of insultingness. A third time the subjects rated the same set of seven stories (in different random orders) on a five-point scale in the same two ways with respect to degree of seriousness (or kiddingness). Thus the four experimental stories within the set of seven stories were randomized both within subjects and between subjects. Finally, a brief questionnaire was administered asking the subjects for age, sex, and grade currently in.

An example of an experimental story in Treatment A is: Joe was sitting in the local pub with his attractive girlfriend and his long-time buddy, Vince. After she left for the powder room, his friend Vince remarked: 'Your girlfriend is badly in need of plastic surgery!'

An example of the equivalent item rewritten for Treatment B is: Joe was sitting in the local pub with his rather unattractive girlfriend. His enemy Vince was seated at the next table. After she left for the powder room, Vince (who intensely disliked Joe) remarked: 'Your girlfriend is plain looking!'

For purposes of testing the present hypotheses only the subjects' second, that is, empathic, judgments were used. The reason each subject was first asked to judge the story from his own point of view was to render it easier for him to follow the instructions regarding the empathic judgments. Also, since nonparametric statistics were used (Chi-Square and exact probability) and the hypotheses were one-tailed, the five judgment categories were collapsed into two for purposes of statistical analyses.

On the first hypothesis, two of the four experimental stories were significantly more insulting on Treatment A than B at the .05 level of significance using Chi-Square. A third item was in the predicted direction and the fourth was quite strongly (almost significantly) in the wrong direction. However, because of the small number of judgments (339, and only a maximum of 85 judgments per item) relevant to each hypothesis in this experiment, a trend would need to be larger than one could reasonably expect for each item to substantiate the hypothesis at .05. But each of the first three hypotheses could be tested at a higher level of abstraction by instead predicting that the number of significant items would be significant. Thus expanding the binomial theorem where $p = .05$ and $q = .95$ and $n = 4$, the probability of two out of four items being each significant at .05 is itself significant at

.05. Therefore we conclude that Hypothesis 1 is substantiated.

However, we still have the problem that one item was almost significantly in the wrong direction. We believe the problem in that item might be that many of our high school subjects might not have known the meaning of a key word in Treatment A for that story - the word lobotomy. Besides, substantiation of this ironic hypothesis is especially significant considering that the cards were very much stacked against its substantiation. After all, Treatment A items were literally much more insulting than Treatment B, yet we found, as predicted, Treatment A items to be judged less insulting.

On Hypothesis 2 all four items were not only in the predicted direction, but significantly so at the .05 level for each item. Thus Hypothesis 2 is substantiated at the .00001 level. In other words subjects believed the 'insultee' to be kidding (or playing) significantly more often in Treatment A than in Treatment B.

On Hypothesis 3 only one of four items was significant. However, the significance level was .0005. But this significance is so high that the probability of at least one of four items being significant at .0005 is itself significant at .05. Therefore, Hypothesis 3 is partially substantiated. That is, Treatment A is more amusing than Treatment B.

Further evidence in favour of Hypothesis 3 is that all four stories scored in the predicted direction. (Such a result is only significant at .07). Of course, the number of experimental stories is too small to get significance at the .05 level in this manner. Further evidence favouring Hypothesis 3 is that over six times as high a proportion of amusing judgments occurred in Treatment A as in Treatment B. An even more basic reason we do not get stronger substantiation than the small number of judgments appears to be the very strong floor effect. Only twenty-one of the three hundred and thirty-nine judgments were amusing. But eighteen amusing judgments were in Treatment A and only three in Treatment B.

Hypothesis 4 was tested by employing a Chi-Square test of whether an amusing-noninsulting-kidding or nonamusing-insulting-nonkidding pattern occurred significantly more often than by chance. Hypothesis 4 is substantiated at .01.

All statistical tests for all hypotheses above are one-tailed and for 1 df. Since all hypotheses were substantiated in this pilot experiment, we therefore tentatively conclude that the theory presented above has won some support. It would probably be stretching the meaning of the word superiority too far to maintain that the judge identifying with the 'victim' in Treatment A feels vicariously superior because there is nothing he compares himself with and feels superior to. Thus we appear to have another criticism of superiority humour theory as insufficiently general.

More appropriate would seem to be McGhee's (1972b, 1974c) application of the word 'mastery' to such ironic humour. Another useful concept would seem to be Rothbart's (1976) notion of arousal-safety or 'nonthreat'. The subject is apparently amused at the incongruity (or cognitive inconsistency) between what he believes to be the literal and the intended meanings. When a friend delivers an extreme insult that is opposite to the insultee's opinion of himself, he believes the friend is only joking. Thus he is not threatened. On the contrary he feels a sense of mastery through having understood the incongruity and also perhaps thinks his friend is complimenting him by realizing that he can 'take a joke'. In consequence we have a sudden happiness increment due to a perceived incongruity - satisfying our working theory for the necessary conditions for amusement (cf. La Fave et al, 1976).

In conclusion, this pilot study seems to establish an important link between the incongruity and superiority humour areas (where the more general term, happiness increment, be substituted for superiority). A central relation of the theory supported in this pilot experiment to ethnic humour, even though ethnic groups were not used, is that it shows an important reason why ethnic humour is often employed in ethnic INTRAgroup relations; because the insults are perceived as disguised compliments between friends.

REFERENCES

See Bibliography for publications on humour, laughter and comedy

La Fave, L., Sense of Humor: A Myopical Illusion? Paper presented at the annual convention of the American Psychological Association, Washington, D.C., September (1971).

Ethnic Humour: Discussion

Lawrence E. Mintz

University of Maryland

The title of one of the presentations, 'Ethnic Humour is No Joke,' states clearly the central issue approached by the Panel on Ethnic Humour. The issue is a controversial, troubling one. In the United States, various ethnic and racial groups (for example, Polish, Italian, Black) have launched campaigns against ethnic humour and stereotyping, and the telling of ethnic jokes in 'polite company' today is more likely to provoke protest than the telling of baldly sexual ones. This has not diminished ethnic humour, it seems, but it does perhaps add a dash of guilt to the draught of laughter, on the part of both the teller and the listener.

The recognition that hostility, aggression, contempt and other unpleasant factors may lie beneath (if not more prominently) ethnic joking should not surprise us. The notion is consistent with all of the theories of humour as a tendentious activity, and all but the most simple of the incongruity theories. Ethnic humour, with specific, hostile purposes, directed in circumstances where the connections with social animosities are obvious, is common enough to force us to dismiss the idea that we are dealing with mere word-play, or image-manipulation for its own sake.

But is ethnic humour entirely a matter of an expression of contempt or hostility? And if so, what is its specific function? Does it mask hostility, defuse hostility, provide a licensed outlet for hostility, perpetuate and justify a group's opinion of another, reinforce a group's own self-definition? Can an ethnic joke be appreciated on structural, aesthetic grounds, independently of prejudicial purposes? These are questions which have been asked — and answered before — but they certainly merit more attention. Since ethnic humour may very well tell us more about the nature of intergroup strife, and since ethnic antagonism is of such crucial importance, both internationally and intra-nationally, the area approached by our panelists is one of the most important ones in humour research.

Since all of the papers except one, which will be dealt with separately and last, involved the experimental method, a discussion of the approaches applied is called for, but since the Discussant (a 'humanities-type') has had virtually no experience with that method, a few, perhaps naive, comments and questions will have to replace a more detailed, knowledgeable critique. Though surely it is a question posed and resolved long ago by experimental psychologists, this observer wondered how we know that an experiment involving a certain very particular group in a highly contrived, limited, artificial environment (for example, a small number of Canadian undergraduate students in a laboratory or auditorium) can tell us, reliably, what ethnic humour is all about. To be sure, it is no less credible than textual analysis, simple observation of the natural environment, or any of the other potential methods, but it takes itself so seriously, with its scientific procedures, terminology, and (more importantly) its confident statement of the results and their implications, that the question should not be tossed aside as blithely as it was during the Panel Discussion.

Moreover, perhaps more disturbing, the lack of quality humour in the experimental material used by all of the experimenters questions the significance of the results. Again this was answered, rather superficially, at the Conference by noting that the experimenters did not wish to prejudice the results by making the jokes too funny, or by arguing that jokes are not inherently funny anyway, so only the situation (with regard to conflict) was relevant. La Fave et al (1976) go so far as to state, 'There are no jokes. The presentation of a "joke" is an insufficient condition to generate amusement.' (p84). But since these aspects (what 'prejudices' the receiver has, and whether the jokes have a structural, aesthetic dimension independent of, or contributory to, the humour) are among the questions at hand, to use banal, unfunny material is to exert an important influence on the result. La Fave's experimental insults (Joe is told, 'Your girlfriend is badly in need of plastic surgery,' and 'your girlfriend is plain looking') and Mannell's cartoons, for example, do help them contrast extreme with more moderate aggression, but do they tell us anything about humour?

Also one wonders about a subject's ability to judge his own reaction (in terms of degree of amusement) as a response to stimuli. Again the experimental environment may interfere, causing the subject to be more self-conscious, more conscious of the social implications of the judgments than they would be in the more natural environment of the locker-room, poker table, cocktail party, etcetera. It has been shown by several researchers (e.g., Chapman, 1976) that laughter, at least, is highly alterable by circumstance, environment, and personality, and though it has also been pointed out that laughter and humour are not at all the same phenomenon, is it unreasonable to suspect, at least, that variables in the environment alter the perception and appreciation of humour? This issue itself demands more attention, specifically as it pertains to ethnic humour. Perhaps these kinds of methodological problems affect the applications or implications of the results more than they do the results themselves, and, as will be suggested below, all of the papers have interesting, useful, and impressive points to make in spite of these questions, but nonetheless, Mannell's bold statement, 'amusement appears to be a direct function of the level of aggression and damage perpetrated by the victor upon the victim' is probably over-confident considering the bases upon which it rests.

The reader can, of course, draw his or her own conclusions concerning the specific papers, but a few direct comments undoubtably are part of the Discussant's 'job description'. Taken as a group, the papers presented provide a useful addition to an inadequate but by no means inconsequential body of literature on the subject. The papers are often direct tests of, comments on, or footnotes to the previous work of such as La Fave (numerous papers), Zillmann and Cantor (1976), Martineau (1972), and several others. The emphasis on the relevance ('saliency') of the ethnic jokes given by Bourhis, Gadfield, Giles and Tajfel is of central importance, and it speaks directly to the previous work of La Fave and his associates (1972, 1976) and Zillmann and Cantor (1976) concerning reference groups, identification classes, and disposition as factors influencing the appreciation of humour, and by implication, the function of the humour-creation. Perhaps it oversimplifies unjustly, considering the close reasoning and careful distinction of terminology found in these papers, but one might say that they all present the thesis, essentially, that ethnic humour has (at least) more of an impact when there is a real hostility, or a sincere dislike, and when the dynamics of superiority/ inferiority are genuine rather than artificial. This does not rule out the impact of the quality of the joke (cleverness of metaphor, aptness, imagination of imagery etcetera), but it does force us to face squarely the functioning of ethnic humour as a device for social expression and social definition. Bourhis et al also make a useful contribution by manipulating the accents of the joke-tellers, thereby calling to our attention the question of the source and manner of presentation of the humour as an associated factor to even the matter of identity and 'saliency.'

La Fave's paper is perhaps justly described as a useful and necessary footnote to his previous work (see, particularly La Fave, 1972, and La Fave, Haddad and Maesen, 1976). His explanation of the irony of the extreme insult's less potent effect protects his previous theories from attack by exception, and it contributes to Mannell's concern with the appropriateness of the response as a factor in the appreciation of insult and aggression humour. It would be lovely if it did 'establish an important link between the incongruity and superiority humour areas', but though it does legitimately show a particular instance of combination of the two aspects (the irony of inappropriateness as an incongruity along with or influencing a superiority situation), it is not quite clear how it actually links the two in a theoretical manner.

Mannell's paper makes a necessary, interesting point concerning the significance of 'serious' and 'judgemental' dispositions to the acceptance of insult and aggression. In this case, a semantic distinction (opposing the above terms to 'fantasy') is intelligently advanced. It contributes to the case made by Zillmann and Cantor (1976), La Fave (1972), La Fave and colleagues (1976, and in the present volume), Bourhis et al (present volume), and others that the attitude of the listener is a crucial element to the appreciation of ethnic humour, though perhaps when added to La Fave's 'reference groups' and 'identification classes,' Bourhis' 'saliency' and Zillmann and Cantor's 'disposition,' it adds up to more terms than desirable to describe a similar, and relatively simple notion. The papers by Issar, Tsang, La Fave, Guilmette and Issar, and by Mutuma, La Fave, Mannell, and Guilmette open up the area of cross-cultural reference, an obviously central element. Ethnic jokes almost always require a set of cultural suppositions - sometimes simple (for example, the X people are stupid, dirty, cheap etcetera) - often more complex and specific (at an International Conference on Elephants, a German presented 'On the Toenails of Elephants,' an Englishman 'The Elephant and the Empire,' an American 'Building Bigger and Better Elephants,' a Frenchman 'The Sex Life of the Elephant,' and so forth). The Canadian research is notable for trying to explore the dynamics of cultural suppositions as they affect ethnic humour.

Husband's paper uses sociological data, rather than experimental methodology, to make the case that ethnic - or more specifically racist - humour reflects the attitudes of its appreciators as well as, or perhaps rather than, its artistic or aesthetic tastes. While there is little doubt that racists can receive support, encouragement, perhaps even motivation

in their views from the programme mentioned, an analysis of 'All In The Family,' the programme
with which this writer is familiar, provokes a number of questions. For one thing, the humour
in 'All In The Family' is almost always separate from both the plot and Archie's prejudice.
It does revolve around his sexism (treatment of Edith) frequently, but his ethnic and racial
slurs are separate from and secondary to the show's jokes and comic situations. Moreover
(and apparently unlike the British programme as it is described by Husband), Ethnics and
Blacks are almost always portrayed favourably (intelligent, confident, capable, strong), so if
there is 'subliminal' learning through image, projection or stereotyping, 'All In The Family'
may have an anti-racist function despite Archie, even if the viewer does identify with, or
agree with him. Archie is a loser, a victim, himself an oppressed member of society, and
while this scarcely justifies identifying with or accepting his dangerous political and social
attitudes, it might well contribute to a willingness to like him, identify with him, and even
agree with him without necessarily either exercising or strengthening one's racial or ethnic
prejudice. But this is a very complex matter that demands far more specific discussion than
can be given here, and certainly it does not detract from Husband's rightful concern for the
potential function of mass media racism or from his proper attention to trying to understand
the role of popular culture in the reflection, articulation, and development of social
opinion and belief. That his paper was virtually by itself in this emphasis at the Conference
is most unfortunate.

To summarize briefly, the papers presented here, despite the inevitable questions and problems,
are particularly valuable because of the tremendous importance of the subject. At the very
least they suggest the need for more work, perhaps (at least) a conference and/or a volume
devoted to ethnic humour in the near future.

REFERENCES

See Bibliography for publications on humour, laughter and comedy

HUMOUR AND COMMUNICATION

Humour and Communication: Introduction to Symposium

Dolf Zillmann

Indiana University

It would appear that a symposium on 'Humour and Communication' potentially encompasses almost all facets of humour - quite independently of the particular definition of humour one endorses. With the possible exception of mirthful reactions in primates and in human infants (cf. McGhee, this volume), humour is primarily a communicative affair. As such, it apparently serves a multitude of psychological and sociological functions. In this symposium, we are certainly not able to exhaust all these conceivable functions of humour as communication. The scope of the coverage of the phenomenon under investigation is, as always, determined by the research interests of the various contributors. As it stands, their contributions span an enormous range of manifestations of humour as communication. The various approaches taken differ in principal ways, and we shall use apparent distinctions to structure the symposium.

Joanne R. Cantor and Christie Davies address manifestations of humour in the so-called mass media of communication. The media involved are television, mass-circulated periodicals, and literary productions published in book form. The type of humour these investigators deal with is characteristically, or almost necessarily, created ahead of time and rehearsed. Although it may well have a spontaneous origin, within the mass communication process it is, so to speak, prefabricated. This is very much in contrast to the type of humour which is addressed by Eric G. Linfeld, Gary A. Fine, and Rita Ransohoff. These investigators deal with spontaneous humour which emerges in different social situations and with the functions that these spontaneous utterances may serve. Last but not least, Jennings Bryant attacks an issue which concerns the appreciation of either spontaneous or nonspontaneous humour. The way in which he has dealt with the issue would seem to place him into the mass communication camp, however.

I shall adopt this division into 'humour in the mass media' and 'spontaneous humour in social settings' and comment on the research in these two domains of interest. And since 'humour in the mass media' was somewhat neglected at the Conference, I will spend a bit more time on that subject.

In the mass media, humour is undoubtedly a ubiquitous phenomenon. Let me illustrate this with a brief look at the mass medium of our times: television. A recent content analysis of television offerings in the United States, conducted by Cantor (in press), shows that humour penetrates virtually all programming. It is employed where one would least expect it: even in religious broadcasts. More than one third of such programmes involve some humour. Other domains of great seriousness, the news, sports competitions, and soap operas, also resort to some 'funny stuff'. About two-thirds of such programmes entail some humorous material. And there is no doubt about the fact that programmes which feature humorous materials reach enormous audiences. Let us consider some data on the American national networks in the Autumn of 1975, which James Webster compiled for me. In prime-time, which is high-exposure time by definition, about fifteen per cent of all programmes are comedies, and these comedies account for about seventeen per cent of the audience. In actual numbers, the average half-hour comedy is watched by about twenty-nine million people. And looking at just one week of comedy programming, the audience drawn to the comedies amounts to five hundred and fifty-one million people. Remember that these figures understate the case. The independent networks and public television should add considerably to the picture.

Given that people in such enormous numbers elect to spend a good portion of their waking hours watching comedy, one would expect that there must be something obvious about comedy which makes for its broad appeal, and that psychologists would have long ago delineated the 'principal ingredients' of successful comedy and their optimal arrangement. As it turns out, both expectations are erroneous. There seems to be a great variety of elements which apparently contribute to or hamper the enjoyment of comedy, and psychologists have delineated numerous factors which either facilitate or impede this enjoyment. But unfailing recipes for combining presumably crucial ingredients have not been uncovered. In other words, a best-seller formula for comedy has not emerged. This fact becomes painfully clear when one serves, as I have done, as a consultant for the communications industry. Experimental-minded investigators have been preoccupied with demonstrating that certain variables help or hinder enjoyment of jokes and miniature comedies - as predicted from some rationale, of course. These investigations point up interesting possibilities. But taken together, the experimental work is rather eclectic. It does not permit a consultant to piece together a formula for comedy in which he can vest much confidence. As academicians we have, no doubt, no obligation whatsoever to help the entertainment industry to a winning formula. The matter might smack of exploitation. On the other hand, if humour is indeed the beneficial activity it is generally held to be, the grand design of comedy which produces maximal gratification, relief, relaxation, recreation, etcetera, may seem an acceptable challenge. Be this as it may, I am under the impression that there is a 'pure' and an 'applied' research interest in humour in the mass media, and that the two interests do not combine too well. The purists have constructed increasingly complex models to account for humour appreciation and its behavioural implications, and they have tested these models under laboratory conditions mainly with college-educated subjects. In talking to investigators in the industry, I have run into criticisms of this approach, the potentially constructive elements of which are the following:

First, research is done on overly educated people who are not representative of the population at large. This is, of course, the old argument that 'sophomores are not necessarily people'. Humour which holds an appeal for large audiences, it is suggested, is far less complex and sophisticated than would be concluded from investigations of subjects with an atypically high level of education.

Second, in evaluating theoretical proposals, academicians generally ignore a wealth of data provided by mass media institutions. Specifically, the data concern comedy and its appeal as measured in the size of the audience drawn. It is suggested that in American commercial television and in economically similar systems, the rule is 'the survival of the fittest'. For comedy, this means that whatever appeals the most, sells the best, and in turn, whatever sells the best, will be put on the most. Assuming that the industry has no scruples about putting on what sells best, the mass media data should reflect a free market-place of humour in which winners and losers are constantly produced by trial and error. The data, then, should tell us not just something, but a lot about the likes and dislikes of 'real' people.

Well, while I think that it is quite true that we have not made the best use of the available data, I am pleased to see that efforts to relate manifestations in the media to theory are now being made. In her paper, Joanne R. Cantor explores the extent to which certain Freudian contentions are reflected in mass media humour. Among other things, she reports data which document a dominance of tendentious humour in media which reach broad audiences, and a lack of this dominance in media which reach smaller audiences associated with above-average levels of education. It should be noticed that such a finding is quite consistent with the claim that general audiences fail to appreciate complex, sophisticated humour.

Let me comment further on this point. Some of my students (Barbara Ball, David Best & Eric Freud) recently did a content analysis of American prime-time commercial television in which they coded the amount of joke-work involved in humorous incidents. Incidents whose humour was immediately apparent, that is, whose decoding required no 'mental effort' to speak of, were classified as 'blunt'. I am speaking of such unsubtle things as the proverbial slip on the banana peel and the pie in the face, and also of direct and raw insult. In contrast to such situations associated with minimal joke-work, humorous incidents which involved some subtleties, that is, some transformations to be executed to get to the point, were classified, for lack of a better term, as 'refined'. I am speaking here of anything which could be construed as mildly ambitious humour: something that involves incongruity, novelty, surprise, ambiguity, polysemy, and the like. Employing this scheme, it was found that in a week's prime-time comedy (situation comedy and comedy-variety combined), fifty-eight per cent of all funny incidents were of the pie-in-the-face variety and the remaining forty-two per cent were more sophisticated. In comedy-variety shows, the dominance of blunt humour rose to sixty-two per cent. These figures should have surprised even Freud (1905) who could have anticipated the dominance of tendentious humour, but who insisted upon the camouflage of the tendentious elements through joke-work. The figures should, of course, be alarming to those who entertain notions in which humour is viewed as primarily resulting from cognitive manoeuvres involved in the resolution of ambiguities and 'problems'. The funny, blunt incidents I am speaking about do not pose problems, are not novel, not ambiguous, etcetera. They are quite predictable - a condition which seems not to detract from their enjoyment. I am, of course, not saying that joke-work is not essential or that it does not contribute to the enjoyment of humour. I am merely trying to point out that when we talk about humour in the mass media, we have to face up to the fact that - to be very conservative about it - a good portion of successful television comedy is rather blunt. Having a good time with humour apparently does not depend upon great cognitive capabilities and skills.

We have just completed an experimental investigation which pertains to this matter. The study explored the relationship between alcoholic intoxication and humour appreciation. The cliché has it that a drink or two makes for a lot of giggles, chuckles, and laughs. Cerebral incompetence, self-inflicted and temporary, as it may be, is thus viewed as enhancing the enjoyment of humorous stimuli. On the other hand, as cognitive functions are impaired, one should expect that much joke-work will go unrecognized and unresolved, and that appreciation will deteriorate as a consequence. The more that humour depends on complex cognitive processes, the more its appreciation should suffer from intoxication. Intoxication which adversely affects cerebral competence, alcoholic intoxication being a case in point, thus seems to favour bluntness in humour.

In our study, which I conducted with Shahin Assadi, subjects drank a constant amount of liquid. In the placebo condition, the liquid was pure orange juice. In a condition of mild intoxication, the juice contained three-quarters of an ounce of vodka per fifty pounds of the subject's body weight. In a condition of severe intoxication, it contained one and a half ounces per fifty pounds of body weight. Subjects in these three conditions watched an extremely blunt piece of slapstick comedy and a routine which involved considerable joke-work and subtleties, and then appraised their enjoyment of these stimuli. Additionally, the subjects were videotaped as they watched, and the tapes were analyzed for smiles and laughs by judges who were naive about the materials the subjects were responding to and about their level of intoxication. The findings leave no doubt about the fact that enjoyment of ambitious, subtle and 'sophisticated' humour deteriorates with increasing alcoholic intoxication. The findings also show that blunt humour, by contrast, gains with intoxication.

If such findings are related to customs of social drinking (I am thinking of the martini or the beer after 'a long day'), one might be inclined to agree with those practitioners who claim that sophisticated humour has no place in prime-time television. Drinking may well take away a portion of the adult audience which potentially would enjoy sophisticated forms of humour. At any rate, the camouflage of tendentious elements of humour, which Freud (1905) considered crucial, seems to be imperative only for the sober respondent. And in a – let us say 'hypothetical' – society in which the social use of drugs that suppress sympathetic activity and cerebral competence is widely accepted, one might expect blunt humour to triumph and to dominate the mass media of communication.

Let me return now to the argument that humour in the mass media is an unbiased testing ground for 'quality humour'. This is quite obviously not so. Content is regulated in one form or another. In the United States, television is quite restricted in carrying sexual humour. If this regulation were not present, tendentious humour, and for that matter, blunt humour, would presumably be far more dominant than it is now. There are less obtrusive regulatory processes, however, which confine humour. Let me illustrate this. It has been established in several experimental investigations (Cantor, 1976; Losco & Epstein, 1975) that disparagement humour in which a female is victimized is funnier to both male and female respondents than, other things equal, when it features the victimization of a male. On the other hand, a recent content analysis (Stocking, Sapolsky & Zillmann, in press) on who-disparages-whom in American television humour shows that females are no more the butt of jokes than males. In fact, males are three times as often the victim of disparaging humour than are females. This circumstance can, of course, be explained in different ways. It may be that the comedy writers have neither knowledge of nor hunches about the anti-female bias in the appreciation of disparagement humour. It may be that male chauvinism (I understand that comedy writers are predominantly male) has prevented the heavy usage of this motif, so that its appeal has not become apparent in the ratings. More probably, however, the female is not discriminated against because, in the waves of the female liberation movement, the American networks follow the self-set, informal policy not to offend prevalent sentiments of their audience. In very practical terms, they apply self-censure to avoid confrontations with politically potent groups. I would assume that a very similar situation exists with regard to the humorous victimization of many other subsections in society, politically potent minorities in particular.

The 'commercial imperative' of American television and of similar systems is thus not quite as compelling as it may appear at first glance. And investigators who want to draw upon the wealth of data out there will have to make allowances for the constraint of the 'free market-place of comedy'.

Before turning away from the mass media, I should briefly comment on two domains of mass communication in which humour has become increasingly popular. While the primary function of comedy per se, dependent upon one's theoretical bent, is to amuse, relieve, relax, pacify, distract, please, gratify, or something to that effect, humour is frequently employed to serve other causes as well. Apparently, humour can attract an audience which is either unwilling or only slightly motivated to watch and listen. This situation prevails in advertising, and also in education.

In America, humour has become a salient element of advertising. So funny are some commercials, that viewers report waiting to see them again and again. It remains to be seen, however, to what extent humorous commercials help sell the products and services they seek to promote (cf. Sternthal & Craig, 1973). The initial fear that the element of ridicule might colour the perception of the product or service advertised has apparently been set aside, and there seems to exist the belief that, independent of the attention-getting function of humour, to amuse and gratify the respondent should positively colour the perception of the product or service advertised. Classical conditioning may be invoked as the mechanism behind the presumed effect: the humour-induced positive affect is consistently paired with brand names and logos; these stimuli, the CS in the paradigm, come to elicit positive affect — a reaction which should enhance the appeal of the product or service in question. Alternatively, Sternthal and Craig (1973) conceive of mirthful reactions to humour as reinforcers in an operant paradigm. Presumably, these reinforcers foster product- and service-related thoughts, which ultimately enhance consumption readiness. However, notwithstanding the apparent popularity of humorous commercials and hypotheses about their effectiveness, at present there is no compelling evidence of the assumed superior effectiveness of the funny as compared to the serious commercial.

The notion that humour can be successfully combined with the teaching of facts, concepts, values, and attitudes is certainly not novel, but within mass communication it has only relatively recently emerged. As it emerged, it has seemed to celebrate triumphs in children's television. 'Sesame Street', as has been acknowledged by its creators, copied the format of the humorous commercial to teach the alphabet and counting. The programme has been a landmark (cf. Lesser, 1974). It sparked numerous similar programmes for children, and it triggered efforts to teach in a humorous fashion such things as health practices and consumerism to adults. While the recipe was successful in attracting children to the screen, its appeal to adults proved to be quite limited. And more recently, some questions have been raised as to whether programmes like 'Sesame Street' can be considered an educational success. Such programmes are undoubtedly meritorious in teaching ethnic integration and cooperation, or at a more basic level, in occupying children in a constructive way. But the scholastic yield (i.e., rote memory of the alphabet and numbers, and some spelling skills) has admittedly been quite modest. Even attracting and holding attention to educational materials through the involvement of humour is not as compellingly efficient as it may appear on first glance. It has been charged that children may selectively attend to the funny stuff, and 'tune out' when the educational message comes on.

There are reasons, then, to question the effectiveness of the use of humour in education. The available evidence on this point tends to support this scepticism. Studies which produced inconclusive findings are abundant, and reliable data are rare (cf. Ann P. Davies, this volume). One of the more elucidating investigations on this subject has been conducted by Weinberg (1974). A lecture was embellished with pertinent examples which were either funny or serious. The students were classified as anxious versus nonanxious and low versus high in intelligence. When all subjects were lumped together, the funniness of examples failed to enhance the acquisition and comprehension of the materials. If there was any indication that humour helped learning, it was found in the bright and nonanxious students. For those who needed help the most, the less intelligent and more anxious students, the involvement of humour had a detrimental effect. This latter finding calls into question the very popular idea that humour puts the nervous student at ease, enabling him to attend and concentrate, and ultimately to learn better.

The psychological mechanism mediating such effects is all but immediately apparent. Other findings make the relationship between humour and the comprehension of educational materials even more puzzling. Let me briefly report on an in-house study of the Children's Television Workshop conducted by Keith W. Mielke of Indiana University. In producing the series 'Feeling Good', a humorous health show for adults which adopted the general format of such shows as 'Sesame Street', the question arose whether or not to employ canned laughter. Canned laughter is an American institution. Its recent substitute, the cue-controlled 'life' laughter of a small audience, keeps the tradition alive. Canned or cued laughter accompanies most televised comedy. In spite of its popular usage, its effect was until very recently virtually unknown (cf. Ray G.C. Fuller, this volume). Faced with uncertainty, it was decided to run a pretest on two versions of the show, one with and one without canned laughter. It was observed that cueing the audience through canned laughter, that is, 'telling them' when it was appropriate to laugh, and possibly, how much to laugh, produced decisively superior appraisals of the show. Specifically, equipped with a laugh track, the show was considered funnier and more enjoyable than without such a track. However, when it came to the comprehension of the health message, it was found that the presence of the laugh track had greatly impaired 'getting the message across'. This impairment was not simply the result of 'distracting noise'. The laughter was, of course, placed in such a way that it did not interfere with the reception of the educational message. If distraction is invoked as an explanation, it must be conceived of as part of the response to humorous materials — not as part of the stimulus per se (cf. Cantor, Mody & Zillmann, 1974).

The concept of combining humour and education thus seems in need of clarifying research. The utilization of humour for educational purposes appears to hold promise as far as attracting audiences and getting and recapturing attention is concerned. But this potential gain in attention does not necessarily further any and every educational effort. The specific conditions in which the involvement of humour helps or hinders the educational message remain to be determined.

There are, of course, many aspects other than appreciation, attention, and comprehension to be considered in the humour-education relationship. For example, humour can be viewed as providing immediate gratifications for attending. Children may 'get hooked' to these gratifications, attending to educational messages only if they are spiced with humour. The last bit of motivation to learn without laughs may thus be undermined. This seems a fundamental problem in education. It is by no means restricted to mass communication processes, however. It extends to direct interpersonal exchanges, that is, to the classroom.

At this point, finally, we leave the field of humour in the mass media and move on to the functions of potentially spontaneous humour in immediate social settings. In education, the rapport between teacher and student has characteristically been viewed to be affected by humour in the classroom. Eric G. Linfeld dealt with this issue, and I would like in this context to make an observation on humour and personal rapport.

It seems to be a truism among teachers that they can improve their rapport with a class by reducing the 'personal distance' presumed to exist between 'their level' and that of the students. In this context, the teacher's humorous disclosure of some rather innocent shortcoming or pratfall of his is said to work wonders. For example, I have an assistant who had been a journalism instructor. She swore by the discussed rapport formula and practised it as follows: Whenever she would stumble over words in an initial lecture, she would pause and comment 'That's why I didn't go into broadcasting.' Reportedly, this always drew a good reaction from the class, and she believed that such self-disparagement had furthered her rapport with the students. She continued to believe this until we conducted an investigation into the implications of humorous self-disparagement (Zillmann & Stocking, 1976; Stocking & Zillmann, in press). We created conditions in which a person disclosed, in a humorous fashion, minor blunders which he himself had committed, or which had been made by either a friend of his or an enemy. Humorous self-disparagement proved to be quite funny to female audiences. Male audiences, in contrast, considered the humorous disparagement of a personal enemy far funnier. Interestingly, however, for male and female audiences alike, the humorous self-disclosure of a pratfall or minor inadequacy had detrimental effects on person perception: compared to the individual who told the same story at someone else's expense (especially at the expense of an enemy), he who displayed 'a sense of humour' by 'laughing at his own expense' was perceived as stupid and lacking in self-confidence. Moreover, the act of self-disparagement, humorous as it was, projected an unwitty personality. It was the disparager of others who, in this comparison, came across as witty, secure, and intelligent.

The display of a sense of humour through self-disparaging humour for the purpose of enhancing rapport, then, seems to be a risky proposition. While these particular findings do not tell us what the use of humour as such can do for rapport, they do tell us that if the reduction of personal distance between teacher and student is imperative, humorous self-disparagement is superior to the humorous disparagement of others. The teacher can effectively reduce the extent to which he is perceived as intolerably intelligent – if this should ever be a problem. But his rapport is likely to be adversely affected because of a perceived lack of security and wittiness. In light of these findings, the teacher's expectation to gain appeal through the humorous disclosure of 'little embarrassing incidents' seems not to be realistic. It may be a faulty truism with its roots in an operant-conditioning process which teachers administer to themselves: Assuming that the class's laughter is gratifying and thus reinforcing for the teacher, the teacher may be especially strongly reinforced for disclosing incidents of self-humiliation. As a consequence, he not only should provide more of this type of information, but he should also interpret the class's good reaction and his ability to trigger it at will as good rapport. This operant mechanism applies, of course, to the teacher's use of humour generally – not just to self-incriminating humour. In fact, the mechanism tends to make a joker out of every teacher who happens to drop a joke here and there.

The teacher-student relationship is, of course, relatively simple when compared to complex interactions in informal and formal groups. In these interactions, humour appears to serve a multitude of functions – social functions as well as psychological ones. Psychologists, it seems, have been preoccupied with Freudian suggestions concerning relief. More recently, the appreciation of humour in its own right has come under scrutiny. In the study of social interaction, these aspects of humour tend to become secondary. In keeping with sociological tradition, manifestations and consequences of humour are analyzed in terms of group cohesion, group efficiency, and social attributes of group members such as social status and power. The pioneering work of Coser and Goodchilds comes to mind. Coser (1959, 1960), for example, disclosed a 'peck order' in the use of humour, especially tendentious humour. Apparently, humour projects downward through a social hierarchy. In a well-defined social system, the status-superior person may use humour to overtly disparage the status-inferior person, but not vice versa. Goodchilds and her co-workers explored characteristics of the wit. A sarcastic wit, for example, tends to be perceived as influential but unpopular, a clowning wit as powerless but popular (Goodchilds, 1959). The deliberate wit in a small group is characterized by high morale and great efficiency (Smith & Goodchilds, 1963). Wits tend to entertain a positive view of themselves and relatively independent minds. According to the findings, the presence of deliberate wits in groups tend to make the group experience more enjoyable for all concerned, but more surprisingly, it tends to facilitate the capacity of a group to solve problems (Goodchilds & Smith, 1964). Potentially, there are many other social or psychological functions of spontaneous humour in groups. The contributions of Gary A. Fine and Rita Ransohoff elaborate these functions. In their presentations, two related notions came up which I find particularly intriguing: the idea that humour may serve to express curiosity about and to deal with taboo topics without undue anxiety, and the fact that humour offers 'a way out' if statements prove controversial. Expressing inquiries and convictions in humorous ways apparently avoids a serious, conflict-generating commitment to a point of view on an issue. It may well function as a trial balloon from which the group member can tell which positions will be well received and which will meet with reproach.

The paper by Jennings Bryant, which concluded our symposium on humour and communication, dealt with the degree of hostility in nonspontaneous and, to a lesser extent, in spontaneous 'aggressive' humour, and with its implications for mirthful reactions. In terms of theoretical speculation, this issue is certainly an old and established one. Plato (in 'Philebus'), Aristotle (in 'Poetics'), Hobbes (in 'Leviathan'), and many more recent writers (e.g., Hazlitt, 1826; Baudelaire, 1855), all have entertained notions which, roughly speaking, project mirth as the consequence of witnessing the humiliation, the disparagement, the debasement, or in short, the victimization of others. And, although there are numerous differences in the various approaches to hostile humour (cf. Zillmann & Cantor, 1976), it appears to have been generally implied that the intensity of mirth varies proportionally with the magnitude of an inadequacy, a mishap, or a putdown. According to Aristotle, however, this relationship is restricted. In his view, the disclosure of ugliness, stupidity, and other weaknesses is ludicrous only when it is not associated with apparent grief or death of the victim. It would thus appear that those who have pondered the secrets of hostile humour have held that such humour is funnier, the more hostility, the more aggression, and the more brutality it involves — with the possible exception of brutality so severe that feelings of pity may be evoked, which then spoil any enjoyment.

The pity reasoning seems to make good common sense and enjoy a considerable following. Who has not witnessed the victim of a 'cruel' putdown turn sour or burst into tears? Such reactions certainly tend to quiet laughter in the on-looker. However, the apparent absence of mirthful reactions under these circumstances, can be viewed as resulting from the witnessed reaction to the severely hostile putdowns, and not from the mere information value of the putdowns themselves. Humour featuring severe hostility may thus motivate mirthful reactions, but expression of these reactions may be effectively inhibited by the social factors involved. It would seem to follow that the removal of such factors would free the individual to enjoy the blatant, cruel, and brutal putdown of others, and of generally respectable, quasi-sacred things as well. The humorous victimization of people whose reactions are not apparent or are concealed is, of course, characteristic of aggressive humour in the mass media. Generally speaking, the newspaper audience does not witness a politicians's potential reaction of annoyance and disturbance to a cartoon which bluntly exaggerates his less desirable traits. At a different level, children usually are spared observation of the misery which a cartoon character would go through after having been booby-trapped in cruel ways. Similarly, in comedy for adult audiences, the aftermath of brutal assaults tends to be played down. It is made nonsalient by skipping adverse reactions, by making such reactions unfitting and inappropriate, or simply by making especially salient the comedy format in which the witnessed events happen. No matter how, specifically, hostility and brutality in humour is made palatable to an audience, a look at political jokes, children's cartoons, and adult comedy should convince anyone that humour which presumably causes considerable enjoyment, thrives on blatantly brutal behavioural exchanges. In political cartoons and children's fare alike, the favourite mirth-makers are as follows (according to my own informal counts on the American scene): (1) blowing up the opponent with the help of dynamite sticks or other types of explosives; (2) pushing or tripping opponents over cliffs; and (3) mutilating them with shotgun blasts. Cruelty in political humour apparently does not prevent mirthful reactions (e.g., Zillmann, Bryant & Cantor, 1974). And children undoubtedly derive great amusement from seeing the bad guy's head blown off and the Cayote in the famous 'Roadrunner' show smashed between rocks, flattened to a disk, stretched out beyond recognition, stripped of his skin, pummelled until his teeth fall down his throat, or simply, once more, pushed into the canyon (e.g., Roussou, 1972). And if one can take the success of recent television shows such as 'Saturday Night Life' and 'Monty Python's Flying Circus' as a measure of the likes of adult audiences, the blatant treatment of grief-and-death motifs seems to do everything but deter merriment. In fact, avant-garde programmes such as these not only do not make any effort to deemphasize

or avoid the pity issue, but build entire routines on grief, death, and convictions held
sacred by large sections of the population.

In the light of the apparent audience preferences, Aristotle's qualification must appear
highly questionable. Brutality in humour seems normatively unlimited. The grief-and-death
motif, in and of itself, does not of necessity inhibit mirthful reactions.

In psychology, Aristotle's stipulation had been largely forgotten anyway. McDougall (1903,
1922) and Freud (1905), among others, proposed rationales which project an unrestricted
correspondence between the degree of hostility in tendentious humour and the intensity of
mirth. McDougall based his propositions on the assumption of an inborn tendency to co-suffer
the noxious experiences of victims, and on the need to ward off such distress through laughter;
Freud based his proposal on the view that the forces upon repression grow along with the
severity of hostile actions, and on the suggestion that enjoyment deriving from witnessing
the expression of repressed behaviour in others is a function of the magnitude of repressive
forces in the witness vis-à-vis the behaviour in question (cf. Cantor & Zillmann, 1973).
While these projections can explain the appeal of extremely hostile and brutal humour, they
falter and fail on the observation that such humour, and at times also far less hostile
exchanges, can strike people as off-colour and distasteful. The question, then, remains:
What, exactly, if not the involvement of grief and death, makes hostile humour unfunny,
detestable, or even 'sick'?

The initial experimental work on this issue has raised more questions than it has answered.
In one of our studies on hostile humour (Cantor & Zillmann, 1973), the severity of
misfortunes suffered by the victim was systematically varied. The findings revealed that,
when the victim was disliked, the greater severity of misfortunes inhibited rather than
enhanced humour appreciation. Such data can be taken as nonsupportive of McDougall's and
Freud's positions, but some caution is indicated in interpreting them as supportive of
Aristotle's qualification. While most of the materials employed in the investigation
involved physical assaults (injurious behaviour was about to be performed, was in progress,
or was clearly implied in the depiction of its devastating consequences), some of the
materials involved only minor mishaps, such as the victim being the apparent target of bird
droppings. Where injury was an issue, it is conceivable that in the condition of severe
victimization feelings of pity inhibited mirthful reactions. However, such an expectation
seems forced when noninjurious, yet embarrassing mishaps are being considered. To salvage
Aristotle's proposal, one would have to assume that the difference between merriment and pity
may lie, for example, between the amount of bird droppings about to hit the victim (which was
the manipulation of severity of misfortune in one set of cartoons). And if one were to
accept that a larger amount of bird droppings may induce mirth-inhibiting feelings of pity,
Aristotle's qualification would seem to become useless as a normative stipulation. Grief
and death would be expanded to feelings of pity for the victim, and since, dependent upon
the circumstances, such feelings can be evoked by trivially sad happenings (e.g., by
witnessing one's favourite athlete win 'only' the silver medal), the presence or absence of
feelings of pity, quite independent of grief and death, would have to be empirically
ascertained before predictions could be made.

A study on political cartoons (Zillmann, Bryant & Cantor, 1974) avoided the conceptual
ambiguities regarding grief and death. At a level of severe brutality of assault, the victim
was shown as either fatally injured or as about to be fatally injured. At minimal brutality,
he was depicted facing a situation which amounted to only a scare. The findings obtained
under these conditions further complicate the grief-and-death issue in humour appreciation.
This time, for the disliked victim, the degree of brutality of the assault upon him proved
of little consequence. For the liked victim, however, humour appreciation increased with
severe brutality. This latter finding is obviously not supportive of Aristotle's view. It
could be construed as supporting the positions of McDougall and Freud. At any rate, while
there are reasons to believe that the latter finding may be unique to political humour (cf.
Zillmann et al, 1974), it should be clear that the available evidence concerning the
implications of the absolute amount of hostility which is involved in tendentious humour, is
highly inconsistent and all but conclusive.

Nonetheless, the data show that the involvement of extremely brutal events in the
disparagement of a victim does not necessarily kill the fun people can derive from hostile
humour. Cruelty can be funny. On the other hand, it certainly does not promote merriment
as a rule. Under these circumstances, it would seem pointless to pursue efforts to
delineate and enumerate conditions of the grief-and-death variety which, for the sake of
humour, have to be avoided at any cost. The normative approach to pityful events thus
appears fruitless. It would seem promising to determine, instead, the specific conditions
under which brutal and cruel actions create or destroy, facilitate or hamper merriment.
Actually, some recent proposals offer a new approach to the old problem.

It has been suggested (Gutman & Priest, 1969) that, to some extent at least, the appreciation
of hostile humour is an inverse function of the social acceptability of the victim. The
putdown of a villain is thus viewed as funnier than the same putdown of a good guy. Villains

are apparently acceptable for humiliating treatments. Well-behaved people are not. And presumably, since villains are acceptable targets for some mistreatment, their victimization should produce mirthful reactions even when it is rather cruel. This is to say that, conceptually, as one steps up the degree of hostility in the disparagement of a victim, one soon might reach a point at which the victimization of a good guy becomes unfunny. The point at which the victimization of a bad guy turns off-colour should be located far higher toward grief and death on this continuum.

The issue here is not restricted, however, to bad guys and good guys, or for that matter, to people with apparent and stable, favourable or unfavourable personality traits. It has been proposed (Zillmann & Bryant, 1974; Zillmann & Cantor, 1976) that the degree to which the victim is perceived as deserving of a misfortune will determine to what extent a witness can accept the mishap without experiencing disturbing feelings of pity, and that the respondent's ability to sanction a misfortune - for anyone who, at this time, appears deserving of such 'punitive' treatment - sets him free to enjoy witnessing it. This model applies, of course, to people of all distinctions. Even a good guy can go wrong on something once in a while, and the rectification of his stray behaviour, potentially through disparagement, would seem in order. Since the sanction of a 'punitive' treatment clearly relates to moral considerations, one might further assume that, dependent upon the on-looker's moral norms, some treatments may be perceived as fitting and fair, and others as inadequate or too severe.

Actually the involvement of moral considerations in humour appreciation, and more generally, in the evocation of mirth, has been experimentally demonstrated. In a first study (Zillmann & Bryant, 1974), the provocation-retaliation format of squelches was manipulated as follows. In a central condition, the victim-to-be annoyed another person who then, in the punchline, applied a disparaging treatment to the victim; this treatment, as empirically determined, was perceived as a prompt and equitable compensation for the annoyer's misbehaviour. In other conditions, the compensation was perceived as far too severe, that is, as uncalled for and inequitable under the circumstances. In yet other conditions, it was perceived as too mild, that is, as inequitable in the sense of inadequate under the circumstances. Involving Heider's (1958) notions on intuitive justice, and equity theory (Adams, 1965; Walster, Berscheid & Walster, 1973), we had proposed that the condition of retaliatory equity would constitute an optimal condition for humour appreciation, and that inequitable putdowns, whether they are too mild or too severe, would impair appreciation because they leave the respondent's sense of justice disturbed. The findings were entirely consistent with these predictions.

The intricate relationship between the sanction of punitive treatments and mirthful reactions has also been documented in research outside the realm of humour. Appreciation of the provocation-retaliation motif in drama, for example, proved to be a function of moral judgment (Zillmann & Bryant, 1975). For a study with children at different levels of moral development, we created audio-visual versions of a highly eventful fairy tale. In the central version, the final turn of events showed a good prince retaliating equitably against his evil brother who had just been subdued after continued devious efforts to deprive the good prince of his rightful share to the kingdom they both had inherited. In this version, the good prince did to the bad prince exactly what the bad prince had meant to do to him. The good prince's reprisal went far beyond this mark of retaliatory equity in the version of overly severe retaliation, and it fell way short of the mark in the version of overly mild retaliation.

Children who had matured to the level of equitable retribution proved highly sensitive to the appropriateness or inappropriateness of the good prince's punitive measures, and they consequently enjoyed most the version in which retaliation was equitable, that is, in which events were in accord with what their moral conviction permitted them to sanction without conflict. In the conditions of both over- and under-retaliation, enjoyment of the drama was clearly impaired. The hero, in his efforts to restore justice, is apparently restricted - if drama is to be appreciated. In dishing out grief, he is confined to a magnitude of punitive measures which can be perceived as an equitable compensation for the magnitude of misdeeds committed by the transgressor. The unnecessarily rough, brutal, and cruel hero is not appreciated. But neither is the one who displays the Christian virtues of forgivingness. To see a transgression go unpunished, or at least, inadequately punished, proves disturbing rather than enjoyable.

All this is different for children who still believe in expiatory punishment. For them, punishment is demanded by unquestionable 'natural' rules, and the consequences of a misdeed rather than its particular motivational circumstances prescribe the magnitude of punishment. To children at this early developmental level, severe punishment appears both necessary and justified. In fact, it has been observed that the sterner the punishment, the more just it seems to be (cf. Piaget, 1948; Johnson, 1962). It should not surprise, then, that these children enjoyed the version of overretaliation the most and the version of underretaliation the least. Such preferences, after all, accord with their moral judgment.

The study of affective reactions to the emotions of others sheds further light on the
individual's willingness to sanction or abhor 'punitive' treatments. It has been shown
(Zillmann & Cantor, in press) that concordant affective reactions presuppose a favourable
disposition toward the person whose emotions are being witnessed. An unfavourable
disposition actually reverses the hedonic value of the affective state induced: witnessing
a disliked or resented person in dysphoria tends to produce euphoria. While considerations
of deservingness help determine such reactions, sheer dislike for a person - negative gut-
reaction, so to speak - apparently promotes discordant affect. The hostile putdown of a
liked person may thus easily turn off-colour humour. Such a putdown of an intensely disliked
person, however, is unlikely to evoke pity and thereby spoil any enjoyment.

All this, of course, is not to say that the enjoyment of hostile humour is entirely controlled
by moral and dispositional factors. Potentially many other determinants are involved.
Following Freudian (1905) suggestions, assaults on established social institutions (e.g.,
marriage, the Church, the police, the 'Establishment', government at large) may well be
motivated by repressions. Moral considerations may have to be retarded, at least temporarily,
to enable the individual to enjoy such derogatory attacks on the forces which influence his
life in crucial ways. The joy of witnessing violations of strictly enforced precepts, the
breaking of taboos, also manifests itself in spite of prevalent moral sanctions. It could
be argued, however, that the enjoyment people derive from seeing their institutions called
into question, and generally accepted precepts violated, is not only based on repression,
but presupposes the individual's moral condemnation of at least some aspect of the
institution or the precept which is being attacked. The individual, then, may well consider
it morally appropriate and 'right' to see a questionable element of an otherwise accepted
institution disparaged. And presumably, he would not be able to enjoy the putdown of an
institution or of a precept which he fully endorses - even when he acutely suffers
from related repressions. The married person, for example, who is badly tempted to engage
in some extra-marital activities, but who nonetheless is faithful to his/her spouse, say,
because of religious convictions, might fail to see the humour in the frequent slurs at the
institution of marriage. Be this as it may, the emphasis on moral considerations and on
dispositional factors in the appreciation of hostile humour appears to hold promise in
explaining the impairment or the total inhibition of mirthful reactions. This emphasis can
guide the exploration of the conditions under which hostile humour is perceived as unfunny,
as off-colour, and as 'sick'. The issue here is obviously very different from that
investigated by Levine and his co-workers (e.g., Levine & Redlich, 1955). These investigators
dealt with misperceptions in humour which serve the purpose of ego-defence. People may
simply 'miss the point' when getting it would bring damage to valued convictions of theirs.
In our case, it is assumed that the humorous message is properly perceived, but that mirth
is hampered by considering a disparagement inappropriate or entirely unwarranted.

As far as the grief-and-death motif in hostile humour is concerned, the notions we
entertained lead to the projection that extremely brutal happenings which bring grief and
death to the situation will be enjoyed when they can be perceived as called for by whatever
preceded them. By the same token, they are unlikely to spark mirth when they simply cannot
be sanctioned by the respondent. In response to a comedy movie, for example, the house may
well roar its approval when seeing the ever-so-evil tormentor of good folks finally break a
leg or two. But no director who would be daring enough to show such a severe mishap befall
a thoroughly sympathetic and liked character would, in his right mind, expect people to find
this hilarious.

In developing the above argument, we have assumed that, notwithstanding the general format
of humour, hostile events and their consequences are depicted with some degree of realism.
As indicated earlier, however, hostile and cruel events, in humour, can take highly
unrealistic and even anti-realistic form. This fact seems to further complicate the
discussion of the effect of extreme hostility and brutality on humour appreciation (cf.
Roger C. Mannell, this volume). Presumably, numerous stylistic means can be employed to
lower the degree of realism of depicted events. And pseudo-realities, which by definition
have a low degree of reality, if any, can readily be created. Through animation, characters
can be mutilated in what, in the real world, would be a most gruesome fashion; and
immediately thereafter, they can be made to recover miraculously. Tom and Jerry, or all the
other cartoon heroes and villains, can be cut up to slices, burned to death, or crushed to
mush - in the next moment they will, of course, pop up alive and well. In much humour,
especially in fare for children, the consequences of brutal actions are highly trivialized.
Hostility, brutality, and cruelty, ultimately have no apparent ill-effects. Under such
conditions of unreality, differentiations as they apply to the real world may be of little
moment. It might be perceived as 'just another little mishap' to the cartoon character to
see a dynamite stick shoved into his mouth and his head go up in smoke. Children, and
certainly adults, may be quite capable of separating a discourse of humour from a discourse
of reality (cf. Morris, 1955), and actions which would be dreadful in real life, when
adequately transformed and placed into the context of humour, may well become acceptable
means of making a putdown. There may be little, if any correspondence between the humour
and reality discourse. Seeing a cartoon figure hit in the mouth so that his teeth crack in

a million pieces may appear cruel to the analyst, but may have little or nothing to do with cruelty in the eyes of all those children looking on.

The fact that children and adults alike are apparently able to derive considerable enjoyment from humour which features high levels of hostility and mayhem, independent of the degree of reality of its depiction, may seem regrettable and even repulsive from an aesthetic perspective. Obviously, people celebrate antisocial acts in humour which are quite generally condemned in their actual social lives. Is this merely a case of poor taste? Or could such celebration of hostile and aggressive behaviour breed actual hostility and aggression? Berkowitz (1970) has addressed this issue and cautioned that hostile humour may indeed promote hostile behaviour.

Berkowitz conducted an experimental investigation in which female college students were either annoyed or not annoyed, listened either to aggressive humour (comedian Don Rickles) or nonaggressive humour (comedian George Carlin), and were then provided with an opportunity to retaliate against their annoyer. The findings show that, while the two types of humour had no differential effect on nonannoyed subjects, annoyed subjects who had been exposed to aggressive humour displayed higher retaliation scores than those who had been exposed to nonaggressive humour. While these data provide strong evidence against the view that hostile humour, compared to other types, is especially beneficial in venting anger and in purging hostile inclinations, they do not necessarily support Berkowitz's view that hostile humour, just like any other message featuring hostile exchanges, stimulates and enhances aggressive behaviour. In the absence of no-humour conditions, it is impossible to tell whether or not the hostile routine produced increments in hostility. The hostile routine, compared to a hypothetical nonhumorous message, may well have reduced the retaliatory behaviour measured. However, while it is not clear what absolute effect on hostility the hostile routine had, it is very clear that the nonhostile humour had a more salutary impact.

It should be pointed out that in the discussed study by Berkowitz, hostile humour was of a highly realistic kind. Don Rickles is known for his blatant brutalization in putting down adversaries and innocent bystanders alike. It is conceivable that less realistic hostility in humour has quite different effects. In fact, an investigation reported by Landy and Mettee (1969) produced findings which oppose Berkowitz's suggestion that hostile humour enhances hostility. Landy and Mettee actually confounded hostile and nonhostile humour, but employed a no-humour control condition. They observed that retaliatory behaviour was less rather than more intense after exposure to humour – compared to no humour. The placement of humour between annoyance and retaliatory opportunities, then, reduced hostile actions, and it did so although half of the materials were of a hostile kind. The aggression-promoting effect of hostile humour, should it exist, thus seems to be quite modest: it apparently was too small to overcome or even just neutralize the aggression-reducing effect of nonhostile humour.

The implications of nonhostile humour for physical aggression have been explored in a decisive study by Baron and Ball (1974). These investigators provoked or did not provoke male and female student subjects, exposed them to nonhostile humour or neutral fare, and then had the subjects aggress against the person who initially interacted with them. The results show that exposure to humour had only a negligible effect on nonprovoked persons, but reduced aggressive behaviour significantly in provoked ones. Nonhostile humour, it appears, has a salutary effect on angry people. And potentially, it can have such an effect on annoyed, irritated, disturbed, and depressed people as well. Humour, at least the nonhostile variety, seems to be capable of producing a pleasant state which then interferes with the return of negative emotions (cf. Baron & Ball, 1974; Tannenbaum & Zillmann, 1975). All this sounds very promising, but unfortunately the available evidence demands some qualifications.

Tannenbaum (cf. Tannenbaum & Zillmann, 1975) found that physiologically arousing humour may facilitate motivated aggression for some time after exposure, and Mueller and Donnerstein (in press) failed to replicate some of the effects reported by Baron and Ball. Specifically, Mueller and Donnerstein found that, compared to a no-humour control condition, neither moderate nor intense and presumably arousing humour had any effect on males. For females, however, they obtained the aggression-reducing effect of moderate humour, while intense humour failed to exert an appreciable influence on aggression.

Looking at the available evidence, then, it would seem that humour, provided that it is not overly intense and arousing, can indeed effectively combat undesirable emotions and their behavioural consequences. Some caution is indicated, however, when it comes to hostile and aggressive humour. Humour is thus not simply a matter of superficial amusement, but it may achieve salutary effects in the individual's household of emotions. About this, we certainly should know more than we do now.

REFERENCES

See Bibliography for publications on humour, laughter and comedy

Adams, J.S., Inequity in social exchange. In: L. Berkowitz (Ed.), Advances in Experimental
    Social Psychology (Vol. 2). Academic Press, New York (1965).

Baudelaire, C., De l'essence du rire. In: Oeuvres Complètes. Gallimard, Paris (1961).
    (Originally published, 1855).

Cantor, J.R., Mody, B. & Zillmann, D., Residual emotional arousal as a distractor in
    persuasion. Journal of Social Psychology, 92, 231-244 (1974).

Hazlitt, W., On the pleasure of hating. In: Essays. Macmillan, New York (1926). (Originally
    published, 1826).

Heider, F., The Psychology of Interpersonal Relations. Wiley, New York (1958).

Johnson, R., A study of children's moral judgments. Child Development, 33, 327-354 (1962).

Lesser, G.S., Children and Television: Lessons from Sesame Street. Random House, New York
    (1974).

Morris, C., Signs, Language and Behaviour. Braziller, New York (1955).

Piaget, J., The Moral Judgment of The Child. The Free Press, Glencoe, Illinois (1948).

Plato., Dialogues (Volume IV). Oxford University Press, London (1892).

Roussou, N.C., Children's appreciation of aggressive contents in televised cartoons.
    Unpublished Master's thesis, Indiana University (1972).

Tannenbaum, P.H. & Zillmann, D., Emotional arousal in the facilitation of aggression through
    communication. In: L. Berkowitz (Ed.), Advances in Experimental Social Psychology
    (Vol. 8). Academic Press, New York (1975).

Walster, E., Berscheid, E. & Walster, G.W., New directions in equity research. Journal of
    Personality and Social Psychology, 25, 151-176 (1973).

Zillmann, D. & Bryant, J., Viewer's moral sanction of retribution in the appreciation of
    dramatic presentations. Journal of Experimental Social Psychology, 11, 572-582 (1975).

Zillmann, D. & Cantor, J.R., Affective responses to the emotions of a protagonist. Journal
    of Experimental Social Psychology, in press.

Tedentious Humour in the Mass Media

Joanne R. Cantor

University of Wisconsin

Much of the empirical research on the psychology of humour has involved the assessment of the effect of particular variables within a humorous communication on the mirth response it evokes. Many researchers have taken the theoretical speculations of philosophers and psychologists as points of departure and have tested whether or not predictions derived from these theories hold up under controlled conditions. These tests have usually employed formalized humorous stimuli, such as the cartoons, jokes, skits, and monologues that appear in the mass media. Typically, the researchers have either manipulated the stimuli along a particular dimension or they have compared responses to intact stimuli which differed along the dimension of interest.

In these studies, then, the findings have been relevant to the question of what effect a particular element of a humorous stimulus has on the mirth response produced by that stimulus. What has not, of course, been produced by these studies is evidence of the frequency with which the elements being studied occur in mass media humour. A carefully planned and rigorously conducted experiment, for example, may reveal that a joke which is heard in one form is rated consistently funnier than the same joke when it is manipulated into another form. It could be, however, that one form of the joke is highly atypical in humour as we know it. Thus the observed lower degree of appreciation of this joke may be due to the fact that it does not fit in with the listener's expectations regarding what a joke is. In other words, the difference in the appreciation of the two stimuli may tell us less about the psychology of humour per se than about generalized notions of what constitutes a humour stimulus.

A method that can be readily applied to determine the typical characteristics of the mass media humour to which we are constantly being exposed is content analysis. In addition to providing us with data regarding the characteristics of current mass media humour, content analyses can be helpful in evaluating theories of mirth. A theory, for example, which states that a particular element in humour is critically important in inducing a mirth response will be challenged if it is shown that this element occurs in only a small proportion of those stimuli which our society reacts to as humorous. Content analyses can also be helpful in understanding the findings of experiments. For example, experimental findings which reveal that particular elements of humour produce the most mirth can be related to the findings of content analyses to determine whether the producers of humour 'intuitively' or through trial and error are turning out stimuli in the most mirth-evoking forms. Additionally, in cases where experimental findings deviate from theoretical expectations or from earlier related results, we can sometimes use content analyses to determine whether the relative frequency or infrequency of specific forms of humour can account for the discrepancy between an expected and an observed outcome.

The research I am presenting here involves several content analyses of mass media humour which were conducted recently. The findings of these studies have been organized to address two specific issues which have arisen out of research and theories of humour: (1) the importance of what Freud termed tendentious, that is, hostile or sexual, wit in the mass media, and (2) the treatment of the two sexes in mass media humour.

With regard to the first issue, Freud (1905) maintained that humour which serves a hostile or sexual purpose is the only intensely funny humour. He stated:

'The pleasurable effect of innocent jokes is as a rule a moderate one; a clear sense of satisfaction, a slight smile, is as a rule all it can achieve in its hearers. And it may be that part even of this effect is to be attributed to the joke's intellectual content, as we have seen from suitable examples. A nontendentious joke scarcely ever achieves the sudden burst of laughter which makes tendentious ones so irresistible. Since the technique of both can be the

same, a suspicion may be aroused in us that tendentious jokes, by virtue of their
purpose, must have sources of pleasure at their disposal to which innocent jokes
have no access.'

'The purposes of jokes can easily be reviewed. Where a joke is not an aim in
itself — that is, where it is not an innocent one — there are only two purposes
that it may serve, and these two can themselves be subsumed under a single heading.
It is either a hostile joke (serving the purpose of aggressiveness, satire, or
defence) or an obscene joke (serving the purpose of exposure).'

Other writers such as Rapp (1951) have taken an even more extreme view, challenging the
very existence of nontendentious humour.

If Freud, Rapp, and others with similar views are correct in assuming that all really intense
mirth derives from humour which involves hostility or sex, we might expect that a large
portion of mass media humour would depict these themes. This, of course, is based on the
assumption that the humour that the media are producing is generally experienced as humorous
by the public and that the types of humour that continue to be represented are those that
have met with some measure of success.

In a study conducted recently, Stocking, Sapolsky, and Zillmann (in press) content analyzed
television humour. Pairs of coders viewed U.S. prime-time television for an entire week,
systematically rotating between the three major commercial networks at ten-minute intervals.
They recorded all incidents which seemed to be intended to be funny. An incident was
classified as 'hostile' if a person or thing was disparaged or put down, or it was recorded
as 'nonhostile' if the incident did not involve disparagement. Their entire programming
sample (which represents one-third of actual programming time) included 852 humorous incidents.
Table 1 shows a breakdown of humorous incidents by type. Out of all humorous incidents, 588

TABLE 1   Frequency of Types of Humour on Prime-Time Television

	Hostile	Nonhostile	Combined
Sexual	63	31	94
Nonsexual	525	233	758
Combined	588	264	852

Data are from Stocking, Sapolsky and Zillmann (in press). Frequencies represent
the number of humorous incidents in each category. All prime-time programmes
were analyzed, but the frequencies represent only one-third of actual programme
time.

or 69% were classified as hostile and only 264 or 31% as nonhostile. Incidents were also
classified according to whether they involved explicit or implied references to sex organs
or sexual intercourse. Ninety-four incidents were classified as sexual, or 11% of the sample.
When the sexual-nonhostile incidents are combined with the hostile incidents, it can be seen
that 619 incidents, or 73% of the sample, involved either sexual or hostile humour. Thus, if
we consider television humour and assume that what appears in prime-time reflects what is
successful with the audience, Freud's notion that tendentious wit evokes the most mirth has
received support.

Quite a different picture emerges if the cartoon humour which appears in popular magazines
is considered. Several years ago, I began a content analysis of the cartoon humour occurring
in magazines. I chose 'The New Yorker' and 'Look' because the cartoons in both magazines
were very well-known and because the main purpose of the content analysis necessitated using
magazines that were not predominantly aimed at one sex or the other. Samples of cartoons
were drawn from both magazines for the years 1955, 1960, 1965, and 1970. In addition, I
recently sampled an additional year from 'The New Yorker' ('Look' having ceased publication
in the interim). Three cartoons were randomly selected from each month of the years in
question, yielding a total sample of 324 cartoons. Last autumn the students in my large mass
media class served as coders in a content analysis of these cartoons which I conducted with
Pat Venus (Cantor & Venus, 1975). For each cartoon in the sample, the coders were asked the
following questions, among others: (a) Is physical violence or aggression engaged in,
threatened, or about to occur? (b) Is nonphysical hostility depicted or implied? (3) Would
you say that sex (sexual behaviour) is a theme in the cartoon? There was an average of
fifteen coders per cartoon, and two-thirds agreement was necessary to place a cartoon in any
or all of these categories. The results of this analysis contrast sharply with those of the
analysis of prime-time television. Out of the entire sample of 324 cartoons, only 18 (or 6%)
were classified as depicting violence, 38 (or 12%) were classified as expressing hostility,

and 17 (or 5%) were said to depict sex. While the definitions of what constituted 'tendentious humour' may have been slightly different in the two studies and the coding procedure seems more conservative in the latter study, the difference between the two samples seems quite substantial. The humour in these two magazines seems to be primarily nontendentious. The proportion of tendentious to nontendentious humour was similar in the two magazines, and no differences emerged over the years in which the cartoons were sampled.

A recent content analysis which I conducted with Carol Richardson (Cantor & Richardson, 1976) provides still a different picture of the degree of tendentiousness in mass media humour. In this study, we looked at four currently popular magazines featuring cartoon humour, two aimed primarily at men and two aimed primarily at women. For each target audience, we chose one magazine reputed to represent the more 'swinging' or sexually 'liberated' point of view, and one known to be more conservative and traditional. We chose 'Playboy' and 'Cosmopolitan' as the "swinging" magazines aimed at males and females respectively, and 'Esquire' and 'Ladies' Home Journal' as their more staid counterparts. Forty-eight cartoons were sampled, that is, four per month for a year (1974) for 'Playboy', 'Cosmopolitan', and 'Ladies' Home Journal'. Only twenty cartoons occurred during the year in 'Esquire', so all were included. The sample was divided into four equal portions, each portion containing the same number of cartoons from the four magazines. A pair of coders (each pair involving a male and a female) was assigned to each of the four portions of the sample. The two coders worked independently, and a fifth male-female pair of judges was used to arbitrate disagreements between coders. The coders were asked to indicate whether each cartoon depicted had as its theme sex, violence, and/or hostility. Sexual themes were described as depicting or relating to sexual relations, body parts related to sexual behaviour, or unorthodox sexual practices or lifestyles. Violent themes included both intentional interpersonal aggression and depictions of accidental bodily destruction. Hostility was defined as explicitly depicted ill-will between characters or between a character and an object or institution. In addition, if a cartoon was seen to depict more than one of these themes, one was to be denoted as the cartoon's major theme. This was done so that in the statistical analysis, a particular cartoon would occur in only one category. Table 2 shows the frequency counts of cartoons depicting tendentious themes, broken down by the magazines from which they were sampled. As can be seen from the table, the number of cartoons depicting the various tendentious themes differed dramatically from

TABLE 2   Frequency of Tendentious Themes in Cartoon Humour

Magazine type	Tendentious theme			Tendentious themes combined	Nontendentious themes	Total
	Sex	Violence	Hostility			
'Liberated'						
Playboy	37	1	3	41[c]	7	48
Cosmopolitan	30	3	3	36[c]	12	48
'Traditional'						
Esquire	1	8	1	10[b]	10	20
Ladies' Home Journal	0	2	6	8[a]	40	48
Total	68	14	13	95	69	164

Frequencies represent the number of cartoons in each category. Distributions of tendentious and nontendentious themes denoted by different letter superscripts differ significantly at p < .05 by chi-square test.

magazine to magazine. The so-called 'liberated' magazines exhibited predominantly tendentious humour ('Playboy': 85%; 'Cosmopolitan': 75%), 'Esquire' contained equal amounts of tendentious and nontendentious humour (50%), and 'Ladies' Home Journal' rarely showed tendency wit (17%). The frequencies show that the tendency wit in the 'liberated' magazines consists almost entirely of sexual themes. In contrast, almost all of the tendency wit in 'Esquire' deals with themes of violence and destruction, and hostility is the predominant source of tendentious themes in 'Ladies' Home Journal'. A chi-square analysis on the distribution of tendentious and nontendentious humour in the four magazines yielded a marked overall difference ($\chi^2(3)=54.68$; p <.001). Individual chi-square comparisons between pairs of magazines revealed that 'Playboy' did not differ from 'Cosmopolitan' in its proportion of tendency wit ($\chi^2(1)=1.64$; p<.20), but that both magazines had significantly higher proportions of tendency wit than both of the other magazines ('Playboy' vs. 'Esquire': $\chi^2(1)=9.44$; p <.01; 'Playboy' vs. 'Ladies' Home Journal': $\chi^2(1)=45.39$; p <.001; 'Cosmopolitan' vs. 'Esquire': $\chi^2(1)=3.96$; p <.05; 'Cosmopolitan' vs. 'Ladies' Home Journal': $\chi^2(1)=32.90$; p <.001). In addition, 'Esquire' exceeded 'Ladies' Home Journal' in the proportion of tendentious humour $(X^2(1)=8.04; p<.01)$. Thus, the data from these four magazines show great differences in the amount of tendentiousness inherent in their cartoons.

The conclusion to be reached regarding Freud's notion of the importance of tendentious humour, then, depends on where we look for data. Freud's notion seems to be confirmed if we consider the humour on prime-time television and in 'hip' magazines, but challenged if we look at magazines oriented toward more of a generalized audience. Freudians might argue, of course, that the two types of humour differ dramatically in their capacity to evoke intense mirth, but the determination of such a difference is beyond the scope of the present research. Suffice it to say that whether or not Freud's speculations regarding intense mirth are true, a good proportion of what our society is labelling and reacting to as humorous does not involve themes which are readily identifiable as tendentious.

The second issue being addressed in this research relates to the well documented tendency for people to 'take sides' for and against protagonists in humour. A respondent's degree of demographic similarity to a joke or cartoon's protagonist has repeatedly been shown to influence the mirth response. Various studies have defined group membership in terms of race, religion, nationality, and political affiliation, and have demonstrated that people tend to find jokes in which members of their own group disparage members of other groups more amusing than jokes in which an alien group disparages their own (cf. La Fave, 1961; La Fave, McCarthy & Haddad, 1973; Middleton, 1959; Priest, 1966; Priest & Abrahams, 1970; Wolff, Smith & Murray, 1934). In 1970, when Zillmann and I tried to demonstrate the same effect using the respondent's sex as the demographic criterion for predicting humour responses, we observed puzzling findings: as expected, males found it funnier to see a male disparage a female than to see a female disparage a male, but, unexpectedly, females showed the same preference. In 1972, Losco and Epstein (1975) observed similar tendencies, and last year, in an expanded replication of our first study (Cantor, 1976) I observed that this apparent anti-female bias still exists. Male and female subjects judged jokes to be funnier when a female protagonist was the victim, whether the disparaging agent was male or female.

Our research (Cantor & Zillmann, 1973; Zillmann, Bryant & Cantor, 1974; Zillmann & Cantor, 1972, 1976) has led us to conclude that a subject's affective disposition toward protagonists leads him or her to 'root' for the protagonist toward whom the strongest affiliative bonds are felt and/or to take sides against the one toward whom the most resentment is held. The logical extension of this reasoning then, is to conclude that women consider themselves more strongly affiliated with the opposite sex than with their own sex, whereas men affiliate themselves more readily with their own sex. If this were true, it would certainly not be encouraging to advocates of the Women's Movement who are trying to promote female solidarity. But other explanations for our findings present themselves. Among these explanations is the notion that humour, throughout history, has been predominantly a male domain. Most humour seems to have been written and performed by males, and perhaps we have become used to seeing, for example, the 'unjustly beleaguered' husband take humorous swipes at his wife, but we are not typically exposed to wives ridiculing their husbands in a humorous vein. It could be that the frequency with which we see males disparage females in humour is much greater than the frequency of disparagement in the opposite direction. Perhaps, then, the findings of these experiments are due to our general expectations regarding humour, independent of our feelings of affiliation or resentment for one sex or the other.

To see whether the female in fact typically receives more than her share of disparagement in mass media humour, we can look again at the findings of content analysis. The study of prime-time television by Stocking, Sapolsky, and Zillmann (in press) dealt specifically with this question. For all incidents of hostile humour in the sample, the sex of the disparager and the victim was noted. Table 3 shows the frequencies with which the four possible combinations of disparager and victim occurred. As expected, males performed disparagement

TABLE 3   Breakdown of Incidents of Hostile Humour in Prime-Time
Television by Sex of Disparager and Victim

Disparager	Victim		Combined
	Male	Female	
Male	255[c]	99[b]	354[B]
Female	104[b]	14[a]	118[A]
Combined	359[B]	113[A]	472

Data are from Stocking, Sapolsky and Zillmann (in press). Differences between frequencies were analyzed separately for the individual cells and for the two pairs of combined frequencies. Frequencies having different superscripts differ significantly at p < .01 by chi-square test. The remaining 116 incidents of hostile humour in the sample were categorized as 'other', meaning that either the disparager or the victim was not identifiable as male or female.

significantly more often than females (354 vs. 118; $X^2(1)=118.0$; p < .001), but contrary to our speculations regarding the reasons for the anti-female bias in humour, male characters were also the victims of humorous disparagement significantly more often than females (359 vs. 113; $X^2(1)=128.2$; p < .001). In fact, disparagement of a male by a male occurred the most frequently (255 incidents). Females disparaged males as frequently as males disparaged females (104 vs. 99, respectively; $X^2(1)=0.123$; p > .7), and females disparaged each other extremely rarely (14 incidents). These data do not help at all, then, to explain the finding that it is funnier to see a male disparage a female than a female disparage a male, or that regardless of the sex of the disparager, it is funnier to see a female than a male be victimized. It is possible, of course, that this apparent equality of men and women in television humour is a recent phenomenon, and that content analyses of earlier times would produce different results.

The study by Cantor and Venus (1975) of cartoons from 'The New Yorker' and 'Look' also provided data relevant to the disparagement of the two sexes. In order to see whether females were depicted more often than males as possessing stereotypical negative characteristics, the coders were asked to indicate whether particular characteristics were attributed to any of the characters in the cartoons. Among these attributes were stupidity, disagreeableness, submissiveness, and unattractiveness. The coders did not know that the sex of the character was at issue. Whenever two-thirds agreement was reached that a protagonist exhibited a particular characteristic, the sex of that protagonist was noted. Independently, the frequencies with which males and females were depicted or mentioned in the cartoons was noted. The top part of Table 4 shows the occurrence of males and females, alone and together, in

TABLE 4   Frequency of Cartoons Involving Male and Female Characters
              in Magazine Humour

Protagonists involved

	Males only	Females only	Both sexes	Neither
Look	71	2	56	15
The New Yorker	83	5	73	19
Combined	154	7	129	34
Playboy	7	0	41	0
Cosmopolitan	3	2	43	0
Esquire	12	0	7	1
Ladies' Home Journal	14	3	30	1
Combined	36	5	121	2

The frequencies refer to the number of cartoons depicting or involving the specified characters. The 'Neither' category refers to cartoons either involving characters whose sex was unidentifiable or involving no animate characters.

the cartoons of our sample. It was found that, in spite of the fact that both 'Look' and 'The New Yorker' are aimed at audiences of both sexes, male characters were involved much more frequently than females. Combining the number of times each sex occurred separately with the number of times the two sexes occurred together, males occurred in 283 cartoons, and females in only 136 ($X^2(1)=51.57$; p < .001). Even more striking is the difference between the number of times males and females occurred without members of the opposite sex. Males occurred in the absence of females in 154 cartoons, whereas females occurred alone in only seven ($X^2(1)=134.22$; p < .001). It is possible to interpret this underrepresentation of the female in two ways. It may be that women are not considered as important as men and that they are particularly unworthy of notice in the absence of men. However, it is also possible that women occur less often because they are considered less deserving of ridicule. Interpretations of these lopsided distributions aside, it is important to keep the frequency of occurrence of males and females in mind when looking at the data regarding the frequency with which members of either sex are ridiculed.

In terms of the stereotyped negative characteristics, 57 males and 31 females were identified as exhibiting the characteristic of stupidity. Comparing this outcome to a theoretical distribution of equal probability, the male exhibits stupidity significantly more often than the female ($X^2(1)=7.68$; p < .01). However, if only the cartoons in which both males and females occur are considered, there are twelve instances of male stupidity and twenty-six instances of female stupidity. In these cartoons, the female is stupid significantly more often than the male ($X^2(1)=5.16$; p < .05). These findings thus present evidence for the overvictimization of both males and females. In cartoons in general, it seems, the image of the stupid male occurs more often than that of the stupid female. However, in cartoons depicting members of both sexes, a female is more likely than a male to be singled out as being stupid.

When the overall sample was considered, more cartoons depicted males than females as being disagreeable (48 vs. 14, respectively; $X^2(1)=18.65$; p < .001) and submissive (46 vs. 10, respectively; $X^2(1)=23.14$; p < .001), but equivalent numbers of cartoons depicted each sex possessing these characteristics when only the cartoons depicting both sexes were involved (disagreeable, male: 17, female: 14; $X^2(1)=0.29$; p > .50; submissive, male: 12, female: 10; $X^2(1)=0.18$; p > .50). The frequency with which male and female characters were depicted as unattractive was equivalent for the entire sample (male: 11, female: 10; $X^2(1)=0.05$; p > .70). For the cartoons involving males and females together, there was a slight tendency for more females than males to be unattractive (males: 3, females: 8), but this tendency was not significant ($X^2(1)=2.27$; p > .10).

The coders in this content analysis were also asked to denote which character appeared to be the object of the cartoonist's ridicule. Out of the entire sample, 121 males and 46 females were so denoted. Thus, significantly more cartoons involved males than females as the butt of the joke ($X^2(1)=33.68$; p < .001). However, in cartoons in which males and females occurred together, the males were perceived as the object of ridicule only twenty-five times and females forty times. This difference approaches significance ($X^2(1)=3.46$; p < .10).

The data from this content analysis thus show that males receive more ridicule in cartoon humour than females. This feature seems to be due primarily to the fact that they occur more frequently than females, however. When only those cartoons in which both males and females occur are considered, the difference is equalized, and in a few cases, the disparagement of the female tends to surpass that of the male.

The content analysis by Cantor and Richardson (1976) also provided data relevant to the issue of male versus female disparagement. As can be seen from the bottom part of Table 4, in the samples drawn from 'Playboy', 'Cosmopolitan', 'Esquire', and 'Ladies' Home Journal', cartoons in which only females were depicted were again the most rare. Cartoons depicting both sexes together were more prevalent than in the earlier content analysis, making the occurrence of males not so much more frequent than that of females (males: 157, females: 126; $X^2(1)=3.40$; p < .10). Females still occurred alone significantly less frequently than males did, however (males: 36, females: 5; $X^2(1)=23.44$; p < .001).

In judging these cartoons, the coders were asked to indicate if one protagonist was seen to disparage another. The responses for all possible male-female combinations were tallied. Table 5 shows the distributions for the four magazines combined. As in the content analysis of television, the male was the disparager more often than the female (28 vs. 18), but this

TABLE 5   Breakdown of Disparagement in Cartoon Humour by Sex of
          Disparager and Victim

Disparager	Victim		Combined
	Male	Female	
Male	9^b	19^b	28^A
Female	18^b	0^a	18^A
Combined	27^A	19^A	36

Data are from the samples drawn from 'Playboy', 'Cosmopolitan', 'Esquire', and 'Ladies' Home Journal'. Frequencies refer to the number of cartoons in each category. For the remaining cartoons in the sample, either the disparager or the victim was not identifiable as male or female, or the depicted events were not considered to depict disparagement.

Differences between frequencies were analyzed separately for the individual cells and for the two pairs of combined frequencies. Frequencies having different superscripts differ significantly at p < .01. Yates' correction for small expected frequencies was used where applicable. Male disparagement of males differs from

male disparagement of females and female disparagement of males at p <.10
($x^2(1)=3.57$ and $x^2(1)=3.00$, respectively).

time the difference was not significant ($x^2(1)=2.17$; p >.10). Again, the male was the
victim more frequently than the female (27 vs. 19), but this difference was also nonsignificant ($x^2(1)=1.39$; p >.20). As in the content analysis of television, the number of
times males disparaged females was equivalent to the frequency with which females disparaged
males (19 vs. 18, $x^2(1)=0.03$; p >.70). Unlike on television, disparagement between males
was not the most frequent type. The most striking aspect of these data is the total lack of
disparagement between females. It will be remembered that the female disparagement of
females was also extremely rare in the content analysis of television. Thus, again, there
is no evidence for the notion that it is more typical to see a man disparage a woman than
vice versa or that female disparagement is highly typical.

When the four magazines were considered separately, there was no difference between the
proportion of male/female to female/male disparagement in the magazines aimed at men and
those aimed at women. For the male-oriented magazines, there were nine instances of male
disparagement of females and eight instances of female disparagement of males. For the
women's magazines, there were ten cartoons of each type. The difference between the two
distributions was, of course, nonsignificant ($x^2(1)=0.04$; p >.70). Even when only the two
more openly 'sexist' magazines, 'Playboy' and 'Cosmopolitan' are compared, the two
distributions do not differ significantly ('Playboy', male/female: 9, female/male: 6;
'Cosmopolitan', male/female: 6, female/male: 8; $x^2(1)=0.80$; p >.30), although perhaps they
would if a larger sample were used.

The coders in this content analysis also were asked to indicate which character seemed to be
the target of the cartoonist's ridicule. The data for this question were tallied for all
cartoons and then separately for the cartoons in which males and females occurred together.
Table 6 shows these data. As can be seen, when all cartoons are considered, male characters

TABLE 6   Sex of Object of Cartoonist's Ridicule in Magazine Humour

	All cartoons Sex of ridiculed protagonist			Cartoons involving both sexes Sex of ridiculed protagonist		
	Male	Female	Both	Male	Female	Both
Playboy	23	16	5	18	16	5
Cosmopolitan	23	12	5	21	11	5
Esquire	13	3	1	2	3	1
Ladies' Home Journal	17	10	4	9	9	4
Combined	76	41	15	50	39	15

Frequencies refer to the number of cartoons in each category. There was one cartoon
(involving both sexes) in which the sex of the target could not be ascertained. In
addition, there were 31 cartoons (of which 17 involved both sexes) in which no
character was identified as the target of ridicule.

are singled out as the object of ridicule more often than females (males: 76, females: 41;
$x^2(1)=10.50$; p <.01). When only humour involving both males and females is considered, the
difference diminishes (50 vs. 39; $x^2(1)=1.36$; p >.20) and is no longer significant. The
distributions of these data did not differ significantly from magazine to magazine.

With regard to the question of why we seem to enjoy the disparagement of females more than
that of males, the findings of these content analyses thus present us with a puzzling picture.
Our expectation that humour would be a predominantly male domain was confirmed. On television,
males figure in hostile humour much more frequently than females, and in magazine humour,
cartoons involving male characters outnumber those involving female characters by far.
However, the fact that males are more frequent participants in humour causes them generally
to be victimized more frequently than females as well as being the source of disparagement
more often. Clearly, if we consider all the humour that was content analyzed in the present
research, it is not more typical to see a woman than a man be disparaged. On the contrary,
it is much more typical to see a man be ridiculed. However, there is some evidence that,
whatever the reason for the male's more frequent presence in humour, it is largely his
overrepresentation that causes him to be overvictimized. In cartoons in which both sexes
occur, the male does not receive more than his share of disparagement, and some findings
suggest a tendency to single out the female for more than her share of the disparagement.
In terms of hostile exchanges between characters, however, females disparage males as

frequently as males disparage females, and females only rarely disparage other females.

Thus we cannot account for the so-called anti-female bias in humour appreciation by the notion that our expectations regarding what is humorous are being shaped by the frequency with which various configurations of dominance occur in the mass media. Further research, perhaps into the social perception of humorous protagonists as a function of their sex (cf. Cantor, 1976) needs to be done before these puzzling findings are understood.

The research reported in this paper was admittedly limited in the mass media sources of humour it sought to analyze. Further analyses involving other popular forms of mass media humour seem called for, to elucidate the theoretical issues currently under review and to attack other issues arising out of humour research.

REFERENCES

See Bibliography for publications on humour, laughter and comedy

Cantor, J. & Richardson, C., Content analysis of the humor in Playboy, Cosmopolitan, Esquire, and Ladies' Home Journal. Unpublished research (1976).

Cantor, J. & Venus, P., Content analysis of the humor in The New Yorker and Look. Unpublished research (1975).

La Fave, L., Humor judgments as a function of reference groups: An experimental study. Unpublished doctoral dissertation, University of Oklahoma (1961).

The Changing Stereotype of the Welsh in English Jokes

Christie Davies

University of Reading

The most remarkable thing about Welsh jokes is their absence. The inhabitants of the British Isles constantly tell jokes about such ethnic minorities as the Scots, the Irish, the Jews and more recently about immigrants from India, Pakistan and the West Indies. Jokes about the Welsh are far less common, and they are far less likely to embody a single distinctive attribute in the way that jokes about the Irish or the Scots do. Anyone familiar with British jokes knows that the Scots are supposed to be stingy and the Irish supposed to be stupid but few people would be able easily and accurately to pin-point a similar distinctive characteristic in jokes about the Welsh.

The Welsh were not always so neglected by the tellers of jokes and the compilers of joke-books, for in the sixteenth and seventeenth century the Welsh were the most common butt of English jokes. In John Ashton's (1883) collection of seventeenth century jokes and joke-books the Welsh appear no less than fourteen times which is far in excess of their nearest rivals, the Scots, with five jokes about them, and the French and Irish with two jokes each.

However, our main concern here is with the stereotype of the Welsh present in the seventeenth century jokes. Four characteristics are repeatedly assigned to the Welsh in these jokes. The Welsh are portrayed as: aggressive and quarrelsome; boastful; speaking English in a peculiar fashion; being excessively fond of eating cheese. The overall stereotype of the Welsh is perhaps best illustrated by quoting one of these jokes verbatim.

> A Welch man in heat of blood, challenged an Englishman
> at Sword and Buckler; but the Englishman giving him
> a lusty blow on the leg which vext him, he threw down
> his Weapon, swearing: Splut, was not her Buckler broad
> enough, but her must hit her on the leg? (Ashton, 1883, p.190)

It would be dangerous, however, to assert that the above are the predominant characteristics of the comic Welshman of the day simply on the basis of a very limited number of jokes from a limited sample of anthologies. It is necessary to provide supporting evidence from other sources to put the suggested elements of the Welsh stereotype on a stronger foundation. Such evidence is readily to be found in the plays of Shakespeare. The Welsh appear in Shakespeare's plays as comic characters more often and more significantly than other nationalities and they are laughed at for essentially the same reasons as the ones I have deduced from anthologies of jokes. The main point to note is that all three of Shakespeare's important comic Welshmen, namely, Fluellen in Henry V, Owen Glendower in Henry IV Part I, and Sir Hugh Evans the Welsh parson in Merry Wives of Windsor, are involved in conflict situations. Fluellen not only beats ancient Pistol in the well-known scene with the leek (Henry V; Act 5) but also quarrels with the Irish Capatain MacMorris (Henry V; Act 3) and is challenged by the English (or Welsh) soldier Williams when he wears the king's glove in his hat (Henry V; Act 4). Owen Glendower spends most of his time on stage wrangling with Harry Hotspur, and Sir Hugh Evans narrowly escapes fighting a duel with the French physician Doctor Caius (The Merry Wives of Windsor; Act 3). Shakespeare's reason for always placing his Welsh characters in the middle of quarrels and conflicts is to extract the maximum humour from the popular stereotype of the Welsh (which presumably he shares with his audience) as being aggressive, touchy, boastful and proud.

This tendency to see the Welsh as proud and boastful - and particularly so about the length of their ancestry - is not confined to Shakespeare. Dodd (1971) says of seventeenth century writers in general that 'If an English dramatist or pamphleteer wanted to raise a good-humoured laugh he had only to conjure up a Welsh "shentleman" poor as a church-mouse but ready to rattle off his pedigree to the ninth generation or even back to Brutus and Adam'.

In Tudor and Stuart times then the English saw the Welsh as the distinctive out-group with certain familiar comic traits. By the late nineteenth and twentieth century all this had changed and anthologies of jokes contain very few references to the Welsh. In terms of numbers of jokes and strength and clarity of stereotyping the main butts of English humour are now the Scots, the Irish and the Jews. There are still some Welsh jokes and a definite though totally changed Welsh stereotype but the Welsh are now on the periphery of English humour.

The paucity of Welsh jokes when compared with jokes about other ethnic minorities can be illustrated by the following statistics based on an analysis of the contents of some eighty-nine 'jokebooks'. Of these books there are eleven which deal exclusively or predominantly with Scottish jokes, three which deal with Irish jokes and three with Jewish jokes. There is no book in English that deals primarily with Welsh jokes and so far as the author knows no such book exists. The author's own Welsh jokebook will be the first in the field (Davies, 1976).

In addition to the above a further six books devote a section to Scottish jokes, a further nine books have an Irish jokes section and five books a section of Jewish jokes. No book has a section of Welsh jokes. The total number of Welsh jokes in all the jokebooks taken together is only eighty-eight which works out at just under one Welsh joke per book. There is a marked contrast with the Scots, the Irish and the Jews, all of whom have over five-hundred jokes (and more) devoted to them.

	Welsh	Scots	Irish	Jews
Number of books specific to the group	0	11	3	3
Number of books with one or more sections on the group	0	6	9	5
Total number of such sections	0	13	13	5
Total number of jokes	88	500+	500+	500+

Despite their relative scarcity, there are, however, enough Welsh jokes in absolute terms for a reasonably clear stereotype of the Welsh to emerge. It is in all respects totally different from that which was earlier depicted in the seventeenth century. In the jokes of the last hundred years (that is, since 1870) the Welsh are very rarely depicted as proud, aggressive or boastful (in four jokes at most) and there is only one reference to the Welsh love for toasted cheese. Furthermore these references are found only in the nineteenth century jokebooks and even there they appear to be anachronisms.

The old image of the Welsh as proud, aggressive and boastful is replaced in modern jokes by a totally different stereotype in which the Welsh are depicted as crafty, devious and evasive. Indeed the new stereotype is almost the opposite of the old one. This new image of the Welsh as crafty or devious is to be found in one form or another in twenty-eight of the eighty-eight Welsh jokes culled from the anthologies (that is, about one third). No other character trait is mentioned anything like as often.

However, a clear, albeit weak, stereotype of the 'devious Welshman' does exist and it takes two forms. The simpler of the two stereotypes depicts the Welsh as crafty, cunning, evasive and that is the end of it. In these jokes the Welshman is usually placed alongside the other inhabitants of the British Isles. He is needed to make up a 'fourth' for the purpose of the joke.

The following example illustrates that this joke stereotype of the crafty Welshman is still alive and flourishing today. An Englishman, a Scotsman, an Irishman and a Welshman were travelling in an aircraft that was going to crash and they had only three parachutes between them. Each man in turn put his case to the others for being given one. The Scotsman pointed out that he was a very important businessman and that if he were to be killed, the stock market would collapse on hearing the news. He was duly given a parachute and he baled out successfully. The Irishman claimed to be an important political figure on whom all hope for peace in Ireland rested. He, too, was allowed to bale out, leaving only the Englishman and the Welshman. 'Here, take this parachute', said the Welshman, handing one to the Englishman. 'But what about you?' exclaimed the Englishman, staggered by such heroism. 'Oh, I'll be all right', said the Welshman, 'I only gave the Irishman my haversack'. This type of crafty-Welshman story, which almost makes the Welshman out to be a kind of super-Scot, is not as truly Welsh as another kind in which the craftiness is allied to a form of naivety, in which the Welshman is devious and open all at the same time. Here are two examples:

A Welshman was playing a golf match in which he was getting the worst of it. He was obviously chagrined, but kept his temper. However, when at last his opponent badly sliced a tee shot, he exclaimed, 'Ah, I'm afraid you're in the bunker, I hope'.

Inquisitive Lady: 'Do you find it a profitable thing to keep a cow?'
Jenkins: 'Oh yes: my cow gives about eight quarts a day'.
Lady: 'And how much of that do you sell?'
Jenkins: 'About twelve quarts'.

It is easy to see what makes us laugh in these jokes but more difficult to pin down the characteristics being ascribed to the Welsh. The actor here is unconscious of the dichotomy in his behaviour patterns; being blissfully unaware of the inconsistencies and contradictions involved either in his behaviour or in his justification of his behaviour. The central Welsh actor is simultaneously crafty and naive, devious and direct, cunning and sincere, evasive and open, both a Scotsman and an Irishman.

One can only speculate as to why the Welsh stereotype in English jokes (a) became less important and (b) changed so radically in content. The reason for the disappearance of the Welsh joke lies partly in the fact that whereas in the sixteenth and seventeenth century they were the most obvious 'foreign' group in England and had no competition as butts for English humour, later they were gradually displaced by new immigrants who were more distinctive, more recent and more comic. The Scotsman of the eighteenth century on the make, the Irishman fleeing the potato famine, the Ashkenazi Jews at the turn of the century were all more exotic, more threatening and more comic from the average Englishman's point of view than the familiar and long established Welshman. In addition the economic and social changes brought about by the industrial revolution made the English and the Welsh more similar as peoples than they had been before. What is sometimes termed the 'Anglicization of Wales' is perhaps better seen as a convergence of the two societies as a result of the forces of modernisation and secularization.

The question of why the content of the stereotype changes is a more difficult one to resolve. A conventional analysis would presumably start from the fact that the Welsh have to live alongside a larger and more powerful neighbour. England is numerically, politically, militarily and economically the dominant partner in the United Kingdom. According to this thesis the old-style aggressive boastful assertiveness and the new-style crafty deviousness of the Welsh can be seen as alternative strategies for dealing with this problem. The Welsh deal with their situation of relative weakness vis-a-vis the English initially by swagger and bluster, then when this fails to impress them, the Welsh are forced instead to try and outwit the English by devious cunning. The English are passive observers of these attempts to manipulate them on the part of the weaker group and the jokes emerge from English observation of Welsh behaviour towards them (that is, the English).

The thesis is plausible but incomplete. It could be a general description of the interaction between any majority and any minority. It leaves out of account the unique qualities of the Welsh historical experience, the inner dynamics of Welsh society which have shaped the Welsh personality just as surely as the presence of their English neighbours. The partial and distorted reality that emerges from the jokes is a product not just of observations of English and Welsh interacting but also of observations made about Welsh behaviour within the confines of their own society.

The roots of Welsh pride and aggressiveness in the seventeenth century can be seen in Gerald of Wales' observation[1] at the end of the twelfth century: "they (the Welsh) do not concern themselves with trade, shipping or manufactures or with hardly any other occupation except the practices of war. The Welsh in the mediaeval period were poor mountain dwelling warriors rather like the Swiss and the Scottish Highlanders were or the Gurkhas are today. When not fighting among themselves they earned their living by hiring out their military skills. When the Tudors came to power after the strife of the Wars of the Roses they began the real pacification of both Wales and England but this process took much longer in Wales; (a) because Wales was more remote; (b) because Wales was economically backward relative to England; (c) because of the tradition of war and soldiering inherited from mediaeval Wales. Even under the Stuarts the Welsh were a relatively turbulent people and Dodd (1971) can speak of the seventeenth century pugnacity and valour of the Welsh (which) was as proverbial as their poverty and their touchiness in point of honour – though it was no doubt they themselves who invented the current proverb, 'Three Welshmen two soldiers; three Englishmen two thieves; three Frenchmen two traitors.'"

Thus the English jokes about the pugnacious Welshman may well be a fairly accurate historical description. The jokes, which on the whole are good-natured, tell us not so much what English-Welsh relations were like but rather describe the intrinsic nature of Welsh society.

Between the seventeenth and the late nineteenth centuries Wales underwent two major connected social changes, the industrial revolution and the growth of Welsh Protestant non-conformity. Both these changes imposed new disciplines on a previously exuberant and unruly people. At one level the Welsh remained an emotional people with a great zest for life, their modal personality remaining relatively unaltered. At another level there is superimposed on this a system of beliefs that is restrictive and puritanical. This is the inner contradiction at the heart of the Welsh character. They continue to desire passionately the very things of the world which are explicitly forbidden. In order to cope with the tensions that this creates certain cultural adaptations have to be made; in particular, the gap between public rhetoric and private behaviour becomes much wider. Men in important positions make high-flown rhetorical statements of principle because that is what men in positions of authority are expected to do. Their actual behaviour will be the same mixture of altruism and self-interest, realism and idealism as anyone else's. The rhetoric has the purely ritual function of helping to hold the community together. It is used or discarded according to whether it is appropriate to the occasion. It is this tension between rhetoric and reality that is ultimately the source of the humour in the new Welsh stereotype for it periodically creates ludicrous conjunctions of opposites. The Welshman in the joke is funny because he is both devious and open, both crafty and naive. Somehow the rhetoric and the reality have caught up with one another and he is left holding the contradiction. The essential Welsh joke concerns a man or woman who tries to be crafty but in providing a justification for his or her behaviour he or she gives the game away. The gap between behaviour and rhetoric mentioned above is suddenly closed and the attempted deceit is revealed by the speaker himself.

The explanations of why the Welsh stereotype weakens and changes over time are necessarily speculative and involve a use of data that is not easily quantifiable. However, one thing does emerge from this diachronic case study which is not always apparent from the more usual synchronic studies: the mutability and malleability of ethnic stereotypes. They are the product of particular historical situations and as the situations change so do the stereotypes, not merely in strength but also in content.

REFERENCES

Davies, C., Welsh Fun. Celtic Educational Press, Swansea. (forthcoming) (1976)

Dodd, A.H., Studies in Stuart Wales. University of Wales Press, Cardiff (1971).

Ashton, J., Humour, Wit and Satire of the Seventeenth Century. Chatto and Windus, London (1883)

FOOTNOTE

1. Giraldus Cambrensis Opera VI, editor J.F. Dimock, quoted in T. Jones Pierce, Medieval Welsh Society, University of Wales Press, p.19 (1972).

Humour in Situ: The Role of Humour in Small Group Culture

Gary Alan Fine

University of Minnesota

Humour is a most delicate flower; a living bud which when plucked quickly dies. However, those engaged in research on humour insist with regularity and stubbornness upon plucking humour from its natural environment - the ongoing flow of social interaction. The naturalistic or 'in situ' approach to humour, while employed upon occasion, has been under-utilized as a method of research.

Humour does not merely occur in the course of interaction; a joke is not just a verbal device that fits in an empty slot in a conversation; rather it is a phenomenon that is created in context, a social construction of participants in an interaction. It is an 'in situ' production of social actors. For a joking sequence to be 'successful', it requires the active, if not always conscious, collaboration of at least two parties - the teller and the audience - and on occasion a third as well, the butt or target.

With the exception of certain preplanned humour before a large audience or in the mass media, most verbal humour occurs within a small group. It is therefore surprising and unfortunate that more humour research has not been devoted to this subject area, particularly when considering the frequency of laughter in such groups - in some cases upwards of one hundred and fifty discrete instances of laughter in an hour. Goodchilds and her colleagues focused on the determinants of wittiness in small groups (Goodchilds, 1959; Goodchilds & Smith, 1964; Smith & Goodchilds, 1963), and other studies more directly relevant to the joking process have analyzed the function of joking in a small group (Bradney, 1957; Coser, 1959, 1960; Goodrich, Henry & Goodrich, 1954; Miller, 1967; Sykes, 1966; Zenner, 1970). This research does not generally treat the group as an on-going entity with a history and a culture, and it is this perspective that shall be explored further in this paper.

Humour arises out of the particular situation and group and is responsive to it. I have proposed elsewhere (Fine, 1976) a concept which seems potentially useful for understanding the development of group content and for understanding how groups differentiate themselves from other groups - the 'idioculture' of a group. The idioculture[1] of a group can be defined as a system of knowledge, beliefs, and customs which are particular to a group to which members can refer and employ as the basis of further interaction. In most small groups this includes such elements as norms, rules, nicknames, repeated insults, local slang, and humour. It is this last element with which this paper will specifically deal.

The concept of idioculture is valuable in that it suggests the means by which a group increases cohesion. The idioculture, including humour, is the mediating element between determinants such as success or threat, which tend to increase group cohesion, and the behavioural outcomes of this unity. The concept emphasizes that group discussion and group humour is not content-free, but that groups are continually engaged in constructing a reality and a sense of meaning (see Berger & Luckman, 1967). Culture and humour are not random agglomerations of items, but directly arise from the group's needs and its social situation.

Five factors are suggested to contribute to determining which elements will become part of a group's idioculture. Since we are emphasizing humour, idioculture is discussed here in terms of a subcategory, termed, for lack of a better word, 'idiowit'. First, for a remark to become part of the humour culture of a group, its components or meanings must be known to members of the group. While the remark need never have been heard before in its particular form or while the particular incongruity may be new to members of the group, it is important that the conversation or action be immediately perceivable as potentially humorous to the group. A humorous remark in German to individuals who do not speak the language will not produce a humour response, unless the humour resided in the act of speaking German and not the meaning structure of the remark.

Second, the remark must be usable as a humour stimulus or set of stimuli, and not considered sacred or taboo. Apparently humour may be more usable than other forms of communication because it allows certain otherwise unutterable comments to be uttered. Thus, in certain groups at certain times, dropping one's trousers might be considered allowable and wildly hilarious; at many other times and with many groups, reactions could range from extreme shock or anger to sexual arousal. The usability of a potential piece of idiowit is determined by both the situation and the audience.

Third, the piece of humour, particularly if it is to be successful and to be repeated in variant forms, must be functional for the group, and for individual members of the group. It must support a goal towards which members are striving, either as individuals or as a group. The example of trouser-dropping is from an instance provided by Stebbins (1976) who cites the occurrence of trouser-dropping by an amateur theatrical company during a performance, and suggests this backstage horseplay serves as social comic relief for the members of the company. Of course, there are many functions that humour may serve: from producing conflict between rival groups, to smoothing over conflict in one's own group (e.g., Stephenson, 1951). Whatever the function, it is assumed, and it must be proved, that successful humour in group settings will be perceived to have functional components - even if these functions are eventually disruptive and counter-productive.

Humour must be appropriate in terms of the friendship and power relationships in a group. Coser (1960) has noted that in psychiatric staff conferences humour is generally directed downward in the structure of the group. It is rare that a low-status member of a group, except the fool, will lampoon a group leader, and when that happens the group frequently does not laugh. In situations in which dropping one's trousers implies an overt lack of respect (coupled with a lack of dignity by the joker) one can predict that it will occur more among equals, or among those who wish to be considered equals, than in other portions of the group social structure.

There are numerous potential items of idiowit which meet the criteria we have suggested for inclusion in the small group's humour repertoire, but rather few instances of humour actually do occur in terms of the vast number possible. The concept of a triggering mechanism is necessary to account for this selection process. A triggering mechanism is any event which produces humour, although only certain classes of happenings are likely to produce humour. Clearly this covers a vast number of potential, public events, including most other pieces of humour (humour notably will be found in bunches), errors, surprises, and incongruities. This fifth component is of course unpredictable, and emphasizes that it is virtually impossible to predict micro-level behaviours with any degree of certainty. It is suggested, however, that the more frequently similar triggering events occur, the more likely will examples of idiowit develop from them. This mechanism is important theoretically in that it stresses the situationally-grounded nature of humour.

These five determinants (that the item be known, usable, functional, appropriate, and triggered) produce the specific humour culture of any group - a culture which for some groups may be quite extensive.

Examples of Group Humour

For the past two years I have been engaged in a participant observation study of Little League baseball teams in the United States. Little League Baseball Inc. is an organization designed to provide preadolescent boys[2] (aged nine to twelve) the opportunity to play baseball under the supervision of adult coaches. Many communities in the United States operate leagues, with each team in the league having about fifteen players.

Humour is common in these teams, and takes many forms, with the preponderance being insulting, teasing, or horseplay (physical humour). Much of the humour that is found in one Little League team could be found in any Little League team, because the essential differences between teams are a different set of triggering mechanisms - in the form of different personnel and events. Since in any one community players have similar backgrounds, they will know much the same items, and will consider the same communications usable. They may differ in terms of the functional aspects of humour in that some teams will have stronger motivation and greater expectation of victory than others, and the social structure in different teams may be distinct, - for example, the presence of isolates or of an elite clique. However, for the most part the team serves as the interactional setting for communications that could reasonably be found among many groups of preadolescents. Teasing or ragging another about an inability at some aspect of life occurs frequently - in this case, baseball-based insults are common - though they are only spoken by one who perceives himself of higher-status to one he perceives of less ability. Thus, one player received the humorous nickname of 'Maniac' when he was eleven years of age and had relatively few close friends on the team. By the time he was twelve and a starting player that nickname had passed out of group usage.

Players on one team thought it immensely amusing when the team's twelve-year-old leader
(Justin) referred to a Black youngster pitching for an opposing team as that 'cross-eyed
monkey on the mound'. This racial slur was known and usable in the group setting (although
the coaches had previously told him to refrain from making racial comments); it was
functional in that it relieved tension for the team, involved in a close game against this
excellent pitcher, and less confident of the ability of their own pitcher. It was functional
at an individual level as an emotional release, particularly because Justin was himself
aggressive, competitive, and frequently given to bursts of emotion. Bad feelings between
the joker and his target made the comment appropriate, and this relationship 'legitimated'
his right to make that remark. The insult was also appropriate because the joker was one of
the acknowledged team leaders, who was able to set 'policy' for the team (and none of the
team members rose to the target's defence on this or other occasions). The comment had been
triggered by a wild pitch which had struck one of the batting team's better (though not best)
players. Justin may have felt a need as the team leader to avenge his fellow team member,
and possibly further disconcert the opposing pitcher.

Boys frequently tease each other about current girl-friends — actual or ascribed. The period
of preadolescence is a time of developing heterosexual relationships, and boys are vulnerable
to teasing about their handling of the transition. On one team three of the high status
players have regular girl-friends of whom the team is aware. These players get ribbed by the
coaches (college students), and more secretly by other players, who because it is the high
status members they are commenting on must be circumspect in their humorous remarks. However,
public reports of these boys' dating behaviour are considered immensely humorous. Once, one
nine-year-old caught one of them 'taking care of personal business' (kissing). He was chased
from the scene, provoking much team laughter. Another player informed me that this same boy
sits in the back of the local movie house with his girl and gives her 'mouth-to-mouth
resuscitation', a comment which produced considerable laughter among the other listeners.
The trigger is my question and the circumstance that I am an adult, the meaning of mouth-to-
mouth resuscitation is known on the overt and symbolic level, and is usable in that situation.
It has been noted (Fasteau, 1974; Jourard, 1974) that it is difficult for boys (and men) to
reveal deep feelings; likewise it is rare for boys to provide clinical descriptions. This
obliqueness substantially complicates life for the participant observer. The above comments
are functional because they express the anxiety and ambivalence felt by nondaters towards the
activities of their more advanced peers, and yet are still appropriate in that they are not
derogatory and admit the target's sexual maturity, and of course are not related in his
presence.

Teasing about sexual matters is also directed downward or across the social hierarchy. One
boy was teased by friends about dating a flat-chested girl (these are twelve-year-olds!),
while a nonpresent other was scornfully derided for only dating his younger sister. The
mirthful response to the latter joke seems to be an example of consensual validation of a
group-held attitude towards this youngster.

At this age naughtiness (sex, bodily functions, behavioural inadequacy) is a prime topic
of humour. Redl (1966) has described preadolescence as the time in which the nicest
children begin to behave in the most awful ways, and this evaluation is supported by their
humour, which contains a large amount of not very thinly disguised aggression. This
aggression is generally directed at low status members, equals who can take it and respond
in kind, or nonpresent higher status members.

Humour by obliquely reinforcing norms and by communicating them to new members strengthens
group ties, and will indirectly control members' behaviours (Stephenson, 1951). Every group,
whether consisting of a loose grouping of members (like an informal friendship group) or a
formally defined body of members (like a Little League baseball team or a laboratory
discussion group), will have an ever expanding set of humorous remarks which, along with
their variants, are appropriate for public expression within the group. These remarks do not
occur randomly in social interaction, but derive from both long-term determinants and the
specific events which affect a group.

As a group develops, certain elements of its humour will be perceived as particularly
characteristic, and may serve as a distinguishing feature of the group for outsiders. One
Little League team took great delight in knocking each other's hats off during a game, and
a preadolescent friendship grouping compared aborted babies to ripe tomatoes. These humour
themes can reveal how the group members respond to each other, their current situation in
the group, and to the environment. By understanding the particular determinants of humour
culture, both situational and trans-situational, we will be able better to understand
fundamental continuities in group dynamics.

FOOTNOTES

[1]This term was chosen rather than the perhaps more conventional term 'group culture', because the latter has been used previously with meanings considerably different from its usage here.

[2]In 1975, due to court challenges, girls were allowed to play Little League baseball; however, with the exception of some softball leagues, few girls have availed themselves of this opportunity.

REFERENCES

See Bibliography for publications on humour, laughter and comedy

Berger, P. & Luckman, T., The Social Construction of Reality. Doubleday Anchor, New York (1967).

Fasteau, M., Why aren't we talking? In: J. Pleck & J. Sawyer (Eds.), Men and Masculinity. Prentice-Hall, Englewood Cliffs, New Jersey (1974).

Fine, G., Perspectives on idioculture. Unpublished Manuscript (1976).

Jourard, S., Some lethal aspects of the male role. In: J. Pleck & J. Sawyer (Eds.), Men and Masculinity. Prentice-Hall, Englewood Cliffs, New Jersey (1974).

Redl, F., When We Deal with Children. Free Press, New York (1966).

Stebbins, R., Comic relief in everyday life: Dramaturgic observations on a function of humor. Presented at the Annual Meeting of the Western Social Science Association. Arizona State University, Tempe, April (1976).

Developmental Aspects of Humour and Laughter in Young Adolescent Girls

Rita Ransohoff

New York University

Some of the developmental functions of humour and laughter in young adolescent girls were studied in the setting of two groups which met weekly in a school environment for a period of seven months. The girls were aged between twelve and fourteen years. A tape-recorder was used for all sessions.

An analysis was made of giggling and laughter in response to the spontaneous recounting of 'real life' events: a story, for example, of a girl who wanted big breasts so much that she stuffed her brassiere with toilet tissue; or the story of a man who approached two of the group members on the street and who offered them money if they would watch him expose himself.

These young adolescents were attempting to deal with the universal and age-specific challenge of physical development and the onset of menstruation. They were trying to cope with the sexual ideation that is a result of internal and external stimulation. A turning toward heterosexuality was found to be one of their responses, but not a very effective one. Reliance on a best friend and the peer group seemed to be more reliable. Among themselves, giggling and laughter served as a special form of communication.

On a cognitive level, when humour worked, the girls were able to reduce awesome words into light, foolish ones. Humour was most successful when it resonated with the young adolescents' developmental tasks: those in the process of mastery. As in the stuffing of the bra, the content dealt with current physical changes, beginning relationships with boys, and pride in developing femininity. Some funny jokes allowed relief in regressive latency-age humour with anal themes. Other developmental issues that could be handled through the medium of humour were sexual curiosity and voyeurism directed to both parents. Ambivalence toward the parent of the same sex could be displayed. Issues of separation and beginning challenge to the latency superego were expressed. Masturbatory wishes could be successfully masked and phallic strivings expressed or derided. In humour that failed and caused the eruption of anxiety, (a) there was a failure to reduce the frightening content to 'size' through 'small' words and foolish disguise, and (b) issues too remote from current developmental ones created anxiety and guilt. These dealt with the destructive power of male penetration, the fearful mystery of the adult female body, and situations or jokes that resonated with the girls' rebudding oedipal wishes and weakened their normal denial of parental sexual activity.

It is necessary to emphasize the group function of giggling and laughter among teenagers. On the level of nonverbal communication, as the group experienced mounting excitement and anxiety laughter communicated a wish to retreat from danger. It served as a signal of the need for auditory reassurance. It showed itself to be an invitation to group aggression, a form of incitement. The contagion effect of hysterical laughter was observed among the girls. Hysterical laughter itself seemed to serve a group function. It offered reassurance which said 'You are not alone; I can hear you.'

Tracking the Intractable – The Analysis of Humour in the Study of Value Systems

C. Edward Hopen

Division of Social Sciences, University of Toronto

In anthropological circles it has long been recognized that the study of humour in a society (via fables, legends, myths, proverbs, poetry, songs, jokes and riddles) will lay-bare core values, philosophical tenants, and beliefs in that social system. It remains to be tested whether people in various societies, which occupy similar ecological niches (for example pastoral nomads), will reflect similarities within the parameters of their humour. Preliminary research reveals tantalizing correlations.

I turn now to an animal fable told to me by the pastoral nomadic Fulani of Northern Nigeria. One day long ago a goat followed a path through the woods which led to a patch of many succulent berries. Arriving at the site he began to pick the berries with his cleft foot. In a short time he chanced to look over his right shoulder and there beheld a large hyena which was watching the goat intently. 'Little goat,' said the hyena, 'If you tell me three truths I will not eat you.' The little goat, serving his own interest, thought swiftly and replied, 'If I return to my family and tell them that I was within touching distance of a hyena and he did not eat me, they will say, "you are a liar."' 'Indeed, that is one truth,' said the hyena, 'Tell me a second.' As the goat was struggling to think of another truth he chanced to look over his left shoulder and at very close quarters stood a large lion. The lion was standing on three feet, for he was rubbing his eye with his right front paw. 'Little goat,' said the lion, 'You have enormous intelligence, you must know an effective medicine for an inflamed eye of a lion.' Again, the goat thought swiftly. 'Indeed, Mr. lion, I certainly know a medicine which will cure the problem that plagues you. You must obtain a long wide strip of raw hide (the fresher the better) from a hyena and apply it to the affected part.' It was not long until the little goat returned, replete with berries, to the warm embrace and good cheer of its happy family.

Wide Fulani ethnographic data support the view that this fable neatly 'fits' Fulani culture. Fulani tell a fable and the listener then examines and discovers the 'messages' or principles embedded within it. Such an approach is in contrast with much of Western teaching where a principle is first mentioned then an example or story is given to support it. The Fulani technique fires the imagination while providing entertainment.

Fables are open to numerous interpretations. I note only several: (a) Scholars of symbolism would see the hyena as the Black peasant (Hausa), the lion as the bureaucrat and, of course, the goat as the vulnerable but wiley Fulani nomad; (2) As a small minority of nomads Fulani are regularly harassed by police, peasant farmers, bureaucrats and politicians. But, the fable tells them, if you apply your wit you can extricate yourself from seemingly impossible situations; (3) The nomads always have at least two enemies – the bureaucrats and the peasants. For survival the strategy is to play one against the other – a craft which they have elevated to an art.

Degree of Hostility in Squelches as a Factor in Humour Appreciation

Jennings Bryant

University of Massachusetts

Many communication-mediated social interactions which are extremely hostile and might be expected to evoke pity, anger or sympathy from an observer, unexpectedly elicit laughter instead. Typically these humorous interchanges begin with a rather blunt insult or hostile attack by a provoking agent, which, in turn, is customarily countered by an equally belligerent retort. The humourizing feature of this antagonistic social exchange is often nothing more than a trivial semantic ambiguity, a gestural exaggeration, or a 'turned phrase' which is embedded in the retaliation portion of the joke - the so-called punchline. It would appear, however, that these simple embellishments, these examples of rather ordinary 'joke work' (Freud, 1905), are sufficient to remove the interaction from the realm of socially adverse and serious disparagement and bestow upon it the quality of being legitimate, socially-sanctioned fun. Effective joke work apparently checks certain of our moral judgmental facilities and allows us to enjoy hostility, aggression and various forms of malicious mischief without undue remorse or regret.

Evidence from a related study on humour appreciation seems to indicate that the presence of joke work does not disinhibit all moral judgment, however. Zillmann and Bryant (1974) examined the potential humour-mediating effect of inequities in social exchanges. In this investigation, squelches employing the familiar format of provocation and retaliation were manipulated to effect a variation in the degree of retaliation achieved, ranging from extreme under-retaliation to extreme over-retaliation. It was found that retaliatory equity - the condition in which the negative consequences inflicted upon the provoker by the retaliator were of a similar magnitude to the negative consequences initially inflicted upon the retaliator - constituted the optimal condition for humour appreciation. Furthermore, both under- and over-retaliation impaired humour appreciation in proportion to the magnitude of the resultant inequity. It would appear that the respondents' moral convictions functioned rather well in modifying the intensity of their mirth responses, in spite of the existence of identical joke work in all versions of the squelches. These findings suggest that any exemption from critical assessment which is allowed by joke work is limited, and that certain judgmental criteria are rather consistently employed by decoders of disparaging humorous communications.

One complementary aspect of disparaging humorous communications which appears to be of theoretical significance is the intensity of the hostility described in the provocation and retaliation portions of this type of joke. Certain theoretical orientations generate expectations for a linear relationship between the ferocity of the social interchanges and humour appreciation, with, depending upon the theoretical orientation chosen, increases in hostility either facilitating or impairing the respondents' mirth. Furthermore, other theoretical notions may be interpreted as predicting that the relationship between hostility in communication-mediated social exchanges and humour appreciation is a curvilinear one, with inordinately intense hostility being appreciated to a lesser degree than more moderate expressions of antagonism. The present study was designed to investigate the relative merit of these theoretical orientations.

Freud's (1905) classic theory of mirth readily lends predictions which relate to the consideration of hostility in social exchanges. Freud proposed that the mechanism underlying the appreciation of hostile or tendentious wit was the release of repressions which are typically derived from censored social activities. It would appear that citizens of contemporary society have become rather permissive toward many rather mild hostilities, such as the almost cursory insults of the commuter manoeuvering for position on the traffic-laden highway; therefore, a modicum of hostility should evoke minimal censorship. More intense expressions of hostility are typically censored however, and therefore it would be anticipated that higher levels of hostility would be associated with stronger repressions. In line with this reasoning, the description of extremely hostile humorous exchanges should lead to a substantial release of inhibitions. If appreciation of tendentious communications

is indeed derived from the release of repressions, then increases in the intensity of the
hostility in jokes should yield concomitant increases in the level of mirth elicited by these
stimuli. According to Freudian reasoning, then, the relationship between the hostility of
a joke and the appreciation of that joke is a simple one: the greater the hostility, the
more the appreciation.

Other predictions can be derived from considerations of social propriety. It may be that
the licence to laugh at the aggression and hostility of others which is purportedly provided
by the respondent-disinhibiting camouflage of joke work is circumscribed by moral and/or
cultural mandates in addition to the previously discussed considerations of equity. Even
when all exchanges between protagonists are perceived as equitable, more extreme hostilities
may offend the sensibilities of decoders by infringing upon their general notions of social
acceptability and good taste (cf. Gutman & Priest, 1969; Zillmann, Bryant & Cantor, 1974).
Certainly in the world of 'serious' interpersonal communication, an intense public shouting
match 'disturbs the peace' (an institutionalization of the norm of propriety) even though
neither party manages to disrupt the equity of the interchange by gaining the upper hand.
Although it may be anticipated that the power of joke work legitimizes a greater magnitude
of hostility in humorous communications than in serious communication-mediated social
exchanges, it is possible that even in humorous communications there are boundaries of
propriety beyond which appreciation of hostility is impaired. Joke work, or other cues
informing the decoder that the social exchange is not to be interpreted as a serious encounter,
may merely function to increase the latitude of hostility that is acceptable. Hostility
beyond these extended boundaries may still disturb the respondent's sense of propriety and
good taste, thereby impairing humour appreciation.

Unfortunately, predictions of humour appreciation relating to varying conditions of
hostility derived from the notion of social propriety are not completely unambiguous. Two
related problems are involved here. First, propriety is a cultural notion of what ought to
exist. As such it is a part of a 'morality of constraint' (Piaget, 1948) which is based
primarily on traditions and conventions rather than on rational or motivational criteria.
This basis in dicta tends to intensify between-group variability, for group mores can make
anything right and prevent condemnation of anything (Sumner, 1960). A second problem is
that even though it may be acknowledged that there are general norms of propriety, specific
criteria for these standards are ill-defined. Unlike other areas of moral and social
judgment, such as equity, in which a great deal of research has been conducted to define the
criteria (e.g., Berkowitz & Walster, 1976), many of the essential dimensions of propriety
are open to speculation, especially as applied to humour appreciation. For example, it
might be argued that any magnitude of hostility other than a bare minimum may violate the
decoder's notion of propriety. After all, if the material of gossip columns, coffee break
discussions or cocktail party conversations is any indication, many people appear to be
aware of even moderate violations of decorum in the behaviour of others. If sensitivity to
these violations is not checked by the joke work of humorous communications, and it may be
that it is not, then any degree of hostility other than the minimal amount which society has
come to accept as normal would be expected to interfere with humour appreciation, because
it violates the decoder's expectations for what 'ought to be' (cf. Zillmann & Bryant, 1974).
More extreme violations of propriety, in this case elicited by increases in the intensity of
hostility in the interchanges, would be expected to impair humour appreciation in proportion
to the magnitude of the abridgement of expectancy. Thus, if decoders' sensitivities to
propriety violations remain rather acute in responding to humorous communications, then the
relationship between intensity of hostility in jokes and humour appreciation is expected to
be an inverse linear one.

If we assume, on the other hand, that the respondent's sensitivity to propriety violations
is mediated by the presence of joke work, then somewhat different predictions can be
obtained from considerations of propriety. It might be argued that if minimal levels of
hostility are acceptable in serious communication-mediated interactions, then moderately
intense hostility is acceptable to decoders of humorous entertainment. Certainly the
humorous exchanges between protagonists in a typical televised situation comedy are more
intensely hostile than those we normally experience in daily interactions. If joke work
serves to increase our latitude of acceptance of hostility, and if we are motivated to enjoy
hostility - because of a need for the release of repressions (e.g., Freud, 1905) or because
of a natural or acquired human propensity to enjoy disparagement, cruelty or hostility in
order to assert one's own superiority (e.g., Hazlitt, 1826; Hobbes, 1651; McDougall, 1903,
1922) - then moderate displays of humorous hostility should be appreciated more than minimal
ones, with the humour-inhibiting effect of violations of considerations of propriety becoming
activated only under conditions of extreme hostility. These considerations lead to
expectations of a curvilinear relationship between degree of hostility and humour
appreciation, with expressions of moderate hostility being appreciated more than depictions
of either minimal or extreme hostility.

Berlyne's (1960, 1972) notions concerning the function of arousal in humour may also be called upon to yield predictions in the present investigation. The most direct application of Berlyne's reasoning is related to the notion of 'arousal jag', defined as the condition in which arousal is suddenly reduced after it has climbed to an uncomfortably high level. This particular type of rapid fluctuation in arousal is said to be rewarding and pleasant. Furthermore, Berlyne (1972) has claimed that the tendentious features of jokes (such as hostility) in combination with certain collative properties of joke work (such as novelty) may induce this arousal jag, thereby yielding pleasure for the joke respondent. Some researchers have interpreted Berlyne's reasoning as lending predictions for humour appreciation based on the level of arousal produced by certain elements of the humorous stimuli. Purportedly following Berlyne's reasoning, Godkewitsch (1972) and Schwartz (1972) postulated humour to vary as an inverted U-shaped function of arousal. That is, humour appreciation is expected to be maximal under moderate levels of arousal and lower under both minimal and extreme arousal. If we assume that so-called moderate hostility in jokes is associated with moderate arousal, then these jokes should be maximally appreciated by the respondents, with jokes featuring either more or less intense hostility in social exchanges yielding less humour appreciation. This reasoning also leads to expectations for a curvilinear relation between the level of hostility of jokes and humour appreciation.

It should be noted that this rationale is not without problems of predictive specificity (cf. Cantor, Bryant & Zillmann, 1974). The arguments advanced herein rely on the assumption that moderate levels of hostility produce the optimal moderate state of arousal. However, without a precise empirical specification of optimal arousal, and without validation of the notion that any humorous communication assumed to contain moderate hostility produces this optimal arousal state, support for or arguments against the value of the model made on the basis of empirical results of this or other investigation must be considered tenuous.

In the present investigation, an effort was made to employ protagonists in the humorous communications towards whom the respondents would be unlikely to hold strong pre-existing affective dispositions. It has often been demonstrated that humour appreciation is modified when the respondent feels pronounced social or experiential affinity for the joke protagonists (e.g., La Fave, 1972; Wolff, Smith & Murray, 1934; Zillmann, Bryant & Cantor, 1974). Therefore, the agents in the jokes presented in the present study were scarcely identified, requiring the respondents to depend almost entirely upon their analyses of the behaviour of the provoker and the retaliator in determining their reactions to the communications. Moreover, the behaviour of the protagonists was controlled in such a manner that the overall outcome of their hostile exchanges was a state of retaliatory equity; that is, the magnitude of the provoker's insult was matched by the intensity of the retaliator's retort. The manipulation of degree of hostility was achieved by making equivalent adjustments in the intensity of hostility of the provoker's insult and the ferocity of the reciprocation in the punchline.

METHOD

Five squelches were either selected or created and were manipulated to effect a three-level variation in the degree of hostility of the interchanges between the provoker and the retaliator (mild hostility, moderate hostility, intense hostility). In an independent-measures design, degree of hostility was factorially varied with sex of respondent. Humour appreciation was assessed by ratings.

The experimental stimuli consisted of six unmanipulated jokes and five manipulated squelches, each presented on a separate page, with a rating scale printed below it. The stimuli were compiled in a constant order in booklet form, with all manipulated squelches in a booklet belonging to the same condition. The manipulated squelches appeared on pages 3, 5, 7, 9 and 11 of the booklet. Each booklet contained a cover sheet labelled 'Humor Study,' and a question assessing the sex of the respondent was included on a final page.

To decrease error variance deriving from individual differences in ratings of humorous communications, the ratings of the first two unmanipulated jokes (positions 1 and 2 in the booklet) were used as a base level against which appreciation of the manipulated squelches could be measured (cf. Zillmann, Bryant & Cantor, 1974). The other unmanipulated jokes served as buffers and as a camouflage to prevent the detection of the repeatedly applied treatment.

The manipulation of degree of hostility in the squelches was accomplished by verbal adjustments in the provocation and retaliation portions of each squelch, increasing or decreasing the magnitude of the insult or mistreatment and the magnitude of the retort or put-down. Retaliatory equity was maintained by making equivalent adjustments in the intensity of the hostility in the provocation and the retaliation.

The manipulation is illustrated in the following two examples. In each example, the squelch is first presented in the moderate hostility version. The mild and intense hostility versions are created by exchanging the appropriate bracketed portion of the provocation and of the retaliation. Both examples involve an insult and a subsequent put-down.

(1) The two ladies were sitting in the living room, waiting for their hostess, who was slightly delayed. The daughter of the family was with them, on the theory that she would keep the visitors occupied during the wait.

The child was perhaps six years old, snub nosed, freckled, and bespectacled. She maintained an unusual silence.

Finally, one of the ladies whispered to the other (rather obtrusively, 'Not at all P-R-E-T-T-Y, I fear,') carefully spelling the key word.

Whereupon the child piped up (in a catty tone, 'But awfully S-M-A-R-T, which seems to be quite rare around here.')

Mild hostility: (quietly, 'not extremely P-R-E-T-T-Y, but she certainly is well-behaved.') (in a seemingly polite manner, 'and very S-M-A-R-T.')

Intense hostility: (haughtily, 'She's downright U-G-L-Y, just like her mother.') (in a belligerent fashion, 'But awfully S-M-A-R-T, which is better'n some old biddies I know!')

(2) A waitress in a diner was serving a customer when a bald-headed gent entered and planted himself at a table in the rear.

'That's old man Snead who eats here every day,' volunteered the waitress. 'He's got a twin brother and they're as much alike as peas in a pod, only this one is stone deaf. Watch me have some fun with him.'

She minced over to him, smiled prettily, and said in a (loud voice, 'Well, you bald-headed old baboon, what kind of food are you going to pour into that fat stomach today?')

The gentleman answered directly, ('I'll have ham and eggs, toast and coffee. And by the way, my brother is the deaf one you nincompoop.')

Mild hostility: (clear voice, 'Well you bald-headed old man, what kind of food are you going to consume today?') ('I'll have ham and eggs, toast and coffee. And by the way, my brother is the deaf one, dearie.')

Intense hostility: (raucous voice, 'Well you stupid, senile, bald-headed old jackass, what kind of slop are you going to pour into that fat gut of yours today?') ('I'll have ham and eggs, toast and coffee. And by the way, my brother is the deaf one you obnoxious, unemployed fool.')

In order to determine whether the stimulus material produced the required differentiation in hostility, a pretest was conducted which measured respondents' perceptions of the level of hostility present in the various versions of the five squelches. Thirty undergraduate subjects, fifteen male and fifteen female, none of whom took part in the later experiment, were given one version of the experimental materials. The order of assignment had been predetermined by a random procedure. The booklets were modified for the pretest by removing all unmanipulated material and replacing the scale designed to measure humour appreciation with one designed to measure perceived intensity of hostility in the interchanges. After the general squelch format was described to them in terms of interaction between antagonists, the subjects were asked to rate the intensity of the hostility of the interchange in each squelch on a unipolar scale ranging from 0, labelled 'no hostility at all', to 100, labelled 'extreme hostility.' The scale was marked and numbered at intervals of ten, but subjects were permitted to intersect the scale at any point. Analyses of variance performed on the ratings for the five individual squelches yielded the required differentiation. For all squelches, the main effect for perceived intensity of hostility was significant, with all F-ratios associated with $p < .05$. For each squelch, the means were directionally differentiated as required, and all adjacent means differed significantly from each other for all squelches ($p < .05$, by Newman-Keuls).

Since it has been demonstrated that inequities in hostile exchanges between protagonists impair humour appreciation (Zillmann & Bryant, 1974), and since such an impairment could constitute a confounding with the present degree-of-hostility treatment, a pretest was conducted in which the appropriateness of the retaliation to the provocation of each version of each squelch was measured. Twenty-four undergraduate subjects, twelve male and twelve female, none of whom participated in the earlier pretest or later experiment, were given one version of the experimental booklets with the unmanipulated material removed. After receiving instructions concerning the squelch format, the respondents were informed that they were to determine the appropriateness of the retaliation to the provocation in the squelches. They rated each stimulus on a scale ranging from −100, labelled 'retaliation falls far too short,' through 0, labelled 'retaliation is just right,' to +100, labelled 'retaliation goes much too far'. The scale was marked at intervals of ten. The scores yielded an overall mean of −6.31 for the appropriateness of degree of retaliation. The mean appropriateness ratings for the various versions of the individual squelches ranged from −9.60 to +8.20. In order to determine whether the mean for any squelch differed significantly from the ideal score of zero, t-tests were conducted (employing the error terms from dummy analyses of variance) to determine the minimal mean value which would differ from zero at $p < .05$. It was determined that the minimal value that would be significantly different from zero for any squelch was 11.13. Since none of the mean appropriateness ratings for the individual squelches equalled or exceeded this value, it was considered that retaliatory equity was established for all squelches.

A final pretest was conducted to determine respondents' abilities to discern the treatment employed. It was anticipated that the extreme verbal hostility presented in the intense hostility condition might sensitize respondents to the nature of the experiment (cf. Gollob & Levine, 1967). If respondents perceived that their appreciation of hostility was being assessed, it is plausible that their ratings of the humorous stimuli would be markedly lower due to evaluation apprehension. Therefore twenty-four subjects, twelve male and twelve female, none of whom participated in any other stage of the experiment, were presented with an intact copy of one version of the experimental booklet in which they rated the unmanipulated jokes and manipulated squelches on the same humour appreciation scale employed in the main experiment. After the subjects had completed their ratings, they were given a separate page that contained a request for a short written explanation of their perceptions of what the experiment was really about. The responses were typed on separate cards which were placed in a random order. Three graduate students were informed of the actual purpose of the experiment and independently determined whether the respondents had accurately concluded that the experiment had to do with hostility or whether they had arrived at erroneous interpretations of the purpose of the study. All three judges identified a single response as an adequate description of the experimental treatment, and that response was from a respondent in the moderate hostility condition. (It might be noted that eleven of the twenty-four respondents failed to construct any plausible explanation as to the purpose of the study, responding with some variation of 'I really can't tell.') Therefore, it was determined that the intense level of hostility presented in the most extreme condition failed to contribute significantly to possible transparency in the procedure.

Subjects

One hundred and ninety-five University of Massachusetts undergraduates, ninety-nine males and ninety-six females, all of whom were enrolled in one of three introductory courses in Communications, served as subjects. The experiment was administered while the students were attending their regular class meetings.

Procedure

The experiment was administered in eight different sections of the three courses by the three regular instructors. The sections ranged in size from fourteen to thirty-five students. The participating instructors had no knowledge of the purpose of the experiment or the hypotheses tested. Each instructor received a set of booklets and a page of instructions to be read aloud to each class. The various experimental conditions were equally represented in each set of booklets, which had been prearranged in a random sequence.

The instructions stated that the class was being asked to participate in a study involving humour appreciation. The subjects were told that they would be rating a series of jokes, and they were shown how to mark the rating scales which they would find in their experimental booklets. Subjects were asked to look at and rate the jokes in the order in which they were presented, not to go back to earlier pages, not to change any ratings once they had been made, and not to laugh out loud or to interact with each other in any way. They were not asked to give any form of personal identification other than to indicate their sex on the final page of the booklet. Booklets were distributed row by row, and each subject was permitted to work at his or her own comfortable speed. When the subjects had finished all ratings, the instructor collected the booklets. After the entire study had been completed, debriefings were carried out in class.

Humour appreciation was rated on a unipolar scale ranging from 0, labelled 'not at all funny,' to 100, labelled 'extremely funny'. The scale was marked and numbered at intervals of ten, but subjects were permitted to intersect the scale at any point. Ratings were recorded to the nearest integer. For each subjects, a base level of humour appreciation was determined as the mean of his or her ratings given to the first two unmanipulated jokes. This basal score was subtracted from each of the subject's ratings of the manipulated stimulus material to form a relative appreciation score for each experimental squelch. The mean of each subject's relative appreciation scores constituted his or her composite score over all five experimental squelches.

RESULTS

The analysis of variance executed on the composite scores of relative humour appreciation yielded a highly significant main effect for degree of hostility ($F=5.31$; $df=2$, 189; $p < .005$). From an examination of Table 1, it can be seen that subjects in the moderate hostility condition appreciated the squelches the most. Either mild hostility or extreme

TABLE 1   Mean Composite Scores of Relative Humour Appreciation of
Squelches Involving Varying Degrees of Hostility

Sex of Respondent	Degree of Hostility		
	Mild	Moderate	Intense
Male	8.90	17.63	9.87
Female	9.18	19.96	7.20
Combined	8.92[a]	18.87[b]	8.58[a]

Note: Means having different superscripts differ significantly at $p < .05$ by Newman-Keuls' test

hostility displayed by the antagonists in the verbal exchanges resulted in significantly lower humour-appreciation ratings, with only trivial differences occurring between the two less humorous conditions. The main effect of sex of respondent was associated with $F < 1$. The degree-of-hostility by sex interaction was also insignificant ($F=1.72$; $df=2$, 189; ns), although there was a slight tendency towards greater humour appreciation for the intense hostility version than for the mild hostility version for the males, whereas the female respondents tended to respond more positively towards the least extreme rather than to the most extreme hostility condition.

In addition to the primary analysis of the composite scores, analyses of variance were performed on the relative appreciation scores of each of the five manipulated squelches. In four of the five squelches, the effect of degree of hostility was significant at $p < .01$. For the remaining squelch, the F-ratio only approached acceptable levels of significance ($F=2.49$; $df=2$, 189; $p < .10$). However, in all five of the squelches, the moderate hostility version yielded the most favourable mean humour appreciation ratings. For each squelch for which a significant F-ratio was reported, the means for the low hostility and high hostility version differed by only a trivial amount, whereas the mean for the moderate hostility version was consistently significantly different from the means of the other versions.

In summary, then, moderate hostility in squelches was found to provide the optimal condition for humour appreciation. The findings were generally consistent for male and female respondents and across stimuli.

DISCUSSION

The findings lend strong support for the notion that, in equitable exchanges of hostile behaviour between protagonists towards whom the respondent holds no strong pre-existing affective dispositions, moderate hostility constitutes an optimal condition for mirth, while mild interchanges or intensely hostile ones impair humour appreciation somewhat.

Predictions based on the Freudian notion of the repression-releasing function of hostility in humorous communications failed to receive support from the present findings. It would appear that joke work may function to eliminate some portion of the social condemnation which typically inhibits the expression of euphoria upon witnessing demonstrations of hostility. However, it apparently does not offer unconditional 'moral amnesty' (Zillmann & Cantor, 1976). Rather, the present findings suggest that the effect of embellishing an exchange of insults by enshrouding a vicious retaliatory comment in a punchline is to protract, not to remove, the boundary of propriety which circumscribes human interaction, never going so far as to sanction the most vehement expressions of hostility. Since from Freudian perspectives it may be assumed that more intense hostilities are associated with more severe societal censorship and, thereby, with more acute repressions, it would appear that joke work fails when it is needed the most. This dilemma casts doubt upon the notion of the role of humour in effectively providing relief from some of humanity's more deep-seated anxieties and thwarted desires.

The findings of this investigation can be adequately accounted for by two of the theoretical notions advanced: Berlyne's considerations of the humour-modifying function of the arousal potential of the tendentious and collative properties of humorous communications, and the version of the social propriety model which endorses the notion that joke work functions to allow the respondent more than a normal amount of tolerance to and appreciation of hostility. It should be noted that the present data do not provide information that would permit adequate determination of the relative explanatory or predictive superiority of these two notions. In fact, it might be argued that neither of these notions considered singularly is better but, rather, that some combination of these rationales is most desirable. For instance, it may be speculated that when an extremely hostile exchange in a joke violates a decoder's expectations of propriety he is unable to empathetically respond to the emotions of the protagonists because their antagonistic behaviour goes beyond the extremes of vicarious involvement permitted by his self-concept (cf. Byrne, 1971), even in fantasy or play. The respondent's inability to empathize with one of the joke protagonists may, in turn, mean that his excitational reactions to the joke may be less intense. This checking of emotional involvement may prohibit the respondent's arousal from climbing beyond the level where the arousal-reduction mechanism of Berlyne's arousal jag may become operative, thereby inhibiting humour appreciation. Or, if we assume that the respondent's arousal in some way becomes elevated to that 'uncomfortably high level' at which arousal reduction must take place in order to induce optimal euphoria, it may be that violations of the respondent's considerations of propriety may prohibit sufficient relaxation for the essential sudden reduction in arousal to occur. Such conjecture is beyond the scope of assessment of the present investigation, of course, since psychophysiological determination was not included in the design. It would appear, however, that the two models which were treated as 'confounded' may be complementary instead.

REFERENCES

See Bibliography for publications on humour, laughter and comedy

Berkowitz, L. & Walster, E. (Eds.), Advances In Experimental Social Psychology: Equity-
      Theory: Towards A General Theory Of Social Interaction. Volume 9. Academic Press, New
      York (1976).

Bryne, D., The Attraction Paradigm. Academic Press, New York (1971).

Hazlitt, W., On the pleasure of hating. In: Essays. McMillan, New York (1926).(Original, 1826).

Piaget, J., The Moral Judgment Of The Child. The Free Press, Glencoe Illinois (1948).

Sumner, W.G., Folkways. Ginn and Company, Boston (1960).

The Function of Humour in the Classroom

Eric G. Linfield

Bath College of Higher Education

Laughter is investigated as a control system by the teacher and as a release system by the pupils, forming a reciprocal interaction. The research on teacher evaluation is reviewed with particular reference to the teacher's sense of humour.

The paper considers the ways in which these control and release systems work in the classroom at varying stages of schooling. Finally, there is an analysis of classroom atmospheres in relation to the teacher's control and pupils laughter-release criteria.

Humour and Communication: Discussion

Gary Alan Fine

University of Minnesota

While researchers agree that humour is preeminently a form of communication, one will discover little agreement on how to treat humour in terms of its communicative aspect. This diversity of viewpoints was well represented in the panel on Humour and Communication, and the disjunctures between presentations were more immediately apparent then were similarities.

In general it appeared that humour as communication was being examined from one of two perspectives. Either humour was seen as interpersonal communication - talk (Ransohoff; Fine; Linfield; Hopen), or it was treated as formal communication spread through the mass media or publishing industry (Cantor; Davies). The interface between these two approaches was not explored, and it may be useful to explore aspects of this interface while critiquing the presentations.

Davies in examining 'The Changing Stereotype of the Welsh in English Jokes' exmphasized a most important, though frequently neglected, aspect of humour. That is, the cultural symbols which are associated with joking behaviour may change over time, although other researchers (Dundes, 1975) have commented upon the remarkable stability of certain joke themes. Davies discovered after examining English jokebooks that over three centuries the perception of the Welsh has changed from a group being preoccupied with aggression, boastfulness, and toasted cheese (a seventeenth century regional delicacy) to one in the nineteenth and twentieth centuries characterized by being crafty, devious (i.e., Welshing on a deal), and evasive. Their stereotype changed from one akin to the Texas cowboy to one more like the Jewish merchant. However, it is not clear the extent to which jokebooks can serve as an indicator of the humour of a period. For a variety of reasons, some of which may not be applicable in this instance, published humour may be systematically different from spoken humour. A case in point might be humour about Blacks on American television.

Because of the power and moral suasion of Civil Rights groups in the United States, the type of humour that can be directed against Blacks has been sharply curtailed. The old negative stereotype of American Blacks as lazy, dishonest, violent, shifty, stupid, sexually promiscuous, and unclean is rarely expressed on television. If Blacks are characterized, it may be as exaggerations of middle-class Whites; thus, Blacks can be shown outsmarting Whites (a traditional motif in Black humour; see Abrahams, 1970: 63-69) or as being cheap, excessively proud, or even crafty. Thus, if one were to examine television comedy to determine the ways in which White society caricatured Blacks, one might be misled by the results. The fact is, much as we may regret it, there still is much humour among Whites which relies on the stereotypes of the past. The classic 'Rastus and Liza' jokes are still being told in the United States.

This is to warn that it can not be assumed that a thematic content analysis based upon an institutionally produced or distributed source will necessarily represent the extent of those themes in a culture (Denzin, 1970). However, analysis based upon textual materials, like that of Davies, may be the best opportunity for insight into these cultural forms in the absence of direct testimony (Carey, 1970). Thus, while we might wish to be cautious about accepting a numerical distribution of themes, in cases in which much of the material reveals particular content, some confidence can be placed in the results.

Davies' central point that the humour themes in a culture may be altered over time is highly significant. While most of the themes from the Sixteenth Century are found in the Twentieth Century, they are no longer associated with the Welsh as targets. We might speculate that there is a need for these motifs to be expressed, but that the symbols which are placed in conjunction with them are mutable. Just how mutable they are is an important topic for inquiry. Noting the spread of certain joke fads - Polish jokes, elephant jokes, or jokes dealing with newsworthy personalities, we expect that joke cycles can start easily and spread rapidly, although their modification or elimination is a much slower process.

Cantor's paper also dealt with printed humour, and, in concession to our modern age, with broadcast humour. In her Conference presentation, Cantor focussed on the importance of tendentious wit in the mass media, although in the formal paper (see this volume) she also discusses the tangentially related question of the treatment of the two sexes in American media humour. It is the first question which seems of more general interest to humour researchers, while the second would perhaps be a central concern to those in American Studies or Women's Studies.

Cantor argues correctly that surface content varies markedly depending on the medium examined. For example, one content analysis of television humour (Stocking, Sapolsky & Zillmann, in press) found that 73% of it contained either sexual or hostile elements. Cantor's own study (Cantor & Venus, 1975) found among cartoons for 'Look' and the 'New Yorker' only 5% depicted sex, 6% implied violence, and 12% indicated hostility. Thus, by this classification at most 23% of the cartoons had tendentious themes. Clearly this is a figure far removed from that found on television. A third study (Cantor & Richardson, 1976) found that tendentious themes in cartoons ranged from 85% in Playboy to 17% in Ladies' Home Journal. Cantor concludes from these findings that a good proportion of what American society is labelling and reacting to as humorous is not based upon themes 'readily identifiable as tendentious' (Cantor, this volume).

There is a problem with this analysis as it relates to a critique of Freudian theory. Does Cantor's schematization of tendentious wit correspond to that of Freud? All of these content studies take a straightforward approach to tendentious wit. In Cantor's magazine studies she merely asks her students if violence, hostility, or sex is depicted or implied. The television content analysis is somewhat more specific, but the categories are defined narrowly. For example, coders scored a remark as being sexual only if it consisted of an implied reference to sex organs or sexual intercourse.

I am not convinced that it is fair to equate the results of these coding schemas with Freud's meaning of tendentious wit. Freudian analysis of wit emphasizes that its aggressive or sexual content is frequently disguised (Freud, 1960). Freud and his followers (e.g., Grotjahn, 1957) have emphasized that jokework is almost identical to dream work. Grotjahn describes the process as:

> 'A foreconscious thought, usually of aggressive nature, perhaps an intended injury, is repressed into the unconscious and left for a moment to unconscious elaboration; symbolically disguised it will reappear in consciousness' (Grotjahn, 1957, p15).

Freud and Grotjahn, while believing the better the disguise, the better the joke, also suggest that on some level the listener must be able to perceive the disguised aggressive tendency. The problem in Cantor's analysis is that we can not determine if this disguised content is being coded. If the presumption on the part of her coders was to score only surface meanings, then the analysis has little relevance to the determination of the maximum extent of tendentious wit in the media. In examining my own collection of 'New Yorker' cartoons I found very few which could not be described as having disguised tendentious themes. It is not clear if Cantor's operationalization of tendentiousness is equivalent to Freud's concept, but I would suspect that a panel of Freudian analysts would find considerably more tendentious jokes than did Cantor's students.

This critique of Cantor's operationalization is not meant to detract from the study which, removed from a Freudian context, is interesting as an analysis of the ecology of humour. Barker (1968, p2) has pointed out the importance of determining the frequency and location of an event in order to determine its significance in the culture and to discover over time the extent of cultural change. Cantor's analysis, dealing with overt and implicit themes in media humour, is a valuable step in this direction. It is also a particularly useful study in documenting the different content of humour directed at specific audiences. It reminds us that, as with individuals, we can learn much about broadcasts and publications by the humour they employ. It will doubtless not come as a surprise that there is more tendentious wit in Playboy than in the Ladies' Home Journal, but it is interesting (for Americans) to learn that Esquire has significantly less tendentious wit than Cosmopolitan.

Here again, we might note the possible disjuncture between humour (or wit) in the media and humour (or wit) in interpersonal interaction. While it is probable that one would find a significant difference in the humour of playboys as opposed to homemakers, we can not assume that the percentage figures based upon magazine content as compared to conversational content will be similar. The content analysis of interpersonal humour is of course much more difficult than analyzing media content — primarily due to immense sampling problems — but a beginning might be for field workers to categorize and quantify the humour that they collect.

The other papers approached humorous communication from a naturalistic perspective and were more interested in process than content. My paper and that of Ransohoff had basic content in common, but they differed in analytic approach. Ransohoff presented a remarkable collection of taped humour from group therapy sessions of early adolescent girls (ages twelve to fourteen). My data were collected through participant observation among preadolescent boys (age nine to twelve) during and after Little League baseball games. Unfortunately in writing this discussion, I do not have access to Dr. Ransohoff's tapes or her formal paper, but I shall attempt to recall her findings as best I can.

Evidence from both studies indicates the prevalence of aggression and sexuality in children's humour. Ransohoff's tapes, which reveal young girls simultaneously interested in and anxious about sexual matters are particularly significant because the assumption has been that women and girls rarely engage in sexual joking. I have been aware for some time that this is no longer (if it ever was) accurate, but the graphic nature of Ransohoff's data disproved this assumption quite directly.

Both papers share the research technique of having an adult collect material from children. I suspect that this may, in part, have influenced the type of data collected, and the type that was considered most appropriate to analyze. Here I will be speaking primarily from my own experience, but having listened to the tapes I suspect that this analysis will probably be valid for Ransohoff as well.

I found that in both years in which I have worked with Little League baseball players it took some time for the players to get accustomed to my presence, and to feel confident that I meant them no harm. After this, there was a long period in which they were willing to treat me as a friendly adult, and to show me many kind indulgences. Yet I felt that I was not being completely accepted into their midst; there was some level at which they could not be completely natural and open in my presence. Eventually I gained sufficient trust to allow them to feel more comfortable with me – particularly in the telling of dirty jokes, obscene teasing, and gross misbehaviour. At first these preadolescents appeared to take great delight in being able to engage in these behaviours in my presence, and perhaps were more risqué than they might have been otherwise (although clearly they could not have invented the humour for my benefit). I felt this aspect of children's behaviour in listening to the early adolescent girls in the presence of their tolerant therapist. The fact that their therapist allowed them to break normal social taboos in her presence may have contributed to their raucous, nearly hysterical laughter. This laughter may have as much to do with the social situation, as with the anxiety-producing content of the humour.

Ransohoff stressed the presence of anxious laughter in group interaction, and at one point she described the group members as 'scared out of their wits'. These girls of lower SES backgrounds are growing up in a dangerous world. This is a world with which they must come to terms, but with which at their stage of emotional development they cannot yet deal properly or maturely. Rape and public exhibitionisms are events that city children may have thrust upon them at an early age, even if the experiences do not happen to them personally. One way of coping with these urban horrors is to make 'light' of them through joking. Yet as the 'hysterical' response to these comments indicate this is not easily done. I have previously suggested that there are occasions of great stress in which humour may serve a counter-productive purpose (Fine, 1975) by revealing to the laugher just how little there is to laugh at and by inducing strong feelings of guilt and shame for having laughed. This is particularly true when the rest of the group does not respond similarly but may also occur when the entire group is for a moment submerged in hideous mirth.

My own research focused on less hysterical humour but humour which also dealt with sensitive social issues. The humour of a small group often comprises a major portion of the communication of that group (Leary, 1975). Joking frequently serves as a means by which members develop rapport with each other on sensitive areas of group life without fearing direct contradiction, since humour can always be retracted as being 'only kidding and not serious'. Further, humour may increase cohesion in a group or may serve to support or restructure the group's status hierarchy. Both the psychiatric perspective of Ransohoff and my own essentially sociological perspective are valuable, though flawed, methods of understanding group interaction.

These approaches lack a systematic indicator of the content of group humour, and must rely upon the intuition grasp of the observer. Neither of us has developed or even has attempted to develop a system of categorization. Our analysis is post hoc and is subject to challenge by those who intuitively disagree with the proposed findings. At least in Cantor's study and those she reports, we know the criteria by which the humour is categorized; in these qualitative analyses we must trust the judgment of the researcher. The richness of the data is being traded for the more sophisticated inference techniques of statistically based analyses.

This difference in methodology frequently occurs between naturalistic studies and those which are based upon 'canned' humour. As mentioned above, a controlled analysis of natural humour, though desirable, would seem to be very difficult, although there have been some attempts at achieving this goal (Coser, 1960; Traylor, 1973). This is not to suggest that these qualitative studies' usefulness is only as a supplement to quantitative data. It is essential to examine humour as it spontaneously occurs in natural settings and to study individual examples as they are created or negotiated in concrete social interactions; I call for more of this type of research, although we must recognize the necessary weaknesses inherent in this approach. It should be obvious that no research tradition is sufficient unto itself for understanding a complex and broadly-based social phenomenon.

The humour analyzed by both Ransohoff and myself seems to be common among children, and similar comments to the ones we discuss are found among many groups of pre- and early adolescents. These humorous remarks and jokes are spread almost entirely by means of word of mouth with great textual conservatism (Brunvand, 1968). Teasing and dirty jokes are not transmitted by means of the media, and most certainly are not communicated by adults to children. They seem to be passed from one generation of children to the next through an informal social network. Since children's activities are not completely age graded (most notably true among boys, Lever, 1976) the older children will communicate these remarks to younger ones, and will be rewarded by being thought mature. Even situational humour, while responding to a specific context, is not created de novo but from previously known elements. Frequently these elements belong to a subterranean children's culture, generally unknown to adults and too overtly tendentious for dissemination by the media. The precise patterns of the diffusion of children's jokelore are not clear and are an area worthy of scholarly analysis in terms of general theories of information diffusion (e.g., Katz and Lazarsfeld, 1955). The humour addressed to children through television, films, and magazines is only a fraction of the humour that is part of children's culture. We would be misled if we examined media humour aimed at children and generalized from that to the domain of items that children laugh at. The humour to which children respond is not for the adult who is faint of heart.

Linfield's paper, 'The Function of Humour in the Classroom,' also deals with humour related to children, but his focus is primarily upon the teacher, and in contrast to the papers of Ransohoff and myself, emphasizes the more overtly positive elements of mirth. Linfield argues that humour is a liberating force, and that teachers who use humour in their classroom instruction are happier than those who refrain from its use. The question that is not directly asked is whether this will affect the performance of the students. There is experimental evidence to suggest that it will not (see Gruner, 1976), but few of these studies have been conducted in naturalistic situations. Perhaps if the educational attainment of classes with comical teachers could be compared with those classes with serious teachers, we would have a better indication of the effect of humour upon education. However, in such a quasi-experiment (Campbell & Stanley, 1963) the many uncontrolled variables would make inferences problematic. Linfield accepts the popular assumption that it is better to be humorous than dull, but it must be remembered that scientifically this is still an assumption.

In considering some of the negative components of humour such as its occasional aggressiveness and obscene sexuality we may even wonder whether a humorist does not contain elements of hostility and sadism. The evaluative perspective accepted is based more on personal prediliction than proven fact.

Hopen ('Tracking the Intractable - The Study of Humour in Value Systems') focuses on the role of humour as a central repository for the values of a culture, and argues that the detailed study of humour will expose the society's values. An ethnological approach has points in common with content analysis in that both attempt to understand the society by means of its products - in other words, a 'cultural reflector' approach to communication, which can apply both to media productions and interpersonal remarks. However, this approach becomes somewhat difficult to employ when applied to humour since humour is not straightforward, but, if successful, is disguised communication. On what level then will the values of a culture be embedded? 'Member's knowledge' would inform us of this, but then presumably with 'member's knowledge' the question of which values are important can be understood by introspection. Hopen is correct in suggesting that central cultural values are being expressed through humour, but it is not entirely clear how these values can be determined, if one does not have some reasonable idea what they are before one begins.

Humour is one element among many which reveals a culture's world-view (Dundes, 1972), but viewed in isolation from other aspects of a group's culture it provides a highly ambiguous perspective on the culture. Humour can only be understood if the incongruity which underlies and creates it is understood, and if the resolution of it is recognized as a legitimate resolution.

In bringing together an anthropologist (Hopen), an educator (Linfield), two sociologists (Fine and Davies), a communications researcher (Cantor), and a psychiatrist (Ransohoff), it is inevitable that this group will to some extent talk past each other. Yet in reviewing these papers, I was impressed by how fascinating they were seen singly and as a group. The topic of humour and communication is a broad one, and these papers represent several different areas; yet they all share the belief that humour is not merely content but serves communicative needs of the group or the society. They all, as good papers inevitably will, reveal an incompleteness which needs to be followed up diligently. Each of the papers has weaknesses based on methodological difficulties, but the papers also indicate the fruitfulness of various methodological approaches.

One point that was not dealt with by any of the papers in the session, and which might be a valuable area of future research is the interface between humour in the media and humour in natural settings. To what extent do scriptwriters, comedians, and jokebook authors employ humour that is already in popular circulation? When they alter it for their particular purposes, do they do this in any systematic way? How does one transform a natural joke to a canned joke? Frequently writers (e.g., Berger, 1975; McMahon, 1976) will credit their own experiences with providing them with comic material; yet, few admit 'stealing' jokes from the public domain. Yet by the redundancy of media humour, this clearly occurs frequently. We do not know if it occurs consciously.

The other side of the issue is that frequently humour in conversation is derived from television. A joke that is told on a popular television programme may be spread interpersonally until it becomes so widely known that it is accepted as part of a culture's jokelore. It is assumed that every joke must have had an inventor at some point, although for most of our humour that inventor remains blessedly obscure. The joke is taken for granted as part of our cultural heritage and is to be used and altered as the situation requires. However, we know very little of the process by which media jokes are transformed to popular jokes, which jokes are most likely to make the transition, and if there are any systematic alterations that standardly occur.

The boundary between media humour and interpersonal humour is clearly a permeable one and one which social scientists and humanists would do well to explore.

REFERENCES

See Bibliography for publications on humour, laughter and comedy

Abrahams, R.D., Positively Black. Prentice-Hall, Englewood Cliffs, New Jersey (1970).

Barker, R.G., Ecological Psychology. Stanford University Press, Stanford, California (1968).

Brunvand, J.H., The Study of American Folklore. Norton, New York (1968).

Campbell, D.T. & Stanley, J.C., Experimental and Quasi-Experimental Designs for Research. Rand-McNally, Chicago (1963).

Cantor, J.R. & Richardson, C., Content analysis of the humor in 'Playboy', 'Cosmopolitan', 'Esquire', and 'Ladies' Home Journal'. Unpublished research (1976).

Cantor, J.R. & Venus, P., Content analysis of the humor in 'The New Yorker' and 'Look'. Unpublished research (1975).

Carey, J.T., The author replies. American Journal of Sociology, 75, 1039-1041 (1970).

Denzin, N.K., Problems in analyzing elements of mass culture. American Journal of Sociology, 75, 1035-1038 (1970).

Dundes, A., Folk ideas as units of world view. In: A. Parades & R. Bauman (Eds.), Toward New Perspectives in Folklore. University of Texas Press, Austin, Texas (1972).

Dundes, A., Slurs international: Folk comparisons of ethnicity and national character. Southern Folklore Quarterly, 39, 15-38 (1975).

Fine, G.A., Humor under stress. Unpublished manuscript (1975).

Katz, E. & Lazarfeld, P.F., Personal Influence. Free Press, New York (1955).

Leary, J.P., Folklore and photography in a small group. In: S. Ohrn & M.E. Bell (Eds.), Saying Cheese: Studies in Folklore and Visual Communication. Folklore Forum Bibliographic and Special Series, No. 13 (1975).

Lever, J., Sex differences in games children play. Social Problems, 23, 478-487 (1976).

INDIVIDUAL DIFFERENCES IN HUMOUR

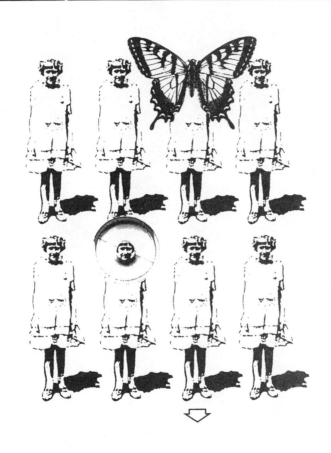

Individual Differences, Personality, and Humour Appreciation: Introduction to Symposium

Howard Leventhal and Martin A. Safer

University of Wisconsin, Madison

It is appropriate to have a session on individual differences at a humour conference if it is true that each of us has a unique 'sense of humour' and that the enjoyment of humour is a personal and subjective affair. But a case by case approach to the study of humour is unlikely to satisfy those who want a scientific orientation with verified fact (Goodchilds, 1972, p174). Indeed, if we did proceed along clinical lines, we might find ourselves accused of developing the '...rank, weedy theories of verbal, literary and clinical psychology... exhibiting every error of scientific conceptualization...' (Hundleby, Pawlik & Cattell, 1965) and adding to the 'Alice-in-Wonderland atmosphere which pervades so much of...' personality psychology (Eysenck, 1952, p8). How then should we proceed?

There are two broadly different strategies one can adopt for the study of individual differences in humour experience. One approach is the traditional individual differences search for factors comprising the humour domain. The other approach is theory directed – personality theory, in the present case. In this chapter we will first briefly discuss the traditional individual differences approach and then discuss three types of theory – (a) social-cultural; (b) cognitive; and (c) affective - which offer guides for the study of individual differences in humour experience. In the final sections we will suggest some new ideas which could guide future research into individual differences and humour.

TRADITIONAL INDIVIDUAL DIFFERENCE APPROACH

A strategy that has been followed by many investigators is to go forth with instruments in hand (jokes, cartoons, recordings, slapstick records, with appropriate rating scales) to conduct empirical studies of what things are funny and what people find them funny. Persons, classes of stimuli, specific stimuli within classes, modes of presentation, occasions for presentation can be sampled, and after obtaining judgments of funniness or observations of laughter, a set of factors can be generated to help describe the data (Cattell, 1966).

Currently, this traditional trait approach is under attack by those who believe traits exist only for the observer, that cross-situational consistency in behaviour is virtually nonexistent, and that situations, not personal dispositions, determine behaviour (Mischel, 1968). The critics claim that traits do not predict behaviour; but in most studies, investigators have used trait measures to predict single, unreliable instances of behaviour (Epstein, 1975). As in the case of predicting behaviour from attitudes (Fishbein & Ajzen, 1975), traits and attitude measures can predict behaviour only if the behavioural measure is reliable and based on multiple observations of behaviour. Assuming that these methodological problems of the trait approach are solvable, it is still necessary to examine the conceptual utility of the trait approach to humour.

Past Studies

Studies of individual differences in humour seem to fall in three clusters: (a) investigations using humorous material to define trait factors of personality or to link factors of humour appreciation with trait factors of personality, presumably enriching our understanding of both (Cattell & Luborsky, 1947; Eysenck, 1947; Kambouropoulou, 1930; Lamb, 1968; Miller & Bacon, 1971; O'Connell, 1960); (b) studies relating humour appreciation to highly general variables, such as age, sex, and intelligence (Ding & Jersild, 1932; Felker & Hunter, 1970; Fry, 1972a,b; McGhee & Grodzitsky, 1975; Perl, 1933; Rothbart, 1973; Prerost, 1975; Young, 1937); and (c) studies where individual differences are used to learn about the dimensions of humour stimuli and humour processing (Abelson & Levine, 1958; T.G. Andrews, 1943; Eysenck, 1943; Kambouropoulou, 1926; Luborsky & Cattell, 1947).

What can be concluded from these studies? With a few exceptions they have added little to the understanding of humour or to the understanding of individual differences in personality. All too often, these investigations were undertaken in a strictly empirical way with no theoretical analysis of the humour process. Because of this, it is seldom clear why particular types of humorous material (or groups of subjects) were selected or if the sampling of material (or subjects) was representative of any particular population of stimuli. In the absence of a theoretical model and a specific hypothesis, there is little way of specifying what populations should be sampled. This is a problem with much humour research, as it is not uncommon for investigators to select a dozen or so from hundreds of contemporary jokes. Also, since what is considered funny changes over time, an investigator who lacks a theoretical model has no basis for selecting new material.

The stimulus dimensions of humour. The area in which individual difference studies have done most to organize our understanding of humour is the study of the stimulus dimensions of humour. Even the very early diary studies of individual differences by Kambouropoulou (1926) suggested categories of events regarded as funny by her Vassar girls. Investigations using factor analysis of jokes, cartoons, etcetera, have defined other categories or dimensions of humour. The early studies of T.G. Andrews (1943), of Eysenck (1942), and of Luborsky and Cattell (1947), as well as the more recent investigation of Abelson and Levine (1958), show agreement on factors such as hostile humour, humour related to immortality, humour involving impudence, and humour involving various forms of sexuality (also in Eysenck, 1942). Eysenck's (1942, 1947) studies have also found higher order factors, such as cognitive, emotional, and motivational humour, suggesting that cognitive, emotional, and motivational (particularly social motivation) processes play an important role in humour. In general, however, there is not a high degree of agreement on more specific lower order factors.

The agreement that appears suggests it may be worthwhile to conduct further investigations into the dimensionality of humorous material. Exploration of lower order factors specific to particular content areas might generate a more consistent view of stimulus dimensions if theories were developed to guide selection of humorous materials and to classify subjects (e.g., Abelson & Levine, 1958). It is also possible that the exploration of stimulus factors could be better approached using contemporary, multidimensional scaling procedures (Carroll, 1972; Shepard, Romney & Nerlove, 1972; Wexler & Romney, 1972). Some multidimensional procedures also permit one to generate factor spaces on individual as well as group data. It might prove of some interest to compare the factor spaces developed in these different ways, as it could give us insight into the heterogeneity or variety of factor spaces for humour and the meaning of individual deviations from modal structures. Successful use of this approach would depend, however, on theoretical analyses capable of predicting individual differences in factor structures.

Individual Differences

Given the multidimensionality of humour stimuli, it seems unreasonable to expect consistent correlations between individual difference measures of personality traits and an overall factor of humour (see Eysenck, 1953, p414). However, a specific personality trait could be linked theoretically to a particular content area of humour, such as the liking of aggressive and hostile humour displayed by persons who score high on the psychopathic deviant subscale of the MMPI (Holmes, 1969). From this perspective, it is not surprising that Nias and Wilson (this volume) failed to find hereditary influence on sense of humour. They might have succeeded had they focused more precisely on linking specific temperamental dispositions, known to be influenced by heredity, to certain specific subsets of humorous material.

If investigators wish to search for correlates of an overall humour factor, we would recommend they use a general measure of mood or joyfulness rather than responses to specific jokes and cartoons. Epstein (1975) reports very high correlations (or reliabilities) for individual differences in mood over twenty-four-day periods (correlations across subjects averaged .88 for unpleasant emotions); and Wessman and Ricks (1966) also reported substantial correlations of life experiences and mood. Both of these investigators used a diary method where the subject reported his overall mood or feeling reaction to the events of his daily life rather than to experimenter-selected humorous stimuli. By rating mood independent of a specific eliciting stimulus or mood related to the self-selected events of the day, one may come closer to recording variance reflecting more permanent, underlying constitutional aspects of personality.

Theory and individual difference research. In summary, we believe that the poor performance of individual difference research in the study of humour reflects a failure to evaluate carefully the kinds of materials and relationships worthy of attention; it reflects a psychometric rather than a scientific, analytic approach (Lewin, 1935; Powers, 1973). Multivariate procedures are extremely powerful, and they seldom fail to account for a substantial proportion of variance in individual difference data. But without a theory of humour, a substantial proportion of 'explained' variance is simply an empirical relationship which usually cannot be integrated with other findings.

PERSONALITY THEORY AND THE STUDY OF HUMOUR

We shall review three classes of personality theory that offer guides for the study of individual differences in humour: (a) social-psychological theories which emphasize interpersonal relationships and informal and formal roles embedded in institutional frameworks; (b) cognitive theories which emphasize the development and the functioning of the structures which determine the individual's understanding of his world; and (c) affective theories which emphasize the contribution of specific affects or emotion to humour. We will briefly review the key variables relevant to humour in each class of theory, pointing out factors relevant to the conference papers which follow.

While these three orientations provide different perspectives on humour, they do not represent three completely independent approaches to personality. Cognitive structure and emotional socialization develop in a cultural context (Labarre, 1947; LeVine, 1973; Tomkins, 1962), and, conversely, social roles and structure reflect internal cognitive and affective organization. Cognitive anthropologists describe cultural grammars or rules for organizing and arranging basic cultural themes (Colby, 1975), such as the functional use of language (Hymes, 1967) and humour for communication.

Social Psychological Approaches to Personality and Humour

Social cultural theories deal with many factors of importance to humour. These include culture and: (a) meaning or content of humour; (b) context or occasion for humour; (c) acceptable form for humour; (d) reciprocal relationships between group structure on the one hand and expressions of humour, joy, and mirth, on the other. Each of these four areas represents a focus for the development of a humour theory and a guide for dealing with individual differences in humour response.

Content. The subject matter or content of humour is obviously conditioned by the sociocultural background of the humorist and his audience. When members of a cultural subgroup tell jokes, the content is relevant to group experience: for example, hospitalized patients joke about nurses, doctors, their subservience in the sick role, and they turn threats into group laughter (Coser, 1959). Psychiatric teams joke about psychoanalysis, physicians, and patients (Goodrich, Henry & Goodrich, 1954); husbands joke about mothers-in-law and brothers-in-law (Radcliffe-Brown, 1940); soldiers joke about snafus, army cooking, and death (Heller, 1961); Jews tell Jewish jokes, Italians specialize in Italian jokes, men joke about women and women are beginning to joke more openly about men (Chapman & Gadfield, 1976). Content also can take subtle, unverbalized forms, such as expectations or schemata respecting the proper role of adult and child; for example, adults walk and eat with utensils, whereas infants crawl and eat with their fingers. An endless set of content subcategories could be elaborated in each of these areas.

Because joke content has so obvious a relationship to events and relationships in the individual's culture and subculture, it is easy to take content for granted. Psychologists have not developed adequate ways of dealing with content in psychological theory or in theories of humour. Many experimental studies of the effects of motive arousal (anger, sex, etcetera) on humour that are now explained in elaborate psychodynamic terms could just as easily reflect individual and sociocultural differences in experience with and salience of different thematic contents (Goldstein, Suls & Anthony, 1972). The underlying themes and concepts which form the base for humour vary by culture, social class, role, sex, and so forth (Martineau, 1972), and these content differences may account for comparisons such as sex differences in response to sexist humour (Nias & Wilson, this volume) and sex differences in preference for male and female comedians (Sheppard, this volume).

Thus, a thorough study of culture with close attention to role relationships could provide a basic vocabulary of humorous themes. But themes alone are insufficient for humour and for dealing with individual and group differences.

Form. Cultures have protocol and role relationships and other rules relating their elements; in short, cultures have grammars or acceptable arrangements of thematic contents (Colby, 1975; Hymes, 1967). In our culture, males are generally supposed to be less emotionally expressive than females but are expected to express aggression overtly rather than covertly (Frodi, Macauley & Thome, in press). Other formal roles define limits and set the stage for emotional reactions. For example, bellboys are supposed to be subservient, and bishops to be revered and feared. Freud (1952, p36) presents the humorous example of the bellboy who responded to the bishop's question, 'Who is it?' by answering, 'The Lord, my boy.' Protocol also calls for symbols and themes to unfold in given sequences, and role relationships also specify sequences of address for communication (Cohen, 1958). And where these complex forms exist, there is the possibility for interesting violation of form.

Culture also provides established humorous forms for both the production and expression of humour. Colby (1975) comments on the tradition of themes and arrangement of themes which provide an underlying vocabulary and grammar for the 'spontaneous', artistic performance of ballad-singing. Similarly, for humour improvisation, there is an underlying vocabulary and grammar which can be used to create variations upon well established themes and forms. Jokes about oneself or one's relative, such as spouse or mother-in-law jokes, are familiar themes in contemporary humour.

The existence of these well established contents and forms are of great aid to the humorist. Knowing these themes, he can anticipate what will and what will not be funny, what will and what will not exceed the limits of propriety, and how to barely exceed and then skilfully withdraw from these unarticulated yet recognizable limits. (For example, see Mark Twain's virtuoso performance in his after-dinner speech for Ulysses Grant, from Eastman, 1936). Culturally defined contents and forms undoubtedly underlie the commonality in audience reactions to humorous plays and films (Pollio, Mers & Lucchesi, 1972). Individual or group differences in familiarity with these themes or dialects of humour may underlie the differences in preference expressed toward specific types of humour and towards male and female comedians (Sheppard, this volume).

Context. Sociocultural factors provide significant contextual cues signifying that specific occasions are appropriate for the generation of humour and the expression of emotion through smiling and laughter (Flugel, 1954; McGhee, 1972b). There are a variety of ways in which culture controls or signals the appropriateness of occasions for affective expression. First, specific roles are defined as relevant for humour; the fool or clown (Klapp, 1950; Levine, 1961), the humorist, the after-dinner speaker, are titles for roles whose occupants are expected to generate the cognitive structures productive of humour (Eastman, 1936). Specific occasions and places such as parties, night clubs, etcetera, serve as signs and instigators for the expression of humour and joyful laughter. These culturally agreed upon cues or signals establish cognitive and emotional sets that are appropriate for the processing of humour-inducing information; for example, they enable the individual to regard as humorous what might otherwise be considered offensive.

Other less permanent cues may function as joke signals or signs of humour. For example, joke fads, such as the Polish joke, involve a set of cognitive elements and arrangements conducive to a particular type of humour, and the term Polish serves as a signal for humour. There must be an infinite number of such 'joke' cues. Groups often develop their own joke cues, and knowledge and use of those cues can identify one as a member of that group. Differences in knowledge and sensitivity to such cues, and not differences in sense of humour or expressiveness, may be responsible for individual differences in humour and humour expression.

Special relationships are another socioculturally specified form prescribing the occasion, content, grammatical organization, and limits for joking. Some long-term relationships follow kinship lines, such as the joking relationships described by Radcliffe-Brown (1940) between a husband and his wife's brothers or between a child and his grandparents. But short-lived joking relationships regularly develop between specific participants at a particular time and place. Coser's (1959) examples of joking among medical patients provide one example — the humour expressed among psychiatric staff members, another (Goodrich, Henry & Goodrich, 1954). There might be important individual differences in the number and quality of a person's face-to-face joking relationships. Having an individual list or describe his face-to-face joking relationships might be a better index of his sense of humour than ratings of standard jokes or cartoons.

The mother (parent)-infant relationship is another close, warm, trusting (Erickson, 1963) situation in which a wide range of potentially distressing stimuli lead to smiles and laughter (Sroufe & Waters, 1976; Sroufe, Waters & Matas, 1974; Sroufe & Wunsch, 1972). This may not be humour in the formal, traditional sense, but the elements of cognition, information processing, and mutual game-playing legitimately define some mother-infant interactions as at least temporary joking relationships.

Proximity and group structure. The papers by Chapman (1973) and Sherman (1976) present evidence for the facilitative effects of proximity on smiling and laughing. But closeness does not always lead to positive affect, it can strengthen many responses (Zajonc, 1965, 1966) — hence, cannot by itself account for the appearance of humour and expressions of mirth in the group context. Other facets - group atmosphere, humour cues, vigorous physical activity in children's groups (Ding & Jersild, 1932; Sherman, this volume) - allow or encourage the expression of pleasure, which can then be magnified by closeness (Freedman, 1975). Aspects of group structure may also affect the balance of positive to negative affects - positive affect being more frequent in democratic than in authoritarian groups (White & Lippitt, 1968) and in groups of friends than in groups of strangers (Chapman, 1976). The evidence is also persuasive in human and nonhuman primates that intent to come near as well as coming near to others stimulate expressive behaviour (R.J. Andrews, 1963; Rowell,

1972; Van Hooff, 1962).

But it is also important to note that proximity may generate emotions which compete with the humour expression; closeness can stimulate embarrassment and social anxiety, and this discomfort and distress may block expressions of pleasure. The observed outcome will likely differ by the individual's social background, by relationship of sex to social training, and so forth (Sutton-Smith, Rosenberg & Morgan, 1963).

Functionally, joking and the expressing of pleasure can generate a sense of group solidarity or belongingness, provide a safety valve or release for dealing with tension generated by conflict internal to the group, and help individuals to cope with various threatening, negative experiences (Martineau, 1972). However, joking may also undermine group structure, since humour by low status participants may be interpreted as an attempt to wrestle group control from high status members (Coser, 1960).

The factors mentioned in this section have counterparts in the cognitive and affective domain, and each of them can be related to individual differences. The investigator of individual differences would be remiss in ignoring differences due to content, form, context, and group structure.

Cognitive Theories of Personality and Humour

An unusually rich number of hypotheses have been suggested to humour researchers by cognitive personality theory, and many of them have been especially helpful in accounting for individual and group differences in humour response. There are two major types of cognitive hypotheses which will be discussed: (a) structural, and (b) processing.

Structural hypotheses. Cognitive theory suggests a variety of factors or predispositional properties which significantly alter humour response. Among these are a host of factors which can be grouped under the heading 'Understanding'. Zigler, Levine and Gould (1966a; 1967) extended earlier work relating age differences to smiling and showed that as mental age increases, more complex forms of humour elicit a humour response (smile or laughter). Only when the concepts and themes of a joke are understood can the joke or cartoon elicit mirth.

Understanding involves more than the structural factor of mental age; to appreciate particular forms of humour, one must possess the informational background with particular themes. For example, Zigler, Levine and Gould (1966b) compared mirth responses of three groups of subjects: institutionalized and noninstitutionalized mental retardates, and normals, all of whom were matched for mental age. Despite the equation of overall mental age, the retardates manifested significantly lower levels of mirth. They speculate that the limited experience of the institutionalized retardates and the wariness of 'evaluation' by noninstitutional retardates lowered the level of their mirth reactions. The experience factor discussed in this comparison is related, of course, to the content factor discussed under sociocultural theories of humour.

A cognitive analysis of humour suggests the need to go beyond mere group comparisons, such as retardate versus normal, male versus female, good-looking woman versus average-looking woman, etcetera. What is needed is to develop hypotheses and methods for disclosing the thematic structures which form the ground work for humour response in each of these classes of individuals.

However, the fact that one understands a joke does not insure that the joke will elicit humour; there are many things we understand which are not at all funny, and there are things we understand that were once funny but are no longer. Zigler, Levine and Gould (1966a) were surprised when they first found a curvilinear relationship between the level of difficulty and the funniness of jokes. Jokes that were too simple failed to generate humour (see also Zelazo, 1972).

The hypothesis that a funny joke must be neither too difficult nor too easy applies to a wide range of observations respecting mirthful behaviour. For example, while a variety of stimuli apparently have the power to innately release infant smiling (Sroufe & Waters, 1976), the smiling response soon becomes controlled by the child's perception and recognition of familiar events. When this happens, the smiling response can serve as an external signal that the child has acquired underlying schemata and developed the skills needed to fit or match the input pattern to these schemata. It has been hypothesized that the arousal induced by the effort and success in fitting input to pattern (McGhee, 1971b, 1972b, 1974a; Sroufe & Waters, 1976) is critical in generating the humour reactions. Harter, Shultz and Blum (1971) reported that when children performed a picture vocabulary test, they smiled more to correct than to incorrect items. However, for the correct items there was no evidence of a linear relationship between item difficulty and smiling.

McGhee (1972b, 1974a) and Shultz and Horibe (1974) believe that age dependent differences in humour response are related to changes in the child's underlying rule structures – that the child acquires the content and Piagetian structural or organizational rules needed to process different types of humour. McGhee (this volume) has argued that children do not really have humour experiences until two or three years of age, since before that they lack the ability to process the information and respond to the particular kinds of relationships, expecially incongruities, that are the essential core of jokes and cartoons. McGhee may be somewhat arbitrary in this definition of humour and his restriction of incongruities to jokes or cartoons. For example, Sroufe and Wunsch (1972) observed smiling reactions in infants who had just learned to crawl when these infants saw their mothers crawling on all fours. Infants who had not yet crawled showed no such response. This seems about as good evidence for incongruity as advanced in most studies.

We would like to comment here on the potential, practical value of research on cognitive difficulty and humour for the investigation and, perhaps, the diagnosis of developmental level and extent of neural damage. The smiling reaction provides a nonverbal signal for understanding, and with careful controls, we can tease out the stimulus features and cognitive structures generating the smile.

Processing. Cognitive forms or rules do not make humour; humour experience and expression arise from particular ways of processing inputs. What are the key features of humour processing, and could these features be responsible for individual differences in humour?

There seem to be three groups of factors important for processing funny material: (a) set or structural readiness; (b) the processing of incongruities, which involves generating an incongruity unit and tolerance for the incongruity unit; and (c) contextual factors indicating safety and humorousness of the incongruous experience (see Eysenck, 1942, for a similar list).

(a) Set or structural readiness. The humour experience is clearly dependent on the respondent set or readiness to encode and structure the stimulus (Suls, 1972). Readiness can be established by factors such as the situational context, which includes the presence of certain roles and joking relationships, as well as the joke or cartoon itself. A critical aspect of set is making salient the structures for perceiving the dual meaning and resolution of the joke or the dual impression and resolution of the cartoon (Shultz, 1974b).

It seems reasonable that the quality of the humour experience depends on the complexity and depth of the structures involved in the incongruous relationship, highly complex structures generating a greater range of incongruous implications. The complexity of the incongruity could affect the duration, intensity, and/or the latency of the humour experience (Pollio, Mers & Lucchesi, 1972).

(b) Incongruity processing. Incongruity appears to be an essential element in humour. Because of McGhee's (1971b, 1972b, 1974a) excellent treatments of this, our discussion can be relatively brief. Incongruity arises when an input is processed so as to fit at least two schemata simultaneously. Role reversals (Freud's pun of boy and bishop), role inappropriate behaviours (mother crawling like an infant), oddities in appearance (mother wearing a funny mask) – all provide grist for the generation of incongruity.

The term 'processing' implies active work, and incongruity processing is an active process. The mere existence of a potentially humorous incongruity does not ensure a humour response. How the incongruity is processed with respect to the factors of 'simultaneity' and 'tolerance' seems of great importance for the experience of humour.

SIMULTANEITY. The concept of simultaneity makes explicit the suggestion that the multiple and incongruous aspects of the joke or cartoon must form a structured whole or unit, with contrasting meanings bound together and viewed simultaneously (Eysenck, 1942; Suls, 1972). The eminent British comedian Ken Dodd also suggests that the incongruity must form a structured unit. For example, in the often quoted jokes – Prof: 'Mr. Twirp, what do you know about French syntax?' Student: 'Gosh, I didn't know they had to pay for their fun.'; or, Prof: 'Name two pronouns.' Student: 'Who, me?' – the unity of the component ideas (1. syntax = grammar, and syntax = pay for sin; 2. 'who me' = fear at not knowing two pronouns, and 'who me' = two pronouns) is essential to funniness. It is essential to funniness that they be rapidly and alternately in view, with their contrasting implications near simultaneous as a structured unit. Freud (1960) referred to this principle when he discussed condensation of form as a way of achieving simultaneity of unconscious ideas. Koestler's (1964) idea of bisociation seems to include the notion of simultaneity. Shultz's (1974a) data suggesting that the order of discovery of incongruity and resolution is irrelevant to funniness also suggests that the critical factor is the temporary regard of the parts as a totality. Shultz (this volume) also provides evidence that an incongruity and its resolution are structural factors in jokes in many different cultures.

These unities of incongruous elements appear to have a fluttering quality; they remind us of experiences of reversible figures on the edge of fluctuation; one gets a sense of vibration while regarding them. This is especially so with incongruities between rich or elaborate themes where varieties of elements enter into the incongruous unity. This 'fluttering' or vibrating quality of these unstable unities may relate to what Berlyne called arousal jags, though I share McGhee's (1972b) opinion that this concept alone does not explain the occurrence or dominance of the humour experience.

TOLERANCE. To generate humour experience, we must do more than accept these incongruous unities; we must tolerate or sustain them! If the juxtaposition is frightening and we attempt to explain it away (see Levine & Redlich, 1955), make sense of it, deal with it analytically, and so on, there is no humour (Kreitler & Kreitler, 1970). While the Kreitlers' data are retrospective, they support the hypothesis that humour depends on tolerating or sustaining these incongruous structures. Failure to tolerate these structures, whether for motivational or for analytic reasons, disrupts the cognitive organization essential for humour reactions.

Other evidence also points to the importance of tolerance for incongruous unities. Gollob and Levine (1967) reported that clarification of the unconscious content of tendentious jokes reduces their funniness. These investigators argue this occurs because making explicit the unconscious content is threatening, and this could be an important factor. But I think their data are also consistent with the suggestion that clarification of the intent of any joke, including low aggressive and nonsense jokes, reduces the joke's funniness. Unfortunately, their experiment was not designed to separate repetition from clarification. Many jokes lose their impact on the retelling and few jokes are funny when explained. We suspect that clarification of intent, retelling, and so forth break apart the incongruous unity by serially exposing and dwelling on the components as entities in themselves.

Much of the funniness of jokes may occur when they are apprehended and stored in 'preconscious', nonverbal, parallel storage. Parallel processing seems to occur up to preattentive stages, before material becomes part of what we label focal attention or consciousness. By parallel processing we mean that the nervous system works simultaneously on a wide range of attributes of a stimulus (Neisser, 1967; Posner, 1973). We are suggesting that affective (Corteen & Wood, 1972; Guthrie & Wiener, 1966), incongruous meaning units are also processed in parallel and that this is critical for generating funniness. Bringing the elements to explicit awareness destroys the parallel processed units and diminishes pleasure unless or until the examination of the separate elements stimulates other, subthreshold, incongruous units.

The 'goodness' of a joke also may be related to the goodness of its incongruous organization. A joke is better not only if its parts are unexpected and contrasting in meaning (Eysenck, 1942), but if they are integrally bound together by some deeper truth; in this case, the joke acquires a solid, emotional significance. Jokes about general life issues, such as marriage, doctors, etcetera, appeal to these deeper themes, and in doing so acquire a good form.

To make systematic use of the conception of good form, we will have to develop ways of describing the implications between joke elements — jokes with a high degree of implication, a symmetrical structure with a central unit, being better forms and funnier (see Garner, 1970).

Eastman's ten commandments of the comic art (1936) seem very relevant to the creation and tolerance of incongruous unities. If a comic is to create incongruous units, he or she must be sudden, use proper timing, appear effortless and unimpassioned, avoid focusing too long on components, and avoid the arousal of conflicting notions that lead to analytic thought, and so forth. Brodzinsky's excellent paper on timing (this volume) relates these processes to the comic's audience; the slow, accurate analyst gets the point but shows less laughter and mirth to forms of humour where the points are laid out in sequential order. These forms require focusing attentively on one point after the other — a process disruptive of incongruous unities. The speedy, playful perceiver may form these structures more easily.

(c) Contextual factors. There is wide agreement that incongruities and surprise are not sufficient to create a humour experience; incongruities and surprise are also conditions for fear (Koestler, 1964; McGhee, 1972b; Sroufe & Waters, 1976). Koestler (1964) points to mood or emotional tension as a contextual factor which is necessary for the humour experience. Eastman says, '...things can be funny only when we are in fun' (1936, p3). Sroufe (Sroufe & Waters, 1976; Sroufe, Waters & Matas, 1974; Sroufe & Wunsch, 1972) writes of the need for contextual signs of safety and the presence of familiar figures such as the mother. McGhee (1972b) argues that the child must regard an incongruity as fantasy in order to perceive it as humorous. Kreitler and Kreitler (1970) suggest that we must see things as funny. While these authors discuss somewhat different concepts, they all seem to be saying that incongruity processing leads to humorous experience only when incongruities

are regarded as funny. If so, we have come full circle and have arrived at the redundant
position that funniness is what is funny.

Emotional Theory Related to Humour

The tautology that the essential element to the funniness of a joke, cartoon, or film is
that we treat and react to it as though it is funny requires explanation. We believe that
the core of this statement is captured by the hypothesis that an emotional response of joy
is what makes a cognitive incongruity humorous. We need, therefore, to specify the nature
of the emotional component of humour. Two different views of emotion have been used in the
humour literature — the cognitive-arousal theory and the specific affect theory.

Cognitive arousal theory. The first of these theories hypothesizes that humour reactions
consist of cognitions of funniness (the incongruities, situational cues, etcetera) combined
with bodily arousal. The papers by Schachter and his students (Schachter & Singer, 1962;
Schachter, 1964; Schachter & Wheeler, 1961) have returned cognition-arousal models to
stage-centre, at least temporarily, though this theory has repeatedly managed the move from
oblivion to popularity. (See Sully, 1902; Russell, 1929; Ruckmick, 1936; or Leventhal,
1974, for a review). The theory's periodic revival stems from dissatisfaction with various
forms of specific affect theories; its return to oblivion remains assured by its failure
to answer a simple question: 'How can the combination of arousal with cognition lead to the
distinctive subjective experience of humour and joy?' Answering this question involves the
following issues. First, there is no clear evidence that arousal is necessary for emotional
experience or emotional behaviour (see Leventhal, 1974). William James (1890) himself
recognized that arousal only was part of turbulent emotions and missing from so-called
aesthetic emotions. And cognition-arousal theory itself argues that bodily arousal is
undifferentiated and cannot account for qualitative differences between emotional states;
it states that arousal cannot differentiate the feeling of fear from the feeling of anger,
joy, shame, etcetera. For this reason, Leventhal (1974), McGhee (1972b), and others have
argued that arousal cannot provide the distinctive quality to define the humour experience.

But can cognition make this differentiation as claimed by the cognition-arousal theory? It
is very hard to see how the content of an idea or perception can by itself provide or create
the phenomenal quality of an emotion. This is not to argue that different cognitions do not
elicit different emotions — they do. But eliciting an emotion is not the same thing as
defining its phenomenal quality. Without some distinctive response to provide or create the
quality of a feeling, we would simply have ideas combined with different levels of excited
feelings; and, as shown in many factorial studies of mood, excitement is not equivalent to
distinctive emotion (Nowlis, 1965). In addition, there is developmental evidence that
emotional experiences exist before the social learning of eliciting conditions and their
labels (Leventhal, 1974). Thus, there is no reason to believe that the combination of
cognition and arousal will do any better than either alone in creating the quality of
different feeling states.

The above conclusion does not mean that arousal is irrelevant to the humour experience.
Godkewitsch (1975) has found substantial correlations between autonomic measures and self-
reports of arousal and between both types of arousal measures and the rated funniness of
cartoons: the higher the level of arousal, the funnier the cartoons. But we cannot tell
from these correlations whether level of arousal influences funniness or is simply a product
of funniness. There is evidence supporting an arousal transfer hypothesis that inducing
arousal in one situation can affect the intensity of the humour experience in a second
situation. Cantor, Bryant and Zillmann (1974) found that subjects made more favourable
ratings of cartoons and jokes if they were previously exposed to material that was high
rather than low in arousal value, and this held whether the prior arousing material was
positive or negative in tone. These and other findings of Zillmann and his collaborators
strongly suggest that arousal has 'transfer value' (Zillmann & Bryant, 1974) — a finding
in accord with traditional Hullian behaviour theory that generalized drive serves as a
multiplier of habits. Arousal generalization also appears to explain the sequence effects
reported in judgments of cartoons, the second cartoon in a pair being rated funnier than the
first (Godkewitsch, 1975). So it is plausible to conclude that arousal can facilitate and
strengthen emotional experience even if it does not give the experience its specific
affective quality.

The above effects strongly suggest that individual differences in arousability need to be
examined in any attempt to evaluate responses to humour. Of course, the problem is how to
measure individual differences in arousability, and that requires a clear conceptualization
of the arousal construct. At present, there is little reason to assume that arousal is
equivalent to any one specific peripheral indicator, since central neural, autonomic, and
behavioural arousal can be completely dissociated (Lacey,1967). Not surprisingly, therefore,
many studies suggest that self-report techniques offer the simplest and best approach to
measuring arousal (Byrne, 1961; Godkewitsch, 1972; Thayer, 1970).

But the data on the effects of arousal on judgment are not so uniform as the above findings would suggest, and measuring individual differences in arousability may not be sufficient to predict the effects of arousal on behaviour. For example, Schachter and Wheeler (1962) found significant differences in expressive reactions but no differences in rated funniness of a slapstick movie for subjects who were injected with epinephrine, placebo, or chlorpromazine prior to seeing the film 'The Good Humor Man.' The data for the Schachter and Singer (1962) study are also weak when we compare ratings of humour and anger for subjects injected with epinephrine to those injected with placebo; the injection of epinephrine has little effect on affective behaviour. In other areas, such as communication research, the evidence is also equivocal for the hypothesis that it is the arousal of fear rather than the objective information in the message that strengthens favourable opinions toward protective health practices (Leventhal, 1970). It is clear that the conditions that encourage and/or discourage arousal transfer need more careful specification (e.g., Calvert-Boyanowsky & Leventhal, 1975), and this will complicate the problem of individual difference measurement.

Specific affect theory. If not arousal, what is the added emotional factor that is important for humour experience? Our work on fear, stress, and humour suggest first of all that emotions should be treated as phenomenally distinct, unique, and self-evident experiences. As Eastman put it, 'Humour is a unique quality of feeling. It belongs with anger, fear, hunger, lust, among the irreducible elements of our affective life' (1936, p27). And he goes on to say, 'Physiologically it is hard to find any difference between anger and fear, but a psychologist who cannot discern the difference between anger and fear seems to me about as brilliant as a zoologist who cannot tell a cow from a hedgehog' (p29). His thoughts on the phenomenal reality and distinctness of emotion are echoed by a host of theorists (Bull, 1951; Darwin, 1965; Graham, Stern & Winokur, 1960; Izard, 1971; Lazarus, 1968; Tomkins, 1962). There are two aspects to a specific affects theory of humour. The first concerns the role of expressive behaviour, the second the role of cognitions.

(a) Expressive behaviour and specific affect. One possible source of the quality of humour and joy is the distinctive feeling generated by the patterns of expressive motor behaviour of smiling and laughing. A distinct pattern of facial expression seems to accompany each emotion; these patterns are detectable in judgments of expression (see Ekman, Friesen & Ellsworth, 1972; Izard, 1971; Osgood, 1966; Tomkins & McCarter, 1964; Woodworth & Schlosberg, 1954). It is not clear how these expressive behaviours contribute to or create the subjective feeling states that make up the phenomenal experiences that we call emotions. The simplest hypothesis is that feeling arises from sensory feedback from facial responses (Tomkins, 1962; Pasquarelli & Bull, 1951; Izard, 1971; Laird, 1974). Our theoretical analysis suggests the feedback hypothesis too simple, and that some kind of central neural outflow process as well as a feedback mechanism is likely to be involved in the generation of emotional qualities (Cannon, 1927; Leventhal, mimeo).

But what about humour? Is there evidence suggesting that facial expressive reactions are involved in the intensity of humorous feelings and/or in humour judgments? Our studies consistently suggest some degree of participation of expression in both feeling and judgment. This involvement cannot be inferred from correlations of judgment and expressiveness to stimuli of different degrees of funniness; high correlations, whether computed subject by subject across stimuli or across subjects, can reflect the differential impact of the stimulus on both judgment and expression, but they do not provide evidence for the mediating role of expressiveness on feelings and judgments (see Figure 1).

Evidence for the mediating role of expressiveness comes from two sources: (i) findings that contextual cues, such as audience laughter, raise the level of expressiveness and also raise the level of judged funniness; and (ii) findings that monitoring of one's own expressiveness results in increases (or no changes) in the level of expressiveness but is associated with lower levels of rated funniness (Cupchik & Leventhal, 1974; Leventhal, mimeo; Leventhal & Cupchik, 1975; Leventhal & Mace, 1970; Panagis, 1973). Neither of these two findings alone is persuasive evidence for the role of expressive reactions in feelings and judgments. The first finding, the elevation of expression and judgment by audience laughter, suggests these responses are linked because each is a product of an underlying feeling state. The second finding suggests that focusing on smiling and laughter breaks the link of expression to feeling, resulting in independence between expression and judgment. Taken together, the findings lend some degree of convergent validity to the hypothesis that the expressive system is usually linked to feeling, and feelings, in turn, linked to judgment. Thus, an exaggeration of expressiveness by contextual cues (audience laughter) leads to increases in feelings and judged funniness, while the separation or the break of the unity between expression and feeling, achieved by paying direct attention to expression, leads to decreases in feeling and lowers the level of judged funniness. (See Figure 1.)

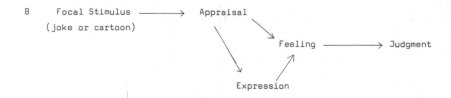

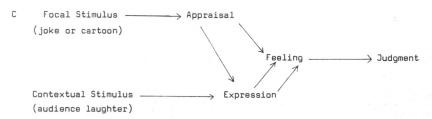

Paths from the humorous stimulus to the humour judgment. The top figure (A)
illustrates objective judgment bypassing feeling. The middle figure (B) illustrates
stimulus appraisal leading to feeling with feeling enhanced by expressiveness and
then leading to judgment. The lower figure (C) illustrates an extraneous stimulus
enhancing expressiveness, then feeling, and finally judgment.

The above findings have suggested the potential importance of measuring individual differences
in expressiveness for both humour judgments (Leventhal & Cupchik, 1975) and judgments of
expressiveness (Cupchik, 1972). The studies also reported that females are more responsive
to both of the independent variables of audience laughter and monitoring of one's own
expressive behaviour. These findings suggest that females make greater use of their inner
feelings in judging humour, and, consequently, their judgments are more influenced by changes
in feeling states. Individual differences in sex-role identification also affect attention
to inner feelings (Caputo & Leventhal, mimeo), though recent data show that situational
factors (and possibly individual differences in self-monitoring) can override these effects.

(b) Cognition and specific affects. Cognitive processes play a crucial role in specific
emotion theory - a role at least as important as that of expressive behaviour. In
discussing cognition and emotion, we are not focusing on the role of cognition as an
elicitor of emotion. Our focus is on two other aspects of cognition: (i) emotion as an
integrative, 'cognitive' category; and (ii) cognitive sets and emotional readiness.

EMOTION AS A CATEGORY. We have advanced the hypothesis that emotions, like phonemes, word
meanings, and other units, exist as categories (Cupchik, 1972; Leventhal, mimeo; Panagis,
1973). When we call emotion a 'category', we are saying that it combines a characteristic
expressive pattern, a memory structure base of acquired images, and a variety of instrumental
actions relevant for coping with a particular feeling state. But how does an emotional
category relate to humour? The answer is that the emotion categories play a key role in
joining the idea content of the joke, the incongruous unity, with joyful expression; when
the incongruity stimulates a humour category, it generates the expressive, emotional
component as well.

EMOTIONAL READINESS. A category such as humour or joy can be activated by a wide range of
cues: for example, the laughter and smiling of a mother (Sroufe & Waters, 1976), socially
defined events signalling the appropriateness of humour (e.g., the joking relationship),
past memories and images of funny happenings, and so forth. Thus, the outer events
(expressive motor, images, instrumental patterns) which cue the categories are similar to
the events coded by the category.

Once a category is aroused, the events activating and grouped within it are pooled. Thus, stimulating a humorous emotional set by an expressive motor event and then by a funny image (e.g., a cartoon) leads to the pooling or adding of these stimulations and to a more intense emotional experience (Leventhal, mimeo; Panagis, Caputo & Leventhal, mimeo). Emotional activation is additive, and there should be positive transfer of activation generated by mirth and imagery from one stimulus episode to another.

Evidence on the lateralization of cerebral activity is beginning to lend credence to the hypothesis that emotional categories or emotional processing may be lateralized in the right hemisphere (Dimond, Farrington & Johnson, 1976; Safer & Leventhal, in press; Schwartz, Davidson & Maer, 1975). Thus, emotional processing, like other perceptual-image types of processing activity, seems differently lateralized than serial, verbal processing (Bogen, 1972; Galin, 1974; Kimura, 1967; Kinsbourne, 1972). The data are suggestive, therefore, of a reasonably high degree of separation of emotional categories and processing from nonemotional cognitive processes. The lateralization data make clear that emotional categorization and processing is only one of several kinds of processing that can be activated by situations, and its dominance over nonemotional processing can be quickly lost in the absence of appropriate situational cues and encouragements and in the presence of barriers to affective experience. The Kreitlers' (1970) data that children must actively tolerate an incongruity in order to find it funny, and our own experiments on attentional sets, strongly support this conclusion.

Finally, emotional processing and responding tends to be spontaneous and stimulus-elicited: the images linked to emotion seem to intrude upon awareness; emotional responses such as laughter, flight, and fight, seem to be triggered by situations that provoke joyful humour, fear, and anger, and so on. There is an impulsive quality to emotionally motivated acts. These properties of emotions reflect their integral organization, which would appear like those of memory cells for episodic experience (Posner, 1973; Tulving, 1972).

Humour and emotion. In summary, the main hypothesis we are offering is that a humorous stimulus (an incongruity generated by a joke or cartoon) creates a humour experience when it is synthesized within an emotion category - when it becomes an instance that gives rise to expressive behaviour, imagery, and instrumental actions that comprise emotional processing. Incongruities, safety signals, cues to special relationships, etcetera, activate emotion categories, and the dominance of emotional processing permits their synthesis within an emotion category. Competing emotions of fear, shame, and guilt (Levine & Redlich, 1955), mechanisms such as denial, social attitudes of conservatism and closed-mindedness (Miller & Bacon, 1971), a variety of sex-linked attitudes (McGhee & Grodzitsky, 1975), beliefs about sexism (Nias & Wilson, 1976; Chapman & Gadfield, 1976), and attitudes regarding processing of material such as an overly analytic approach to tasks (Kreitler & Kreitler, 1970) - all can block the elicitation of an appropriate positive, affective category and/or block the synthesis of funny material with the humour-joy category.

Just as factors can block the involvement of emotion, so, too, can factors enhance emotion activation and synthesis. We all have experienced occasions of laughter over the most silly jokes - jokes we have long 'outgrown'. This should warn us that findings which are now seen as universal properties of humour information processing, such as the curvilinear relationship between complexity of jokes and humour responses, may be true primarily in laboratory settings where the emotional component of humour must be elicited by the joke itself, as the subject may feel that silliness and hilarity are inappropriate behaviour in a scientific experiment. The curvilinear effect may be absent in a setting where situational cues permit or demand silliness, cautioning us again of the difference between theoretical and empirical generalizations. Indeed, this line of reasoning suggests we can create humorous incongruities by provoking emotional responses of joyful funniness in inappropriate situations. We have in mind the Monty Python skit where the most banal remark of a most ordinary man provokes uncontrollable mirth in his listeners; and their outburst of mirthful joy and the similar reaction it stimulates in us create the contrast and incongruity between our feeling state and the total banality of the situation. Mirth can create humour.

Humour and unconscious motivation. It would take more space than we have been granted to review the role of Freudian (1960) theory in humour research. Even a brief summary of the studies of aggression and catharsis of aggressive feelings in hostile humour would take pages (cf. Gollob & Levine, 1967; Lamb, 1968; Leak, 1974; Hetherington & Wray, 1966; Singer, 1968). The issues raised by these studies concern the enhancement of humour by generalization from specific prior emotional states and from contact of incongruities with psychoanalytically potent themes. It is interesting to compare the results to those of Zillmann and Cantor, as together they begin to suggest some of the conditions for emotional facilitation and inhibition of humour. In this paper, we have proposed that social factors establish themes as the basis for incongruous units which are synthesized with emotion categories in situations signalled as humorous. We believe this theoretical framework can readily incorporate these Freudian phenomena.

Implication of Emotion Theory for the Measurement of Individual Differences in Humour

The affective aspect of humour emphasizes a whole new set of individual differences
variables ranging from individual differences in expressiveness on the one hand to salience
of and tolerance for different types of affective categories on the other. It also suggests
that we study mood and general temperament as preconditions for affective experience and
humour and that we do not ignore factors such as attentional styles that make some individuals
more responsive than others to internal feeling states rather than external states.

For example, our studies of sex differences in humour ratings suggested that female subjects
are very sensitive to internal feeling states. Because dieting creates an unpleasant
internal state that one is highly motivated to ignore, we expected that dieting women would
be motivated to ignore their internal states and that any exaggeration of feeling – for
example, by emotional arousal provoked by audience laughter – would key off a motive to
ignore or not attend to this feeling. As a consequence, we expected dieting females to be
unresponsive to audience laughter in making cartoon ratings. A re-analysis of some old data
and an experiment that compared cartoon ratings between subjects exposed to audience laughter
and subjects not exposed to audience laughter showed that only nondieting females gave higher
ratings of funniness in the audience laughter condition; dieting women actually gave somewhat
lower ratings in the audience than in the no audience condition.

The introduction of the emotional factor makes clear the need to assess separately judgments
of funniness and expressions of mirth and provides an internal mechanism for the well-
grounded sociocultural observation that smiling, laughter, and humour judgment can be (and
remain) highly correlated even though the level of one of the factors is moved about by some
selected independent variable to which the other responses are insensitive. It is obvious
that we may laugh heartily at poorly structured incongruities, rate them as poor and silly,
and recognize that we had one hell of a good time.

CONCLUSION

We concluded that the traditional individual difference approach to humour has not been
fruitful for both methodological and conceptual reasons and instead suggested that humour
research should apply personality models to the sociocultural, cognitive, and affective
factors in humour. In reviewing these models, we stressed that each looks at the humour
experience from a different perspective: the sociocultural model describes from an external
perspective the factors dealt with by the cognitive and emotion models from an internal,
mediating perspective.

Second, the models suggest a sequential theory of the humour experience – the social
situation establishing the conditions (initial perception and readiness) for the action of
cognitive processes that construct incongruity units (perceptual interpretation) and then
integrate these units at a second stage with an affective category. These factors taken
together make up the humour experience.

Finally, individual differences exist in each of these domains – in sociocultural background,
in roles and role relationships, in cognitive factors for the understanding of rule
structures, in intellectual tempo responsible for forming incongruity units, and in
expressiveness and willingness to enjoy or sustain emotional experience. The study of
individual differences in each of these areas will require the development of refined
measuring devices and the use of these measures in an experimental setting where situational
factors are varied. Only when we can predict which subjects will be affected by specific
situational variables and not by others can we be sure that our individual difference
measures are assessing a specific, underlying, conceptual factor. If the study of humour
now seems overwhelmingly complex, we can take heart in the fact that our efforts will be
long-term and hopefully bring us more than a few laughs and a good deal of enlightenment on
the nature of emotional processes and their relationship to thought.

REFERENCES

See Bibliography for publications on humour, laughter and comedy

Bogen, J.E., The other side of the brain. II: An appositional mind. Bulletin of the Los
    Angeles Neurological Societies, 34, 135–162 (1969).

Bull, N., The attitude theory of emotion. Nervous and Mental Disease Monographs, 81 (1951).

Calvert-Boyanowsky, J. & Leventhal, H., The role of information in attenuating behavioral
    responses to stress: A reinterpretation of the misattribution phenomenon. Journal of
    Personality and Social Psychology, 32, 214–221 (1975).

Cannon, W.B., The James-Lange theory of emotions: A critical examination and an alternative theory. American Journal of Psychology, 39, 106-124 (1927).

Caputo, G.C. & Leventhal, H., Sex differences in lateralization effects for holistic-subjective processing. Unpublished manuscript, University of Wisconsin.

Carroll, J.D., Individual differences and multidimensional scaling. In: R.N. Shepard, A.K. Romney & S.B. Nerlove (Eds.), Multidimensional Scaling, Volume I. Seminar Press, New York (1972).

Cattell, R.B., The data box: Its ordering of total resources in terms of possible relational systems. In: R.B. Cattell (Ed.), Handbook of Multivariate Experimental Psychology. Rand McNally, Chicago (1966).

Cohen, A.R., Upward communication in experimentally created hierarchies. Human Relations, 11, 41-53 (1958).

Colby, B.N., Culture grammars. Science, 187, 913-914 (1975).

Corteen, R.S. & Wood, B., Autonomic responses to shock associated words in an unattended channel. Journal of Experimental Psychology, 97, 308-313 (1972).

Cupchik, G.C., Expression and impression: The decoding of nonverbal affect. Unpublished dissertation, University of Wisconsin (1972).

Dimond, S.J., Farrington, L. & Johnson, P., Differing emotional response from right and left hemispheres. Nature, 261, 690-692 (1976).

Ekman, P., Friesen, W. & Ellsworth, P., Emotion in the Human Face. Pergamon Press, New York (1972).

Epstein, S., Traits are alive and well. Paper read at Symposium on International Psychology, Stockholm (1975).

Erickson, E.H., Childhood and Society. W.W. Norton, New York (1963).

Eysenck, H.J., Dimensions of Personality. Routledge and Kegan Paul, London (1947).

Eysenck, H.J., The Scientific Study of Personality. Routledge and Kegan Paul, London (1952).

Eysenck, H.J., The Structure of Human Personality. Wiley, New York (1953).

Fishbein, M. & Ajzen, F., Belief, Attitude, Intention, and Behavior: An Introduction to Theory and Research. Addison-Wesley, Reading, Massachusetts (1975).

Freedman, J.L., Crowding and Behavior. W.H. Freeman, San Francisco (1975).

Freud, S., A General Introduction to Psychoanalysis. Washington Square Press, New York (1952).

Frodi, A., Macauley, J. & Thome, P., Are women always less agressive than men? A review of the experimental literature. Psychological Bulletin, in press.

Galin, D., Implications for psychiatry of left and right cerebral specialization. Archives of General Psychiatry, 31, 572-583 (1974).

Garner, W.R., Good patterns have few alternatives. American Scientist, 58, 34-42 (1970).

Graham, D.T., Stern, J.A. & Winokur, G., The concept of a different specific set of physiological changes in each emotion. Psychiatric Research Reports, 12, 8-15 (1960).

Guthrie, G. & Wiener, M., Subliminal perception or perception of partial cue with pictorial stimuli. Journal of Personality and Social Psychology, 3, 619-628 (1966).

Heller, J., Catch 22. Modern Library, New York (1961).

Hooff, J.A.R.A.M. van., Facial expressions in higher primates. Symposia of Zoological Society of London, 8, 97-125 (1962).

Hundleby, J.D., Pawlik, K. & Cattell, R.B., Personality Factors in Objective Test Devices: A Critical Integration of a Quarter of a Century's Research. R.R. Knapp, San Diego (1965).

Hymes, D., Models of the interaction of language and the social setting. Journal of Social
     Issues, 23, 8–28 (1967).

Izard, C.E., The Face of Emotion. Appleton–Century–Crofts, New York (1971).

James, W., The Principles of Psychology. Holt, New York (1890).

Kimura, D., Functional asymmetry of the brain in dichotic listening. Cortex, 3, 163–178
     (1967).

Kinsbourne, M., Eye and head turning indicates cerebral lateralization. Science, 176,
     539–541 (1972).

Labarre, W., The cultural basis of emotions and gestures. Journal of Personality, 16, 49–67
     (1947).

Lacey, J.I., Somatic response patterning and stress: Some revisions of activation theory.
     In: M.H. Appley & R. Trumbull (Eds.), Psychological Stress. Appleton–Century–Crofts,
     New York (1967).

Laird, J.D., Self–attribution of emotion: The effects of expressive behavior on the quality
     of emotional experience. Journal of Personality and Social Psychology, 29, 475–486
     (1974).

Lazarus, R.S., Emotions and adaptation: Conceptual and empirical relations. In: W.J. Arnold
     (Ed.), Nebraska Symposium on Motivation. University of Nebraska Press, Lincoln (1968).

Leventhal, H., Findings and theory in the study of fear communications. In: L. Berkowitz
     (Ed.), Advances in Experimental Social Psychology. Academic Press, New York (1970).

Leventhal, H., Emotions: A basic problem for social psychology. In: C. Nemeth (Ed.), Social
     Psychology. Rand McNally, Chicago (1974).

Leventhal, H., A perceptual motor theory of emotion. Unpublished manuscript, University
     of Wisconsin.

LeVine, R.A., Culture, Behavior, and Personality. Aldine, Chicago (1973).

Lewin, K., A Dynamic Theory of Personality. McGraw–Hill, New York (1935).

Mischel, W., Personality and Assessment. Wiley, New York (1968).

Neisser, U., Cognitive Psychology. Appleton–Century–Crofts, New York (1967).

Nowlis, V., Research with the mood adjective checklist. In: S.S. Tomkins & C.E. Izard (Eds.),
     Affect, Cognition, and Personality. Springer, New York (1965).

Osgood, C.E., Dimensionality of the semantic space for communication via facial expressions.
     Scandinavian Journal of Psychology, 7, 1–30 (1966).

Panagis, D.M., Sex differences in the evaluation of cartoons: The role of attentional style
     and self–observation. Unpublished master's thesis, University of Wisconsin (1973).

Panagis, D.M., Leventhal, H. & Caputo, G.C., Sex differences in integrating focal and
     contextual cues. Unpublished manuscript, University of Wisconsin.

Pasquarelli, B. & Bull, N., Experimental investigation of the body–mind continuum in
     affective states. Journal of Nervous and Mental Diseases, 113, 512–521 (1951).

Posner, M.I., Cognition: An Introduction. Scott, Foresman, Glenview, Illinois (1973).

Powers, W.T., Feedback: Beyond behaviorism. Science, 179, 351–356 (1973).

Rowell, T., The Social Behavior of Monkeys. Penguin, Harmondsworth (1972).

Ruckmick, C.A., The Psychology of Feeling and Emotion. McGraw–Hill, New York (1936).

Russell, B., An Outline of Philosophy. Meridian Books, New York (1960).

Safer, M.A. & Leventhal, H., Ear differences in evaluating emotional tones of voice and
     verbal content. Journal of Experimental Psychology: Human Perception and Performance,
     in press.

Schachter, S., The interaction of cognitive and physiological determinants of emotional
    state. In: L. Berkowitz (Ed.), Advances in Experimental Social Psychology, Volume 1.
    Academic Press, New York (1964).

Schachter, S. & Singer, J.E., Cognitive, social, and physiological determinants of emotional
    state. Psychological Review, 69, 379-399 (1962).

Schwartz, G.E., Davidson, R.J. & Maer, F., Right hemisphere lateralization for emotion in
    the human brain: Interactions with cognition. Science, 190, 286-288 (1975).

Shepard, R.N., Romney, A.K. & Nerlove, S.B., Multidimensional Scaling, Volume I. Seminar
    Press, New York (1972).

Sroufe, L.A., Waters, E. & Matas, L., Contextual determinants of infant affective response.
    In: M. Lewis & L. Rosenblum (Eds.), The Origins of Fear. Wiley, New York (1974).

Sutton-Smith, B., Rosenberg, B.G. & Morgan, E.F. Jr., Development of sex differences in
    play choices during preadolescence. Child Development, 34, 119-126 (1963).

Thayer, R.E., Activation states as assessed by verbal report and four psychophysiological
    variables. Psychophysiology, 7, 86-94 (1970).

Tomkins, S.S., Affect, Imagery, Consciousness: Volume I, The Positive Affects. Springer,
    New York (1962).

Tomkins, S.S. & McCarter, R., What and where are the primary affects? Some evidence for a
    theory. Perceptual and Motor Skills, 18, 119-158 (1964).

Tulving, E., Episodic and semantic memory. In: E. Tulving & W. Donaldson (Eds.),
    Organization of Memory. Academic Press, New York (1972).

Wessman, A.E. & Ricks, D.F., Mood and Personality. Holt, Rinehart & Winston, New York (1966).

Wexler, K.N. & Romney, A.K., Individual variations in cognitive structure. In: A.K. Romney,
    R.N. Shepard & S.B. Nerlove (Eds.), Multidimensional Scaling, Volume II. Seminar Press,
    New York (1972).

White, R. & Lippitt, R., Leader behavior and member reaction in three 'social climates.'
    In: D. Cartwright & A. Zander (Eds.), Group Dynamics. Harper & Row, New York (1968).

Woodworth, R.S. & Schlosberg, H., Experimental Psychology. (Revised Edition). Henry Holt,
    New York (1954).

Zajonc, R.B., Social facilitation. Science, 149, 269-274 (1965).

Zajonc, R.B., Social Psychology: An Experimental Approach. Wadsworth, Belmont, California
    (1966).

Zillmann, D. & Bryant, J., Effect of residual excitation on the emotional response to
    provocation and delayed aggressive behavior. Journal of Personality and Social
    Psychology, 30, 782-791 (1974).

Conceptual Tempo as an Individual Difference Variable in Children's Humour Development

David M. Brodzinsky

Rutgers University

To anyone who has taken the time to reflect on the nature of humour, one fact is inescapable — there exists a wide range of individual variation in humour responsiveness. For example, consider the following observation which I recently made in a fourth grade classroom. As part of an oral recitation assignment children were asked by their teacher to tell a funny story or relate a favourite joke to the rest of the class. One boy told the following joke:

> Did you hear about the woman who got married four times? Her first husband was a millionaire; her second was a famous actor; her third was a well-known minister; and her fourth was an undertaker. Oh, I see. One for the money; two for the show; three to get ready; and four to go.

As one might expect, there was mixed reaction to the joke. While some children laughed uproariously, others chuckled or smiled broadly, and still other children showed little or no response. However, when asked by the teacher to indicate how funny the joke was, nearly 80% of the class agreed that it was very funny. The obvious question that comes to mind is what determines these varied reactions. Why do some children consistently show higher levels of mirth than other children? Moreover, why do some children show relatively little humorous laughter even though they rate jokes as being funny?

While between—subject response variation often constitutes a major portion of the total variance in humour experiments, few developmental researchers have attempted to explore the source of this variation systematically. With the exception of those studies focusing on the role of sex of subject (Felker & Hunter, 1970; Groch, 1974; Leventhal & Mace, 1970), psychopathology (Waterman, 1972), and atypical patterns of development (Hetherington, 1964; Zigler, Levine & Gould, 1966b), there have been few direct investigations of individual difference factors associated with the widely divergent reactions manifested by children in response to humour stimuli (see the paper by Leventhal in this volume for a general review of the individual difference approach to the study of humour).

Recently, the programme of research which I have been engaged in has centred specifically on individual differences in children's humour. The focus of the studies has been the dimension known as conceptual tempo or reflection-impulsivity. The conceptual tempo variable represents a cognitive style or disposition that children adopt in processing task-related information in problem-solving situations involving moderate to high response uncertainty (see Messer, in press). Operationally, this dimension is defined by the child's performance on the Matching Familiar Figures test (MFF) which was developed by Kagan and his colleagues (Kagan, Rosman, Day, Albert & Phillips, 1964). The MFF is a match-to-standard task in which the child is presented with a standard familiar figure and six variants, only one of which exactly matches the standard. The goal of the task is to find the exact match. While some children approach the task in a slow and systematic manner, and therefore are relatively accurate (reflectives), other children are quick and cursory in their analysis of problems, and subsequently are more often inaccurate (impulsives). Still other children appear to be able to retain a high level of accuracy even though their response is relatively quick (fast-accurates), while a fourth group of children display both cautiousness in responding and a low level of accuracy (slow-inaccurates).

The rationale for focusing on this specific individual difference dimension was the assumption that the ability to experience humour may be related to the style that the child adopts in processing information inherent within the humour stimulus. Humour by its very nature poses a type of stimulus ambiguity for the individual in the form of perceptual, linguistic, and/or logical incongruities. The level of ambiguity may vary, however, as a function of the degree to which incongruous stimulus features are embedded within the humour context. Thus, humour that contains subtle defining characteristics (for example, cartoons or jokes based upon logical discrepancies) may be more likely to be identified and resolved, although not necessarily enjoyed, by children who are cautious and detailed in their approach to processing information. In contrast, humour material that openly portrays incongruous features (for example, cartoons based upon perceptual discrepancies) may be easily recognized and comprehended regardless of the child's information processing style.

Indirect support for these assumptions can be found in the sizable body of research that has accumulated on the conceptual tempo dimension (Messer, in press). In general, it has been found that impulsive children scan stimuli in a more global fashion, and ignore a greater percentage of relevant task information than reflective children. Furthermore, the impulsive child is also more likely to adopt a less successful problem-solving strategy than his reflective counterpart. On the other hand, as a result of his cautious, systematic, and detailed approach to problems, the reflective child is more likely to pick out the nuances of stimuli that often escape the impulsive child, which in turn, presumably leads to more accurate performance.

In the immediate sections to follow, I shall outline the preliminary results of the research programme relating children's conceptual tempo and humour development. The basic hypothesis guiding the research was the following: If reflective and impulsive children display their typical scanning and information processing strategies in the analysis of humour material, then one would expect the reflective group to be more successful in identifying and resolving humorous incongruities. The relationship between conceptual tempo and mirth and/or funniness ratings is less clear, however, since humour appreciation is a complex phenomenon, and is not linearly related to humour comprehension (Zigler, Levine & Gould, 1967). Furthermore, since little attention has been paid to fast-accurate and slow-inaccurate children in the conceptual tempo literature (Messer, in press), their relationship to humour development is also unclear. As a result, these latter two questions have formed an exploratory part of the research programme.

COMPREHENSION AND APPRECIATION OF CARTOON HUMOUR

The initial study in this programme of research (Brodzinsky, 1975) attempted to answer several basic questions: (1) Do children from various conceptual tempo groups differ in their ability to identify and resolve cartoon humour? (2) Do these children display different levels of mirth and/or funniness ratings in response to humorous cartoons? (3) Are there differences in mirth and rating behaviour in response to control stimuli as a function of conceptual tempo? (4) Is the relationship between conceptual tempo and children's humour constant across different age levels?

Six-, eight-, and ten-year-old boys were classified into one of four conceptual tempo groups (reflective, impulsive, fast-accurate, slow-inaccurate) on the basis of their performance on Kagan's Matching Familiar Figures test. These subjects then were individually presented with cartoons varying in cognitive complexity and affective salience. Half of the cartoons contained highly salient visual incongruities, while the other half contained more subtle, conceptually-based incongruities. Further, the level of affective salience varied within each of these structural cartoon categories such that half of the cartoons openly portrayed high levels of aggression, hostility, and/or danger, while the remaining cartoons were relatively neutral with respect to these affective dimensions. In addition to these four categories of humorous cartoons, subjects also received control stimuli, composed of cartoons in which all incongruous and affectively-laden content had been removed. These stimuli served to control for individual differences in sensitivity to social demand factors and/or differences in baseline emotionality.

The first thing to note is that reflective children comprehended the cartoon humour to a greater extent than impulsive and slow-inaccurate children at six and eight years of age, but not at ten years of age. The major difference in comprehension among these groups occurred for the visually-determined, high affective cartoons, and for the more subtle, conceptually-determined, low affective cartoons. Furthermore, while humour comprehension decreased for all children in response to aggressive and hostile cartoons, the decrease was significantly less for reflective subjects than for all other children. This suggests two things: (a) that high levels of cartoon aggression may distract children to the point where they fail to attend to relevant stimulus features that are crucial for successful comprehension, and (b) that the reflective child's cautious and detailed manner of responding overcomes at least part of the distractive potency of aggressive material. Thus, the basic hypothesis of the study was confirmed: the ability of children to identify and resolve cartoon humour is dependent upon the manner in which they attempt to process the information inherent within the stimulus.

What about the children's appreciation of the cartoon stimuli? While there was no difference among conceptual tempo groups for the funniness rating data, a significant relationship was found between children's mirth level and conceptual tempo. In contrast to the comprehension data, it was the impulsive children who showed the highest levels of mirth to humorous cartoons, followed by slow—inaccurate, reflective, and fast—accurate children. Moreover, the increased mirth of impulsive children was particularly evident in response to cartoons containing high levels of aggression and hostility.

How is one to interpret these data? Impulsive children smile and laugh more than other children, and yet they show less comprehension of the stimuli. One explanation may be that impulsive children simply are more appreciative of pure incongruity as opposed to resolvable incongruity than are other children (Shultz, 1976). If so, then they would have less need to locate and explain the resolution elements of the stimuli. On the other hand, the impulsive children's increased mirth may simply reflect a higher baseline level of emotionality and/or a greater sensitivity to perceived social demand factors. In fact, this interpretation is supported by the differential mirth response of conceptual tempo groups to the control stimuli. Impulsive children also showed the highest level of mirth to control cartoons, although only the comparison between impulsive and fast—accurate children was significant.

To summarize, children's conceptual tempo was significantly related both to humour comprehension and appreciation (mirth). While reflective children generally showed the highest comprehension scores, it was the impulsive subjects who showed the greatest mirth.

DETECTION OF LINGUISTIC AMBIGUITY

While the results of the initial study strongly suggest that children's humour development is related to conceptual tempo, many questions remain unanswered. One in particular concerns the differential sensitivity of conceptual tempo groups to linguistic aspects of humour stimuli. Shultz (1976) has noted that much of the humour in jokes, riddles, and captioned cartoons depends on the ability to identify and resolve various types of linguistic ambiguity. For example, consider the following joke:

> Okay class, we are going to have a vocabulary test. Billy what is the meaning of the word 'unaware'?
> That's easy teacher. It's the last thing I take off at night.

Here the humour is based upon a phonological ambiguity surrounding the word 'unaware'. Only when the individual recognizes that the boy has mistaken the word 'unaware' for the similar sounding word 'underwear' will he comprehend, and possibly appreciate the joke.

Various types of linguistic ambiguity have been identified (Kessel, 1971; Shultz & Pilon, 1973), and related to children's humour (Shultz, 1974a, 1976; Shultz & Horibe, 1974), including not only phonological ambiguity, but also lexical, surface—structure, and deep— structure ambiguity. Generally, these studies have found that phonological and lexical ambiguities are easier to detect than surface— and deep—structure ambiguities, although the results have varied somewhat depending upon the type of stimuli used (i.e., ambiguous sentences, jokes, or riddles).

In the second study, which was only tangentially related to children's humour (Brodzinsky, Feuer & Owens, in preparation), the following question was the focus of attention: Do children from various conceptual tempo groups display differences in ability to detect and comprehend various types of linguistic ambiguity?

Fourth— and seventh—grade children (mean age = 9 years, 11 months and 13 years, 0 months, respectively) were presented with a series of tape-recorded sentences, half of which contained phonological, lexical, surface—structure, or deep—structure ambiguities. Following the procedures of Shultz and Pilon (1973), subjects were asked to paraphrase the meaning or meanings of each sentence (spontaneous comprehension). In addition, whenever the child did not spontaneously provide more than one interpretation for a sentence, the examiner asked several nonleading probe questions in order to elicit additional information (prompted comprehension). The results of the study were quite interesting. While reflective children were more successful than impulsive and slow—inaccurate children in spontaneously detecting and comprehending the various types of linguistic ambiguity (even with IQ controlled), the difference among these groups was eliminated when children were prompted by the examiner to consider the possibility of alternative meanings for the sentences. These findings suggest that the performance difference among the conceptual tempo groups for the spontaneous paraphrase measure reflects a 'production deficiency' stemming from their general behavioural style rather than their cognitive ability. Further, one can interpret the data as indirectly

supporting the position that differences in humour comprehension among conceptual tempo groups
is also a function of their information processing styles. In the final study to be outlined
in this paper, the latter speculation is examined in more detail.

COMPREHENSION AND APPRECIATION OF VERBAL JOKES

In the preceding section, it was observed that reflective children, when left to their own
accord, spontaneously detected the double meaning of linguistic ambiguities to a greater
extent than impulsive and slow-inaccurate children. This finding lead to the present study
which was concerned with the role of conceptual tempo in children's comprehension and
appreciation of verbal jokes (Brodzinsky, 1976). The focus of the research was guided by
the following questions: (1) Does the reflective child's superiority in spontaneously
detecting linguistic ambiguities manifest itself in increased humour comprehension for jokes
based upon similar ambiguities? (2) Do impulsive children show increased mirth to verbal
jokes (and verbally presented control stimuli) as previously found in response to cartoons?
(3) Do children from various conceptual tempo groups display differential humour appreciation
as a function of joke type?

Fourth grade children from the various conceptual tempo groups (mean age = 9 years, 5 months)
were presented with a series of tape-recorded jokes containing either phonological, lexical,
surface-structure, or deep-structure ambiguities. In addition, a set of control stimuli,
composed of jokes whose punchlines had been altered so as to eliminate all incongruous or
emotionally-laden content, also were presented. These latter stimuli served the same purpose
as the control stimuli in the cartoon study.

Generally, the results were consistent with the first two studies. Reflective and fast-accurate
children spontaneously comprehended verbal jokes based upon linguistic ambiguities to a greater
extent than impulsive and slow-inaccurate children. However, when prompted by the examiner
to consider alternative explanations for the depicted humour, the difference among these
groups was eliminated.

It was also observed that impulsive children displayed a higher level of mirth than reflective
and fast-accurate children both to humorous jokes and control stimuli. Yet, when children's
mirth scores for humorous jokes were covaried for their response to control stimuli, there
were no differences among conceptual tempo groups. This finding raises the question whether
affective responding in children from the different conceptual tempo groups reflects the same
type of process, at least within the context in which it was measured in these studies. In
other words, the various groups of children may have been smiling and laughing for different
reasons. While some children may have been responding to the specific humour of the joke
(or cartoon), other children may have been responding more to the presence of the examiner,
as a result of greater affiliative needs. This issue is highlighted even more when one
examines the mirth response of children to the different types of verbal jokes. Only the
reflective group showed differential mirth responding as a function of joke type. That is,
reflective children smiled and laughed more at phonological and lexical ambiguity jokes than
to the more complex, subtle, surface- and deep-structure ambiguity jokes. The other groups
of children showed approximately equal levels of mirth to the different joke types, although
for fast-accurate children, this may have been partly due to a floor effect since these
subjects showed relatively little affective responding. This issue is discussed in more
detail in the next section.

SUMMARY, CONCLUSIONS AND IMPLICATIONS FOR FURTHER RESEARCH

What do the results of these studies tell us about children's humour development? First, it
is clear that humour comprehension is determined not only by factors such as intelligence
and operativity level (McGhee, 1974a), but also by the child's conceptual tempo. Left to
their accord, reflective children (and possibly fast-accurate children) are more likely to
identify and resolve humorous incongruities than are other groups of children. This is not
to say, however, that these other children lack the ability to comprehend the same type of
humour as reflective children. On the contrary, when prompted by the examiner to analyze
the stimuli in a more systematic and detailed fashion (similar to the style spontaneously
adopted by reflective children), there were no differences in humour comprehension among
conceptual tempo groups. Thus, in the present studies, it was the child's style of
responding and not his ability to respond which determined humour comprehension.

It is also apparent that children's mirth responding is related to conceptual tempo.
Impulsive children generally displayed higher levels of mirth to humour material than
reflective and fast-accurate children, while slow-inaccurate children scored between these

groups but were not different from them. However, the fact that impulsive children also showed increased mirth to control stimuli, and that impulsive and slow-inaccurate children showed no difference in mirth as a function of joke type, indicates that these subjects may be more affectively labile than other children. That is, they may display increased levels of smiling and laughter to humour material because of higher baseline levels of emotionality, and/or because they possess a greater need for approval which is expressed as increased positive affect in the presence of the examiner. At this point, however, these explanations are purely speculative, and in need of further research.

On the other hand, the fact that reflective children displayed differential mirth as a function of joke type suggests that affective responding in these children is modulated by their cognitive processes to a greater extent than is the case for other children. This position is partially supported by other research. Brodzinsky and Rightmyer (in press) found that while children from the various conceptual tempo groups showed equal levels of positive affect in response to correct solutions on the Matching Familiar Figures test, reflective children displayed the least pleasure when their initial choice was incorrect.

In concluding, it is clear that conceptual tempo is an important individual difference dimension in children's humour development. Many questions, however, remain to be examined. Specifically, additional research is needed to examine the processes which mediate the increased mirth observed in impulsive, and to some extent, slow-inaccurate children. Further, it would also be interesting to explore social processes in humour in relation to conceptual tempo. If, in fact, impulsive children are more affectively labile than other children, or if they possess a lower threshold for affective responding, then one might expect them to display a greater social facilitation response with respect to mirth, than would be the case for other conceptual tempo groups. Finally, while a relationship between conceptual tempo and humour has been established for children, it is unclear whether it holds for adolescents and adults. It is quite conceivable that not only the nature, but the very existence of the relationship might change across the life-span.

REFERENCES

See Bibliography for publications on humour, laughter and comedy

Brodzinsky, D.M. & Rightmyer, J., Pleasure associated with cognitive mastery as related to children's conceptual tempo. Child Development (in press).

Kagan, J., Rosman, B.L., Day, D., Albert, J. & Phillips, W., Information processing in the child: significance of analytic and reflective attitudes. Psychological Monographs, 78, (1, Whole No. 578) (1964).

Kessel, F.S., The role of syntax in children's comprehension from ages six to twelve. Monograph of the Society for Research in Child Development, 35, (Whole No. 6) (1971).

Messer, S.B., Reflection-impulsivity: a review. Psychological Bulletin (in press).

Shultz, T.R. & Pilon, R., Development of the ability to detect linguistic ambiguity. Child Development, 44, 728-733 (1973).

Waterman, J.M., Humor in young children: Relationships of behavioral style and age with laughter and smiling. Unpublished doctoral dissertation, University of California, Los Angeles (1972).

Ecological Determinants of Gleeful Behaviours in Two Nursery School Environments

Lawrence Sherman

Miami University, Ohio

This study concerns itself with an affective behaviour noted as 'group glee'. McGhee (1971b) makes a distinction between laughter which may be attributed to humour, and laughter which may only be '...a mere expression of heightened pleasure' (p341). It is McGhee's later description which is felt to be related to the group glee phenomenon. Although laughter is one of its components, glee is believed to be a more global phenomenon which encompasses three behavioural manifestations: joyful screaming, intense physical behaviour and laughter, all of which may be going on simultaneously in a group of children. One previous study reported evidence which distinguished laughter from glee by noting several differences in the antecedent conditions precipitating group glee (Sherman, 1975). These previous findings indicated a strong social interdependence factor operating to produce group glee.

The objective of the present study was to investigate some other ecological determinants of nursery school children's gleeful behaviour. When the video-tape archive was initially collected, thirty-seven of the children were individually taped throughout their three-hour day during their open freeplay activities. The children's behaviours in this setting were less influenced by teachers and other adults in the environment than in the short, well structured formal lessons where glee was originally examined. Two previous papers (Houseman, 1972; Rosenthal, 1973) have documented the children's activities in a variety of behaviour settings throughout this open freeplay time. One might expect to find differences in group glee between the lesson and the freeplay settings. Exploration of these data is of a comparative nature. Is the rate of gleeful behaviour greater in the formal lesson setting than in the open freeplay setting? What are the influences of individual differences such as age and sex in the production of gleeful behaviours? To answer these and other questions gleeful behaviours of the same thirty-seven children were examined in both their formal lesson and freeplay behaviour settings.

METHODOLOGY

In earlier reports on group glee (Sherman, 1971, 1973, 1975; Kounin & Gump, 1973, 1974) an event sampling technique was used in which a critical incident of group glee was the unit of analysis. This study will make use of the aggregated glee events for each of the observed children (n=37) as the unit of analysis. Altmann (1974) has described seven types of sampling methods in the non-manipulative, observational study of behaviour. The sampling procedures used in the present study would be described by Altmann as either 'focal animal sampling' or 'sampling all occurrences of some behaviour'.

The thirty-seven focal children had a mean age of 51.7 months of age and ranged from thirty-four to sixty-five months. There were eighteen males (eight who were Non-Caucasian and ten who were Caucasian) and nineteen females (eight who were Non-Caucasian and eleven who were Caucasian). These target children were followed by a mobile video-camera throughout their activities in an open environment where they were free to choose from a variety of activities described in great detail by Rosenthal (1973) and Houseman (1972). The dimensions of the freeplay environment were 8.8 x 11.1 m. Regular and student teachers who were available in this environment gave only minimal assistance and guidance, and they rarely intruded into the children's activities unless requested.

The video-taping of the 596 structured lesson settings was done in a small (2.2 x 2.7 m.) room equipped with a stationary, somewhat concealed camera. The technician was not present in the lesson room at all. For further descriptions and details of this setting, see Sherman (1971, 1975) and Kounin and Gump (1974).

In their previous study Kounin and Gump (1974) generically categorized nursery school lessons. Utilizing the concepts of signal sources, intrusiveness, and insulation, they categorized all

lessons as belonging to one of six lesson types which are used in the present study as a
major independent variable. (For further delineation of these lesson types refer to their
study).

Because of differences between the structured lesson and freeplay habitats, many parts of the
original group glee code (Sherman, 1975) are not included in the present analysis. The only
criterion for glee recognition in the present study is the overt behavioural manifestation.
In the freeplay environment information regarding the numbers of males and females present
when gleeful events happened, how glee was behaviourally manifested, the behavioural contagion
and the duration and frequency of gleeful events in the six lesson types for each child was
coded. The primary issue of concern was to utilize this global information regarding glee
frequency and duration to test differences among the various lesson structures and between
the lesson settings and the freeplay environment.

The 596 video taped lessons taught by thirty-six student teachers each teaching approximately
sixteen different lessons were collected over a two year period. The thirty-seven children's
freeplay day tapes were collected only for the complete first year's population. Thus, in
order to compare group glee in these two different settings (lesson versus freeplay), a
stratified random sample of glee from each of the six lesson types, of approximately equal
time duration, was obtained for each of the thirty-seven children. A trained rater went
through each of the randomly selected six lesson types in which one of the thirty-seven target
children was participating and coded his/her gleeful behaviour. Each child had both frequency
and duration data in both settings.

Throughout the ensuing analyses the primary dependent variable used is the rate-per-hour of
group glee. The method of calculating this quantity was to divide the frequency of gleeful
events by the number of seconds the child was observed and multiply this quotient by 3600
seconds, i.e., the number of seconds in an hour. Separate rates were calculated for each of
the six lesson types. The rate for all glee in lesson settings, not taking the six lesson
types into consideration, was also computed. In addition the overall rate in freeplay
environment was calculated.

The analysis used in this study was a three-way repeated measures ANOVA design (Winer, 1974),
with sex and ethnicity being unrepeated factors and environmental condition being the third
and repeated measure. In addition, certain descriptive and correlational analyses are
reported.

RESULTS

From 682 separate incidents of glee in the lesson environment, an average of 18.4 incidents
per child was noted. The highest frequency of gleeful incidents was 45 for one child while
only one child exhibited no glee whatsoever. Table 1 breaks down the rate-per-hour of glee
in the six lesson types and freeplay environment by sex and ethnicity. Table 2 presents the
results of a 2 (sex) by 2 (ethnicity) by either 6 (six lesson types) or 2 (lesson versus
freeplay environment) three-way ANOVA, with repeated measures on the lesson type or environment
factors utilizing an unweighted means solution according to Winer (1974). The only main
effect to reach statistical significance in the first analysis was the lesson type. Post hoc
analysis of mean rates-per-hour of glee among these six lesson types, using Tukey's (Winer,
1974) 'honestly significant difference' procedure, revealed that lesson type six is
significantly greater than the other five types ($p < .01$). Lesson type one, though not
significantly different from type two or type four, was significantly less than type three,
five, and six ($p < .01$). In addition, lesson type five was found to be significantly greater
than lesson type two ($p < .05$) and lesson type three was significantly greater than lesson
type two ($p < .01$). In a previous report (Kounin & Gump, 1974) of glee rate-per-hour
aggregated for teachers in the six lesson types, a similar pattern was noted. The largest
amount of glee in lessons comes from lesson type six and the least from lesson type one. The
sex by ethnicity by environment analysis where the lesson habitat is contrasted with the
freeplay setting is also reported in Table 2. The lesson environment was found to have
significantly ($p < .01$) greater rate-per-hour of glee than the freeplay environment.

Sex compositions of the groups in which freeplay glee occurred were also examined. For each
of those children who were gleeful (n=23), glee rates were computed separately for their
events which occurred in homogeneous and heterogeneous sex composition groups. A correlated
t-test between homogeneous and heterogeneous glee revealed the heterogeneous glee rate
(mean = 2.12) to be greater than homogeneous glee (mean = 1.05) (t=2.45; df=22; $p < .01$,
one-tail test). This is similar to the findings of the previous study of lesson settings
(Sherman, 1975).

TABLE 1   Mean Rate-Per-Hour of Gleeful Behaviour for 37 Male and Female
Caucasian and Non-Caucasian Children in Two Nursery School
Environments

(Data are expressed in terms of mean number of incidents per hour)

		Environment						Freeplay
		Lesson Type						
Sex	Race	1	2	3	4	5	6	
Male	Non-Caucasian (n=8)	1.1	3.3	9.6	6.2	6.2	19.2	2.7
	Caucasian (n=10)	1.1	2.0	4.4	3.2	7.6	13.8	0.6
Female	Non-Caucasian (n=8)	2.2	4.7	8.1	6.9	5.9	32.1	1.7
	Caucasian (n=11)	1.1	1.2	8.7	3.2	9.2	10.6	2.8

TABLE 2   Three-Way Repeated Measures ANOVA of Thirty-Seven Children's
Rate of Glee for Sex by Race by Six Lesson Types and by Lesson
versus Freeplay Environments

Source of Variation	SS	df	MS	F	p
Analysis of six Lesson Types					
Between Subjects	3680.025	37	99.460		
A (Sex)	49.295	1	49.295		
B (Race)	290.716	1	290.716	2.666	ns
AB	28.629	1	28.629		
Error(b)	3598.737	33	109.053		
Within Subjects	13097.315	185	70.796		
C (6 Lesson Types)	3560.551	5	712.110	9.725	.001
AC	113.216	5	22.643		
BC	618.021	5	123.604	1.688	ns
ABC	314.466	5	62.893		
Error(w)	12081.603	165	73.222		
Analysis Contrasting Lesson versus Freeplay Environments					
Between Subjects	343.029	36			
A (Sex)	11.043	1	11.043	1.093	ns
B (Race)	31.586	1	31.586	3.126	.10
AB	1.111	1	1.111		
Error(b)	333.384	33	10.103		
Within Subjects	334.701	37			
C (Environment)	201.876	1	201.876	23.592	.001
AC	2.472	1	2.472		ns
BC	17.709	1	17.709	2.070	ns
ABC	15.260	1	15.260	1.783	ns
Error(w)	282.371	33	8.557		

Several correlational findings were also examined in attempting to relate rate of glee to
age of the children. Within the lesson setting this correlation was 0.35 ($p < .01$), while in
the freeplay setting it was 0.37 ($p < .01$). It was felt that since these two correlations
are not significantly different, a look at an overall glee rate as correlated with age might
be useful. To accomplish this we simply computed the rate using total frequency of glee
regardless of environmental setting and total observation time across both settings. When
the glee rates are combined from both settings, the correlation with age is 0.43 ($p < .01$).

Also, it should be noted in the previous three-way ANOVA that ethnicity was not a significant factor, although Non-Caucasian children did appear to be somewhat more gleeful than Caucasian children (p < .10). Therefore a stepwise multiple regression procedure was applied to the data to see if the linear combination of age and ethnic heritage would yield a greater prediction than either variable by itself. Ethnicity was found to predict 18% of overall glee variance. When age and ethnic background were combined a squared multiple correlation of 0.31 was found. Also, using age and ethnicity as predictors of glee rate in only lesson type six, the lesson type accounting for the highest rates of glee, the squared multiple correlation is 0.47. One interpretation of these squared multiple correlations is that older Non-Caucasian children are likely to be more gleeful than younger Caucasian children, especially so for lessons which utilize intense props and vigorous physical behaviours.

DISCUSSION

In summary, a naturalistic observational study of thirty-seven preschool children in two nursery school environments examined differences in rate of gleeful behaviours. The children's behaviours were recorded on video tapes in their freeplay activities in an open environment and also while attending short, teacher-directed, structured lessons. While sex differences were not statistically significant, groups homogeneous according to sex were found to have significantly lower glee rates than heterogeneous groups. This finding may be related to a Darwinian theory of differentiating vocal signals in animals and man (Eibel-Eibelsfeldt, 1970 and Wickler, 1972). It is suggested that the heterogeneous groups may be more sexually arousing than homogeneous groups. Multiple regression analysis revealed a significant multiple r of 0.69 predicting glee rate from age and ethnic heritage. Socialization practices are suggested as an explanation for the glee rate differences in ethnic backgrounds of Caucasian and Non-Caucasian children. The Non-Caucasian children appeared to be less inhibited in the expression of their emotions than did Caucasian children regardless of the habitat they were observed in; i.e., structured lessons or freeplay environments. The freeplay environment was found to have significantly lower rates of glee than the lesson environment. Within the lesson habitat significant differences among six distinct types of lessons were also noted. Lessons utilizing intense physical behaviours and also having competing and intrusive signal sources contained significantly more glee than lessons which were insulated from social behaviours amongst the children. Children's glee is believed to be a socially interdependent phenomenon. These differences in habitat are believed to be explained in terms of the potential for social interactions which the various environments offered.

REFERENCES

See Bibliography for publications on humour, laughter and comedy

Altmann, J., Observational study of behaviors: Sampling methods. Behavior, 49, Parts 3-4, 227-265 (1974).

Eibel-Eibelsfeldt, I., Ethology, The Biology of Behavior. Holt, Rinehart, Winston, New York (1970).

Houseman, J.A., An ecological study of interpersonal conflicts among preschool children. Unpublished doctoral dissertation, Wayne State University (1972).

Kounin, J.S. & Gump, P.V., Input systems of lesson settings and the task related behavior of preschool children. In: W. Ambinder (Chrmn.), The Preschool Environment: An Ecological Study of Structured Lessons and Free-play in an Integrated Preschool. Symposium presented at the meetings of the American Psychological Association, Montreal (1973).

Kounin, J.S. & Gump, P.V., Signal systems of lesson settings and the task-related behavior of preschool children. Journal of Educational Psychology, 66, 554-562 (1974).

Rosenthal, B.L., An ecological study of freeplay in the nursery school. Unpublished doctoral dissertation, Wayne State University (1973).

Sherman, L.W., Glee in small groups of preschool children. Unpublished doctoral dissertation, Wayne State University (1971).

Winer, B.J., Statistical Principles in Experimental Designs. McGraw-Hill, New York (1974).

Wickler, W., The Sexual Code. Doubleday, New York (1972).

Individual Differences in Children's Social Responsiveness in Humour Situations

Hugh C. Foot, Jean R. Smith and Antony J. Chapman

University of Wales Institute of Science and Technology

A major aim in the programme of research which we are currently conducting is to examine the social responsiveness of children in humour situations, in particular to investigate the ways in which laughter, smiling and other nonverbal behaviours reflect the intimacy of the interactive situation. This paper is, therefore, more concerned with individual differences in reactions to social situations than it is with individual differences in humour responsiveness per se. Inevitably, though, in any humour situation these two kinds of reactions augment each other, and it is an intractable problem to differentiate the extent to which overall responsiveness is attributable to humorous or social stimuli.

In the research to be discussed the effects of friendship and sex upon the responsiveness of children in interacting pairs was analyzed. The work has its theoretical foundations in the context of social intimacy theory. The compensatory model of interpersonal intimacy proposed by Argyle and Dean (1965) is well-known; in any dyadic situation there is a stable equilibrium of tolerated intimacy such that if one individual disrupts that stable level by increasing intimacy along some dimension, then the other person takes corresponding compensatory steps to restore the accepted balance by reducing his intimacy behaviour in some way. Thus, if person A initiates an increase in gaze at the other, person B compensates by moving farther away or averting his gaze. The compensatory process has been likened by Patterson (1973) to a hydraulic model in which the total pressure in the system remains constant but can be differentially distributed through the system. Levels of intimacy deemed to be comfortable vary between different people and across different settings. Support for the model comes from a number of investigations in which factors such as physical proximity, eye-contact, body orientation and intimacy of conversational topic have been varied.

Patterson (1976), however, has noted a number of research reports in which not only has the Argyle and Dean model not been confirmed, but in fact directly contradicted. Jourard and Friedman (1970) and Breed (1972), for example, found that subjects increased the intimacy of their responses when trained confederates raised the level of their intimacy behaviours. Chapman (1975a) found that children sitting closer together when listening to a humorous recording engaged in more eye-contact. These studies suggest that as person A raises his level of responsiveness, or varies intimacy, on some dimension, so person B reciprocates by matching up his own level of responsiveness appropriately to that of person A. To explain the difference in results Patterson notes that many of the studies in which compensatory reactions were found involved a somewhat artificial or 'sterile' laboratory environment with procedures involving the use of stooges or where at best the subjects are strangers. Studies in which reciprocating reactions have been found are, on the other hand, characterized by more naturalistic and pleasurable conditions, often with individuals who were acquainted with each other.

Patterson invokes an arousal model of interpersonal intimacy. He argues that when person A changes his level of intimacy to any noticeable degree, this creates arousal in B which is either negatively or positively valued by B. If the situation is artificial, embarrassing or has other unpleasant connotations, then the arousal thus generated is uncomfortable and negative in value, and the Argyle and Dean compensatory model holds. If, on the other hand, the situation is naturalistic and pleasurable, then the arousal is positive and reciprocation or response matching will occur. The outcome, in behavioural terms, is therefore wholly dependent upon the nature of the affect associated with the arousal changes.

Our studies involve children in watching comedy cartoon films or listening to amusing stories. They are situations which are typically pleasurable and on which, therefore, response matching in the children's behaviour is theoretically more probable than response compensation. Indeed, our studies characteristically show that the more the subject laughs, smiles, looks, etcetera, the more his companion will engage in the same activities. This accords well with Patterson's model, but, on the basis of measures of total responsiveness alone the results might equally be interpreted in terms of socially facilitating processes.

In the studies to be discussed here we varied the relationship between the children by pairing them either in friend pairs or in stranger pairs. The purpose of the analysis was to assess whether more reciprocation (response matching) occurs amongst friends than amongst strangers. This would be expected on the basis of the assumption that arousal induced by the change in intimacy behaviours of a friend is likely to have more positive value than arousal induced by the change in intimacy behaviours of a stranger. The critical feature of the Patterson model is not just that friends should enhance interactive behaviours in each other relatively more than should strangers (social facilitation theory would predict this too), but that there should be closer actual response matching among each of the friend pairs than among the stranger pairs - irrespective of whether their overall level of responsiveness is high or low.

Results come from two studies and although there are differences in some aspects of the design of these two studies, these differences are not relevant for the purposes of the present analysis. A more detailed description of the design of the two studies is given in Foot, Chapman and Smith (1976).

The research was carried out using a mobile-laboratory on location in a local Junior school. Subjects were drawn from a pool of 192 seven- and eight-year-old children who had been thoroughly familiarized with the testing environment. Essentially, and in both studies, the children were placed into pairs of friends (based upon a simple sociometric technique) or into pairs of strangers (made up across classes). In one study the children were in same sex pairs, boys with boys and girls with girls; in the other study there were also mixed-sex pairs. All children watched a six-and-a-half minute 'Tom and Jerry' colour cartoon film and were video-recorded as they did so. Measures of laughing, smiling, looking (at companion) and talking were extracted from the video-recordings - in terms of the duration and frequency of each emission of each behaviour by both children in each dyad.

The data used for analysis were not the overall levels of responsiveness by the children which have been analyzed and reported elsewhere (Foot, Chapman & Smith, 1976), but the similarity of response level (or lack of it) that existed between subject and companion in each dyad. If Patterson's model is valid, then it is to be expected that friends would show greater similarity of response on each measure than would strangers, because of the greater positive affect associated with arousal increases brought about by changes in intimacy behaviour by a friend. The analysis, therefore, consisted of taking the overall duration in seconds of each measure from the subject (S) and companion (C) in each dyad and expressing whichever value was the smaller as a proportion of the larger. Thus, if S smiled for a total of fifteen seconds and C for a total of twenty seconds, or vice versa, then the proportion of the smaller to the larger was 15/20 = 0.75. This measure will be referred to as the RM - the Response Match value. For each S-C pair, a set of RMs was thus generated, indicating the proportion of time one spent laughing, smiling, looking and talking in relation to the other. The nearer to 1.0 these RMs are, the more they represent perfect response matching between S and C; the nearer to 0, the more totally dissimilar are S's - C's responses.

TABLE 1   Average Response Match (RM) Values

	Laughing (Study 1)			Smiling (Study 1)		
	Boys	Girls	Mixed	Boys	Girls	Mixed
Strangers	-	-	0.03	0.28	0.36	0.31
Friends	0.26	0.40	0.34	0.72	0.41	0.60

	Looking (Study 2)			Talking (Study 2)		
	Boys	Girls		Boys	Girls	
Strangers	0.20	0.33		0.31	0.12	
Friends	0.44	0.62		0.29	0.56	

Table 1 shows the mean RMs obtained for each measure. The data for laughing and smiling are drawn from Study 1 and include mixed-sex pairs, whereas the data for looking and talking are taken from Study 2 and only include same-sex pairs. In fact Table 1 represents the bulk of the significant data from both studies: in Study 1, looking and talking are not significant to the extent that they are in Study 2, and in Study 2 laughing and smiling are not significant to the extent that they are in Study 1. Basically, though, differences are in the same direction on all measures in both studies.

Laughing: the gaps in the data here are because of the large proportion of zero scores with strangers, making the mean RMs very unreliable and meaningless. For this reason no statistical tests of comparison were made.

Smiling: the main difference is that, overall, the RMs for friends are significantly higher than those for the strangers (F=5.67; df=1,24; p <.025). The effect is particularly noticeable for boys and mixed-sex pairs but less so for girls, although there was no interaction effect with sex (F=0.11; df=2,24; ns).

Looking: RMs for looking are significantly higher for friends than they are for strangers (F=6.90; df=1,32; p <.025).

Talking: RMs for talking are also significantly higher for friends than for strangers (F=5.63; df=1,32; p <.05), but this is largely a function of the significant friendship x sex interaction effect (F=6.50; df=1,32; p <.025). Amongst girls RMs are substantially higher amongst friends than strangers; amongst boys the difference is nonexistent: if anything it is slightly in the reverse direction.

The overall pattern clearly confirms Patterson's model with respect to the measures taken here: there is more response matching amongst friends than amongst strangers, suggesting that friends are reciprocating each other's levels of responsiveness on each behaviour more than are strangers. Amongst pairs of strangers there is greater independence in levels of responsiveness.

With respect to sex differences, the only significant difference to emerge is the friendship by sex interaction on talking: girls appear to show significantly higher RMs when with friends than do boys (p <.05), and significantly lower RMs when with strangers than do boys (p <.05). It is curious why only talking should be sensitive to these sex differences. It is quite likely that since talking is more overtly communicative than the other measures studied, it is a behaviour over which the individual exercises greater conscious control. It is also very plausible that there are social norms governing the amount of talking appropriate in different social situations. If these assumptions can be accepted then it would be necessary to postulate that the appropriate norms concerning volume of speech for females are different from those for males, or that females are more sensitive to the social situation and more prone to modify their volume of speech accordingly. There is substantial evidence both from our own work and from that of other researchers that females are more sensitive to the social situation than are males (cf. Garai & Scheinfeld, 1968) so this latter hypothesis at least may be valid. Thus, in relation to the present results with talking, it is argued that whereas the behaviour of a boy does not vary very much whether he is with a friend or stranger, the behaviour of a girl does vary substantially: girls who are strangers and have no or little interest in each other make no attempt to reciprocate their volume of speech; girls who are friends and have a strong interest in each other preserve and cement their friendship by sharing the conversation equally, hence matching their volume of speech to each other. Although it is going well beyond the present data, it might even be the case that girls adopt as their friends others whose general 'speech output' or loquaciousness is similar to their own, if only because this is one quickly apparent index of how equitable (on one dimension at least) their relationship might become.

A further analysis of the talking data was undertaken to ascertain whether the S-C pairs who showed the greatest degree of similarity in amounts of talking were also those who talked the most in any case. Pearson Product-Moment correlation coefficients were calculated between the RM measures and the total durations of talking by subjects in all S-C pairs (data for friends and strangers were pooled). In the case of boys there was no relationship (r = -0.04) between RMs and actual amounts of talking by subjects; in the case of girls, however, the relationship was very high (r = 0.77; p <.01). In other words, the more that the girl subjects talked, the more similar their speech volume became to that of their companion. This result again lends some support to the foregoing interpretation of the sex differences. The more speech that occurs the more capable are the girls in sensing the appropriate level of speech necessary for them to achieve an equitable exchange and the more likely they are to be able to gauge their own level of talkativeness to that of their companion. Taken together these data strongly suggest that in the case of girls some kind of delicate balancing of overt communicative behaviour is occurring in exchange situations, whereas amongst the boys no such process is at work.

Returning to the general issue, the reciprocity notion of Patterson could, and indeed should, be extended further than it has been extended in this paper. If friends are responding in step with each other, then this should not only be reflected by their similarity in overall levels of responsiveness but also in their momentary behaviours. If a microanalytic analysis of the sequential patterning of subject and companion behaviours were conducted, it might well be found that they respond in closer temporal unison as the relationship between them grows stronger. Evidence of this kind would serve to strengthen substantially the reciprocity model of social intimacy.

REFERENCES

See Bibliography for publications on humour, laughter and comedy

Argyle, M. & Dean, J., Eye-contact, distance and affiliation. Sociometry, 28, 289-304 (1965).

Breed, G., The effect of intimacy: reciprocity or retreat? British Journal of Social and Clinical Psychology, 11, 135-142 (1972).

Foot, H.C., Chapman, A.J. & Smith, J.R., Friendship and social responsiveness in boys and girls. Unpublished report (1976).

Garai, J.E. & Scheinfeld, A., Sex differences in mental and behavioral traits. Genetic Psychology Monographs, 77, 169-299 (1968).

Jourard, S.M. & Friedman, R., Experimenter-subject "distance" and self-disclosure. Journal of Personality and Social Psychology, 15, 278-282 (1970).

Patterson, M.L., Compensation in nonverbal immediacy behaviors: A review. Sociometry, 36, 237-252 (1973).

Patterson, M.L., An arousal model of interpersonal intimacy. Psychological Review, 83, 235-245 (1976).

ACKNOWLEDGEMENT

This research is part of a series of studies on children's responsiveness in humour situations, sponsored by the Social Science Research Council, U.K. (Grant No. HR 3043/1).

Sex-Role Attitudes, Sex Differences, and Comedians' Sex

Alice Sheppard

California State University

Comedians vary a good deal in the types of material which they present and in their manner of presentation — aspects which, together with the comedian's physical appearance, constitute their unique personal styles. I have been interested in assessing the reactions of people to different comedians because their appreciation appears related to personality factors and attitudes, as well as serving to reveal some fundamental dimensions of comedy itself.

The research reported here was conducted using a set of comedy tapes, selected on the bases that they contained routines or excerpts of similar durations, were consistently rated funny in pilot studies, and represented both male and female comedians. It was intended that they thus be representative of popular comedy, judged both by their availability on commercial recordings and by their appeal to college audiences.

To give an idea of the nature of the material to be discussed, the following descriptions are provided, although it must be realized that such characterizations are scarcely adequate, and apologies are extended to the artists for any misrepresentations.

1. Lily Tomlin: The marriage counsellor — a helpful telephone operator aids a woman trying to phone her husband who is conversing with his wartime lover in Korea.
2. George Carlin: The confessional — candid reflections on life in a Catholic high school and the trials of meeting puberty in this setting.
3. Fannie Flagg: Press conference — a caricature of an outspoken, bungling politician's wife.
4. Joan Rivers: The fat girl — facts and fantasies in the childhood of a young overweight girl.
5. Don Rickles: Hello dummy — Don Rickles with audience, where he succeeds in putting down everyone and every group that he can.
6. Rusty Warren: Rusty lays it on the line — recollections of adolescence in the days when big breasts were essential.
7. David Steinberg: Take my wife please — personal recollections of a Jewish neighbourhood and comments on the marriage service.
8. Bill Cosby: Planes — a discussion of air travel and of expressing one's feelings and fears in that situation.
9. Phyllis Diller: Hypochondria — a put-down of people who treasure their illnesses.
10. Herman Schnitzel: Pennsylvania Dutch festival — an episode concerning a foolish gentleman and a little white house in 'the back.'

SEX DIFFERENCES IN RATINGS OF COMEDY ROUTINES

The first question investigated in the studies was whether men and women differed in their ratings of comedy routines. Three psychology classes listened to the tapes in class, assigning each routine a score ranging from one to five on a 'like/dislike' scale. The classes contained a total of sixty-four men and seventy women; two were from a Community College, the third from a small, Liberal Arts College. The stimulus tape consisted of the ten selections described above, plus two others by female comedians which were subsequently eliminated as the least appreciated routines, and which will not be discussed further.

The comparison of the ranking for the top five comedians gave a rather similar picture for men and women subjects, as shown in the table.

| | Ranked Rating | | |
	Total	Men	Women
Bill Cosby	1	1	1
George Carlin	2	2	3
Don Rickles	3	3	4
Lily Tomlin	4	5	2
Herman Schnitzel	5	4	5

In short, the ranked preferences are nearly identical — the main difference being that Lily Tomlin ranks second for women, but fifth for men. Moreover, four of the top-ranked five are men — despite the fact that the original set contained seven women prior to the deletion of two!

Statistical analyses of the ratings indicated significant differences between men's and women's ratings of the comedy routines, reflecting the fact that men rated all male comedians higher than did women, while, similarly, women rated four of the five women higher than did men (the last showing little difference). These differences were most pronounced in men's preferences for Don Rickles, George Carlin, and David Steinberg; in women's appreciation of Lily Tomlin and Joan Rivers.

The existence of sex differences in humour has been documented in a number of studies, though largely dealing with response to cartoons (e.g., Brodzinsky & Rubien, 1976; Chapman & Gadfield, 1976; Groch, 1974; Landis & Ross, 1933). However, other media have not been studied extensively, and minimal effects have been found when sex of cartoon character has been varied (Felker & Hunter, 1970; Losco & Epstein, 1975). In this respect, the comedy tapes appeared to differ, in that comedian's sex was the major basis serving to distinguish male and female patterns of appreciation.

Appreciation of comedians by each sex appears related to some level of identification — whether mediated by physical appearance, style of delivery, or commonality of life experiences. In Pollio's terms (Pollio, Edgerly & Jordan, 1972), either surface or style traits could account for these differences. Style traits were reflected in themes used, since it appeared that men tend to talk more frequently about themselves, their feelings, their sexuality, and their experiences, while women's self-references refer more often to weight or physique (e.g., Joan Rivers and Rusty Warren) — a subject not mentioned by any of the male comedians in the study. Two other women played stereotyped roles of weak or bungling women — Tomlin's telephone operator and Flagg as a politician's wife. Phyllis Diller's routine was in fact the only one by a female not involving caricature or physique. Her routine, moreover, was appreciated equally by men and women.

Nevertheless, while the differences between sexes paralleled sex of comedian, both men and women in the study agreed that the male comedians were more enjoyable, a fact reflected in mean ratings and overall rankings. The preference for male comedians is consistent with the finding that recordings by males were much more readily available, and with the fact that in a list of thirty-seven well-known comedians compiled by a research team (Pollio et al., 1972), only five appear to be women.

I would suggest that this male bias may be related to cultural expectations. That is, because men are supposed to be competent, strong, and unemotional, their admission of weakness is perceived as funnier than the same admission by a woman. Similarly, aggression as a form of wit — and most humour is to some degree aggressive — is accepted and serves to release repressed emotion from the audience when the comedian is male, whereas a display of hostility from a female comedian is suspect and therefore renders her less effective as a comedian.

SEX-ROLE ATTITUDES AND COMEDY PREFERENCES

Because it was believed that response to male versus female comedians was reflective of general cultural attitudes, a second aspect of the research concerned the relationship between individuals' responses to the comedy tapes and their general sex-role attitudes. To assess the relationship, the same subjects described above also completed the Attitudes Toward Women Scale, a measure of sex-role attitudes developed by Spence and Helmreich (1972). This questionnaire was filled out immediately after the comedy study.

To facilitate analysis, twenty men and twenty women above the ninetieth percentile (liberal pole) were compared to twenty men and twenty women scoring below the sixtieth percentile (conventional pole). This comparison revealed a significant relationship between sex-role attitude and comedy preference, but one affecting preference for both male and female comedians. Specifically, liberal students enjoyed Lily Tomlin and George Carlin more than did students who were conventional in sex-role outlook, while conventional students rated Don Rickles and Rusty Warren higher.

Some of this relationship appears explained by an analysis of the specific routines. For example, Don Rickles and Rusty Warren, preferred by the conventional group, are both much older than George Carlin and Lily Tomlin, and additionally present very traditional views in their material. Don Rickles describes the 'broads' he likes, alludes to traditional honeymoon activities, and puts down just about everyone he can - an acceptable pattern of male hostile-aggressive behaviour. Rusty Warren's routine concentrates on the teenage anxieties of the girl with small 'boobs,' suggesting parenthetically that lack of physical endowment is the cause of heightened mental development for girls.

George Carlin's routine appears to some extent analogous - that of the adolescent male's moral dilemmas - yet his discussion of the confessional and the issue of thought versus deed lends itself to a questionning of the entire system's validity. That is, if thought is sufficient to generate sin, then concern over choice or behaviour appears superfluous. Also complex is Lily Tomlin's role as telephone operator. On the one hand she plays a traditional feminine role, and an extremely stereotyped one at that. However, under the guise of simplicity and bungling intrusions, she catches a husband's conversation with his wartime Korean lover, gets a lawyer on the line, and guarantees a settlement amidst the contention that, '..believe me, it's just like a man. They're all animals.'

To summarize, what an individual thinks is funny is related to the attitudes and beliefs which he or she holds regarding sex-roles. Among contemporary comedians, certain ones seem to offer styles consistent with the values of liberal or conventional sex-role outlooks.

ADJECTIVE RATINGS OF COMEDIANS

In a final check on the perception of various comedians, twenty additional students were asked to rate each routine on the degree to which the comedian's routine was: blunt, self-confident, outspoken, showing commonsense, aggressive, foolish, active, self-derogatory, hostile, oriented to sex, competent, masculine (feminine), emotional, assertive, knowing the way of the world, and feeling superior. The results showed that comedians as a group averaged high ratings as outspoken, confident, assertive, active, feels superior, and foolish. There were some differences along gender lines, with female comedians tending to surpass males as blunt, outspoken, and foolish; men were judged higher as competent, non-self-derogatory, and masculine. These comparisons are somewhat difficult to evaluate, since it is unclear whether, for example, the females were actually more blunt than the males, or whether ones who are funny stand out as being exceptionally blunt as women. This question cannot be answered at present.

A comparison of the four comedians whose evaluation correlated with sex-role attitudes yielded some interesting patterns. Don Rickles surpassed George Carlin as masculine, aggressive, active and assertive - clearly masculine values, whereas Lily Tomlin led Rusty Warren in confidence, feelings of superiority, and activity. Since most of these traits can be described as traditionally male-valued, Rickles would be traditional by subscribing to them, whereas Tomlin must be said to deviate from the traditional pattern when the same standards are used. In short, Rickles and Warren are preferred by conventional individuals because they meet implicit expectations, whereas Carlin and Tomlin do not conform to sex-role stereotypes and thus appeal to those who are less conventional in their outlooks.

CONCLUSIONS AND FUTURE DIRECTIONS

In conclusion, the findings support the view that differences between male and female comedians are intimately connected with sex-role stereotypes, and that both the type of material selected and the manner in which it is presented differ for each sex. The adjective ratings indicated the nature of some of these stereotypes, while the finding that each sex was better able to laugh at itself seems to add an optimistic note concerning the process underlying humour appreciation, as well as suggesting the importance of ability to identify with the comedian. The fact that routines by female comedians were not as highly appreciated as those by men calls for further investigation into factors underlying audience response to female comedians.

A. Sheppard

ACKNOWLEDGEMENTS

My appreciation is expressed to Steve Daugherty, Barney Goldstein, Bob Hung, and Carma Park for their assistance in the study, and to Kalamazoo College and Kalamazoo Valley Community College for their cooperation.

REFERENCES

See Bibliography for publications on humour, laughter and comedy

Spence, J.T. & Helmreich, R., The Attitudes Toward Women Scale. JSAS Catalogue of Selected Documents in Psychology, 2, 66 (1972).

Female Responses to Chauvinist Humour

David K. B. Nias and Glenn D. Wilson

University of London Institute of Psychiatry

ATTRACTIVENESS AND HUMOUR

Wilson and Brazendale (1973, 1974) attempted to demonstrate the relevance to psychology of sexual attractiveness. They found that a girl's beauty is more than skin deep, since it influences her social attitudes and sense of humour. Female student teachers were given the Conservatism Scale and asked to rate their amusement at each of forty-two cartoon postcards collected from seaside resorts in England. Their sexual attractiveness was rated by two lecturers; the interjudge agreement was .60.

There was a tendency for the unattractive girls to be more idealistic (tender-minded), religious (puritanical), and opposed to sexual freedom. Their sense of humour, however, provided a marked contrast to their negative attitude about sex. In particular, they liked cartoons which depicted sexually attractive girls at the centre of lecherous male attention. The pretty girls were more broad-minded in their attitude to sex, but did not like so many of the jokes. Among the few they did like were 'female-offensive' cartoons in which the joke is on the man, or where the female character is taking the initiative in an explicitly sexual situation, that is, female chauvinist jokes. Relative to the plain girls, they did not like the 'female-passive' cartoons in which a girl is being ogled by men.

This study was criticized on the grounds that the method for assessing attractiveness (observer ratings) was too subjective. It was argued that an improvement would be to base attractiveness on objective criteria. Other critics, however, argued rather the opposite: saying that subjective ratings of how a girl perceives herself (i.e., her self-image) would be more appropriate than how others view her (observer ratings). Therefore, a subsequent study was designed to meet both these criticisms (Wilson, Nias & Brazendale, 1975). The measurement of attractiveness was extended in both objective and subjective directions. This was done by using 'vital statistics' as the objective measure, and self-ratings of sex appeal as the subjective measure; they were asked to rate themselves according to how physically attractive they thought they were to the opposite sex.

Female student teachers were asked to rate the same set of seaside postcards as before. Consistent with the previous study it was the unattractive girls who were relatively more appreciative of the sexy cartoons, although the results were not as clear as before. Twenty-nine of the forty-two correlations with self-rated attractiveness were negative (p < .05), but only one cartoon attained individual significance. This depicted a busty girl passing a bookshelf in a library with a sign 'Thrillers' apparently indicating her breasts.

THE COMPONENTS OF SEXUAL HUMOUR

A principal components analysis of the results revealed an important general factor in sense of humour. This first dimension, which accounted for thirty per cent of the variance, was identified and labelled as 'sexual risqueness' or 'chauvinist humour'. Cartoons with high loadings tended to define the typical seaside postcard, being prime exemplars of this 'art form'. Jokes referring to 'erogenous zones' and sexual practices had the highest loadings, especially where the humour was directed at the female. Lavatorial humour and jokes about pregnancy and maternity had lower and sometimes quite negligible loadings. Instead these areas were represented on subsequent factors; that is, they formed separate categories. There is clearly a distinction to be made between the different jokes portrayed in seaside postcards.

SHAPELINESS

A measure of shapeliness of the female form was derived from the vital statistics. It was decided to use the bust/waist ratio, even though this index was uncorrelated with self-rated attractiveness. This analysis revealed that shapely girls tended to prefer the sexy jokes, especially those involving lecherous males; thirty-four of the forty-two correlations were positive (p < .01). Another finding was that the cartoons characterizing the shapely girls had high loadings on the 'chauvinist' factor. Cartoons that were most closely related to shapeliness all load on the factor of chauvinism.

WOMEN'S LIBERATION

A study by Chapman and Gadfield (1976) included a measure of self-rated attractiveness. Although not significant, the results were consistent with the above study. For example, there was a .49 correlation between attractiveness and liking for a male impotence cartoon (i.e., female chauvinism), and a correlation of -.23 with a male chauvinist joke.

The girls were also assessed for their views on Women's Liberation. Those in sympathy expressed little amusement at cartoons involving rape and male chauvinism. Of special interest, however, were the relatively high ratings they gave to cartoons portraying male impotence and homosexuality, that is, female chauvinism. While having a poor opinion of jokes that ran counter to Women's Liberation, they took special delight in the opposite, that is, jokes denigrating men.

INTERPRETATION

How can these results best be interpreted? It is tempting to apply Freud's (1905) theory of humour. This theory is ideally suited to explain the paradoxical finding that plain girls are anti-sex but enjoy sexy jokes. Plain girls may be anti-sex in their attitudes in order to protect themselves from painful jealousy feelings - because of their disadvantage in a permissive society. If sex can be classified as 'sinful', then there is less need to feel jealous of those with greater opportunity to indulge. Adopting puritan attitudes, or denying the value of sex, may thus be seen as defence mechanisms.

Their paradoxical liking for sexy jokes may reflect unconscious sexual longings finding an outlet through humour. Cartoons depicting male attention may be liked by plain girls - because they derive vicarious gratification through identification with the female character. In other words, deprived of male attention the plain girl may imagine herself in the place of the female character, and so share in the kind of pleasure that in real life is gained by attractive girls. In this way she may find the cartoons funny for sexual reasons but remain unconscious of this motivation, interpreting it only as amusement.

Before accepting Freud's interpretation it is necessary to consider alternative explanations. For example, attractive girls may find male chauvinist jokes annoying because they receive an excess of in vivo male attention; that is, tiring of too many male advances in real life, they no longer see the funny side of it.

Most of the results in this field (the present paper reviews only a selection of them) can be explained in terms of a 'trait/interest generalization' theory. For example, the plain girls who denounce sex may be seen as acting in their self-interest, in that they play down the importance of an area in which they are disadvantaged.

The finding that shapeliness as measured by the 'large bust/small waist' indicator is not equivalent to self-rated attractiveness is not surprising bearing in mind the many other attributes that contribute to sex appeal; for example, facial features. Nevertheless we are left with the finding that girls who are 'built' in the sense of having a desirable female shape expressed a relative liking for cartoons concerned with intercourse and treating the female as a sex toy. Perhaps girls who are shapely but otherwise unattractive come into their own during sex play, that is, their shapely form will be most appreciated at this time. If this is so then it is understandable why they should appear to be endorsing the 'Playboy philosophy' in their reactions to humour.

REFERENCES

See Bibliography for publications on humour, laughter and comedy

A Genetic Analysis of Humour Preferences

David K. B. Nias and Glenn D. Wilson

University of London Institute of Psychiatry

Many studies have been concerned with individual differences in response to all kinds of humour. It is, of course, already well-known that people vary greatly in their sense of humour. Rather than directly establishing this point, researchers have usually shown that the particular type of humour enjoyed by a person depends on factors such as age and sex (e.g., Wilson, 1973). An interesting study of this type was carried out by Terry and Ertel (1974). Sexual jokes were preferred by males, especially those with high intelligence and a 'group-dependent' personality. On the other hand, nonsense jokes were preferred by females, especially those with low intelligence.

To date no one has investigated the question of whether these individual differences in humour appreciation are predominantly genetic or environmental. It might well be predicted that a sense of humour as well as the type of humour that a person prefers would be partly, if not largely, inherited. This appears likely in view of the fact that appreciable heritability has been found for the established correlates of humour, such as personality and social attitudes (Eaves & Eysenck, 1974; Shields, 1976). A study on the genetics of aggressiveness has been conducted by Selmanoff and his colleagues (1975) in the Biobehavioral Sciences Department at Connecticut. Active genes on the Y chromosome of males have long been recognized to contribute to the trait of aggressiveness. Males with an extra Y chromosome (i.e., XYY males) have an increased tendency to be tall and violent. Anyway, Selmanoff et al demonstrated that Y chromosomes in mice predispose to aggression in varying degrees; that is, there is heritable variation. This helps explain how an XY male can be more aggressive than an XYY male, and of course why the reverse is more usual. They also noted that the Y chromosome was associated with hairy ears.

The present study was an attempt to compare the relative importance of heredity and environment in the development of humour preferences. For this purpose we used the classical technique of comparing responses from identical and fraternal twins.

METHOD

The sample consisted of one hundred pairs of same-sex twins, who were attending the psychology department for laboratory investigations. There were a roughly equal number of male and female pairs, and a similar number of identical and fraternal pairs. They were mostly aged around the mid-twenties. The twins had been previously classified as identical or fraternal by blood tests or fingerprinting.

A humour test was specially constructed from cartoons representing four intuitive categories: (1) Nonsense, (2) Satirical, (3) Aggressive, and (4) Sexual. There were twelve cartoons in each category, thus making up a total of forty-eight cartoons, which were presented in booklet form. The twins were independently asked to rate the cartoons on a five-point scale ranging from 'Not at all funny' (scored 1) to 'Extremely funny' (scored 5). The test scores were summarized by simply adding the ratings given to the cartoons in each of the four categories; that is, each person was given four scores. A shortened version of the test has been published by Eysenck and Wilson (1975).

RESULTS

The traditional method of testing for genetic effects is to compare the two types of twin in terms of concordance rates or correlations between the pairs within each type. Evidence for a genetic contribution is provided only if identical twins are more similar than fraternals. Thus correlations were computed for the two types of twin in each of the four

categories of humour, and are presented in Table 1. The coefficients average .45 and are at
a similar level for both types of twin. Only for the aggressive category is there an
indication that identical twins are more alike than fraternals in their preferences. This
result indicates that a liking for aggressive humour may, in part, be genetically determined,
but the differences between the two coefficients is in fact not significant (t = 1.56).
Therefore, we are left with the possibility that for all four types of humour there is no
genetic contribution.

TABLE 1   Correlations Between Twin Pairs

Humour category	Correlations	
	Identical	Fraternal
Nonsense	.40	.49
Satirical	.43	.44
Aggressive	.59	.34
Sexual	.52	.51

With fifty pairs in each group, the difference between the coefficients
for aggressive humour is not significant (t = 1.56).

The average level of the coefficients, .45, may be taken to indicate that environmental
influences shared by both members of a pair play a fairly substantial role in the development
of their humour preferences. Apart from the environmental contribution a coefficient of .55
(i.e., 1 - .45) is left to cover chance factors affecting one twin and not the other, and
errors of measurement.

A more detailed method of analysis has been reported elsewhere (Wilson, Rust & Kasriel, 1976).
This method, which was developed by Jinks and Fulker, would take too long to describe here.
Anyway, the results were consistent with the present interpretation. In addition, it was
noted that sex was not a significant source of variance, thus providing some justification
for pooling the humour scores of males and females. Moreover, the genotype-environment
interaction was not significant, so there was no evidence for one type of twin being
differentially affected by the environment.

Another method of analysis is to look at scores for the individual cartoons rather than
category scores. The cartoons can be rank-ordered in terms of the difference between the
correlations for the type types of twin. Yet another method of analysis would be one based
on factor analytic categories from the humour test. A principal components analysis yielded
a general factor loading on all the cartoons but especially aggressive ones, and a second
bipolar factor contrasting sexual with nonsense jokes. Nevertheless, the method of analyzing
each cartoon separately is safer than any method based on categories.

DISCUSSION

This study is somewhat unique in that it fails to provide evidence of a genetic contribution
to a psychological characteristic. Countless studies have been reported in other areas of
psychology - and invariably show that both heredity and environment play their part. Why has
a genetic component not been demonstrated for a sense of humour? The sample size of the
present study is of course a limitation - but with a total of two hundred subjects it compares
favourably with most of the other studies. Another explanation might be that the subjects
did not take the research seriously. This is unlikely, however, since they were volunteers
in the true sense of the word. Also, the correlations between the pairs, which averaged .45,
indicates that they were at least paying attention to the task and not responding in any
random fashion.

Thus we are left with the possibility that the psychological trait of a sense of humour is
environmentally determined to the exclusion of heredity. Our knowledge that the correlates
of humour, such as personality and attitudes, involve a genetic component suggests that
humour also does - but it is not sufficient proof in itself. Anyway, we must now wait to
see if subsequent studies succeed in demonstrating a genetic component.

Finally the important role of the environment in determining humour preferences is indicated
by the size of the correlations between the twin-pairs. The correlations, averaging .45,
may represent a slight overestimate since the sample was not entirely homogeneous with
respect to variables such as age and intelligence. For example, if humour preferences change
during the age range represented in this study (most of the subjects were in the range
twenty to thirty years) then the 'true' correlation between the twin-pairs (who were of
course the same age) would be slightly less. On the other hand, correction for the

unreliability of the humour test would act to give a slightly higher 'true' correlation. Thus we are left with a coefficient of about .45 to represent the shared learning experiences that have contributed to the twins similarity in sense of humour.

REFERENCES

See Bibliography for publications on humour, laughter and comedy

Eaves, L.J. & Eysenck, H.J., Genetics and the development of social attitudes. Nature, 249, 288–289 (1974).

Eysenck, H.J. & Wilson, G.D., Know Your Own Personality. Temple Smith, London (1975).

Selmanoff, M.K., Jumonville, J.E., Maxson, S.C. & Ginsburg, B.E., Evidence for a Y chromosomal contribution to an aggressive phenotype in inbred mice. Nature, 253, 529–530 (1975).

Shields, J., Heredity and environment. In: H.J. Eysenck & G.D. Wilson (Eds.), A Textbook of Human Psychology. Medical and Technical Press, Lancaster (1976).

Wilson, G.D., Rust, J. & Kasriel, J., Genetic and family origins of humour preferences. In preparation (1976).

Individual Differences in Humour: Discussion

Paul Kline

University of Exeter

In considering the papers which we have heard in this session, a number of difficulties and problems general to the study of humour and applicable to some of these researches have to be explicated. In addition some more specific points will be raised. There are four general problems:

1. In research into humour we must be aware of the distinction between making or creating humour and responding to it. All these studies, in as much as they refer to humour at all, refer to the second category only.

2. It is not easy to define what is a humour response. This can clearly be seen in the work of Foot, Smith and Chapman. Their work seems to be concerned with a more general social response. Indeed, in as much as the factors apparently facilitating it are those facilitating other social responses, it is manifestly not about humour. What is needed is some kind of differential facilitator for humour but not for other responses (unless of course part of the claim of the research is that humour is not different from other social responses). Similarly as Sherman admits, his 'gleeful' behaviour may well not be humour.

3. In sampling our humorous stimuli, we have to ensure as far as possible that we have a representative sample. It is conceivable that a man who richly enjoyed the humour of the Dunciad, for example, would be left cold by the cartoons used in the studies by Nias and Wilson. Even among seaside cartoons it is not easy to argue that these pictures are a good sample. Furthermore the categories of humour in the cartoons were only intuitive (not established statistically), and it is notoriously difficult to get agreement among judges on such categorizations, as the early work on humour by Cattell and colleagues at Illinois showed.

4. There is a logical problem in studying the comprehension of humour as a guide to understanding the nature of humour. Thus, while it is true that if a joke is not comprehended, it is no joke, the converse is not the case, as we saw in some of the examples from Brodzinsky's study where the jokes were understood but not laughed at.

We have shown how these four problems which are general in humour research apply to the papers we have heard. It is obviously important to consider how these should affect our interpretation of their results. However, in addition we must now look at some of the more specific difficulties, particular to these papers:

1. Brodzinsky's paper is well-designed and carefully carried out. However, the construct of 'conceptual tempo' is not altogether convincing. What we need to know is where this dimension falls in factorial space whether of ability or of personality. By now the major dimensions of personality are reasonably well established — dimensions which have some considerable psychological meaning and which have been empirically determined. Our reason for putting forward this argument is that it is relatively simple to form scales which can screen out certain groups as in the MMPI or the criminality scale of the EPI. However, such scales have no necessary psychological meaning, unlike factorial scales, and psychological interpretation of results is therefore difficult and dubious. The status of 'conceptual tempo' needs further clarification.

2. Statistical inadequacies, alas, are common to all research not just humour. However, Sherman's multiple correlations based on small n's of less than forty have to be treated with great caution.

   Sheppard's work has a more subtle problem of research design which makes interpretation of the meaning of the data difficult. Each of the comedians gave different performances (i.e., used different scripts) and must have been truly different on a notional variable of 'absolute funniness'. Thus, script and individual comedian are confounded in this design. Ideally, but impossibly, each comedian should have delivered the same script or scripts and perhaps done it in transvestite costume as well!

3. Nias and Wilson's studies require little comment. There would appear little a priori reason to examine genetic differences in humour (although a humour gene should presumably be on the x or y chromosome) and in any case the efficacy of twin studies in genetic research can be called into question.

The main point raised in the general discussion that followed was that although the rigorous approach of the Discussant was doubtless laudable, in practice it would put an end to most humour research! After all, it was better to study attitudes to comedians despite the difficulties, than not to study them at all. In reply, it was argued that in any event it was the privilege of a discussant to point out flaws in research without necessarily having to suggest his own improved versions. However, it was necessary to recognize that these difficulties exist, and to interpret all results with due caution, a quality that had not always been exhibited in these papers. It was concluded that what was necessary in research into individual differences in humour was a combination of experimental rigour, imagination and caution. No wonder such research appears difficult!

THE WORLD OF COMEDY

The World of Comedy: Introduction to Symposium

William F. Fry, Jr.

Department of Psychiatry, Stanford University

Listening to the words behind the winds of August, one hears an implacable message for all mankind. Each harvest is determined by what has been sown.

Two major forces oppose each other in Nature. One is variously called creation, construction, anabolism, synthesis, formation, the beginning. The other is known as annihilation, destruction, catabolism, analysis, erosion, the end. These forces are ubiquitous; they manifest their influences in all the world of human experience. During all previous epochs of history, their potentials have been basically equal. Lately, in the hands of Biology's foundling — the human race — potential for annihilation has undergone a nuclear escalation, so that the long-blessed stand-off is now out of balance.

This awesome development affects all human enterprises. Its shadow can be seen cast into every formula, every conjecture, every dream. There are few worlds of human experience where this umbra is more intense, and more relevant, than it is in the World of Reality. That intensity, and relevance, has much more than passing significance for the 'World of Comedy'.

Introducing a discussion on the World of Comedy with the statement that comedy and humour and mirth have crucial importance to all present and future organic existence on earth could expose one to an accusation of melodramatic overstatement — if it were not for the peculiar contemporary circumstances of Reality. As it actually stands, that statement is but a modest exposition and can be easily defended.

The 'World of Reality' has, historically, enjoyed an excellent reputation. At times, its impact may be stern and oppressive, but generally reality is unprejudiced and just and even-handed. By and large, the effects of reality are considered beneficial and desirable. It is a world consisting of facts, units, measurements, revealed truths, numbers, principles, molecules and palpable substance. It is characterized by its devotees as immutable, concrete, inflexible, thoroughly reliable, predictable. It lends its strength and rigour in one fashion or another to every human life. But the peculiar contemporary circumstances of reality have added a new dimension. Reality has, through the agency of potential for destruction, become pregnant with threat, heavy with danger. Certain of its facts illuminate that reality.

It is forecast that, by 1980, thirty nations across the globe will have capacity for waging nuclear warfare. Approximately half of the world's scientists are engaged in military weapons development. Over sixty million people serve in the world's military forces or related occupations. The total value of weapon stockpiles on earth during 1976 exceeded the equivalent of one trillion dollars. Expenditures for military uses during that year were close to the equivalent of three hundred billion dollars. The USA and USSR together spend each year on military purposes a total exceeding the gross national product of all Africa, with its population of three hundred and fifty million.

Commenting on this distressing state of affairs, the 1976 World Military and Social Expenditures report stated, '.... munitions is one ofthe largest industries in the world today.... Economic growth has stopped, worsening the plight of hundreds of millions of people who live at the margin of existence. There is hunger to be found throughout the world; one third of the world's adults are illiterate.'

Many people are appalled by these circumstances. Pundit Norman Cousins expressed the anguish of many, 'The line between ultimate absurdity and reality is getting thinner all the time. What gives our age its bitter flavor is precisely the triumph of irrational behavior in the operation of society. Total power is being wedded to total madness. The official delusion persists that we can buy security with superbombs. What we are buying instead is a colossal suicide pact. Nuclear stockpiles protect nothing. They are the means by which radioactive firestorms can sweep over a large part of the world, consuming not only human beings but also any access to the future.'

The World of Reality is ill-served, and is made grotesque, by this destructive potential. But also, like all entities, reality has never been perfect; it has its inherent flaws. One prominent flaw is the curious reputation, within Reality, of the World of Comedy. It is a sad fact that humour is usually regarded scornfully, even contemptuously, by the arbiters of reality. They question how one can justify spending one's time and energy so foolishly. They spend their time seriously, in counting and measuring the universe and all eternity — and designate a frivolous corner for comedy and mirth. In Reality, there are so many things 'far too important for a laugh, for a smile'. Generally, this humourless myopia is not recognized as the flaw that it is.

Measured with Reality's cold, hard steel, the World of Comedy may indeed appear foolish, trivial, inconsequential. But there are several reasons to think that these 'trivia' and the pursuits thereof are less of an embarrassment to our humanity than various serious and calculated endeavours of Reality.

Counting and measuring give cause for self-congratulation. We quantify yet another aspect of Reality. Immediately reproducible and communicable knowledge of the universe is thus extended. Our time and space and event-binding senses are enhanced.

It is a terrible irony that much of this knowledge has contributed crucially to the dilemma of destruction. Further agony is found in the ways by which quantifying skills are continuously used, blindly and stubbornly and irrationally, to expand the destructive potential and fix our dreadful trap ever more tightly. Naturalist Jacques-Yves Cousteau recently commented on this tragedy. 'The tragic irony of the social systems we live in is that such a monumental hypocrisy is forged by very sincere people. (They) are all working for scientific institutes; the results will be published in learned magazines. It is none of the scientists' business to deal with what may be done with their findings. The geologist and the nuclear physicist work for the advancement of knowledge and wash their hands of any responsibility. This "Pilatic syndrome" has been institutionalized, so that inventors and finders simply surrender all their substance to the elected adventurers who rule our world.. Madness could go no farther...... We are living a nightmare, when our hands desperately reach for an easy, accessible cure, while incomprehensible forces paralyze us.'

In these words, Cousteau keenly and bitterly cuts to the heart of the matter. He also illustrates, in usage, his awareness of the power of humour — by introducing wit, satire, sarcasm, and other humour mechanisms into his presentation. Without these mechanisms, his statements would be no less accurate, but would suffer with insipidity and pallor. His wisdom in humour has practical significance, as well as aesthetic richness.

What Cousteau seems to know, what citizens of the World of Comedy realize, what is generally ignored in the World of Reality: humour and comedy and mirth are not trivial in human life. And since the crystallization of the potential for total and eternal destruction, they are not trivia against the grandeur of the entire living earth. Yesterday and today and tomorrow, they sustain and protect and encourage hope and inspire and strengthen resolution. They constitute one of the most important forces making possible further global viability.

The power of the World of Comedy is ultimately derived from the various effects humour creates within the context of a single individual's life. This power is most apparent, though, when humour is active in the social, political, tribal, cultural, diplomatic, national and international context. When an individual laughs, he signifies discovery and surprise. When a parliament or international congress laughs, life is protected and we all are sustained once again.

Through its cathartic effects and its functions as a coping experience, humour can produce resolution or relaxation of social tensions, international crises, cultural anxieties. These tensions are escalated by emotions of frustration and indignation and vindictiveness. Hatred and rampage are nurtured by the sour wine of 'inferiority' and 'vulnerability'. Humour dealing with economic imbalances, class conflicts, racial disputes, sexual discrimination and exploitations diminishes the escalation pressures generated by negative emotions.

Not an opiate that dulls the sensitivities, humour instead plays the dynamic role of defusing negative emotions, thus offsetting their tendency to prevent intelligent, creative and productive approaches and solutions to various social and cultural conflicts and difficulties. Being able to enter a community — sharing in the World of Comedy, not being paralyzed by rage or paranoid brooding, members of any group are blessed with a liberation which enhances the possibilities of functioning closer to their highest, most creative, most inspired potentials.

There are many mechanisms whereby this liberation by mirth is activated. Probably the most common, as life proceeds these days in the communities of mankind, is that spontaneous burst of shared amusement and mirth, which is marked by laughter and glistened eyes. Hardly trivia, this experience is one of great significance and complexity. The significance is already apparent; the complexity is more extensive than quickly recognized.

Part of that complexity is a product of the remarkable structure of humour - the intricately interactive paradoxes of the contextual 'play frame' and the paradox of reality content suddenly turned upside-down at the humour climax or punchline. My book, 'Sweet Madness: A Study of Humor', presents an extensive discussion of the interactive force of these paradoxes, beyond what can be delineated at this point.

That complexity is one of 'nature', as in 'it is the nature of the beast'. That complexity is of structure, formal cognitive character. It is integral to humour phenomena as we know humour at this stage of our evolution. Lord only knows what sophistications will develop in the structure of humour as we continue our mental evolution.

Another major source of the complexity of mirth is that peculiar environmental context which offers the potentiality for a bursting forth of the comic spirit. This is a Janus-type environment, looking in opposite directions at the same time. One direction leads to danger, threat, challenge, stress, duress. The other proceeds to a state of security and comfort. If either prevail separately, unopposed by the other, the possibility for mirth is defeated; some other mood-state would establish. If threat or challenge prevails, the emotion might be fear, or anger. A supremacy of security would bring forth a surfeit of complacency, unsuitable ground for that spark of anxiety essential to the tension build-up just prior to release of mirth. This balanced state is similar to the 'ambivalent' context described by Ambrose in his studies of the beginnings of social smiling in human infants. It is also similar to the environmental character pertaining when that appeasement display named 'social grimace' is presented by primates - as described by several behavioural scientists, including Pinneo and myself.

It is informative to explore the actual operation of these Janus-like trends in the humour context, as they exist during that 'spontaneous burst of shared amusement and mirth' during a parliamentary debate, a confrontation at United Nations, negotiations between leaders or world powers - or any interpersonal transaction scaled down from those lofty, and hazardous, levels. Examples quickly come to mind of either extreme, where threat dominates and defeats humour, or where complacency smothers wit and laughter. A vivid example of overwhelming threat is provided in that famous episode at United Nations when Soviet Premier Nikita Khrushchev removed his shoe during an empassioned speech and began to hammer the lectern with its heel. That act could have been experienced as hilarious, but the dangers were too pronounced to be received by the audience in that fashion. Examples of dominant security are notably common in any governmental or social body, when the issue is very low key, perhaps even somniferous. There is no stimulus leading to laughter. In such circumstances, many of the distinguished personages can be observed snoring, hardly chuckling.

Implicit in the similarity between this Janus environment and the 'ambivalent' environment surrounding early infant mirth responses is the concept that a long human history exists for the association of this context and the outbursting of mirth. For justification of this view, we turn to the history of the World of Comedy, and can consider some honoured customs of that world.

The jester and the clown - nobility in the World of Comedy - have served for centuries their 'betters' in the World of Reality. In this serving, they have manifested a skill in creating that balance of anxiety and security, as if their lives depended on this skill. And, in all too many instances, their lives did in fact depend upon the level of skill they exercised in their art. To pique the king, without causing outrage; to provoke, without humilation; to agitate, without inflaming: these are the goals - and obligations - of the royal fool. A miscalculation of the ingredient, causing a disruption of the delicate balance, could be fatal.

But consider the privilege, and implied power, of the fool. He possessed prerogative to express - in 'humorous' form - truths which no one else was permitted even to contemplate. Traditionally, he had privy to the ruler's innermost experiences, both personal and those of State. He might even be called upon to speak for a ruler those facts or sentiments for which the ruler would not wish his own responsibility. Small wonder that many jesters have been famed as diplomats in motley.

It is quite clear, in this setting, that ambivalent balance is crucial to the environment for humour. The fool's dilemma highlights our perception. Less clear, in the annals of Comedy, is this same necessity for the performances of those travelling drolls, who constituted the other major force in historic humour. Often associated with more serious actors, troubadours or balladiers, acrobats, and the odd fire-eater, these merry-makers made their way through the centuries, from town to town, manor to manor, fortress to fortress, exchanging amusement for livelihood. 'Make 'Em Laugh' was the injunction of survival.

Farce and slapstick have been the preferred media of exchange for these troupes, both during early, almost prehistoric days of Attic Comedy and Dionysian festivity and during later, more sophisticated times of Middle Ages Carnival, Renaisssance commedia dell 'arte, music hall and vaudeville, cinema and television. Although the vulnerable, tenuous position of the king's fool makes more apparent the importance of a balance between inflammation and tedium, the nature of the drolls' act carries within it the message of that balance.

Farce is noted as that form of humour granted the greatest degree of licence. Outrageous events mark the unfolding of farcical presentation; farce moves from one atrocity to the next — all with accompaniment of millenial laughter. The safety of farce is in its rigorous, codified structure. Even highly repetitious at times, farce is mostly predictable, conservative in its format. Infamy terrorizes the audiences and sure confidence that the farce will follow time-humoured tradition soothes, calms and reassures them. The product in this golden mean is mirth.

Slapstick is farce's country cousin. Its outrages are customarily so obvious as to be crude; slapstick usually makes no pretence of subtlety. Most of its devices would, in the World of Reality, cause crippling, agony, or even death. But, the safety side of a balanced environment is inherent in the comedic performance; screams or groans, rather than laughter, would accompany bloody slapstick gone wild. A recent example of that unbalancing was the Mike Nichols production of Joseph Heller's 'Catch 22', in which gory anguish so dominated as to obviate most of the story's hilarity. Usually, however, slapstick's format keeps to the security of a custard pie.

Recorded laughter, orchestrated to the production, is an innovation of the electronic sector of the World of Comedy. There are several reasons for its introduction and rapidly-spread use, but one speaks to this issue of the Janus-headed context. A chorus of pre-arranged laughter cues the audience in their mood. Some modern-day descendant of a witty jester utters, with scathing sincerity, a bon mot insult or salty observation. Any hesitancy about how this aggressive jibe is to be understood will be quickly dissipated by a rousing volley of Tape 37, from the Laughter Library, entitled 'Appreciative Crowd Guffaws'. Canned laughter ensures a slapstick device is not taken as authentic mayhem. Abuses of this technology occur — as in any other human endeavour — but the reassurance of hearing laughter behind the sturm und drang is compelling. Poetic justice is found that one form of abuse is excessive gelastic input. The audience is assaulted by this excess. The golden balance is tipped thus by what is designed to foster it.

Shared amusement and mirth, in the communities of mankind, is obviously an important experience in these communities, evidenced by its frequency, emotional power, and ubiquitousness. It is no simple event in the lives of its participants; its complexity is derived from several sources. This communion of perception, sensation and thought contributes a liberating force for humans confronted with various momentous problems of their gregarious way of life. When brought together in comedic fellowship, the sharp edge of 'different' is dulled and the surge of opposition is checked.

Liberation is thus enhanced by humour's centripetal tendency. But also, a centrifugal force lends power to liberation. This force originates in humour's succinct incisiveness. A group can find a common theme in shared humour; those members may also use humour to isolate, even deviate, errant elements of their group or immediate environment. Certain cultures, exemplified by the Soviet use of its semi-official humour magazines, 'Krokodil', carry out this latter function on a broad scale, extending the communication to an entire people. Other cultures reserve this corrective influence for family use, in service of child-raising objectives.

These uses, whether broad or limited, are usually directed downwards in a hierarchy structure. The liberation is from abrasion and oppression less apparent than when the force is directed upwards, towards a blatantly oppressive tyrant. It is an unfortunate aspect of human life that tyrany can exist in many modes. The fortunate side of humour is that ridicule, satire, irony and burlesque are equally effective against any form of tyrany.

Demagogues generally attempt to fix their positions by drawing parallels between themselves and divinities; they aspire to various degrees of perfection, all pointed towards 'greater', rather than 'lesser'. They confuse the populace — and usually themselves — with an elitism, of which they are the prime representatives. Adolph Hitler was a vivid example of this demagoguery in recent times. The ages have contained thousands of this type; others, of happily lesser scale, exist today.

A person oriented to the perpetation of tyrany seeks to disguise his or her humanness. They are 'godlike', not people. They wear cosmetics to hide the warts, dye their faded

hair, shave again and again to avoid the facial hirsutism which reminds us of our kinship
with other furry creatures; they hoist sagging tissues, cinch in bulges, straighten angles,
brighten eyes and practise deep and throaty vocal tones. All this artifice is necessary to
dupe their subjects - and to give themselves the degree of conceit and self-deception
essential for committing their multitudinous outrages.

This aspiration towards divinity may be a necessary deception, but it is also the ultimate
hole in the tyrant's bag. His elitism is vulnerable, and no more vulnerable then to humour's
thrust. The surgical sharpness of jest probes for that hole: the warts are unveiled and
the imperfections which make us all kin are revealed. Unlike sober, convoluted, legalistic,
serious-minded procedures for unseating a tyrant, humour cannot be offset by invective or
destroyed by fiat or legislation. In the last analysis, humour is only truly vulnerable to
opposing humour - for Hitler, Goebbels provided that strength. Most tyrants or would-be
tyrants are either too shortsighted or intellectually deprived to have access to antagonistic
humour.

The World of Comedy is an essentially democratic society. We are brought together in common
experience and we are found, in the balance, to be equal. As I have stated, these group
(social, cultural, national, familial, etcetera) effects are based on the participation of
individuals in the network of Comedy. Ultimately, we recognize humour as communication,
within individuals, between individuals, and among individuals.

There can be no doubt that humorous communication grows from a multitude of sources, and
has a multitude of consequences. The World of Comedy is a busy world, quick and filled with
characters and mirthful devices. The central element is mercury, rather than iron or lead.
And like that quality implied in the name 'quicksilver', the theme is liberation. Christopher
Fry once stated, 'Comedy is an escape, not from truth but from despair; a narrow escape
into faith.'

Society is liberated from tyranny of involuted, defeating emotions and can use humour to
shake loose malevolent domination by usurping rulers. Individuals are similarly freed from
the ever-circling traps of emotions such as hatred, guilt, envy, jealousy. But also, a
deeper freedom within each individual is associated with the creative force of humour. Each
bit of humour is a discovery for the individual; previously unrecognized relationships are
discovered in mirth. This experience is a creative act for each person participating. From
this creation and discovery comes expansion of knowledge. Greater knowledge results in
deeper freedom. Ultimately, any progression in a person's life depends on expansion of
knowledge.

Creativity, by definition, is the germinal source of all human advance. From several
standpoints, humour is definable and recognizable as a creative act. The argument is well
detailed in Arthur Koestler's 'Act of Creation', the chapter Melanie Allen and I contributed
to 'Humour and Laughter' (Edited by Chapman & Foot), and in our own book, 'Make 'Em Laugh'.
The crucial factor is discovery, by participants in mirth, of relationships between entitites
which had not previously been recognized as associated in that fashion.

'Lateral thinking' has been described by Jacques-Yves Cousteau as 'the process by which the
mind scans events or facts that are apparently uncorrelated to see if there is not a hidden
correlation.' He contrasts this with deduction, or 'vertical thinking' which 'rarely leads
to breakthrough discoveries.' Another way of labelling these two procedures would be to
identify them as analogue and digital processes.

Humour is clearly, in its cognitive nature, an analogue event - and finds in this
characteristic its kinship with all other metaphoric experience, including play, myths,
poetry, rites of reversal, fairy tales. These are magic elements in life, without which we
would all be pedestrian slaves; counting and measuring with digital skill, yes, but not
laughing, or dreaming, or making music.

On occasions, humour may be common, it may be coarse, perhaps unsophisticated, even
unintellectual. It may be flawed, and subject to the human capacity for error and/or
mischief. It may appear in simple surroundings or rough gatherings or even as a deliberate
tool to manipulate human emotions for egocentric aims. It is certainly not our only answer
to all problems; and in certain instances, not even the preferred resolution. But, it is
creative. It may be the most creative experience available each day in the lives of millions
of humans. And it possesses the grace and skill of self-correction. There always is this
hope in the World of Comedy.

By reason of these many values - and many others - humour is a highly important part of
each person's life. It may be discounted as trivial in the World of Reality, and not given
its due for that importance. But, observe the indignation arousal if one is told that he
has no sense of humour; a deeper awareness of that importance is touched.

An eloquent — and poignant — expression of what humour means in an individual's life is found in an anecdote about Abraham Lincoln, a deep-feeling humanist with a keen appreciation of the World of Comedy. He is well-known to have found in humour much solace from personal tragedy and especially his agony for the bloody and rending Civil War through which he was leading his nation. On one occasion, he attempted to share this relief with his heavy, moody, oppressed Cabinet. He read some passages from a favourite humorist, contemporary Artemus Ward — with no effect on the Cabinet's mood. After his own solitary laughter died down, he pleaded with these solemn associates, 'Gentlemen, why don't you laugh? With the fearful strain that is upon me night and day, if I did not laugh, I should die. And you need this medicine as much as I do.'

REFERENCES

See Bibliography for publications on humour, laughter and comedy

Heller, J., Catch 22. Modern Library, New York (1961).

Laughter and Joking — The Structural Axis

Paul Taylor

University of Leicester

In this paper an approach to the study of humour is suggested which bypasses and ignores the vast majority of work on the subject, namely that work which can be loosely grouped under the heading 'the psychology of humour' and subtitled 'the individual in spite of himself'. The individual holds the key to a number of problems but I would prefer to broaden the scope and look upon the individual as a 'social' being - one who participates whether voluntarily or involuntarily, in social interaction as a member of certain groups and classes. Martineau (1967, 1972) has suggested that a sociology of humour should entail the study of group processes and group structures but as yet that sociology remains a very much barren field. A lack of research data bedevils the subject[1] and leaves theories groundless and vague, or subject to criticism (both lay and academic) as being commonsensical - a criticism to which there is rarely any reply.

If we take as a starting point the individual in society then the tools of analysis which appear best suited to tackling the problem of understanding humour are those taken from communication theory (see de Fleur, 1966; Riley, 1959; Shannon & Weaver, 1963). By seeing any joke or humorous act as a message one is automatically forced to view that joke as part of a larger process - a process which both forms, and is formed by, the message it conveys. Many writers have emphasized the importance of 'cues' in classifying that which follows the cue as humorous (e.g., Berlyne, 1972; Chapman, 1973a; Emerson, 1973; McGhee, 1972b; Suls, 1972). Too few writers, in my opinion, have realised that these cues, as meta-communication, exist as an integral part of the message and are, of necessity, of a paradoxical nature (Bateson, 1953, 1956; Fry, 1968). How much these paradoxes influence humour is beyond the scope of this paper - they are concerned with the actual technique of the joke and, as such, an attempt to understand them is an attempt to answer the question 'Why is something funny?' The question I would like to ask is 'What other factors influence the nature of the joke?'

THE CREATOR'S PERCEPTION OF THE AUDIENCE

My research into comedy and humour in the mass media, with a special reference to television, has given me the opportunity to interview both scriptwriters and producers or directors who are involved with the creation of half-hour situation comedies. Much research[2] into the production side of the mass media has stressed the importance of the producer's conception of the audience he hopes to reach when making decisions which will alter the nature or style of the end product (e.g., Bauer, 1958; McQuail, 1969; Pool & Shulman, 1959). Thus, Cantor (1971) writes of American television producers that 'The basic philosophy expressed by those in the industry is giving the public what it wants...' (p27), and in the same work quotes two different producers as saying: 'If it appeals to me in a broad sense it will appeal to the audience' (p172), and 'I think of myself as audience. If it pleases me - I always think it is going to please the audience' (p172).

Riley and Riley (1959) suggest that the sender of any message assumes the attitude of the other - the generalized other being the audience[3]. From my own research, a successful scriptwriter has clearly stated his own approach to writing:

> 'I do think of the audience but through me. If I write a scene that I find funny
> I've got to believe that the audience will... in a way, I am the audience and I
> know if a scene is going to work or not and if it doesn't work for me then it
> won't work for the audience. That's the only criterion that you can base on - that
> you are a member of the audience and you've got to write it for your own
> satisfaction first and believe that that's right and you'll soon be proved wrong
> if you are wrong'.

The most commonly used phrases in reply to a question about perceptions of the audience were synonymous with 'I just know', 'it's just a feeling', or 'it's an instinct'. Both writers and producers certainly do not have a clear picture of an imaginary audience — the only element of certainty is the size of the audience, though everybody in the industry seems to be well aware of the vagaries of audience research[4]. However, the creators of television comedy, especially those working for the commercial channels, must 'give the audience what it wants' — and if their perceptions of audience wants are based on assuming the attitude of the other, 'gut' reactions, or comments from friends and neighbours then it would appear obvious that their perception, although probably correct, is based on very imperfect and incomplete information. The creators are sending messages into a void about which they know so little though in saying 'I know that's funny' they are effectively saying 'I know that that will make people laugh'[5].

Whether it is possible for a scriptwriter or a producer to discover anything about the audience for the mass media apart from 'headcounts' is irrelevant here. The point I am trying to stress is that the creator's perception of the audience will, to some extent, dictate the nature and style of the material presented. I may think a particular joke funny, but as a creator my only guide can be either based on experience or prediction. In either case, I do not have access to audience response, except that of the studio audience which is unreliable for a number of reasons[6]. An interview with a prodigious script-writer gave the following comments on the dilemma:

> 'I write what pleases me and I hope that it also pleases the audience. I think that if you're in a creative profession... you do it to please yourself basically and if you're talented and creative enough you'll please other people'.

Another writer told me his views on the home audience; he said:

> 'You never think about them. You can't. It's such an amorphous mass of five to ten to twenty million people. You can't say that they're going to like this or they're not going to like it. You have to write what you think is funny and hope that they think it's funny as well'.

MEDIA VARIATIONS

A model of humour as communication has the advantage of flexibility. Communications theory can be expanded to include both face-to-face interaction and the mass media, together with the range of variations between the two extremes — and, more importantly I believe, can tell us something about both humour and communication in general.

I would like to discuss, very briefly, the impact of certain organizational elements of television which impinge on the area of comedy — elements which are, to a large extent absent from face-to-face interaction.

The Passage of Time

A half-hour situation comedy usually takes anything between a week and a fortnight to write — sometimes longer but rarely shorter. It will then be rehearsed and revised for about a week prior to one day in the studios. A rehearsal in the morning and one in the afternoon are the final preparations before recording the show in the evening. The actual recording can take anything up to two hours. There are breaks for the actors, scene-changes, and the almost inevitable re-takes. A producer told me that, 'some producers automatically do the first scene twice. Unless it goes exceedingly well they pretend that technically they want to do it again because very often you get more and better laughs the second time'. The show will then be edited, usually by the producer or director, in readiness for transmission at a predetermined date in the future.

The television half-hour is about 24 and 28 minutes long on the commercial channels and the BBC respectively — a very definite limitation on creativity as an assumption is made that comedy can be compartmentalized into equal segments[7]. There is a further restraint peculiar to the commercial channels in that every writer must be aware that he needs to build a climax just before the commercial break to carry the audience over the advertisements into the second half of the programme. A dramatic play on television can be anything from 25 to 90 minutes long: a situation comedy, with the rare exceptions of 'Christmas specials', has definite temporal boundaries which can only act as a restraint to the creative writer or producer.

Finance

One producer told me: 'We may find that there's a lovely subject we'd like to do on boats but it would mean filming so much...' His comment is indicative of the views of many.

Budgets vary enormously, not only between the channels but also between different shows. The restrictions of any particular budget operate in four main areas:

(1) 'Stars', who will hopefully attract more viewers, cost more to contract than less famous actors or actresses. The size of the cast must also depend on the amount of money available — one writer I spoke to commented that the ideal situation comedy would be based on one man spending half an hour in a telephone kiosk.

(2) Studio sets are limited in number, usually to three or four per episode — obviously the same sets will be re-used for future programmes. The cost of building materials has risen enormously, the budgets for the shows have not. There is also a spatial limitation in that all the sets must be built and contained in one studio: it would be impractical to manoeuvre the cast, technicians, props, the production staff, and most importantly, the audience from studio to studio.

(3) Outdoor location filming must be kept to a minimum. Whereas it was possible in the late fifties and early sixties to film a complete show for about £3,000, a similar enterprise today would cost in the region of £60,000.

(4) There is a definite limitation on experimentation. With a possible budget (excluding overheads) of about £10,000, the television companies must be guaranteed returns whether in the size of audience or in advertisement revenue. Tried and trusted formulas have become the staple diet.

The root problem with situation comedies, both as humour and as communication, is that there is an almost total reliance by the programme companies on the studio audience. Everything in the process is geared to making an audience, varying in size from about two- to four-hundred people, react to the recording of the show[8].

THE STRUCTURAL AXIS

Any discussion of humour inevitably leads to the question of what are suitable (in the sense of relevant rather than morally acceptable) subjects for comedy. It would appear to be fairly well documented (e.g., Bergson, 1911; Daninos, 1952; Pearsall, 1975) that variations in subject matter exist, both in time and space. Whilst there are certain recognized minority tastes that television feels obliged to cater for, the basic maxim is to reach the widest and largest audience possible, whether to inform, educate, or entertain.

In the vast majority of jokes there will be found both a social (or a structural) axis and a humorous one — the latter giving the joke its funniness, usually by some incongruous mixing or juxtaposition of the elements of the social axis, these elements being symbolically loaded by their reference to structural groups or categories. Jokes which lack the humorous axis will tend to reveal their derisory nature; those that lack the social axis will be nonsensical or judged to be 'childish'. The mass media have generally been criticized for their breadth of approach — as they are supposedly out to capture the largest number of people, their conception of the audience has been seen as that of a large, undifferentiated mass. To reach this mythical body the products offered tend to rely on the principle of the lowest common denominator. The humour, for the most part, will lack subtlety and finesse. The social axis of the humour will refer to the dominant symbols and values of that society, partly because the mass media have been shown to demonstrate conservative tendencies (cf. Miliband, 1973; Murdock & Golding, 1974), but more importantly because those symbols and values exhibited must have some relevance and meaning for the greatest number of viewers. The overwhelming abundance of humorous material on sex and marriage depends on its existence not only on psychological principles but also on the presence of structural conflicts which are inherent in the social fabric. While marriage is seen as essential to the continuation of society it automatically creates certain strains and stresses concomitant with the changes of status and the creation of new (to the individual) structural categories. It is certainly conceivable to regard mother-in-law jokes as somehow being expressive of Oedipal desires; I would maintain, however, that one is missing a large part of the picture if the socially ambivalent position of mothers-in-law is ignored.

Douglas (1968) has argued the point before. She suggests that

'a joke is seen and allowed when it offers a symbolic pattern of a social pattern occurring at the same time.. all jokes are expressive of the social situations in which they occur...if there is no joke in the social system, no other joking can appear.'

Jokes are essentially a revolt against the structure of a society — they suggest that there is a possibility that mothers-in-law are human after all. There is a strong parallel with the work of Levi-Strauss (1955, 1967) on mythology. Levi-Strauss suggests that a myth is an attempt to reconcile the irreconcilable — a mother-in-law is (supposedly) sexually desirable and (certainly) sexually prohibited. The potential of a joke lies in its ability to personalize stereotypes; to make the revolt against structure essentially one of liberation. To make a joke which reinforces stereotypes and makes them concrete is to ignore that potential.

THE AUDIENCE AS FEEDBACK GENERATORS

In a recent interview a popular husband and wife acting team talked about their relationship with the audience (John Alderton and Pauline Collins interviewed in the Radio Times, 19th April, 1975, p7): 'You embrace them into your moves and move with them...you dance with them'. Both partners agreed that, for them, it is nearly impossible to play comedy without a studio audience — if there isn't one, the wife relies on the reactions of the cameramen or anyone else who happens to be about.

There are two distinct types of performer in situation comedies. Certain people are primarily known as comedians in their own right; they have usually been stand-up comics with a history of working in clubs and theatres. The majority, however, are actors first and comic actors second. Both types are used to playing in front of live audiences, and, in a sense, have come to depend on audience reaction as an integral part of their performance[9]. 'Timing' is continually stressed by the performers as one of the key elements of successful comedy (see Nathan, 1971) — and timing is absolutely dependent on a reaction to any given joke or line. The reactions of the millions of viewers at home cannot be tapped so a surrogate audience must be set up to represent them.

Apart from the apparent necessity of the studio audience for the cast they are also, in the opinion of many producers and writers, essential in supplying the viewing audience with cues. Research has tended to show that hearing other people laugh (whether that laughter be 'canned' or 'natural') has a heightening effect on one's own laughter (Chapman, 1973a, 1974; Fuller, 1976, this volume; Fuller & Sheehy-Skeffington, 1974; Smyth & Fuller, 1972). How true this is in relation to television remains to be demonstrated though it can be stressed that most people working in television are firmly convinced of the contagion of laughter and tend to think, therefore, that they are justified in using canned laughter or turning the volume up a bit[10] if the end result will be a large audience viewing with increased pleasure. Face-to-face interaction is characterized by a very high level of immediate feedback[11]. There are constant opportunities for the audience to respond and a process of negotiation (Emerson 1973) is feasible.

There is a constant communication about the joke throughout its narration and each sequence of the whole process has inbuilt potential terminations. The situation in broadcasting is entirely different. The creator of comedy will get some feedback from colleagues[12], friends, and the studio audience but he must remain largely ignorant of the response of the vast viewing public. Letters from the public are rare and tend to be purely congratulatory or obscene[13]. The lack of any significant feedback has led to some controversy in the field of race relations — the creator of television comedy can have no control at all over the uses the public makes of his material. Humour in television is characterized by very imperfect feedback between the creator and the audience — the high level of 'noise' in the channel seriously inhibits communication.

CONCLUDING REMARKS

Flugel (1954) wrote that:

> 'Where so many eminent minds have failed to agree it would be presumptuous to suppose that any satisfactory explanation or classification of the causes and nature of humour can be easily achieved' (p709).

It is impossible to quibble with his supposition and even after over twenty years further research into the subject, it does seem that Flugel was really rather mild in what now appears to be an under-estimation of the situation. Academic research has a long history of getting the wrong answers because of the pure and simple fact that it has asked the wrong questions. The study of laughter and humour has thankfully progressed from the search for a universal and eternal formula but it has not yet escaped from the fundamental error of positing the same questions as to 'causes and nature'. Laughter is social communication and until we start to seek answers in the social structure and in the relationships between groups and organizations then we can only expect to hear and read the well-worn conclusions that have littered the field of study for so long.

FOOTNOTES

[1] Among those works containing data are Douglas (1968), Fletcher (1974), Gabbard (1954), Goodlad (1969, 1971), Greenberg and Kahn (1970), La Fave (1972), Pearsall (1975), Sacks (1974), Seymour-Ure (1974, Ch.8), Victoroff (1953, 1969), BBC (1973/4), Surlin (1973), and Wilhoit and de Bock (1975).

[2] Tracey (1976) has quite clearly demonstrated, however, that a conception or perception of the audience is almost totally absent in the production of television political programmes.

[3] Their debt to Mead (1934) is acknowledged.

[4] See Croll (1975) for a discussion of the adequacy of current audience research techniques, and for a comparison between the approach of the IBA and the BBC.

[5] Successful scriptwriters are rarely proved wrong; unsuccessful scriptwriters tend not to have their work broadcast.

[6] Although the commercial companies differ to some extent there is a strong tendency for tickets to be allocated in much the same way as the BBC - on a first come, first served basis. Producers and scriptwriters alike appear to have recurrent nightmares, usually based on experience, of large groups of Women's Institute members, Polish students plus their interpreter, deaf and dumb coach parties etcetera. The studio audience is rarely, if ever, a representative sample of the viewing audience, to the extent that approximately 70% of the audience will be female. The audience viewing at home will be split roughly 50:50 between the sexes. The people who make up the studio audience are placed under a certain obligation to react 'properly'. The tickets are free and everybody from the cast to the production crew is being so nice and stressing how important their presence is for the success of the show. A warm-up man invariably succeeds in generating a cheerful atmosphere.

[7] The time period of half an hour seems to have derived from early radio comedy shows which themselves owed something to the 'American Invasion' of radio during the war. It was thought by the advertisers that half an hour was long enough to keep someone amused.

[8] As a postscript to this paragraph it must be stressed that the problem has been vastly oversimplified. Very many other factors play important parts in determining, for example, why some scripts are chosen and not others.

[9] Comics and comic actors learn how to 'milk' laughter, to build it up step by step. It is conventional wisdom that theatre audiences vary tremendously in their appreciation or willingness to laugh - the comic, or comic actor, must know how to 'ride' a laugh and how to carry on when laughter is unexpectedly absent.

[10] Producers are quite defensive about how much canned laughter they use. They seem to realise that it is a form of artistic cheating and use the (often valid) excuse that 'it's done for technical reasons'.

[11] As should now be apparent I am using the term feedback in a much broader sense than the definition postulated by Shannon and Weaver (1963).

[12] Burns (1970) writes of BBC staff that, 'it was said with great firmness that what counted was judgement by fellow professionals of a programme's quality' (p152). Tracey (1976) stresses that this view is overly simplistic.

[13] Elliott (1972) makes some valid observations on unsolicited correspondence: 'It was no use to the production team in suggesting programme ideas for the future, because of its content, the way the team reacted to it and because by the time most of it arrived, the production team had disbanded...' (p141).

REFERENCES

See Bibliography for publications on humour, laughter and comedy

Adorno, T.W., Television and the patterns of mass culture. In: B. Rosenberg & D.M. White (Eds.), Mass Culture - The Popular Arts in America. Free Press, New York (1964).

Bateson, G., The message 'This is Play'. In: B. Schaffner (Ed.), Group Processes. Josiah Macy, New York (1956).

Bauer, R., The communicator and the audience. Conflict Resolution, 2, 66–76 (1958).

BBC, Annual Review of BBC Audience Research Findings: 1973/4. British Broadcasting Corporation, London (1974).

Burns, T., Public service and private world. In: J. Tunstall (Ed.), Media Sociology. Constable, London (1970).

Cantor, M., The Hollywood TV Producer. Basic Books, New York (1971).

Croll, P., Audience Research in British Broadcasting. Mimeograph CMCR, University of Leicester (1975).

Daninos, P., Le Tour du Monde du Rire. Hachette, Paris (1952).

de Fleur, M., Theories of Mass Communication. David McKay, New York (1966).

Elliott, P., The Making of a Television Series. Constable, London (1972).

Fletcher, C., Beneath the Surface. Routledge & Kegan Paul, London (1974).

Gabbard, E.G., An Experimental Study of Comedy. Unpublished doctoral dissertation, University of Iowa (1954).

Goodlad, J.S.R., An Analysis of the Social Content of Popular Drama, 1955–1965. Unpublished doctoral dissertation, London School of Economics (1969).

Goodlad, J.S.R., A Sociology of Popular Drama. Heineman, London (1971).

Levi-Strauss, C., The structural study of myth. Journal of American Folklore, 68, No. 270 (1955).

Levi-Strauss, C., The story of Asdiwal. In: E.R. Leach (Ed.), The Structural Study of Myth and Totemism. Tavistock, London (1967).

McQuail, D., Towards a Sociology of Mass Communications. Collier-Macmillan, London (1969).

Mead, G.H., Mind, Self and Society. University of Chicago Press (1934).

Miliband, R., The State in Capitalist Society. Quartet, London (1973).

Murdock, G. & Golding, P., For a political economy of mass communications. In: R. Miliband & J. Saville (Eds.), Socialist Register (1974).

Pearsall, R., Collapse of Stout Party: Victorian Wit and Humour. Weidenfeld & Nicolson, London (1975).

Pool, I. de S. & Shulman, I., Newsmen's fantasies, audiences and news-writing. Public Opinion Quarterly, 23, 145–148 (1959).

Riley, J. & Riley, M., Mass communication and the social system. In: R. Merton, L. Broom & L.S. Cottrell (Eds.), Sociology Today. Basic Books, New York (1959).

Seymour-Ure, C., The Political Impact of the Mass Media. Constable, London (1974).

Shannon, C.E. & Weaver, W., The mathematical theory of communication. University of Illinois, Urbana (1963).

Surlin, S.H., Bigotry on air and in life: the Archie Bunker case. Public Telecommunications Review, 18, 97–107 (1973).

Tracey, M., Determinations: the Production of Political Television. Routledge & Kegan Paul, London (1976, in press).

Tunstall, J., Media Sociology. Constable, London (1970).

Victoroff, D., Le Rire et Le Risible. Universitaires de France, Paris (1953).

Wilhoit, G.C. & de Bock, H., Archie Bunker in a Foreign Culture. Paper presented at IAMCR Conference, Leicester (1976).

A Structural Approach to Humour in Farce

Jessica R. Milner Davis

University of New South Wales, Australia

LIVE COMEDY AS COMMUNAL JOKING

Comedy in the live theatre is a social activity which in one form or another has commanded popular audiences in Western societies since before the Golden Age of Greek Civilization. It constitutes a communal version of the basic joking triangle described by both Freud (1905) and Bergson (1911); the jokester, the butt of the joke and the audience of listeners. The joke, however, is not merely recited to the audience; it is acted out and rendered dramatic, communicating visually as well as verbally.

According to Freud, one of the functions of joking is to satisfy, in a more or less disguised way depending on the degree of sophistication of the audience, those hostile and aggressive impulses which are barred from open expression by social rules. Another is to approach forbidden but gratifying topics. Yet another, to give rein to innocent feelings of playfulness. All of these functions may be ascribed to comedy.

WHAT KINDS OF JOKING?

Freud's response to the age-old dispute over the nature of the comic was to admit the existence of both hostile and harmless jokes. As a matter of common-sense, it is clear that many more different varieties, or 'flavours' of jokes exist and audiences are evidently capable of recognizing these distinctions. The range of comedy in the theatre demonstrates this, passing from hostile wit and practical joking to romance and sympathetic festivity; from obscenity to nonsense; from satirical criticism, to ironic indulgence. The parameters of such distinctions are artistic ones and therefore do not usually figure in experimental work on humour. They are, briefly: the presence or absence of empathy; the degree of taboo-violation; and the presence or absence of an implied moral comment or criticism. From an artistic point of view, these parameters should be used to gauge the humour of a particular joke, or of a comic incident, or, cumulatively, of the sequence of incidents and jokes which make up an evening's entertainment, whether it be in the theatre, on film, or on television.

JOKING AND FARCE

Introduction to Farce

Of all types of comedy, farce is regarded as the simplest. It is also the oldest and most popular form, which pre-dated Athenian Old Comedy of the fifth century B.C. and which has flourished in most ages of the European theatre. It survived brilliantly the transition first from the theatre to the film, and then from the silent film to the talking movie. The materials of farce may be found in all comedy, used for many different kinds of humour in, for example, Molière, in Shakespeare, in Chekhov, in the Theatre of the Absurd and in the Flying Circus of Monty Python. But at its simplest, farce is merely the theatrical form of practical joking. It is that form of comedy which depends upon visual acting out of its jokes and not upon their expression in distanced and witty dialogue. It is therefore the most directly aggressive comic form, using both physical violence and scatological joking. It is not highly regarded by literary critics, although any man of the theatre will tell you that it is characterized by extreme discipline, both in its construction and in its acting. It is a very difficult genre in which to succeed. It is this aspect which has struck me most forcibly in my studies of farce: that the most aggressive, the most atavistic form of comedy is also the most rigid in its internal rules.

Measuring the Humour of Farce

If we apply the artistic parameters I have postulated to farce, the genre falls more on the side of hostile and aggressive joking than on that of festive romance (although the two are by no means mutually exclusive); on the side of taboo-violation rather than on that of mere nonsense-humour (although nonsense for the sheer fun of it is not entirely excluded); but, on the side of an ironic acceptance of human frailty, rather than on the side of social satire. When farce, with its violence and obscenity, leans towards a serious comment upon its targets, it passes into social satire and risks a diminution of laughter and the gradual awakening of a social conscience. The result may be social outrage, as, for example, in the famous case of Molière's 'Tartuffe', in which the satirical message about religious hypocrisy is too strong to be ignored.

FARCE AND ITS LICENCE

It is nevertheless surprising what farce is able to get away with. In Imperial Rome, where a father held power of life and death over his household, Plautus chose as his most consistent farce-theme the deception and humiliation of miserly old fathers, cheated out of their money by their rebellious son and his wily slave. The audience's reaction was apparently laughter. In mediaeval Europe, where wives were chattels and the word of the Church was law, the French farces and German 'Fastnachtspiele' celebrated the triumph of wife over husband, often with the assistance of a philandering priest. During the century of Victoria's reign, London audiences amused themselves with the spectacle of respectable gentlefolk passing the night under suspicious circumstances in seedy hotels, or dining apart from their spouses in private rooms, while their adolescent sons made passes at the maids.

In effect, farce-plots abound in taboo-violations and in violence: sons deceive their fathers, slaves terrify their master, wives maltreat their husbands and vice-versa, magistrates suffer at the hands of their own police-officers, trousers are removed, limbs torn off, food, drink and even shit is flung, and every conceivable weapon of attack, from fisticuffs to cannon-balls and steamrollers, is brought into play. What is the secret of this privileged licence which allows farce freely to admit the animality and egotism of human nature without offence to even the most strictly 'civilized' of societies? If it does not disguise its hostility behind a highly-wrought literary facade, what are its artistic techniques?

BRIEF DESCRIPTION OF FARCE TECHNIQUES

Festive Licence

All comedy shares a festive element; an audience enters the theatre in an expectant state of willingness to be entertained which prepares it to take the comedy 'as a joke' and not as the materials of a tragedy. It is understood that this period of indulgence will be limited to the duration of the evening's entertainment. Within a farce itself, however, the licence extended to the rebels and jokers is of a similarly limited nature. Farce-plots display a fundamental movement towards restoration of the authority figures under attack and towards a reconciliation between the warring camps, no matter how superficial it is. The period of revelry is thus no serious challenge to normal social order.

Mechanical Plotting

Even within the licensed period of rebellion, balancing devices distribute the aggression amongst a series of competing victims. The roles of jokester, victim and audience circulate among the characters of a farce and neither side can be quite certain of his triumph until the final turn of the story. The theme of 'the robber robbed', or the social outcast on whom the tables are turned with a vengeance, is the simplest form of this kind of balance. A fully circular movement is displayed in 'Le Tre Becchi': each of three husbands takes the stage in turn as the triumphant cuckolder of his neighbour, only to be exposed in the next sequence as an irate victim. In 'Les Boulingrin' there is a skilful example of the 'quarrel-farce', in which the balance of aggression directed between two partners is so exact that the two are locked into an equilibrium which can only be broken by an external representative of sanity. In 'Les Boulingrin', this figure merely becomes the victim of an escalating snowball of violence.

Type-Characterization

The predictability created by mechanical patterning of events in farce is reinforced by the recognizability of the characters. They are comic types, not complex psychological beings and are repeated from one play to another. They are rigid because each is identified with his role and thus with a fixed motivation which drives him forward, denying him the flexibility to adapt to changing circumstances and even preventing the luxury of self-awareness. Type-characters and mechanical plots mesh perfectly: the clash of rigidities between types motivates the plot, which in turn imposes its balanced patterns. The impression is often created that only a temporary truce has been declared and that battle will erupt again in the next episode, where we are likely to find Gilles, for example, infuriating Arlequin with yet another piece of inconvenient bestiality. This power of type-characters to create an illusion of their existence beyond a brief stage-appearance is one of the most appealing aspects of farce, as anyone who is a devotee of Monty Python will admit.

Stylization of Acting

The presentation of such puppetry requires a special mode if the actor is to hold his audience's attention. The distance between what is 'normal' for the audience and what is normal for the characters on stage must be signalled by what is called 'stylization'. Type-characters are essentially theatrical and larger-than-life: they deal in extremes of behaviour and gesticulation, not in introspection and instrumental action. The messages of stylized acting are as broad as the characterization and since there is no need for subtlety, they are mediated principally through the actor's body and not through his face. It is for this reason that the wearing of masks is often associated with farce. The actor becomes an embodiment of his type and its dominant rigidity; he communicates through gesticulation, through mime and through body-language which is so disciplined that it often extends to acrobatics. The result is that he treads a borderline between the living and the inanimate, presenting a character who is governed by conventions so unlike our own that we can only classify him as dehumanized, although his traits are only too human and familiar.

Stylization also permits the actor to signal suspension of some or all of the laws of nature regarding physical and mental suffering on the part of his character. The speed of action can either be accelerated or retarded, especially when approaching a climax. If the pace increases with the level of violence, neither the characters nor the audience are permitted the leisure to reflect upon the effects of each blow; if it slows down, a general air of unreality pervades the scene. The snowball of violence which gathers in 'The Boulingrin Family' explodes during a total blackout, in which the normal visual linkage between activity and sound is destroyed. The opposite kind of dissociation characterizes farce in the silent movie, where blows are seen to fall without sound, or are received by the victims without apparent effect. The actor's sensory perception may even be reversed, so that as one critic puts it, 'prongs of the rake in the backside are received as pinpricks' (Bentley, 1974), while pinpricks produce wails of pain. This kind of distortion of normal cause and effect carries over to the emotional responses of the characters, producing absurdly inverted reactions to serious and trivial events. Such effects are the chief reason for labelling farce as fantastic.

Farce and Obscenity

Rabelaisian jokes about the three basic needs of the body -- for comfort, food and sex -- provide a realistic counterpoint to the extreme stylization of farce. These puppets, we observe, are in the grip of the same human condition that is common to us all. They struggle against social rules; against each other; against the independent wills of their children, servants and spouses; against the unpredictable nature of what should be predictable; against machines of which they should be the master; against unlucky coincidences; and, above all, they struggle against the inconvenient tendency of the body to assert its needs at the worst possible time.

In this sense, farce is more realistic than society, daring to assert that obnoxious people deserve to be fooled; that neighbours enjoy hating each other; that husbands and wives deceive, torment, and even shoot at each other; and that we are more preoccupied with satisfying the basic wants of our bodies than with seeking the higher refinements of affection and a purposeful life. Aspiration, in farce, is a joke. As an audience, we laugh and admit the justice of the observation.

SUMMARY: FARCE AND THE PARAMETERS OF HUMOUR

Empathy and Taboo-Violation

Given the combination of type-characterization, stylized acting and mechanical plots, it is difficult for the audience in farce to feel a deep sympathy for puppets who lack more than an elementary self-awareness and who are certainly incapable of controlling or altering their nature. When, for example, the merchant in 'Le Merchand de Merde' mourns his fate, smeared with his own merchandise and spurned by his lady-friend, our laughter may be touched ever so lightly with pity; but that is all. For the parasitical des Rillettes, the victim of a humiliation that arrives by misdirection, rather than by deliberate aim, sympathy is even less possible: he is after all responsible for choosing to remain in the line of fire. Sympathy is more likely in the case of those who are true representatives of the life-force and we may well feel more for the young wife, Cintia and her lover than for old Pantalone, as he is clasped to the ample bosom of the washer-woman. By and large, farce is hostile in its joking. Such an attitude is reinforced by the fact that the taboo-violations take place in direct and physical forms, which require, even more than verbal obscenities, that the audience be distanced from the events on stage. On these two scales, therefore, farce registers hostile and dangerous.

Moral Comment

In this case, it is clear that farce studiously avoids any implication of a need to change social rules or human behaviour. In its acceptance of limits to a period of indulgence, and in its movements to distribute humiliation equally and to restore conventional authorities, farce is essentially conservative. At the same time, it manages to be extraordinarily tolerant of the devilry which motivates its leading characters and is most realistic about the causes of their downfall. Our three cuckolds are not punished for their adultery, but for their vanity and sheer blockheadedness in boasting about their triumphs while leaving their own wives unattended.

The view-point of farce is that of realpolitik: to those who can use them go the spoils; to the young and eager go the triumphs of sex; to the old, and the timid, the frustrations; to the slow-witted, defeat; to the clever, the temporary advantage; but to the powerful, finally, the right of victory. If farce is tendentious joking, its subversion is limited to a sharing of the open secret that we are all sadly no better than we should be.

REFERENCES

See Bibliography for publications on humour, laughter and comedy

Bentley, E., The Life of the Drama. Atheneum, New York (1974).

Uses and Abuses of Canned Laughter

Ray Fuller

Trinity College, Dublin

Although the term canned laughter (CL) could be used to refer to the exuberant mirthful outbursts of the inebriated, its more conventional use is for prerecordings of laughter which are edited onto comedy material that has been recorded in the absence of a live audience. Apart from this application in the television and radio industry, prerecorded tapes of laughter have also been used in a variety of psychological experiments, principally to determine whether laughter per se is capable of modifying subjects' overt expressions of mirth and/or their evaluations of the funniness of the material to which the CL has been added. Such studies do not simply have a practical relevance in evaluating the effects of the broadcaster's use of CL but may also throw light on the relationship between overt mirth and humour judgements.

The most reliable effect of adding CL to humorous materials is an increase in subjects' overt expressions of mirth. Thus CL increases the frequency of laughs (Nosanchuk & Lightstone, 1974; Smyth & Fuller, 1972), the duration of laughs (Smyth & Fuller, 1972) and scores on a mirth scale which measure both smiles and laughs (Chapman, 1973a; Cupchik & Leventhal, 1974; Fuller & Sheehy-Skeffington, 1974; Leventhal & Mace, 1970). The reliability of this effect is perhaps all the more remarkable when one considers that the humorous materials used have included a slapstick movie, recordings of professional comedians, jokes, slides of cartoons and even materials rated as non-humorous by independent subjects. Furthermore, the nature of the CL has also varied markedly between experiments including tapes of laughter used in broadcasting by dubbing editors, recordings of a group of eighteen students asked to laugh consistently at the end of a joke and laughter recorded at a party. The effect has also been found to occur in subjects tested individually with the experimenter present and in subjects tested alone but under the impression that other subjects could hear their audible humour responses (Nosanchuk & Lightstone, 1974). Various forms of CL, then, are associated with increased overt expressions of mirth under a wide variety of experimental conditions.

Adding CL to various materials is associated also with increased evaluations of the funniness of those materials, but the effect is not quite so reliable as for smiles and laughs. Although in all eight studies under review some increase in funniness ratings in the CL condition has been observed, this has not always been statistically significant (e.g., Chapman, 1973a), has not applied to certain combinations of subjects and materials or instructions (see below) and in one experiment a significant decrease in ratings was found for male high school subjects who were categorized as having high mirth levels while watching a control film (Leventhal & Mace, 1970).

Cupchik and Leventhal (1974) found no effects of CL on funniness ratings by male subjects rating high quality cartoons or by females asked to attend to their own overt expressions of amusement during the experiment. Nosanchuk and Lightstone (1974) added to this list by reporting that a low level of CL added to a high humour joke also had no effect on ratings.

If one can make any general statements at all about the effects of CL on ratings of humorous and other material, and the vast differences in experimental procedures makes that a most precarious exercise, it appears that under certain conditions CL may enhance funniness ratings of both sexes for both high (Fuller & Sheehy-Skeffington, 1974; Smyth & Fuller, 1972) and low humour material (Fuller & Sheehy-Skeffington, 1974; Nosanchuk & Lightstone, 1974) but that the effect is more reliable in females (Cupchik & Leventhal, 1974; Leventhal & Cupchik, 1975), low mirth males (Leventhal & Mace, 1970), males rating poor quality materials and low mirth males rating poor quality materials (Cupchik & Leventhal, 1974). Thus one might predict that the strongest effects of CL on ratings would be where the audience was predominantly female or, if not, where the humorous material itself was not very funny and the males present were not particularly disposed to laugh anyway.

It is not surprising that these different observations of the effects of CL have led authors
to provide a range of different explanations. Thus where CL has increased mirth scores but
not ratings it has been suggested that CL is a funny thing in itself (Chapman, 1973a),
especially where it is seen as incongruous (Sheehy-Skeffington, 1973); or that laughter
rather than evaluation is more vulnerable to social pressures to conform (Chapman, 1973a);
or that necessary and sufficient conditions for laughter are elevated arousal and a humour
stimulus and that CL elevates arousal (for evidence consistent with this see Cantor, Bryant
& Zillmann, 1974; Chapman, 1975b; Morrison, 1940; Schachter & Wheeler, 1962; Young &
Frye, 1966); or that the overt expression of mirth is normally inhibited but CL disinhibits
it (Chapman, 1973a, and see also Young & Frye, 1966); or that laughter is an Unconditioned
or Conditioned Stimulus for laughter (Foot, Smith & Chapman, 1975; Sheehy-Skeffington, 1973).
Alternatively one might simply characterize smiling and laughter as essentially nonverbal
communicative acts which provide feedback to others about one's current state. Thus if
amused one is more likely to exhibit this in a group context than when alone (see Chapman,
1975b), unless aversive consequences would be a result, and CL simply provides an artificial
group context for humour expression.

Where CL has increased both mirth scores and ratings of funniness, authors have suggested,
in conjunction with one or more of most of the above hypotheses, that subjects' ratings
conformed either to the implicit evaluation of others represented by the CL (Nosanchuk &
Lightstone, 1974; Smyth & Fuller, 1972) or to the evaluation implied by their own expressions
of mirth which were increased with CL (Cupchik & Leventhal, 1974; Leventhal & Cupchik, 1975;
Smyth & Fuller, 1972). These latter authors, in line with Leventhal and Mace (1970), have
suggested further that this effect may be one of cognitive dissonance reduction or simply
persuasion due to exposure to one's own actions.

However, despite these brave attempts at explanation for the correlated increase in mirth
scores and ratings with CL, the finding of Young and Frye (1966) and Chapman (1973a) that
overt expressions of mirth can be manipulated without changes in evaluations makes it
possible to conclude that subjects do not necessarily use either their own laughter or an
implicit group appraisal in rating humorous materials. It has been argued elsewhere by
Fuller (1974) and by Fuller and Sheehy-Skeffington (1974) that CL and more generally the
laughter of others may act rather as a cue which directs the listener or viewer to search
for a humorous interpretation of whatever is associated with the laughter, prompting the
perceiver to see the 'funny side' of things. Thus with CL present the attention of subjects
may be focussed on missing aspects of humour stimuli (Tolman, 1968) and in the more extreme
case subjects may interpret a stimulus as humorous, and laugh more, even if the stimulus
itself is not intentionally funny.

This hypothesis is consistent with the general conclusion that in the humour situation cues
are important which facilitate a fantasy rather than a reality mode of assimilation (Berlyne,
1972; McGhee, 1971b, 1972b), a conclusion substantiated by the work of Martin (1905) who
found that pre-exposure to silly or funny pictures enhanced the reported amusement for
subsequently presented humour while pre-exposure to serious or sad pictures reduced it.
Cues to fantasy assimilate appear to be well established in professional comedy. The circus
clown sports a traditional costume and style of make-up which strongly dispose us to see
only the funny side of his antics, even though the same behaviour in a different context
might be quite distressing. Comedians have adopted similar and other cues which dispose us
to perceive humour rather than take their words or actions seriously, including frequent
grinning and even accompanying their own performances with bursts of laughter. And of
course most people when they tell a joke provide an appropriate set by saying things like,
'Did you hear the one about...' and 'A funny thing happened to me on the way to the...'

If this interpretation of the effects of CL on ratings of humorous material is correct then
it could be predicted that CL would be most effective in situations where no set to perceive
humour had been established. This does indeed appear to be the case. In studies which
provided no set (e.g., Fuller & Sheehy-Skeffington, 1974; Smyth & Fuller, 1972) CL produced
unambiguous increases in ratings; in studies which initially established a set, no
significant effect of CL on ratings was found (e.g., Chapman, 1973a) or reduced effects were
recorded (e.g., Cupchik & Leventhal, 1974) or the effect obtained only in low mirth subjects
or to intrinsically low humour material (e.g., Cupchik & Leventhal, 1974; Leventhal & Mace,
1970; Nosanchuk & Lightstone, 1974). It might also be predicted that the effect of CL
would decrease over trials once a humour set was established and this has also been found
in the one experiment where it has been examined (Cupchik & Leventhal, 1974), but for some
unknown reason the effect applied only to males. However, despite this and other
interpretations of the effects of CL, critical experiments have yet to be carried out.

The use of CL in the television and radio industry is often criticised because it sounds
awkward and inappropriate and some stations have even dispensed with its use as a matter of
policy. This state of affairs reflects more the frequent abuse of CL rather than questions
the merit of CL per se. However, it is worth emphasizing that whenever the use of CL sounds
unnatural the implication is that overt group responses to humorous events have characteristics

which are sufficiently regular to enable us to formulate expectations about them and recognize when these expectations have not been realised.   Clearly this aspect of the humour process warrants further attention and in particular the determination of the precise relationships between various categories or qualities of humour stimuli and characteristics of the overt humour response.

The functional abuse of CL has been explored in a preliminary study by Pollio, Mers and Lucchesi (1972) which used a thirty-minute recording of the television programme 'I Love Lucy'. The authors were interested in determining whether there were identifiable differences in the properties of CL as used in the programme compared with naturally occurring group laughter. They found no correlation between duration and amplitude in the CL whereas the laughter of live audiences was found to have a correlation between these variables of between 0.47 and 0.67. They also found marked differences between CL and live laughter in latency following punchlines. The modal values for the CL were between zero and 330 msec and for live laughter between 660 and 1000 msec. Furthermore, the distribution of latencies for CL approximated a reversed J-shape whereas for live laughter the latency distribution approximated a normal curve. Pollio et al concluded that the distribution of latencies for CL were rather like a distribution of simple reaction times, and probably did indeed reflect the psychomotor performance of the dubbing editor.

It was also noted in this study that the shape of the curve relating amplitude to time for CL was highly regular whereas for live audience laughter it took on a variety of forms which the authors called early, middle and late 'risers'. Finally it was observed that in the CL film a no-sound period frequently preceded the CL whereas with live audiences there was always some non-laugh-related sound occurring during this period.

Clearly, if CL is to be used effectively it should replicate as closely as possible the characteristics of a live audience and be more or less indiscriminable from it. Pollio et al have identified some characteristics which may be important. However, detailed specifications for dubbing editors await a systematic research investment and until that occurs they will still have to rely largely on their own intuitions.

The implications of this research for the CL studies reviewed earlier are important because those studies employed a striking variety of CL sources and procedures for incorporating CL with humorous material. How realistic each use of CL actually was appears to have depended on the whim of each experimenter and is rarely discussed in the experimental reports. However, in the light of the observations of Pollio et al on latency of real group laughter one might be forgiven for being a little suspicious of the technique used by Cupchik and Leventhal (1974) who reported that their CL always followed the spoken caption to projected slides of cartoons by 200 msec.

Apart from functional abuse, CL could be used somewhat unethically by dubbing it onto material which was originally serious in intent, such as recorded interviews with ministers, politicians, clerics and so on. Although the effects of adding CL to such materials have not been studied experimentally, a television demonstration of the effects of CL on non-humorous materials in the Republic of Ireland, which used two recorded interviews with politicians as examples, produced a derisive reaction in the studio audience and was reported in the national press as a 'send up' of the two politicians involved. Minutes after the item the television station switchboard was jammed with over 700 protest calls and the programme producer faced a row with the journalists who had carried out the interviews in good faith. This anecdotal evidence provides an indication that CL could be used unethically to ridicule public figures as well as confirming that CL can direct the attention of the listener to a humorous interpretation of otherwise serious material.

In conclusion, it is worth emphasizing to humour researchers that CL provides a highly flexible technique for exploring group laughter as an independent variable and for eliciting reliable increases in the frequency of smiling and laughter in experimental subjects. To professional programme editors it must be admitted that we simply do not yet know enough about how to use CL effectively. However, it does have the potential to enhance comedy programmes by boosting mirth reactions and perceived funniness, effects which could surely be described as worthwhile.

REFERENCES

See Bibliography for publications on humour, laughter and comedy

Foot, H.C., Smith, J.R. & Chapman, A.J., Investigating social aspects of children's laughter. Paper presented at the Annual Conference of the British Psychological Society, Nottingham, April (1975).

Fuller, R.G.C., Effects of group laughter on responses to material of varied humour content. Paper presented at the Annual Conference of the British Psychological Society, Bangor, April (1974).

Sheehy-Skeffington, A., An investigation of some determinants of the humour response. Unpublished Bachelor's thesis, University of Dublin (1973).

Tolman, C.W., The role of the companion in the social facilitation of animal behaviour. In: E.C. Simmel, R.A. Hoppe & G.A. Milton (Eds.), Social Facilitation and Imitative Behavior. Allyn & Bacon, Boston (1968).

Funny Ha Ha or Funny Peculiar

Anthony Buffery

Institute of Psychiatry, University of London

```
(The Speaker is a tall, curly-haired, male neuropsychologist with an eye-patch).

Professor Chairperson Junior, Doctors, M.A.s, B.A.s, Ladies and Gentlemen....B.Sc.s and
Students.
Professor Chairperson Junior, Doctors, M.A.s, B.A.s, Ladies and Gentleman....B.Sc.s and
Students.

Had the Convenors of this the International Conference on Humour and Laughter,
Had the Convenors of this the International Conference on Humour and Laughter,

Doctors Chapman and Foot,
Doctors Chapman and Foot,

realized that I suffer from a rare, nay unique,
realized that I suffer from a rare, nay unique,

speech disorder,
speech disorder,

I feel sure that they would not have invited me
I feel sure that they would not have invited me

to speak,
to speak,

but they didn't so they did so thats
but they didn't so they did so thats

that.
that.

My speech disorder is called
My speech disorder is called

Echolia.
Echolia.

I say things twice,
I say things twice,

or, if I shout,
or, if I shout,

thrice (shouted).
thrice (normal).
thrice (whispered).

Though listeners are all too aware of my speech disorder
Though listeners are all too aware of my speech disorder

I am not.
I am not.
```

People have told me about it
People have told me about it

but to no avail.
but to no avail.

My formal address will be boring enough
My formal address will be boring enough

and does not bear
and does not bear

repetition.
repetition.

Consequently, I'm afraid that you, my audience, are going to become very bored,
Consequently, I'm afraid that you, my audience, are going to become very bored,

all of you that is except for
all of you that is except for

my grandmother
my grandmother

who is unable to be with us this evening,
who is unable to be with us this evening,

and even if she could be with us is mercifully deaf
and even if she could be with us is mercifully deaf

and dead
and dead

and has been for the past twenty-nine years.
and has been for the past twenty-nine years.

Echolia is a congenital abnormality
Echolia is a congenital abnormality

found only in tall, curly-haired, male one-eyed neuropsychologists,
found only in tall, curly-haired, male one-eyed neuropsychologists,

so that lets me out (the Speaker removed the eye patch to reveal a second normal eye –
a long pause during which the Speaker looks much relieved – but...)

so that lets me out.

Who said that?
Who said that?

Me?
Me?

So much for miracle cures.
So much for miracle cures.

By the way occasionally I do not repeat precisely what I have just said,

Sometimes I do not say exactly the same thing twice,

Though the meaning is more or less the same.

but the sense is similar.

This usually immediately precedes a cessation of echolia (there is a silence followed by a
sigh of relief from the Speaker).

but it also usually immediately precedes some other form of speech disorder such as
stam.........mering or stutt... stutt... stutt... stutt... stuttering or even complete
amnesia (the Speaker develops a dazed look and then a blank expression. He then says, as if
for the first time.....)

Professor Chairperson, Doctors, M.A.s, B.A.s, Ladies and Gentlemen..... B.Sc.s and Students. My formal address to this the International Conference on Humour and Laughter has a title somewhat simpler than those preceding it:

> 'Sex differences in the ontogeny and phylogeny of the neuropsychological development
> of verbal and non-verbal cathartic codes in solitary, dyadic and group interaction:
> towards a heuristic theory of client-centred merriment (Jolly Rogers) Part I.
> Contextual Arousal Schemata.'

This study is inspired by the first paper ever to be presented to the British Psychological Society (Sully, 1902).*

A funny thing happened to me on my way to the Conference, and I am using the word 'funny' in the sense of both 'ha ha' and 'peculiar'.

(During the recounting of the following 'adventure' on British Rail the Speaker notices that his pulse is weak, perhaps even stopped! He searches for other pulses and eventually feels his chest for a heartbeat - all to no avail. Towards the end of the 'adventure' the Speaker jumps on top of the table before him, rolls up his right trouser leg and reveals a pulsating right knee-cap painted with a red heart - 'Ace of Hearts'. Much pleased he climbs down and continues with his formal address rather than his informal undress.)

On leaving Paddington for Cardiff I found myself in a British Rail restaurant car seated opposite a passenger who was hidden behind a copy of the Times. The passenger in question was wearing what I took to be a pair of fur gloves. It was only later, when I was hiding beneath the table to avoid paying a monstrous bill for an indifferent luncheon and noticed that the passenger in question was also wearing what I took to be a pair of fur boots, that I realized that the passenger in question was without question a coypu. A coypu is an aquatic rodent native of South America immigrant to East Anglia. A coypu is rather like a large rat or small horse. Now until that moment I hadn't realized that a coypu could read. I knew that they glanced at the Beano and occasionally page 3 of The Sun but for a coypu to have completed two-thirds of The Times Crossword struck me, and indeed continues to strike me, as somewhat surprising. The coypu on hearing my gasp of amazement put down The Times and proceeded to squat with me beneath the table. He... for I could see that the coypu was male from his long brown cigar.... he then spoke to me in a soft, slow coypu-like voice.

> 'I say, I say, I say
> stop me if you've heard it,
> Do you know the one about...'

We then entered upon the following routine.

> 'What is it that hangs on a wall, is green and whistles?'
> 'I don't know; what is it that hangs on a wall, is green and whistles?'
> 'A kipper.'
> 'A kipper doesn't hang on a wall.'
> 'You can hang it on a wall, can't you?'
> 'A kipper isn't green.'
> 'You can paint it green can't you?'
> 'But a kipper doesn't whistle.'
> 'Alright! alright! so it doesn't whistle.'

With that the disgruntled coypu jumped out of the window leaving me to pay not only for my luncheon but also for his cigar. Coypus have never been noted for good manners.

So much for the historical introduction and review of the literature. Now let me move on to the experimental evidence for sex differences in the ontogeny and phylcgeny of the neuropsychological development of verbal and non-verbal cathartic codes in solitary, dyadic and group interaction, and towards a heuristic theory of client-centred merriment (Jolly Rogers) Part I. Contextual arousal schemata.

My first slide (the Speaker snaps his fingers as if to signal the projectionist) must be studied most carefully as it is rather small (the Speaker produces a 2 x 2 inch slide from his breast pocket and holds it up to the light) in fact very, very tiny indeed. The ordinate is human heart rate per minute and the abscissa human laughter as measured by a laughometer - a laughometer being a device for measuring laughter. Notice the inverted-U curve - proving conclusively that for someone to have either zero heart beats per minute or 3,000 heart beats per minute is no laughing matter. Optimum heart rate correlates with optimum laughter; therefore heart rate equals laughter and laughter is heart rate - we live to laugh and vice versa, so much for the hard data.

My next slide (the Speaker produces a 'hair slide') is a German skier!

---

* Sully, J., The evolution of laughter. Proceedings of the Psychological Society, February 15th (1902). (Cited in The British Journal of Psychology, Volume 1, Part 1, p116, January, 1904).

My third slide (the Speaker produces another 2 x 2 inch slide) is of my mother-in-law on holiday. It looks as if she is holding up the Leaning Tower of Pisa. She is not, of course, but merely pretending to do so - which was a pity because the tower fell and crushed mother-in-law to pieces. I have one of her pieces here in my pocket (the Speaker searches himself but without luck). Sorry it must be in the suit I sent to the cleaners...UGH!

My last slide (the Speaker produces a slide-rule) provides the statistical analysis for my data and shows a sex difference of 'basically about four inches' - thus replicating the findings of a recent advertisement for The Metropolitan Police entitled 'What's the difference between a policeman and a policewoman?'

Talking about the police reminds me that much has been said at this Conference about transgression of taboo as a source of tension reduction and thence laughter. Let me now give a demonstration of taboo transgression induced laughter or, to put it more scientifically, TTIL. (The Speaker picks up a newspaper and a plastic bottle with a 'squirting' spout, similar to that used for dampening linen prior to ironing). In this bottle is a very mild acid, sulphuric I think (the Speaker touches the nozzle and the 'acid' apparently burns him) well quite mild, perhaps more medium to strong than mild per se, let us say strongish sulphuric acid. Now, if I squirt a little of this strongish sulphuric acid onto this copy of The Times .. (the Speaker does so and exhibits the obviously charred newspaper which, in fact, he had prepared unbeknown to the audience in the Gentlemen's lavatory with the help of a borrowed cigarette lighter). So much for the coypu's crossword. Taboo transgression would occur, however, if I squirted the strongish sulphuric acid over people rather than a newspaper, over you for example (the Speaker squirts the audience with the 'acid' - several people scream then laugh on discovering the 'acid' to be water). Behold TTIL! When attempting to replicate this experiment it is important to remember to use water and not, repeat NOT, sulphuric acid. The control condition using sulphuric acid, though methodologically sound, is ethically dubious and, I can assure you from my own personal experience, simply ruins carpets. So don't do it - unless of course you happen to have a captive audience of coypus.

Each of you now has a smile on your face because you think that I did not transgress the taboo of wiping a smile off your face by wiping off your face. My audiences usually think like that, they desperately need to believe that tragedy is comedy, that death is life, that acid is water - well it was in fact acid, but I'm probably lying ... probably, so I will not say anything else - except don't leave anything behind in the auditorium ... particularly fingers, and be sure to count your ears before you go to bed.

Finally, Professor Chairperson, Doctors, M.A.s, B.A.s, Ladies and Gentlemen..... B.Sc.s and Students, I had hoped to attempt a new world record of weightlifting but unfortunately (the Speaker squirms as if kicked below the belt) I have misplaced by dumb-bells. Instead let me leave you with this thought -

(the Speaker takes on a pensive pose - a long pause - then again the Speaker cannot find his pulse, but this time when he rolls up his right trouser leg the 'Ace of Hearts' knee-cap shows only a dysrhythmic twitch. Eventually it stops completely and in mounting desperation the Speaker rolls up his left trouser leg only to reveal a knee-cap painted with a motionless 'Ace of Spades' - the death card. In horror and utterly doomed the Speaker exits holding up both trouser legs and muttering something about, 'I haven't a leg to stand on', and 'coypus go home!')

ACKNOWLEDGEMENTS

This study was supported by grants from the M.R.C. (Multidisciplinary Research on Coypus), the S.S.R.C. (Silly Science Research Council), and the Co-op (dividend number 58872).

The data, which were lifted from the unpublished thesis of Hugo Beltempo, Universita di Bologna, were first presented at the International Conference on Dichotic Listening (Hear, Hear) and have been submitted for publication to the Quarterly Journal of Tachistoscopic Exposure (Flash!).

I am pleased to acknowledge the guidance in inebriation from Jack Durac, the squirting spout of Mrs. Roselyn Clark and help with the mortgage from her husband Peter.

The following refused to have anything to do with my research; Winifred, George, Rosalind, Kenneth, Bill, Liz, Kate, Alice, Jo, Lucy, Jennifer, Joanna and Ian Buffery...... not to mention Miss Anna Faith Wright, but I promised not to mention Miss Anna Faith Wright.

I humbly dedicate this work to the one man who can analyze the deep structure of sign language in non-human primates... Professor No-name Chimpsky.

Humour as a System of Communication

Arthur Asa Berger

San Francisco State University

Humour was described in terms of its being a kind of communication. A model was presented
which shows A, the creator of the humour (the sender); B, the information sent (the content);
C, the audience (the receiver); D, how it is transmitted (the medium); E, the kind of
humour (the form); F, the methods employed (the techniques, taken from a list of forty-five
provided); X, the consequences (the effects) and Y, the purposes the humour serves (the
functions). A structuralist analysis of a joke was made, listing the elements of the jokes
serially (a syntagmic analysis) and expanding the meaning via eliciting bi-polar oppositions
found in the joke (a paradigmatic analysis). It was suggested that humour is generated by
the punchline when a switch from the syntagmic structure to the paradigmatic one is suddenly
effected. Helping disentangle the various elements in a joke, and in humour in general,
helps us understand what it is and how it works.

FURTHER STUDIES ON HUMOUR
AND LAUGHTER

INDIVIDUAL PAPERS

Favourite Jokes of Children and Their Dynamic Relation to Intra-Familial Conflicts

Atalay Yörükoğlu

Hacettepe University, Turkey

INTRODUCTION

Freud (1928) viewed humour as a basic mechanism of adaptation to human suffering. He stressed that in humour the ego turns away from harsh reality and enjoys a partial return to a guilt-free narcissistic existence of childhood. The momentary escape from the control of the superego gives one a feeling of strength. As he stated: 'Humour signifies the triumph not only of the ego but also of the pleasure principle'.

In his book, Freud (1960) examined in detail the various forms of humour and elucidated their psychodynamic meanings: in short, jokes disguise the unconscious tendencies and afford an outlet for them. In jokes, as in dreams, conflicting tendencies are expressed in a condensed and masked form. However, in a successful joke, unlike in dreams, the unconscious tendency remains intelligible and it can be perceived by the listener. A play on words, or 'wit-work' as Freud termed it, serves to remove repression and suppression. Thus forbidden impulses escape censorship and are expressed in a socially acceptable way. Laughter occurs when the energy no longer needed to repress forbidden impulses and painful affects is discharged suddenly. As Freud noted: 'The resultant pleasure corresponds to the economy of psychic expenditure'.

On the basis of Freud's contributions humour constitutes an important key to the understanding of dynamic forces within the personality. By studying a person's humour appreciation much can be said not only about his inner conflicts, but also about his ego-resiliency with which he copes with them. If the dream is the royal road to the unconscious, humour certainly is the most enjoyable path leading to the human psyche.

The use of favourite jokes, as shown by the studies of Brill (1940), Zwerling (1955) and Yörükoğlu (1974) can be a productive approach in detecting the unconscious conflicts of emotionally disturbed adults as well as children.

In my diagnostic and therapeutic interviews, school-age children are encouraged to tell the 'favourite', 'funniest' or 'best' joke they have ever heard or read. It is ascertained that the joke is not a recently heard one. If the joke is a 'last joke heard' then the child is asked to remember the best joke he heard before. The favourite joke is written down exactly as it is narrated by the 'child-patient'. After he tells the joke, he is asked what strikes him as funny about the joke. This favourite joke is then analyzed dynamically in the light of family history, patient's personality and psychopathology; thus, the favourite joke is used as an adjunctive tool of evaluation. The favourite joke can be discussed with the patient as soon as he reports it, or it may be brought up at an appropriate time in a subsequent session. It may also be discussed with the parents, provided that the patient gives his/her consent.

The present report is a continuation of a previously published study on the same subject and it focuses only on those favourite jokes of children with emotional problems that are related to intra-familial conflicts. In the following case vignettes, the psychodynamic relationship between the child's favourite joke and intra-familial conflicts, is illustrated. The utilization of favourite joke in psychotherapy with children as well as their parents is discussed.

CASE EXAMPLES

Case 1

Ozden, a boy of eleven years and the elder of two sons in a family, was brought to the clinic because of various facial tics. He was described as an affectionate boy who was very much attached to his mother. The mother, although seemingly annoyed at his clinging, still helped him to get dressed and fed him at every meal. After school she kept him home and did not allow him to mingle with his peers. The mother complained of carrying the burden of the entire family. Her husband, a very passive and quiet man, worked in his father's shop. He would come home in the evening, eat his meal, pick-out a detective story and read it until bedtime. He hardly spoke a word unless asked a direct question. Although he was very soft-hearted, he did not seem to show any interest in his sons' upbringing. The paternal grandfather lived in the same house and was respected and feared by everybody. The mother had difficulty in bringing the father to the clinic because meeting strangers was such an ordeal for him. Finally, when she managed to bring him to one of the interviews, he turned out to be exactly the way his wife pictured him. He spoke in a soft voice and answered briefly only the questions posed to him. Throughout the hour he avoided looking the therapist in the eye.

In the interview the patient proved himself to be an intelligent but very immature boy. Almost all of his responses to the picture story test dealt with separation anxiety. One ran as follows: 'A young man wants to go to a big city. He heads for the railroad station. He turns and looks at his home for the last time. By doing this he misses the train and has to come back home. Everybody makes fun of him because he missed the train. But his family is also glad to see him back, because his parents did not want him to go away in the first place!' In this story the patient's ambivalent feelings regarding the separation from the family are clearly expressed. When asked to tell his favourite joke he related the following:

> An old man was crying. A passer-by asked him what he was crying for. He said,
> 'My father spanked me'. Astonished, the man asked him again: 'How old is your
> father?' 'He is one hundred years old'. 'Why did he spank you?' The old man
> replied: 'Because I stuck my tongue out to my Grandpa!'

The dependent relationship between grandfather, father and the grandson is reflected in this joke in a striking way. Figuratively speaking, in this case, the immaturity and dependency seem to run in the family! Upon hearing the joke the therapist responded with laughter and remarked that it was as if this joke were made up to show their situation at home. The patient smiled and acknowledged the similarity. Since the father never came back the joke was made use of in the interviews with the mother to modify her overprotective attitide toward her son. With the help of the patient's favourite joke the mother began to realize that she has been discouraging her son from being more independent.

Case 2

Sevim, a girl of twelve years, was referred because of tomboyish behaviour. She posed no problem at home except she preferred the company of boys and engaged in rough games with them. She played only with guns and wore trousers all the time. She irritated her mother by refusing to wear dresses even on special occasions. She wanted to take judo lessons and hoped to become a pilot or astronaut when she grew up. She was enuretic up until the age of seven years. The mother stated that the father treated Sevim like a son and would buy her guns, trucks and other boys' toys.

Sevim's mother was an attractive woman who favoured the younger sibling, a more easy-going sister, who was anxious to please her parents. The mother was rather obsessive and according to the father, intolerant of Sevim. The father was a well-dressed and stern-looking man. He became angry over trivial matters and criticized his wife. He also belittled her because she was not interested in reading books as he was. He spoke very little at home and wanted everything to be done his way. The mother, except for her occasional attempts to assert herself, seemed to accept her husband's unconditional authority.

When asked to draw a human figure, Sevim drew a picture of a boy. Her responses to the Sentence Completion Test were all concerned with the rivalry between the sexes: 'The boys think girls cannot do anything good... I wish I were a boy so I could do anything I want....' On a projective test she related stories which dealt with sibling rivalry and oedipal conflict. It became evident that Sevim felt that she could neither compete with her attractive mother nor with the gratifying sister for her father's love. Her only solution to her conflicts was to give up her feminine identity. In that way she could win her place with the father who treated her as a boy before her sister was born. In her 'masculine protest', in a sense she seemed to identify herself with the mother and rebel against her low status in the family, When asked if she had a favourite joke, she reported the following joke:

> A girl asked her father what the word 'war' meant. The father began to explain,
> 'Suppose one of our neighbouring countries tried to occupy our land....' Right at
> this moment the mother entered the room and told the father to explain it in as

few words as possible. So they got into an argument over how to explain it
best. Then the girl said, 'That's enough, now I know what war means!'

The patient's favourite joke clearly expressed the intra-familial conflict she had been
experiencing. Although the joke did not add anything new to the dynamic understanding of
the case, it was most useful in therapy with all family members, especially with the parents.
They, seeing in it clear evidence of their child's dilemma, accepted the therapist's
interpretations without resistence.

Case 3

Deniz, a girl of nine years, was referred because of nervousness, stubbornness and poor
school performance. She was the oldest child and the only girl in a family of three children.
According to the parents, Deniz did the opposite of what she was asked to do, or took her
time doing what her parents told her to do. She threw a temper tantrum whenever she could
not have her own way. At school she was a quiet pupil who day-dreamed a lot. Although her
teacher thought Deniz capable of doing much better academically, she made little effort to
achieve.

The father was a passive man who favoured his sons. Deniz wanted to get close to her father
but he did not return her love. The mother was an emotionally cold woman who openly
expressed her dislike for the patient. The mother stated that this might be due to the fact
that she did not take care of Deniz as a baby. The paternal grandmother who did not approve
of this marriage in the first place, took the baby away and returned her at the age of two.
Neither of the parents could explain satisfactorily why they could not keep the child. The
only thing they did say was that they were not so sure themselves that this marriage could
last. Although the marriage lasted, the home-life was far from peaceful. There was constant
tension and arguments because of the mother-in-law's interference into family affairs. The
mother complained that her husband took his mother's side on every issue except divorcing
her. Even after quarrels over trivial matters the couple would not talk to each other for
days. Deniz reported the following as her favourite joke:

> One evening a farmer and his wife were sitting in their home. The farmer told
> his wife to get up and feed the horse. His wife said, 'I can't feed the horse,
> it is your job, you go and feed it'. To determine the one who was going to feed
> the horse they found a solution: they would stop talking, and the one who then
> spoke first was supposed to feed the horse. Shortly after that argument, a
> burglar broke into the house and began to collect everything worth taking before
> the eyes of the silent couple. Finally, the wife broke the silence and shouted,
> 'What are you waiting for? The man is stealing everything we have!' The
> farmer replied, 'You spoke first; you are going to feed the horse!'

The joke describes a couple who are passive-aggressive to the extreme. They are ready to
sacrifice anything to win an argument. In this respect they are like the patient's parents
who had given up their first baby passively. Deniz was the one who paid the price for her
parents' passivity and stubbornness. Therefore, her antagonistic behaviour, at home and
at school, seemed to be her reaction to the parents' rejection of her. This joke was not
interpreted to the patient fully: only the similarity between this joke and their family
relationship was pointed out. However, in the interview with the parents the patient's
feelings of rejection thatwere related to marital discord were brought up and discussed. The
therapist had the impression that the parents, who enjoyed the joke very much, seemed for
the first time to realize the ridiculousness of their peevish antagonism toward each other.

Case 4

Omer, a boy of thirteen years, and the second child in a family of three sons, was brought
to the clinic because of fainting spells. The patient had fainted for the first time about
a year ago after being insulted and beaten by the father. The mother who brought Omer to the
clinic stated that these spells occurred usually during family fights. The father, a very
aggressive man, would come home drunk and start an argument with his wife. He would throw
things and beat up his wife and sons because of minor faults. He had threatened his wife
with a knife several times. The wife was once hospitalized on account of a head injury she
suffered in one of these beatings. The mother who appeared depressed, had received psychiatric
treatment following a suicidal attempt. The mother described Omer as an affectionate boy who
got along well with everybody. He felt so sorry for his mother that he helped her with
household chores. He was eager to please her and very careful not to do things to upset her.
Omer, not a very masculine boy, tried to play the role of a big sister who was the best
helper of a sickly mother. Although he was very much afraid of his father, on several
occasions he had tried to stop him in order to protect his mother.

His responses to a picture story test dealt with the fear of losing the mother and violence
of various kinds. When asked to tell his favourite joke he reported the following:

One day Nasreddin Hoca and his wife were eating soup. Forgetting that the soup
was very hot, the wife took a spoonful. Tears came to her eyes. Hoca asked
his wife why she was crying. She said, 'All of a sudden I remembered my
deceased brother'. Next Hoca took a spoon of hot soup which brought tears to his
eyes too. His wife asked him innocently, 'Why are you crying?' Hoca replied:
'Why shouldn't I cry; my beloved brother-in-law died instead of you!'

This favourite joke which describes a provocative wife and an aggressive husband, reflects
very well the tense and hostile atmosphere at home. The meaning of the joke was so obvious
that neither the child nor the mother needed any interpreting. The discussion of the joke
might have been useful in the interview with father, but he could not be brought to the
clinic.

Case 5

Metin, a boy of eleven years, was referred because of behaviour problems and a sudden drop
in school performance. The mother stated that the onset of all these problems dated back to
the time when her husband deserted the family to live with a young woman. Metin reacted so
strongly to his father's desertion of the family, he became unmanageable at home and lost
interest in going to school. He wrote letters begging his father to come back. But at home
and in the interviews he expressed his anger openly and claimed that he did not want to see
his father again, since the latter preferred 'a whore' to his family. On the other hand, he
kept torturing his mother by accusing her of having made his father's life at home miserable.
The mother who was much older than her husband said that he used to run around with women
but that he had never left them before. She was very much hurt and felt so helpless that
she did not know how to handle her son's temper tantrums and rebellious behaviour. When
asked if he had a favourite joke, Metin reported the following:

A flirting man, while travelling on an aeroplane, offers to the young woman
sitting beside him ten Liras to see her legs. She readily agrees and after a
while pulls her skirt higher up in return for twenty Liras. When the man
hesitates to make another offer, she says: 'Would you pay me fifty Liras if
I show you my place of operation?' Excited, the man says, 'Yes'. The young
woman then points to a hospital way down and says: 'That is the place of my
operation!'

When asked what strikes him as funny in this joke, Metin, a very intelligent boy, had these
comments to make: 'The joke shows how stupid men can get! The guy is like my stupid father,
he thinks he is smart but he gets cheated at the end. Soon that "whore" will get tired of
my father and throw him out. Then she will find herself another sucker!' The therapist had
nothing to add to this interpretation.

DISCUSSION

The favourite joke, as it was shown in the case examples, could be used as an adjunctive
method for elucidating child psychodynamics. In a previously published study (Yörükoğlu,
1974), the favourite jokes of children were found to be dynamically related to emotional
conflicts. Moreover the favourite joke, in most instances, seemed to stress the core
conflict that the patient was experiencing. In the present study, all the children came
from the families in which the marital conflict stood out. Their favourite jokes primarily
touched upon the intra-familial conflicts rather than the intra-psychic ones. Thus these
jokes contributed to the dynamic understanding of the relationships between family members.

When exposed to jokes, a particular child picks one out unconsciously which corresponds to
his/her inner needs, and he/she begins to use it repeatedly to express a certain conflict.
Naturally this becomes possible only when the child develops a rich enough repertoire of
jokes to select one which is suitable for his conflict. As a condensed form of the emotional
conflict, the favourite joke serves as a means to escape the censorship. Thus the internal
conflict breaks through into the consciousness in a disguised form. In other words the
favourite joke represents an attempt, on the part of the patient's unconscious, to resolve
the conflict. As a healthy defence mechanism, the joking affords a pleasurable discharge
for the painful affect which is related to the repressed conflict. Since the selection of
a favourite joke is an unconscious dynamic process, the favourite joke may, in time, be
replaced by new and different jokes, whenever the different conflicts come to the foreground.
Also various types of preferred jokes may correspond to different kinds of conflicts within
a particular person.

On the other hand, some deep-seated conflicts may not find an expression in the language of
jokes. They may be represented in jokes only tangentially. Whether or not the favourite
joke is closely related to the patient's core conflict, it certainly serves the function of
relieving anxiety.

As it is described in the case examples, even when the favourite joke does not provide a new insight into the child's inner conflicts, it may be utilized as an effective tool in psychotherapy. The discussion of the joke creates a relaxed atmosphere which lowers the resistance to the interpretations made by the therapist. Especially in initial interviews the joke telling eases the patient's apprehension and improves the communication between the patient and the therapist.

In the course of therapy, some children tend to bring new jokes and riddles into the sessions. These children may try to turn the therapeutic hour into an occasion for intellectual competition at sharing jokes. In fact a few children, after relating their joke, asked the therapist to tell his favourite joke. Occasionally, a child, after having told his favourite joke, volunteered to tell another one he liked. These 'second best jokes', interestingly enough, were complementary to the favourite ones in indicating the emotional conflicts. Usually no child could be expected to tell, spontaneously, a joke unless he had been in therapy for some time. But, curiously, one boy's response on the Sentence Completion Test ran as follows: 'The thing I never forget is a joke!' By this he seemed to invite the therapist to ask him to tell it. Indeed, this joke turned out to be one that reflected his anxiety over his most disturbing symptom, namely, the fear of dying!

As the scarcity of studies concerning humour productions of emotionally disturbed children indicates, humour does not receive the attention it deserves in psychotherapy. In other words, humour, as an important aspect of human interaction is not taken seriously by therapists, old or young. It is observed frequently that the beginning therapists fail above all others to bring their patients' humorous remarks into the supervisory hour; some of them actively discourage their patients' joke-telling. A pertinent example is the case of a bright boy who was being interviewed by a new trainee, asked him if he could tell a joke. But the patient was discouraged because the trainee believed that the psychiatric interview was a solemn affair, not an occasion for telling jokes!

REFERENCES

See Bibliography for publications on humour, laughter and comedy

Humour and Fairy Tales: Quests for Wider Worlds

Julius E. Heuscher

Stanford University

Golux: 'Remember laughter! you'll need it even in the blessed isles of Ever After', (Thurber, 1950).

In this paper, I explore the hypothesis that both humour and fairy tales lift us beyond the ordinary, blindly accepted limits of the everyday world. I also focus upon some differences between humour and fairy tales, and attempt to understand how various forms of humour assist in the function of fairy tales. A succinct list of examples of various ways in which humour is incorporated in folklore precedes the discussion of this main topic, and some pertinent excerpts from Thurber's charming tale 'The 13 Clocks' follows it.

HUMOUR IN FAIRY TALES

The ways in which humour is expressed in fairy tales can be listed: (a) by considering the portions of the tale taken up by jokes, jests or witty asides; (b) by identifying various kinds of comical connotations which are sometimes expressed in riddles or symbolical representations; and (c) by focusing on the role of laughter that often occurs in a tale.

(a) Occasionally the entire tale is a joke. Typical examples are the master-thief stories of which there are innumerable variants dating back as far as ancient Egypt (Heuscher, 1974). Sometimes certain sections of a story are jokes - often but not always practical jokes - as illustrated, for instance, by many of the funny adventures of Wakdjunkaga in the American-Indian Winnebago trickster cycle. At other times humour is limited to brief, witty asides, like Perrault's comment in regard to Sleeping Beauty's prince who had the courtesy not to mention how out of fashion her hundred-year-old dress was. In addition there are the frequent introductory and terminating statements in fairy tales that at first sight seem sheer nonsense, such as, 'There is no if or maybe, the tripod has always three legs' (Luthi, 1964). Finally we find numerous fairy tales that are enlivened by the insertion of witty verses such as Jack's giant, 'Be he live or be he dead, I'll grind his bones to make my bread'.

(b) A comical connotation linked to a challenge or riddle is exemplified by Anderson's bean underneath the seven mattresses, felt keenly by the sensitive, true princess. Comical connotations of some tricks are frequent, such as the little tailor's emblem, boasting, 'Seven with one stroke!' (Grimm & Grimm, 1945). It frightens the giant who does not know that the boast refers to seven flies rather than seven men. Comical are also such symbolical representations as that of the overly ambitious fisherman's wife sitting on a two-mile-high throne while all the emperors and kings are on their knees kissing her toe (Heuscher, 1976). And sometimes a mildly comical connotation may pervade the entire narrative: for instance in the tale of Abu Kasem's old slippers that stubbornly keep returning to their stingy owner, causing him great grief.

(c) Laughter is frequently mentioned in fairy tales; more often, it seems, as manifestation of cruel delight by the evil ones than as expression of pure joy. In the Winnebago trickster cycle, Wakdjunkaga laughs both at himself and at his victims; and Juan in Castaneda's mystic novels frequently laughs uproariously during the most crucial moments of rites of transition. Finally, there are some tales in which laughter is the central topic. Such are the many variants of the Grimms' tale in which the hand of the princess is promised to the hero who can make her laugh.

HYPOTHESIS: FAIRY TALES AND HUMOUR AS WORLD-WIDENERS

(a) Modalities of World-Expansions: interpretations of the meaning and function of humour
     are numerous and often overlapping: pleasurable release of suppressed emotions or
     instincts; satisfaction in a one-upmanship game; joy in sudden discovery or in
     being defeated by a good punchline, etcetera. Here I wish to emphasize but one
     important, apparently universal feature of humour - and especially of jokes - that
     is implicit in most interpretations and which consists in a sudden widening of the
     recipient's experiential horizon. We can observe this widening (i) in 'canned jokes',
     (ii) in situational humour, as well as (iii) in practical jokes.

   (i)   As an example of a 'canned joke', we may take the story of the Italian whose
         friends accompany him home after he has won the local spaghetti-eating contest,
         and who admonishes them, 'per favore, don't tell my wife, or she won't serve
         me dinner!'

   (ii) A humorous situation occurred one freezing, windy day when a man from Milan
         and I were the only skiers in a small, Swiss ski resort. After commiserating
         with each other and agreeing that only a crazy person would ski in such
         weather, we discovered to our amusement that both of us were psychiatrists.

   (iii) Many 'question-jokes' are a variant of practical jokes. A person may be asked,
         'Do you know the difference between a cauliflower and a piano?' And when he
         naively or dutifully replies 'No', he is told, 'In that case you better never
         buy a piano, or you might bring home a cauliflower!'

We now notice that the sudden widening of the experiential horizon can take on various
characteristics. In the spaghetti-eating contest joke the expansion is simply beyond the
expected possible limit; in the situational humour involving the two skiers the widening
consists mostly in the new twist given to the 'craziness' by the fact that only psychiatrists
would venture out into such horrid weather. In the 'practical joke-question' concerning a
cauliflower and a piano, however, the widening is accomplished by suddenly shifting the entire
frame of reference from one of playful fantasy to concrete reality. Again and again jokes
surprise us pleasantly by showing us how narrow our preconceptions are, and how easily they can
be transcended or modified.

In other words, the recipient's 'world-design', the way he has structured his existence, is
suddenly, albeit only temporarily, modified as a result of the punchline of the joke. This
'world-design', however, is a crucial aspect of an individual's identity, and often
considerable anxiety is aroused when it is suddenly altered in other than witty situations.
What is it, then, that causes mirth rather than fright when a joke is told?

Though one is justified in equating a person's 'world-design' with his identity, one must keep
in mind that equally important in vouchsafing his identity are those genuine, warm human
relationships that, in contrast to merely technical, manipulative or interobjective ones, are
termed intersubjective. They are sincere, non-exploitative and characterized by unconditional
respect and tolerance. It is primarily when reassured of his identity by such a relationship
that the human being is willing to explore new and wider 'world-designs'.

I believe that we find some of the qualities of intersubjective relationships in those social
gatherings that produce various forms of humour. Mutual respect, permissiveness, warmth and
absence of exploitative endeavours create an atmosphere in which jokes are most pleasantly
appreciated.

(b) Analogies and differences between fairy tales, humour and related phenomena: some of
     the above observations concerning humour are also applicable to fairy tales. Yet,
     as a matter of fact, epos, sagas and a considerable number of fairy tales contain
     little if any genuine humour. Knowing, then, that humour is not indispensable in
     folklore, we must ask ourselves what the essential features of fairy tales are, and
     what role humour plays in regard to these essential features when it is woven into a
     story.

Folk as well as artistic fairy tales are spontaneous human creations that have distinctly
revolutionary aspects in as much as they turn to some extent against the established and rigid
religious, political, social and moral order, thereby opening new sources of vitality.
Whether Theseus kills the Minotaur that has decimated the youths of Athens, whether Beowulf
defeats Grendel so that life may return to the king's castle, whether the fairy tale hero
solves three riddles or accomplishes three impossible tasks and thus overcomes the holdfast
king, or whether the American Indian Wakdjunkaga breaks every taboo before he begins his
bizarre journey - the established order is always overthrown, expanded or revitalized.

Similar in this regard to humour, folklore aims at the widening of overly rigid 'world-designs'; but it portrays the widening as a lasting achievement rather than a transitory glimpse.

Probably because of the warm, positive and profoundly optimistic atmosphere that pervades them, fairy tales — much more than myths and sagas - avail themselves of various kinds of humour in order to enhance their basic intent to lift the reader or listener out of his everyday, stifling existence, and to lead him into a wider, 'secondary' (Tolkien, 1966), or 'spiritual' world within which his yet hidden potentials can thrive. Though aesthetic considerations unquestionably are involved in the introduction of humour in fairy tales, it is humour's manifold skills of pleasantly disrupting our conventional views that makes it a most effective ingredient of those tales that open new worlds of meaning for us.

ILLUSTRATION OF MAIN HYPOTHESIS

Because of its exceptional charm and richness, I shall try to illustrate our hypothesis with Thurber's story of 'The 13 Clocks'. Its basic theme is the overcoming of the holdfast, cold 'Duke of Coffin Castle' and the liberation of beautiful Saralinda with whom the young prince, then, lives happily ever after. The successful dénouement in a fairy tale is almost always linked with the paradox that only he who risks everything in face of a seemingly impossible task can succeed. In Thurber's tale this paradox is magnified when the hero must place his trust in Golux, a bizarre, befuddled, amusing and totally unreliable creature. Yet Golux is on the side of laughter: he knows that laughter can free us again and again from being trapped by a deadly world where time has stopped. Their antagonists are the cold Duke and Todal: blind greed and unfeeling rigidity lead towards total nothingness which, nevertheless, is the necessary background for any meaningful endeavours. Whereas the spies and guards agonize in terror at the mere mention of Todal, a shapeless monster, the prince's identity is safeguarded in this utterly unpredictable and insecure world by his reciprocated love for Saralinda.

The cold Duke — we may well recognize in him aspects of ourselves — tries to maintain his identity by clinging to a rigid, unchanging world which thereby becomes ever more oppressive and deadly. Yet only a trusting, loving relatedness to another (a friend, a sweetheart, God) permits us to step back from our accustomed world without panicking, to accept life's paradoxes, and to consider new options seriously. It is especially in dreams and daydreams, in art, philosophy and psychotherapy, as well as in wit and folklore, that we find ways of stepping back in order to gain a broader, detached view of the dance of life; but it is our destiny to re-enter this dance again and again.

In 'The 13 Clocks' we find many instances and forms of humour: Golux's apparel and his weird sayings; limericks and light ballads; grotesque exaggerations; ridiculous, perverted logic; jokes intended to bring forth tears; situation jokes; cold, sardonic laughter; and diffuse, gentle humour. They all contribute to the fairy tale's intent of letting a new, wider, happier and richer world emerge. We now must ask ourselves in what ways this 'stepping back' provided by humour differs from the other mentioned forms of transcending everyday existence.

All wit, humour or laughter is, in the last analysis, directed at ourselves, even where another human being is the recipient of our jest. In as much as we like him we share with him the sense of exhilaration; and if we trick him, we share the embarrassment of being exposed as having clung to all-too-narrow horizons. Wit, jests, laughter, jokes or humour are probably the first and oldest steps in achieving detachment from dreariness that invades everyday existence. 'Remember laughter!' is Golux's parting remark.

The smiling Buddha, the jesting Zen Master, the tricked Trickster, Juan in Castaneda's novels, they all manifest their authenticity by various qualities of laughter. Without this basic potential, without humour, all the other forms of transcendence would become unreliable. True enough, dreams, philosophy, art, psychotherapy and folklore need not always include humour, in as much as they are more complex, enduring and committed endeavours. Yet the dreamer, the therapist, the bard, the philospher, or the artist who is incapable of laughter, of wit, is bound to be quite ineffective in expanding, deepening and enriching his or his fellow men's world.

REFERENCES

Grimm, J. & Grimm, W., Grimms' Fairy Tales. Grosset & Dunlap, New York (1945).

Heuscher, J.E., A Psychiatric Study of Myths and Fairy Tales. Thomas Company, Springfield, Illinois (1974).

Heuscher, J.E., The Fisherman and His Wife. Unpublished Manuscript (1976).

Luthi, M., Es War Einmal. Vandenhoeck & Ruprecht, Göttingen (1964).

Thurber, J., The 13 Clocks. Simon & Schuster, New York (1950).

Tolkien, I.R.R., The Tolkien Reader. Ballantine Books, New York (1966).

Nonverbal Communication Among Friends and Strangers Sharing Humour

Jean R. Smith, Hugh C. Foot and Antony J. Chapman

University of Wales Institute of Science and Technology

This paper reports three experiments which were designed as part of a research project investigating children's nonverbal behaviours in humour situations (Chapman, Foot & Smith, 1976)[1]. The majority of studies on nonverbal behaviour and nonverbal communication have used adult subjects engaged in conversation and/or in task-orientated and artificial laboratory settings; many of these studies, like our own, relate to Argyle and Dean's (1965) model of social intimacy.

We adopt a rigorous experimental approach but, at the same time our subjects are provided with a naturalistic and pleasant environment (Foot, Smith & Chapman, 1975). They are presented with humour material in a mobile-laboratory. The laboratory is specifically designed for on-location studies in schools and the main part of it is fitted-out as a children's playroom.

The subjects in the three studies reported here were aged between seven-and-a-half and nine years. Behavioural responsiveness was defined in terms of duration scores for laughter, smiling, 'looking' (that is, looking at the other child's face), eye-contact, mutual-laughter, and mutual-smiling (cf. Foot, Chapman & Smith, 1977). In Experiment I additional dependent measures were, distance between subjects, seating orientation and the time which was spent looking away from the film. All measures were extracted from the video-tape-recordings by three observers.

EXPERIMENT I

The first study was designed to demonstrate that behavioural responsiveness of children in dyads is determined in part by the prior relationship existing between the members of the dyad. Thirty-six boys and thirty-six girls attended the mobile-laboratory, sited in their school grounds: for purposes of statistical analyses, twelve boys and twelve girls were treated as subjects, and the remainder were treated as companions. Each subject was observed during three visits to the laboratory; once on his/her own, once with a chosen friend of the same sex, and once with a stranger of the same sex. 'Strangers' were chosen by the experimenter from classes other than the subjects', and care was taken to ensure that the children did not know one another, except possibly by sight.

Order of testing in the three social conditions was randomized across subjects. In each condition the children watched two films, one humorous (a 'Tom and Jerry' film, from three available), and one nonhumorous (from a children's documentary about Sri Lanka, edited into three self-contained units). Humorous and nonhumorous films were presented in a counter-balanced design. The children were permitted to sit wherever they chose on the floor of the playroom, the experimenter retiring to the room adjacent immediately before the films began.

Experiment I hypotheses were: (1) girls would look more at their companions and engage in more eye-contact than boys. This is a robust finding for adults (cf. Argyle & Cook, 1976), and there is evidence suggesting a corresponding difference for children (Chapman, 1973b, 1974b; Levine & Sutton-Smith, 1973); (2) the presence of a companion would enhance responsiveness in subjects and this effect would be most marked when the companion was a friend; (3) during the presentation of nonhumorous films subjects would look relatively less at the screen and relatively more at their companions, especially when paired with a friend.

RESULTS AND DISCUSSION

Hypothesis 1.   As predicted, girls looked at their companions more than boys (F=9.01; df=1,22; p < .01) and engaged in more eye-contact (F=7.31; df=1,22; p < .025). There were no other sex differences.

Hypothesis 2.   A preponderance of zero scores prevented data from the solitary condition being combined in parametric statistical analyses with data from the two other social conditions. Hence analyses of variance were $2 \times 2 \times 2$ (instead of $3 \times 2 \times 2$, as originally intended). As hypothesized, children were more responsive with a friend companion than with a stranger companion: that is, they laughed more ($F=5.35$; $df=1,22$; $p<.05$), smiled more ($F=8.56$; $df=1,22$; $p<.01$), looked more ($F=19.06$; $df=1,22$; $p<.001$), engaged in more mutual-smiling ($F=18.95$; $df=1,22$; $p<.001$), and engaged in more eye-contact ($F=16.37$; $df=1,22$; $p<.001$). They also looked at the films less ($F=8.78$; $df=1,22$; $p<.01$), and friends sat closer together than strangers ($F=15.64$; $df=1,22$; $p<.001$).

Hypothesis 3.   During the nonhumorous films, as predicted, there was more looking ($F=18.72$; $df=1,22$; $p<.001$) and eye-contact ($F=8.76$; $df=1,22$; $p<.01$). Children looked at the humour films more than at the nonhumour films ($F=28.62$; $df=1,22$; $p<.001$).

There were two-way statistical interactions, for sex by social conditions, on looking ($F=5.37$; $df=1,22$; $p<.05$) and eye-contact ($F=4.47$; $df=1,22$; $p<.05$), and these were attributable to girls with friends being relatively more responsive than other groups. Interactions for social conditions by film material on looking ($F=13.24$; $df=1,22$; $p<.01$) and eye-contact ($F=7.94$; $df=1,22$; $p<.025$) resulted from subjects with friends in the nonhumour film condition being relatively more responsive.

In Experiment I, the three hypotheses therefore were confirmed. Also, friends showed a clear preference for a side-by-side seating arrangement, one which has been taken to be more intimate than most (Argyle, 1969; Chapman, 1976). Strangers usually sat one behind the other, and invariably facially out of sight of one another.

EXPERIMENT II

Experiment II and Experiment III focused upon relationships between interpersonal distance and nonverbal behaviours; two distances were employed. The experiments examined how children react when their 'natural' level of intimacy is disturbed by an external agent. In Experiment II seating position was varied systematically in order to observe the effect this had upon levels of responsiveness, particularly the responsiveness of friends when seated apart, their natural inclination being to sit close together. Independent groups of children from a second school (forty-eight boys and forty-eight girls) were tested in same-sex pairs of friends/strangers and seated at one of two interpersonal distances defined by the position of their chairs (near = 0.38 metres; far = 1.60 metres). The children were again video-tape-recorded while watching a 'Tom and Jerry' cartoon film. (Nonhumour material was not used after Experiment I because strangers had responded minimally during its presentation).

Experiment II hypotheses were: (1) as in Experiment I girls would respond more than boys on measures of looking and eye-contact; (2) again a companion would enhance responsiveness, particularly when the companion was a friend rather than a stranger; (3) when seated farther apart, children in order to compensate for diminished intimacy would look more and engage in more eye-contact than when seated near together (cf. Argyle & Cook, 1976), and this would be especially so when they were friends.

RESULTS AND DISCUSSION

Hypothesis 1.   Girls did look at each other more than boys ($F=4.60$; $df=1,40$; $p<.05$), but in this experiment the tendency for them to engage in more eye-contact was nonsignificant ($F=3.95$; $df=1,40$; $p<.10$).

Hypothesis 2.   As predicted and in confirmation of Experiment I, the companionship of a friend increased responsiveness in the subject more than the companionship of a stranger on all measures: that is, with a friend they laughed more ($F=4.55$; $df=1,40$; $p<.05$), smiled more ($F=20.04$; $df=1,40$; $p<.001$), looked more ($F=16.22$; $df=1,40$; $p<.001$), and engaged in more mutual-smiling ($F=12.82$; $df=1,40$; $p<.01$) and eye-contact ($F=12.35$; $df=1,40$; $p<.01$).

Hypothesis 3.   When seated relatively far apart, children looked more ($F=14.75$; $df=1,40$; $p<.01$) and engaged in more eye-contact ($F=12.35$; $df=1,40$; $p<.01$).

There was a two-way, sex by social conditions, interaction on looking ($F=8.18$; $df=1,40$; $p<.01$) and a nonsignificant trend on eye-contact ($F=3.85$; $df=1,40$; $p<.10$): girls with friends were again more responsive than any other group. There was a social conditions by distance interaction on eye-contact ($F=4.61$; $df=1,40$; $p<.05$), and a nonsignificant trend on looking: these were attributable to friends when seated apart being relatively more responsive than other subjects.

Experimental hypotheses were again confirmed, therefore. For friends it appeared that the far seating position was not sufficiently intimate: their increased looking and eye-contact

presumably served to restore intimacy to an acceptable level. Other measures of responsiveness showed similar though nonsignificant trends, lending some support to the compensation
hypothesis.

However, these two studies used film material and, in a study using auditory material,
Chapman (1975a) found that children who respond most are those who sit as close as possible
to one another. In his study, the children sat face-to-face, and not side-by-side as here,
but the crucial factor underlying the disparity between those two studies is probably mode of
presentation of humour stimuli. With auditory material, children have more freedom to
interact because there are no stimuli demanding visual fixation for appreciation of humour.
Auditory material therefore might promote a more intimate social environment than a 'Tom and
Jerry' film, which is predominantly visual. Experiment III was designed in part to examine
this possibility.

EXPERIMENT III

The subjects had all taken part in Experiment II. Forty boys and forty girls were tested in
like-sex pairs of friends/strangers. Friendship pairs remained unchanged but new stranger
pairings were generated. The children were seated at the same interpersonal distances as
before. However children who previously sat near together now sat far apart and vice versa.
Video-tape-recordings were made while the children listened to a humorous recording by Ken
Dodd, taken from his album 'Ken Dodd and the Diddymen' (MFP 1367); it was presented through
a cassette-tape-recorder.

Experiment III hypotheses were: (1) with the introduction of auditory humour enhancing the
intimacy of the social milieu, girls would smile more than boys. In earlier studies we have
found evidence to support the notion that girls at this age are more concerned than boys in
sharing the social situation and that they engage in proportionally more nonmirthful smiling.
They would be expected therefore to be relatively more sensitive than boys to a situation in
which intimacy cues are heightened (Chapman, 1973b; Smith, Chapman & Foot, 1976); (2) as
before, the companionship of a friend would enhance responsiveness more than the companionship
of a stranger.

RESULTS AND DISCUSSION

Hypothesis 1.   As predicted, girls did smile more than boys (F=9.84; df=1,32; p< .01).
There were no sex differences on any other measure. The absence of sex differences on looking
and eye-contact behaviours appear to be a function of humour being presented auditorily.
Although Chapman (1975a) using auditory material did find a sex difference on eye-contact,
levels of responsiveness in his study were generally much higher than in the present experiment.

Hypothesis 2.   As in Experiment I and Experiment II, children were more responsive with a
friend companion than with a stranger companion: that is, they smiled more (F=17.62; df=1,32;
p <.001), looked more (F=10.82; df=1,32; p <.01), engaged in more mutual-laughter (F=5.21;
df=1,32; p <.05), engaged in more mutual-smiling (F=9.14; df=1,32; p <.01), and engaged in
more eye-contact (F=11.48; df=1,32; p <.01).

As far as the distance variable is concerned, children looked more when seated apart (F=4.49;
df=1,32; p <.05) but, contrary to expectations arising from Experiment II, there was no
corresponding effect for eye-contact; neither were there any distance effects for any other
measure.

Summarizing Experiment III, hypotheses were confirmed and levels of responsiveness were found
to be indiscriminable at the two distances. In conjunction with Experiment II, Experiment III
data indicate that auditory material more than film material (visual/auditory) enhances humour
and social responsiveness. The failure to replicate Chapman's findings may be primarily
attributable to mode of presentation and children's seating orientations; in the present
experiment subjects sat side-by-side whereas in Chapman's study they sat face-to-face. The
latter situation is likely to have been the more intimate.

CONCLUSION

We have shown in some of our studies that intimacy is not static and this has led us to
deduce that Argyle and Dean's (1965) model is not satisfactory for all circumstances. Their
model states that in any two-person situation intimacy is static. It is in a state of balance
and if this balance is disturbed by altering the distance between subjects, for example, then
social responsiveness is changed along other dimensions in an effort to restore the 'natural'
level of intimacy.

The present findings are consonant with Patterson's (1976) model of social intimacy: in part this states that if a situation is positively rewarding then intimacy increases. In our studies intimacy does appear to increase and the basal levels are varied in a number of ways; for example, by changing prior relationships, seating positions, amount of interaction feasible, amount of eye-contact, proximity, and so on. As intimacy increases so in humour situations laughter and smiling increase, but the relationship between intimacy and so-called humour responsiveness is not linear. At low levels of intimacy, increments have very little effect upon responsiveness, but at high levels of intimacy a slight increase (e.g., through adopting a more intimate front-on seating orientation) can have a marked boosting effect until a ceiling is attained for laughter and smiling.

The data collected in these studies and in our others, coupled with our informal observations, leave us in no doubt that social intimacy promotes responsiveness to humour and vice versa: the one feeds on the other, particularly when social intimacy is very high. Our observations are of children, but we can see no reason why our conclusions should not relate to adults also. Indeed, data from Osborne and Chapman (this volume) suggest that adults are even more sensitive than children to a companion's presence. Also, in all our experiments, humour is presented to social groups from external sources such as auditory tape-recorders, and video-cassette-players. Outside the laboratory in their everyday interactions, our subjects may make even greater use of humour (self-generated) to enhance the intimacy of the social situations in which they find themselves.

FOOTNOTE

1.   This research is part of a series of studies on children's responsiveness in humour situations, sponsored by the Social Science Research Council, U.K. (Grant No. HR 3043/1). We express our sincere gratitude to Mr. E. Powell (Llanedeyrn Junior School, Cardiff), Mrs.K.Jones (Marlborough Junior School, Cardiff), and to their teaching staffs for making possible the research reported here.

REFERENCES

See Bibliography for publications on humour, laughter and comedy

Argyle, M., Social Interaction. Methuen, London (1969).

Argyle, M. & Cook, M., Gaze and Mutual Gaze. Cambridge University Press, Cambridge (1976).

Argyle, M. & Dean, J., Eye-contact, distance and affiliation. Sociometry, 28, 289-304 (1965).

Chapman, A.J., Laughter and social intimacy. Paper presented at the Social Psychology Meeting of the British Psychological Society London Conference, December (1974) (b).

Chapman, A.J., Foot, H.C. & Smith, J.R., The psychology of laughter: A review. Invited Paper presented at the Annual Conference of the British Psychological Society, York, April (1976).

Foot, H.C., Smith, J.R. & Chapman, A.J., Investigating social aspects of children's laughter. Paper presented at the Annual Conference of the British Psychological Society, Nottingham, April (1975).

Levine, M.H. & Sutton-Smith, B., Effects of age, sex and task on visual behavior during dyadic interaction. Developmental Psychology, 9, 400-405 (1973).

Patterson, M.L., An arousal model of interpersonal intimacy. Psychological Review, 83, 235-245 (1976).

Smith, J.R., Chapman, A.J. & Foot, H.C., Friendship and sex as variables in children's social interactions. Paper presented at the Annual Conference of the Social Psychology Section of the British Psychological Society, York, September (1976).

The Effects of Humour on the Flow of Social Conversation[1]

John La Gaipa

University of Windsor, Canada

A social encounter is unlikely to be satisfying if one finds it difficult to get a word in
edgewise. The need to take turns in speaking and listening is perhaps the most obvious
aspect of conversation. Various mechanisms are used such as vocal amplitude, eye gaze and .
other turn-taking signals (Yngve, 1970). Social laughter is also used for '... maintaining
the flow of interaction ... filling in pauses in our conversation and maintaining the
interest and attention of our conversational partners' (Foot & Chapman, 1976, p188). A more
systematic approach requires that we determine what kinds of humour have what kinds of
effects under what kinds of conditions. What is needed to demonstrate the social functions
of humour are indicators of its objective, observable consequences (Bateson, 1953). If
humour does affect group processes, its consequences should be apparent in the interaction
sequences immediately following the injection of wit. Because of its temporal aspects,
change in conversation seemed useful for this purpose.

This study examined some of the factors facilitating or inhibiting the effects of humour on
social interaction: (1) the type and target of humour; (2) mirth responses, and (3) social
situation. The content of the humour was of interest because of earlier findings that the
stimulus properties of humour influence the intensity of the responses to it (cf. La Gaipa,
1968). The category of mirth responses was of interest as part of the broader problem on
the relationship between humour and laughter (La Fave, Haddad & Maesen, 1976). If humour
does serve a regulatory function, are its effects mediated by laughter? The social
situation was examined because prior research has shown that the social setting influences
the expressive response to humour (cf. Pollio & Edgerly, 1976). Are the regulatory functions
of humour also influenced by social variables?

An attempt was made to design a research paradigm for studying humour and laughter. Research
in this area is likely to remain at an embryonic stage until more effective paradigms are
developed. The main features of the paradigm include: (1) the use of cohesive friendship
groups instead of ad hoc groups of strangers; (2) the study of situational jokes instead
of written jokes or canned humour; (3) the conducting of the research in naturalistic
settings instead of in a laboratory; (4) the analysis of temporal sequences of conversation
rather than ad hoc interpretations, and (5) the use of video-recordings instead of
participant observers.

Existing friendship groups were used instead of artificially created groups because of what
we found in the early phases of this research. There was little variation in the kind of
humour and most of the laughter appeared to be evoked by the tensions arising out of the
formal tasks (La Gaipa, 1971). Jocular gripes require some common experiences. Teasing
requires knowledge about the butt of the joke and an acceptance and accurate perception of
intent. Hostile wit is often not expressed unless the group has achieved a level of
cohesiveness to be able to tolerate it. Such conditions are seldom found in a new group.
The assumption underlying the use of situational humour is that spontaneous jokes in
reflecting the common concerns of the group are likely to facilitate change. Situational
jokes have their origin in the ongoing interpersonal process (Fry, 1963). Such jokes are
likely to reflect the dynamics underlying the social interactions at any given point in
time.

Free social interaction under naturalistic conditions was achieved by leaving the social
psychology laboratory and going to the college pub. The one-way mirrors were substituted
by the murals of nudes. (See Chapman 1976, for a discussion of the inhibiting effects of
the lab on the expression of laughter and some attempts made to overcome such problems).

The video-recording of behaviour made possible the microscopic analysis of each of the
humour episodes. The group processes could be studied in considerable detail by replaying
the video-tapes. This procedure helped to achieve quite adequate reliabilities in the

coding of the humour content, and the mirth responses to the humour. (See Foot & Chapman, 1976). Needless to say, the use of video-recordings permits other investigators to look at the same event with possibly different theoretical perspectives and techniques.

METHOD

The data are based on 22 groups, each containing between four and six males. A graduate student observed a large number of groups of university students in their eating and drinking environments. Those groups engaged in lively conversation were approached and asked to participate; the rationale was that he was doing research on informal, sociable groups. Groups were not included that involved casual acquaintances; relatively cohesive groups were sought.

Eleven of the groups were selected and videotaped at a local tavern frequented mainly by students. Free beer was provided during the videotaping in the basement of the pub. The other eleven groups were selected from the university cafeteria and videotaped in a small room nearby. The groups were instructed to avoid discussing serious topics, and to continue what they were doing in front of the TV camera (the minimal effects of the TV were established early in this research). The average time spent by each group was about twenty to thirty minutes.

A series of playbacks was required. In brief, the humour and non-humour episodes were identified. Then, each of the humour episodes was classified by type and target of humour. Next, each person was rated by means of mirth response measures. Finally, the conversation rate preceding and following each occurrence of wit was determined.

The mirth response measures were as follows:

'Smiling' was measured by a five-point scale ranging from no expression to a strong smile.

'Body movement' was measured by a five-point scale ranging from no movement to increasing use of head, shoulders, trunk and limbs.

'Vocal intensity' was measured by a five-point scale ranging from minimal response to hearty laughter.

'Number laughing' was a group score for tapping the amount of participation.

'Duration of laughter' was a group score measured in seconds by a stop watch.

Type of humour was classified as follows:

'Cognitive wit' involves novelty, incongruity or surprise and includes the funny story, puns and word games.

'Jocular gripes' are jokes expressing some kind of frustration that is shared by and experienced by others, and evoke a sympathetic response in the group.

'Teasing' focuses on a negative quality or weakness of the butt of the joke but in the spirit of fun rather than malice.

'Hostile wit' is characterized by cutting or sarcastic language with the intention of hurting or rejecting another person or his ideas.

Each of these types of humour were further classified in terms of the butt of the joke, i.e., as ingroup or outgroup humour. An ingroup joke is one in which the butt was a member of the immediate group or the entire group itself. An outgroup joke is one where the member was not physically present, or an entire group, such as professors. Preliminary analysis indicated that finer distinctions within each group were impractical.

The criterion for classifying an attempted joke as humorous was that at least half of the members of the group exhibited a moderate response on at least two of the mirth measures. The mean duration of laughter in 369 episodes was 3.56 seconds.

Both the humour and the nonhumour episodes involved thirty second time periods divided into pre- and post. The pre-humour episode was defined as the fifteen seconds after the mirth response ceased. The nonhumour episodes were also divided into two time periods to have equivalent pre- and post measures. All nonhumorous episodes were identified in most of the groups. When there were long lapses of time without humour, every other thirty second period was classified as nonhumorous.

The temporal aspects of the social conversation were examined by using the Bales recorder
to approximate the data generated by the Chapple Interaction Chronograph. While the video-
monitor was playing, a felt pen was applied to the moving paper tape of the Bales recorder.
Each horizontal line represented one person talking without interruption. The length of the
line was translated into seconds to provide a measure of how long a person talked. A shift
from one person to another was shown by a vertical line. The number of vertical lines in
each fifteen second time period was used as an index of the rate of conversation.

The interaction rate for each individual was computed. These data were used to compute
group scores. The twenty-two groups were ranked on the basis of the average group score.
The groups above the median were designated as fast tempo and the groups below the median
were designated as slow tempo groups.

RESULTS

Mirth Responses

Table 1 presents data on the relationships among the various mirth response measures, as
well as the degree of agreement between the two coders. These data were based on 369 humour
episodes. The highest reliability was obtained for duration of laughter, probably due to
the use of a stop-watch. Subsequent analyses were limited to duration of laughter since
this mirth response was found to be the only one related to changes in social interaction.

TABLE 1   Median correlations among mirth response measures and
           inter-coder reliabilities

Mirth Responses	Intercorrelations				Reliabilities
	2	3	4	5	
1 Smiling	.66	.67	.63	.39	.63
2 Body movements		.70	.57	.44	.76
3 Vocal intensity			.83	.42	.73
4 Number laughing				.38	.85
5 Duration of laughter				--	.92

Analysis of Groups

The mean conversation rate was computed for each kind of humour for each group. This was
necessary for treating each of the twenty-two groups as providing one degree of freedom.
The conversation rate was subjected to a series of analyses of variance. Different sets of
independent variables were used, including episode, group tempo, social setting, type of
humour, target of humour, and pre-post conditions. The last three variables were subjected
to repeated measures design. Simple main effects were examined by the Newman-Keuls test in
order to locate the sources of the interactions.

The overall impact of humour on social interaction is apparent from the significant main
effect found for episode ($F=11.83$; $df=1,21$; $p <.01$). The episode X pre-post interaction
($p <.05$) is critical. This interaction is due to the lack of any significant difference in
the means in the pre- condition of humour and nonhumour ($\bar{X} = 2.97$ versus $\bar{X} = 2.76$), and the
significant differences in the post- condition ($\bar{X} = 3.29$ versus $\bar{X} = 2.68$). Essentially,
what this indicates is that there was an increase in the number of interaction sequences
immediately following the humorous event. The lack of any significant difference in the
conversation rate in the pre- condition is also important. What this suggests is that the
increase following humour cannot be explained simply in terms of the frequency of exchange
preceding the humour.

The analysis of variance that included group tempo as one of the variables revealed a
significant tempo X target interaction ($p < .01$). In order to account for this interaction,
the fast tempo and the slow tempo groups were separately analyzed. The reason for the
interaction is that the target was important in the fast tempo but not in the slow tempo
groups. In the fast tempo groups the flow of conversation was more rapid following the
injection of ingroup humour than outgroup humour. Cognitive humour speeded up the
conversation, regardless of the target. Jocular gripes speeded up the conversation when
the ingroup was involved. Hostile wit, however, slowed down the flow when the ingroup was
the target, and speeded it up when the outgroup was the target. Teasing had no impact on
the conversation.

The analysis of the slow tempo group data indicated that cognitive wit increased the flow,
whereas hostile wit decreased the flow of conversation. No significant results were
obtained with either teasing or jocular gripes.

Analysis of Episodes

To supplement the analysis of the twenty-two groups, the more than 1,000 episodes were
examined. A sequential analysis was done involving the onset of the humour and changes in
conversation. Table 2 provides some descriptive data showing where increases and decreases
occurred in relation to the form of humour irrespective of the degree of change.

TABLE 2   Percent of episodes with increases and decreases in rate of
           conversation by type and target of humour

Type of Humour	Target	Increases %	Decreases %	No. of Episodes
Cognitive Wit	Ingroup	66	9	59
	Outgroup	58	19	93
Jocular Gripes	Ingroup	51	27	49
	Outgroup	28	33	54
Teasing	Ingroup	43	18	101
	Outgroup	35	43	23
Hostile Wit	Ingroup	25	50	28
	Outgroup	45	41	58
Total Humour	Ingroup	50	22	237
	Outgroup	45	31	228
Non-Humour	--	29	40	556

What is revealing about this method of analysis is that it calls attention to the amount and
direction of change, in particular, the ratio of increases to decreases by type and target
of humour. The most pronounced change occurred for cognitive humour in speeding up the
conversation. Jocular gripes was also instrumental in increasing the exchange for ingroup
humour. Similarly, the impact of hostile wit was most dramatic in slowing down the interaction
when the ingroup was involved. A finding not evident in the analysis of variance was that
teasing increased the conversation when someone in the group was involved. Overall, ingroup
humour appeared to be more instrumental than outgroup humour, and the results paralleled what
was found by group analysis.

Table 2 also presents the number of different kinds of humour generated in the twenty-two
groups. About two-thirds of the humorous episodes involved some element of aggression.
Teasing was the most common ingroup form of humour (42%), whereas hostile wit toward the
ingroup was relatively scarce (12%).

Role of Laughter

Table 3 presents the mean duration of laughter in seconds by type and target of humour.
Analysis of variance revealed only a significant type X target interaction ($p < .01$). This
was due to a lack of any significant difference among the ingroup jokes, and significant
differences among some of the outgroup jokes. In particular, hostile wit directed toward an
outgroup generated longer laughter than either teasing ($p < .01$) or jocular gripes ($p < .05$).
It may also be observed in Table 3 that hostile wit directed toward the outgroup generated
longer laughter than hostile wit directed toward the ingroup. The reverse was found for
teasing. The laughter was longer when teasing an insider than when teasing an outsider.
These results suggest, then, that the intensity of mirth response does vary with the stimulus
characteristics of spontaneously generated humour.

TABLE 3   Mean duration of laughter in seconds and correlations (r)
           between laughter and post-humour rate of conversation

Type	Ingroup Humour		Outgroup Humour	
	Mean	r	Mean	r
Cognitive wit	4.27	.07	4.17	.28**
Jocular Gripes	4.25	.04	3.14	.36**
Teasing	3.97	.29**	3.61	.29
Hostile wit	3.64	.05	4.62	.31**

**p .01 (one-tail test)

Because the role of laughter was still unclear, further analyses were necessary. It has been shown that the content of the humour influences both change and the duration of the laughter, but no one-to-one relationship exists between these effects. Analysis of covariance was done. The covariate used was the duration of laughter. The criterion employed was the change scores derived by obtaining the difference in the rate of interaction before and after humour. The type X target interaction was significant (p < .005). The within group regression coefficient was only −.20 indicating that the degree of adjustment by using duration of laughter was negligible. This was evident when the adjusted means were examined to find out if they differed from the unadjusted means from the previous analysis of variance. The results obtained with the adjustment were essentially the same. This suggests that changes in interaction following humour are minimally affected by duration of laughter. The differential effects of humour, as a function of type and target, cannot be accounted for by differences in the intensity of this mirth response.

Social Situation

No difference was found in the kind of spontaneous humour as a function of the social setting. The type and target of humour that emerged in the more formal 'dry' atmosphere was quite similar to what was observed in the more informal 'wet' atmosphere. For example, in the tavern setting, 14% of the humour consisted of hostile wit, whereas in the university setting, 15% of the humour was of this type. Next, the effects of different kinds of humour on conversation were examined in both social settings. No significant main or interaction effects were found. Finally, we sought to determine if the social setting enhanced or inhibited the expression of laughter. The analysis of duration of laughter produced a significant main effect (p < .05). Contrary to expectations, the duration of laughter was longer in the formal than in the informal setting.

DISCUSSION

A four-fold classification scheme is apparent by looking at the possible combinations of humour and laughter. Laughter models can include or exclude humour. Similarly, humour models can include or exclude laughter. This scheme will be used to make explicit some of the theoretical assumptions; to place the data in some kind of perspective, and to call attention to some of the problems in testing these models.

Laughter Models that exclude Humour

The basic assumption made here is that nonhumorous stimuli can generate laughter having various social consequences. Giles and Oxford (1970) have classified such experiences under the category of social laughter. The social cues in the situation are viewed as the crucial determinants rather than the stimulus properties of the humour. The present study has limited application to this model. An adequate test would require the identification of laughter episodes not preceded by humour, and the isolation of social cues instigating the laughter. This kind of analysis of the video-recordings was beyond the scope of this study.

Laughter Models that include Humour

Models in this category go beyond the notion that humour appreciation is arousing. This property of humour lends itself to the deliberate use of humour as a tactic for achieving certain objectives. La Gaipa (1970) has looked at humour as a manipulative technique. More recently, Chapman (1975) has suggested that humour-generated laughter can serve such purposes as a safety-valve to protect the individual against excessive 'social arousal'. This kind of model also assigns a higher priority to conditions under which humorous stimuli lead to laughter than to the content of the humour. Situational factors enhancing or inhibiting laughter are of particular interest. Such social aspects of the situation as the presence of companions has been examined by Chapman (1975). The finding in the present study that social variables influence laughter but not the tempo of the conversation is consistent with an observation by Chapman (1976) that laughter as an expressive response is more susceptible to situational factors than are other responses to humour.

The play or 'fun' aspects of the situation are emphasized in the arousal-safety model proposed by Rothbart (1976). 'Laughter may occur when an arousing stimuli is judged to be safe, when a problem is solved or when an incongruity or improbable act has occurred and we can do nothing about it (p52).'

The finding that people laughed longer in the more formal than in the less formal situation could be interpreted in terms of this arousal-safety model. The greater tension in the formal situation might be reflected in the higher need for laughter-type messages communicating safety and the fun aspects of the situation. A similar interpretation by the more traditional tension-reduction model would be that the longer laughter resulted from the greater tension that had to be drained off. A more parsimonious explanation was suggested by a female graduate student. 'It is risky to laugh a lot when drinking beer unless you have good bladder control.' (Personal communication).

Humour Models that exclude Laughter

Such models assume that the stimulus properties of the humour induce arousal, and that increases or decreases in arousal can occur without the expression of laughter. This is not to say that laughter may not arise. Rather, this mirth response is treated as unnecessary to the model. Laughter is viewed as an insensitive index of humour appreciation.

Berlyne's (1969) theory of collative motivation postulates that changes in momentary level of arousal influences the quality and intensity of affective responses. Collative factors such as novelty, incongruity and surprise tend to increase the level of arousal. The cognitive wit in the present study was coded in terms of such collative factors. It seems to follow that increase in the conversation rate following the occurrence of cognitive wit is consistent with this theory of arousal.

The finding that verbal self-reports of arousal following humour are correlated with physiological indices (Godkewitsch, 1976) may have some relevance here. Are the changes in the conversation following humour also related to physiological indices? If so, the rate of verbal responses in a group following humour might be interpreted as an indicator of the level of arousal instead of reduction of arousal.

A somewhat different approach focuses on the target or directionality of the humour rather than its cognitive qualities. The basic assumption is that the responses to humour depend on the attitudes or dispositions toward the protagonist. La Fave, Haddad and Maesen's (1976) theory of vicarious superiority calls attention to the classes of persons with whom identification exists. The degree of amusement depends in part on whether jokes dealing with these classes are self-esteeming or ego-deflating. Martineau (1972) is more concerned with the perceived intent of the initiator, specifically whether the humour is perceived as esteeming or disparaging of the group. Zillmann and Cantor (1976) focus instead on the affective dispositions toward the butt of the joke.

The results of the present study using laughter as one of the dependent measures are fairly consistent with research using humour appreciation as the dependent measure (cf. La Gaipa, 1968). More laughter was evoked by hostile wit aimed at the outgroup than aimed toward the ingroup. Moreover, the finding that hostile wit toward the ingroup decreased the rate of conversation might be interpreted by the model developed by Martineau. Hostile wit might have dampened the social interaction because such wit endangered the cohesiveness of the group.

No claim is made as to the adequacy of the tests of such models. No independent measures were used to determine any momentary changes in cohesiveness or self-esteem. The extent to which attitudes toward the outgroup were negative was not established. And interpretations made as to the perceived intent of persons initiating humour were not examined. The collection of these kind of data would be difficult without interrupting the ongoing interaction. Such intervention would also have a disrupting effect in making the subjects 'interaction-conscious'.

Humour Models that include Laughter

An assumption of drive reduction models is that of a direct relationship between humour and laughter, and between laughter and its effects. In the Freudian version of this model, the higher the arousal, the more intensive the affective response in terms of laughter. Laughter is a major vehicle for seeking relief. The intensity of the mirth response is seen as a response to the evaluation of the humorous stimuli. And the magnitude of the change would reflect the intensity of the response.

The finding that the effects of humour on the flow of conversation does not covary with the intensity of the mirth response offers little support to a tension-reduction model. After controlling for the duration of laughter, the contribution of humour was still quite evident and unchanged. Berlyne (1969) suggests that one can experience pleasure from increases in arousal by humour independently of any decreases in arousal by laughter. Another possibility is that changes in the affective state of the group are communicated by laughter. But beyond a certain level, further increases in intensity make little difference in the message transmitted by laughter.

The cognitive models of humour that include laughter assume that the effects of the laughter evoked by humour depend on the cognitive responses to the humour. One such model emphasizes the encoding and decoding processes (Giles, Bourhis, Gadfield, Davies & Davies, 1976).

Humour can be encoded for a variety of reasons, such as to maintain group solidarity. But the decoding of the humour determines the behavioural response to it. The joke may not be understood or even appreciated. Instead of humorous laughter, the result may be no laughter or ignorance laughter.

This cognitive model offers one possible explanation to the finding of little effect of laughter on the tempo of conversation. Perhaps some laughter that we assume to be evoked by humour was evoked by something else. What the initiator of the joke intended, how the audience decoded, and how it was scored by the raters may not always have coincided.

Finally, it is possible to defend a multi-motive model of either humour or laughter. It could be argued, for example, that laughter is merely one of various behaviours instigated by humour which serve similar or different functions. Talking might serve to reduce tension as well as laughter. Whereas some people laugh when nervous, others may reduce tension by talking.

A multi-motive model would be useful for dealing with some of the inconsistent results in this study. The effects of humour on conversation did vary with the stimulus properties of the humour, and some jokes evoked more laughter than others. But the amount of change did not vary with the amount of laughter elicited by the humour. Perhaps laughter served other functions not measured in this study.

In conclusion, humour served as a social mechanism in facilitating and inhibiting the flow of conversation. The effects of humour varied with such stimulus properties as type and target. Changes in conversation following humour were found to operate independently of laughter.

Change in the rate of interaction appears to be a sensitive and reliable indicator of responses to humour. Further use of this index requires understanding of the mechanisms involved and the functions served by momentary fluctuations in interaction sequences.

FOOTNOTE

[1]This research was supported by a grant from the Canada Council (68-1238).

REFERENCES

See Bibliography for publications on humour, laughter and comedy

La Gaipa, J.J., Methodological problems in the study of the social function of humor in small groups. In: Social Aspects of Humor: Recent Research and Theory. Symposium proceedings of the Western Psychological Association, Vancouver, June (1969).

La Gaipa, J.J., Humor as a manipulative technique. Paper presented at meeting of the Southeastern Psychological Association, Louisville, April (1970).

La Gaipa, J.J., Social psychological aspects of humor. Paper presented at meeting of the Midwestern Psychological Association, Detroit, May (1971).

Yngve, V.H., On getting a word in edgewise. Paper presented at the sixth regional meeting of the Chicago Linguistic Society, Chicago (1970).

Suppression of Adult Laughter: An Experimental Approach

Kate Osborne and Antony J. Chapman

University of Wales Institute of Science and Technology

It is commonly said that if you laugh the world laughs with you. The results of this research show the veracity of this aphorism and in particular of its extension. They demonstrate that an adult's smiling and laughing is markedly suppressed in the presence of a dour, unresponsive partner.

These findings provide a clear distinction between the responses of children and those of adults in humour situations. When children are presented with material that they find funny, they laugh and smile far more when in the presence of a companion than when alone; their expressive responses are equally evident whether the companion is also laughing and smiling or whether he/she is not responding (Chapman, 1976). Laughter occurs in children even when a companion reacts blankly to the humour and ignores the subject's presence. It has therefore been argued that the presence of a companion and the sharing of the social environment, is a fundamental determinant of children's humour responsiveness in humour situations.

The present study was designed to investigate the extent to which the presence of a companion is sufficient to enhance 'humorous laughter' in adults. Common experience would suggest that, in contrast to children, adults often do not laugh when a companion fails to respond to humour. The experiment shows in adults that laughing and smiling can be suppressed and it can be released or triggered, depending on whether a companion is responsive or unresponsive to the subject and to the humour material. Past research into adults' humour appreciation concentrated on subjective ratings of funniness rather than on overt expressive responses (cf. Goldstein & McGhee, 1972). There has been some observational research of very large groups, which has established that in spite of its variability and the changing nature of the humour stimuli a theatre audience's laughter bears a positive relationship to its size (cf. Pollio, Mers & Lucchesi, 1972).

In addition, several experimental studies have shown that canned laughter can be a powerful releasing influence (cf. Chapman, 1976). On the other hand, the social inhibition of laughter has been demonstrated (Young & Frye, 1966) in a situation where sexual jokes were presented to male students in the presence of a confederate female. When the confederate appeared to be acutely embarrassed there was a decrease in the appreciation of the jokes and of the accompanying laughter.

In the present experiment young female adults were paired with a confederate female (viz K.O.). They were asked to listen to humour tape-recordings which were neither embarrassing nor offensive. Experimental sessions were video-tape-recorded through a one-way viewing screen and measures were taken of laughter and smiling. The subjects were thirty-one females, aged between eighteen and twenty-five years; the confederate was also in this age-range. Selection of subjects was from a volunteer pool on the basis of age and sex, and they were paid a token sum of money for participating.

Subjects were assigned randomly to three experimental conditions. In a 'responsive-companion' condition the confederate attempted to match her smiling and laughter to responses of the subject. She did not initiate such behaviour, but 'replied' whenever the subject looked at her, smiled or laughed. In an 'unresponsive-companion' condition, the confederate remained unsmiling and straight-faced, did not seek eye-contact, and displayed no reactions to the humour material. In a third condition, subjects sat alone listening to the tapes to provide a baseline measure against which the enhancement or suppression of responses could be compared. The tape-recorder was placed on a table near to where the subject, or subject and confederate pair, was seated. The volume was adjusted so that the sound level was comfortable. The programme lasted for approximately twenty-five minutes and contained two recordings by Peter Cook and Dudley Moore ('Superstitions' and 'Command Performance') and one from Bob Newhart ('Merchandizing the Wright Brothers'). At the end of each experimental session both

VARIATION OF SMILING AND LAUGHING WITH COMPANIONSHIP

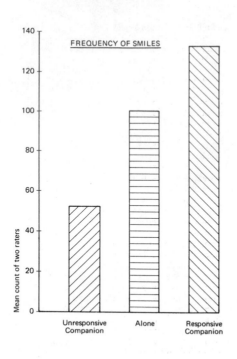

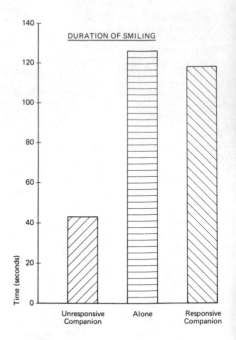

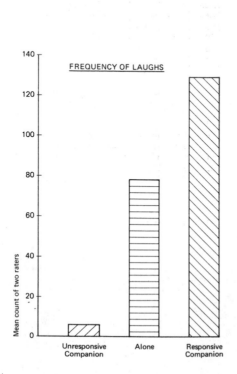

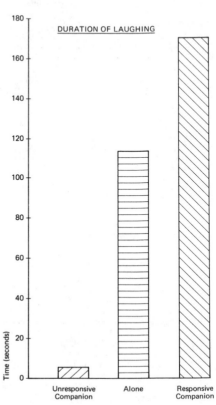

subject and confederate filled in humour rating-scales, showing for example how funny subjects normally found such material, how much they laughed during the tape, and whether they had heard any of the recordings before.

The video-tape-recordings were analyzed by two raters who scored independently the frequency and duration of smiles and laughter of subjects in each condition; the scores of the raters were averaged. There were significant differences between conditions both in the number of times subjects smiled (Kruskal-Wallis, $H = 10.12$; $df = 2$; $p < 0.01$) and in the time spent smiling during experimental sessions ($F = 4.92$; $df = 30$; $p < 0.025$). Further analyses between pairs of conditions showed that the subjects in the 'unresponsive-companion' condition smiled significantly less frequently than did the subjects in the 'alone' condition ($U = 30.5$; 1-tailed $p < 0.05$) and less frequently than subjects in the 'responsive-companion' condition ($U = 6$; $p < 0.001$). A similar pattern occurred for the duration measure. Subjects in the 'unresponsive-companion' condition smiled for shorter periods of time than those in either the 'alone' condition ($t = 1.42$; $df = 20$; 1-tailed $p < 0.05$) or the 'responsive-companion' condition ($t = 1.63$; $df = 19$; 1-tailed $p < 0.05$). Statistical analyses of laughing scores were not possible due to the high number of subjects in the 'unresponsive-companion' condition who did not laugh at all. However, it can be seen in the histograms that laughing is dramatically decreased (in duration and frequency) when an adult is with an unresponsive companion rather than on her own or with a responsive companion.

An analysis of the subjective ratings solicited at the end of the sessions showed no significant differences between the three groups in terms of the perceived funniness of the tape-recordings. Similarly there were no treatment effects in how much the subjects judged themselves to laugh during the tape, nor in how funny they claimed normally to find such material. Most subjects had not heard these recordings before, and those that had heard them were evenly distributed between the three groups.

It can be concluded that the social situation in which young adults receive funny material affects their responsiveness. Taking behaviour when alone as a baseline, there is a facilitation of expressive responses in the presence of another adult when that adult responds in a similar way to the material. This is in marked contrast to the suppression of such behaviours occurring in the presence of a straight-faced, unresponsive companion. Remembering that children in a comparable situation continue to laugh and smile, it is interesting to speculate about the age at which the alteration of these responses occurs.

During adolescence, many changes occur both in an individual's self-perception and in his/her behaviour in the company of others. From being invariably a facilitator of behaviours such as laughing and smiling, the presence of another has to be first evaluated and appraised before the behaviour considered to be appropriate is emitted. Argyle (1969) discusses these developmental changes in terms of increasing social awareness and the acquisition of social skills. He cites, for example, unpublished data from McPhail who studied the process of developing social competence during adolescence. Solutions selected to problem-solving tasks varied with the age of adolescent subject. Younger children gave many crude, aggressive, dominating responses, which McPhail called 'experimental' attempts to acquire by trial and error the social skills necessary for dealing with new situations. The older adolescents were able to use more skilful, sophisticated social techniques similar to those used by adults.

Presumably children learn gradually that the release of laughter is highly dependent on the humour responses and social responsiveness of others. Further developmental research should provide information about the time-span of such adaptation to social situations involving laughter and smiling. New research should also be directed towards providing insights into pathological behaviour where laughing and smiling is inappropriately released by adults.

REFERENCES

See Bibliography for publications on humour, laughter and comedy

Argyle, M., Social Interaction. Methuen, London (1969).

Sex Differences in Humour Appreciation: A Question of Conformity?

Nicholas J. Gadfield

University of Wales Institute of Science and Technology, Cardiff

Sex differences apparently existing in appreciation of sexual and aggressive humour have recently been questioned by Chapman and Gadfield (1976). They point out that most studies have used published cartoons and jokes and they argue that these tend to be created by men for a predominantly male audience. The authors' discussion of this male-orientated bias may be particularly relevant to studies examining the relationship between expressive and evaluative responses to humour. The present study considers the extent to which both these types of response may be facilitated by the presence of a companion and by the experimenter.

It has been suggested by Leventhal and colleagues that the sex of a subject is one factor governing the strength of the relationship between subjective ratings of humour funniness, and expressive responses to that humour, (e.g., Cupchik & Leventhal, 1974; Leventhal & Cupchik, 1975; Leventhal & Mace, 1970). While the laughter of a subject is usually positively facilitated by the presence of a companion's laughter, whether live or on tape, the corresponding effect on subjective ratings is not as straightforward. The argument put forward by Leventhal and colleagues is that female subjects make 'emotionally' based judgments of the funniness of cartoons and jokes. They incorporate their own laughter, facilitated or not, as a part of the information available to judge the funniness of all types of material. Male subjects, however, apparently make judgments which are more 'objective' and generally ignore outside influences including their own laughter, when viewing high quality material. Where low quality material is presented, male subjects who have been encouraged to laugh apparently subsequently moderate their rated criticism of the humour (Leventhal & Cupchik, 1975).

Despite arguments that these sex differences in reactions to humour are fundamental, it seems likely that subjects may be aware of the sexist nature of many of the cartoons and jokes in current use, especially the sexual ones (Chapman, 1975c). This, together with a lack of objective cues as to what constitutes the humour in a set of stimuli, could lead to considerable conformity pressure. The potency of such a situation could be further strengthened by the behaviour of a companion, and by the behaviour of the experimenter.

Having a keen sense of humour is socially desirable, but subjects need not respond favourably to all humour stimuli in order to demonstrate such a trait. In fact, they may not wish to reveal their attitude towards embarrassing materials such as sexual jokes and cartoons, particularly if there is a victim who is of the same sex as the subject. Since not responding to a stimulus is almost as revealing as favourably responding, a subject may attempt to match his or her responses to those of a companion. This matching will depend on a number of factors, including the extent to which the subject respects the judgment of the companion. Thus when faced with nonsexist sexual humour, female subjects may be just as appreciative as male subjects. However, if the material is derogatory to female values, but the subject is unwilling to show a dislike for the material, then she may use her companion's responses as a cue as to how to react. The extent to which the subject's laughter and subjective ratings are matched may then become a function of the sex and status of the companion and the sex and status of the experimenter, as well as of the sex of the subject.

To investigate the extent to which the sex and level of humour responsiveness of a companion influences a subject's reactions to humour stimuli, a 2 x 2 x 2 factorial study was designed; the factors were subjects' sex, companions' sex, and companions' responsiveness. For the test session, each subject viewed eight selected cartoons in a different randomized order, evaluating each in turn on a ten-point rating scale for funniness.

The cartoons were from Chapman and Gadfield (1976), selected in the following manner. In their study, five male and five female judges independently sorted three hundred and twenty so-called seaside postcards into thematic categories. Those cards which satisfied only one theme, and were allocated to a category with total interjudge agreement, were presented to fifteen male and fifteen female subjects aged between twenty-four years and fifty years. Six sex-related cartoons elicited sex differences in subjective ratings, and these six cards together with two nonsexual cards were the ones used in the present study.

Thirty-eight male and thirty-eight female first-year undergraduates were tested in the present study. They were randomly assigned to the experimental conditions so that ten subjects of each sex were in an alone session, and the remaining subjects performed in dyadic sessions with a companion. The companion was, in fact, a confederate of the same or opposite sex as the subject. The behaviour of the companion was predetermined so that he or she, after apparently reading the captions to each cartoon in the study, either laughed or made no reaction at all to each item.

During the test sessions, the subjects were video-tape-recorded through a concealed camera, and their expressive responses to the cartoons were later scored on a five-point scale similar to that of Zigler, Levine and Gould (1966). None of the subjects revealed any suspicion with respect to either the behaviour of the confederate or the possibility of being observed.

The results for the alone condition did not yield any sex differences in either expressive or evaluative responses to any of the six sexual or either of the nonsexual cartoons. This contrasts with the sex differences in subjective ratings obtained in the previous study for the sexual cartoons ($p < .01$). The difference between the studies lies in the reduced appreciation of male subjects for the sexual material in this study, compared with the previous one. This in turn may be attributable to a number of factors including the age difference between the two samples, or their different life-styles. In particular, the older group were mostly full-time workers and part-time students.

In dyads, confederate laughter significantly increased subjects' expressive responses to sexual cartoons, ($F=46.1$; $df=1,48$; $p < .002$) and significantly enhanced subjective ratings of funniness of these cartoons ($F=22.9$; $df=1,48$; $p < .002$). Male confederates elicited higher ratings of funniness than did female confederates ($F=16.5$; $df=1,48$; $p < .002$), a difference which did not emerge in the expressive responses. For the nonsexual cartoons, expressive responses were again facilitated by confederate laughter ($F=9.0$; $df=1,48$; $p < .02$), as were subjective ratings, ($F=6.9$; $df=1,48$; $p < .05$) but the latter were not affected by the sex of the confederate. There was, however, a significant sex difference in the subjective ratings given to the nonsexual cartoons ($F=6.6$; $df=1,48$; $p < .05$) which apparently resulted from considerably lower male subjective ratings. Overall, the extent to which subjects responded to confederate behaviour seems to have been less for nonsexual cartoons than for sexual ones. This result suggests that subjects were making greater use of the confederates' behaviour to gain information as to how to react when they were looking at sexual cartoons, whereas they did not need this information for the nonsexual cartoons.

The strength of the relationship between the two measures of humour appreciation taken was calculated using Pearson Product Moment Correlations. Male subjects alone showed a slight positive correlation between the measures for sexual cartoons ($r=.41$; $df=8$; ns), while females alone showed a slight negative relationship between measures ($r=-.37$; $df=8$; ns). This could not be reasonably expected on the basis of previous work, and it may be that female subjects experienced some form of evaluation apprehension concerning the experimenter's presence (cf. Chapman, 1974); this could have led them to give lowered funniness ratings for the sexual cartoons. The fact that the nonsexual cartoons, presumably not as threatening, produced positive response measure correlations from both male and female subjects alone (male $r=.64$; $df=8$; $p < .025$; female $r=.46$; $df=8$; ns) supports an explanation of this form.

In the dyadic conditions, there were only two significant correlations for the sexual cartoons, from male subjects with a responsive male confederate ($r=.71$; $df=5$; $p < .05$) and female subjects with a responsive female confederate ($r=.79$; $df=5$; $p < .025$). Viewing the nonsexual cartoons, only the male subjects produced any significant correlations and this was in the situation with a responsive male confederate ($r=.75$; $df=5$; $p < .05$).

In conclusion, it would seem that the extent to which any subject makes an 'objective' assessment of a humorous item depends very much on the subject's knowledge of the material, and his or her self-assurance in reacting to it. Where subjects are embarrassed or confused, the reaction of a companion provides extra information or simply acts as a facilitative pressure to make the subject respond in a certain fashion. Whether the expressive response of smiling and laughing is followed by a similarly enhanced subjective rating seems to depend on whether the judgment or behaviour of the companion is respected sufficiently by the subject to overcome the evaluation apprehension instilled by the presence of the experimenter.

REFERENCES

See Bibliography for publications on humour, laughter and comedy

Chapman, A.J. Sexism in sexual humour. Paper presented to the British Psychological Society, Social Psychology Section Conference, London, December (1975c).

Teasing and Joking in Isolated Societies

Gordon Burnand

Buckinghamshire College of Higher Education, England

A number of isolated societies were examined in terms of 'problems'. Any problem may be thought to generate two types of behaviour: restrained behaviour which helps diminish the problem, and unrestrained behaviour which risks magnifying it. Unrestrained behaviour includes teasing, joking, fantasy and play. The problems examined corresponded to a lack of one of the six basic requirements of a supportive relationship: unity of purpose, fairness, stability, freedom, reward in the sense of favourable outcomes for the individual, and optimism or morale, a positive approval from others (cf. Burnand, 1977). It is possible to specify, to some extent, the conditions that would sensitise a person to each problem and the behaviour patterns that would help diminish each problem. For example, if someone important in one's life unpredictably comes and goes, ignores one, moves away, threatens to move, etcetera, one would expect a person to become sensitised to stability. The problem of stability would be helped by searching out and holding onto stable groups, trying to understand and predict change, religious belief, conservatism, etcetera. It appeared possible to link societies with particular problems.

With the unrestrained, humorous behaviour, as represented mostly by teasing, descriptions were usually brief and inconspicuous. Thus usually it was possible to classify a society in terms of its restrained behaviour before one encountered evidence of the unrestrained behaviour. When reported, the nature of teasing in societies appeared always very specific and reasonably clearly classifiable in terms of the six problems. Thus the Ilicano of Tarong were classified as being sensitised to the 'optimism or morale' problem, and were capable of great restraint when people's emotions were involved. Their teasing caused great emotional upset to one another. The Navaho were classified as having a 'unity' problem which they dealt with by integration or segregation. Their teasing and joking involved accusations of inferiority, failing to maintain distinction between humans, animals and objects, buffoonery, where ridicule was invited by not conforming to the appropriate role, and playing practical jokes where people acted outside the appropriate role category, thus going against the normal practice of careful conformity and segregation of different groups. The Gusii were categorized as having a physical 'reward' problem, associated with sensible care over food and property. Among children teasing was always a provocation to fighting, for example, by shooting a berry with a sling or the use of derogatory names. Among adults teasing sometimes took the form of threat of physical abuse, and stealing was an accepted pastime for youths below ten or at initiation. With all these three societies teasing seemed reasonably distinctive and descriptions were encountered only after the society had been classified on the basis of its restrained behaviour.

The 'mirror-image' relationship between restrained behaviour and teasing for the Ilicano is illustrated by the following observations of Nydegger & Nydegger (1967) at a small dance. An impromptu programme began while the band rested. One shy youth who could only sing very badly was forced into participating. He sang horribly in terror and increasing misery. The audience showed a 'polite respectful silence they would have accorded the mayor had he decided to sing at a similar gathering. No movement that could have been construed as derisive was made: each face was carefully blank. When the boy finished he was applauded heartily — the decrease in tension was almost audible' (p861). They also observe: 'At evening porch gatherings, parties, prayer meetings — anywhere groups gather — the most common and most interesting activities are gossip about people not present and teasing of those who are among the group. This teasing although friendly is accurate in regard to facts and mercilessly embarrassing' (p761).

There was also reasonably clear evidence that the Kwakiutl, classed as having a fairness problem, leading to the sub-problem of establishing a credible image, so that claims for fairness would receive a hearing, teased through attacking and distorting people's images. Other people were satirized and jokes were often involved in an element of 'You should not

437

be able to understand that'.

The Eskimo clearly resembled the Ilicano in having an optimism problem. Some sketchy
evidence of teasing came to light later. Two reports of children teasing others to the point
of distress were found. While having the good opinion of others seemed the most important
concern for adults, and one would expect teasing to be an important factor, actual reports
of Eskimo teasing and humour were not encountered.

With the Balinese, who were classed as having a freedom-frustration problem, the pattern of
teasing was one of restraining others and of stimulation followed by frustration. While the
pattern of teasing was known before the society was classified, the nature of the restrained
behaviour and teasing seemed beyond dispute. With three other societies the pattern of
teasing seemed more obscure. The Ojibwa, the North American Indians who were very isolated
in winter were classed as having a stability problem. They appeared to cope with this via a
kind of 'private' religion, where each had his own guardian spirit and destiny. Possibly the
competitions that occurred in the brief summer reunions threatened the person's belief in his
guardian spirit and destiny and thus constituted a form of teasing. With the Yurok Indians,
who were classed as having a reward problem, it seemed possible that statements that property
was damaged and quarrels over property and litigation may have represented forms of teasing.
The Rajputs like the Navaho, were classed as having a unity problem. There was some use of
accusation of inferiority, using the names of inferior castes, in the discipline of children,
and it seems likely that teasing followed a similar pattern. With the Nyakusas, who seemed
concerned about the unfairness of inequality, there was favouritism in the home and this could
reflect teasing.

There appeared to be a great deal of continuity between teasing behaviour and the happy
confident behaviour within the home. Among the Ilicano and Navaho the pattern of teasing
between adults also appeared to be used to discipline children. The Gusii used physical
punishment to discipline children more than other societies. Among the fairness-credibility-
respect sensitive Kwakiutl there was no respect for elders in the home.

Thus it appeared possible to match cultures to particular problems of social relationships.
Where teasing behaviour was fully reported it seemed to be clear and distinctive of the same
problem that appeared to underly restrained behaviour.

REFERENCES

Burnand, G., Problems We Create. Harper & Row, London, in press (1977).

Nydegger, W.F. & Nydegger, C., Tarong an Ilocos Barrio in the Phillipines. In: B. Whiting
     (Ed.), Six Cultures. Wiley, New York (1967).

Environmental Conditions Affecting the Humour Response: Developmental Trends

Frank J. Prerost

Lewis University, Illinois

This paper investigates the effects of crowding on humour appreciation between the ages of ten to twenty years of age. Research on the effects of crowding has been differentiated into two types by Loo (1973). Spatial density research compares the behaviour of groups of the same number in spaces of differing sizes. Social density research compares behaviour of groups with differing numbers in the same sized space. This paper utilizes both concepts of crowding to determine their individual effects on humour appreciation.

Considering the first type of crowding, a number of reactions to high spatial density conditions have been reported suggesting that it is an unpleasant stressful state of experience. McBride, King and James (1965) found that galvanic skin responses increased for subjects in high spatial density conditions, and Dosey and Meisels (1969) reported an increase in feelings of anxiety among crowded subjects. Subjects in high spatial density situations became more irritable and antagonistic in a study by Cozby (1973). Further evidence of the stress-producing nature of high spatial density has been provided by Ross, Layton, Erickson, and Schopler (1973) who also noted that males were most affected by the high spatial density. Stress reactions have also been noted in an adolescent population in a study by Freedman, Levy, Buchannan and Price (1972) when spatial density increased.

Research with humour has demonstrated that feelings of anxiety or threat will adversely affect humour appreciation. Hammes and Wiggins (1962) found decreases in the appreciation of humour as manifest anxiety scores increased. Levine and Redlich (1960) reported that as perception of threat from the environment increased, humour appreciation decreased. Prerost and Brewer (1973) found that as feelings of threat increase, the appreciation and satisfaction with humour decreases significantly.

If high spatial density is indeed an unpleasant stress-producing situation, the appreciation of humour should be adversely affected. The present paper attempted to determine if humour appreciation is affected by high spatial density in such a way as to reflect the theorized negative effects of such conditions. The humour utilized throughout this study was categorized into three types: neutral, aggressive, and sexual. These three types of humour content were selected because results reported by Prerost (1972) indicate differential appreciation of such humour by males and females. Humour appreciation was predicted to decrease in high spatial density conditions as a result of stressful qualities present.

Concerning social density, a general belief appears to exist that the presence of other persons will increase humour appreciation as number of individuals increase. But little actual empirical evidence supportive of this notion exists. Humour appreciation has been reported to increase with the size of audiences in a theatre by Andrus (1946) and Morrison (1940). Also children's laughter has been found to be facilitated when another child is present in a study by Chapman (1973b). Thus, although widespread supportive evidence is lacking, indications are that high social density would increase humour appreciation.

There were one hundred and forty-four male and female students utilized in this investigation of spatial density effects. Twenty-four male and twenty-four females participated at each of three age levels. The three age groups were pre-adolescents, middle adolescents and young adults. The age ranges for the three age levels were as follows: pre-adolescents: ten to twelve years; middle adolescents: fourteen to sixteen years; and young adults: eighteen to twenty years. Selection of these three age levels was made because: (1) of the significance of puberty in development of social behaviours; (2) the same type of humour could be employed for all three groups - McGhee (1972b) demonstrated that by the age of ten years children comprehend written forms of adult humour; and (3) there is a general lack of research during this adolescent period concerning humour appreciation. All of the subjects were students from parochial schools who shared a White middle socioeconomic background. Subjects were randomly assigned to the different experimental conditions. An additional like number of subjects from the three age groups participated in the social density conditions.

Spatial Density

Subjects from the three age levels were examined in either high or low spatial density conditions. Male and female subjects were run in same-sexed groups of six persons. Subjects completed booklets containing thirty-six jokes (twelve neutral, twelve aggressive, twelve sexual, randomly intermixed) to be rated for funniness on a seven-point scale from 0 ('not at all funny') to 6 ('extremely funny'). Written forms of humour appreciation were employed to eliminate any obtrusive instruments in the experimental setting. The basic design for the study was a 2 x 2 x 3 x 3 factorial design crossing density (high, low), sex, age, and humour type.

For the low density condition, the group of six subjects was run in a room measuring 3.50 metres by 3.10 metres; these dimensions allow 1.81 square metres per person. Under the high spatial density setting, the subjects were in a space 2.51 by 1.20 metres; this area allowed 0.50 square metre per person. These figures are comparable to the areas used in the studies cited above. No furniture except for chairs was in the experimental area.

Four judges from each of the three age levels aided in the selection of the jokes used. They rated a master list of one hundred and twenty jokes along the dimensions of aggression and sexuality on a six-point scale from 0 ('not at all') to 5 ('extremely'). The twelve jokes receiving zeros on aggression and sexuality were neutral jokes. The twelve jokes with the highest aggressiveness ratings, and the twelve jokes with the highest sexuality ratings were selected as the aggressive and sexual jokes respectively.

Social Density

Subjects from the three age levels were examined in high or low social density situations. All the subjects were tested in a standard-sized classroom. In the low social density condition three same-sexed individuals completed the booklets containing the thirty-six jokes to be rated on the dimension of funniness. In the high social density condition, the group size was nine individuals who independently completed the joke ratings. Once again a 2 x 2 x 3 x 3 factorial design resulted crossing density, sex, age and humour type.

RESULTS AND DISCUSSION

The analyses indicated that density did significantly affect the appreciation of humour, but a differential effect occurred depending on the type of density. As spatial density increased humour appreciation significantly diminished ($F=45.74$; $df=1,132$; $p < .001$), yet when social density increased humour appreciation likewise increased significantly ($F=28.35$; $df=1,132$; $p < .001$). Thus, high spatial density had an inhibitory effect on the appreciation of humour while high social density produced a facilitating effect on humour appreciation.

It was revealed in the data that density had a differential effect on males and females. This Sex by Density interaction indicated that males were more sensitive to increases in spatial density than were the female subjects. Their appreciation of humour declined to a much greater extent during high spatial density than did the female appreciation scores. But it was the females who demonstrated greatest reactance to the condition of high social density. The female humour appreciation scores increased to a greater degree during high social density than did the male scores ($F=15.11$; $df=1,132$; $p < .001$). Thus a different sensitivity to the type of density occurred depending upon the sex of the subject, with males being most influenced by the spatial density ($F=16.97$; $df=1,132$; $p < .001$).

The appreciation of humour was found to be significantly different across the three age levels for both spatial and social density ($F=21.69$; $df=2,132$; $p < .001$ and $F=19.55$; $df=2,132$; $p < .001$, respectively). For spatial density humour appreciation increased from pre-adolescence to a peak during middle adolescence (fourteen- to sixteen-year-olds). Both the appreciation of humour and the effect of spatial density was most profound during the middle adolescent period, while the pre-adolescent group was least influenced by fluctuations in spatial density. A different picture occurred in the social density conditions. The greatest social density effects occurred in the pre-adolescent group. The ten- to twelve-year-olds, especially the female subjects, exhibited the greatest degree of increases in the appreciation of humour as the social density became high. This age group appeared to be most sensitive to the high social density.

Although humour ratings were significantly different for the three types of humour ($F=31.49$; $df=2,264$; $p < .001$), no changes in preferences for a particular type of humour content between spatial density conditions was noted. What did occur in both spatial and social density conditions was that a particular type of humour content was most affected by the shifts in density. In the spatial density, the male appreciation of aggressive humour was particularly inhibited. In the social density conditions, the female appreciation of sexual humour was facilitated to the greatest degree.

The effects of density on the appreciation of humour reported in this paper suggest the possible use of a social learning approach in the development of the humour response. The maximum affect of social density during the pre-adolescent years may indicate the children's attempts to determine exactly what should be considered as humorous. During this age children are still undergoing a search to prepare themselves for their entry into the adolescent transitional phase to adulthood. Thus children of this age would be particularly susceptible to what other children their own age consider as funny. In a high social density situation there are more inputs (that is, humorous reactions) upon which a child can make a judgment as to the degree of funniness of different jokes. Thus different reactions such as a giggle, laugh, or smile would be merely added together to establish degree of funniness. Differential sensitivity of sexual humour by females and aggressive humour among males may indicate cultural peer factors acting upon the child at that age. Reactions discovered in the high spatial density situations, may signify when a group becomes too stressful to continue to serve its social learning function. Since the time of middle adolescence is already particularly stressful due to identity problems, reactions to crowding would be expected to be most pronounced during these ages. And the data indicate that humour appreciation is most inhibited during this period as a function of high spatial density.

REFERENCES

See Bibliography for publications on humour, laughter and comedy

Cozby, P.C., Effects of density, activity, and personality on environmental preferences. Journal of Research in Personality, 7, 45-60 (1973).

Dosey, M. & Meisels, M., Personal space and self protection. Journal of Personality and Social Psychology, 11, 93-97 (1969).

Freedman, J., Levy, A., Buchannan, R. & Price, J., Crowding and human aggressiveness. Journal of Experimental Social Psychology, 8, 528-548 (1972).

Loo, C.M., Important issues in researching the effects of crowding in humans. Representative Research in Social Psychology, 4, 219-226 (1973).

McBride, G., King, M. & James, J. Social proximity effects on galvanic skin responses in adult humans. Journal of Personality, 61, 153-157 (1965).

Ross, M., Layton, B., Erickson, B. & Schopler, J. Affects, facial regard, and reactions to crowding. Journal of Personality and Social Psychology, 28, 69-76 (1973).

Vulgarity in Humour

William Hodgkins

Cardiff

VULGARITY

When one considers vulgarity one assumes that it belongs to a lower level of language. To Partridge (1975) low language and vulgarisms are not the same. He suggests that low language springs from the proletariat, a word he dislikes using but prefers it to the phrase, 'the lower classes', but also, and this is more important, low language is the thrusting of words from a social class of a lower order into the conversation of other classes. 'Low words' he says, 'are those which, used by the poorest and meanest classes, are yet neither cant nor "good" colloquialisms' (p355). This is a language full of the immediacy of life, strong, vivid, and to the user emotionally satisfactory, but belonging to a part of society and not the whole.

Vulgarisms, on the other hand, do not spring from the lowest or lower classes; they are not used by one class only, but are idiomatic English. They are not mentioned in so-called polite society; they are not drawing room verbal currency. They require an atmosphere of convivial freedom or intimacy to release them.

> 'Vulgarisms are words that denote such objects or processes or functions or
> tendencies or acts as are not usually mentioned in polite company and are never
> under those names mentioned in respectable circles'. (Partridge, p356).

For the more personal organs of the body we have two vocabularies. On the one hand the Latinized and Grecized words such as 'penis' and 'prudend' and on the other 'prick' and 'cunt'. These latter are part of the structure of the English language. They are words which belong to us because for centuries they were Standard English in everyday use. We are more deeply involved in them than in the Latinisms and clinical speech forms of this century. Words become vulgarisms and fall into social disuse because they can arouse emotions which are socially embarrassing. Hoggart in his Introduction to D.H. Lawrence's 'Lady Chatterley's Lover' (Penguin, 1975 Edition) says:

> 'Most of us know these "four letter words" from an early age. We know them as
> swear words or as parts of dirty jokes. If we wish to speak simply and naturally
> about sex we are baffled. We tend to take roundabout ways, most of which are
> ashamed escape-routes. There is an old war-time story which illustrates both
> these characteristics. A soldier on leave from abroad was charged with assaulting
> another man. He explained why he had done it: "I came home after three fucking
> years in fucking Africa, and what do I fucking-well find? My wife in bed, engaged
> in illicit cohabitation with a male".' (pix).

When people hear vulgarisms they are shocked on the surface, shaken in their superficial social values. But they laugh at jokes because underneath in the deeper life of the mind they are not shocked.

CONVIVIALITY

Proximity is essential to human beings for sustenance, safety and sanity. In this nearness to each other we are offered continually the choice between conformity or dissent. The social pressures, especially the benefits of proximity, make for conformity. The response to humour has as its background the unconscious desire to share in the general well-being.

'Conviviality' is the word used by Polanyi (1958) to describe that atmosphere of social encouragement which is marked by friendliness and co-operation.

'The sentiments of trust and the pursuasive passions by which the transmission
of our articulate heritage is kept flowing, bring us back once more to the
primitive sentiments of fellowship that exist previous to articulation among
all groups of men and even among animals. (p209).

There is a physical pattern in communication which is prior to speech. It is as if
physically we hurl meanings at people and then use words to express more explicitly what we
mean by our physical behaviour. The speech pattern is not a package to be opened out by the
recipient who takes each word and examines it, but a stirring of meanings within the listener
who accepts the message given to him by his own meanings. The process of gathering meanings
is not a conscious one to the speaker or the listener. The moment the process becomes
conscious and the speaker is concentrating on how he is speaking, hesitation comes into the
speaking and if the concentration continues the speaking will stop. In a similar way the
listener must fully accept the process of the stirring and enlivening of his meanings, for,
if he concentrates on each meaning separately he will soon lose the comprehensive import of
what is being said.

Conviviality is an important element in communication. It facilitates awareness and attention,
it inhibits ego tendencies, it makes possible that enlivening and selection of meanings which
is the process by which we inform each other. A lack of conviviality makes communication
difficult and the telling of jokes and the arousing of laughter impossible.

The nurturing of friendship within the family is the basis of fellowship in school,
neighbourhood and society. Our institutions find their emotional roots in this friendship;
the well-being of our society is only possible on the basis of its continuation. When we
discuss humour and its contribution to our well-being we are entering spheres of responsibility,
for the despoiling of humour is the destruction of friendship. To say that something is
obscene is to say that it is detrimental to the good within society. The difference between
obscenity and vulgarity is that obscenity is destructive and vulgarity is creative.

HUMOUR

Humour to be satisfactory has its own sophistication. The presentation of the joke must be
competent. The use of language must be confident. A vulgarism ceases to be funny if it is
presented in a sneaky apologetic manner. With the confidence there must be a hard core of
certainty. The laughter response may be elicited by the contradictory nature of the same
idea used in two different ways. The well-known story used by Freud illustrates this.
'Chamfort tells a story of a Marquis at the court of Louis 14th who, on entering his wife's
boudoir and finding her in the arms of a Bishop, walked camly to the window and went through
the motion of blessing the people in the street. "What are you doing?" cried the anguished
wife. "Mon seigneur is performing my functions", replied the Marquis, "so I am performing
his".' (Koestler, 1964, p33). Koestler uses this story to point out that 'unexpectedness
alone is not enough to produce a comic effect. The crucial point about the Marquis' behaviour
is that it is both unexpected and perfectly logical – but of a logic not usually applied to
this type of situation. ... It is the clash of two mutually incompatible codes, or
associative contexts, which explodes the tension'. (p33).

In his analysis of humour Koestler makes the 'dual concepts of matrices and codes' central
to his consideration. There are other ways of differentiating humour, such as that between
two people, face-to-face, or the semi-private humour of the family, or that of the club
audience, or the large audience of radio and television. All these influence the choice of
humour, the way it is presented and the reactions of those sharing in the humour situation.
In addition to the frames of reference there are circles of behaviour interaction, each
circle separately conditioning the humour situation. The comedian with a studio audience
before him drops his joke like a stone into a pond, watching groups are widening circles
until they are universal.

DIALECT AND VULGARISMS

Dialect is a local language. It may have roots as deep as the Gothic language as, for
example, in the Rossendale Forest dialect. Most dialects have been studied in great detail;
glossaries and grammars have been published, and their value as contributions to colloquial
English recognized. The general usage of local languages is declining, mostly because of the
necessity today of a universal serviceability of language. The world has become a
neighbourhood, and a language which can be understood by everybody is a necessity for its
continued existence. The assertion of the importance of national and local language and
culture is a reaction to the continued movement towards a universal language. The general
effect of education is to lessen the value of dialect because of its limited application.

Although there is a similar effect upon vulgarisms it is not so strong because vulgarisms belong to the structure of the language and have a place in a whole group of languages.

CONCLUSION

Vulgarity belongs to the social inheritance of all English-speaking peoples. It is not alien but has been passed over in verbal currency which, like old coins having served their purpose, remain mostly unused in corners and cupboards. Vulgarity is essentially different from obscenity, for it is creative where obscenity is destructive. The value of vulgarity is not only in a release of energy repressed through inadequate social expression, it is also an affirmation of the rightness of the ordinary, the common-place, and the plebeian. This is a true value in the social interaction of humour because it provides a creative perspective.

REFERENCES

Partridge, E., Usage and Abusage. Penguin, Harmondsworth (1975).

Polanyi, M., Personal Knowledge. Routledge & Kegan Paul, London (1958).

The Measurement of Humour Appreciation

Alan Sheehy-Skeffington

Trinity College, Dublin

At some stage in most humour studies, it becomes necessary to assess the degree of amusement experienced by the subject. Naturally, any measure used should be reliable, objective, and capable of fairly precise quantification. Two methods are commonly employed: either we observe the subject to see if he shows signs of amusement, or we ask him if he is amused. By the first method, certain characteristics of the overt mirth response are measured, the mirth response generally being taken to include both laughs and smiles. The amplitude or the frequency of the response, may, of course be measured, but reliable quantification of these variables is technically difficult. The most common practice is to record the total duration of the response in the course of an experimental session. This should represent an expression of the perceived funniness of the material presented. The overt mirth response, however, appears to be influenced by variables other than the humour content of the material, such as the presence of others laughing, or the presence of alcohol in the bloodstream. Even the mere presence of others has been shown, for example by Chapman (1975b), to facilitate the response of laughter. Presumably, we would not usually wish to say that the presence of another person is itself something amusing, although perhaps there are persons of whose presence this might often be said. Although the 'strength' of the overt response is a simple and obvious measure of amusement, it is a fairly crude one, and a more reliable measure is needed.

It might be supposed that a subject's verbal behaviour is less susceptible to the influence of extraneous variables than is the more primitive and instinctive behaviour of laughing. Hence, we ask the subject how amused he was at the material presented to him. This is generally done by requiring him to rate the material for humour content on, for example, a five-point scale.

In certain circumstances, the two measures have been found to show a degree of independence. The addition of 'canned' laughter to recorded humorous material, for example, has been found by Leventhal and Mace (1970), among others, to strengthen the overt mirth response without raising subjects' ratings of the humour content of the material. But this result has not been consistently obtained. For example, Smyth and Fuller (1972) found that the addition of canned laughter to humorous recordings raised both measures and, when Chapman (1975b) found that the presence of an expressionless confederate augmented subjects' laughing behaviour, he also found that funniness ratings were raised.

Researchers cannot yet be confident about the quantitative aspects of any measure of amusement. Perhaps the difficulty is compounded by the fact that much reference is made outside the psychological laboratory to both the fore-mentioned aspects of the humour response. People tend to use overt expressions of mirth and verbal behaviour about equally as indicators of amusement. The finding that they do not always co-vary poses something of a problem. The psychologist must take account of normal linguistic usage, and cannot arbitrarily define one or other as 'the' humour response. The trouble is that the best answer to the question 'What sort of thing is amusing?' is still 'The sort of thing that people laugh and smile at'. And yet it is still tempting to say that there are aspects of the humour response which are somehow independent of other determinants of laughter and smiling. No doubt some of these problems arise from the difficulty of defining humour stimuli or responses without some degree of circularity. It is perhaps impossible to define one satisfactorily without some reference to the other.

It is true that these theoretical considerations do not preclude the possibility of heuristic research. Certainly, these considerations are unlikely to perturb us if all we want to do is to ascertain whether or not a subject is amused. But if we want to quantify and compare various degrees of amusement, there is no doubt that the issues in measurement will have to be clarified.

Meanwhile, however, to return to the consideration of the effects of canned laughter, perhaps exploration of a rather different avenue of inquiry would be fruitful. So far, we have been asking whether or not subjects find material to which canned laughter has been added more amusing than the same material without canned laughter. Alternatively, to circumvent the issue of the quantification of amusement, we might ask whether subjects prefer to listen to or watch humorous material with or without canned laughter. The producer of comic films may, after all, be less interested in amusing his audience than in inducing the greatest possible number of people to watch his films. The two objectives do not necessarily coincide, and the relationship of the amusement value of humorous material to its reinforcement value should be of some scientific interest.

This is the sort of question that fits an operant paradigm. One common method for determining subjects' preferences is the use of concurrent schedules of reinforcement. Concurrent schedules are two or more schedules operating simultaneously and independently, each for a different response. The use of this method to assess differences in reinforcement value has been shown by Catania (1963). In this case, it had been found that the rate of pigeons' key-pressing was not significantly affected by relatively large changes in the duration of presentation of food reinforcement. This was contrary to expectation, since one would suppose that the longer the duration of presentation, the greater the reinforcement value, and hence the higher the rate of response. Given a choice of durations programmed on the same schedule but on different keys, however, a clear separation could be obtained, with rate of response linearly related to duration of reinforcement. Concurrent schedules thus seem to be well suited to the demonstration of preferences between reinforcers.

Humour response rate is not really a viable measure for our purposes. There are ways, however, in which concurrent schedules can be used to show preferences between recorded materials. For example, the subject may be offered the choice of pressing one of two telegraph keys, to obtain one of two humorous tape-recordings. The schedule of reinforcement, in other words the response requirement, might be the same for both keys, in which case the experiment is reduced to a fairly simple choice situation, the relative time spent listening to each recording being a measure of preference. A more satisfactory arrangement is to vary at frequent intervals the recording corresponding to a given key. Thus the subject is required to make a continuous series of choices. Alternatively, the schedules of reinforcement may be different for each response, the response requirement being higher for one than for the other. Again, the key requiring the higher response rate may be varied in the course of a session. This last procedure should provide a fairly fine discrimination between the reinforcing values of, for instance, a humorous recording with added laughter and the same recording without.

Another operant technique which may be of value in studying attitudes to canned laughter is what is known as a titration schedule. This is a schedule in which one response changes a variable in one direction, and either a second response or the nonoccurrence of the first response changes the same variable in the opposite direction. The classic description of this type of schedule is that of Blough (1958) who used this procedure to determine psychophysical thresholds in the pigeon. The procedure is useful in determining the level of intensity of a reinforcer which is preferred by a subject. Stein and Ray (1959), for example, used a titration schedule to allow rats to set the intensity of brain-stimulating electric current at a preferred level. In a similar way, subjects' preferred intensity of canned laughter may be determined.

The point of these procedures, as in all operant studies, is that the subject must do something in order to obtain reinforcement. It is not enough for him to state that he prefers A to B; he is forced, we might say, to speak with his feet. He must express his preference by his behaviour, which is drawn out somewhat in time with the hope of increasing the accuracy of the measure.

One expects that an operant analysis should be able to tease out some further relationships between stimulus, subject and response variables. Increased accuracy of measurement may enable us to extend some of our earlier investigations. For example, the effects of canned laughter on humour ratings were found by Cupchik and Leventhal (1974) to be greatest when the humour content of the material was low. This result, however, is not consistently obtained with any degree of significance. Of some interest in this context would be the measurement of preferences between various combinations of low- and high-humour material with and without canned laughter. The greater flexibility of operant measures may afford new insights into this problem.

Again, it has been suggested by Fuller and Sheehy-Skeffington (1974) that the reason for increased humour ratings resulting from the addition of canned laughter may be that the laughter serves as a situational cue, conditioning the listener to search for a humorous interpretation of the material. In other words, canned laughter may serve as a discriminative stimulus for the perception of humour. If this is the case, it should be possible for a perfectly arbitrary discriminative stimulus, such as a coloured light, to acquire the same function. A systematic investigation of the operation of discriminative stimuli in the context of humour situations is possible using operant techniques.

In conclusion, the value of trying an operant approach to the study of humour lies in the new aspects of old problems which may be revealed. We may hope that this will prove to be a useful step towards the solution of some of these problems.

REFERENCES

See Bibliography for publications on humour, laughter and comedy.

Blough, D.S., A method for obtaining psychophysical thresholds from the pigeon. Journal of the Experimental Analysis of Behavior, 1, 31-43 (1958).

Catania, A.C., Concurrent performances: a baseline for the study of reinforcement magnitude. Journal of the Experimental Analysis of Behavior, 6, 299-300 (1963).

Stein, L. & Ray, O.,Self-regulation of brain-stimulating current intensity in the rat. Science, 130, 570-572 (1959).

An Anatomical and Psychological Examination of Eye-Pouches

John Kirkland, Michael Mair and Michael Couzens

University of London Institute of Education

Small shifts in the orientation of a viewer or of a viewed object can produce quite dramatic perceptual shifts. This phenomena is not limited to 'classical' two-dimensional configurations such as the Necker cube. They are, we suspect, evidenced on the human face as well. It has been shown that small changes on the human face can affect perception out of proportion to that change. For instance in his now well-known demonstration Hess (1965) manipulated pupil-sizes on one of two otherwise indentical pictures. Since these Hess-prints were each originally taken from a single negative it is certain that the only variations were the touched-up, dilated, pupils. Additionally, equal-interval computer-generated mirth-like faces affect perception non-linearly (Kirkland, this volume).

The mechanisms underlying such perceptual shifts have not been fully explicated; the present study is another description. It is an attempt to examine the perceptual effect of minor human-face changes. This time it is directed toward perception of 'genuine' mirth. When some people smile and/or laugh, small horizontal bulges appear under the skin beneath the lower eye-lids. These are not 'air conditioning' bags, neither are they the obvious 'age-sags' of older people. They are labile pouches often accompanying the simultaneous occurrence of eye-narrowing and lip-corner retraction. We call these bulges 'eye-pouches.' It has been suggested (Brannigan & Humphries, 1972; Grant, 1969) that eye-pouch production is a hallmark of 'genuine upper-smiles,' the smiles in which upper but not lower teeth are displayed. These writers claim that eye-pouch manipulation is not volitional. We set about to test one aspect of these claims - that their presence is critical for interpreting smile genuineness. Besides examining eye-pouches we are toying with applying catastrophe theory (Thom, 1975) to face-perception.

Our approach was two-fold. First, one of us (Mair) undertook an anatomical examination of a face to find out just how it is that eye-pouches are produced. And, secondly, we arranged for the artistic removal of eye-pouches from four portrait pictures (after much the same manner as Hess attended to his pupils) and requested subjects to rate these, the originals, and filler-portraits for smile 'genuineness.'

The aim was to reveal insertion of fibres of Orbicularis Occuli into the skin. In conventional dissection the skin is the first to be removed. Actual facial appearance is however the appearance of the skin and the effect of underlying structures upon it. Unless the face is dissected from behind, demonstration of insertion of fibres into the skin depends upon folding back small skin flaps. This latter procedure was adopted. The area of skin about six square centimetres beneath each eye was dissected, in three cadavers. An eliptical incision through the dermis was performed, from medial to lateral canthus. The flap was dissected upwards, to remain attached at the lash margin. In each case, small fibres of the Orbicularis Occuli were seen diverging from the main course of this muscle which runs concentrically around the eye from its origin near the medial palpebral ligament. These small fibres splayed out to be inserted into the underside of the skin flap (that is, the dermis). Contraction of these fibres would account for the fleeting appearance and disappearance of the eye pouches, and indeed it is hard to account for them in any other way.

METHOD

Forty students, including both undergraduates and graduates, volunteered to participate in the study. Subjects, half male, were drawn from two educational institutions in and close to London. Neither payment nor course credit was available for participants.

A set of twenty-four high quality polychrome portraits from an advertising poster were each
mounted on stiff card. These were given to ten adults (half male) in varying orders who were
individually instructed to allocate pictures to one of three piles labelled: definite
'eye-pouch' present, not sure, no 'eye-pouch' present. By omitting children, a dog, and
pictures receiving less than ninety per cent interjudge agreement four pictures remained (two
male and one of each sex showing an 'upper' smile). In addition to these 'critical pictures'
fourteen others were included as buffer stimuli. These eighteen pictures were then copied to
give large monochrome negatives (9.16 x 12.7 cm). Matt-finish enlargements (18.32 x 25.4 cm)
were produced from these negatives, including a dual set of the critical ones. An artist
removed eye-pouches from one of these sets. All twenty-two enlargements were then
rephotographed, twice, onto 35 mm film (using Ajfa dia-direct), to produce monochrome
positives which were mounted and subsequently displayed as slides. A single carousel magazine
was loaded with two sets of eighteen slide-pictures. One set was in random order and the
other reversed so as to reduce order effects. Critical pictures occupied positions three,
seven, thirteen and fifteen in the randomly ordered set. For half the subjects these pictures
were exchanged for the alternative ones in each set. Slides were displayed against a white
wall 2.5 m from the projector lens. Subjects were seated 0.5 m in front and slightly to the
right of the projector. Illumination by a 60 watt, 250 volt white-lamp was maintained through
out each testing session. Response sheets, each with twenty equally-spaced seven-point
numerical scales, were mimeographed and one each given subjects. A cassette-tape-synchroniser
was used to advance the projector automatically.

The following instructions were read aloud by a single male experimenter to each individually-
tested subject.

> This study will take about six minutes for you to complete. Several head-and-shoulder
> pictures of different people will be projected onto the wall. Each picture shows
> a person smiling; some of these smiles are bigger than others. Your task is to
> rate each person's smile according to how genuine you think it is. Try to disregard
> the smile size when making your genuineness ratings. Enter your ratings on the
> seven-point scales provided; use one scale for each smile. Each scale is a
> continuum ranging from one (false smile) to seven (genuine smile). To record your
> judgement circle one number on the relevant scale; use the top scale for the first
> smile, the next scale for the second, and so on. Following the projection of each
> smile-face which will last only for two seconds, is a blank, grey like, slide which
> will last for seven seconds. Record your genuineness ratings during this period.
> In all there are about twenty smiles for you to rate. Do you have any questions
> about your task? Are you ready?

Following the rating phase additional instructions were provided: 'Now please turn over your
rating-paper and describe how you interpreted genuineness.' Subjects were thanked for
volunteering their time and dismissed.

A two-factor randomized block design was employed with the following factors: sex of
respondent (male, female); condition of 'critical' stimuli (original, modified); while the
order of presentation of stimuli (forward or reverse) provided the blocking. To avoid the
problems of multiple testing with four dependent variables - the 'critical' picture ratings -
a multivariate analysis of variance (MANOVA) was used with factorial discriminant analysis
(Cooley & Lohnes, 1971) to differentiate amongst dependent variables, within any resultant
effects. A computerized procedure (Baughan, 1972) is available for this purpose.

RESULTS AND DISCUSSION

MANOVA results show neither significant main effects nor their interaction; (see Table 1).

TABLE 1

Effect	Approximate 'F' Ratio	Probability of 'F'
SEX	0.11	0.98
CONDITION	1.37	0.27
SEX/CONDITION	1.26	0.31
ORDER	1.68	0.18

Clearly the null hypothesis of no differences between 'genuineness' ratings and the different conditions is not shaken by these data. Taken independently there are no differences for the 'uppersmile' faces either. Consequently it is unnecessary to interpret discriminant functions.

These anecdotal data indicate 'genuineness' is related to warmth, spontaneity, naturalness, sincerity and sparkle. It is noteworthy that the comments did not produce any reference to actual facial features, thus completely bypassing the salience of eye-pouches, or the quality of the artwork.

The present research had dual objectives. First, anatomically we have shown that eye-pouches are produced by contraction of fibres of the obicularis occuli muscle which are inserted directly into the skin below the eye. The 'skin-flap' technique employed for this phase of the research may be useful for other workers probing the face instrumentally. It is not known at present whether voluntary control can be exercised over these fine thread-like muscles. Secondly, we have produced some data on evaluating an effect of these eye-pouches. Our data suggest that the presence of eye-pouches is, in fact, unimportant to the perception of smile genuineness. A similar nonsignificant outcome has been reported for photographic modification of pupil dilation, (Hicks, Reaney & Hill, 1967). It should be noted that we are not claiming that these sort of small alterations cannot affect the perception of faces. By viewing our original and modified pictures as pairs, one is struck (and others are too) by a feeling that something strange has occurred. The lack of differences in smile genuineness ratings found in this study must therefore be placed in context.

Between group designs such as the present one, are usually avoided in psychology for fear of confounding treatment and group differences, regardless of random assignment. Using the same subjects to rate modified and original faces however, was seen as involving potentially differential carry-over effects. Clearly, the modifications made to photographs could not be done, even by the most able artist, equally well for all faces. In addition, consideration must also be given to our measuring instruments; it may be that such differences as do exist, are not sensitive to a scale requiring ratings for smile genuineness. Perhaps differences will emerge with alternative experimental designs or measurement devices, and to this end further work is currently being considered.

ACKNOWLEDGEMENTS

This research was funded by Minor Research Fund, University of London Institute of Education. Support by a grant to Michael Mair from the Social Science Research Council is acknowledged. We gratefully acknowledge the Post Office for supplying the original pictures. A. Gillies at University of London Audio Visual Centre carefully and artistically removed the eye-pouches from photographs.

REFERENCES

Baughan, B., Gumma - the universal multivariate analyser. University of London Institute of Education (1972).

Brannigan, C.R. & Humphries, D.A., Human non-verbal behaviour, a means of communication. In: N.G. Blurton Jones (Ed.), Ethological Studies of Child Behaviour. University Press, Cambridge (1972).

Cooley, W.W. & Lohnes, P.P., Multivariate Data Analysis. Wiley, London (1971).

Grant, E.C., Human facial expression. Man, 4, 525-536 (1969).

Hess, E.H., Attitude and pupil size. Scientific American, 212, 46-54 (1965).

Hicks, R.A., Reaney, T. & Hill, L., Effects of pupil size and facial angle on preference for photographs of a young woman. Perceptual and Motor Skills, 24, 388-390 (1967).

Thom, R., Structural Stability and Morphogenesis, (translated D.H. Fowler). Benjamin, Massachusetts (1975).

Perception of Computer-Drawn Animated-Movie Smiles

John Kirkland

University of London Institute of Education

As Disney's Empire attests, cartoon animation is a popular form of entertainment. Animation does lead to the perception of movement. By plotting computer-generated faces onto sixteen-millimetre film it is possible to simulate dynamic configurative changes of the face. In the present investigation the mirth response is selected for analysis. The principal issue is whether the important variables for guaging mirth-intensity includes duration and time taken to return to the original baseline rest-face as well as amplitude. If these other factors, or combinations of them, are important then mirth-researchers who record actual expressional changes will need to take cognizance of them when planning their research projects.

It is essential that a method be developed for investigating dynamic components of the mirth response. This way commonsense can be replaced by reliable criteria. One method is presented in this study. Briefly, computer-generated schematic-face stimuli were plotted directly onto 16 mm film and displayed as animated movies.

One of the more complete analyses of the dynamic aspect of the mirth-response is provided by Pollio, Mers and Lucchesi (1972). By transcribing the vocal component of laughter onto print-outs that could be visually scanned, they identified three indices of humour: onset, duration and amplitude. This is one instance where dependent measures were selected on the basis of unrefutable evidence rather than referral to commonsense. The main objective of the present study is to follow-up the lead provided by Pollio's group and investigate visual aspects of dynamic smiles. Three variables (smile amplitude, duration and wane) are combined orthogonally to produce eight different smiles, when they are each at two levels. By having subjects view and then make rating judgments (for smile-intensity), salient variables or their combinations will emerge. This research is seen as an important link in the systematic analysis of mirth (and other dynamic) behaviours.

METHOD

Ten naive subjects (five males and five females) volunteered for participation in this study. The sample included faculty, secretaries, graduate students and clerks. These subjects were different from those participating in the other study. All were English nationals aged between nineteen and forty-five years. Schematic-face stimuli were computer-generated from the same data-deck used in the other study (Kirkland, this volume). This time stimuli were plotted directly onto 16 mm double-sprocketed film. Smile amplitude, duration and wane (each of two levels) were combined. Details for duration and wane were obtained from Pollio. These three terms are defined as follows: 'Amplitude' is the peak mirth displayed on any particular film-sequence - the two levels are called, simply, Full, and Half; 'Duration' is the time for which amplitude is maintained - it is determined by the number of amplitude frames, and is either short (8 frames, or 0.5 seconds with a 16 frames per second projector) or long (32 frames, or 2.0 seconds); 'Wane' is the time taken for a smile to recede from amplitude to baseline rest-face. It is either fast (16 frames, 1.0 second) or slow (64 frames, or 4.0 seconds). A continuous film loop was spliced. Thus all subjects saw the same series in the same order. But each subject commenced viewing from different places on the loop.

Each subject was tested individually. They were seated on a chair behind a table (1.3 m from the projection area) in front of the projector. A Spectro Mark II 16 mm projector was positioned on another table, 2.4 m from a plain white wall that served as the projection area. A white-on-black image of 18 cm (ear to ear) by 23 cm was displayed. The experimenter sat to the right of the projector and immediately behind each subject. The illumination in the test-room was dimmed throughout the session by drawing heavy curtains across the windows.

Instructions for Phase I, outlining the introductory settling-down, were provided for each subject to read. When subjects indicated readiness to proceed the complete film loop was projected, showing all eight animated smiles. Instructions for Phase II were given to subjects immediately following the initial viewing provided in Phase I. In Phase II, subjects were asked to rank-order the eight smiles for 'intensity'. A visual aid was provided. It consisted of a sheet of white card (48 cm wide, by 19 cm) upon which the letters 'a' through 'h' (lettraset number 718;19.3 mm) were evenly spaced (4 cm apart and 4.5 cm from the card top). The eight numbers '1' through '8' (lettraset number 1286;11.7 mm) were each mounted on a white card (8.0 cm long by 2.5 cm wide). Just prior to a smile display, the experimenter called out the relevant identifying letter ('a' through 'h'). After viewing, subjects placed the number indicating the rank for the previously viewed smile adjacent to the identifying letter on the large card. This procedure continued for at least four complete cycles and until subjects indicated the rank-ordering had stabilized. There-a-upon the large card was removed with the rank numbers still in place and the next set of instructions given.

In Phase III, subjects were instructed to rate each smile using seven-point scales. They were reminded that the scale numbers were equally spaced, in preparation for subsequent parametric analysis. Previous phases were designed to build-up for this final rating phase. By requesting an activity, such as the rank-ordering, subjects became acquainted with the film piece. In an earlier run, in which the second phase was omitted, subjects reported confusion. Essentially then, the second phase is an extended familiarization session.

RESULTS AND DISCUSSION

The outcome calculated by application of Kendall's Coefficient of Concordance to data obtained in Phase II is 0.496. When tested for statistical significance ($X^2 = K(N-1)W$; Siegel, 1956) it is found to be highly significant ($X^2 = 34.72$; df = 7; p <.001). Thus subjects demonstrated consistency in their rank ordering of the eight smiles for 'intensity'. Just one significant effect emerged from the three-way analysis of variance computation. This was the main effect for amplitude (F = 280.09; df = 1,9; p <.001). All remaining main effects and their interactions did not reach acceptable levels of statistical significance. The sole factor emerging from the analysis of intensity-ratings given toward computer-generated schematic-face animated-smiles is amplitude. Neither duration nor wane nor any of the interactions was statistically significant.

These results are important. They clearly show that, for stimuli used in the present study, only amplitude is related to 'intensity'. Since subjects were exposed to all smiles at least five times it is unlikely that duration or wane were overlooked. When subjects were casually asked at the end of the study to list their criteria for distinguishing between the various smiles, almost all included mouth-width and over half mentioned duration or wane. Further, if subjects were only responding to total smile display (the time for which each smile-piece was projected) then both wane and duration would have emerged as significant in the statistical analyses. It appears that subjects distinguished between the various smile components and selected amplitude as the best indicator of mirth intensity. Should these results have an implication for analysis of actual rather than schematic-faces they suggest mirth-intensity can be represented by amplitude. This extrapolation is limited by two considerations. First that amplitude is a useful variable in a research design. And, secondly, that mirth-recorders are aware of possible bias when transposing smiles into hard data.

It has already been noted that coarse-grained 'present/absent' type decisions absolve mirth-researchers from some of the bias of more complete and finely graded scales. By recording total smile- or laugh- times (as, for example, Chapman, 1975b, does) the sole decision is couched in detection rather than assessment of degree of change. Thus, given a reliable distinction between smile and laugh and their onsets it seems that a viable measure of duration is available. Perhaps, like the implicit assumption of 'intensity' on subject-rating scales, cumulative records also implicitly acknowledge an 'intensity' measure. Intensity may be a ubiquitous measure for humour researchers.

In the present study 'intensity' was manufactured by tight stimulus control. Rival explanations based on either smile-time or display-time can be dismissed. First, total smile-time can be readily calculated from a straightforward count of film-frames for each smile piece. Whereas the difference between the two 'amplitude' levels is 78 frames, this is less than the difference between either the levels for 'duration' (96 frames) or for 'wane' (98 frames). Secondly if overall display-time was a significant variable for assessing 'intensity' then its effects would have been evident in all three factors. However, the results obtained for both the ranking and rating phases do not support this extrapolation. Only 'amplitude' is selected by subjects as the sole contributor to intensity.

REFERENCES

See Bibliography for publications on humour, laughter and comedy

Siegel, S., Nonparametric statistics. McGraw-Hill, New York (1956).

Perception of Equally-Different Computer-Drawn Mirth-Like Schematic Faces

John Kirkland*

University of London Institute of Education

This study investigates the relationship between computer-generated schematic-faces and how these are perceived. Under examination is the assumed isomorphism between several machine-generated face-stimuli and their perception. That is to say whether the change between equally-different stimuli appear uniform to persons arranging them.

The procedure used in this study is a reversal of Simpson and Crandall's (1972) ratio-scaling technique. These writers were initially faced with the task of determining absolute differences between many smile stimuli. Eighteen subjects were instructed to arrange selected smile-pictures into a sequence and then separate the pictures so that distances between adjacent members would be indicative of smile magnitude. By averaging across all subjects' results a final set of pictures was obtained. According to these authors each smile-picture was quantitatively distinct from the remainder. Whilst the Simpson and Crandall smile-pictures were assumed to reflect smile-magnitude it is not reported which facial characteristics were selected by subjects to make their judgments. Further it is not possible to adequately measure absolute differences between several naturalistic pictures.

The reversed technique used in the current study depends initially upon having available quantified stimuli. Of interest is the distribution of these stimuli by naive judges. This method of discerning psychological scaling between members of a stimulus set with known parameters is not altogether unknown in established areas of perceptual scaling. Correspondence is usually assumed between equal-interval scales used in the recording of mirth behaviours and what is observed on people's faces. But this assumption has not been tested. In the present study the amount of agreement between the absolute differences among members of a computer-generated schematic-face series and personal, subjective, reports of these differences is examined.

The study is executed in two complementary phases. In the first, subjects order seven (the magical number) computer-generated schematic-face stimuli. These stimuli are arranged according to the mirth displayed. In phase two, stimuli are spread apart so as to make distances between adjacent members proportional to mirth magnitude (after Simpson & Crandall, 1972). Following the outcome of the first study it is anticipated that subjects will be consistent in ordering these stimuli. Subsequently, it is expected that the smile-face stimuli will be unequally distributed. That is, the perception of equally-spaced machine-generated schematic-face stimuli will not be uniform.

METHOD

Seven male and four female subjects were each invited to volunteer for participation in this study. The sample included faculty members, technicians, secretaries and graduate students. All were English nationals aged between nineteen and forty-five years. Several symmetrical comic-like schematic-faces were constructed by computer and plotted directly onto microfilm. Each face was made up of forty independent lines. From original pencil drawings of a face on mm graph paper, co-ordinates for each line determine both position and shape in two-dimensional space.

Since the proposed investigations involve mirth it is necessary to determine the stable and dynamic characteristics of relevant facial features. To this end several still picture sets of the same person were scrutinized. Other sequences were obtained from the unobtrusively filmed movie-watchers. Available literature about mirth descriptions were also consulted. As one might expect changes in eye-closure, mouth broadening and lip compression were observed. Although additional facial elements may be important for smile perception these were omitted from the present study. In the absence of other elements observers are limited to those utilized. For the present research, absolute representation is not sought. Instead it is sufficient to present consistent elements which are systematically manipulated.

Extreme positions for each of the selected features were plotted on graph paper and entered as numerical co-ordinates on punch-cards for the computer programme to deal with. This programme generates one hundred equal-interval steps between extremes. From the many thousands of possible combinations particular ones are nominated and individualized faces drawn. Additional details about the general functioning of this programme are obtainable elsewhere (Frith, 1974). Two identical sets of seven schematic-faces were generated using the computerised object-drawing technique. All faces in each set differed by equal amounts. Each stimulus was mounted onto stiff plain card (measuring five cm by six and a half cm). Stimuli were randomly numbered on the reverse side. Subjects were exposed either to one fixed sequence set or the other arranged in a reverse order. Use of two similar sets lessened the likelihood that stimulus differences could be attributed to irregularities in Xerox photocopying.

Subjects were tested either individually or in back-to-back pairs in a room devoid of visual or auditory distractors. Instructions relevant to the ordering task were given to each subject. In Phase I, subjects were asked to arrange the seven schematic stimuli in a single line which would show gradual mirth increase when scanned in a left-to-right direction. A second set of instructions was provided for subjects in Phase II, as soon as they indicated the ordering task was completed. This time subjects were instructed to separate the seven face-stimuli so that distances between them were proportional to differences in the perceived magnitude. When subjects indicated completion distances were measured (in mm) between the edges of adjacent stimuli. The order of stimuli was also recorded.

Subjects were not restricted by a predetermined scale length. To standardize individual scales for statistical purposes a ratio between the sum of six distances of each individual's scale and one hundred mm was calculated. All distances were then adjusted using this ratio. Finally, standard mean scores were calculated across all subjects. If standard mean scores are equivalent to the computer-generated differences they would fall along a horizontal straight line when plotted graphically against each other. Amount of departure can be tested by analysis of variance. Further, by using a repeated design, a trend analysis will fit the best curves to these data. A trend analysis is justified because the differences between stimuli are equal. (Note: Results obtained from subjects not matching the known order would be discarded from additional analysis in the second phase as their results would violate the design).

RESULTS AND DISCUSSION

Complete agreement was reached by all subjects for ordering the seven stimuli. Thus the concordance analysis was not applied, and no data had to be discarded. Standard mean scores obtained in the second phase were, for each interval: 7.37; 13.94; 20.50; 24.16; 17.00, and 17.18 (mm). The repeated measures one-way analysis of variance indicated these standard means were significantly different ($F = 4.41$; df = 5,50; $p < .01$) from each other. Two components of the trend analysis reach an acceptable level of statistical significance. The quadratic trend ($F = 9.36$; df = 1,30; $p < .02$) accounts for 54.37% of the variance and the linear trend ($F = 8.83$; $p < .02$) accounts for 33.12% of the variance. Adjacent members of the schematic-face set differed by equal amounts. This certainty was guaranteed by the computer.

Clearly absolute agreement for ordering the seven stimuli into a single line, ranging from least- to greatest-expressed mirth, was demonstrated. Even though actual differences between adjacent stimulus members are slight, subjects reliably perceived these differences in the correct order. Secondly, when subjects were requested to separate the previously ordered stimuli so as to make distance between members proportional to perceived mirth differences, a consistent pattern emerged. The pattern, obtained by plotting perceived distances (on the ordinate) against actual differences, is an inverted U-shape.

The first five stimuli in the series were spread further and further apart by subjects until a critical point was reached. Beyond this point remaining stimuli were placed closer together. Thus it seems that a slight change has a much greater impact on central stimulus members than it has on peripheral ones. Perhaps a single expressional series also has 'holes', such as the ones which Osgood (1966) reports when several expressions are mapped with his semantic differential. A similar outcome may occur with different facial expressions as well. For example, a sequence depicting an increasingly 'angry' expression may reveal a crucial range within which slight changes are perceptually magnified. Thus, just-perceptible-differences in a central range of face-pattern continually tend toward greater perceived alteration than the end members of a series when all are adjusted by the same amount.

The present study demonstrates effects obtained from slight alterations of simple-face elements. Above all else the present research indicates that reliable mirth-scale categorization may, at this stage, be an oversimplification of what occurs on faces.

FOOTNOTE

*Now at Education Department, Massey University, Palmerston North, New Zealand.

REFERENCES

See Bibliography for publications on humour, laughter and comedy

Frith, C.D., A programme for drawing objects varying along a number of independent dimensions. Technical Report CDF/A1, University of London, Institute of Psychiatry (1974).

Osgood, C.E., Dimensionality of the semantic space for communication via facial expressions. Scandanavian Journal of Psychology, 7, 1-30 (1966).

Penry, J., Looking at Faces and Remembering Them. Elek, London (1971).

Laughter in the Basement

S. G. Brisland, R. A. Castle, J. W. Dann, D. McGarry, R.N. Smith and A. J. Snow

King Alfred's College, Winchester

Our interest in the subject of humour led us to consider the practical uses to which humour
could be put, and we finally focused upon creating a 'Humour Environment'. The idea in
essence was that people should feel better after passing through a specially designed laughter
chamber - rather like a car is 'refreshed' after passing through a car-wash. We hoped to
provide a place where people could relax and enjoy themselves, revelling in an atmosphere
where everybody could 'exercise' their own particular sense of humour. The sense of humour
is delicate and can be distorted and seriously restricted if analyzed too persistently;
however we recognized that we required some objective means of assessing our success or
otherwise.

Turning to practicalities, a room was found: the boiler room under the College theatre!
Having cleared and cleaned out this basement area, it was obvious that our ideas would have
to be developed to suit the structure of the room and available equipment; any ugly or
seemingly hopeless shapes within the room were used to form incongruous elements — the basis
of a great deal of the humour. The painting of a wall set the transformation in motion, and
the room was then divided up into different areas:

(1) A Spaceship. This stemmed from the existence of a small air duct with a central
     'control panel' at about chest height. Two walls were constructed to enclose the
     area and, after painting, they took on the outward appearance of a small cottage
     which we named 'Happy Daze'. Inside there was a silver wheel-chair, space helmet,
     television screen (annotated to look like a map of space), numerous buttons, levers
     to play with, port-holes suggesting a bizarre exterior, a pair of headphones linked
     to a three-minute loop tape with science fiction sound effects plus limited
     dialogue. A typewriter was also made available in the craft.

(2) A Submarine. This was a narrow corridor built from hardboard alongside the metal
     ventilation duct at a particular confluence of smaller heating pipes. At eye-level,
     standing on the top of the duct, were several obsolete electronic control panels
     to which headphones were connected emitting submarine and sonar sound effects.
     On a six-inch back-projection-screen at eye-level were displayed in sequence
     eighty 'periscope views', ranging from the Mediterranean Sea to 'rural farmyard
     locations'. The panels were rewired to control lights and other taped sounds.

(3) The Toilet. The finished product evolved from the notion that the toilet evokes
     its own type of humour, often demonstrated by scribbled graffiti decorating the
     walls, and is the basis for many a dirty joke. It became an elongated room
     containing a lavatory bowl with an adjoining theatre seat, a cistern with a cast
     bottom and blow-up plastic legs hanging down. A car steering-wheel was positioned
     in front of the seated subject who looked at a television screen. To his left
     was positioned an elaborate shelving system comprising a cocktail cabinet and
     bookcase — complete with suitable props. On the floor was a black duckboard which
     added to the overall toilet atmosphere created by the avocado green walls. On the
     sides of the walls were six red boxes for dispensing toilet paper. A small white
     graffiti board was hung on one of the walls to accommodate any writing. As it
     happened the board was ignored and subjects covered the walls with extensive
     graffiti!

(4) A Theatre for One. The idea was conceived on a visit to a gallery housing Gerald
     Newman's 'Orders 1'. He has attempted to convey the 'landscape tradition' in art
     by displaying on a board at one end of a white room - the words 'view'(in white),
     'west', 'sunset' (in black) underneath each other. At the other end of the room one
     could sit on a black couch in between two white speakers through which taped

evening bird calls etcetera came through. In the basement environment we wanted
to adapt this idea to convey a comic performance by providing the basic requirements.
Thus, at the end of a long passage underneath the ventilation duct was placed a
lighted sign — with the words Watch (in red), Performance, Smile (in green). The
subjects sat on a car seat and listened to a comedy performance through headphones
taped on a one-minute loop tape. Through a combination of soundtrack and visual
stimuli it was hoped that subjects could use these basic ingredients to create
their own personal comedy performance.

(5) The Central Area. The ceiling was covered with selected bill-board posters which
     were chosen for their colours and facial expression. The floor was carpeted
     throughout, walls and ducts were covered with pictures and posters which added to
     the colourful surroundings. Two cylindrical pillars were covered with jokes and
     cartoons which could be viewed without commitment. One of these cylinders was
     fairly large and had the inside lined with pictures on which people could write
     their own captions. In the main entrance there was a large roll of paper for people
     to contribute to a continuing story. In the 'play area' there was a large trunk
     containing hats, masks and dressing-up clothes for people to rummage in. Mirrors
     were provided for this purpose. There was a chaise-longe, a table with plasticene
     and crazy foam and a large collection of novelties such as rattles, false moustaches,
     noses, bubbles, glasses, etcetera. A roller tube on the floor proved very successful;
     this was a kind of rocking cradle for one, or two. Throughout the environment
     subjects were encouraged to use the felt pens available to contribute their thoughts
     and opinions. The only specific instructions to the subjects were 'feel free to do
     as you please'.

This combination of stimuli for one or for a group enabled participants to experience
individual enjoyment and/or social interaction. For some people participation with others may
not be desired, and the dual purpose nature of the environment took account of this.

To test the effect of the 'Humour Environment' upon subjects, some method of measurement was
necessary. An adaptation of the Vincent Nowliss Mood Scale was selected, in the form of a
questionnaire administered before and after visiting the environment. In addition to this
objective impersonal analysis, the subjects were observed in a variety of other ways. A
concealed camera and video-tape-recorder filmed the general activity within the central area.
A one-way screen, positioned at the opposite end to the camera, enabled us to observe and
take notes of occurrences of particular interest, whilst one member of the group was always
concealed behind a ventilation duct — being able to observe not only the whole area — but also
to pay special attention to the behaviour of subjects in the Theatre for One.

A random sample of a hundred people was chosen. We also selected year groups, peer groups,
subject groups, staff, ancillaries, members of the general public, school children, eight-
and nine-year-olds, twelve- and thirteen-year-olds, fifteen- and sixteen-year-olds. Some of
them were aware that they were coming to an exhibition of humour, some had no such knowledge.
The environment was open for just one week. The first three days were spent specifically on
observational testing, after which time the environment was open as a College amenity, and
advertized as such.

As far as effectiveness was concerned we were more than satisfied. It is fair to say that a
vast majority of the subjects thoroughly enjoyed themselves. This was apparent from our
video-tape observations and mood scale results, as well as informal comments received such as:
'Well ... I can only stay two minutes' — then leaving forty-five minutes later; 'I wish I
could stay longer'; 'I really enjoyed it'; 'I reckon we ought to do this every afternoon'.

The mood scale results in particular confirmed our views about the success of the environment.
We found that groups of close friends scored significantly higher and their moods became more
positive than those groups of people unknown to each other. It was also apparent that the
size of the group (providing it was over about three or four) bore no relation to the degree
of change. There were vast individual differences in mood change but seventy per cent of a
testing sample of one hundred and three came out 'feeling better'. In conclusion, we feel
that the concept of a humour environment as a social amenity has distinct possibilities and
implications for future communities. Whilst not suggesting our environment should serve as
a model, we do believe the basic concept could be used to structure further developments
(cf. Atkin, this volume).

A Designed Locale for Laughter to Reinforce Community Bonds

John R. Atkin

North York Board of Education, Toronto

Laughter could be the human experience which binds neighbourhoods together if an appropriate
chamber were constructed. The parish church during feudal times and in feudal places was a
unifunctional chamber which optimized the reception of a spoken message. The public library
was and is a similar building. A new building, a possible design of which was discussed,
could stimulate laughter and reduce anomie – the feeling of the effect of diminishing
national and neighbourhood consciousness – to a major degree. Some form of community centre
seems to be a social need. A Laughter Centre, specially designed to optimize reception of
jokes was proposed.

Culture Bias in Attitudes to Humour

Tim Healey

Barnsley, England

The study of humour is inseparable from considerations of history and geography. Mere topicality is less important than whole cultural attitudes, which are best expressed in folk humour, songs, jokes and slang expressions. These often cross language barriers rather more easily than the less tangible difficulties of remoteness in distance and time. Thus our modern English humour is closer to that of say Denmark than to the United States, though the early clowns and jesters were often forced back upon tumbling, dexterity, dancing and piping to transcend language difficulties. A clever pun is incomprehensible to a dull wit or to even an intelligent foreigner, if he does not understand the tongue. The invention of printing, the standardization of spelling, the forming of nations, the availability of education, the development of radio and television — all tend to work in the same direction, so that we can appreciate the other fellow's humour. As with all art forms, much depends on conventions, but with scholarship and adequate records, the field of humour is continuing to expand.

The Fool and His World, As Exemplified in the Fool of the Tarot Pack

Tim Healey

Barnsley, England

The joker in the pack of playing cards is a recent intruder, being only about a century old. His lineage is direct however from the Fool of the old Tarot decks, and a study of his relationships with the other trump cards in the Tarot deck shows many parallels with the lessons of life. The emergence of the Tarot Fool from his beginnings as a court jester attending upon the four court cards (King, Queen, Knight and Valet) shows the influences of Biblical and classical myth, of the Commedia Dell'Arte, of mediaeval mystery plays (and hence of Punch and Judy shows), of Morris dancers, and of Shakespearian Fools. Illustrations were given of famous jesters and fools from all times and examples were shown from the author's extensive collection of Tarot cards.

Humour Among the Au Pairs

Alice Heim

University of Cambridge

Some examples were given of humorous remarks from au pair girls who have worked with me. They are humorous in the sense that they evoke laughter in the hearer – and, later, when the girls have become more used to the English language they often prove retrospectively amusing to the perpetrator. Thus the illustrations offered were of humour that is unintentional and that depends largely on linguistic peculiarities and national customs. The following distinctions were briefly discussed: that between intentional and unintentional humour, between humour and wit; and between malicious and benign humour.

Humour and the Deprived Child

Winifred Hunter

Cleveland, England

Educational neglect of the children who most need help must be one of the nation's most critical social problems. It is hardly surprising that pupils become alienated from school and society and feel hostility to any authority outside their families or their gangs. School success is not for them. To survive, they live in their own world, create their own rules, and follow their own set codes. Very few teachers have been disadvantaged to the extent that typically disadvantaged children are. But does an educational training prepare teachers to cope? Are schools alerted, aware, or even concerned about the disadvantaged child?

Is the basic aim of education to control emotions, to nourish them, to refine them, or to provide therapeutic release for inhibited feelings? Should educationalists help children to achieve sincerity of emotion, to develop self-awareness, and to make them more considerate of others? How far is this the responsibility of the teacher, the psychologist or the parent? Surely education must attend to all these matters. Teachers with a sense of proportion do confidently attempt to make children into truly developed adults. But it appears that in society, homogenized culture does not make people more aware of their relations with one another as persons, but the contrary. The secondary school usually provides examples of hostility between the intelligence streams; but a moral education would teach more about the diversity of gifts and the need to respect each man for himself. Perpetual misunderstandings occur and there is a complete rejection by one group of another. Common culture of the kind which now prevails even among the educated does not seem to unite people. It only depersonalizes people and turns them into so much material for receiving impressions.

Society battles to maintain stability in the face of change; measurement and categories are needful, but so too is meaning; and those who are not easily measured or put into commercially successful categories need to be given meaning quite as much as their successful rivals. There is not much point in a joke which covers only sorrow or failure, but it is even such a joke which some schools are making of themselves and of their most problematical children. There appears to be in every school a group who regard school as a 'laugh'; violence as a form of entertainment, and perversity and perversion as amusing.

In working with children whose restricted code of language confines them to subculture, it is essential to possess a sense of humour and to bring it into some flexible relationship with that of one's children. Experience of these problems would suggest, however, that their neglect is no laughing matter.

Humour as a Facilitator of Learning in Primary School Children

Ann P. Davies

University College, Cardiff

Despite many claims that the introduction of humour to a lesson or lecture should facilitate learning, experimental evidence in support of this view remains equivocal. The author's work suggests that this may be because the amount of learning material has not been great enough to overcome novelty effects of experimental situations which bear little resemblance to a classroom. In the present work, children aged between 8 and 11 years are shown a five-minute teaching programme (either humorous or nonhumorous). Prior to seeing the programme they are given a pre-test for knowledge in the area. The same test is re-administered immediately afterwards, together with an 'attitude to the programme' questionnaire. Not surprisingly, it has been found that the novelty of a new teacher on the screen, is sufficient to maintain interest and motivation for at least five minutes. Studies are now in progress in which children are shown four, twenty-minute, slide-tape programmes during one school day (either humorous or nonhumorous). The effects of showing programmes on four consecutive days are also being examined, and so too are the effects of various personality factors.

Humour, Laughter and Comedy: A Bibliography of Empirical and Nonempirical Analyses in the English Language

Jeffrey H. Goldstein, Paul E. McGhee, Jean R. Smith, Antony J. Chapman and Hugh C. Foot

Abelson, R.P. & Levine, J., A factor analytic study of cartoon humor among psychiatric patients. Journal of Personality, 26, 451–466 (1958).

Abrahams, R.D., The literary study of the riddle. Texas Studies in Literature and Language, 14, 188–189 (1972).

Abrahams, R.D. & Dundes, A., Riddles. In R.M. Dorson (Ed.), Folklore and Folklife: An Introduction. University of Chicago Press, Chicago (1972).

Adams, W.J., The use of sexual humor in teaching human sexuality at the university level. Family Coordinator, 23, 365–368 (1974).

Adelson, J., Ethnocentrism and humor appreciation. American Psychologist, 2, 413 (1947).

Adler, B., How To Be Funny In Your Own Lifetime. Playboy Press, Chicago (1973).

Aiken-Sneath, B., Comedy in Germany in the First Half of the Eighteenth Century. Clarendon Press, Oxford (1936).

Alderson, F., Comic Postcard in English Life. Tuttle, London (1970).

Allchin, A.M., The true substance of joy: A study of Fr Congreve. Theology, 62, 465–505 (1959).

Allen, S., The Funny Men. Simon and Schuster, New York (1956).

Allen, S., Bigger than a Breadbox. Paperback Library, New York (1967).

Allen, S., The uses of comedy. Journal of Creative Behavior, 6, 83–85 (1972).

Allin, A., On laughter. Psychological Review, 10, 306–315 (1903).

Allport, G.W., Patterns and Growth in Personality. Holt, Rinehart and Winston, 292–294 (1963).

Almack, J.C., Sense of Humor Test (Form 1). Gregory, Cincinnati (1928).

Alston, J.P. & Platt, L.A., Religious humor: A longitudinal content analysis of cartoons. Sociological Analysis, 30, 217–222 (1969).

Altman, S., The Comic Image of the Jew. Associated University Presses, Cranbury, New Jersey (1971).

Ambrose, A., The development of the smiling response in early infancy. In B. Foss (Ed.), Determinants of Infant Behaviour I. Wiley, New York (1961).

Ambrose, A., The age of onset of ambivalence in early infancy: indications from the study of laughing. Journal of Child Psychology and Psychiatry, 4, 167–181 (1963).

Ames, L.B., Development of interpersonal smiling responses in the preschool years. Journal of Genetic Psychology, 74, 273–291 (1949).

Anderson, J.F. & Berdie, D.R., Effects on response rates of formal and informal questionnaire follow-up techniques. Journal of Applied Psychology, 60, 255–257 (1975).

Andrew, R.J., Evolution of facial expression. Science, 142, 1034–1041 (1963).

Andrew, R.J., The origin and evolution of the calls and facial expressions of primates. Behavior, 20, 1–109 (1963).

Andrew, R.J., The origins of facial expressions. Scientific American, 213, 88–94 (1965).

Andrews, T.G., A factorial analysis of responses to the comic as a study of personality. Journal of General Psychology, 28, 209–224 (1943).

Andrus, T.C., A study of laugh patterns in the theatre. Speech Monographs, 13, 114 (1946).

Annis, A.D., The relative effectiveness of cartoons and editorials as propaganda. Psychological Bulletin, 36, 628 (1939).

Anonymous, The nature of a joke. New Statesman, 191-193, June 15th (1926).

Anonymous, Laughter and blood pressure. Literary Digest, 95, 22 (1926).

Anonymous, Famous faces by Oscar Berger. American Artist, 27, 45-59, 65-67 (1963).

Anonymous, My Son the Teenager: A Cartoon Satire. Belmont, New York (1963).

Arieti, S., New views on the psychology of wit and the comic. Psychiatry, 13, 43-62 (1950).

Aristophanes, The Comedies. Translated by B.B. Rogers (6 vols). London (1902-1916).

Arlin, M.N. & Hills, D., Comparison of cartoon and verbal methods of school attitude assessment through multitrait-multimethod validation. Educational and Psychological Measurement, 34, 989-995 (1974).

Armstrong, M., Laughing: An Essay. Harper, New York (1920).

Arnez, N.L. & Anthony, C.B., Contemporary Negro humor as a social satire. Phylon, 29, 339-346 (1968).

Arpad, J.J., The fight story: Quotation and originality in native American humor. Journal of the Folklore Institute, 10, 141-172 (1973).

Arya, S., Riddles, proverbs and magical practices of Western Uttar Pradesh. Folklore (Calcutta), 13, 220-233 (1972).

Ashbee, C.R., Caricature. Chapman & Hall, London (1928).

Asher, R. & Sargent, S., Shifts in attitude change caused by cartoon caricatures. Journal of General Psychology, 24, 451-455 (1941).

Ashton, J., Humor, Wit and Satire of the Seventeenth Century. Dover, New York (1968).

Athey, C., Let us laugh. The Link, No. 64, 48-54 (1974).

Auden, W.H., Notes on the comic. Thought, 27, 57-71 (1952).

Austin, M., The sense of humor in women. The New Republic, 41, 10-13 (1924).

Averill, J.R., Autonomic response patterns during sadness and mirth. Psychophysiology, 5, 399-414 (1969).

Azimov, I., Jokester. The Penguin Science Fiction Omnibus.

Azimov, I., Treasury of Humor. Houghton Mittlin, Boston (1971).

Babad, E.Y., A multi-method approach to the assessment of humor: A critical look at humor tests. Journal of Personality, 42, 618-631 (1974).

Baillie, J., Laughter and tears: The sense of incongruity. Studies in Human Nature, 9, 254-293 (1921).

Bailey, J., Intent on Laughter. New York, Quadrangle (1976).

Barcus, F.E., A content analysis of trends in Sunday comics, 1900-1959. Journalism Quarterly, 38, 171-180 (1961).

Barley, N.F., Structural aspects of the Anglo-Saxon riddle. Semiotica, in press.

Baron, R.A. & Ball, R.L., The aggression-inhibiting influence of nonhostile humor. Journal of Experimental Social Psychology, 10, 23-33 (1974).

Barrick, M.E., Racial riddles and the Polack joke. Keystone Folklore Quarterly, 15, 3-15 (1970).

Barrick, M.E., The newspaper riddle joke. Journal of American Folklore, 87, 253-257 (1974).

Barrie, A., The importance of not being earnest. Good Housekeeping, 72, 164, 165 (1975).

Barron, M.L., A content analysis of intergroup humor. American Sociological Review, 15, 88-94 (1950).

Barrow, I., Sermon against foolish talking and jesting. Extract in Hunt's 'Wit and Humour'.

Barry, H. Jr., The role of subject-matter in individual differences in humor. Journal of Genetic Psychology, 35, 112-128 (1928).

Barshay, R., The cartoon of modern sensibility. Journal of Popular Culture, 523-533 (197?).

Bascom, W., Literary style in Yoruba riddles. Journal of American Folklore, 62, 1-16 (1949).

Basgoz, I., Functions of Turkish riddles. Journal of the Folklore Institute, 2, 132-147 (1965).

Bateson, F.W., English Comic Drama 1700-1750. Russell, London (1929).

Bateson, G., The role of humor in human communication. In: H. von Foerster (Ed.), Cybernetics. Macey Foundation, New York (1953).

Baudelaire, C., The Essence of Laughter. Introduction, P. Quennell. Meridian Books, New York (1956).

Bawdon, H.H., The comic as illustrating the summation-irradiation theory of pleasure-pain. Psychological Review, 17, 336-346 (1910).

Beattie, J., Essay on laughter and ludicrous composition. In: Essays. Edinburgh (1776).

Beatty, J., Humor versus taboo: The sorrowful story of the cartoon. The Saturday Review, 40, 11-13 (1957).

Becker, S.D., Comic Art in America. Simon & Schuster, New York (1959).

Beerbohm, M., Laughter. North American Review, 214, 33-49 (1921).

Beerbohm, M., The humour of the public. In: Yet Again. Chapman & Hall, London (1959).

Behrens, R.R., On creativity and humor: An analysis of Easy Street. Journal of Creative Behavior, 8, 227-238 (1974).

Ben-Amos, D., The 'myth' of Jewish Humor. Western Folklore, 32, 112-131 (1973).

Ben-Amos, D., Solutions to riddles. Journal of American Folklore, 89, 249-254 (1976).

Bender, L. & Lourie, R.S., The effect of comic books on the ideology of children. American Journal of Orthopsychiatry, 11, 540-551 (1941).

Bender, L., The psychology of children's reading and the comics. Journal of Educational Sociology, 24, 34-53 (1944).

Bennett, D.J., The psychological meaning of anti-Negro jokes. Fact, 1, 53-59 (1964).

Berger, A.A., What makes people laugh. ETC, 32, 427-428 (1975).

Berger, A.A., Authority in the comics. Transaction, 22-26 (Dec.) (1966).

Berger, P., The Last Laugh. Morrow, New York (1975).

Bergler, E., A clinical contribution to the psychogenesis of humor. Psychoanalytic Review, 24, 34-53 (1937).

Bergler, E., Infantile and adult forms of reducing to absurdity. Samiska, 8, 69-75.

Bergler, E., Laughter and The Sense of Humor. Intercontinental Medical Book Corporation, New York (1956).

Bergson, H., Laughter: An Essay on the Meaning of the Comic. Macmillan, New York (1911).

Berkowitz, L., Aggressive humor as a stimulus to aggressive responses. Journal of Personality and Social Psychology, 16, 710-717 (1970).

Berlo, D.K. & Kumata, H., The investigator: The impact of a satirical radio drama. Journalism Quarterly, 33, 287-298 (1956).

Berlyne, D.E., Laughter, humor and play. In: G. Lindzey & E. Aronson (Eds.), Handbook of Social Psychology (2nd edition), Vol. 3. Addison-Wesley, Reading, Massachusetts (1969).

Berlyne, D.E., Humor and its kin. In: J.H. Goldstein & P.E. McGhee (Eds.), The Psychology of Humor. Academic Press (1972).

Bernard, H.R., Otumi obscene humor: Preliminary observation. Journal of American Folklore, 88, 383-392 (1975).

Beuchat, P.D., Riddles in Bantu. African Studies, 16, 189-190 (1957).

Bhagwat, D., The riddle in Indian life, lore and literature. Popular Prakashan, Bombay (1965).

Bier, J., The Rise and Fall of American Humor. Holt, Rinehart & Winston, New York (1968).

Bird, G.E., An objective humor test for children. Psychological Bulletin, 22, 137-138 (1925).

Bissett,   A touch of humor. Elementary English, 52, 617-619 (1975).

Blacking, J., The social value of Venda riddles. African Studies, 20, 1-32 (1961).

Blair, W., Horse Sense in American Humor, from Benjamin Franklin to Ogden Nash. University of Chicago Press, Chicago (1942).

Blair, W., Native American Humor. Chandler, San Francisco (1960).

Blatz, W.E., Allen, K.D. & Millichamps, D.A., A Study of Laughter in the Nursery School Child. University of Toronto Press, Toronto (1936).

Bliss, S.H., The origin of laughter. American Journal of Psychology, 26, 236-246 (1915).

Blistein, E., Comedy in Action. Duke University Press, Durham N.C. (1964).

Blurton Jones, N.G., An ethological study of some aspects of social behaviour of children in nursery school. In D. Morris (Ed.), Primate Ethology. Doubleday, New York (1969).

Blurton Jones, N.G., Categories of child-child interaction. In: N.G. Blurton Jones (Ed.), Ethological Studies of Child Behaviour. Cambridge University Press, Cambridge (1972).

Blyth, R.H., Oriental Humor. Hokuseido Press, Tokyo (1957).

Boatright, M.C., Folk Laughter on the American Frontier. Peter Smith, Gloucester, Mass., (1949).

Bogardus, E., Sociology of the cartoon. Sociology and Social Research, 30, 139-147 (1945).

Bogart, L., Comic strips and their adult readers. In: B. Rosenbert & D.M. White (Eds.), Mass Culture. Free Press, Glencoe, Illinois (1957).

Boskin, J., Good-by, Mr. Bones. New York Times Magazine, May 1, 30 ff, (1966).

Bowman, H.A., The humor of primitive people. In: Studies in the Science of Society. Yale University Press, New Haven (1939).

Boyle, D.G., Comments on the theory of laughter by Giles and Oxford. Bulletin of the British Psychological Society, 23, 317-318 (1970).

Brackbill, Y., Extinction of the smiling response in infants as a function of reinforcement schedule. Child Development, 29, 115-124 (1958).

Brackett, C.W., Laughing and crying of preschool children. Journal of Experimental Education, 2, 119-126 (1933).

Brackett, C.W., Laughing and crying of preschool children. Child Development Monographs, No. 14, 119-126 (1934).

Bradney, P., The joking relationship in industry. Human Relations, 10, 179-187 (1957).

Brake, R., The lion act is over: Passive/aggressive patterns of communication in American Negro humor. Journal of Popular Culture, 9, 548-560 (1975).

Branch, A.Y., Fine, G.A. & Jones, J.M., Laughter, smiling, and rating scales: An analysis of responses to tape-recorded humor. Proceedings, American Psychological Association, 8, 189-190 (1973).

Brant, C.S., On joking relationships. American Anthropologist (New Series), 50, 160-162 (1948).

Brant, C.S., A preliminary study of cross-sexual joking relationships in primitive societies. Behavior Science Notes, 7, 313-329 (1972).

Brenman, M., On teasing and being teased: The problem of moral masochism. Psychoanalytic Study of the Child, 7, 264-285 (1952).

Bricker, V.R., Ritual Humor in Highland Chiapas. University of Texas Press, Austin & London (1973).

Bridges, K.M., Emotional development in early infancy. Child Development, 3, 324-341 (1932).

Brigham, J.C., Ethnic humor on television: Does it reduce/reinforce racial prejudice? Proceedings, American Psychological Association (1975).

Brill, A.A., Freud's theory of wit. Journal of Abnormal and Social Psychology, 6, 189 ff (1911).

Brill, A.A., The mechanism of wit and humor in normal and psychopathic states. Psychiatric Quarterly, 14, 731-749 (1940).

Brinkman, D., Do editorial cartoons and editorials change opinions? Journalism Quarterly, 45, 724-726 (1968).

Broadhead, R.S., Notes on the sociology of the absurd. Pacific Sociological Review, 17, 35-46 (1974).

Brody, E.B. & Redlich, F.C., The response of schizophrenic patients to comic cartoons. Folia Psychiatrica Neurologica at Neurochirurgica Neerlandica, 56, 623-635 (1953).

Brody, M.W., The meaning of laughter. Psychoanalytic Quarterly, 19, 192-201 (1950).

Brodzinsky, D.M., The role of conceptual tempo and stimulus characteristics in children's humor development. Developmental Psychology, 11, 843-849 (1975).

Brodzinsky, D.M & Rubin, J., Humor production as a function of sex of subject, creativity, and cartoon content. Journal of Consulting and Clinical Psychology, in press.

Brown, J.R., Shakespeare and his Comedies. Methuen, London (1957).

Brown, T.G., Note on the physiology of the basil ganglia and mid-brain of the anthropoid ape, especially in reference to the act of laughter. Journal of Physiology, 49, 195-207 (1915).

Broyev, Y.B., The world will never die if it dies laughing. UNESCO Courier, April, 22-24 (1976).

Bruce, H.A., Why do we laugh? Outlook, August (1913).

Brukman, I., Tongue play: Constitutive and interpretive properties of sexual joking encounters among the Koya of South India. In: M. Sanches & B.G. Blount (Eds.), Sociocultural Dimensions of Language Use. Academic Press, New York (1975).

Brumbaugh, F., The place of humor in the curriculum. Journal of Experimental Education, 8, 403-409 (1940).

Brumbaugh, F. & Wilson, R.T., Children's laughter. Journal of Genetic Psychology, 57, 3-29 (1940).

Brunvand, J.H., As the saints go marching by: Modern jokelore concerning Mormans. Journal of American Folklore, 85, 53-60 (1970).

Brunvand, J.H., Some thoughts on the ethnic-regional riddle jokes. Indiana Folklore, 3, 128-142 (1970).

Burma, J.H., Humor as a technique in race conflict. American Sociological Review, 11, 710-715 (1946).

Burns, T.A., Riddling: An occasion to act. Journal of American Folklore, 89, 139-165 (1976).

Burns, W.J. & Tyler, J.D., Appreciation of risqué cartoon humor in male and female repressors and sensitizers. Journal of Clinical Psychology, 32, 315-321 (1976).

Burrow, M.L., A content analysis of intergroup humor. American Sociological Review, 15, 88-89 (1950).

Burrows, A.S., Carroll, C., Moore, S. & Quinn, D., Radio comedy in war time. In: Writers' Congress, Proceedings. University of California Press, Berkeley (1944).

Burt, C., The psychology of laughter. Health Education Journal, 3, 101-105 (1945).

Burton, R.F., Wit and Wisdom From West Africa. New American Library, New York, (Original 1865) (1969).

Bynan, J., Riddle telling among the Berbers of central Morocco. African Language Studies, 85 (1966).

Byrne, D.E., The relationship between humor and the expression of hostility. Journal of Abnormal and Social Psychology, 53, 84-89 (1956).

Byrne, D.E., Drive level, response to humor, and the cartoon sequence effect. Psychological Reports, 4, 439-442 (1958).

Byrne, D.E., Some inconsistencies in the effect of motivation arousal on humor preferences. Journal of Abnormal and Social Psychology, 62, 158-160 (1961).

Byrne, D.E., Terrill, J. & McReynolds, P., Incongruency as a predictor of responses to humor. Journal of Abnormal and Social Psychology, 62, 435-438 (1961).

Cahn, W., Pictorial History of the Great Comedians. Grosset & Dunlap, New York (1957).

Cameron, W.B., The sociology of humor and vice versa. In: Informal Sociology. Random House, New York (1963).

Cantor, J.R., Bryant, J. & Zillmann, D., Enhancement of humor appreciation by transferred excitation. Journal of Personality and Social Psychology, 30, 812-821 (1974).

Cantor, J.R. & Zillmann, D., Resentment toward victimized protagonists and severity of misfortunes they suffer as factors in humor appreciation. Journal of Experimental Research in Personality, 6, 321-329 (1973).

Carl, L.M., Editorial cartoons fail to reach many readers. Journalism Quarterly, 45, 533-535 (1968).

Carpenter, R., Laughter, a glory in sanity. American Journal of Psychology, 33, 419-422 (1922).

Carpenter, W.R., Experiments on the comic. American Journal of Psychology, 36 (2), 309-310 (1925).

Carr, P., Can comic books be used in education? Education, 79, 57-61 (1958).

Carritt, E.F., A theory of the ludicrous. Hibbert Journal, 21, 552-564 (1923).

Carus, P., On the philosophy of laughing. Monist, 8, (1897-8).

Cassell, J.L., The function of humor in the counseling process. Rehabilitation Counseling Bulletin, 17, 240–245 (1974).

Cattell, R.B. & Luborsky, L.B., Measured response to humor as an indicator of personality structure. American Psychologist, 1, 257–258 (1946).

Cattell, R.B. & Luborsky, L.B., Personality factors in response to humor. Journal of Abnormal and Social Psychology, 42, 402–421 (1947).

Cattell, R.B. & Luborsky, L.B., The validation of personality factors in humor. Journal of Personality, 15, 283–291 (1947b).

Cattell, R.B. & Tollefson, D.L., The Handbook for the IPAT Humor Test of Personality. Institute for Personality and Ability Testing, Champaign, Illinois (1963).

Cavanagh, J.R., The comics war. Journal of Criminal Law, Criminology and Police Science, 42, 28–35 (1949).

Cazamian, L., Development of English Humour. AMS Press, London (1952).

Chandler, K.A., The sense of humor in children. Century, 42, 959–960 (1902).

Chapman, A.J., Funniness of jokes, canned laughter and recall performance. Sociometry, 36, 569–578 (1973a).

Chapman, A.J., Social facilitation of laughter in children. Journal of Experimental Social Psychology, 9, 528–541 (1973b).

Chapman, A.J., An experimental study of socially facilitated "humorous laughter". Psychological Reports, 35, 727–734 (1974).

Chapman, A.J., Eye-contact, physical proximity and laughter: A re-examination of the equilibrium model of social intimacy. Social Behavior and Personality, 3, 143–155 (1975a).

Chapman, A.J., Humorous laughter in children. Journal of Personality and Social Psychology, 31, 42–49 (1975b).

Chapman, A.J., Social aspects of humorous laughter. In: A.J. Chapman & H.C. Foot (Eds.), Humour and Laughter: Theory, Research and Applications. Wiley, London (1976).

Chapman, A.J. & Chapman, W., Responsiveness to humour: Its dependency upon a companion's humorous smiling and laughter. Journal of Psychology, 88, 245–252 (1974).

Chapman, A.J. & Foot, H.C. (Eds.), Humour and Laughter: Theory, Research and Applications. Wiley, London (1976).

Chapman, A.J. & Gadfield, N.J., Is sexual humor sexist? Journal of Communication, 26, 141–153 (1976).

Chapman, A.J., Smith, J.R. & Foot, H.C., Language, humour and intergroup relations. In: H. Giles (Ed.), Language, Ethnicity and Intergroup Relations. Academic Press, London, in press (1977).

Chapman, A.J. & Wright, D.S., Social enhancement of laughter: An experimental analysis of some companion variables. Journal of Experimental Child Psychology, 21, 201–218 (1976).

Chapman, J.J., The comic. Hibbert Journal, 8, 862–872 (1910).

Charles, L.H., The clown's function. Journal of American Folklore, 58, 25–34 (1945).

Chatterji, N.N., Laughter in schizophrenia and psychotic disorders. Samiska, 6, 32–37 (1952).

Cherfras, J., What is the difference between humorous research and research on humour? New Scientist, 431, February 20th (1975).

Chesterton, G.K., On the comic spirit. In: S. Barnet et al (Eds.), Eight Great Comedies. New American Library, New York (1958).

Clark, M., Humour and incongruity. Philosophy, Journal of the Royal Institute of Philosophy, 45, 20–32 (1970).

Clark, T.D., Humor in the stream of Southern history. Mississippi Quarterly, 13, 176–188 (1960).

Claxton, G., Why can't we tickle ourselves? Perceptual and Motor Skills, 41, 335–338 (1975).

Cleland, R.S., Creative humor in relation to authoritarianism. American Psychologist, 14, 375 (1959).

Cloyd, J.S., Patterns of behavior in informal interaction. Sociometry, 27, 161–173 (1964).

Clubb, M.D., A plea for an eclectic theory of humor. University of California Chronicle, 34, 340–356 (1932).

Coates, J.F., Wit and humor: A neglected aid in crowd and mob control. Crime and
    Delinquency, 18, 184-191 (1972).

Cohen, H. & Dillingham, W.B., Humor of the Old Southwest. Houghton Mifflin Company,
    Boston, (1974).

Cohn, R., Forced crying and laughing. Archives of Neurology and Psychiatry, 66, 738-743
    (1951).

Cole-Beuchat, P.D., Riddles in Bantu. African Studies, 16, 133-147 (1957).

Cole, W., Punch Lines: Twenty Five Portfolios of English Comic Artists. Simon & Schuster,
    New York (1969).

College Laughs, 1, No. 36 (August 1964), Major Magazines, Holyoke, Mass. (1964).

Collier, M.J., Popular cartoons and prevailing anxieties. American Imago, 17, 255-269 (1960).

Congreve, W., The Comedies. Mermaid Series, London (1887).

Congreve, W., Essay upon humor in comedy. In: J.E. Spingarn (Ed.), Critical Essays of the
    Seventeenth Century. Oxford (1908).

Cook, A., The Dark Voyage and the Golden Means: A Philosophy of Comedy. Norton, New York,
    (Original 1949) (1966).

Cooper, E. & Jahoda, M., The evasion of propaganda: How prejudiced people respond to
    anti-prejudice propaganda. Journal of Psychology, 23, 15-25 (1947).

Cooper, L., An Aristotelian Theory of Comedy. Harcourt, New York (1922).

Corbin, H., Mysticism and humour. Spring, 24-34 (1973).

Coriat, I.H., Humor and hypomania. Psychiatric Quarterly, 13, 681-688 (1939).

Cornford, F.M., The Origin of Attic Comedy. Doubleday, New York (1914).

Corrigan, R.W., Comedy: Meaning and Form. Chandler, San Francisco (1965).

Corrigan, R.W. & Loney, G.M., Comedy: A Critical Anthology. Houghton Mifflin, Boston (1971).

Coser, R.L., Some social functions of laughter. Human Relations, 12, 171-182 (1959).

Coser, R.L., Laughter among colleagues. Psychiatry, 23, 81-95 (1960).

Coulter, S.K., Wundeleigh, R.A., Ball, M.F. & Canary, J.J., Humor ratings as a function of
    weight and food deprivation. Psychological Reports, 32, 1099-1105 (1973).

Crane, W.G., Wit and Rhetoric in the Renaissance. Peter Smith, Gloucester, Mass. (1964)
    (Original 1937).

Crile, J.W., The Origins and Nature of the Emotions. Saunders, Philadelphia (1915).

Cunningham, A., Relation of sense of humor to intelligence. Journal of Social Psychology,
    57, 143-147 (1962).

Cupchick, G.C. & Leventhal, H., Consistency between expressive behavior and the evaluation
    of humorous stimuli: The role of sex and self-observation. Journal of Personality and
    Social Psychology, 30, 429-442 (1974).

Daniels, A.K. & Daniels, R.R., The social function of the career fool. Psychiatry, 27,
    218-229 (1964).

Daniels, E.B., Some notes on clowns, madness and psychotherapy. Psychotherapy and
    Psychosomatics, 24, 465-470 (1974).

Darwin, C., A biographical sketch of an infant. Popular Science Monthly, 57, 197-205 (1900).

Darwin, C., The Expression of the Emotions in Man and Animals. John Murray, London (1890).

Davis, H.T., The Fine Art of Punning. Principia, Evanston, Illinois (1954).

Davis, J.M. & Farina, A., Humor appreciation as social communication. Journal of Personality
    and Social Psychology, 15, 175-178 (1970).

Davison, C. & Kelman, H., Pathologic laughing and crying. Archives of Neurology and
    Psychiatry, 42, 595-643 (1939).

Day, H.I. & Langevin, R., Curiosity and intelligence: Two necessary conditions for a high
    level of creativity. Journal of Special Education, 3, 263-268 (1969).

Dearborn, G.V.N., The nature of the smile and laugh. Science, 2, 851-856 (1900).

Deckers, L. & Kizer, P., A note on weight discrepancy and humor. Journal of Psychology, 86,
    309-312 (1974).

Deckers, L. & Kizer, P., Humor and the incongruity hypothesis. Journal of Psychology, 90,
    215-218 (1975).

Deikel, S.M., The life and death of Lenny Bruce: A psychological autopsy. Life Threatening Behaviour, 4, 176-192 (1974).

Dennis, W., An experimental test of two theories of social smiling in infants. Journal of Social Psychology, 6, 214-233 (1935).

Derks, P.L., Leichtman, H.M. & Carroll, P.J., Production and judgment of "humor" by schizophrenics and college students. Bulletin of the Psychonomic Society, 6, 300-302 (1975).

Desai, M.W., Surprise: A historical and experimental study. British Journal of Psychology (Monograph Supplement), No. 22 (1939).

Ding, G.F. & Jersild, A.T., A study of laughing and crying in preschool children. Journal of Genetic Psychology, 40, 452-472 (1932).

Diserens, C.M., Recent theories of laughter. Psychological Bulletin, 23, 247-255 (1926).

Diserens, C.M. & Bonifield, M., Humor and the ludicrous. Psychological Bulletin, 27, 108-118 (1930).

Dobree, B., Restoration Comedy: 1660-1720. Clarendon, Oxford (1924).

Dobree, B., Comedy. In: S. Barnet et al (Eds.), Eight Great Comedies. New American Library, New York (1958).

Domash, L., The use of wit and the comic by a borderline psychotic child in psychotherapy. American Journal of Psychotherapy, 29, 261-270 (1975).

Donaldson, I., The World Upside-Down. London (1970).

Dooley, L., A note on humor. Psychoanalytic Review, 21, 49-58 (1934).

Dooley, L., Relation of humor to masochism. Psychoanalytic Review, 28, 37-46 (1941).

Doris, J. & Fierman, E., Humor and anxiety. Journal of Abnormal and Social Psychology, 53, 59-62 (1956).

Douglas, M., The social control of cognition: Some factors in joke perception. Man, 3, 361-376 (1968).

Doyle, C.C., Title-author jokes, now and long ago. Journal of American Folklore, 86, 52-54 (1973).

Draper, J.W., Theory of the comic in eighteenth-century England. Journal of English and Germanic Philology, 37, 207-223 (1938).

Dresser, N., The metamorphosis of the humor of the black man. New York Folklore Quarterly, 26, 216-228 (1970).

Druckman, R. & Chao, D., Laughter in epilepsy. Neurology, 7, 26-36 (1957).

Du Bois, A.E., Comedy, an experience. English Literary History, 7, 199-214 (1940).

Ducharte, P.L., Italian Comedy. Dover, New York (1965).

Duckworth, G.E., The nature of Roman Comedy. Princeton University Press, Princeton (1952).

Duncan, H.D., Language and Literature in Society. University of Chicago Press, Chicago (1953).

Dundes, A., A study of ethnic slurs: The Jew and the Polack in the United States. Journal of American Folklore, 84, 51-61 (1971).

DuToit, B.M., Riddling traditions in an isolated South African community. Journal of American Folklore, 79, 471-475 (1966).

Durgnat, R., The Crazy Mirror. Dell, New York (1969).

Dworkin, E.S. & Efran, J.S., The angered: Their susceptibility to varieties of humor. Journal of Personality and Social Psychology, 6, 233-236 (1967).

Eastman, M., The Sense of Humor. Scribners, New York (1921).

Eastman, M., Enjoyment of Laughter. Simon & Schuster, New York (1936).

Easton, R., Humor of the American Indian. Mankind, 2, 37 ff (1970).

Ecker, J., Levine, J. & Zigler, E., Impaired sex-role identification in schizophrenia expressed in the comprehension of humor stimuli. Journal of Psychology, 83, 67-77 (1973).

Eckerman, C.O. & Whatley, J.L., Infant's reactions to unfamiliar adults varying in novelty. Developmental Psychology, 11, 562-566 (1975).

Edwards, S., The function of laughter. Psyche, 22-32 (1926).

Ehrle, R.A. & Johnson, B.G., Psychologists and cartoonists. American Psychologist, 16, 693-695 (1961).

Eidelberg, L., A contribution to the study of wit. Psychoanalytic Review, 32, 33-61 (1945).

Eijerveld, A.C., Jokes and their relation to social reality. Social Research, 35, 286-311 (1968).

Eisenbud, J., The oral side of humor. Psychoanalytic Review, 51, 57-73 (1964).

Elliot, R.C., The Power of Satire, Magic Ritual, Art. Princeton University Press, Princeton (1960).

Ellis, G.T. & Sekyra, F., The effect of aggressive cartoons on the behavior of first grade children. The Journal of Psychology, 81, 37-43 (1972).

Emde, R.N. & Koenig, K.L., Neonatal smiling and rapid eye movement states. Journal of the American Academy of Child Psychiatry, 8, 57-67 (1969).

Emerson, J.P., Negotiating the serious import of humor. Sociometry, 32, 169-181 (1969).

Enck, J.J., Jonson and the Comic Truth. University of Wisconsin Press, Madison (1957).

Enck, J.J., Forter, E.T. & Whitley, A., The Comic in Theory and Practice. Prentice-Hall, Englewood Cliffs, New Jersey (1960).

Enders, A.C., A study of the laughter of the preschool child in the Merrill-Palmer nursery school. Papers of the Michigan Academy of Science, Arts, and Letters, 8, 341-356 (1927).

Epstein, S. & Smith, R., Repression and insight as related to reaction to cartoons. Journal of Consulting Psychology, 20, 391-395 (1956).

Erskine, J., Humor. Century, 115, 421-426 (1928).

Esar, E., The Humor of Humor. Horizon, New York (1952).

Escarpit, R., Humorous attitudes and scientific creativity. Impact of Science on Society, 19, 253-258 (1969).

Escovar, L. & Escovar, P.L., Achievement motivation and power motivation in the content of comics. Revista Interamericana de Psicologia, 7, 233-238 (1973).

Esslin, M., The Theatre of the Absurd. Doubleday, New York (1961).

Etzel, B.C. & Gewirtz, J.L., Experimental modification of caretaker-maintained, high-rate operant crying in a 6- and 20-week-old infant (Infans tyrannotearis):Extinction of crying with reinforcement of eye-contact and smiling. Journal of Experimental Child Psychology, 3, 303-317 (1967).

Evans, B., Shakespeare's Comedies. Clarendon, Oxford (1960).

Evans, D., Riddling and the structure of context. Journal of American Folklore, 89, 166-188 (1976).

Everett, C.C., The Philosophy of the Comic: Poetry, Comedy and Duty. Houghton Mifflin, New York (1893).

Eyles, A., American Comedy Since Sound. Barnes, Cranbury, New Jersey (1969).

Eysenck, H.J., The appreciation of humour: An experimental and theoretical study. British Journal of Psychology, 32, 295-309 (1942).

Eysenck, H.J., An experimental analysis of five tests of appreciation of humor. Educational and Psychological Measurement, 3, 191-214 (1943).

Eysenck, H.J., National differences in "sense of humor": Three experimental and statistical studies. Character and Personality, 13, 37-54 (1944-1945).

Fadiman, C., Humor as a weapon. Journal of Creative Behavior, 6, 87-92 (1972).

Farzan, M., Another Way of Laughter. Dutton, New York (1973).

Feeney, L., 'The menace of puns' from 'you'd better come quickly'. In:P.J. Phelan (Ed.), With a Merry Heart. Longmans Green & Company (1944).

Feibleman, J.K., In Praise of Comedy. Macmillan, New York (1939).

Feibleman, J., In Praise of Comedy: A Study in its Theory and Practice. Russell & Russell, New York (1962).

Feinberg, L., The Satirist. Citadel, New York (1965).

Feinberg, L., Introduction to Satire. State University Press, Ames, Iowa (1967).

Feinberg, L., Asian Laughter. Weatherhill, New York (1971).

Feldmann, S., Supplement to Freud's theory of wit. Psychoanalytic Review, 28, 201-217 (1941).

Feleki, L., Keeping laughably up with science. Impact of Science on Society, 19, 279-290 (1969).

Feleky, A., The influence of emotions on respiration. Journal of Experimental Psychology, 1, 218-246 (1916).

Felheim, M., Comedy: Plays, Theory and Criticism. Harcourt, Brace, New York (1962).

Felker, D.W. & Hunter, D.M., Sex and age differences in response to cartoons depicting subjects of different ages and sex. Journal of Psychology, 76, 19-21 (1970).

Ferenczi, S., The psychoanalysis of wit and the comical. In: Further Contributions to Psychoanalysis. Hogarth, London (1911).

Ferguson, J., Wit of the Greeks and Romans. International Publications Service, New York, (1968).

Ferguson, S.M., Schwartz, M.L. & Rayport, M., Perception of humor in patients with temporal lobe epilepsy. Archives of General Psychiatry, 21, 363-367 (1969).

Ferris, D.R., Humor and creativity: Research and theory. Journal of Creative Behavior, 6, 74-79 (1972).

Ferris, D.R. & Bewsey, D.K., A selected, annotated bibliography on humor. Journal of Creative Behavior, 6, 80-82 (1972).

Feshbach, S., The drive-reducing function of fantasy behavior. Journal of Abnormal and Social Psychology, 50, 3-11 (1955).

Fine, G.A., In search of the quadrennial perennials. Folklore Forum, 7, 203-205 (1974).

Fine, G.A., Components of perceived sense of humor ratings of self and others. Psychological Reports, 36, 793-794 (1975).

Fine, G.A., Popular culture as humor: The psychology of cultural evaluation. Proceedings, Popular Culture Association, in press.

Fleet, F.R., Theory of Wit and Humor. Kennikat, (Original 1890) (1970).

Flemming, R., Of contrast between tragedy and comedy. Journal of Philosophy, 36, 543-553 (1939).

Flugel, J.C., Humor and Laughter. In: G. Lindzey (Ed.), Handbook of Social Psychology. Addison-Wesley, Cambridge, Mass. (1954).

Foot, H.C. & Chapman, A.J., Laugh and the world laughs with you. Psychology Today (U.K.), 1, 42-45 (1975).

Foot, H.C. & Chapman, A.J., The social responsiveness of young children in humorous situations. In: A.J. Chapman & H.C. Foot (Eds.), Humour and Laughter: Theory, Research and Applications. Wiley, London (1976).

Foot, H.C., Smith, J. & Chapman, A.J., Boys and girls come out to play: Sex differences in the social interaction of young children. New Behaviour, 1, 418-420 (1975).

Foss, B., The functions of laughter. New Scientist, 11, 20-22 (1961).

Foster, J.R. (Ed.), Folktales of Wit and Humor. Harper, New York (1955).

Frank, J., What's in the comics? Journal of Educational Sociology, 18, 214-222 (1944).

Freud, S., Humour. In: Collected Papers, Vol. 5. Basic Books, New York, (1959). (Also International Journal of Psychoanalysis, 9, 1-6 (1928)).

Freud, S., Jokes and their relation to the unconscious. Norton, New York (1960). (Originally Der Witz und seine Beziehung zum Ubewussten. Deuticke, Leipzig & Vienna (1905)).

Froeschels, E., Philosophy in Wit. Philosophical Library, New York (1948).

Fry, C., Comedy. Tulane Drama Review, 4, 70-79 (1960).

Fry, W.F. Jr., Sweet Madness: A Study of Humor. Pacific, Palo Alto (1963).

Fry, W.F. Jr., Humor in a physiological vein. Beckman Instruments Newsletter (1969).

Fry, W.F. Jr., Now you see it, now you don't: The magic of humor. Perspectives in Biology and Medicine, 14, 173-175 (1970).

Fry, W.F. Jr., Laughter: Is it the best medicine? Stanford MD, 10, 16-20 (1971).

Fry, W.F. Jr., Psychodynamics of sexual humor: Women's view of sex. Medical Aspects of Human Sexuality, 6, 135-139 (1972a).

Fry, W.F. Jr., Psychodynamics of sexual humor: Sexual views of children. Medical Aspects of Human Sexuality, 77-80, September (1974b).

Fry, W.F. Jr., Psychodynamics of sexual humor: Man's view of sex. Medical Aspects of Human Sexuality, 6, 128-134 (1972b).

Fry, W.F. Jr., Psychodynamics of sexual humor: A look at adultery. Medical Aspects of Human
    Sexuality, 32, 35, 39, 41, April (1975).

Fry, W.F. Jr., Psychodynamics of sexual humor: Sex and the elderly. Medical Aspects of Human
    Sexuality, 145-148, February (1976).

Fry, W.F. Jr. & Allen, M., Make 'em laugh. Science & Behavior Books, Palo Alto (1976a).

Fry, W.F. Jr. & Allen, M., Humour and creativity. In:A.J. Chapman & H.C. Foot (Eds.),
    Humour and Laughter: Theory, Research and Applications. Wiley, London (1976b).

Fry, W.F. Jr. & Stoft, P.E., Mirth and oxygen saturation levels of peripheral blood.
    Psychotherapy and Psychosomatics, 19, 76-84 (1971).

Frye, N., The argument of comedy. English Institute Essays, Columbia University Press,
    New York (1948) (1949).

Frye, N., The structure of comedy. In: S. Barnet, et al (Eds.), Eight Great Comedies. New
    American Library, New York (1958).

Fujima, T.H., Restoration Comedy of Wit. Princeton University Press, Princeton (1952).

Fuller, R.E., Headshrinker: The psychiatrist in cartoons. Bulletin of the Menninger Clinic,
    36, 335-345 (1972).

Fuller, R.G.C. & Sheehy-Skeffington, A., Effects of group laughter on responses to humourous
    material: A replication and extension. Psychological Reports, 35, 531-534 (1974).

Garfield, E., Of smiling dogs and laughing people and why they can't tickle themselves.
    Current Contents, No. 47, 5-8, November 24th (1975).

Garth, T.R., The psychology of riddle solutions. Journal of Educational Psychology, 11,
    16-33 (1920).

Garth, T.R., Riddles as a mental test. American Journal of Psychology, 47, 342-344 (1935).

Georges, R.A. & Dundes, A., Toward a structural definition of the riddle. Journal of American
    Folklore, 76, 111-118 (1963).

Gerasimov, B., The gift of the Gabrovo. UNESCO Courier, 9-11, April (1976).

Gerber, W.S. & Routh, D.K., Humor response as related to violation of expectancies and to
    stimulus intensity in a weight-judgment task. Perceptual and Motor Skills, 41, 673-674
    (1975).

Gewirtz, J.L., The course of infant smiling in four child-rearing environments in Israel.
    In: B.M. Foss (Ed.), Determinants of Infant Behaviour, Vol. III. Methuen, London (1965a).

Gewirtz, J.L., The course of smiling by groups of Israeli infants in the first eighteen
    months. Scripta Hierosdymitana, Vol. XIV. Studies in Psychology, Magnes Press, Hebrew
    University, Jerusalem (1965b).

Ghosh, R., An experimental study of humour. British Journal of Educational Psychology, 9,
    98-99 (1939).

Giles, H. & Oxford, G.S., Towards a multidimensional theory of laughter causation and its
    social implications. Bulletin of the British Psychological Society, 23, 97-105 (1970a).

Giles, H. & Oxford, G.S., Laughter: A reply. Bulletin of the British Psychological Society,
    23, 319-320 (1970b).

Giles, A., Bourhis, R.Y., Gadfield, N.J., Davies, G.J. & Davies, A.P., Cognitive aspects
    of humour in social interaction: A model and some linguistic data. In: A.J. Chapman &
    H.C. Foot (Eds.), Humour and Laughter: Theory, Research and Applications. Wiley,
    London (1976).

Gilman, B., A Clinic on the Comic. Nice, France (1926).

Glantz, R., The Jew in Early American Wit and Graphic Humor. KTAV Publishing House, New
    York (1973).

Glazier, J. & Glazier, P.G., Ambiguity and exchange: The double dimension of Mbeere
    riddles. Journal of American Folklore, 89, 189-238 (1976).

Godkewitsch, M., The relationship between arousal potential and funniness of jokes. In:
    J.H. Goldstein & P.E. McGhee (Eds.), The Psychology of Humor. Academic Press, New York
    (1972).

Godkewitsch, M., Correlates of humor: Verbal and nonverbal aesthetic reactions as a
    function of semantic distance within adjective-noun pairs. In: D.E. Berlyne (Ed.),
    Studies in the New Experimental Aesthetics. Hemisphere Press, Washington, D.C.
    (1974).

Godkewitsch, M., Physiological and verbal indices of arousal in rated humour. In: A.J. Chapman & H.C. Foot (Eds.), Humour and Laughter: Theory, Research and Applications. Wiley, London (1976a).

Godkewitsch, M., Thematic and collative properties of written jokes and their contribution to funniness. Canadian Journal of Behavioural Science, 8, 88-97 (1976b).

Goldstein, J.H., Repetition, motive arousal, and humor appreciation. Journal of Experimental Research in Personality, 4, 90-94 (1970a).

Goldstein, J.H., Humor appreciation and time to respond. Psychological Reports, 27, 445-446 (1970b).

Goldstein, J.H., Humour. In: S. Krauss (Ed.), Encyclopaedic Handbook of Medical Psychology. Butterworth, London (1976).

Goldstein, J.H., Theoretical notes on humor. Journal of Communication, 26, 102-112 (1976).

Goldstein, J.H., Harman, J., McGhee, P.E. & Karasik, R., Test of an information-processing model of humor: Physiological response changes during problem- and riddle-solving. Journal of General Psychology, 92, 59-68 (1975).

Goldstein, J.H. & McGhee, P.E. (Eds.), The Psychology of Humor. Academic Press, New York (1972a).

Goldstein, J.H. & McGhee, P.E., An annotated bibliography of published papers on humor in research literature and analysis of trends: 1900-1971. In: J.H. Goldstein & P.E. McGhee (Eds.), The Psychology of Humor. Academic Press, New York (1972b).

Goldstein, J.H. & McGhee, P.E. Humor and laughter: A supplementary bibliography. JSAS/Catalog of Selected Documents in Psychology, 4, 81 (1974).

Goldstein, J.H., Suls, J.M. & Anthony, S., Enjoyment of specific types of humor content: Motivation or salience? In: J.H. Goldstein & P.E. McGhee (Eds.), The Psychology of Humor. Academic Press, New York (1972).

Goldstein, K., The smiling of the infant and the problem of understanding the 'other'. Journal of Psychology, 44, 175-191 (1957).

Goldstein, K.S., Riddling traditions in northeastern Scotland. Journal of American Folklore, 76, 330-336 (1963).

Goldstein, K.S., The verse competition jest in northeastern Scotland. Journal of American Folklore, 83, 351-353 (1970).

Gollob, H.F. & Levine, J., Distraction as a factor in the enjoyment of aggressive humor. Journal of Personality and Social Psychology, 5, 368-372 (1967).

Goodchilds, J.D., Effects of being witty on position in the social structure of a small group. Sociometry, 22, 261-272 (1959).

Goodchilds, J.D. & Smith, E.E., The wit in his group. Human Relations, 17, 23-31 (1964).

Goodchilds, J.D., On being witty: Causes correlates and consequences. In: J.H. Goldstein & P.E. McGhee (Eds.), The Psychology of Humor. Academic Press, New York (1972).

Goodenough, F.L., The expression of the emotions in infancy. Child Development, 2, 96-101 (1931).

Goodlad, S., On the social significance of television comedy. In: C.W. Bigsby (Ed.), Approaches to Popular Culture. Edward Arnold, London (1976).

Goodman, P., Comic plots. In: The Structure of Literature. University of Chicago Press, Chicago (1954).

Goodrich, A.J., Henry, J. & Goodrich, D.W., Laughter in psychiatric staff conferences: A sociopsychiatric analysis. American Journal of Orthopsychiatry, 24, 175-184 (1954).

Gopala-Swami, M.V., The genesis of the 'laughter' instinct. Psychological Studies of the University of Misore, 1, 1-25 (1926).

Gordon, A., Cataplexy. Diseases of the Nervous System, 8, 11-14 (1947).

Gowlett, D.F., Common Bantu riddles. African Studies, 34, 79-146 (1975).

Graeven, D.B. & Morris, S.J., College humor in 1930 and 1972: An investigation using the humor diary. Sociology and Social Research, 59, 406-410 (1975).

Graham, L.R., The maturational factor in humor. Journal of Clinical Psychology, 14, 326-328 (1958).

Grandgent, C.H., Getting a Laugh. Harvard University Press, Cambridge (1925).

Granfield, A.J. & Giles, H., Towards an analysis of humor through symbolism. International Journal of Symbology, 6, 17-23 (1975).

Grant, M.A., The ancient rhetorical theories of the laughable. University of Wisconsin Studies in Language and Literature, No. 21 (1924).

Gray, D.J., The uses of Victorian laughter. VS, 10, 135-176 (1966).

Greenberg, B.S. & Kahn, S., Blacks in 'Playboy' cartoons. Journalism Quarterly, 47, 557-560 (1970).

Greenwald, H., Humor in psychotherapy. Journal of Contemporary Psychotherapy, 7, 113-116 (1975).

Gregg, A., Miller, M. & Linton, E., Laughter situations as an indication of social responsiveness in young children. In: D.S. Thomas (Ed.), Some New Techniques for Studying Social Behaviour. Teachers' College, New York (1929).

Gregory, J.C., Some theories of laughter. Mind, 32, 328-344 (1923).

Gregory, J.C., The Nature of Laughter. Kegan Paul, London (1924).

Greig, J.Y.T., The Psychology of Laughter and Comedy. Dodd, Mead, New York (1923a).

Greig, J.Y.T., Freud's theory of wit. British Journal of Medical Psychology, 3, 51-58 (1923b).

Grimes, W.H., A theory of humor for public address: The mirth experience. Speech Monographs, 22, 217-226 (1955).

Groch, A.S., Generality of response to humor and wit in cartoons, jokes, stories and photographs. Psychological Reports, 35, 835-838 (1974).

Groch, A.S., Joking and appreciation of humor in nursery school children. Child Development, 45, 1098-1102 (1974).

Grossman, S.A., The use of sexual jokes in psychotherapy. Medical Aspects of Human Sexuality, 4, 35-46 (1970).

Grote, B. & Cvetkovitch, G., Humor appreciation and issue involvement. Psychonomic Science, 27, 199-200 (1972).

Grotjahn, M., Laughter in dreams. Psychoanalytic Quarterly, 14, 221-227 (1945).

Grotjahn, M., Laughter in psychoanalysis. Samiska, 3, 76-82 (1949).

Grotjahn, M., Laughter in psychoanalysis. In: S. Lorand (Ed.), The Yearbook of Psychoanalysis, Vol. VI. International University Press, New York (1950).

Grotjahn, M., The inability to remember dreams and jokes. Psychoanalytic Quarterly, 20, 284-286 (1951).

Grotjahn, M., Beyond Laughter. McGraw-Hill, New York (1957).

Grotjahn, M., Laughter and sex. In: W. Mendel (Ed.), A Celebration of Humor. Mara Books, Los Angeles (1970).

Grotjahn, M., Laughter in group psychotherapy. International Journal of Group Psychotherapy, 21, 234-238 (1971).

Grotjahn, M., Smoking, coughing, laughing and applause: A comparative study of respiratory symbolism. International Journal of Psychoanalysis, 53, 345-349 (1972a).

Grotjahn, M., Sexuality and humor: Don't laugh. Psychology Today, 6, 50-53 (1972b).

Grotjahn, M., Jewish jokes and their relation to masochism. In: W.H. Mendel (Ed.), A Celebration of Humor. Mara Books, Los Angeles (1970).

Grove, M. & Eisenman, R., Personality correlates of complexity-simplicity. Perceptual and Motor Skills, 31, 387-391 (1970).

Gruner, C.R., An experimental study of the effectiveness of oral satire in modifying attitude. Speech Monographs, 31, 231-232 (1964).

Gruner, C.R., An experimental study of satire as persuasion. Speech Monographs, 32, 149-154 (1965a).

Gruner, C.R., Is wit to humor what rhetoric is to poetic? Central States Speech Journal, 16, 17-22 (1965b).

Gruner, C.R., A further experimental study of satire as persuasion. Speech Monographs, 33, 184-185 (1966).

Gruner, C.R., Editorial satire as persuasion: An experiment. Journalism Quarterly, 44, 727-730 (1967a).

Gruner, C.R., Effect of humor on speaker ethos and audience information gain. Journal of Communication, 17, 228-233 (1967b).

Gruner, C.R., The effect on speaker ethos and audience information gain of humor in dull and interesting speeches. Central States Speech Journal, 21, 160-166 (1970).

Gruner, C.R., Ad hominem satire as a persuader: An experiment. Journalism Quarterly, 48, 128–131 (1971).

Gruner, C.R. & Lampton, W.E., Effects of including humorous material in a persuasive sermon. Southern Speech Communication Journal, 38, 188–196 (1972).

Gruner, C.R., Wit and humour in mass communication. In: A.J. Chapman & H.C. Foot (Eds.), Humour and Laughter: Theory, Research and Applications. Wiley, London (1976).

Gruner, C.R., The Psychology and Communication Function of Wit and Humor. Nelson-Hall, Chicago, in press.

Grziwok, R.K. & Scodel, A., Some psychological correlates of humor preferences. Journal of Consulting Psychology, 20, 42 (1956).

Gundappa, R., The psychological background of laughter. Indian Journal of Psychology, 13, 188–191 (1938).

Guthrie, W.N., A theory of the comic. International Quarterly, 7, 254–264 (1903).

Gutman, J. & Priest, R.F., When is aggression funny? Journal of Personality and Social Psychology, 12, 60–65 (1969).

Haggard, E.A. & Sargent, H., Use of comic strip characters in diagnosis and therapy. Psychological Bulletin, 38, 714 (1941).

Haggard, E.A., A projective technique using comic strip characters. Character and Personality, 10, 289–295 (1942).

Hall, G.S. & Allin, A., The psychology of tickling, laughing and the comic. American Journal of Psychology, 9, 1–42 (1897).

Hall, W., The Smiling Pheonix: Southern Humor from 1865–1914. University of Florida Press, Gainesville (1965).

Hammes, J.A., Suggestibility and humor evaluation. Perceptual and Motor Skills, 15, 530 (1962a).

Hammes, J.A. & Wiggins, S.L., Manifest anxiety and appreciation of humor involving emotional content. Perceptual and Motor Skills, 14, 291–294 (1962b).

Hammond, P.B., Mossi joking. Ethnology, 3, 259–267 (1964).

Hamnett, I., Ambiguity, classification and change: The function of riddles. Man, 2, 380–391 (1967).

Handelman, D. & Kapferer, B., Forms of joking activity: A comparative approach. American Anthropologist, 74, 484–517 (1972).

Hannay, D., Humour. Encyclopaedia Brittanica (Eleventh Edition), Cambridge (1910).

Hansen, A.J., Entropy and transformation: Two types of American humor. American Scholar, 43, 405–421 (1974).

Hanser, R., Wit as a weapon. Saturday Review, 35, 13 ff, November 8th (1952).

Haring, L., On knowing the answer. Journal of American Folklore, 87, 197–207 (1974).

Harlow, H.F., The anatomy of humour. Impact of Science on Society, 19, 225–240 (1969).

Harms, E., The development of humor. Journal of Abnormal and Social Psychology, 38, 351–369 (1943).

Harrelson, R.W. & Stroud, P.S., Observations of humor in chronic schizophrenics. Mental Hygiene, 51, 458–461 (1967).

Harries, L., The riddle in Africa. Journal of American Folklore, 84, 377–393 (1971).

Harries, L., On the deep structure of riddles. African Studies, 35, 39–44 (1976).

Harrower, M.R., Organisation in higher mental processes. Psychologische Forschung, 17, 56–120 (1933).

Harsh, P.W., A Handbook of Classical Drama. Stanford University Press, Stanford (1944).

Hart, D.V., Riddles in Filipino Folklore: An Anthropological Analysis. Syracuse University Press, Syracuse (1964).

Harter, S., Shultz, T.R. & Blum, B., Smiling in children as a function of their sense of mastery. Journal of Experimental Child Psychology, 12, 396–404 (1971).

Hartmann, G.W., Personality traits associated with variations in happiness. Journal of Abnormal and Social Psychology, 29, 202–212 (1934-5).

Hauck, W.E. & Thomas, J.W., The relationship of humor to intelligence, creativity, and intentional and incidental learning. Journal of Experimental Education, 40, 52–55 (1972).

Hausdorff, D., Magazine humor and popular morality, 1929-1934. Journalism Quarterly, 41, 509-516 (1964).

Hayworth, D., The social origin and function of laughter. Psychological Review, 35, 367-384 (1928).

Hazen, B.B., Humor in uniform. Cornell Journal of Social Relations, 7, 1-10 (1972).

Hazlitt, W., On wit and humor. In: Lectures on the English Comic Writers. Taylor, London (1819).

Hazlitt, W.C., Studies in Jocular Literature. Gale, Detroit (Original 1890) (1969).

Heckel, R.V. & Kvetensky, E.D., The development of humor in children. Psychology, 9, 17-21 (1972).

Heim, A., An experiment on humour. British Journal of Psychology, 27, 148-161 (1936).

Hellyar, R.H., Laughter and jollity. Contemporary Review, 132, 757-763 (1927a).

Hellyar, R.H., The meaning of the comic. Psyche, 8, 78-99 (1927b).

Helson, R., The heroic, the comic, and the tender: Patterns of literary fantasy and their authors. Journal of Personality, 41, 163-184 (1973).

Henderson, J., The Maculate Muse: Obscene Language in Attic Comedy. Yale University Press, New Haven (1975).

Henigman, J.J., An interpretation of the social psychological functions of the ritual clown. Character and Personality, 10, 220-226 (1942).

Herrick, M.T., Tragic comedy, its Origin and Development in Italy, France and England. University of Illinois Press, Urbana (1955).

Herrick, M.T., Comic Theory in the Sixteenth Century. University of Illinois Press, Urbana (1964).

Herrick, M.T., Italian Comedy in the Renaissance. University of Illinois Press, Urbana (1966).

Hertzler, J.O., Laughter: A Socio-Scientific Analysis. Exposition Press, New York (1971).

Hes, J.P. & Levine, J., Kibbuts humor. Journal of Nervous and Mental Disease, 135, 327-331 (1962).

Hess, A.G. & Mariner, E.A., On the sociology of crime cartoons. International Journal of Criminology and Penology, 3, 253-265 (1975).

Hetherington, E.M., Humor preferences in normal and physically handicapped children. Journal of Abnormal and Social Psychology, 69, 694-696 (1964a).

Hetherington, E.M. & Wray, N.P., Aggression, need for social approval, and humor preferences. Journal of Abnormal and Social Psychology, 68, 685-689 (1964b).

Hetherington, E.M. & Wray, N.P., Effects of need aggression, stress, and aggressive behavior on humor preferences. Journal of Personality and Social Psychology, 4, 229-233 (1966).

Highet, G., The Anatomy of Satire. Princeton University Press, Princeton (1962).

Hines, E., Cartoons as a means of social control. Sociology and Social Research, 17, 454-464 (1933).

Hinson, M., The assessment of children's appreciation of humorous verses. Educational Review, 22, 198-204 (1970).

Hinton, J., Seggar, J., Northcutt, H. & Fontes, B., Tokenism and improving imagery of blacks in television drama comedy. Journal of Broadcasting, 18, 423-432 (1974).

Hitoshi, U. & Fujiko, U., Joking relationships among the Kamba. Japanese Journal of Ethnology, 40, 169-191 (1975).

Hodgart, M., Satire. McGraw-Hill, New York (1969).

Hoglund, J.S., In search of a theory of comedy. New Orleans Review, 3, 315-319 (1973).

Holland, N.N., The First Modern Comedies. University of Indiana Press, Bloomington (1959).

Holliday, C., The Wit and Humor of Colonial Days. Ungar, New York (Original 1912) (1970).

Hollingworth, H.L., Experimental studies in judgment: Judgment of the comic. Psychological Review, 18, 132-156 (1911).

Holmes, D.S., The development of measures of the sensing of humor. California Mental Health Research Digest, 3, 27-28 (1955).

Holmes, D.S., Sensing humor: Latency and amplitude of responses related to MMPI profiles. Journal of Consulting and Clinical Psychology, 33, 296-301 (1969).

Hom, G.L., Threat of shock and anxiety in the perception of humor. Perceptual and Motor
    Skills, 23, 535–538 (1966).

Holt, E., Wit and humor. In: D. Robinson (Ed.), Readings in General Psychology. University
    of Chicago Press (1916).

Holt, R.R., Cognitive controls and primary processes. Journal of Psychological Research, 4,
    105–112 (1960).

Hooff, J.A.R.A.M. van., A comparative approach to the phylogeny of laughter and smiling.
    In: R. Hinde (Ed.), Nonverbal Communication. Cambridge University Press, Cambridge (1972).

Hooker, E.N., Humour in the age of Pope. Huntington Library Quarterly, 11, 361–386 (1948).

Horowitz, L.S., Attitudes of speech defectives toward humor based on speech defects. Speech
    Monographs, 24, 46–55 (1957).

Horowitz, M.W. & Horowitz, L.S., An examination of the social psychological situations of
    the physically disabled as it pertains to humor. American Psychologist, 4, 256–257
    (1949).

Hoult, T., Comic books and juvenile delinquency. Sociology and Social Research, 33, 279–284
    (1949).

Howard, J.E., Peyote jokes. Journal of American Folklore, 75, 10–14 (1962).

Howe, I., The nature of Jewish laughter. New American Mercury, 72, 211–219 (1951).

Humes, J.C., Podium Humor. Harper & Row, New York (1974).

Hunt, L., Wit and Humour. London, 1882 (Reprint 1910).

Hurrell, J.D., A note on farce. Quarterly Journal of Speech, 45, 426–430 (1959).

Huizinga, J., Homo Ludens: A Study of the Play Element in Culture. Beacon, Boston (1955).

Hutcheson, F., Reflections Upon Laughter. Glasgow (1750).

Hyers, C., Zen and the Comic Spirit. Westminster, Philadelphia (1974).

Isager, H., Factors contributing to happiness among Danish college students. Journal of
    Social Psychology, 28, 237–246 (1948).

Jacobson, E., The child's laughter: Theoretical and clinical notes on the function of the
    comic. The Psychoanalytic Study of the Child, 2, 39–60 (1947).

Jacobson, E., On the child's laughter and the function of the comic. In: Depression.
    International Universities Press, New York (1971).

Janoff, B., Black humor, absurdity and technique. Studies in the Twentieth Century, 39–49
    (197?).

Janus, S.S., The great comedians: Personality and other factors. American Journal of
    Psychoanalysis, 35, 169–174 (1975).

Jekels, L., On the psychology of comedy. In: Selected Papers. International University Press,
    New York (Original 1926) (Also Imago, London, 1952) (1952).

Jones, J.M. & Harries, P., Psychophysiological correlates of cartoon humor appreciation.
    Proceedings, American Psychological Association, 6, 381–382 (1971).

Jones, J.M. & Liverpool, H.V., Calypso humor in Trinidad. In: A.J. Chapman & H.C. Foot
    (Eds.), Humour and Laughter: Theory, Research and Applications. Wiley, London (1976).

Jones, J.M. & Zelazo, P., Cognitive developmental factors in children's appreciation of
    cartoon humor. Child Development, in press.

Jonson, B., Every man out of his humour. In: P. Lauter (Ed.), Theories of Comedy. Doubleday,
    New York (1964).

Kadis, A.L. & Winick, C., The cartoon as therapeutic catalyst. In: H. Mosak (Ed.), Alfred
    Adler: His Influence on Psychology Today. Noyes Press, Park Ridge, New Jersey (1973).

Kahn, S., Why and How We Laugh. Philosophical Library, New York (1975).

Kallen, H.M., The aesthetic principle in comedy. American Journal of Psychology, 22, 137–157
    (1911).

Kambouropoulou, P., Individual differences in the sense of humor. American Journal of
    Psychology, 37, 268–278 (1926).

Kambouropoulou, P., Individual differences in the sense of humor and their relation to
    temperamental differences. Archives of Psychology, 19, 1–83 (1930).

Kant, O., Inappropriate laughter and silliness in schizophrenia. Journal of Abnormal and
    Social Psychology, 37, 398–402 (1942).

Kanzer, M., Gogol — A study on wit and paranoia. Journal of the American Psychoanalytic Association, 3, 110 (1955).

Kao, G., Chinese Wit and Humor. Sterling, New York (1946).

Kaplan, H.B. & Boyd, I.H., The social functions of humor on an open psychiatric ward. Psychiatric Quarterly, 39, 502-515 (1965).

Kappas, K.H., A developmental analysis of children's responses to humor. Library Quarterly, 37, 67-77 (1967).

Karstetter, A.B., Toward a theory of rhetorical irony. Speech Monographs, 31, 162-178 (1964).

Katz, N. & Katz, E., Tradition and adaptation in American Jewish humor. Journal of American Folklore, 84, 215-220 (1971).

Kauffmann, S.P. & Dwyer, F.M., Effectiveness of cartoons and photographs in in-service training. California Journal of Educational Research, 25, 197-204 (1974).

Keith-Speigel, P., Early conceptions of humor: Varieties and issues. In: J.H. Goldstein & P.E. McGhee (Eds.), The Psychology of Humor. Academic Press, New York (1972).

Keller, W., Humour, irony, sarcasm. Heilpadogogishe Werkblatter, 35, 228-230 (1966).

Kelling, G.W., An empirical investigation of Freud's theory of jokes. Psychoanalytic Review, 58, 473-485 (1971).

Kelly, J. & Solomon, P., Humor in television advertising. Journal of Advertising, 4, 31-35 (1975).

Kenerdine, M., Laughter in the preschool child. Child Development, 2, 228-230 (1931).

Kenny, D.I., The contingency of humor appreciation on the stimulus-confirmation of joke-ending expectations. Journal of Abnormal and Social Psychology, 51, 644-648 (1955).

Kernan, A., The Cankered Muse. Yale University Press, New Haven (1959).

Kernan, A., The Plot of Satire. Yale University Press, New Haven (1965).

Khumalo, J.S.M., Zulu riddles. African Studies Quarterly, 33, 193-226 (1974).

Kilbride, J.E. & Kilbride, P.L., Sitting and smiling behavior of Baganda infants. Journal of Cross Cultural Psychology, 6, 88 ff (1975).

Kimmins, C.W., An investigation of the sense of humor in children. Reports of the British Association for the Advancement of Science, No. 449 (1921).

Kimmins, C.W., The sense of humour in children. Strand Magazine, 63, 52-57 (1922a).

Kimmins, C.W., Visual humour: Sights that children laugh at. Strand Magazine, 63, 294-299 (1922b).

Kimmins, C.W., The Springs of Laughter. Methuen, London (1928).

Kincaid, J.R., Dickens and the Rhetoric of Laughter. Oxford University Press, Oxford (1971).

King, P.V. & King, J.E., A children's humor test. Psychological Reports, 33, 632 (1973).

Kinnosuke, A., What makes Japan laugh? Outlook, 146, 49-51 (1927).

Kirkland, J., Warm-up and fatigue effects in jokes rated by concrete and abstract persons. Social Behavior and Personality, 2, 161-165 (1974).

Kirkland, J., Epistemic curiosity and cartoon preference. Psychological Reports, 38, 354 (1976).

Klapp, O.E., The fool as a social type. American Journal of Sociology, 55, 157-162 (1950).

Klein, J.P., On the use of humour in counseling. Canadian Counselor, 8, 233-239 (1974).

Kleivan, I., Examples of Greenlandic humour with regard to culture contacts and inter-ethnic relationships. Folk, 16-17, 189-192 (1974-1975).

Kline, L.W., The psychology of humor. American Journal of Psychology, 18, 421-441 (1907).

Knights, L.C., Notes on comedy. In: F.R. Leavis (Ed.), Determinations: Critical Essays. Chatto & Windus, London (1934).

Koch, M., Constitutional variants of wittiness. Psychotherapy and Medical Psychology, 5, 203-214 (1955).

Koestler, A., Insight and Outlook. Macmillan, London (1949).

Koestler, A., The Act of Creation. Hutchinson, London (1964).

Kohn, A., The journal in which the scientists laugh at a science. Impact of Science on Society, 19, 259-268 (1969).

Kolaja, J., American magazine cartoons and social control. Journalism Quarterly, 30, 71-74 (1953).

Kole, T. & Henderson, H.L., Cartoon reaction scale with special reference to driving behavior. Journal of Applied Psychology, 50, 311-316 (1966).

Koppel, M.A. & Sechrest, L., A multitrait-multimethod matrix analysis of sense of humor. Educational and Psychological Measurement, 30, 77-85 (1970).

Kramer, C., Stereotypes of women's speech: The word from cartoons. Journal of Popular Culture, 8, 624-631 (1974).

Kramer, H.C., Laughing spells in patients after lobotomy. Journal of Nervous and Mental Diseases, 119, 517-522 (1954).

Kreitler, H. & Kreitler, S., Dependence of laughter on cognitive strategies. Merrill-Palmer Quarterly, 16, 163-177 (1970).

Kris, E., The psychology of caricature. International Journal of Psychoanalysis, 17, 285-303 (1936).

Kris, E., Ego development and the comic. International Journal of Psychoanalysis, 19, 77-90 (1938).

Kris, E., Laughter as an expressive process. International Journal of Psychoanalysis, 21, 314-341 (1940).

Kris, E., Psychoanalytic Explorations of Art. International University Press, New York (1962).

Kris, E. & Gombrich, E., The principles of caricature. British Journal of Medical Psychology, 17, 319-342 (1938).

Krishna Menon, V.K., A Theory of Laughter: With Special Relation to Comedy and Tragedy. George Allen & Unwin, London (1931).

Kristol, I., Is Jewish humor dead? The rise and fall of the Jewish joke. Comentary, 12, 431-436 (1951).

Kronenberger, L., Some prefatory notes on comedy. In: The Thread of Laughter. Knopf, New York (1952).

Krutch, J.W., Comedy and Conscience After the Restoration. Columbia University Press, New York, (1924).

Kubie, L.S., The destructive potential of humor in psychotherapy. American Journal of Psychiatry, 127, 861-886 (1971).

Kwang, L.L., Theories of laughter. Chinese Students' Monthly, 17, 102-111 (1921).

La Fave, L., Comment on Priest's article: 'Election jokes: The effects of reference group membership'. Psychological Reports, 20, 305-306 (1967).

La Fave, L., Humor judgments as a function of reference group and identification classes. In: J.H. Goldstein & P.E. McGhee (Eds.), The Psychology of Humor. Academic Press, New York (1972).

La Fave, L., Haddad, J. & Maesen, W.A., Superiority, enhanced self-esteem, and perceived incongruity humour theory. In: A.J. Chapman and H.C. Foot (Eds.), Humour and Laughter: Theory, Research and Applications. Wiley, London (1976).

La Fave, L., Haddad, J. & Marshall, N., Humor judgments as a function of identification classes. Sociology and Social Research, 58, 184-194 (1975).

La Fave, L., McCarthy, K. & Haddad, J., Humor judgments as a function of identification classes: Canadian versus American. Journal of Psychology, 85, 53-59 (1973).

Laffal, J., Levine, J. & Redlich, F.C., An anxiety reduction theory of humor. American Psychologist, 8, 383 (1953).

La Gaipa, J.J., Stress, authoritarianism, and the enjoyment of different kinds of hostile humor. Journal of Psychology, 70, 3-8 (1968).

Laing, A., The sense of humour in childhood and adolescence. British Journal of Educational Psychology, 9, 201 (1939).

Lamb, C.W., Personality correlates of humor enjoyment following motivational arousal. Journal of Personality and Social Psychology, 9, 237-241 (1968).

Landis, C. & Ross, J.W.H., Humor and its relation to other personality traits. Journal of Social Psychology, 4, 156-175 (1933).

Landy, D. & Metee, D., Evaluation of an aggressor as a function of exposure to cartoon humor. Journal of Personality and Social Psychology, 12, 66-71 (1969).

Langer, S.K., The comic rhythm. In: S. Barnet et al (Eds.), Eight Great Comedies. New American Library, New York (1958).

Langevin, R. & Day, H.I., Physiological correlates of humor. In: J.H. Goldstein & P.E. McGhee (Eds.), The Psychology of Humor. Academic Press, New York (1972).

Lariar, L. (Ed.), Best Cartoons of the Year 1965. Crown, New York (1965).

Lauter, P., Theories of Comedy. Doubleday, New York (1964).

Lax, E., On Being Funny: Woody Allen and Comedy. Charterhouse, New York (1975).

Layton, M.J., Luba and Finnish riddles: A double analysis. Journal of American Folklore, 89, 239-248 (1976).

Leacock, S., Humour as I see it. In: Laugh with Leacock, Dodd, Mead, New York (1913).

Leacock, S., Further Foolishness. London (1917).

Leacock, S., Humour: Its Theory and Technique. John Lane, London (1935).

Leacock, S., Humour and Humanity. Butterworth, London (1937).

Leak, G.K., Effects of hostility arousal and aggressive humor on catharsis and humor preference. Journal of Personality and Social Psychology, 30, 736-740 (1974).

Lee, J.C. & Griffith, R.M., Forgetting of humor: Repression? American Psychologist, 15, 436 (1960).

Lee, J.C. & Griffith, R.M., Time error in the judgment of humor. Psychological Reports, 11, 410 (1962).

Lee, J.C. & Griffith, R.M., Forgetting jokes: A function of repression? Journal of Individual Papers, 19, 213-215 (1963).

Lefcourt, H.M., Antrobus, P. & Hogg, E., Humor response and humor production as a function of locus of control, field dependence and type of reinforcements. Journal of Personality, 42, 632-651 (1974).

Lefcourt, H.M. & Sordoni, C., Locus of control and the expression of humor. Proceedings, American Psychological Association, 8, 185-186 (1973).

Lefcourt, H.M., Sordoni, C. & Sordoni, C., Locus of control and the expression of humor. Journal of Personality, 42, 130-143 (1974).

Lefebvre, L.M., Encoding and decoding of integration in modes of smiling and gaze. British Journal of Social and Clinical Psychology, 14, 33-42 (1975).

Legman, G., Toward a motif-index of erotic humor. Journal of American Folklore, 75, 227-248 (1962).

Legman, G., Rationale of the Dirty Joke. Grove, New York (1968).

Legman, G., No Laughing Matter: Rationale of the Dirty Joke. Second Series, Wharton, Breaking Point, New Jersey (1975).

Leroy-Boussion, A., Study of the emotional behavior of children during the projection of a comic film. Revue International de Filmologie, No. 5, 103-123 (1954).

Lerup, L., Riddles and unriddling. Ekistics, 39, 300-305 (1975).

L'Estrange, A.G., History of English Humour. B. Franklin (1878).

Leuba, C., Tickling and laughter: Two genetic studies. Journal of Genetic Psychology, 58, 201-209 (1941).

Leventhal, H. & Mace, W., The effect of laughter on evaluation of a slapstick movie. Journal of Personality, 38, 16-30 (1970).

Leventhal, H. & Cupchik, G.C., The informational and facilitative effects of an audience upon expression and evaluation of humorous stimuli. Journal of Experimental Social Psychology, 11, 363-380 (1975).

Leventhal, H. & Cupchik, G.C., A process model of humor judgment. Journal of Communication, 26, 190-204 (1976).

Lever, K., The Art of Greek Comedy. Methuen, London (1956).

Levin, G., Children's smiles and laughter. Ofakim, 14, 128-131 (1960).

Levin, M., Wit and schizophrenic thinking. American Journal of Psychiatry, 113, 917-923 (1957).

Levine, J., Responses to humor. Scientific American, 194, 31-35 (1956).

Levine, J., Regression in primitive clowning. Psychoanalytic Quarterly, 30, 72-83 (1961).

Levine, J., Humor and mental health. In: A. Deutsch & H. Fishman (Eds.), Encyclopaedia of Mental Health, Vol. 3 (1963).

Levine, J., Humor and play in sports. In: R. Slovenko & J.A. Knight (Eds.), Motivation in Play, Games and Sports. Thomas, Springfield, Illinois (1967).

Levine, J., Humor. In: D.E. Sills (Ed.), International Encyclopaedia of the Social Sciences, Vol. 7. Macmillan, New York (1968).

Levine, J. (Ed.), Motivation in humor. Atherton, New York (1969).

Levine, J. & Abelson, R., An anxiety reduction theory of humor. American Psychologist, 8, 383 (1953).

Levine, J. & Abelson, R., A factor analytic study of cartoon humor among psychiatric patients. Journal of Personality, 26, 451-466 (1958).

Levine, J. & Abelson, R., Humor as a disturbing stimulus. Journal of General Psychology, 60, 191-200 (1959).

Levine, J. & Rakusin, J., The sense of humor of college students and psychiatric patients. Journal of General Psychology, 60, 183-190 (1959).

Levine, J. & Redlich, J., Failure to understand humor. Psychoanalytic Quarterly, 24, 560-572 (1955).

Levine, J. & Redlich, J., Intellectual and emotional factors in the appreciation of humor. Journal of General Psychology, 62, 25-35 (1960).

Levinson, R.M., From Olive Cyl to Sweet Polly Purebread: Sex role stereotypes and television cartoons. Journal of Popular Culture, 9, 561-572 (1975).

Leyburn, E.D., Satiric Allegory. Yale University Press, New Haven (1969).

Lieber, M.D., Riddles, cultural categories, and world view. Journal of American Folklore, 89, 255-264 (1976).

Lieberman, J.N., Playfulness in play and the player: A behavioral syndrome viewed in relationship to classroom learning. Contemporary Educational Psychology, 1, 197-205 (1976).

Lilly, W.S., Theory of the Ludicrous. Fortnightly Review, 59, 724-737 (1896).

Lindeman, H., Humor in politics and society. Impact of Science on Society, 19, 269-278 (1969).

Lloyd, E.L., The respiratory mechanism in laughter. Journal of Genetic Psychology, 10, 179-189 (1938).

Lloyd, J.A.T., Humour and mechanism. Fortnightly Review, 118, 244-254 (1922).

Lloyd-Morgan, C., Laughter. Encyclopaedia of Religion and Ethics, 7, 803-805 (1915).

Loftis, J., Comedy and Society from Congreve to Fielding. Stanford University Press, Stanford (1959).

Logre, B.J., The neuro-vegetative aspect of laughter. Psyche, 7, 657-664 (1952).

Losco, J. & Epstein, S., Humor preference as a subtle measure of attitudes toward the same and the opposite sex. Journal of Personality, 43, 321-334 (1975).

Lowenthal, M.M., The laughter of detachment. Dial, 66, 133-135 (1919).

Luborsky, L. & Cattell, R., The validation of personality factors in humor. Journal of Personality, 15, 283-291 (1947).

Ludovici, A.M., The Secret of Laughter. Gordon Press, London (1932).

Lull, P.E., The effects of humor in persuasive speech. Speech Monographs, 7, 26-40 (1940).

Lumley, F.E., Means of Social Control. Century, New York (1925).

Lundberg, C.C., Person-focused joking: Pattern and function. Human Organization, 28, 22-28 (1969).

Luomala, K., Humorous narratives about individual resistance to food-distribution customs in Tabiteuea, Gilbert Islands. Journal of American Folklore, 78, 28-45 (1965).

Lynch, K.M., The Social Mode of Restoration Comedy. Macmillan, New York (1926).

Lynn, K., The Comic Tradition in America. Doubleday, New York (1958).

Maclachlan, J.M., Southern humor as a vehicle of social evolution. Mississippi Quarterly, 13, 157-162 (1960).

Macnaughton, S., Humour. Nineteenth Century and After (1913).

Mahony, P., Barbed Wit and Malicious Humor. Citadel, New York (1956).

Maier, N.R.F., A gestalt theory of humour. British Journal of Psychology, 23 69-74 (1932).

Main, D.C. & Schillace, R.J., Aversive stimulation and the laughter response. Psychonomic Science, 13, 241-242 (1968).

Malpass, L.F. & Fitzpatrick, E.D., Social facilitation as a factor in reaction to humor. Journal of Social Psychology, 50, 295-303 (1959).

Mandel, O., What's so funny: The nature of the comic. Antioch Review, 30, 73-89 (1970).

Manuel, E.A., Bagobo riddles. Asian Folklore Studies, 21, 123-185 (1962).

Maranda, E.K., Theory and practice of riddle analysis. Journal of American Folklore, 84, 51-61 (1971).

Maranda, E.K., The logic of riddles. In: P. Maranda & E.K. Maranda (Eds.), Structural Analysis of Oral Tradition. University of Pennsylvania Press, Philadelphia (1971).

Maranda, E.K., Riddles and riddling: An introduction. Journal of American Folklore, 89, 127-138 (1976).

Marcos, L.R., The emotional correlates of smiling and laughter: A preliminary research study. American Journal of Psychoanalysis, 34, 33-41 (1974).

Markiewicz, D., Effects of humor on persuasion. Sociometry, 37, 407-422 (1974).

Martin, J.P., Fits of laughter (sham mirth) in organic cerebral disease. Brain, 73, 453-464 (1950).

Martin, L.J., Psychology of aesthetics: Experimental prospecting in the field of the comic. American Journal of Psychology, 16, 35-116 (1905).

Martineau, W.H., A model for a theory of the function of humor. Research Reports in the Social Sciences, 1, 51-64 (1967).

Martineau, W.H., A model of the social functions of humor. In: J.H. Goldstein & P.E. McGhee (Eds.), The Psychology of Humor. Academic Press, New York (1972).

Masson, T.L., Our American Humorists. Moffat, New York (1922).

Mathewson, L., Bergson's theory of the comic in the light of English comedy. University of Nebraska Studies in Language, Literature and Criticism, No. 5 (1920).

Maw, W.H. & Maw, E.W., Differences between high- and low-curiosity fifth-grade children in their recognition of verbal absurdities. Journal of Educational Psychology, 63, 558-562 (1972).

McAllester, D.P., Riddles and other verbal play among the Comanches. Journal of American Folklore, 77, 251-257 (1964).

McCall, R.B., Smiling and vocalization in infants as indices of perceptual-cognitive processes. Merrill-Palmer Quarterly, 18, 341-347 (1972).

McCarthur, H., Tragic and comic modes. Criticism, 3, 36-45 (1961).

McComas, H.C., The origin of laughter. Psychological Review, 30, 45-55 (1923).

McConnell, J., Confessions of a scientific humorist. Impact of Science on Society, 19, 241-251 (1969).

McConnell, J.V., Worm breeding with tongue in cheek. UNESCO Courier, 12-15, April (1976).

McCrary, L.H., Why We Laugh. Courier Print, Woodbury, Tennesse (1934).

McDougall, W., The theory of laughter. Nature, 67, 318-319 (1903).

McDougall, W., A new theory of laughter. Psyche, 2, 292-303 (1922a).

McDougall, W., Why do we laugh? Scribners, 71, 359-363 (1922b).

McDougall, W., New light on laughter. Fortnightly Review, 148, 312-320 (1937).

McGhee, P.E., Cognitive development and children's comprehension of humor. Child Development, 42, 123-138 (1971a).

McGhee, P.E., The development of the humor response: A review of the literature. Psychological Bulletin, 76, 328-348 (1971b).

McGhee, P.E., The role of operational thinking in children's comprehension and appreciation of humor. Child Development, 42, 733-744 (1971c).

McGhee, P.E., Methodological and theoretical considerations for a cross-cultural investigation of children's humor. International Journal of Psychology, 7, 13-21 (1972a).

McGhee, P.E., On the cognitive origins of incongruity humor: Fantasy assimilation versus reality assimilation. In: J.H. Goldstein & P.E. McGhee (Eds.), The Psychology of Humor. Academic Press, New York (1972b).

McGhee, P.E., Birth order and social facilitation of humor. Psychological Reports, 33, 105-106 (1973).

McGhee, P.E., Cognitive mastery and children's humor. Psychological Bulletin, 81, 721-730 (1974a).

McGhee, P.E., Development of children's ability to create the joking relationship. Child Development, 45, 552-556 (1974b).

McGhee, P.E., Moral development and children's appreciation of humor. Developmental Psychology, 10, 514-525 (1974c).

McGhee, P.E., Children's appreciation of humor: A test of the cognitive congruency principle. Child Development, 47, 420-426 (1976a).

McGhee, P.E., Sex differences in children's humor. Journal of Communication, 26, 176-189 (1976b).

McGhee, P.E. & Goldstein, J.H., Advances toward an understanding of humor: Implications for the future. In:J.H. Goldstein & P.E. McGhee (Eds.), The Psychology of Humor. Academic Press, New York (1972).

McGhee, P.E. & Goldstein, J.H., The Sense and Nonsense of Humor, In preparation.

McGhee, P.E. & Grodzitsky, P., Sex-role identification and humor among preschool children. Journal of Psychology, 84, 189-193 (1973).

McGhee, P.E. & Johnson, S.F., The role of fantasy and reality cues in children's appreciation of incongruity humor. Merrill-Palmer Quarterly, 21, 19-30 (1975).

McGoldrick Orfanidis, M., Children's use of humor in psychotherapy. Social Casework, 147-155, March (1972).

McRae, C.R., Laughter. Australasian Journal of Psychology and Philosophy, 8, 263-270 (1930).

Meadows, C.M., The phenomenology of joy, an empirical investigation. Psychological Reports, 37, 39-54 (1975).

Meerloo, J.A.M., The biology of laughter. Psychoanalytic Review, 53, 189-208 (1966).

Melland, M.C., Psychological causes of laughter. Popular Science Monthly, 53, 398-403 (1895).

Mendel, W.M. (Ed.), A Celebration of Laughter. Los Angeles, Mara Books (1970).

Mendel, W.M., Humor as an index of emotional means. Worm Runner's Digest, 13, 53-61 (1971).

Menon, V.K., A Theory of Laughter. Allen & Unwin, London (1931).

Merchant, W.M., Comedy. Barnes & Noble, New York (1932).

Meredith, G., An Essay on Comedy. Charles Schribner's Sons, New York (1918).

Messenger, J.C., Anang proverb-riddles. Journal of American Folklore, 73, 225-235 (1960).

Mettee, D.R., Hrelec, E.S. & Wilkens, P.C., Humor as an interpersonal asset and liability. Journal of Social Psychology, 85, 51-64 (1971).

Mettee, D.R. & Wilkins, P.C., When similarity 'hurts': Effects of perceived ability and a humorous blunder on interpersonal attractiveness. Journal of Personality and Social Psychology, 22, 246-258 (1972).

Middleton, R., Negro and white reactions to racial humor. Sociometry, 22, 175-183 (1959).

Middleton, R. & Moland, J., Humor in Negro and white subcultures: A study of jokes among university students. American Sociological Review, 24, 61-69 (1959).

Mikes, G., Humor in Memorium. Routledge & Kegan Paul, London (1970).

Mikes, G., Laughing Matter: Towards a Personal Philosophy of Wit and Humor. Library Press, New York (1971).

Mikes, G., The importance of NOT being earnest. UNESCO Courier, 5-8, April (1976).

Mikhail, E.H., Comedy and Tragedy: A Bibliography of Critical Studies. Whitston, New York (1972).

Miller, D.L., Achelous and the butterfly: Toward an archetypal psychology of humor. Spring 1-23 (1973).

Miller, F.C., Humor in a Chippewa tribal council. Ethnology, 6, 263-271 (1967).

Miller, G.R. & Bacon, P., Open- and closed-mindedness and recognition of visual humor. Journal of Communication, 21, 150-159 (1971).

Milner, G.B., Homo ridens: Towards a semiotic theory of humour and laughter. Semiotica, 1, 1-30 (1972).

Mindess, H., Laughter and Liberation. Nash, Los Angeles (1971a).

Mindess, H., The sense in humor. Saturday Review, 10-12, August 21st (1971b).

Mindess, H., The Chosen People? Nash, Los Angeles (1972).

Mindess, H., Shut up you fool! Your doctor is laughing! The use and abuse of humour in psychotherapy. In:A.J. Chapman & H.C. Foot (Eds.), Humour and Laughter: Theory, Research and Applications. Wiley, London (1976).

Mockheimer, S.H., Laughter in military life. Egypt Journal of Psychology, 5, 31-48 (1949).

Mones, L., Intelligence and a sense of humor. Journal of Exceptional Child Psychology, 5, 150-153 (1939).

Monro, D.H., Argument of Laughter. Melbourne University Press, Melbourne (1951).

Monson, D., Children's test responses to seven humorous stories. Elementary School Journal, 334-339 (196).

Montague, A., Why man laughs. Think, 30-32, April 26th (1960).

More, D.M. & Roberts, A.F., Societal variations in humor responses to cartoons. Journal of Social Psychology, 45, 233-243 (1957).

Moore, F.H., The Nobler Pleasure. University of North Carolina Press, Chapel Hill (1963).

Moreau, R.E., The joking relationship (utani) in Tanganyika. Tanganyika Notes and Records, 12, 1-10 (1941).

Moreau, R.E., Joking relationships in Tanganyika. Africa, 14, 386-400 (1944).

Morris, D., The Naked Ape, Jonathon Cape, London (1967a).

Morrison, J.A., A note concerning investigations on the constancy of audience laughter. Sociometry, 3, 179-185 (1940).

Morrison, M., Wedding night pranks in western New Brunswick. Southern Folklore Quarterly, 38, 285-297 (1974).

Mukherji, N., The psychology of laughter. Indian Journal of Psychology, 10, 95-110 (1935).

Mull, H.K., A study of humor in music. American Journal of Psychology, 62, 560-566 (1949).

Mumford, L., The mood of satire. Freeman, 224, November 14th (1923).

Murphy, B. & Pollio, H.R., I'll laugh if you will. Psychology Today, 7, 106-110, December (1973).

Murphy, B. & Pollio, H.R., The many faces of humor. Psychological Record, 25, 545-558 (1975).

Murray, H.A., The psychology of humor. Journal of Abnormal and Social Psychology, 29, 66-81 (1934).

Mussen, P. & Rutherford, E., Effects of aggressive cartoons on children's aggressive play. Journal of Abnormal and Social Psychology, 62, 461-464 (1961).

Muthayya, B.C. & Mallikarjunan, M.A., A measure of humour and its relation to intelligence. Journal of Psychological Research, 13, 101-105 (1969).

Myers, H.A., The analysis of laughter. Sewanee Review, 43, 452-463 (1935).

Myers, L., Psychiatric Glossary: A Cartoon View of the World of Psychiatry. Dutton, New York (1962).

Nathan, P., Laughter Makers. Fernhill New York (1971).

Nerhardt, G., Humor and inclination to laugh: Emotional reactions to stimuli of different divergence from a range of expectancy. Scandinavian Journal of Psychology, 11, 185-195 (1970).

Nerhardt, G., Rated funniness and dissimilarity of figures: Divergence from expectancy. Scandinavian Journal of Psychology, 16, 156-166 (1975).

Nerhardt, G., Incongruity and funniness: Towards a new descriptive model. In: A.J. Chapman & H.C. Foot (Eds.), Humour and Laughter: Theory, Research and Applications. Wiley, London (1976).

Nevo, R., Toward a theory of comedy. Journal of Aesthetics and Art Criticism, 21, 328 ff (1963).

Nicolson, H., The English Sense of Humour. Constable, London (1956).

Norris, D., Crying and laughing in imbeciles. Developmental Medical Child Neurology, 13, 756-761 (1971).

Norwood, G., Greek Comedy. Hill & Wang, New York (Original 1931) (1963).

Nosanchuk, T.A. & Lightstone, J., Canned laughter public and private conformity. Journal of Personality and Social Psychology, 29, 153-156 (1974).

Nussbaum, K. & Michaux, W.W., Response to humor in depression: A predictor and evaluator of patient change? Psychiatric Quarterly, 37, 527-539 (1963).

Oberndorf, C.P., Kidding. International Journal of Psychoanalysis, 13, 479 (1932).

Obrdlik, A.J., 'Gallows humor' - A sociological phenomenon. American Journal of Sociology, 47, 709-716 (1942).

O'Connell, W.E., The adaptive functions of wit and humor. Journal of Abnormal and Social Psychology, 61, 263-270 (1960).

O'Connell, W.E., An item analysis of the wit and humor appreciation test. Journal of Social Psychology, 56, 271-276 (1962).

O'Connell, W.E., Multidimensional investigation of Freudian humor. Psychiatric Quarterly, 38, 97-108 (1964a).

O'Connell, W.E., Resignation, humor and wit. Psychoanalytic Review, 51, 49-56 (1964b).

O'Connell, W.E., The humor of the gallows. Omega, 1, 31-32 (1966).

O'Connell, W.E., Humor and death. Psychological Reports, 22, 391-402 (1968a).

O'Connell, W.E., Organic and schizophrenic differences in wit and humor appreciation. Diseases of the Nervous System, 29, 275-280 (1968b).

O'Connell, W.E., Creativity in humor. Journal of Social Psychology, 78, 237-241 (1969a).

O'Connell, W.E., Humor: The therapeutic impasse. Voices, 5, 25-27 (1969b).

O'Connell, W.E., Freudian humour: the eupsychia of everyday life. In: A.J.Chapman & H.C.Foot (Eds.), Humour and Laughter: Theory, Research and Applications. Wiley, London (1976).

O'Connell, W.E. & Covert, C., Death attitudes and humor appreciation among medical students. Existential Psychiatry, 6, 433-442 (1967).

O'Connell, W.E. & Cowgill, S., Wit, humor, and defensiveness. Newsletter for Research in Psychology, 12, 32-33 (1970).

O'Connell, W.E. & Peterson, P., Humor and repression. Journal of Existential Psychology, 4, 309-316 (1964).

O'Connell, W.E., Rothaus, P., Hanson, P.G. & Moyer, R., Jest appreciation and interaction in leaderless groups. International Journal of Group Psychotherapy, 19, 454-462 (1969).

Oliver, E.J., Hypocrisy and Humor. Sheed & Ward, London (1960).

Olson, E., Theory and Comedy. Indiana University Press, Bloomington (1970).

Omwake, L., A study of sense of humor: Its relation to sex, age and personal characteristics. Journal of Applied Psychology, 21, 688-704 (1937).

Omwake, L., Factors influencing the sense of humor. Journal of Social Psychology, 10, 95-104 (1939).

Omwake, L., Humor in the making. Journal of Social Psychology, 15, 265-279 (1942).

Orben, R., Comedy Technique. Wehman, Hackensack, New Jersey (1951).

Oreglia, G., Commedia dell'Arte. Hill & Wang, New York (1968).

Orel, H., The World of Victorian Humor. Appleton-Century-Crofts, New York (1961).

Oring, E., 'Hey, you've got no character' - Chizbat humor and the boundaries of Israeli identity. Journal of American Folklore, 86, 358-366 (1973).

Oster, H., Negro humor: John and old marster. Journal of the Folklore Institute, 5, 42-57 (1968).

Palmore, E., Attitudes toward aging as shown by humor. The Gerentologist, 11, 181-186 (1971).

Panagis, D.M. & Leventhal, H., The interaction of short term set and sex differences in altering funniness judgments. In preparation.

Parachini, A., Social protest hits the comic pages. Columbia Journalism Review, 13, 4-7 (1974).

Parsons, E.C. & Beals, R.L., Sacred clowns of the Pueblo and Mayor-Yaqui Indians. American Anthropologist, 36, 491-514 (1934).

Parton, J., Caricature and Other Comic Art. Harper, New York (1877).

Partridge, E., The 'Shaggy Dog' Story - Its Origin, Development and Nature. Faber & Faber, London (1953).

Paskind, H.A., Effect of laughter on muscle tone. Archives of Neurology and Psychiatry, 28, 623-628 (1932).

Paul, S.E., The musical surprise: A discussion of the elements of the unexpected in the humour of Haydn. Music, Cambridge Review, 171-175, May 30th (1975).

Paulson, R., Satire: Modern Essays in Criticism. Prentice-Hall, Englewood Cliffs, New Jersey (1971).

Pearson, H., Humour. In: H. Kingsmill (Ed.), The English Genius. Eyre & Spottiswoode, London (1938).

Pedler, F.J., Joking relationships in East Africa. Africa, 13, 170-173 (1940).

Pendleton, W.K., How To Win Your Audience With Humor. Essandess, New York (1969).

Pennell, E.R., Why the world grins. Western American Review, 218, 537-544 (1923).

Penrod, J.H., Minority groups in old southern humor. Southern Folklore Quarterly, 22, 121-128 (1958).

Perl, R.E., The influence of a social factor upon the appreciation of humor. American Journal of Psychology, 45, 308-312 (1933a).

Perl, R.E., A review of experiments on humor. Psychological Bulletin, 30, 752-763 (1933b).

Perlis, M.E., The social function of marriage wit. Marriage and Family Living, 16, 49-50 (1954).

Perry, H.T.E., Masters of Dramatic Comedy and Their Social Themes. Harvard University Press, Cambridge (1939).

Peto, E., Weeping and laughing. International Journal of Psycho-Analysis, 27, 129-133 (1946).

Piddington, R., The Psychology of Laughter: A Study in Social Adaptation. Figurehead, London (1933) (Reissued, Gamut Press, New York (1963)).

Pien, D. & Rothbart, M.K., Incongruity and resolution in children's humor: A re-examination. Child Development, in press.

Pines, L.N., Laughter as an equivalent of epilepsy. Soviet Psychology and Psychiatry, 2, 33-38 (1964).

Plass, P., Freud and Plato on sophistic joking. Psychoanalytic Review, 59, 347-360 (1972).

Plessner, H., Laughing and Crying: A Study of Border Situations of Human Behaviour. Arnheim, Netherland (1940a).

Plessner, H., The problem of laughing and crying. Tijdschr Phil., 2, 317-384 (1940b).

Pokorny, G.F. & Gruner, C.R., An experimental study of the effect of satire used as support in a persuasive speech. Western Speech, 33, 204-211 (1969).

Poland, W.S., The place of humor in psychotherapy. American Journal of Psychiatry, 28, 635-637 (1971).

Pollio, H.R. & Edgerly, J., Comedians and comic style. In: A.J. Chapman & H.C. Foot (Eds.), Humour and Laughter: Theory, Research and Applications. Wiley, London (1976).

Pollio, H.R., Edgerly, J. & Jordan, R., The comedian's world: Some tentative mappings. Psychological Reports, 30, 387-391 (1972).

Pollio, H.R. & Mers, R.W., Predictability and the appreciation of comedy. Bulletin of the Psychonomic Society, 4, 229-232 (1974).

Pollio, H.R., Mers, R. & Lucchesi, W., Humor, laughter, and smiling: Some preliminary observations of funny behaviors. In: J.H. Goldstein & P.E. McGhee (Eds.), The Psychology of Humor. Academic Press, New York (1972).

Posen, I.S., Pranks and practical jokes at children's summer camps. Southern Folklore Quarterly, 38, 299-309 (1974).

Potter, S., The Sense of Humour. Penguin, London (1954).

Potter, S., British humour for the middle class. Saturday Review, 28-29, May 7th (1955).

Potts, L.J., Comedy. Putnam, New York (1948).

Prentice, N.M. & Fatham, R.E., Joking riddles: a developmental index of children's humor. Developmental Psychology, 11, 210-216 (1975).

Prentice, N.M. & Fatham, R.E., Joking riddles: A developmental index of children's humor. Proceedings, American Psychological Association, 7, 119-120 (1975b).

Prerost, F.J., The indication of sexual and aggressive similarities through humor appreciation. Journal of Psychology, 91, 283-288 (1975).

Prerost, F.J. & Brewer, R.E., Choice of humor after aggression arousal: A search for relief. Proceedings, American Psychological Association, 8, 187-188 (1973).

Prerost, F.J. & Brewer, R.E., The common elements of sex and aggression as reflected in humor preferences. Personality and Social Psychology Bulletin, 1, 189-191 (1974).

Preston, K.A. & Preston, M.J., A note on visual Polack jokes. Journal of American Folklore, 86, 175-177 (1973).

Priest, R.F., Election jokes: The effects of reference group membership. Psychological Reports, 18, 600-602 (1966).

Priest, R.F., Sexism, intergroup conflict and joking. JSAS/Catalog of Selected Documents in Psychology, 2, 15 (1972).

Priest, R.F. & Abrahams, J., Candidate preference and hostile humor in the 1968 elections. Psychological Reports, 26, 779-783 (1970).

Priest, R.F. & Wilhelm, P.G., Sex, marital status, and self-actualization as factors in the appreciation of sexist jokes. Journal of Social Psychology, 92, 245-249 (1974).

Priestly, J.B., English Humour. London (1929).

Pustel, G. & Siegel, L., Humor products of high grade institutionalized retardes. Art Psychotherapy, 1, 67-68 (1973).

Pustel, G., Sternlicht, M. & Siegel, I., The psychodynamics of humor as seen in institution- alized retardates. Journal of Psychology, 80, 69-73 (1972).

Radcliffe-Brown, A.R., On joking relationships. Africa, 13, 195-210 (1940).

Radcliffe-Brown, A.R., A further note on joking relationships. Africa, 19, 133-140 (1949).

Raley, A.L., A psychometric study of humor. American Psychologist, 1, 265 (1946).

Raley, A.L. & Ballmann, C., Theoretical implications for a psychology of the ludicrous. Journal of Social Psychology, 45, 19-23 (1957).

Ramsey, B.A., Lloyd, I.F. & Waterson, N.C., The variable of wit in Anglo-American argumentation. Quarterly Journal of Speech, 59, 474-476 (1973).

Ranke, K., European Anecdotes and Jests. Rosenkilde & Bagger, Copenhagen (1972).

Ransohoff, R., Some observations on humor and laughter in young adolescent girls. Journal of Youth and Adolescence, 4, 155-170 (1975).

Rapp, A., Toward an eclectic and multilateral theory of laughter and humor. Journal of General Psychology, 36, 207-219 (1947).

Rapp, A., The dawn of humor. Classical Journal, 43, 275-280 (1948).

Rapp, A., A phylogenetic theory of wit and humor. Journal of Social Psychology, 30, 81-96 (1949).

Rapp, A., The Origins of Wit and Humor. Dutton, New York (1951).

Rappaport, E.A., From the keystone of comedy to the last of the clowns. Psychoanalytic Review, 59 333-346 (1972).

Redlich, F.C., Intellectual and emotional factors in appreciation of humor. Journal of General Psychology, 62, 25-35 (1960).

Redlich, F.C., Levine, J. & Sohler, T.P., A mirth response test: Preliminary report on a psychodiagnostic technique utilizing dynamics of humor. American Journal of Orthopsychiatry, 21, 717-731 (1951).

Reed, G.E., Comic book ideology. Journal of Criminal Psychopathology, 5, 779-785 (1944).

Reich, A., The structure of the grotesque-comic sublimation. Bulletin of the Menninger Clinic, 13, 160-171 (1949).

Reik, T., Freud and Jewish wit. Psychoanalysis, 2, 12-20 (1954).

Reik, T., Jewish Wit. Gamut Press, New York (1962).

Rensbergern, B., An uncommon inquiry into the nature of a common phenomenon. New York Times Magazine, 63, August 10th (1975).

Repplier, A., Humor: English and American. The Cosmopolitan, 16, 361-369 (1894).

Repplier, A., In Pursuit of Laughter. Houghton Mifflin, Boston (1936).

Reutener, D.B. & Kazak, A.E., The effect of cognitive task difficulty on humor ratings of captioned cartoons. Bulletin of the Psychonomic Society, 7, 275-276 (1976).

Rexroth, K., Humor in a tough age. The Nation, 188, 211-213 (1959).

Rinder, I.D., A note on humor as an index of minority group morale. Phylon, 26, 117-121 (1965).

Roback, A.A., Sense of Humor Test (Second Edition). Sci-Art Publishers, Cambridge, Mass. (1943).

Roberts, A.F. & Johnson, D.M., Some factors related to the perception of funniness in humor stimuli. Journal of Social Psychology, 46, 57–63 (1957).

Roberts, J.M. & Forman, M.L. Riddles: Expressive models of interrogation. Ethnology, 10, 509–533 (1971).

Roecklelein, J.E., Auditory stimulation and cartoon ratings. Perceptual and Motor Skills, 29, 772 (1969).

Rose, G.J., 'King Lear' and the use of humor in treatment. Journal of the American Psycho-analytic Association, 17, 927–940 (1969).

Rosen, V., Varieties of comic caricature, and their relationship to obsessive compulsive phenomena. Journal of the American Psychoanalytic Association, 11, 704–724 (1963).

Rosenberg, B. & Shapiro, G., Marginality and Jewish humor. Midstream, 4, 70–80 (1958).

Rosenheim, E., Humor in psychotherapy: An interactive experience. American Journal of Psychotherapy, 28, 584–591 (1974).

Rosenthal, F., Humor in Early Islam. Leiden Brill (1955).

Rosenwald, G.C., The relation of drive discharge to the enjoyment of humor. Journal of Personality, 32, 682–698 (1964).

Rosenzweig, S., The treatment of humorous responses in the Rosenzweig picture-frustration study: A note on the revised instructions. Journal of Psychology, 30, 139–143 (1950).

Rothbart, M.K., Laughter in young children. Psychological Bulletin, 80, 247–256 (1973).

Rothbart, M.K., Incongruity, problem-solving and laughter. In: A.J. Chapman & H.C. Foot (Eds.), Humour and Laughter: Theory, Research and Applications. Wiley, London (1976).

Roubicek, J., Laughter in epilepsy, with some general introductory notes. Journal of Mental Science, 92, 734–755 (1946).

Rouff, L.L., Creativity and sense of humor. Psychological Reports, 37, 1022 (1975).

Rourke, C., American Humor: A Study of National Character. Harcourt, Brace, New York (1971).

Rovit, E., Jewish humor in American life. American Scholar, 36, 237–245 (1967).

Rowe, W.W., Observations on black humor in Gogol and Nabokov. Slavic and East European Journal, 18, 392–399 (1974).

Rubin, L.D. Jr., The Comic Imagination in American Literature. Rutgers University Press, New Brunswick, New Jersey (1973).

Sachs, L.T., On crying, weeping and laughing as defenses against sexual drives, with special consideration of adolescent giggling. International Journal of Psychoanalysis, 54, 477–481 (1973).

Saenger, G., Male and female relations in the American comic strip. Public Opinion Quarterly, 19, 195–205 (1955).

Salutin, M., The impression management techniques of the burlesque comedian. Sociological Inquiry, 43, 159–168 (1973).

Salzen, E.A., Visual stimuli eliciting the smiling response in the human infant. Journal of Genetic Psychology, 102, 51–54 (1963).

Salzi, P., Laughter as enjoyment of art. Psyche, 7, 684–688 (1952).

Samuels, C. & Samuels, L., Once Upon a Stage. Dodd, Mead, New York (1974).

San Francisco Public Library, Catalog of the Schmulowitz collection of wit and humor, San Francisco (1962).

Schachter, S. & Wheeler, L., Epinephrine, chlorpromazine and amusement. Journal of Abnormal and Social Psychology, 65, 121–128 (1962).

Scheerer, M., An aspect of the psychology of humor. Bulletin of the Menninger Clinic, 30, 86–97 (1966).

Schick, C., McGlynn, R.P. & Woolam, D., Perception of cartoon humor as a function of familiarity and anxiety level. Journal of Personality and Social Psychology, 24, 22–25 (1972).

Schiller, P., A configurational theory of puzzles and jokes. Journal of Genetic Psychology, 18, 217–234 (1938).

Schilling, E.N., The Comic Spirit: Boccaccio to Thomas Mann. Wayne State University Press, Detroit (1965).

Schipper, K.M., The Chinese have a word for (w)it. UNESCO Courier, 28-31, April (1976).

Schmalhausen, S.D., Some marginal notes on laughter, Open Court, 35, 361-370 (1920).

Schmidt, H.E. & Williams, D.I., Humor and its relation to creativity. Psychologica Africana, 13, 34-49 (1969).

Schmidt, H.E. & Williams, D.I., The evolution of theories of humour. Journal of Behavioural Sciences, 1, 95-106 (1971).

Schmidt, W., The analysis of laughter by means of paper-model experiments: A contribution to the solution of the problem of communicative functions of human expression. Psychologische Beitrage, 3, 223-264 (1957).

Schneider, H.K., Pokot folktales, humor and values. Journal of the Folklore Institute, 4, 265-318 (1967).

Schoel, D.R. & Busse, T.V., Humor and creative abilities. Psychological Reports, 29, 34 (1971).

Schuman, S., Out of the fryeing pan and into the pyre: comedy, myth and the Wizard of Oz. Journal of Popular Culture, 302-304 (197?).

Schwartz, B.E., Telepathic humoresque. The Psychoanalytic Review, 61, 591-606 (1974-75).

Schwartz, S., The effects of arousal on appreciation for varying degrees of sex-relevant humor. Journal of Experimental Research in Personality, 6, 241-247 (1972).

Scott, C.T., New evidence of American Indian riddles. Journal of American Folklore, 76, 236-241 (1963).

Scott, C.T., Amuzgo riddles. Journal of American Folklore, 76, 242-244 (1963).

Scott, C.T., On defining the riddle. Genre, 2, 129-142 (1965).

Scott, J.R., Practical jokes of the Newfoundland seal-fishery. Southern Folklore Quarterly, 38, 275-283 (1974).

Segal, E., Roman Laughter: The Comedy of Platus. Harvard University Press, Cambridge (1968).

Sein, M.T. & Dundes, A., Twenty-three riddles from central Burma. Journal of American Folklore, 77, 69-75 (1964).

Senf, R., Huston, P.E. & Cohen, B.D., The use of comic cartoons for the study of social comprehension in schizophrenia. American Journal of Psychiatry, 113, 45-51 (1956).

Seward, S.S. Jr., The Paradox of the Ludicrous. Stanford University Press, Stanford (1930).

Sewell, E., The Field of Nonsense. Chatto & Windus, London (1952).

Shaffer, L.F., Children's interpretations of cartoons. Teachers College Contributions to Education, No. 429 (1930).

Shapiro, E., Biber, B. & Minuchin, P., The cartoon situations test: A semi-structured technique for assessing aspects of personality pertinent to the teaching process. Journal of Projective Techniques, 21, 172-184 (1957).

Sharman, A., 'Joking' in Padhola: Categorical relationships, choice and social control. Man, 4, 103-117 (1969).

Shaw, F.J., Laughter: Paradigm of growth. Journal of Individual Psychology, 16, 151-157 (1960).

Sheridan, M., Comics and Their Creators. Luna, New York.

Sherman, L.W., An ecological study of glee in small groups of preschool children. Child Development, 46, 53-61 (1975).

Shukur, A., Dakhani riddles of Kurnool district. Folklore (Calcutta), 14, 343-346 (1973).

Shultz, T.R., The role of incongruity and resolution in children's appreciation of cartoon humor. Journal of Experimental Child Psychology, 13, 456-477 (1972).

Shultz, T.R., Development of the appreciation of riddles. Child Development, 45, 100-105 (1974a).

Shultz, T.R., Order of cognitive processing in humour appreciation. Canadian Journal of Psychology, 28, 409-420 (1974b).

Shultz, T.R., A cognitive-developmental analysis of humour. In: A.J. Chapman & H.C. Foot (Eds.), Humour and Laughter: Theory, Research and Applications. Wiley, London (1976).

Shultz, T.R. & Horibe, F., Development of the appreciation of verbal jokes. Developmental Psychology, 10, 13-20 (1974).

Shultz, T.R. & Scott, M.B., The creation of verbal humour. Canadian Journal of Psychology, 28, 421–425 (1974).

Shultz, T.R. & Zigler, E., Emotional concomitants of visual mastery in infants: The effects of stimulus movement on smiling and vocalizing. Journal of Experimental Child Psychology, 10, 390–402 (1970).

Shurcliff, A., Judged humor, arousal, and the relief theory. Journal of Personality and Social Psychology, 8, 360–363 (1968).

Sidis, B., The Psychology of Laughter. Appleton, New York (1913).

Simmons, D.C., Protest humor: Folkloristic reaction to prejudice. American Journal of Psychiatry, 120, 567–570 (1963).

Simmons, D.C., Anti-Italian-American riddles in New England. Journal of American Folklore, 79, 475–478 (1966).

Simmons, D.C., Cultural functions of the Efik tone riddle. Journal of American Folklore, 129, 22–28 (1958).

Simpson, H., Excursions in Comedy. Besant, London (1930).

Simpson, W.E. & Crandall, S.J., The perception of smiles. Psychonomic Science, 29, 197–200 (1972).

Singer, D. & Berkowitz, L., Differing 'creativities' in the wit and the clown. Perceptual and Motor Skills, 35, 3–6 (1972).

Singer, D.L. Aggression arousal, hostile humor, catharsis. Journal of Personality and Social Psychology, 8, 1–14 (1968).

Singer, D.L., Gollob, H.F. & Levine, J., Mobilization of inhibitions and the enjoyment of aggressive humor. Journal of Personality, 35, 562–569 (1967).

Singh, R. & Jack, R.M., Personal evaluations, laughter and affective judgments. Journal of Social Psychology, 97, 53–59 (1975).

Sinnott, J.D. & Ross, B.M., Comparison of aggression and incongruity as factors in children's judgments of humor. Journal of Genetic Psychology, 128, 241–250 (1976).

Skells, D., The function of humor in three Nez Perce Indian myths. American Imago, 11, 294–361 (1954a).

Skells, D., Classification of humor in Nez Perce mythology. Journal of American Folklore, 67, 57–63 (1954b).

Smith, C.M. & Hamilton, J., Psychological factors in the narcolepsy-cataplexy syndrome. Psychosomatic Medicine, 21, 40–49 (1959).

Smith, E.E. & Goodchilds, J.D., Characteristics of the witty group member: The wit as a leader. American Psychologist, 14, 375–376 (1959).

Smith, E.E. & Goodchilds, J.D., The wit in large and small established groups. Psychological Reports, 13, 273–274 (1963).

Smith, E.E. & White, H.L., Wit, creativity, and sarcasm. Journal of Applied Psychology, 49, 131–134 (1965).

Smith, N.V. & Vinacke, W.E., Reactions to humorous stimuli of different generations of Japanese, Chinese, and Caucasians in Hawaii. Journal of Social Psychology, 34, 69–96 (1951).

Smith, H.A., The Complete Practical Joker. Arthur Barker, London (1954).

Smith, R.E. The use of humor in the counterconditioning of anger responses: A case study. Behavior Therapy, 4, 576–580 (1973).

Smith, R.E., Ascough, J.C., Ettinger, R.F. & Nelson, D.A., Humor, anxiety, and task performance. Journal of Personality and Social Psychology, 19, 243–246 (1971).

Smith, W.M., The Nature of Comedy. Gorham, Boston (1931).

Smits, G.J., Mobilized inhibition and the appreciation of hostile humor. Psychological Reports, 35, 900 (1974).

Smyth, M.M. & Fuller, R.G.C., Effects of group laughter on responses to humorous material. Psychological Reports, 30, 132–134 (1972).

Sop, I., Nasrudin Hodja, The man who rode his ass backwards. UNESCO Courier, 16–21, April (1976).

Sorrell, W., Facets of Comedy. Grossett & Dunlap, New York (1972).

Spencer, H., The physiology of laughter. Macmillan's Magazine, 1, 395-402 (1860).

Sperling, S.J., On the psychodynamics of teasing. Journal of the American Psychoanalytic Association, 3, 458-483 (1953).

Speigel, D., Brodkin, S.G. & Keith-Speigel, P., Unacceptable impulses, anxiety and the appreciation of cartoons. Journal of Projective Techniques and Personality Assessment, 33, 154-159 (1969).

Speigel, D., Keith-Speigel, P., Abrahams, J. & Kranitz, L., Humor and suicide: Favorite jokes of suicidal patients. Journal of Consulting and Clinical Psychology. 33, 504-505 (1969).

Speigelman, M., Terwilliger, C.& Fearing, F., The content of comics: Goals and means to goals of comic strip characters. Journal of Social Psychology, 37, 189-203 (1953).

Speroni, C., Wit and Wisdom of the Italian Renaissance. University of California Press, Berkeley (1964).

Spitz, R.A. & Wolf, K.M., The smiling response: A contribution to the ontogenesis of social relations. Genetic Psychological Monographs, 34, 57-125 (1946).

Sroufe, L.A. & Waters, E., The ontogenesis of smiling and laughter: A perspective on the organisation of development in infancy. Psychological Review, 83, 173-189 (1976).

Sroufe, L.A. & Wunsch, J.P., The development of laughter in the first year of life. Child Development, 43, 1326-1344 (1972).

Starer, E., Reactions of psychiatric patients to cartoons and verbal jokes. Journal of General Psychology, 65, 301-304 (1961).

Steams, F.R., Laughing: Physiology, Pathophysiology, Psychology and Development. Thomas, Springfield, Illinois (1972).

Stephenson, R.M., Conflict and control functions of humor. American Journal of Sociology, 56, 569-574 (1951).

Sterling, P., Laughing On The Outside. Grosset & Dunlap, New York (1965).

Stern, A., Laughter and tears as philosophical problems. Folia Humanistic, 14, 255-266 (1976).

Sternthal, B. & Craig, C.S., Humor in advertising. Journal of Marketing, 37, 12-18 (1973).

Stolnitz, J., Noes on comedy and tragedy. Philosophy and Phenomenological Research, 16, 45-60 (1955).

Stowe, W.F. & Grimested, D., White-black humor. Journal of Ethnic Studies, in press.

Streicher, H.W., The girls in the cartoons. Journal of Communication, 24, 125-129 (1974).

Strickland, J.F., The effect of motivation arousal on humor preferences. Journal of Abnormal and Social Psychology, 59, 278-281 (1959).

Strother, G.B., Barnett, M.M. & Apostolakos, P.C., The use of cartoons as a projective device. Journal of Clinical Psychology, 10, 38-42 (1954).

Stuart, I.R., Iconography of group personality dynamics: Caricatures and cartoons. Journal of Social Psychology, 64, 147-156 (1964a).

Stuart, I.R., Primary and secondary processes as reflections of catastrophe: The political cartoon as an instrument of group emotional dynamics. Journal of Social Psychology, 64, 231-239 (1964b).

Stump, N.F., Sense of humor and its relationship to personality, scholastic aptitude, emotional maturity, height and weight. Journal of General Psychology, 20, 25-32 (1939).

Styan, J.L., The Dark Comedy: The Development of Modern Comic Tragedy. Cambridge University Press, Cambridge (1962).

Sully, J., Prolegomena to a theory of laughter. Philosophical Review, 9, 365-383 (1900).

Sully, J., An Essay on Laughter: Its Forms, Its Causes, Its Development, and Its Value. Longmans Green, London (1902).

Suls, J.M., A two-stage model for the appreciation of jokes and cartoons: An information-processing analysis. In: J.H. Goldstein & P.E. McGhee (Eds.), The Psychology of Humor. Academic Press, New York (1972).

Suls, J.M., The role of familiarity in the appreciation of humor. Journal of Personality, 43, 335-345 (1975).

Suls, J.M. & Miller, R.L., Humor as an attributional index. Personality and Social Psychology Bulletin, in press (1976).

Summo, A.J., Humor in review. Journal of Social Therapy, 4, 201-208 (1958).

Sutherland, J., English Satire. Cambridge University Press, Cambridge (1958).

Sutton, M.K., 'Inverse sublimity' in Victorian humor. VS, 10, 177-192 (1966).

Sutton-Smith, B., A developmental structural account of riddles. In: B. Kirschenblatt-Gimblett (Ed.), Speech, Play and Display. Mouton, Hague (1975).

Svebak, S., A theory of sense of humor. Scandinavian Journal of Psychology, 15, 99-107 (1974a).

Svebak, S., Revised questionnaire on the sense of humor. Scandinavian Journal of Psychology, 15, 328-331 (1974b).

Svebak, S., Three attitude dimensions of sense of humor as predictors of laughter. Scandinavian Journal of Psychology, 15, 185-190 (1974c).

Svebak, S., Respiratory patterns as predictors of laughter. Psychophysiology, 12, 62-65 (1975a).

Svebak, S., Styles in humour and social self-images. Scandinavian Journal of Psychology, 16, 79-84 (1975b).

Swabey, M.C., Comic Laughter: A Philosophical Essay. Yale University Press, New Haven (1961).

Sykes, A.J.M., Joking relationships in an industrial setting. American Anthropologist, 68, 188-193 (1966).

Tallman, R.S., A general approach to the practical joke. Southern Folklore Quarterly, 38, 259-274 (1974).

Tandy, J., Crackerbox Philosophers in American Humor. Columbia University Press, New York (1925).

Tarachow, S., Remarks on the comic process and beauty. Psychoanalytic Quarterly, 18, 215-226 (1949).

Taylor, A., The riddle. California Folklore Quarterly, 2, 129-147 (1943).

Taylor, A., Riddles among the North American Indians. Journal of American Folklore, 57, 1-15 (1944).

Taylor, A., English Riddles from Oral Tradition. University of California Press, Berkeley (1951).

Taylor, P.M., The effectiveness of humor in informative speaking. Research Reports, Central States Speech Journal, 15, 295-296 (1964).

Tave, S.M., The Amiable Humorist. University of Chicago Press, Chicago (1960).

Terry, R.L. & Ertel, S.L., Exploration of individual differences in preferences for humor. Psychological Reports, 34, 1031-1037 (1974).

Thomas, D.R., Shea, J.D. & Rigby, R.G., Conservatism and response to sexual humour. British Journal of Social and Clinical Psychology, 10, 185-186 (1971).

Thompson, R., Popular reading and humour in Restoration England. Journal of Popular Culture, 9, 653-671 (1975).

Thomson, A.A., Anatomy of Laughter. Epworth, London (1966).

Thorndike, R.L. & Stein, S., An evaluation of the attempts to measure social intelligence. Psychological Bulletin, 34, 275-285 (1937).

Thorp, W., American Humorists. University of Minnesota Press, Minneapolis (1964).

Tibbetts, S.L., What's so funny? Humor in children's literature. California Journal of Educational Research, 24, 42-46 (1973).

Time Magazine, American humor: Hardly a laughing matter. Time, 26-27, March 4th (1966).

Tollefson, D.L. & Cattell, R.B., Handbook for the IPAT Humor Test of Personality. Institute for Personality and Ability Testing, Champaign, Illinois (1963).

Trachtenberg, S., The economy of comedy. Psychological Review, 62, 557-578 (1976).

Traylor, G., Joking in a bush camp. Human Relations, 26, 479-486 (1973).

Treadwell, Y., Bibliography of empirical studies of wit and humor. Psychological Reports, 20, 1079-1083 (1967).

Treadwell, Y., Humor and creativity. Psychological Reports, 26, 55-58 (1970).

Trueblood, E., Humor of Christ. Harper & Row, New York (1964).

Tubau, I., The political and satirical cartoon. UNESCO Courier, No. 4, 25-27 (1976).

Turner, A., The many sides of southern humor. Mississippi Quarterly, 13, 155-156 (1960).

Ullman, L.P. & Lim, D.T., Case history material as a source of the identification of patterns of response to emotional stimuli in a study of humor. Journal of Consulting Psychology, 26, 221-225 (1962).

Urewitch, M., Comedy: The Irrational Vision. Cornell University Press, Ithica, New York (1975).

Van Hemert, N.A., Semantic transformations in the structure of the intellect model and cartoons. Nederlands Tijdschrift voor de Psychologie en Haar grensgevieden, 30, 113-138 (1975).

Vasey, G., The Philosophy of Laughter and Smiling. London (1875).

Ventis, W.L., Case history: The use of laughter as an alternative response in systematic desensitization. Behavior Therapy, 4, 120-122 (1973).

Verinis, J.S., Inhibition of humor enjoyment: Differential effects with traditional diagnostic categories. Journal of General Psychology, 82, 157-163 (1970a).

Verinis, J.S., Inhibition of humor enjoyment: Effects of sexual content and introversion-extraversion. Psychological Reports, 26, 167-170 (1970b).

Veth, C., Comic Art in England. Gale, Detroit (Original 1930) (1974).

Victoroff, D., New approaches to the psychology of humour. Impact of Science on Society, 19, 291-298 (1969).

Vidulich, R.M. & Wilson, D.J., The environmental setting as a factor in social influence. Journal of Social Psychology, 71, 247-255 (1967).

Walker, H., English Satire and Satirists. London (1925).

Walker, M.A. & Washburn, M.F., The Healy-Fernald Picture Completion Test as a test of the perception of the comic. American Journal of Psychology, 30, 304-307 (1919).

Wallace, J., The role of humor in the Hupa Indian Tribe. Journal of American Folklore, 66, 135-141 (1953).

Wallis, W.D., Why do we laugh? Scientific Monthly, 15, 343-347 (1922).

Walsh, J.J., Laughter and Health. Appleton, New York (1928).

Washburn, R.W., A study of the smiling and laughing of infants in the first year of life. Genetic Psychology Monographs, 6, 397-535 (1929).

Wasson, M., What is humor?   Forum, 76, 425-429 (1926).

Watson, J.S., Smiling, cooing, and 'the game'. Merrill-Palmer Quarterly, 18, 323-339 (1972).

Watts, A.W., The Meaning of Happiness. Harper Row, New York (1970).

Watts, H.H., The sense of regain: A theory of comedy. University of Kansas City Review, 13, 19-23 (1946).

Weightman, J., Humour and the French. Twentieth Century, 170, 117-126 (1961).

Weiskrantz, L., Elliott, J. & Darlington, C., Preliminary observations on tickling oneself. Nature, 230, 598-599 (1971).

Weller, L., Amitsour, E. & Pazzi, R., Reactions to absurd humor by Jews of eastern and western descent. Journal of Social Psychology, 98, 159-164 (1976).

Wells, C., Outline of Humor. Putnam, New York (1923).

Wells, R.E., A study of tastes in humorous literature among pupils of junior and senior high schools. Journal of Educational Research, 28, 81-92 (1934).

Welsch, R.L., A note on practical jokes. Southern Folklore Quarterly, 38, 253-257 (1974).

Welsford, E., The Fool: His Social and Literary History. Faber & Faber, London (1935).

Welsh, D.I., Russian Comedy, 1765-1823. Humanities, New York (1966).

Wharton, M., Beyond a joke. Twentieth Century, 170, 10-15 (1961).

White, E.B. & White, K.S. (Eds.), Subtreasury of American Humor. Putnam, New York (1962).

Willeford, W., The Fool and his Scepter: A Study in Clowns and their Audience. Northwestern University Press, Evanston, Illinois (1969).

Williams, C. & Cole, D.L., The influence of experimentally induced inadequacy feelings upon the appreciation of humor. Journal of Social Psychology, 64, 113-117 (1964).

Williams, J.M., An experimental and theoretical study of humour in children. British Journal of Educational Psychology, 16, 43-44 (1946).

Williams, T.R., The form and function of Tambunan Dusan riddles. Journal of American Folklore, 76, 95-110 (1963).

Willmann, J.M., An analysis of humor and laughter. American Journal of Psychology, 53, 70-85 (1940).

Wilson, G.D., Conservatism and response to humour. In: G.D. Wilson (Ed.), The Psychology of Conservatism. Academic Press, New York (1973).

Wilson, G.D., What ever turns you on: The psychology of sexual attraction. New Behaviour, April 24th (1975).

Wilson, G.D. & Brazendale, A.H., Sexual attractiveness, social attitudes and response to risqué humour. European Journal of Social Psychology, 3, 95-96 (1973).

Wilson, G.D. & Brazendale, A.H., Psychological correlates of sexual attractiveness: An empirical demonstration of denial and fantasy gratification phenomena? Social Behavior and Personality, 2, 30-34 (1974).

Wilson, G.D. & Maclean, A., Personality, attitudes and humor preferences of prisoners and controls. Psychological Reports, 34, 846-854 (1974).

Wilson, G.D. & Nias, D.K.B., Sexual types: Differences in attitudes and behaviour, New Behaviour, 330-332, August 28th (1975).

Wilson, G.D., Nias, D.K. & Brazendale, A.H., Vital statistics, perceived sexual attractiveness and response to risqué humor. Journal of Social Psychology, 95, 201-205 (1975).

Wilson, G.D. & Patterson, J.R., Conservatism as a predictor of humor preferences. Journal of Consulting and Clinical Psychology, 33, 271-274 (1969).

Wilson, J.H., Court Wits of the Restoration. Octagon, New York (1967).

Wilson, K.M., The sense of humour. Contemporary Review, 131, 628-633 (1927).

Wilson, S.A.K., Pathological laughing and crying. In: Modern Problems in Neurology. William Wood, New York (1929).

Wilson, W., Sex differences in response to obscenities and bawdy humor. Psychological Reports, 37, 1074 (1975).

Wimsatt, W.K., The Idea of Comedy. Prentice Hall, Englewood Cliffs, New Jersey (1969).

Winick, C., Space jokes as indication of attitudes towards space. Journal of Social Issues, 27, 43-49 (1961).

Winick, C., Teenagers, satire, and 'Mad'. Merrill-Palmer Quarterly, 8, 183-203 (1962).

Winick, C., A content analysis of orally communicated jokes. American Imago, 20, 271-291 (1963).

Winick, C., Outer Space Humor. Peter Pauper Press, Mount Vernon (1963).

Winick, C., USSR Humor. Peter Pauper Press, Mount Vernon (1964).

Winterstein, A., Contributions to the problem of humor. Psychoanalytic Quarterly, 3, 303-316 (1934).

Winterstein, A., Children's Humor: A Psychological Analysis. Free Press, Glencoe, Illinois (1954).

Wisse, R.R., The Schlemiel as Modern Hero. University of Chicago Press, Chicago (1971).

Witty, P., Children's interest in reading the comics. Journal of Experimental Education, 10, 100-104 (1941a).

Witty, P., Reading the comics - a comparative study. Journal of Experimental Education, 10, 105-110 (1941b).

Witty, P., Some observations from studies of the comics. Bull. Ass. Arts in Childhood (1942).

Witty, P., Those troublesome comics. Nat. Parent Teacher, 36, 29-30 (1942).

Wolfe, W.B., How to be Happy Though Human. George Routledge & Sons, London (1932).

Wolfenstein, M., A phase in the development of children's sense of humor. The Psychoanalytic Study of the Child, 7, 336-350 (1951).

Wolfenstein, M., Children's understanding of jokes. The Psychoanalytic Study of the Child, 9, 162-173 (1953).

Wolfenstein, M., Children's Humor. Free Press, Glencoe, Illinois (1954).

Wolfenstein, M., Mad laughter in a six year old boy. The Psychoanalytic Study of the Child, 10, 381-394 (1955).

Wolff, H.A., Smith, C.E. & Murray, H.A., The psychology of humor.I. A study of responses to race-disparagement jokes. Journal of Abnormal and Social Psychology, 28, 341-365 (1934).

Wolff, P.H., Observations on the early development of smiling. In: B.M. Foss (Ed.), Determinants of Infant Behaviour II. Methuen, London (1963).

Wolosin, R.J., Cognitive similarity and group laughter. Journal of Personality and Social Psychology, 32, 503-509 (1975).

Worcester, D., The Art of Satire. Harvard University Press, Cambridge (1940).

Worthen, R. & O'Connell, W.E., Social interest and humor. International Journal of Social Psychology, 15, 179-188 (1969).

Wright, M., What's Funny and Why. McGraw-Hill, New York (1939).

Wynn-Jones, L., The appreciation of wit. Report of the British Association for the Advancement of Science, 373 (1927).

Yarnold, J.K. & Berkeley, M.H., An analysis of the Cattell-Luborsky Humor Test into homogenous scales. Journal of Abnormal and Social Psychology, 49, 543-546 (1954).

Yates, M.W., The American Humorist. Iowa State University Press, Ames (1964).

Yörükoğlu, A., Children's favorite jokes and their relation to emotional conflicts. Journal of Child Psychiatry, 13, 677-690 (1974).

Yörükoğlu, A. & Silverman, J.S., Responses of psychiatric patients to a battery of cartoons and jokes. Psychiatric Communications, 6, 9-16 (1963).

Young, P.T., Is cheerfulness-depression a general temperamental trait? Psychological Review, 44, 313-319 (1937a).

Young, P.T., Laughing and weeping, cheerfulness and depression: A study of moods among college students. Journal of Social Psychology, 8, 311-334 (1937b).

Young, R.D. & Frye, M., Some are laughing, some are not: Why? Psychological Reports, 18, 747-755 (1966).

Zelazo, P.R., Smiling to social stimuli: Eliciting and conditioning effects. Developmental Psychology, 4, 32-42 (1971).

Zelazo, P.R., Smiling and vocalizing: A cognitive emphasis. Merrill-Palmer Quarterly, 18, 349-365 (1972).

Zelazo, P.R. & Komer, M.J., Infant smiling to non-social stimuli and the recognition hypothesis. Child Development, 42, 1327-1339 (1971).

Zemach, S., A theory of laughter. Journal of Aesthetics and Art Criticism, 17, 311-329 (1959).

Zenner, W., Joking and ethnic stereotyping. Anthropological Quarterly, 43, 93-113 (1970).

Zigler, E., Levine, J. & Gould, L., Cognitive processes in the development of children's appreciation of humor. Child Development, 37, 507-518 (1966a).

Zigler, E., Levine, J. & Gould, L., The humor response of normal, institutionalized retarded and noninstitutionalized retarded children. American Journal of Mental Deficiency, 71, 472-480 (1966b).

Zigler, E., Levine, J. & Gould, L., Cognitive challenge as a factor in children's humor appreciation. Journal of Personality and Social Psychology, 6, 332-336 (1967).

Zijderveld, A.C., Jokes and their relation to social reality. Social Research, 35, 286-311 (1968).

Ziller, R.C., Behringer, R.D. & Goodchilds, J.D., Group creativity under conditions of success or failure and variations in group stability. Journal of Applied Psychology, 46, 43-49 (1962).

Zillman, D. & Bryant, J., Retaliatory equity as a factor in humor appreciation. Journal of Experimental Social Psychology, 10, 480-488 (1974).

Zillmann, D., Bryant, J. & Cantor, J.R., Brutality of assault in political cartoons affecting humor appreciation. Journal of Research in Personality, 7, 334-345 (1974).

Zillmann, D. & Cantor, J.R., Directionality of transitory dominance as a communication variable affecting humor appreciation. Journal of Personality and Social Psychology, 24, 191-198 (1972).

Zillmann, D. & Cantor, J.R., A disposition theory of humour and mirth. In: A.J. Chapman & H.C. Foot (Eds.), Humour and Laughter: Theory, Research and Applications. Wiley, London (1976).

Zinsser, W.K., Pop Goes America. Harper & Row, New York (1966).

Zippin, D., Sex differences and the sense of humor. Psychoanalytic Review, 53, 209-219 (1966).

Zug, C.G. III, The nonrational riddle: The Zen Koan. Journal of American Folklore, 80, 81-88 (1967).

Zuk, G.H., A further study of laughter in family therapy. Family Process, 3, 77-89 (1964).

Zuk, G.H., On the theory and pathology of laughter in psychotherapy. Psychotherapy: Theory, Research and Practice, 3, 97-101 (1966).

Zuk, G.H., Boszormenyi-Nagy, I. & Heiman, E., Some dynamics of laughter during family therapy. Family Process, 2, 302-314 (1963).

Zuver, D., Salvation by Laughter. Harper & Row, New York (1933).

Zwerling, I., The favorite joke in diagnostic and therapeutic interviewing. Psychoanalytic Quarterly, 24, 104-114 (1955).

ADDENDUM TO:-
HUMOUR, LAUGHTER AND COMEDY:
A BIBLIOGRAPHY OF EMPRICAL AND NONEMPIRICAL ANALYSES IN THE ENGLISH
LANGUAGE

Jeffrey H. Goldstein, Paul E. McGhee, Jean R. Smith,
Antony J. Chapman and Hugh C. Foot

Anonymous, Seeing the gag. New Behaviour, Volume 2, No. 2, July 10th (1975).

Anonymous, The science of humour and the humour of science. Impact of Science on Society, 3, 19 (1969).

Bateson, G., The position of humour in human communication. In: J. Levine (Ed.), Motivation in Humour. Atherton Press, New York (1969).

Berger, A.A., Anatomy of the joke. Journal of Communication, 26, 113-115 (1976).

Berlyne, D.E., Conflict, Arousal and Curiosity. McGraw-Hill, New York (1960).

Boskin, J., 'Black'/black humor: The renaissance of laughter. In: W.M. Mendel (Ed.), A Celebration of Laughter. Mara Books, Los Angeles (1970).

Brodzinsky, D.M., Feur, V. & Owens, J., Direction of linguistic ambiguity by reflective, impulsive, fast accurate, and slow inaccurate children. In preparation (1976).

Byron, C., Killing laughter. Time, 58, August 2nd (1976).

Cantor, J.R., What is funny to whom? Journal of Communication, 26, 164-172 (1976).

Cantor, J.R., Humor on television: A content analysis. Journal of Broadcasting, in press.

Chapman, A.J., An electromyographic study of apprehension about evaluation. Psychological Reports, 33, 811-814 (1973).

Douglas, M., Do dogs laugh? In: M. Douglas (Ed.), Implicit Meanings. Routledge & Kegan Paul, London (1975).

Durgnat, R., The Crazy Mirror: Hollywood Comedy and The American Image. New York (1970).

Fine, G.A., Obscene joking across cultures. Journal of Communication, 26, 134-140 (1976).

Furlong, W., The flow experience: The fun in fun. Psychology Today, 10, 35-38, 80 (1976).

Grey, E., Some riddles of the Nyanja people. Bantu Studies, 13, 25 (1949).

Harries, L., Some riddles of the Makua people. African Studies, 1-2, 275 (1942-43).

Hobbes, T., Humane Nature. Anchor, London (1651).

Hobbes, T., Leviathan. Crooke, London (1651). (Reprinted Harmondsworth, Penguin, 1968).

Hyers, C. (Ed.), Holy Laughter: Essays on Religion in the Comic Perspective. Seabury, New York (1969).

Jette, J., Riddles of the Ten'a Indians. Anthropos, 8, 181, 630 (1913).

Justin, F., A genetic study of laughter provoking stimuli. Child Development, 3, 114-136 (1932).

Kennedy, J.G., Bonds of laughter among the Tarahumara Indians: Toward a rethinking of joking relationship theory. In: H. Hoijen (Ed.), The Social Anthropology of Latin America. University of California Press, Los Angeles (1970).

Koestler, A., Humour and Wit. In: The Encyclopaedia Britannica. H.H. Benton, Chicago (1974).

La Fave, L. & Mannell, R.C., Does ethnic humor serve prejudice? Journal of Communication, 26, 116-123 (1976a).

La Fave, L. & Mannell, R.C., Ethnic humour as a function of reference groups and identification classes. In: D.F. Lancy & B.A. Tindall (Eds.), The Anthropological Study of Play: Problems and Prospects. Leisure Press, New York (1976b).

Levine, J.B., The feminine routine. Journal of Communication, 26, 173-175 (1976).

MacRae, D., National Humour. Stokes, New York.

Mannell, R. & La Fave, L., Humor judgements and the 'playful attitude'. In: D.F. Lancy & B.A. Tindall (Eds.), The Anthropological Study of Play: Problems and Prospects. Leisure Press, New York (1976).

Mueller, C. & Donnerstein, E., The effects of humor-induced arousal upon aggressive behaviour. Journal of Research in Personality, in press.

McMahon, J., Funny is funny. New Woman, 23, March-April (1976).

Nast, G., The Comic Mind: Comedy and The Movies, New York (1973).

O'Mahony, M. & Brown, M., The interstimulus humour effect. European Journal of Social Psychology, in press.

Preston, W.D., Japanese riddle materials. Journal of American Folklore, 61, 175 (1948).

Sacks, R.A. & Wolf, K.M., The origin of the smiling response. In: D.C. McClelland (Ed.), Studies in Motivation. Appleton-Century-Crofts, New York (1955).

Sherman, L.W., An analysis of group glee in formal preschool lessons. In: W. Ambinder. The Preschool Environment: An Ecological Study of Structured Lessons and Free-Play in an Integrated Preschool. Symposium presented at the meetings of the American Psychological Association, Montreal (1973).

Starr, F., Japanese riddles. Transactions of the Asiatic Society of Japan, 38, 1 (1910-1912).

Stocking, S.H., Sapolsky, B. & Zillmann, D., Is there sex discrimination in humor on prime-time television? Journal of Broadcasting, in press.

Stocking, S.H. & Zillmann, D., Effects of humorous disparagement of self, friend, and enemy. Psychological Reports, in press.

Suls, J.M., Humor and misattribution: A comment on 'Enhancement of humor appreciation by transferred excitation'. Journal of Personality and Social Psychology, in press (1976).

Sypher, W., Comedy. New York (1956).

Ullian, J.A., Joking at work. Journal of Communication, 26, 129-133 (1976).

Wilde, L., The Great Comedians Talk About Comedy. Citadel Press, New York (1968).

Winick, C., The social contexts of humor. Journal of Communication, 26, 124-128 (1976).

Zillmann, D. & Stocking, S.H., Putdown humor. Journal of Communication, 26, 154-163 (1976).

Conference Contributors

ALLEN, M., Department of Psychology, California State University, Northridge, California 91324, U.S.A.

APTER, M.J., Psychology Department, University College, P.O. Box 96, Cardiff CF1 1XB, Wales, U.K.

ATHEY, C., Froebel Educational Institute, Grove House, Roehampton Lane, London SW15 5PJ.

ATKINS, J.R., Box 6, Whitevale, Ontario, L0H 1M0, Canada.

BARIAUD, F., Ecole Practique des Hautes Etudes, Laboratoire de Psycho-Biologie de l'Enfant, 41, Rue Gay Lussac, 75005 Paris Veme, France.

BARSHAY, R., Department of English Studies, Prince George's Community College, 301 Largo Road, Largo, Maryland 20870, U.S.A.

BERGER, A.A., Behavioural and Social Sciences Cross-disciplinary Programs, San Francisco State University, 1600 Holloway Avenue, San Francisco, California 94132, U.S.A.

BOUISSAC, P., Department of French, Victoria College and Graduate Department of Linguistics, University of Toronto, Toronto M5S 1K7, Canada.

BOURHIS, R.Y., Psychology Department, Bristol University, 8-10 Berkeley Square, Bristol BS8 1HH, Avon, U.K.

BRADSHAW, J., Department of Educational Enquiry, The University of Aston in Birmingham, Gosta Green, Birmingham B4 7ET, U.K.

BRISLAND, S.G., King Alfred's College, Winchester, Hampshire, U.K.

BRODZINSKY, D.M., Department of Psychology, Douglass College, Rutgers University, New Brunswick, New Jersey 08903, U.S.A.

BRYANT, J., Department of Communication Studies, University of Massachusetts, Armherst 01002, U.S.A.

BUFFERY, A.W.H., Institute of Psychiatry, University of London, De Crespigny Park, Denmark Hill, London SE5.

BURNAND, G., Buckinghamshire College of Higher Education, School of Education and Social Sciences, Queen Alexandra Road, High Wycombe HP11 2JZ, U.K.

CANTOR, J.R., Department of Communication Arts, Vilas Communication Hall, 821, University Avenue, Madison, WI 53706, U.S.A.

CASTELL, P.J., Quarters D. National Naval Medical Center, Bethesda, Maryland 20014, U.S.A.

CHAPMAN, A.J., Department of Applied Psychology, UWIST, Llwyn-y-Grant Road, Penylan, Cardiff CF3 7UX, Wales, U.K.

COHEN, D., Department of Psychology, Bedford College, University of London, Regent's Park, London NW1 4NS.

COUZENS, M.R.J., Institute of Education, University of London, Malet Street, London WC1E 7HS.

DAVIES, A.P., Department of Psychology, University College, Cardiff CF1 1XB, Wales, U.K.

DAVIES, G.C.H., 12 Glanybrydan Avenue, Uplands, Swansea, Wales, U.K.

DAVIES, J.C.H., Faculty of Letters and Social Sciences, University of Reading, Whiteknights, Reading RG6 2AA, U.K.

DAVIS, J.R.M., University of New South Wales, Australia.

DODD, K.A., Knotty Ash University, c/o Forrester George Ltd., Suite 34, 140 Park Lane, London W1.

FINE, G.A., Department of Sociology, 1114 Social Sciences Building, Minneapolis, Minnesota 55455, U.S.A.

FOOT, H.C., Department of Applied Psychology, UWIST, Llwyn-y-Grant Road, Penylan, Cardiff CF3 7UX, Wales, U.K.

FOSS, B.M., Department of Psychology, Bedford College, University of London, Regent's Park, London NW1 4NS.

FRY, W.F., 888 Oak Grove Avenue, Menlo Park, California 94025, U.S.A.

FULLER, R.G.C., Department of Psychology, Trinity College, 25-26 Westland Row, Dublin 2, Eire.

GADFIELD, N.J., Department of Applied Psychology, UWIST, Llwyn-y-Grant Road, Penylan, Cardiff CF3 7UX, Wales, U.K.

GALE, M.A., Department of Psychology, University of Southampton, Southampton, U.K.

GOLDSTEIN, J.H., Department of Psychology, Temple University, College of Liberal Arts, Philadelphia, PA 19122, U.S.A.

GREENWALD, H., 5135 Pacifica Drive, San Diego, California 92109, U.S.A.

GROSSMAN, S.A., 33, Split Rock Road, South Norwalk, Connecticut 06854, U.S.A.

HANDELMAN, D., Department of Sociology and Anthropology, The Hebrew University of Jerusalem, Jerusalem, Israel.

HANSEN, A.J., Department of English, University of The Pacific, Stockton, California 95211, U.S.A.

HEALEY, T., Northfield, Salisbury Street, Barnsley, South Yorkshire, U.K.

HEIM, A., Psychological Laboratory, Downing Street, Cambridge CB2 3EB, U.K.

HERSHKOWITZ, A., 2700 Harry Hudson Parkway, Riverdale, New York 10463, U.S.A.

HEUSCHER, J.E., 18500 Hillview Drive, Monte Sereno, California 95030, U.S.A.

HODGKINS, W., 7 Leven Close, Cardiff CF2 6DN, Wales, U.K.

HOPEN, C.E., Division of Social Sciences, Scarborough College, University of Toronto, West Hill, Ontario MIC 1A4, Canada.

HUNTER, W., Kathakali, 16 Roseberry Crescent, Norton-on-Tees, Cleveland TS20 1JS, U.K.

HUSBAND, C., School of Social Work, University of Leicester, 107 Princess Road, Leicester LE1 7LA, U.K.

HYDE, D.M.G., The American University in Cairo, Sociology-Anthropology-Psychology Department, 113, Sharia Kar El Aini, Cairo, Egypt, A.R.E.

KANE, T.R., Department of Psychology, SUNY at Albany, 1400 Washington Avenue, Albany, New York 12222, U.S.A.

KEEN, S., Elm Cottage, Upton Pyne, Exeter, Devon, U.K.

KILLINGER, B., Graduate Programme in Psychology, York University, 4700, Keele Street, Downsview, Ontario M3J 1P3, Canada.

KING, J., Department of Psychology, Bristol University, 8-10 Berkeley Square, Bristol BS8 1HH, Avon, U.K.

KIRKLAND, J., Department of Education, Massey University, Palmerston North, New Zealand.

KLINE, P., Department of Psychology, University of Exeter, Exeter EX4 4QG, Devon, U.K.

LA FAVE, L., Department of Psychology, University of Windsor, Ontario N9B 3P4, Canada.

LA GAIPA, J.J., Department of Psychology, University of Windsor, Ontario N9B 3P4, Canada.

LEE, T.R., Department of Psychology, University of Surrey, Guildford, Surrey, U.K.

LEVENTHAL, H., Department of Psychology, W.J. Brogden Psychology Building, 1202 West Johnson Street, University of Wisconsin, Madison 53706, U.S.A.

LEVINE, J., Veterans Administration Hospital, West Spring Street, West Haven, Connecticut 06516, U.S.A.

LINFIELD, E.G., Bath College of Higher Education, Newton Park, Newton St. Lowe, Bath BA2 9BN, Somerset, U.K.

MAIR, M.W., University of London Institute of Education, Department of Child Development, 24-27 Woburn Square, London EC1H 0AA.

MANNELL, R.C., Centre of Leisure Studies, Acadia University, Wolfville, Nova Scotia B0P 1X0, Canada.

McGhee, P.E., The Fels Research Institute, Yellow Springs, Ohio 45387, U.S.A.

MINDESS, H., 337 South Beverly Drive, Beverly Hills, California 90212, U.S.A.

MINTZ, L.E., American Studies Program, University of Maryland, College Park, Maryland 20742 U.S.A.

MUTUMA, H.L., Department of Sociology, University of Windsor, Windsor N9B 3P4, Ontario, Canada.

NERHARDT, F.K.G., Psychological Laboratories, University of Stockholm, Box 6706, S-11385 Stockholm, Sweden.

NEWCOMB, T.M., Department of Psychology, University of Michigan, Ann Arbor, Michigan, U.S.A.

NIAS, D.K.B., Institute of Psychiatry, University of London, De Crespigny Park, Denmark Hill, London SE5 8AF.

O'CONNELL, W.E., Veterans Administration Class Ark Drug Dependency Center, 2120 Travis, Houston, Texas 77002, U.S.A.

O'MAHONY, M., Department of Psychology, Bristol University, 8-10 Berkeley Square, Bristol BS8 1HH, Avon, U.K.

OSBORNE, K.A., Department of Applied Psychology, UWIST, Llwyn-y-Grant Road, Penylan, Cardiff CF3 7UX, Wales, U.K.

PALMER, R., Department of Psychology, Bristol University, 8-10 Berkeley Square, Bristol BS8 1HH, Avon, U.K.

PAULOS, J.A., Department of Mathematics, Temple University, Philadelphia, Pennsylvania 19122, U.S.A.

PIEN, D., Department of Psychology, College of Liberal Arts, Eugene, Oregon 97403, U.S.A.

POWELL, C., Department of Sociology, University of Stirling, Stirling, Scotland, U.K.

PREROST, F.J., Department of Psychology, Lewis University, Route 53, Lockport, Illinois 60441, U.S.A.

RANSOHOFF, R., 343 E 30th Street, New York, New York 10016, U.S.A.

ROBINSON, J.O., Department of Psychology, University College, Cardiff, Wales, U.K.

ROTHBART, M.K., Department of Psychology, College of Liberal Arts, Eugene, Oregon 97403 U.S.A.

SCHUMAN, S., Department of English, Cornell College, Mount Vernon, Iowa 52314, U.S.A.

SCHUTZ, C.E., Department of Political Science, Albion College, Albion, Michigan 49224, U.S.A.

SHEEHY-SKEFFINGTON, A., Department of Psychology, Trinity College, 26 Westland Row, Dublin 2, Eire.

SHELLEY, D., c/o 71 Boyne Road, London SE13.

SHEPPARD, A.G., Department of Psychology, Kalamazoo College, Kalamazoo, Michigan 49007, U.S.A.

SHERMAN, L.W., Department of Educational Psychology, 201 McGuffey Hall, Miami University, Oxford, Ohio 45056, U.S.A.

SHULTZ, T.R., Department of Psychology, McGill University, P.O. Box 6070, Station A, Montreal, Quebec, H3C 3G1, Canada.

SMITH, J.R., Department of Applied Psychology, UWIST, Llwyn-y-Grant Road, Penylan, Cardiff CF3 7UX, Wales, U.K.

SMITH, K.C.P., 14 Howard Road, Bristol BS8 7UT, Avon, U.K.

SNOW, A.J., King Alfred's College, Winchester, Hampshire, U.K.

SULS, J.M., Department of Psychology, SUNY at Albany, 1400 Washington Avenue, Albany, New York 12222, U.S.A.

SVEBAK, S., University of Bergen, Psykologisk Institutt, Postboks 25, 5014 Bergen - U, Norway.

TAYLOR, P., Centre for Mass Communication Research, University of Leicester, 104 Regent Road, Leicester LE1 7LT, U.K.

TSANG, S.Y.W., Department of Psychology, University of Windsor, Ontario N9B 3P4, Canada.

WILSON, G.D., Institute of Psychiatry, De Crespigny Park, Denmark Hill, London SE5 8AF.

WRIGHT, D.S., School of Education, University of Leicester, University Road, Leicester LE1 7RH, U.K.

YORUKOGLU, A., Division of Child Psychiatry, Department of Psychiatry, University of Hacettepe, Faculty of Medicine, Ankara, Turkey.

ZILLMANN, D., Institute for Communication Research, Indiana University, Bloomington, Indiana 47401, U.S.A.